PRAISE FOR *HEARING VOIC*

CW00922585

'A gripping, fascinating tale, told here with elegance, enthusiasm
crafted, highly readable, impeccably researched, beautifully ill
important social history in more than a decade'
Professor Ivor Browne, *Irish Times*

'Magisterial'
Alan Gilsenan, *Irish Times*

'Fascinating ... As Kelly asks, how much has really changed?'
Valerie Flynn, *Sunday Times*

'Masterpiece. Monumental in every way'
Dr Maurice Gueret, *Sunday Independent*

'A *tour de force* by one of Ireland's leading psychiatrists, encompassing every psychiatric
development from the Middle Ages to the present day'
Dr Muiris Houston, *Irish Medical Times*

'The definitive work ... a *vade mecum* for anyone with an interest in the history of Irish
psychiatry and the care of the mentally ill'
Liam Hennessy, *Dublin Review of Books*

'A gift to future scholars ... masterful work'
Dr John S. McIntyre, *American Journal of Psychiatry*

'Comprehensive and scholarly'
Dr Barry O'Donnell, *The Letter*

'The book is about hearing the voices of the past, present and future: Professor Kelly's voice
rings with integrity and resonates with truth. It deserves to be heard'
Dr Maureen McCourt, *Studies*

'A truly fascinating read'
Dr Triona Waters, *Critical Social Policy*

HEARING VOICES

This book is dedicated to Meabh

Brendan Kelly is Professor of Psychiatry at Trinity College Dublin, and Consultant Psychiatrist at Tallaght University Hospital, Dublin. In addition to his medical degree (MB BCh BAO), Professor Kelly holds masters degrees in epidemiology (MSc), healthcare management (MA) and Buddhist studies (MA); and doctorates in medicine (MD), history (PhD), governance (DGov) and law (PhD). He is also UCD Clinical Professor at University College Dublin (UCD) School of Medicine; a fellow of the Royal College of Psychiatrists (London) and Royal College of Physicians of Ireland; and a member of the College of Psychiatrists of Ireland. He has served on various government committees relating to psychiatry and mental health law, and was editor of the *Irish Journal of Psychological Medicine* from 2010 to 2016. Professor Kelly has authored and coauthored over 250 peer-reviewed publications and 500 non-peer-reviewed publications, as well as a number of book chapters and books, including *Ada English: Patriot and Psychiatrist* (Irish Academic Press, 2014). He is Editor-in-Chief of the *International Journal of Law and Psychiatry*.

HEARING VOICES

THE HISTORY OF PSYCHIATRY
IN IRELAND

Brendan Kelly

IRISH ACADEMIC PRESS

First published in 2016 by
Irish Academic Press
10 George's Street
Newbridge
Co. Kildare
Ireland
www.iap.ie

ISBN: 9781788550864 (Paper)
ISBN: 9781911024422 (Kindle)
ISBN: 9781911024439 (PDF)
ISBN: 9781911024446 (Epub)

British Library Cataloguing in Publication Data
An entry can be found on request

Library of Congress Cataloging in Publication Data
An entry can be found on request

Typeset in Garamond Premier Pro 10.5/14 pt
Front cover image: Courtesy of Úna Spain with permission from the HSE.
Back cover image: St Ita's Hospital, Portrane (1900). Source: *Building News and Engineering Journal* (78, 2364, 27 April 1900, pp. 572–3). Courtesy of the Irish Architectural Archive.

CONTENTS

ABBREVIATIONS

ADHD	Attention deficit hyperactivity disorder
APA	American Psychiatric Association
BILD	British Institute of Learning Disabilities
CMH	Central Mental Hospital
CRPD	Convention on the Rights of Persons with Disabilities
DBS	Deep brain stimulation
DETECT	Dublin and East Treatment and Early Care Team
DPM	Diploma in Psychological Medicine
DSM	Diagnostic and Statistical Manual of Mental Disorders
ECHR	European Convention on Human Rights
ECT	Electroconvulsive therapy
EEC	European Economic Community
EU	European Union
GLEN	Gay and Lesbian Equality Network
GNC	General Nursing Council
GNP	Gross national product
GP	General practitioner
GPI	General paralysis of the insane
HSE	Health Service Executive
IMG	Independent Monitoring Group
IRA	Irish Republican Army
KC	King's Counsel
LGB	Lesbian, gay and bisexual
LGBT	Lesbian, gay, bisexual and transgender
LSD	Lysergic acid diethylamide

MB	Medicinae Baccalaureus (Latin; Bachelor of Medicine)
MD	Medicinae Doctor (Latin; Doctor of Medicine)
MHID	Mental health of intellectual disability
MP	Member of Parliament
MPA	Medico-Psychological Association
MPhil	Masters in philosophy
NCHD	Non-consultant hospital doctor
NHS	National Health Service
NICE	National Institute for Clinical Excellence
NOSP	National Office for Suicide Prevention
NSW	New South Wales
OCD	Obsessive compulsive disorder
OECD	Organisation for Economic Co-operation and Development
PTSD	Post-traumatic stress disorder
RCSI	Royal College of Surgeons in Ireland
RIC	Royal Irish Constabulary
RMPA	Royal Medico-Psychological Association
RMS	Resident Medical Superintendent
RTA	Road traffic accident
RTÉ	Raidió Teilifís Éireann
SJ	Society of Jesus
TB	Tuberculosis
TD	Teachta Dála
UCC	University College Cork
UCD	University College Dublin
UK	United Kingdom
UN	United Nations
US	United States
WHO	World Health Organisation

FOREWORD

Of the many national histories of psychiatry, Brendan Kelly's well-researched and compellingly written history of Irish psychiatry leads the pack. This is the first comprehensive history of psychiatry in Ireland.

Kelly, who is an historian as well as the Professor of Psychiatry at Trinity College, Dublin, shares the historian's preference for primary sources, often unpublished, in order to let the people of the time speak for themselves. And here, in a story that begins in 1745 with author Jonathan Swift providing in his will for the establishment of a proper hospital for the mentally ill, the psychiatrists of the day as well as the patients find their voices heard loudly and clearly.

Kelly's main theme is that 'the asylums were primarily social creations, reflecting social and political change far more than they ever reflected changes in the practice of medicine and psychiatry'. The story is driven for the most part by changes in the real world, such as the Famine, rather than by internal motors such as the introduction of new concepts or medications – though Kelly gives the internalist moments their full due.

This is not 'antipsychiatry' history at all, in which we learn that there is no such thing as mental illness and that the physicians were mainly intent upon increasing their 'power'. Kelly, himself a senior figure, respects the magnitude of the therapeutic power that psychiatry often brings to bear, and ventilates fully the sufferings of the patients in the hope that future patients who encounter this work might bear away some measure of encouragement.

Ireland in the nineteenth century groaned under often unimaginable poverty, and Kelly notes that, 'the asylums functioned as a vast, unwieldy social welfare system for patients and possibly some staff'. Before the 1960s, in other words, psychological medicine was centred in asylums, and this, says Kelly, left an indelible stain on Irish psychiatry as the psychiatry of confinement.

The central issue in the Irish history, Kelly argues, is not why the rate of mental illness was higher in Ireland than elsewhere (Kelly definitively shows it was not). Rather, the big question is why Ireland's asylums were larger in size – and slower to decrease in size – than elsewhere. The answer lies in a society that has 'an apparently insatiable hunger for institutionalization'. This would be an Irish theme, there was no comparable hunger in Italy, for example.

Yet Irish psychiatry reflects other themes that are global in scope. It was true in many lands that admission to an asylum in the nineteenth century could be a death warrant, because tuberculosis (TB) was endemic and spread easily from patient to patient. Kelly finds that 16 per cent of the Irish general population died of TB, 25 per cent of the asylum population.

Everywhere in the nineteenth century, 'insanity' was thought to be increasing. Yet the consensus among historians of other countries was that it was not. Kelly finds an increase unlikely for Ireland as well. What did change was the 'presentation', or ascertainment, of mental disorder, which shifted from what we now call 'intellectual disability' (formerly, 'idiots') to psychotic disorder (formerly, 'lunatics'). Moreover, the Famine may have tipped mentally precarious individuals into outright insanity, thus increasing the rate for a short time. What makes the notion of a long-term increase in mental illness unlikely is that the major disorders in psychiatry are heavily influenced by genetics, and genetic factors are unlikely to change much over time. Was there more 'stress' in modern urban life than previously? Every generation lives with the idea that it is more subject to stress than the previous generation. This belief is likely a constant in the human condition.

Were more Irish in fact mentally ill than elsewhere? Kelly says that in 1901 the Irish rate of insanity in the population outside of institutions was 11 per 100,000, which on a comparative basis is probably quite low (comparing these international statistics is like quicksand). The 'Mad Irishman' was thus an unjust stereotype, an urban myth, not a firm national reality.

As we approach the present, asylum stays become much shorter. One reason is the introduction of the antipsychotic drug chlorpromazine (Largactil) in 1954 and its successors. The antipsychotics do not abolish hallucinations and delusions entirely but make it possible for patients to tolerate their disorders with less anxiety and agitation, and thus to be able to cope once again with life outside the asylum.

Yes, of course, this is a social plus. Yet one advantage of the traditional long stays was the ability of the staff to ensure that the patient was in fact quite well before discharging him or her. It is a historical reality that suicides post-discharge today are much higher than they were in the nineteenth century – and this despite the introduction of psychopharmacological agents that supposedly reduce suicidality. So, before we pat ourselves too smugly on the back for the wonderful progress we've made in reducing 'institutionalisation', let us keep in mind that these old, and today much maligned, asylums did serve a social purpose that we have been unable to replace.

This, therefore, is the story of Irish psychiatry, told by a scholar who is both a historian and a clinician, and has both skill sets. The book is an exhaustively researched look at the past; it concludes with a speculative glance at the future of Irish psychiatry, and is well worth the price of admission for those interested in Irish mental health issues in the present.

Prof. Dr Edward Shorter, PhD FRSC
Jason A. Hannah Professor of the History of
Medicine and Professor of Psychiatry
Faculty of Medicine, University of Toronto

PROLOGUE

In 1905, a brother-in-law of Irish writer, Sean O'Casey, was committed to the Richmond District Lunatic Asylum at Grangegorman in Dublin, part of the vast network of mental hospitals that sprawled across Ireland for much of the 1800s and 1900s. 'Benson' (not his real name) suffered from general paralysis of the insane (GPI), a neuropsychiatric disorder caused by late-stage syphilis which often presented with psychiatric symptoms. Commonly fatal, GPI was a substantial problem in asylums in Ireland[1] and elsewhere.[2]

'Benson' died in Grangegorman two years later, leaving a widow and five young children.[3] In his autobiography, *Drums Under the Window*, O'Casey described 'Benson's' initial arrival at Grangegorman in vivid, affecting terms:[4]

> Between the keepers, with Sean opposite to see him safe home, Benson, grinning helplessly, was driven to the house of strident shadows, to dress in the rough grey tweed of the loony pauper, to wear the red woollen neckerchief so tied that when one became restless, a keeper could seize it, pull, and choke all movement, quench all fire out of the gurgling, foam-lipped madman; to where he would be dust to dust and ashes to ashes before he was dead, withered grass that hadn't yet been cast into the oven, to Grangegorman. Wide gates of heavy, dull, heartless lead opened to let them in, and the black cab rolled silently along the drive, drawn by a horse with a sly and regular trot as if he felt and feared anything else might entitle him for companionship with the dread life of the still-twitching dead. Dotted here and there in the grounds were the dismal brothers of disorders grey, their red mufflers making them look as if their tormented heads had been cut off, and pushed crookedly back on to their necks again. The cab stopped slowly before the building, wide and long, built like a bully that had suddenly died shrugging his shoulders. Long rows of lifeless windows mirrored long rows of lifeless faces, their silence hymning a fading resurrection of Velazquez's idiots[5], a whole stonily-grinning gallery of God's images turned to dull grey clay, the emptiness of a future age in every face. Now and again, some of them would vent a laugh that rippled a shudder along the walls of the asylum. The grass everywhere grew brown and long, and fell to dust whenever it was touched; the trees twisted their branches like limbs in pain, and grew grey leaves that never seemed to move, a cold immortal grey, as if under the blight of the fig tree Christ had cursed. Flowers that tried to grow beneath the windows were slimy stalks, crawling along the grey ground like slugs tantalizing the rim of a festering lily,

lost amid the quiet storm of lunacy distilling a sour air everywhere. In a corner a chestnut tree dropped worm-worn fruit like leaden balls, and riven church bells rang out a raucous angelus three times a day, carolling rakishly mid the mindless chatter and the rasping laugh. Only ghosts of things and men were here ...

INTRODUCTION

The history of psychiatry is a history of therapeutic enthusiasm, with all of the triumph and tragedy, hubris and humility that such enthusiasm brings. This book presents this history in the very particular context of Ireland, and tells the story of early psychiatric care, the emergence of Ireland's remarkable asylum system in the 1800s, its demise in the 1900s, and the development of 'community care'. It is an extraordinary tale.

What is Psychiatry?

Psychiatry, according to Professor Anthony Clare (1942–2007; Chapter 6), one of the outstanding Irish figures in its history,[1] is 'the branch of medicine that is concerned with the study and treatment of disorders of mental function'.[2] More specifically, a *medical* disorder is a disease or ailment,[3] and a *mental* disorder, according to the World Health Organisation (WHO), is a clinically recognisable group of symptoms or behaviours associated in the majority of cases with distress and with interference with personal functions.[4] If personal dysfunction is not present, social deviance or conflict on their own are not sufficient to constitute mental disorder: the person's mood, thoughts, judgement, relationships or personal function must be disturbed.

Throughout history, the evolution of this concept of 'mental disorder' has been, and continues to be, a highly contested process.[5] Mental disorders are variously conceptualised as spiritual or religious manifestations, legal conundrums, medical diseases, social issues, or all of the above, with the balance between competing conceptualisations varying over time.[6] In recent decades, re-definition and expansion of diagnostic categories within psychiatry have proven especially controversial.[7]

This book, however, is a history of *psychiatry* rather than a history of mental disorder, madness, the mentally ill, asylums or even psychiatrists.[8] Of necessity, all of these concepts feature strongly in the story, but this book is primarily a history of, to use Clare's definition, that 'branch of medicine that is concerned with the study and treatment of disorders of mental function'. It is, quite simply and quite complicatedly, a history of psychiatry in Ireland.

Why Write a History of Psychiatry in Ireland?

In March 1817, Robert Peel (1788–1850), Chief Secretary, prevailed upon the House of Commons of the United Kingdom of Great Britain and Ireland to set up a Select Committee to look into the need to make greater provision for 'the lunatic poor in Ireland'.[9] The Right Honourable Denis

Browne (a Mayo Member of Parliament) gave evidence about the plight of the mentally ill in rural areas of early nineteenth-century Ireland:

> There is nothing so shocking as madness in the cabin of the peasant, where the man is out labouring in the fields for his bread, and the care of the woman of the house is scarcely sufficient for the attendance on the children. When a strong young man or woman gets the complaint, the only way they have to manage is by making a hole in the floor of the cabin not high enough for the person to stand up in, with a crib over it to prevent his getting up, the hole is about five feet deep, and they give the wretched being his food there, and there he generally dies. Of all human calamity, I know of none equal to this, in the country parts of Ireland which I am acquainted with.[10]

When presented to the Select Committee in 1817, this picture – the mentally ill person kept in a pit until he or she dies – was a searing one and it still retains its power to shock today, some two centuries later. This image and the reaction it evokes highlight the importance of the history of psychiatry in Ireland. Can an examination of this history help us to understand why such a situation was allowed to develop? How did matters change (if at all) following a seemingly endless succession of official reports such as that of the 1817 Select Committee? Did the emergence of psychiatry in the 1800s improve matters? How much of this situation was specific to Ireland and how much was continuous with the broader, international histories of mental disorder, the treatment of the mentally ill by various societies, and the emergence of the profession of psychiatry internationally?

The history of psychiatry in Ireland is located within both the history of Ireland as a country and the broader history of psychiatry internationally. From the international perspective, there are as many versions of the history of psychiatry as there are historians, each presenting varying, often competing narratives about the development of psychiatric practice, psychiatric institutions and psychiatrists. Ireland features in such histories to varying degrees, generally linked with Ireland's high rates of psychiatric institutionalisation during the 1800s and early 1900s.[11] In a dedicated volume, Brennan, in particular, deftly explores Ireland's high committal rates which substantially outpaced those in England, Wales and Scotland, and by the 1950s resulted in Ireland having the highest rate of psychiatric bed availability internationally.[12] Why?

As will become apparent throughout the present book, I am not convinced that core epidemiological rates of mental disorder rose in Ireland during the 1800s or are rising today, or that Ireland has ever had an exceptionally high rate of mental disorder compared to other countries. It is certainly true that there were increased rates of *admission* to psychiatric institutions throughout the 1800s in various countries, including Ireland, England, France and the United States (US),[13] and that Ireland's rates were especially high at their peak, and particularly slow to decline.[14] But Ireland's increase in committals was influenced by such a broad range of social, political, legal, economic and demographic factors that it is difficult to determine definitively whether or not a true increase in the incidence of mental disorder really occurred. On balance, it is my view that it did not, and this view is explored at various points throughout this book (especially Chapter 3).

Reaching firm conclusions on this point is, admittedly, rendered extremely complex by the fact that diagnostic systems in psychiatry are continually changing, principally owing to psychiatry's dependence on symptom based diagnosis rather than biological testing. There is, in addition, considerable ambiguity of the numbers of persons with mental disorder who resided outside asylums during the 1800s and 1900s (Chapter 4), and the picture is further clouded by continual changes in legislation and institutional practices in Ireland and elsewhere. Notwithstanding these interpretative complexities, this book does not present a history of psychiatry based on the idea that rates of mental disorder were especially high or truly increasing in Ireland, but rather emphasises the roles of other factors in driving up admission rates.

The Emergence and Roles of
Psychiatric Professionals

Another version of the history of psychiatry which seeks to explain institutional expansionism in Ireland and elsewhere places strong emphasis on the emergence of the psychiatric profession and its proposed role in generating increased committal rates. This narrative is supported by the fact that the complex, evolving psychiatric classification system used by medical superintendents during the 1800s undoubtedly reflected, at least in part, their growing desire for specialization and recognition,[15] adding the search for professional prestige to the complex of factors affecting practices over this period.[16] Links between doctors' pay and asylum size in the late 1800s further underline the role of the new professionals in the growth of the asylums (Chapter 3).

This book supports this view to the extent that the emergence of clinical professionals, both medical and nursing, throughout the 1800s and 1900s was inevitably a factor in shaping psychiatric practice in Ireland, as it did elsewhere.[17] There is, however, little evidence that the search for professional prestige was the main driver of increased committal rates in Ireland, or that it was unconnected with broader societal concerns driving up admission rates.

In the first instance, the medical and nursing professions were by no means the only or even the main stakeholders in the Irish asylums. In 1951, the town of Ballinasloe in the west of Ireland had a population of 5,596, of whom no fewer than 2,078 were patients in the mental hospital.[18] As a result, virtually everyone in the area was a stakeholder in the hospital in one way or other, and there is growing evidence that communities and families were powerful users and shapers of the system, acting in complex and often subtle ways, according to community and family needs.[19] Most committals were instigated by hard pressed families, rather than governmental agencies or doctors,[20] and it was not uncommon for families to remove relatives from the asylums to work in the summer months and then return them in the winter ('wintering in').[21] The situation was similar in England, where families used asylums strategically and often with considerable thought.[22]

Indeed, for much of the nineteenth century, medical opinion was not even required for committal in Ireland, as many admissions were certified by justices of the peace, clergymen or others, and decided by hospital boards or courts. As a result, doctors were frequently obliged to admit, 'treat' and attempt to discharge people whom they did not believe to be mentally ill in the first instance.[23]

There is also evidence that asylum board members used their privileges to facilitate admissions from their own localities, adding further to non-medical factors shaping admission practices.[24]

Second, while asylums sometimes declined to discharge patients despite family requests, it is also the case that the archives of many asylums are replete with letters from asylum doctors urging families and governmental authorities to cooperate with the discharge of patients, often to little avail. Some families were simply too poor to receive home someone with enduring mental illness or intellectual disability, and argued that that person was better off in the asylum. And when a family could not be found to accept a patient home, the patient might well die in the asylum, confirming asylum doctors' views that confinement after recovery was actively harmful.[25] Some of the stories in this book are moving in the extreme.

Finnane quotes a letter sent to Omagh asylum by a family member in the 1800s, declining the asylum's request that they take their relative, a patient in the asylum, home: the family member outside the asylum explicitly requested that their relative be let die in the asylum, and that the asylum should only contact them again when the relative died.[26] Similar cases are presented by Cox[27] and yet more are outlined in Chapter 2 of the present book, as archival case notes demonstrate medical officers at the Central Criminal Lunatic Asylum pleading with the Inspector of Lunatics to permit the release of three brothers who showed signs of physical rather than mental illness; not only did these brothers not need to be in the asylum, the asylum environment was clearly unhealthy – and possibly fatal – for them.[28]

This issue was again highlighted in the *Irish Times* in June 2016, which recounted the history of a young man admitted to the asylum in Portrane in 1901, who wrote to his father in 1912 noting that the doctors were keen he be discharged, but that his father refused to accept him home.[29] The young man begged his father to take him home, as the doctors recommended, but his father did not or could not yield, and suggested instead that his son should remain in the mental hospital indefinitely. That is precisely what occurred: this unfortunate patient died in the hospital in 1949 and was buried in a little wooden coffin, with no relatives at his funeral. There are two key issues here: the family declining to accept the patient home, and the mental hospital, after robustly trying to send him home, eventually acquiescing with the family's decision. The doctors were progressive to the extent that they recommended and pressed for discharge, but this was not yet enough: the asylum framework still (in 1912) facilitated long term institutionalisation and, too often, that became the default position. Once again, psychiatry acquiesced to the roles pressed upon it by others (families, judges, the police, and the state in various forms), despite highly progressive voices within psychiatry who sought and worked for change but did not always achieve enough.

There has always been a strong, historiographically neglected progressive tradition within Irish psychiatry, with doctors such as Dr Conolly Norman (1853–1908) at the Richmond Asylum, Dublin in the late 1800s and early 1900s strongly urging alternatives to inpatient care.[30] Later analogous figures include Dr Robert McCarthy,[31] Dr Dermot Walsh and Professor Ivor Browne, among others.[32] The reasons why Norman, for example, did not succeed in his plans for care outside the asylum walls lay not within the medical profession, but within government, which repeatedly frustrated doctors' efforts to deinstitutionalise, in response to powerful, non-medical vested interests in the asylums. The stigma of mental illness was also relevant: an apparent link between mental illness and danger was indelibly underlined by the Dangerous Lunatic Act 1838 and as long as the asylum stood behind large, grey walls at the edge of the local town, the public felt secure.

Finally, no matter how many doctors, public representatives and other reformers sought to dismantle Ireland's asylum system, their task was rendered even more difficult by the fact that the asylums also functioned as a vast, unwieldy social welfare system for patients and possibly some staff. In the absence of more extensive, systematic provision for the destitute or working poor, asylums were always going to be full: in 1907, 30 per cent of admissions to the Richmond Asylum came directly from workhouses.[33] Exactly a century later, in 2007, the psychiatric service in the Mater Misericordiae University Hospital, just up the road from Grangegorman, reported that 35 per cent of emergency psychiatry assessments were of homeless persons: *plus ça change, plus c'est la même chose*.[34]

As a result of these factors, the Irish asylums appeared, for all intents and purposes, immovable, immutable and apparently inevitable features of Irish life for almost 150 years, from the mid-1850s onwards. The only events that produced slight, temporary declines in admission rates were the two world wars, and, once the wars ended, admission rates resumed their seemingly inexorable upward trajectory.[35] Much, although by no means all, of this book is concerned with elucidating why this was so.

The Asylums: Social or Medical Creations?

The history presented in this book leads to the conclusion that the Irish asylum system was a social creation as much as it was a medical one, if not more so. The psychiatric profession was certainly complicit to the extent that asylum doctors permitted and even facilitated the growth of the asylums through their (reluctant) acquiescence to the questionable roles pressed upon them by broader society, and their recurring therapeutic enthusiasms for the broad range of treatments discussed throughout this book, ranging from the moral management of the 1800s to the pharmaceutical innovations of the late 1900s.

Throughout the 1880s and 1900s, determined efforts at reform and moves away from large asylums were continually frustrated by a society with an apparently insatiable hunger for institutionalisation. From the perspective of the early twenty-first century, it is a matter of regret that even greater objections to this state of affairs were not raised by more asylum doctors, attendants or nurses, as legislation such as the Dangerous Lunatic Act 1838 visibly drove up admission rates and the poor conditions within asylums became ever more indefensible. While doctors commonly did indeed object, both publicly and strongly, this book argues that their objections were insufficiently strong and often to no avail.

Ultimately, the end of the institutions, when it finally commenced in the 1960s, was attributable only in part to advances in clinical psychiatry (e.g. antipsychotic medication) and was more substantively shaped by broader changes in Irish society, such as the opening up of Ireland to greater outside sociopolitical influences in the 1960s and 1970s, an increasingly free press, the growth of the language of human rights across Europe, and Ireland's accession to the European

Economic Community (EEC; later European Union (EU)) in 1973. All of these themes are explored throughout this book.

As ever, psychiatry in Ireland came to reflect these broader changes in society as they occurred, as well as advances in psychiatric care in other countries, and so the asylums finally began to empty in earnest in the 1960s. And, as usual, Irish psychiatry was not short of reform-minded doctors enthusiastic for change, as a fresh generation of psychiatrists and other mental health professionals gave shape to a new, post-institutional psychiatry in Ireland. While the pace of reform was slow, the changes were definite and duly reflected in the 1966 *Report of the Commission of Inquiry on Mental Illness*[36] and all subsequent governmental mental health policies (which have, essentially, been re-statements of the 1966 report).[37]

All of these events are explored in some detail throughout this book. Inevitably, much of the book is devoted to the emergence and ultimate demise of the Irish asylum system owing to both its magnitude and its remarkable, absorbing character. Attention is also given, however, to Irish psychiatry prior to the asylums of the 1800s, and Irish psychiatry since the demise of the large hospitals in the late 1900s, as well as current and future trends.

The precise roles of psychiatry and psychiatrists in all of this are interesting, engaging and occasionally alarming. Rather than psychiatry shaping its own history as a distinct discipline within medicine, it often seems as if psychiatry in Ireland was, for the most part, shaped by broader social and historical trends, as opposed to developing as an autonomous, readily identifiable entity on its own terms. As a result, it is difficult, although by no means impossible, to trace out a clear identity for Irish psychiatry over past centuries.

Notwithstanding these challenges, I hope that the historical events explored throughout the book set out the parameters for establishing such an identity, and that the analyses presented provide perspectives on both how psychiatry has evolved in Ireland and how the path to today's psychiatry is likely to influence its future.

Gaps in the Story

While a growing quantity of research has focused on various aspects of the history of psychiatry in Ireland, substantial lacunae remain.[38] Walsh, in his positive review of Reynolds's invaluable book, *Grangegorman: Psychiatric Care in Dublin since 1815*, noted that Reynolds's 'worthwhile' and 'meticulous contribution' did not 'pretend to be a scholarly analytical academic work analysing the various forces shaping the intellectual and emotional attitudes to lunacy policy and its administration in Ireland in the 19th and 20th centuries'.[39] Clearly, further work, likely by a range of researchers, was needed to build on the accounts of Reynolds and others and provide a clearer picture of the history of psychiatry in Ireland.

Looking more broadly, there are, in fact, very many gaps in the historiography of Irish psychiatry. One of the key features of the literature to date is that it demonstrates a remarkably strong focus on the history of *institutions*, understandably echoing the emphasis that government traditionally placed on asylums as a key element in resolving the social problems presented by people with apparent mental disorder or intellectual disability. There has been particular engagement with the histories of earlier, larger institutions such as St Brendan's Hospital, Dublin;[40] St Patrick's Hospital, Dublin;[41] St Vincent's Hospital, Fairview;[42] St Davnet's Hospital, Monaghan;[43] Our Lady's Hospital, Cork;[44] St. Mary's Hospital, Castlebar;[45] Holywell Hospital, Belfast;[46] St Fintan's Hospital, Portlaoise;[47] St Luke's Hospital, Clonmel;[48] and Bloomfield Hospital, Dublin,[49] among others. There is also a growing literature relating to the Central Criminal Lunatic Asylum (later Central Mental Hospital [CMH]) in Dundrum, Dublin.[50]

In addition to this focus on institutions, the historiography of Irish psychiatry also shows a strong focus on the evolution of mental health *legislation*. This, again, is entirely understandable and largely attributable to both the existence of laws permitting criminal and civil detention on the grounds of mental disorder,[51] and the fact that the development of Ireland's psychiatric institutions throughout the 1800s and 1900s[52] was rooted in endless, obsessional revisions of legislation, including committal laws.[53]

There are, however, other stories to be told and other perspectives to be explored, many of which are challenging to uncover. St Patrick's Hospital in Dublin, for example, was founded following the benevolent bequest of Jonathan Swift (1667–1745), as a private, charitable institution aiming to provide high quality care to a finite number of the afflicted, without the broader, population level responsibilities of government run institutions.[54] Malcolm, in her excellent, detailed history of St Patrick's, however, found that it was noticeably difficult to reconstruct the living conditions of the patients there.[55] There was a wealth of information regarding details of the building, the provision of food and so forth, but, from a clinical and historical perspective, the patients themselves proved remarkably elusive.[56]

This elusiveness may reflect a lack of governmental interest in individual patients and an exuberance of interest in psychiatric hospitals *as institutions*. Dr William J. Coyne, chief psychiatrist and resident governor at the CMH in Dundrum, who resided at the hospital from 1949 to 1965, was, every year, in the words of his grandson, Dr Maurice Guéret, 'hauled before politicians on the public accounts committee to explain matters like failures of the carrot crop on the hospital farm, low prices from sales of hospital sheep, victualling rations for staff and the late delivery of spring seeds. Never once was he asked a single question about his patients'.[57]

As a result of these factors, the historiography of psychiatry in Ireland, as elsewhere, focuses largely on the histories of institutions and legislation, and the patients themselves remain ephemeral, elusive and largely unknown. Despite their vast numbers, patients' voices are astonishingly distant and frequently inaudible to today's historians. How can this be remedied?

Searching for Patients' Voices

Recent decades have seen some progress towards seeking out the patients' voices in the history of Irish psychiatry, commonly through analysis of official clinical records in certain establishments, including St Brigid's Hospital, Ballinasloe,[58] the Central Criminal Lunatic Asylum,[59] St Brendan's Hospital,[60] and Enniscorthy Lunatic Asylum, County Wexford,[61] among others. These are, however, analyses of *official* medical records, with all of their associated narrative and interpretative ambiguities.

One of the key merits of historical research based on clinical records is that such records are uniquely useful for identifying shifts in clinical practice over time and conveying the complexity of hospital life.[62] Compared to approaches framed by institutional or legislative perspectives, which are so common in the historiography of Irish psychiatry, approaches based on clinical notes move somewhat towards Porter's conceptualisation of 'medical history from below',[63] although they still rely on official records written by medical superintendents and others, rather than direct patient accounts, such as patients' own correspondence or memoirs.[64] Official medical records can be manipulated, consciously and unconsciously, by the individuals writing the records, to demonstrate, for example, that staff always behaved in a fashion appropriate to the doctor-patient relationship (even if they did not).[65] But such accounts do, at least, seek to tell that patient's story at the individual level, as it was experienced.

Given these methodological issues, it is apparent that constructing an 'authentic' account of patient experience is a complex, challenging and possibly impossible task.[66] Be that as it may, the case record still reflects both the patient's behaviour and the interpretation of such behaviour by hospital authorities and, as such, presents a unique and crucial account of the patient's experience – an account which generally played an important role in determining how the patient was treated in and by the institution. Archival case records are used to present patient histories throughout this book (e.g. the cases of three brothers committed to the Central Criminal Lunatic Asylum in the 1890s in Chapter 2, and that of Mary in Chapter 3).

Other limitations with approaches based on archival case notes include unclearness about how systematic medical notetaking was in the nineteenth century; potentially inconsistent use of medical terms; and inclusion of clinical descriptions which may be challenging or impossible to interpret today.[67] These issues, however, present both challenges and opportunities. In relation to individuals with apparent intellectual disability, for example, an enquirer with experience of both historical and clinical work can at least attempt to move beyond the diagnostic labels used loosely throughout historical case records and focus on more objective descriptions of clinical symptoms (many of which are readily recognisable today), in order to provide a *clinical* analysis of the extent to which such patients in nineteenth- and early twentieth-century Ireland were truly intellectually disabled by today's standards.[68]

Therefore, while extreme caution must be exercised when associating archival clinical descriptions with contemporary diagnoses ('presentism'),[69] this approach can nonetheless prove fruitful if archival accounts of patients' experiences can meet the careful 'clinical gaze',[70] with an emphasis on descriptive pathology rather than loosely applied diagnoses, and a focus on the clinical rather than institutional or legislative dimensions of patients' histories. The case study of Michael in Chapter 4 presents an example of this approach from the 1890s.

Patients' Symptoms, Letters and Belongings

Even with careful interpretation and analysis, however, official clinical records are still at least one step removed from the voices and thoughts of patients themselves. In order to move closer to the patient's voice, recent international attention has focused on other materials such as patients' letters, journals and first-person accounts of incarceration and treatment.[71] Beveridge, for example, studied letters written by patients admitted to the Royal Edinburgh Asylum and found evidence of commonality between symptoms in the letters and symptoms commonly seen in clinical practice today.[72] Similarly, Smith studied letters from families and some patients at Gloucester Asylum between 1827 and 1843.[73] While some admissions and discharges were undoubtedly problematic, there was also evidence of dialogue between asylum staff, families and patients, and by no means were all interactions conflictual, with certain patients very grateful for their care. There have also been studies of correspondence related to the York Retreat in England[74] and the colonial asylums of New Zealand and Australia.[75]

Not all discharged patients described positive experiences, of course, and patient accounts of treatment in England and the US during the 1800s and 1900s were often highly critical.[76] In Ireland, the past few decades have seen interesting initiatives seeking out patients' voices in different ways, including through the reminiscences that accompanied the closure of St Senan's Hospital in Enniscorthy.[77] Other patient voices from recent decades were presented by Prior[78] and McClelland,[79] with the latter providing a fascinating account of *Speedwell* magazine, and its 'insider view' of Holywell Psychiatric Hospital, Antrim, from 1959 to 1973. Another mental hospital magazine, *The Corridor Echo*, of St Mary's Hospital, Castlebar, provides further insights from 1966 onwards.[80]

Notwithstanding these records, accounts and publications, however, there remains a real paucity of detailed patients' accounts of psychiatric admission and treatment in Ireland in the 1800s and early 1900s. Despite the general dearth of such literature in Ireland, this book includes, where possible, patients' voices, with particular consideration of patient accounts of treatment in Irish psychiatric hospitals, such as those provided by the Reverend Clarence Duffy (1944)[81] and Hanna Greally (1971)[82] (Chapter 6).

In the absence of a plentiful supply of such accounts, however, it is worth speculating if there are other routes to the patient's voice from past decades and centuries that merit exploration. What about delusions or hallucinations, which are often recorded in some detail in archival case notes? Delusions are convictions which are strongly held despite evidence to the contrary and hallucinations are perceptions without appropriate external stimuli (e.g. hearing voices).[83] Can such phenomena be gainfully understood or decoded by the historian or clinician today, up to two centuries after they were recorded?

In other words, even though delusions and hallucinations are, in most conventional senses, 'false', might they also reflect truths, possibly unspeakable truths, in disguised or metaphorical form? Certainly, in contemporary clinical practice, both delusions and hallucinations are rarely random in their content and are commonly, demonstrably shaped by context. This is surely equally true when they are sourced from archival case notes.

Finnane, for example, recounts the case of a young woman in the Richmond Asylum in the early 1890s, who was brought up as an orphan in the workhouse but then went to prison and was later admitted to the asylum.[84] According to the asylum case book, she was frightened when she believed she saw three nuns on a ladder beating their own foreheads with stones, and when distressed she believed herself to be dead. Might not this young woman have had good reason to fear nuns, or at least view them as difficult to understand and somewhat strange? And, following a difficult childhood, imprisonment and, now, incarceration in an asylum, was she entirely incorrect to consider herself, in a certain sense, 'dead'?

At the Central Criminal Lunatic Asylum in 1892, a 34-year-old servant from Dublin was admitted after being charged with the murder of her 8-month-old child. Her previous five children had all died young.[85] The asylum's case book records that, 'on the morning of the crime, she took the child in her arms and left the house. She wandered off some distance from home, did not know where she was or what she was doing. She imagined that she was followed by a large crowd of soldiers and people'. A distressed young mother in late nineteenth-century Ireland, mourning the loss of her five children, feels persecuted and alone? True, there were no soldiers following her that morning, but surely there is still a very compelling truth in her delusions of persecution? Her feelings of being lost? Her hopelessness?

The ultimate truth about what this or other patients thought about their committal and treatment may lie hidden somewhere in these evolving delusions and hallucinations, or in the patients' own stories (wherever they may be), or even in the physical objects and personal effects that patients left behind when they died or finally left Ireland's asylums behind them.[86] Some of these objects and possessions are explored with particular power and poignancy in 'Personal Effects: A History of Possession' by Irish artist Alan Counihan, focusing on patients' personal effects found in the attic of a disused hospital building at Grangegorman Mental Hospital in Dublin (later St Brendan's).[87] A profound sense of tragedy is palpable in many of these found objects and images, as is a sense of loss and, more often than one might expect, a real sense of survival, hope and life.

For the historian, the methodological challenges inherent in hearing patients' voices from the asylums of the past are all opportunities, complicated to navigate but by no means impervious to exploration, and certainly not impossible to understand. As a result, while the voices of patients from the 1800s and early 1900s might presently remain largely unknown, they are certainly not unknowable. Maybe we just need to listen harder and, perhaps, listen better. This book sets out to do so, insofar as possible, with particular focus on case histories and various other accounts and analyses of patients' experiences inside and outside the asylums.

The Title, Approach and Structure of this Book

This book is titled 'Hearing Voices: The History of Psychiatry in Ireland'. There are three reasons for this choice of title. First, 'hearing voices' (auditory hallucination) is one of the classic symptoms traditionally associated with mental disorder, so it inevitably features in any history of psychiatry. Second, as I've just discussed, this book is an attempt to hear voices that have not often been heard: not only the voices of patients in the asylums, but also those of clinical staff[88] who lived their lives behind asylum walls, in circumstances that differed significantly, although by no means completely, from those of their patients.

Third, evolving attitudes towards the experience of 'hearing voices' reflect important, iconic changes in psychiatry in recent decades, which I am very keen to highlight. In Chapter 8, I explore the international 'hearing voices' movement, which is based on an exceptionally powerful reinterpretation of the experience of hearing voices which used to be routinely associated with major mental disorder but is now subject to more nuanced interpretations, formulated chiefly by those having such experiences themselves (rather than mental health professionals).[89] This is an important and arguably iconic shift in the societal approach to such symptoms, and this is an important element of the story that I seek to tell in this book.

From a methodological perspective, there are many possible approaches to my task and to the history of medicine in general, ranging from exclusively medical perspectives, charting the evolution of treatments over time, to exclusively sociological approaches, which prioritise the social and political contexts in which medicine and healthcare develop and are practiced. Like most historical texts, this book lies somewhere between these extremes.

From a thematic perspective, Burnham identified five key 'dramas' in the history of medicine, relating to the histories of (a) the healer; (b) the sick person; (c) various diseases; (d) discovery and communication of knowledge; and (e) interactions between medicine and health on the one hand, and society on the other.[90] All of these 'dramas' are reflected in a variety of ways throughout this book, with particular emphasis on interactions between psychiatry and society, owing to the intrinsically societal basis of the Irish asylums of the 1800s and 1900s, and the social roles commonly foisted upon (and all too often accepted by) psychiatry, no matter how unsuitable those roles are. This regrettable feature of the history of psychiatry is a recurring theme in my story.

Chapter 1 of the book commences by exploring the 'birth of psychiatry in Ireland' and covers the Middle Ages and early modern era, *Gleann na nGealt* and Mad Sweeney (in the twelfth century), and Brehon Law (up to the seventeenth century). The emergence of new forms of institutional care is explored, as are the lives and work of Sir William Fownes and Jonathan Swift, especially in the context of St Patrick's Hospital, Dublin (1746). Burnham's 'drama' of the healer features strongly in the form of Dr William Saunders Hallaran and the succession of therapeutic enthusiasms for new treatments that emerged in the late 1700s and early 1800s in Ireland, as was also the case elsewhere.

Chapter 2 moves on to examine the growth of the asylums in nineteenth-century Ireland, commencing with the Richmond Asylum (1814) and examining the work of pivotal figures such as Dr Alexander Jackson, Robert Peel (Chief Secretary, 1812–17) and Dr John Mollan at the Richmond. Other notable developments included the Select Committee on the Lunatic Poor in Ireland (1817), the Dangerous Lunatic Act 1838, the Private Lunatic Asylums (Ireland) Act 1842, the 1843 report on the 'State of the Lunatic Poor in Ireland', the 1851 census and the 1858 Commission of Inquiry on the State of Lunatic Asylums in Ireland. The 'drama' of the patient is explored through the use of archival case records and case studies of restraint, 'neglect and cruelty', as well as *folie à plusieurs*, an unusual psychiatric syndrome which, in these cases, was associated with the killing of family members. This chapter also examines treatments for mental disorder, life and death in the institutions, and the experiences of women in nineteenth-century asylums.

Chapter 3 moves explicitly to the 'drama' of the interactions between psychiatry and society, looking at the effects, if any, of the Great Irish Famine (1845–52) on admission rates, workhouses, treatment of the intellectually disabled, and widespread alarm about the alleged 'increase of insanity in Ireland' during the late 1800s and early 1900s. This chapter also reflects on why the Irish asylums grew so large; outlines (in detail) psychiatric diagnoses from the archives of Carlow Lunatic Asylum in the late 1800s; explores the histories of Bloomfield (1812) and Hampstead Hospitals (1825); and examines Burnham's 'drama' of the healer by looking at the contributions of Dr Thomas Drapes, Dr Conolly Norman and Dr Eleonora Fleury, a remarkable republican doctor and first woman member of the Medico-Psychological Association (MPA, 1894).

Chapter 3 also presents the case of Mary, a 40-year-old 'housekeeper' with seven children who was charged with the manslaughter of her 4-year-old child in the mid-1890s. Mary was 'acquitted on the grounds of insanity' and detained at the Central Criminal Lunatic Asylum (later Central Mental Hospital, Dundrum) 'at Her Majesty's Pleasure' (i.e. indefinitely). Mary's admission diagnosis was 'chronic melancholia', and examination of her archival case records in this chapter questions the nature of this diagnosis and uses Mary's story to illustrate diagnostic challenges in the late 1800s, along with difficulties separating mental disorder from social and economic problems, especially among women, during this difficult period in Irish psychiatric history.

Chapter 4 explores 'early twentieth-century psychiatry', setting the scene with consideration of the remarkably insightful (but sadly ignored) *Reports of the Committee Appointed by the Lord Lieutenant of Ireland on Lunacy Administration* (1891).[91] Chapter 4 then outlines the fate of the mentally ill outside the asylums in the early 1900s, the Conference of the Irish Asylum Committees (1903) and key issues at the Richmond District Asylum (Grangegorman) in 1907. In terms of the links between psychiatry and broader sociohistorical events, this chapter outlines the effects of the 1916 Easter Rising on Dublin's asylums; the story of the Richmond War Hospital (1916–19); the remarkable life and career of Dr Ada English, patriot and psychiatrist in Ballinasloe; and the broader relevance of nationalist sentiment throughout the asylum system during Ireland's revolutionary years.

Again, Burnham's 'drama' of the sick person is explored throughout this material, especially through the case study of Michael, a 35-year-old man committed to the Central Criminal Lunatic Asylum in the 1890s, charged with 'assault'; declared 'insane on arraignment'; and diagnosed as a 'congenital imbecile'. Michael's story, based on archival clinical records, demonstrates many important features of Irish asylum life in the late 1800s and early 1900s, especially as they relate to persons with apparent intellectual disability. The experiences of the intellectually disabled feature repeatedly (and disturbingly) throughout the story told in this book.

Chapter 5 moves on to examine efforts at reform of Ireland's mental health services in the early 1900s, looking at multiple sources of evidence including media articles, developments relating to the intellectually disabled, and accounts of industrial unrest (e.g. the Monaghan Asylum Soviet, 1919). Burnham's 'drama' of the healer is explored through the work of Professor John Dunne in Grangegorman and, in relation to occupational therapy, Drs Eamonn O'Sullivan in Killarney and Ada English in Ballinasloe. This chapter also explores therapeutic enthusiasms for some of the most controversial treatments in the history of psychiatry (psychotherapy, malarial treatment, insulin coma, convulsive therapy, lobotomy); the reforming efforts of the Mental Treatment Act 1945 and the Commission of Inquiry on Mental Illness (1966); and, in the independent sector, the development of St Patrick's Hospital, Dublin during the twentieth century.

Chapter 6 documents the 'decline of the institutions' in the late 1900s and explores various factors that contributed to this, including the advent of effective antipsychotic medication, and changing public and press perceptions of psychiatry. The patient's voice is heard through first-person accounts of psychiatric hospitalisation provided by the Reverend Clarence Duffy (1944) and Hanna Greally (1971).

This chapter also examines Irish psychiatry in relation to homosexuality, explores the remarkably persistent idea that mental illness was more common in certain parts of Ireland than elsewhere, and looks at the figures who led various reforms within Ireland's mental health services, including, but by no means limited to, Dr Dermot Walsh, Professor Ivor Browne, Dr Des McGrath, Professor Thomas Lynch, Professor Thomas Fahy, Dr Robert McCarthy, Professor Robert Daly, Dr Brian O'Shea, Professor John P. (Seán) Malone, Professor Noel Walsh, Professor Marcus Webb and Professor Eadbhard O'Callaghan. These figures speak not only to Burnham's 'drama' of the healer, but also the emphasis Burnham places on the discovery and communication of knowledge as a key factor in the history of medicine, as well as interactions between psychiatry and broader society.

Attention is also devoted in Chapter 6 to the emergence of military psychiatry in Ireland, the ill-fated Health (Mental Services) Act 1981, the opening of new acute psychiatric units in general hospitals, issues relating to mental health nursing, the 1984 policy, *Planning for the Future*, and the outstanding contribution of Professor Anthony Clare to psychiatry in Ireland and beyond. Chapter 6 incorporates considerations of the emergent emphasis on human rights in mental health in Ireland and the role of international human rights movements in creating a context for changes in policy, law and social perceptions of mental illness and psychiatry.

Chapter 7 explores the recent history of psychiatry in Ireland in the early twenty-first century, looking at the Mental Health Act 2001; the 2006 policy, *A Vision for Change*; the development of child and adolescent psychiatry; the *Irish Journal of Psychiatry* (1982), the *Irish Journal of Psychological Medicine* (1982) and other professional journals in Irish psychiatry; the emergence of the College of Psychiatrists of Ireland (2009); and the 2015 review of the Mental Health Act 2001. Important service developments are explored, including the ongoing move to community care, the evolution of the National Forensic Mental Health Service and mental health services for the deaf.

The final chapter, Chapter 8, focuses on the future of psychiatry in Ireland in light of the historical analyses presented in earlier chapters, as well as recent data. This concluding section focuses particularly on interactions between psychiatry and society; societal 'structural violence' and social exclusion of the mentally ill; postpsychiatry and other reformist movements; suicide; ongoing issues relating to human rights; and likely future developments in clinical, academic and historical psychiatry. The book concludes with a consideration of the overall future of psychiatry in Ireland, based on events and trends over past centuries and informed by the state of psychiatry in early twenty-first century Ireland.

Throughout the book, extensive details of primary and secondary sources are provided for readers who seek further information on any topic. I have devoted particular attention to citing and quoting primary material and cross referencing to the secondary literature, with an especially strong emphasis on publications relating directly to psychiatry in Ireland. It is hoped that this extensive quotation, citation and referencing will assist future researchers.

For the most part, practicing psychiatrists are not discussed in depth, although some are mentioned. For recently retired or recently deceased psychiatrists who are discussed (especially in

Chapter 6), it is too soon to present a historically informed, critical appraisal of their contributions. As a result, my accounts of recent figures should not be read as critical, historical analyses of their lives and work, which would be premature at this short remove, but as summaries of their careers and achievements (with some brief comments). Future historians will be better placed to comment critically on the enduring effects of their work, and hopefully the brief accounts presented here will assist in informing such assessments.

Finally, throughout this book, original language and terminology from the past and from various archives and reports have been maintained, except where explicitly indicated otherwise. This represents an attempt to optimise fidelity to historical sources and does not represent an endorsement of the broader use of such terminology in contemporary settings.

1

𝕏

THE BIRTH OF PSYCHIATRY IN IRELAND

It is not considered desirable in certain circumstances to have a flat-footed man dealt with as lame, but in other circumstances it is considered desirable and it is done. In like manner, in certain circumstances, it is not considered desirable to have a particular kind or degree of mental unsoundness dealt with as lunacy, but in different circumstances this is considered desirable, and it is done.

It is thus plain that the number of registered lunatics in a country is not a fixed figure, which cannot be increased or diminished. On the contrary, it is a figure which can be made to change greatly through the operation of many and varying causes; and it is obvious that this should not be forgotten by those who are deciding what ought to be the relations and duties of the State to the insane.

Committee on Lunacy Administration (Ireland),
*Second Report of the Committee Appointed by the
Lord Lieutenant of Ireland on Lunacy
Administration (Ireland)* (1891)[1]

The history of psychiatry is interesting, important and complicated to unravel.[2] In Ireland, this history commences with the prehistory of psychiatry in the Middle Ages and early modern era, and continues with explorations of *Gleann na nGealt* (Glenn of the Lunatics) and Mad Sweeney (in the twelfth century), and Brehon Law (up to the seventeenth century). The emergence of new forms of institutional care is explored, as are the lives and works of Sir William Fownes and Jonathan Swift, both of whom were connected with the establishment of St Patrick's Hospital, Dublin, in 1746. Burnham's 'drama' of the healer[3] features strongly in the form of Dr William Saunders Hallaran and the succession of enthusiasms for new treatments that emerged in Ireland (and elsewhere) in the late 1700s and early 1800s. This is how it all began.

The Middle Ages and Early Modern Era

Early understandings of mental illness in Ireland, as in other countries, focused on supernatural and religious explanations for the unusual beliefs and behaviour displayed by persons who would later be regarded as mentally ill.[4] In pre-Christian Ireland, it was believed that druidic priests, acting for pagan deities, could induce madness by throwing a 'madman's wisp' (a ball of grass or straw) in a person's face.[5] Fullon, a druid of Leinster around 600 BC, was reputedly the first to cast such a spell, initially making incantations on the wisp of straw and then throwing it at his victim.[6] A similar fate befell Comgan, son of Maelochtair, King of the Decies in Munster in the seventh century, when a young woman he spurned persuaded a druid to throw a magic wisp on him, leading to skin ulceration, baldness and madness, interspersed with periods of lucidity during which the unfortunate but still articulate Comgan robustly declaimed poetry and prophecies.[7]

The moon was commonly linked with madness in early Ireland and there was a belief that a seaside rock in Dunany, County Louth, known as *Cathaoir Ana* (Madman's Chair), attracted the mentally ill, who could be cured by sitting on it three times.[8] Conversely, those who were not mentally ill and sat on it might become mad. According to another account, if a mad person sat on the rock during a period of lucidity, that lucidity would be maintained because the mental state of the person at the time he or she sat on the rock would be so fixed for life. Early Irish literature and folklore are full of other references to madness and various unusual psychological states. Stories such as the Cattle Raid of Cooley (*Táin Bó Cúalnge*), the central epic of the Ulster cycle, as well as many other strands of Irish folklore, present vivid descriptions of altered states of mind and diverse kinds of madness.[9]

The arrival of Christianity saw the emergence of beliefs that insanity was attributable to possession by the devil or punishment by God, and the phrase *duine le Dia* (person of God) came into common use for persons with intellectual disability. One story claims that St Mochuda cured a man of madness (owing to demonic possession) by interceding with God.[10] Another tells how a Norman archer became mad after entering the sacred area surrounding a perpetually burning fire lit by St Brigid in Kildare.[11] This man blew on the fire and became insane, blowing into people's mouths and running from house to house blowing on every fire he could find. He was seized by his comrades and, at his request, brought to water where, thirsty from all the blowing, he drank so much that he burst and died on the spot. Another man tried to enter the circle around St Brigid's fire and put one of his legs across the hedge, but was dragged back by his comrades, only to find his leg and foot had withered away; he was lame and intellectually disabled for the rest of his life.

Early Irish law outlined a series of rights for persons of unsound mind and the intellectually disabled, specifying an obligation for families to look after the insane, the elderly and those with physical disabilities.[12] Law texts from the seventh and ninth centuries distinguished between a person who was deranged (*mer*), a person who was violently insane (*dásachtach*) and a person with intellectual disability (*drúth*).[13] There was a clear distinction drawn between madness and intoxication due to alcohol.[14] A person with epilepsy *(talmaidech)* was regarded as possessing legal competence once he or she was of sound mind; it was, however, imperative that he or she was minded in order to prevent injury to self or others during seizures.

Exploitation of the insane was forbidden; a contract with a person of unsound mind was invalid; anyone inciting a *drúth* to commit a crime had to pay the fine himself; and there were specific provisions dealing with land owned by the insane.[15] There were also provisions dealing with offences committed by persons of unsound mind or a *drúth*, and provisions governing issues related to childbirth and responsibility for offspring of the mentally ill. Overall, the main concern of these laws was to protect the mentally ill and intellectually disabled from exploitation and ensure that any children were looked after appropriately.

For much of this period, there was a widespread belief that mental illness conferred lightness of body such that affected persons could move from one spot to the next at high speed by merely touching the ground here and there; i.e. essentially flying.[16] This was consistent with the belief that madness induced by battle resulted in warriors becoming as light as air and simply floating away from the battlefield, as reportedly occurred to Bolcáin, King of France, at the battle of Ventry when he beheld the ferocious Oscar, son of Oisín, rushing towards him.[17]

This interesting belief persisted up to the thirteenth century and contributed to the mythic figure of Mad Sweeney (*Suibhne Geilt*), whose remarkable tale is told in *Buile Suibhne*, an epic story written in the twelfth century but with origins in the ninth century or earlier. The story of Sweeney is a vivid one, magically retold by Seamus Heaney (1939–2013)[18] and brilliantly reimagined in comic form by Flann O'Brien (1911–1966).[19] Sweeney, a chieftain, was cursed by Ronan the Fair, abbot of Drumiskin, and condemned to a life of madness, flying and wandering through the world. After wandering for many years, the curse was tragically fulfilled when he was killed with a spear.

Maddened by the slaughter at the battle of Moyrath in 637 AD, Sweeney (*Suibhne*) flew into the air from the battlefield[20] and in this altered state decided to turn away from mankind and live with the birds and animals in the wilderness.[21] For many years he wandered from tree to tree (commonly the yew tree), having strange, disturbing visions. In the end, he joined a community linked with St Moling but was speared to death by a swineherd who falsely accused him of adultery with his kindly, charitable wife.

Sweeney's story is a powerful one, full of tragedy and loss, and for many centuries it underlined the idea of the mentally ill person as a wandering loner, misunderstood, persecuted and cast out. This was a feature of the history and mythology of mental illness in many cultures, not just Ireland.[22] In all of its torment, tragedy and isolation, Sweeney's story reflected not only contemporary views of the dislocation and loneliness of madness, but also tensions between pre-Christian and Christian Ireland, demonstrated vividly in Sweeney's unresolved disturbance and dislocation.

There were various other local stories and traditions concerning mental illness and intellectual disability. In Kerry, a valley became known as *Gleann na nGealt*, Glenn of the Lunatics, as it was believed that all the mentally ill would, like Bolcáin and Sweeney, come to live there eventually, if left to their own devices.[23] It was thought they would drink the water and eat watercress from the well, *Tobar na nGealt*, which were said to have cured the madness of Gall, king of Ulster, as well as that of Bolcáin. Those who lost their minds owing to being jilted in love could also seek solace in *Gleann na nGealt*. There is a nearby stone with a hollow in its centre, known at the Mad Stone, and a river crossing known as Fool's Crossing.

The valley is still a site of local and tourist interest, as well as the subject of research, most notably in relation to the lithium content of its water.[24] This is of interest not only because lithium is now used in the treatment of bipolar affective disorder (manic depression), but also because international studies have suggested that higher concentrations of lithium in drinking water might be associated with lower rates of suicide at population level.[25]

Biochemical analysis performed for the purpose of this book, however, showed that the lithium content of water from *Tobar na nGealt* is less than 5 micrograms of lithium per litre of water.[26] The same result was obtained for water from a stream near the village of Inch (on the other side of the Dingle peninsula, also in County Kerry); water from Our Lady's Holy Well at Dromore near Kenmare, County Kerry; and Dublin tap (drinking) water. These concentrations of lithium are significantly lower than the concentrations apparently associated with lower rates of suicide in Austria[27] and Japan.[28]

The concentration of lithium in the water in *Tobar na nGealt* is also too low to have any detectable therapeutic benefits at the individual level. Even if the water had a concentration more than 200 times greater than it has (i.e. if it had a concentration of 1 milligram of lithium per litre), and a person drank two litres per day, that would still correspond to a daily dose of just 13.8 milligrams of lithium carbonate,[29] which is less than two per cent of the usual therapeutic dose for bipolar affective disorder (approximately 900–1,200 milligrams per day for an adult).

Biochemical analysis is, however, neither the only nor the best way to examine the therapeutic value of *Tobar na nGealt* or other folk cures for mental illness, which find their true value as embedded elements of local traditions and beliefs, and reflect subtle, powerful cultural interpretations of mental illness and human suffering. In Inishowen, Donegal, a well with similar properties was known as *Srubh Brain* and there was another well at *Port an Doras*, near Inishowen Head.[30] Cures were also reported at *Cloc na Madaidh* near Malin Head and the sixth-century oratory of St Barry in County Roscommon, where three nights spent in the ruins followed by mass on Sunday were reputed to alleviate madness.[31]

From a social perspective, the image of the wandering lunatic reflected in the traditions of Sweeney and *Gleann na nGealt* was a largely accurate one (except for the flying). Although chieftains were said to protect the mentally ill of their kin group, society was generally unwelcoming and unsympathetic.[32] Some accommodation was provided for the mentally ill in Irish monasteries during this period, but this was erratic, limited in scope, and did not endure. One such monastic hospital was the relatively large Hospital of St John without the New Gate of Dublin, founded by Ailred the Palmer in the twelfth century.[33] The Hospital of St Stephen (where Mercer's Hospital later stood) may also have housed the mentally ill, although it is unclear to what extent such establishments catered for the mentally ill and intellectually disabled as opposed to those with medical or surgical needs, and the poor.

Overall, since Brehon law focused on protection from abuse rather than neglect, and provision in monastic hospitals was patchy at best, the mentally ill and intellectually disabled in the Middle Ages and Early Modern Ireland tended to live harsh, difficult, brief lives characterised by vagrancy, illness, imprisonment and neglect, especially in times of hardship and famine.[34] The dissolution of the monasteries changed this landscape further, resulting in even less accommodation and greater neglect. Interestingly, though, while dedicated provision for the mentally ill was very limited, there is no compelling evidence of widespread witch-hunts against the mentally ill in Ireland, as were reported in other countries during this period.[35]

Nonetheless, as the 1600s drew to a close, the mentally ill in Ireland tended to be either homeless or confined in prisons, and, despite isolated initiatives,[36] their plight clearly presented increasing cause for concern. This concern ultimately led to the beginnings of systemic reform in the early 1700s. One of the key figures in this process was Sir William Fownes, a wealthy, philanthropic landowner whose initiatives were to shape institutional mental health care in Ireland for many decades to follow.

Sir William Fownes:
Providing for the Mentally Ill

Sir William Fownes was a pivotal figure in the history of care for the mentally ill in Ireland. A member of the Irish House of Commons for Wicklow Borough from 1704 to 1713, Fownes became Lord Mayor of Dublin in 1708 and the Fownes Baronetcy, a title in the Baronetage of Ireland, was created for him on 26 October 1724.

Fownes was one of Dublin city's patriarchs and a wealthy landowner, with a villa adjoining Phoenix Park, a townhouse off College Green, and an estate in Wicklow. Notwithstanding his privileged background, Fownes's interest in providing for the destitute mentally ill was matched with actions: in 1708, while mayor of Dublin, he initiated the provision of cells for the mentally ill in the workhouse at St James's Gate.

Some years earlier, in 1684, the master of the City of Dublin House of Correction had requested and received additional payment for maintaining mentally ill persons there[37] and, in 1699, an anonymous donor acting through Dr Thomas Molyneux (later state physician), offered Dublin city corporation £2,000 towards maintaining a hospital for aged lunatics and diseased persons.[38] While the corporation initially accepted the offer and even agreed to donate £200 themselves, they reallocated the site for the Dublin workhouse, which opened in 1703. In 1701, the problem of mentally ill persons in the House of Correction was again highlighted by its Master, Robert Parkes, and financial support was provided to the tune of two shillings per person per week.[39]

The six additional cells provided by Fownes for the most disturbed of the mentally ill in 1708 represented the first definite beginning of organised care for the destitute mentally ill in Dublin. In parallel with Fownes's initiative, in 1711 Lord Justice Ingoldsby persuaded the governors of the Royal Hospital in Kilmainham to provide dedicated accommodation for soldiers who developed mental illness. Mentally ill soldiers continued to be accommodated at Kilmainham until 1849, when provision moved to Yarmouth.

In 1729, the governing body of the Dublin workhouse decided to cease admitting persons with mental illness to the cells that Fownes had established. At that point, there were approximately forty 'lunatics' in the workhouse but by then the overall establishment had taken on more of the characteristics of a foundling hospital – albeit one in which children were sometimes locked into cells with disturbed mentally ill persons when they had broken the hospital rules.

It was against this background that, in 1731, Jonathan Swift, author of *Gulliver's Travels* (1726) and various other classics of eighteenth-century literature, announced his intention to provide in his will for the establishment of a hospital for the mentally ill. He consulted Fownes, who wrote at length to Swift on 9 September 1732, starting with an account of the current plight of the mentally ill and his own efforts to ameliorate matters at the workhouse at St James's Gate.[40] Fownes went on to tell Swift that he had been initially reluctant to consider the establishment of a public asylum in Dublin along the lines of Bethlem Hospital in London (one of the first asylums in the world, founded in 1247), but had changed his view and now supported such a venture:

> I own to you, I was for some time averse to our having a publick Bedlam, apprehending we should be overloaded with numbers, under the name of mad. Nay, I was apprehensive our case would soon be like that in England; wives and husbands trying who could first get the other to Bedlam. Many, who were next heirs to estates, would try their skill to render the possessor disordered, and get them confined, and soon run them into real madness. Such like consequences I dreaded, and therefore have been silent on the subject till of late. Now I am convinced that regard should be had to those under such dismal circumstances; and I have heard the primate and others express their concern for them; and no doubt but very sufficient subscriptions may be had to set this needful work on foot. I should think it would be a pleasure to any one, that has any intention this way, to see something done in their lifetime, rather than leave it to the conduct of posterity.[41]

Thus reformed, Fownes suggested a site for the proposed establishment, behind Aungier Street, later site of Mercer's Hospital.[42] He proposed that the new asylum should be surrounded by a high wall, have appropriate staff quarters and contain space for patients to walk around, as well as dedicated accommodation for the most disturbed and scope for enlargement.[43] Fownes recommended that the establishment should be supported by subscriptions and that the College of Physicians should advise on the work.

When Fownes wrote his letter to Swift in 1732, he was pushing at an open door with the great author: both men were trustees of Steevens' Hospital in Dublin and both were deeply concerned with the plight of the destitute mentally ill.[44] On 3 April 1735, however, less than three years after he wrote to Swift, Fownes died and was buried in St Andrew's in Dublin. By this time, Swift was already engaged in planning his iconic hospital, later known as St Patrick's.[45] Today, over three centuries after Fownes established his cells for the mentally ill at the Dublin workhouse, there is a ward in the psychiatry unit of St James's Hospital in Dublin named in his honour, commemorating Fownes's unique contribution to early psychiatric care.

Jonathan Swift: Author, Churchman, Pioneer

On his death in 1745, Jonathan Swift famously and generously bequeathed his entire estate to establish a hospital for 'idiots and lunaticks' in Dublin, consistent with Fownes's initiative.[46] This establishment would duly become St Patrick's Hospital, the first formal asylum in Ireland. As a result of his benevolent bequest, Swift occupies a unique position in the history of psychiatry in Ireland.

Swift was born in Dublin in 1667 and gained a Doctor of Divinity degree from Trinity College in 1702. He went on to become a celebrated essayist, novelist, poet, satirist and cleric, serving as

Dean of St Patrick's Cathedral in Dublin from 1713 to 1745. Swift's interest in madness may have stemmed from family experiences: Swift was raised by an uncle who developed mental disorder and died when Swift was 21.[47]

Professor Anthony Clare, who himself became medical director of St Patrick's Hospital in 1989, studied Swift's writing on madness in *A Tale of A Tub* (1704) and *Gulliver's Travels* (1726) and found much to comment upon.[48] *A Tale of A Tub*, for example, was Swift's first major work and in it Swift divided madness into three types: religious, philosophical and political. In book three of *Gulliver's Travels*, Swift portrays people trying to extract sunbeams from cucumbers and an architect who seeks to build houses from the roof downwards. In *The Legion Club* (1736), Swift treats the Irish Houses of Parliament as an asylum, complete with madhouse keeper. Clearly, madness and its management were key concerns for Swift and emerged as recurring motifs in his literary and satirical work.

In addition to his writings about madness, Swift was acutely aware of the reality of the plight of the mentally ill. On 26 February 1714, he was elected as a governor of Bethlem Hospital ('Bedlam') in London.[49] There is no record that Swift actually attended any meetings but in 1722 it is recorded that he used his position as governor to nominate a certain Mr Beaumont for admission, as Mr Beaumont was reportedly riding through the streets on a horse, throwing money around.[50] Swift himself, in a characteristic burst of satire, asked whether, once incurable wards were established in Bedlam, he might possibly be admitted there, on the grounds that he was an 'incurable scribbler'?[51]

Swift's interest in madness and its causes was by no means unique among writers of the day: John Locke, Thomas Hobbes, Alexander Pope, Laurence Sterne and Samuel Johnson all wrote about the subject, sometimes at great length. But Swift was notable for the extent to which he matched his writings with concrete actions, most obviously by becoming a governor of Bethlem Hospital and bequeathing his estate for the foundation of an asylum in Dublin.

By 1733, Swift had made the momentous decision to devote his estate to public benefaction and by 1735 he had settled his entire fortune on Dublin city in trust for the erection of an asylum. The following year, Swift's London publisher, Benjamin Motte, praised his benevolent intentions but warned sternly against permitting the kinds of abuses and maltreatment reported in English private asylums of the times.[52] This was a real issue: English private asylums of the 1700s were the subject of considerable concern in relation to the balance between custody and care. The conditions in which patients were kept, as well as their treatment, were the subject of repeated scandal and outrage.[53] Swift was fully aware of the risks and took considerable care with his bequest, frequently redrafting his will in order to ensure, as best as possible, that the institution would be run to a high standard.[54]

Swift's own mental state was the subject of considerable speculation and discussion both during his life and ever since. Malcolm recounts several opinions that Swift developed mental illness, based on the views of Samuel Johnson, William Makepeace Thackeray and Sir Walter Scott, among others.[55] The idea that Swift became a lunatic gained considerable currency following his death, along with the belief that Swift had, in later life, become a patient at the very hospital he founded. In 1849, Dr (later Sir) William Wilde (1815–1876), an eye and ear surgeon, and distinguished author on the subjects of medicine, folklore and archaeology, wrote an entire book about Swift's health and recounted that it was rumoured that Swift was the first patient at St Patrick's, although this was not true.[56]

These tales about Swift had their roots not only in contemporary gossip and innuendo, but also in the fact that, in 1742, a writ, *de Lunatico Inquirendo*, was issued, declaring Swift 'a person of unsound mind and memory, and not capable of taking care of his person or fortune'.[57] This writ was issued following a petition from Swift's friends and consideration of medical evidence, and the declaration made by a jury.

Notwithstanding this writ, it is clear that Swift was not truly mentally ill: a lunacy enquiry was the only legal means by which a person incapable of conducting their own business affairs or looking after themselves could be effectively protected.[58] As a result, the writ did not necessarily mean that Swift had become a 'lunatic', but simply that he was no longer in a position to manage his own affairs and required assistance, most likely as a result of age-related decline. In fact, Swift lived just three years after these events, largely in isolation, and did not write during these later years.

With regard to the specifics of Swift's health and possible diagnoses, there were suggestions that Swift may have been afflicted with a form of syphilis,[59] but it now appears clear that Ménière's Disease was most likely the central diagnosis.[60] Ménière's Disease is a disorder of the inner ear that affects hearing and balance, and symptoms include vertigo, tinnitus and hearing loss. Various medical examinations of Swift's life have concluded that he experienced giddiness, nausea, dizziness and tinnitus, all of which are consistent with Ménière's Disease, especially from the 1730s onwards. In 1736, Swift complained explicitly about some of these symptoms to his friend Alexander Pope, noting that he could no longer write, read or think clearly because of them.[61]

Swift also experienced severe memory loss from 1739 onward and may have suffered from cerebrovascular disease (impaired blood supply to the brain), further reducing his abilities and cognitive function. Sir Russell Brain (1895–1966), a British neurologist, was of the view that this was the root cause of Swift's symptoms in later life, especially his aphasia (impairment of language).[62] Ultimately, a great number of opinions have been expressed about Swift's health and the emergent consensus appears to be that he suffered from Ménière's Disease during his life and cerebrovascular disease towards the end, possibly contributing significantly to his death.[63]

It is beyond doubt, however, that, towards the end of his life, Swift did not recognise people familiar to him and lost the ability to express himself.[64] This must have been an extraordinary frustration for a man so accustomed to thinking, writing and speaking with outstanding passion, clarity and, in relation to the mentally ill, charity.

St Patrick's Hospital, Dublin: 'Swift's Hospital'

Following Swift's bequest and his death in 1745, on 8 August 1746 a royal charter was granted to St Patrick's by King George II (1683–1760) and St Patrick's became the first psychiatric hospital in Ireland, and one of the first in the world.[65]

On 29 August 1746, the board of governors held its first meeting and the first patients, four women, were admitted on 26 September 1757, at which point the hospital had just sixteen admissions rooms.[66] They were joined by five male patients in early October.[67] The hospital expanded significantly over the following decades and admitted growing numbers of patients, although reports from the early 1800s indicated difficulties providing treatments and concern about lengths of stay.[68]

Such concerns were by no means unique to St Patrick's and, in March 1817, Robert Peel, Chief Secretary, persuaded the House of Commons to set up a select committee to look into the need to make greater provision for 'the lunatic poor in Ireland'.[69] The committee considered all such establishments, including St Patrick's, and concluded that 'the extent of the accommodation which may be afforded by the present establishments in the several counties of Ireland' was 'totally inadequate for the reception of the lunatic poor'.[70]

During the course of its deliberations, the committee received a letter from 'Mr James Cleghorn', 'medical attendant' at 'Saint Patrick's or Swift's Hospital', dated 17 March 1817, with interesting information about the hospital.[71] Cleghorn pointed out that recent years had seen 'very considerable improvements' at St Patrick's, which, by that time, housed 96 'paupers' and 53 'boarders'.[72] Cleghorn was 'fully aware of the advantages to be derived from dividing the different description of insane persons into classes, according to the nature and stage of the disease', but noted that 'the original construction of Swift's Hospital does not admit of their separation, as it consists of six very long corridors or galleries, each containing twenty-eight cells'.

Cleghorn 'was very anxious to have some separate cells for the noisiest of the patients, built apart from the principal building' but the government did not grant money for this development, citing the 'great accommodation for the insane, which the Richmond Lunatic Hospital would afford, which was then in progress'.[73] Cleghorn regretted the government's decision:

> ... the reasonableness of enabling us to adopt the system of classification in the most material point would have ensured to us more extensive aid; medical treatment in maniacal persons, and the insane in general, except in the very early stages of the disease, has ever appeared to me to be of little service towards the cure of it ... moral treatment, as it is called, is of much more moment than medical, and I am sure that in this particular, much improvement has taken place of late years; and that the late investigations will contribute much to the amelioration of the state of lunatics.[74]

Cleghorn was at pains to point out the infrequent use of restraint at St Patrick's:

> The system observed in Swift's Hospital, before I was concerned in it, was of the most humane kind; and it has always been my object to avoid any other coercion or restraint but what was required for the safety of the patients and those around them. The strait waistcoat and handcuffs are seldom resorted to, and we prefer the latter to the former, as being more convenient for cleanliness, and not so heating; occasional confinement to the cell is the principal restraint which we employ.[75]

Cleghorn reported, with satisfaction, that he had 'succeeded, last spring, in prevailing on the governors to take a lease of the ground on the east side of the hospital, containing two acres and a half, and affording a good view into the Phoenix Park, where the greater number of the patients are at liberty to walk about and to take exercise'. Many were also 'employed, with their own consent, in working the ground, and have been much happier and freer from their malady in consequence of it'.

Cleghorn also addressed distressing allegations regarding transport of mentally ill persons to Dublin from elsewhere in Ireland:

> I wish, while writing to you on this subject, to take notice of certain statements which I have seen in the public prints, as having been lately made in the House of Commons, relative to the conveyance of mad persons to Dublin from the country. It has been said, that they have been tied to cars, and so bruised as to render the amputation of their limbs necessary, and that death has ensued from the mortification occasioned by this cruel mode of conveyance, During fourteen years I have attended Swift's Hospital, I have never known an instance of the kind where any ill consequences have followed.[76]

Cleghorn heard 'it rumoured, that it is intended to have either provincial or county asylums for lunatics and idiots: such a design is founded in wisdom and humanity, and will be a great relief to the pressure on the establishments in the capital'. This rumour was correct and, having taken account of the evidence of Cleghorn and others, the 1817 Committee duly recommended that 'there should be four or five district asylums capable of containing each from one hundred and twenty to one hundred and fifty lunatics'.[77]

Notwithstanding the later development of these public asylums during the 1800s, numbers at St Patrick's continued to rise and, by 1857, the profile of patients had changed significantly: in 1800 there had been 106 'free' patients and 52 'paying' patients; by 1857 this balance had reversed, with fewer 'free' patients (66) and more 'paying' patients (83).[78] The Lunatic Asylums, Ireland, Commission of 1858 was not pleased:

> We cannot consider this as indicating a satisfactory application of [Swift's] endowment. It is true that the average payment by boarders is somewhat less than their actual cost in ordinary years, and so far they may be considered as maintained in part by the charity; but if the diminution of free patients and the increase of paying patients are to continue, it may one day result that no inmates of Dean Swift's Hospital will be maintained entirely out of his bequest, which certainly does not appear to have been in the contemplation of the founder.
>
> It appears by the evidence that the reception of paying patients has been so profitable, that the governors have been enabled to accumulate the sum of £20,000 thereby, the interest of which is available for the support of the institution. We cannot but think that the objects of the endowment would have been more properly carried out, if the income had been entirely appropriated to the maintenance of free patients.[79]

As regards conditions for patients, although a library was introduced in 1851, along with various other changes and innovations, there were persistent problems with infectious diseases in the hospital.[80] The 1858 Commission had several further concerns, including that there was 'only one fixed bath for 150 patients of both sexes' and that was 'out of order', so that 'patients wash in tubs in the day-rooms'; 'the hospital is not lighted with gas'; 'the hospital cannot be sufficiently warm in the winter months'; and various other issues, which led the Commission to the conclusion that St Patrick's was, 'in many respects, one of the most defective institutions for the treatment of the insane which we have visited'. [81]

To remedy matters, the report recommended that 'the master of the hospital should be a member of the medical profession', and that greater control and inspection were needed:

> On the whole, the condition of this hospital satisfied us that it is absolutely necessary it should be placed under the control of the Central Board, which may be established for the direction of lunatic asylums in Ireland, and that it should be subject to the visits of the Commissioners as frequently as the district asylums. It is, no doubt, a private endowment, but in former times received large aid (£24,194) from the state; and what, in the interest of the public, we have suggested, should be done for its better government, will be in furtherance of the benevolent intentions of the founder.[82]

Notwithstanding these concerns, many of which were equally relevant to most other asylums of the day, there is still plentiful evidence that the 'benevolent intentions of the founder' of St Patrick's were being observed in important ways in the early 1800s, although the latter part of the century was to bring more significant problems for the hospital, relating to patient care, financial challenges and structural dilapidation of the building.[83]

In many respects, the story of St Patrick's from the mid-1700s to the late 1800s was typical of the trajectory of early asylum care in Ireland, commencing with noble intentions, followed by enthusiasm, and then difficulty sustaining the enthusiasm and standards so clearly required for care of the mentally ill. St Patrick's was, however, a private, charitable establishment as opposed to a government run institution. The network of public asylums that developed alongside St Patrick's during the 1800s merits consideration from this perspective too and its inception, was, in significant part, attributable to the work of one especially dominant figure in Irish asylum medicine, Dr William Saunders Hallaran (1765–1825).

Dr William Saunders Hallaran: Treating the Mentally Ill

The most prominent and prolific Irish asylum doctor of the late eighteenth and early nineteenth centuries,[84] William Saunders Hallaran was born in 1765 and studied medicine at Edinburgh. He spent much of his working life as Senior Physician to the South Infirmary and Physician to the House of Industry and Lunatic Asylum of Cork. Hallaran established the Cork Lunatic Asylum during the late 1780s and early 1790s,[85] and Citadella, a private asylum in Douglas, County Cork, in 1799 ('Bull's Asylum').[86] Throughout his career, Hallaran was not only an industrious, progressive administrator, clinician and teacher, but also a tireless advocate for a more systematic approach to mental disorder and its treatment.

In 1810, Hallaran published the first Irish textbook of psychiatry, titled *An Enquiry into the Causes producing the Extraordinary Addition to the Number of Insane together with Extended Observations on the Cure of Insanity with Hints as to the Better Management of Public Asylums for Insane Persons.*[87] This book outlined many of the central themes that defined his approach to the mentally ill, including explicit recognition of the roles of physical or bodily factors as causes of mental disorder in certain cases; deep concern about the apparent increase in mental disorder in nineteenth-century Ireland; and systematic, scientific engagement with the causes, courses and outcomes.

The recognition of physical or bodily factors (such as infections) rather than just psychological or 'moral' factors in causing mental disorder was an especially key theme:[88]

> A principal object of this essay is to point out what heretofore seems to have escaped the observation of authors on the subject, namely, the practical distinction between that species of insanity which can evidently be referred to mental causes, and may therefore be denominated *mental insanity*, and that species of nervous excitement, which, though partaking of like effects, so far as the sensorium [i.e. mind] may be engaged, still might appear to owe its origin merely to organic [i.e. physical or bodily] injury, either idiopathically [i.e. by unknown mechanisms] affecting the brain itself, or arising from a specific action of the liver, lungs or mesentery [i.e. inside the abdomen]; inducing an inflammatory disposition in either, and thereby exciting in certain habits those peculiar aberrations, which commonly denote an unsound mind. That this distinction is material in the treatment of insane persons, cannot well be denied, any more than that the due observance of the causes connected with the origin of this malady, is the first step towards establishing a basis upon which a hope of recovery may be founded.[89]

This was consistent with preexisting theories linking mental disorder with, for example, disorders of the spleen – a theory outlined with particular enthusiasm by Sir Richard Blackmore of the Royal College of Physicians in London in 1726.[90] Almost a century later, Hallaran's distinction between causes 'of the mind' and physical or bodily causes of mental disorder held clear importance when planning treatment:

> In the mode of cure, however, I would argue the necessity of the most cautious attention to this important distinction, lest as I have often known to be the case, that the malady of the mind which is for the most part to be treated on moral principles, should be subjected to the operation of agents altogether more foreign to the purpose; and that the other of the body, arising from direct injury to one or more of the vital organs, may escape the advantages of approved remedies ... this discrimination has been found to be of the highest importance where a curative indication was to be looked for, nor need there be much difficulty in forming a prognosis, where either from candid report, or from careful examination, the precise nature of the excitement shall be ascertained.[91]

In his incisive, often witty, textbook, Hallaran paid particular attention to the role of the liver in causing mental disorder, recommending that 'the actual state of the liver in almost every case of mental derangement should be a primary consideration; even though the sensorium should be largely engaged'.[92] Hallaran finished the opening discussion of his 1810 text by reemphasising both the distinction and the links between the 'sensorium' and the body:

> Here we have sufficient evidence of the existence of insanity on the principle of mere organic [i.e. physical or bodily] lesion; holding a connection as it would appear, with the entire glandular system. Hence we may be led to suppose than an imperfect or a specific action in certain portions of this important department tends to lay the foundation of that affection, which I would under such circumstances, denominate the 'mania corporea' of Cullen; including at the same time within this species, the different varieties of the complaint as described by authors, depending upon the various causes, whether mechanical or otherwise, as affecting the sensorium, and the other important organs of the animal economy.[93]

'Cullen' was Dr William Cullen (1710–1790), a prominent Scottish physician who had substantial influence on an entire generation of prominent asylum doctors including Hallaran, John Ferriar, Benjamin Rush and Thomas Trotter, author of *A View of the Nervous Temperament*.[94] Cullen was the first asylum doctor to use the term 'neurosis' which, in contrast with later usage, he used to denote a range of psychiatric disorders that occurred in the absence of pyrexia (i.e. in the absence of raised body temperature).[95] Consistent with Cullen's approach, Hallaran's distinction between organic (physical) and non-organic (psychological and moral) factors in causing mental disorder was to consolidate the foundation for much subsequent work on determining causes of insanity throughout the nineteenth and twentieth centuries.

Syphilis, for example, was cited as a major cause of admission to psychiatric institutions throughout nineteenth-century Europe,[96] despite the fact that accurate diagnosis was not possible prior to the work of August Paul von Wassermann (1866–1925), the German bacteriologist who developed a complement fixation test for syphilis in 1906.[97] Nevertheless, Hallaran undertook to gather the first systematic data on the causes of psychiatric admissions in Ireland, and identified, as best he could, that venereal disease accounted for a lower proportion of admissions in Ireland than elsewhere.[98]

Towards the end of the nineteenth century, several decades after Hallaran's textbook appeared, the classification of mental disorders underwent further revision as Emil Kraepelin (1856–1926), a German psychiatrist, divided all mental disorders into 13 groups, including two groups of 'functional psychosis' (i.e. mental disorders involving a loss of contact with reality but without demonstrable organic or physical cause).[99] These two groups were: affective psychosis (in which loss of contact with reality was accompanied by disturbance of mood) and non-affective psychosis (in which it was not).

Kraepelin's classification, like Hallaran's approach, recognised the key role of organic or physical factors in producing certain cases of mental disorder, but went a step further by dividing 'functional psychosis' into these two separate groups. This classification duly led to the emergence of 'manic depression' (bipolar disorder, sometimes involving psychosis with prominent mood disturbance) and 'dementia preacox' (schizophrenia, or psychosis without prominent mood disturbance) as substantive diagnostic entities which are broadly still retained in current classification systems.[100] The distinction between organic and functional disorders, as emphasised by both Hallaran and Kraepelin, is also retained in diagnostic and clinical practices some two centuries after Hallaran's text first appeared.

Unsurprisingly, Hallaran was, like virtually all of his peers, deeply concerned with 'the extraordinary increase of insanity in Ireland', which he, characteristically, attributed to both 'corporeal' (i.e. bodily) and 'mental excitement',[101] and which he also related to the effects of social unrest,[102] 'terror from religious enthusiasm',[103] and 'the unrestrained use and abuse of ardent spirits',[104] among other factors. Unlike many of his peers, however, Hallaran brought a great deal of systematic and critical thought to the treatment of mental disorders, expressing scepticism about many of the established remedies of the times and notable enthusiasm for others.

Treatments in the Late 1700s and Early 1800s: Spin Doctors

In his 1810 textbook, Hallaran provided a careful consideration of many traditional physical treatments for mental disorder (e.g. bloodletting); a detailed exploration of novel treatments (e.g. Dr Cox's Circulating Swing, which is explored shortly); and a re-evaluation of traditional medicinal remedies (e.g. opium) and various other approaches (e.g. shower baths, diet and exercise).[105]

These treatments, and Hallaran's relatively scientific approach to them, represented a shift from older, more traditional practices which, according to Lady Jane Wilde (1821–1896), included placing the mentally ill person in a pit in the ground (three feet wide and six feet deep), with only the head uncovered, and leaving him or her alone for three days and three nights, without food or contact with anyone.[106] A harrow-pin (from a harrow, an agricultural instrument) was placed over the person, owing to the alleged mystical properties of harrow-pins. If the unfortunate person survived this dreadful ordeal, it was reported that a cure might be effected, although Lady Wilde conceded that the majority of those who survived emerged from the pit cold, hungry and mentally worse than ever.

Lady Wilde also recounted folk beliefs that madness was both hereditary and caused by demonic possession, and could be cured by drinking honey, milk and salt in a seashell before sunrise.[107] Other treatments included exorcism by witch doctor, which involved the local witch doctor drinking whiskey, speaking unintelligibly at some length, throwing holy water over the patient and room, hitting the patient repeatedly with a blackthorn stick (while the patient was held down), and then swirling the blackthorn stick wildly around the room hitting any people or objects it encountered.[108] Particular attention was paid to hitting the door through which the demon would allegedly escape. The exorcist was comprehensively fortified with whiskey throughout this elaborate, alarming, brutal process.

It is not entirely clear when this ritual dates from, how long it persisted, or whether it occurred at all, but Lady Wilde goes on to describe a specific example which, she says, took place 'lately' (her book appeared in 1890).[109] If Lady Wilde's sources are to be regarded as reliable, this is a most disturbing case. It concerns a man in Roscommon who apparently became mentally ill and was bound hand and foot, foaming at the mouth. He was described as 'elf-stricken' as it was believed he had been replaced by a fairy demon. The witch doctor was summoned and concluded that the unfortunate man had been replaced by a horse which needed to be fed oats in order to keep the horse alive and, thus, keep the real man (now in Fairyland) alive too.

At this, the patient was forcibly fed a sheaf of oats while the exorcist and the general company sent for five kegs of *poitín* (poteen, a strong, distilled, alcoholic Irish beverage) to fortify themselves for the exorcism ahead. A bucket of cold water was thrown on the patient's head and the exorcism began. In the midst of the ritual, however, the patient was untied and immediately made as if to attack the witch doctor, with the result that the witch doctor and all the others fled the house, pursued by the extremely irate patient. The patient was, however, soon overpowered and again tied up, after which a magistrate ordered that he be brought to Roscommon Lunatic Asylum, where he is said to have died.

By way of contrast with these disturbing, dramatic tales, Hallaran's treatment techniques in Cork in the early 1800s were significantly less punitive, although they were not entirely without drama either. Turning to traditional physical treatments first, Hallaran expressed particularly little faith in venesection (bloodletting) which was a common treatment for a range of conditions, including mental illness, for many centuries.[110] While acknowledging the usefulness of venesection in certain circumstances, Hallaran generally felt that 'bleeding to any great extent does not often seem to be desirable, and except in recent cases, does not even appear to be admissible'.[111] This was consistent with the views of Dr William Battie (1703–1776), influential author of *Treatise on Madness*, who had written in 1758 that bloodletting was positively harmful if the patient was feeble or suffering from convulsions.[112]

The administration of emetics, to make the patient vomit, was another common treatment for a range of disorders,[113] but while Hallaran acknowledged 'the use of emetics in all febrile affections' (i.e. infections producing high body temperature),[114] he was cautious about their use in mental disorder: 'I have been a witness to very disagreeable consequences arising from the want of necessary precaution on this head, which have deterred me from directing full emetics in any case'. Battie was similarly circumspect about vomiting.[115]

Notwithstanding these views, emetics and purgatives were commonly used for a range of physical and mental disorders in Ireland and elsewhere: in 1810, the same year that Hallaran published his textbook, Dr Martin Tuomy, Fellow of the Royal College of Physicians of Ireland, produced his *Treatise on the Principal Diseases of Dublin*[116] in which he explicitly endorsed the use of purgatives and emetics, which might be administered daily for up to 21 days. As was the case with bloodletting, these treatments were aimed at evacuating noxious 'humours' from the body in order to produce clinical improvement. There was, however, growing disenchantment with the indiscriminate use of emetics and purgatives throughout the nineteenth century, and prescriptions for more violent emetic and purgative agents declined as the century progressed.[117]

Hallaran noted that patients occasionally exhibited 'excessive obstinacy'[118] and, in such circumstances, he recommended the use of the 'circulating swing' which had been recently developed by Dr Joseph Mason Cox (1763–1818), a Bristol-born mind doctor.[119] Building on the work of Dr Erasmus Darwin (1731–1802) who described a 'rotative couch' aimed at inducing sleep,[120] Cox suggested suspending a chair from the ceiling by means of ropes; seating a patient securely in the chair; and instructing an asylum attendant to rotate the chair at a given speed, thus spinning the patient around a vertical axis for a given period of time.[121] This technique was employed at many asylums throughout nineteenth-century Europe, especially in German-speaking countries.[122] It was, according to Cox, 'both a moral and a medical mean in the treatment of maniacs'.[123]

In Ireland, Hallaran 'was not slow in taking advantage of Dr Cox's observations'[124] and assembled an apparatus that was 'so contrived, that four persons can if necessary, be secured in it at once'.[125] Hallaran used this 'Herculean remedy' for patients 'who have been recently attacked with maniacal symptoms, and who, previous to its employment, had been sufficiently evacuated by purgative medicines'.[126]

In the 'obstinate and furious' the swing reportedly generated 'a sufficiency of alarm to insure obedience', while in the 'melancholic' it generated 'a natural interest in the affairs of life'.[127] Hallaran warned against indiscriminate use of the apparatus, advising particular caution with tall patients and noting that certain patterns of rotation could produce 'sudden action of the bowels, stomach and urinary passages, in quick succession'.[128] Despite these drawbacks, the swing was also a source of entertainment for certain patients who 'used it sometimes when permitted, as a mode of amusement, without any inconvenience or effect whatever'.[129]

Despite Hallaran's awareness of the adverse effects of the swing, his insistence on 'careful superintendence'[130] and his belief that he was acting in his patients' best interests, it is clear that Cox's Circulating Swing belonged to an era prior to the development of more humane treatments for the mentally ill and prior to clear enunciation of their rights.[131] From today's perspective, Hallaran's use of the swing appears misguided: some two hundred years later, it is to be hoped that increased emphasis on the rights of the mentally ill will ensure sustained emphasis on the dignity of patients during treatment and enhance the provision of evidence based therapies that are humane, safe, effective and acceptable to patients and their families.[132]

Hallaran's 1810 textbook concluded with detailed evaluations of a range of therapeutic approaches to mental disorder, including traditional medicinal remedies (digitalis, opium, camphor and mercury) and physical treatments for insanity (shower baths, diet and exercise). Digitalis,[133] which appeared to act by 'restraining the inordinate action of the heart and arteries',[134] had, according to Hallaran, substantial 'merits as an anti-maniacal remedy, on as high a scale as can well belong to any one subject of *materia medica*'.[135] The current understanding of the action of digitalis (chiefly on a sodium pump enzyme) suggests that digitalis may indeed have had an effect on the brain,[136] but it was not until the work of Dr William Withering (1741–1799) that the issues of standardised preparation and dose-response characteristics were identified as critical for the safe and effective use of the drug.[137]

Hallaran believed that opium[138] had 'deservedly obtained a principal character amongst anti-maniacal remedies'[139] but that camphor, another common treatment,[140] 'frequently failed altogether' in the treatment of mania.[141] He had similar doubts about mercury[142] except, perhaps, 'as a preparative for the commencement of the digitalis'.[143]

Hallaran was notably enthusiastic about water treatments,[144] maintaining that the shower-bath worked 'by immediately tranquilising the high degree of febrile action'[145] and 'answers an extremely good purpose in enforcing cleanliness at all seasons' (a real consideration in large, unhygienic asylums).[146] Other water treatments of the day primarily aimed at inducing shock and terror, and included the 'bath of surprise' whereby the mentally ill person was thrown from a bridge into running water and caught with a net; being dragged through a river; or being forced into a dark room, one half of which comprised a cistern of water into which the person would inevitably fall while seeking to escape.[147]

In 1756, Charles Lucas (1713–1771), a radical Irish physician, apothecary and politician, had published an enthusiastic, influential *Essay on Waters* dealing with 'simple waters', 'cold medicated waters' and 'natural baths':

> It will appear strange to every attentive reader, that the most useful and necessary part of the creation, whether economically, physically, or medicinally considered, has been so far, and so long neglected, as to make it, at this day, necessary to compile so large a volume as this, to rectify men's notions in so interesting a point!
>
> [...] Warm bathing, for the like reasons, had long been an established and approved remedy amongst the ancients, in all kinds of mania or madness; though in this, as well as other respects, it has become so much neglected by the moderns.[148]

In 1772, a year after Lucas's death, a similarly themed volume was published in Dublin, titled *The Theory and Uses of Baths, Being an Extract from the Essay on Waters by the Late Charles Lucas, Esq., MD, with Marginal Notes by Dr Achmet, Illustrated by Some Annexed Cases.*[149] The distinctly enterprising 'Dr Achmet' (also known as Patrick Kearns and Patrick Joyce) ran the Royal Patent Baths at Bachelors Walk in Dublin, offering a range of water therapies, including hot and cold baths flavoured with putrefying horse manure.[150] In the 1772 volume, 'Dr Achmet', perhaps unsurprisingly, recounted excellent testimonials from his clients, including the following fulsome account of one water cure:

> My case when I began the use of the vapor baths was as follows; the disorder in my head had arose to such a degree, that I was in almost a constant state of delirium, and my mind so full of inquietude and uneasiness, that I could not stand or sit any length of time in one place, and at certain times, my bowels seemed full of pains and inflammations, and an almost constant burning painfulness in my fundament, with a callous lump below my groin; in short, my situation was such, that rest, either day or night, I was a stranger to.
>
> I have now been one month under the doctor's care ['Dr Achmet'], in which time he has treated me with the utmost tenderness, attention and care; and since the first week of my residence with him, I have daily continued recovering the use of my senses, and faculties, and my disease seems, in every place that it affected me, to have submitted to the salutary effects of his medicines and vapor baths; in such a manner

am I now, that I hope, through the blessing of God, of being as well as ever I was in my life. I must here observe, that when I first went into the vapor, or steaming bath, my time was limited every other day to about an hour, and that in the last week of my being there, I generally spent every day from three to four hours in the said bath ...

... I have continued to recover my strength, and am light, supple, and full of spirits at this time ...[151]

Back in Cork, Hallaran, in addition to promoting water treatments, also recognised the importance of diet and described the asylum's 'farinaceous diet' (i.e. consisting of meal or flour)[152] in some detail. 'Animal food' was carefully restricted to 'certain seasons of the year' owing to its tendency to produce a 'disposition to riot' and 'aggravation of insanity'.[153] This was an intriguing objection to meat, given the centrality of alcohol (wine, beer, porter, etc.) in asylum diets – for both patients and attendants – throughout much of the 1800s.[154] ('The cost of wine and spirits could be included in the budget for 'medicines', which was helpful).[155]

Regulation of diet was a key element in programmes of 'moral management' which were employed in most Irish asylums throughout the nineteenth century.[156] Other elements included regular exercise and gainful occupation.[157] This therapeutic approach, along with the principle of the 'panopticon' (having a point from which an unseen governor could see all), had a critical influence on the design of many Irish asylums constructed during the great 'asylum-building era' of the nineteenth century,[158] The 'moral management' paradigm actively informed the 'Kirkbride Plan', advocated by Thomas Story Kirkbride (1809–1883), a Philadelphia mind doctor.[159]

Hallaran also paid considerable attention to exercise and gainful activity. He suggested 'removing the convalescent, and incurable insane, to convenient distances from large cities and towns, to well enclosed farms, properly adapted to the purposes of employing them with effect, in the different branches of husbandry and horticulture'.[160] Over the following two hundred years, various developments in the practice of psychiatry (including the introduction of neuroleptic medication) were to tilt the balance away from this broad based, multi-modal approach to treatment recommended by Hallaran. The late twentieth century, however, saw the re-emergence of reenergised models of biopsychosocial psychiatry which emphasised the role of occupational therapies in the process of recovery,[161] consistent with the approach outlined by Hallaran almost two centuries earlier.

Developments in England, France and the United States

As these developments and innovations in treatment were unfolding in late eighteenth- and early nineteenth-century Ireland, especially in Hallaran's establishments in Cork, they coincided, to greater or lesser extents, with significant shifts in practice elsewhere. In England, the asylums that emerged during the 1700s were mostly highly custodial places and, although there were inevitably pockets of enlightened practice, there were also clear, systematic problems across the emergent system. At Bedlam in London, there were continual reports of abuse and poor conditions, albeit accompanied by contrasting reports of good treatment at times, with the result that Bedlam was subject of interminable speculation among journalists, politicians and the public, to whom it provided endless cause for concern and morbid fascination.[162]

More broadly, the asylums of eighteenth-century England included a range of different establishments including, for example, St Luke's Hospital in London, which accepted its first patients in July 1751.[163] In what would be a remarkably consistent pattern across institutions and across countries, numbers at St Luke's rose steadily following its opening. Battie, its founding medical officer and the leading asylum doctor of his day, duly wrote in strong support of confinement as a key element in management of the mentally ill, stating that confinement was always necessary and sometimes sufficient to effect a cure.[164] Battie's uncompromising stance strongly reinforced the emphasis on asylums in the treatment of the mentally ill over the following decades.

In addition to its allegedly unique therapeutic potential, the asylum was also, according to Battie, essential for the education of physicians.[165] England's first provincial subscription asylum was duly established in Newcastle in 1765, and many others followed (e.g. Manchester in 1766, York in 1777). While regulations governing various specific practices were in place in these establishments, restraint, coercion and punishment still featured strongly, at least until evidence of abuses in Bedlam and York were later exposed.[166]

The most palpable sign of change appeared in the 1790s, when William Tuke (1732–1822), a Quaker tea merchant, founded and opened The Retreat at York following the death of a Quaker woman in York Asylum.[167] The Retreat aimed to provide care for the mentally ill in a humane and nurturing setting, and patients were allowed access to the grounds, housed in comfortable settings, and generally treated with sympathy.[168]

Tuke was an admirer of Dr Philippe Pinel (1745–1826)[169] of the Salpêtrière Hospital in Paris, who published an influential textbook promoting principles similar to those that underpinned Tuke's initiative.[170] Many of Pinel's proposals were later championed by Dr Jean-Étienne-Dominique Esquirol (1772–1840) in Charenton, Paris and at the Salpêtrière. Pinel was an inveterate reformer, rejecting the established practices of bloodletting and purging, and concluding that mental disorder stemmed from heredity or 'passions' such as sadness, fear, anger or elation.

Most famously, Pinel became known for removing the chains from female patients at the Salpêtrière in 1800, some three years after his assistant, Jean-Baptiste Pussin (1746–1811), had done so for male patients at the Bicêtre. In fact, Pinel's initiative commenced in the early 1790s and built steadily over the following years.[171] More broadly, it was Pinel's sympathetic writings about the mentally ill, portraying them as unfortunate persons deserving of respect and sympathy, that likely had the greatest impact on public perceptions of the mentally ill in France and other parts of Europe.[172]

These shifts in approach, exemplified by Tuke in England and Pinel in France, resulted in greater recognition of the idea that mental illness was a problem for which society had responsibility, and that the mentally ill should be treated with dignity. This idea did not rest easily, however, with the traditions of coercion, punishment and poor treatment that had evolved in many eighteenth-century English asylums.

In Ireland, Hallaran, like Tuke and Pinel, was a key figure in developing progressive, humane approaches to the mentally ill, warning strongly against reliance on simple force, and promoting the idea of speaking with each patient as an individual human being:

Maniacs, when in a state to be influenced by moral agents, are not to be subdued *ex officio*, by measures of mere force, and he who will attempt to impose upon their credulity by aiming it at too great a refinement in address or intellect, will often find himself detected, and treated by them with marked contempt ... I have in consequence made it a special point on my *review days*, to converse for a few minutes with each patient, on the subject which appeared to be most welcome to his humour. By a regular attention to the duties of this *parade*, I am generally received with as much politeness and decorum as if every individual attached to it, had a share of expectancy from the manner in which he may happen to acquit himself on the occasion. The mental exertion employed amongst the convalescents by this species of address is very remarkable, and the advantages flowing from it are almost incredible.[173]

Hallaran's engagement with each patient on the subject the patient wished to speak about was entirely consistent with the more humane, respectful approach recommended by Tuke and Pinel. In retrospect, Hallaran's approach is also consistent with twenty-first century ideas about engaging with patients' symptoms in direct ways,[174] as reflected in, for example, the increasing use of cognitive behaviour therapy (a talking therapy focused on thoughts and behaviours) for psychosis in the late twentieth century, focusing on understanding and interpreting symptoms, with patients and therapists working together to co-create a shared dialogue.[175]

In parallel with developments in Europe, the 1700s also saw several significant moves towards organised care for the mentally ill in the US. In 1729, the first identifiable psychiatric ward was created in the Boston alms house when persons with mental illness were separated from other inmates.[176] The mid-1700s saw the establishment of the Pennsylvania Hospital in Philadelphia, which took its first admissions in 1752 and was devoted to the care of the sick and mentally ill.[177] Conditions for the mentally ill were, however, generally poor and an admission fee was charged for members of the public who wished to visit the insane wing of the establishment as spectators.

The first hospital devoted exclusively to mental illness in the US, Virginia Eastern Lunatic Asylum in Williamsburg, was established in 1770, and the first patients admitted three years later.[178] Notwithstanding these developments, most of the care and support needs of the mentally ill in colonial America were still met by families and communities, albeit increasingly backed up by the alms houses and hospitals that emerged in the later 1700s.[179]

Subsequent developments in the US during the 1800s, especially the drive to establish mental hospitals, were driven by a range of diverse factors, including demographic changes, growing awareness of the social problems presented by the mentally ill, the philanthropic impulses of various elite groups, and developments in psychiatric practice in Europe and elsewhere. In France, for example, the 1700s had seen care of the mentally ill chiefly located in general hospitals, workhouses and hospices,[180] although the Salpêtrière and Bicêtre in Paris would later lead the way in reforming conditions for the mentally ill. Clearly, a time of substantial change had arrived in France, the US, England and Ireland, focusing – chiefly and regrettably – on well-meaning institutional provision for the mentally ill.

Asylums for the Mentally Ill:
Inevitable, Inexorable, Unstoppable?

Given these developments in Ireland and elsewhere during the late 1700s and early 1800s, and the long standing, unresolved problems presented by the mentally ill, it is useful to pose the question: was there any alternative to the asylums that emerged so resolutely throughout the 1800s and dominated the history of psychiatry until the late 1900s? Were they inevitable? Inexorable? Unstoppable?

There can be no doubt about the need for some kind of solution to the urgent problems presented by the destitute mentally ill in eighteenth-century Ireland.[181] No sooner had a House of Industry been opened in North Brunswick-Street in Dublin in 1773, for example, than it needed to deal with an extraordinary influx of destitute persons with mental disorder.[182] In 1776, 10 cells were specifically dedicated for the mentally ill; in 1778, an entire extra house was taken over for persons with mental disorder; in 1798, 32 additional cells were required; and 10 years later, 4 more cells were added. Between 1799 and 1802, some 3,679 persons died in this House of Industry, many of them mentally ill.

Nationwide, the Houses of Industry, by 1804, contained disturbingly large numbers of persons with mental disorder or intellectual disability, including 118 in the Dublin House of Industry, 90 in Cork, and 25 in Waterford.[183] Conditions in the Limerick House of Industry were particularly brutal, with one 1806 report indicating that mentally ill persons were kept naked, chained, handcuffed and exposed to the elements.[184] More specifically, John Carr, in *The Stranger in Ireland*, described disturbing scenes of mistreatment, neglect and cruelty in the Limerick establishment, which he visited in 1805:

Under the roof of this house, I saw madmen *stark naked* girded only by their irons, standing in the rain, in an open court, attended by *women*, their cells upon the ground-floor, scantily supplied with straw, damp, and ill-secured. In the wards of labour, abandoned prostitutes, in rags and vermin, each loaded with a long chain and heavy log, working only when the eye of the superintending officer was upon them, are associated throughout the day with respectable old female housekeepers, who, having no children to support them, to prevent famishing, seek this wretched asylum. At night, they sleep together in the same room; the sick (unless in very extreme cases) and the healthy, the good and the bad, all crowded together. In the venereal ward, the wretched female sufferers were imploring for a little more covering, whilst several idiots, squatted in corners, half naked, half famished, pale and hollow-eyed, with a ghastly grin, bent a vacant stare upon the loathsome scene, and consummated its horror. Fronting this ward, across a yard, in a large room, nearly thirty feet long, a raving maniac, instead of being strapped to his bed, was handcuffed to a stone of 300lbs [136 kilograms] weight, which, with the most horrible yells, by a convulsive effort of strength, he dragged from one end of the room to the other, constantly exposed to the exasperating view and conversation of those who were in the yard. I have been well informed that large sums of money have been raised in every county for the erection of mad-houses: how has this money been applied?[185]

Clearly, despite the Inspector General of Prisons having the power, since 1787, to inspect all places where the mentally ill and intellectually disabled were kept,[186] there were still real problems with conditions of confinement. Walsh summarises the position:

> By the closing decades of the 18th century lunacy had become a problem not only for families of property but also for those responsible for maintaining civil order. The first action was taken against lunatics who were vagrants, beggars or thieves. These were sent off to bridewells or jails and left to languish there often until they died. Their general state and condition was subject to the scrutiny of the Inspectors of Prisons, a role which had been created around 1770. Prisons were plentiful in Ireland and no town with any pretensions towards importance lacked one. With the coming of the 19th century, public lunacy became a social problem of some magnitude.[187]

Against this rather bleak background, it was increasingly clear that the twin problems of destitution and mental illness in nineteenth-century Ireland needed to be addressed both urgently and systematically. But what, precisely, was to be done?

Looking at the management of mental disorder in particular, Battie, in his 1758 *Treatise on Madness*, set out clear views that while mental illness was still poorly understood,[188] it was clear that asylums were absolutely essential for both the treatment of patients and the education of physicians.[189] Battie had particular views about the causes of 'madness',[190] chiefly related to the brain, and emphatically recommended confinement in asylums, ideally far distant from the patient's home, with spectators banished from the buildings along with any other persons that might excite the patients and impede recovery.[191] This regime would bring considerable benefits, according to Battie, who also warned against confining the mentally ill in prisons or regarding them as public nuisances: mental illness was, in his view, both manageable and curable.[192]

In addition to confinement, Battie dutifully devoted attention to the roles of specific treatments in the management of the mentally ill, such as bleeding, opium, mineral waters and vomiting.[193] But the chief argument in his *Treatise on Madness* concerned asylums, which he felt should be places of treatment rather than simple confinement, and where conditions should be hygienic, therapeutic and markedly different to those prevailing in prisons.

Battie was a leading figure of his time, a fellow of the Royal College of Physicians in London and physician at St Luke's Hospital, and his views were highly influential. Shorter goes as far as to argue that the birth of psychiatry commenced in earnest with Battie.[194] Given his strong promotion of asylums, his broad professional influence, the clear social problems presented by the mentally ill, and the philanthropic impulses of the governing classes of the 1800s, the die was soon very firmly cast in the form recommended by Battie: the 1800s were to be the century of the asylum.

2

THE NINETEENTH CENTURY: GROWTH OF THE ASYLUMS

... it is of the utmost importance that cases of insanity should as speedily as possible be removed to an asylum.

Lunatic Asylums, Ireland, Commission, *Report of the Commissioners of Inquiry into the State of the Lunatic Asylums and Other Institutions for the Custody and Treatment of the Insane in Ireland: with Minutes of Evidence and Appendices* (1858)[1]

For the mentally ill, the tone of the turbulent nineteenth century was set firmly by the Criminal Lunatics Act 1800, implemented following the attempted assassination of King George III at the Drury Lane Theatre, London in May 1800 by James Hadfield, a dragoon suffering from mental disorder and, possibly, brain injury.[2] The legislation established a procedure for the indefinite detention of mentally ill offenders and led to state funding of accommodation for apparent criminal lunatics at Bethlem in London.

In Ireland, the Hospitals and Infirmaries (Ireland) Act 1806 enabled Grand Juries to present money for wards for lunatics in connection with County Infirmaries and for the maintenance of asylums in connection with the Houses of Industry.[3] There was still enormous pressure on the House of Industry in Dublin and in 1810 monies were made available for the building of a public asylum, named the Richmond Asylum, in honour of the Duke of Richmond, Lord Lieutenant of Ireland. The establishment was later known as the Richmond District Lunatic Asylum (from 1830), then as Grangegorman Mental Hospital and, from 1958, as St Brendan's Hospital.

In the early days of the Richmond, Dr Alexander Jackson (1767–1848), a physician at the House of Industry, had an especially keen interest in the mentally ill, having visited asylums abroad and provided advice on the new Richmond building.[4] The architect was Francis Johnston, whose other work includes Dublin General Post Office, and the asylum was built on a plan similar to that of Bethlem. The first patients from the House of Industry were transferred in 1814 and the Richmond was officially opened the following year, when an act was passed establishing its governors as a corporation with perpetual succession.[5]

The new Richmond Asylum, with Jackson and Hugh Ferguson as physicians, and Andrew Jackson as surgeon, was determined to provide enlightened care to the mentally ill and avoid the use of physical restraint wherever possible. Initial reports were duly positive, noting that no more than one patient in twenty was confined to his or her room, and in most of those cases the reason for confinement was physical illness rather than disturbance due to mental disorder.[6] In the early 1830s, the Richmond Asylum, valued with its furniture at £80,000, was handed over from the government to the District, comprising counties Meath, Wicklow, Louth and Dublin.[7] In 1846, the Inspector of Lunatic Asylums reported positively:

> I have been in the habit of visiting this institution frequently during the last year, and of inspecting it very minutely, and have also had the pleasure of attending the Board of Governors on various occasions. It is unnecessary for me to add, that the general business is most satisfactorily performed [...]. The Asylum continues to maintain its high character as being one of the best-managed institutions in the country; and also for the great order, regularity, and state of cleanliness in which it is kept. The beds and bedding are kept always very clean.[8]

The Inspector, Dr Francis White, felt it was 'necessary to enlarge the Richmond Asylum by the addition of a wing to accommodate 100 patients, and also of an infirmary, so that the Asylum, when enlarged, may altogether be adequate to the accommodation of 400'.[9]

Throughout the early decades of the 1800s, the Richmond Asylum was at the forefront of both therapeutic enthusiasm and efforts to reform and expand Ireland's emerging asylum system. This initiative built on progress elsewhere, especially the humanitarian approach of Pinel in Paris, who pioneered less custodial approaches to asylum care, and Tuke's York Retreat, based on policies of care and gentleness, as well as medical supervision.[10]

From its establishment, the Richmond pioneered 'moral management' in Ireland. Esquirol, in France, had defined moral management as 'the application of the faculty of intelligence and of emotions in the treatment of mental alienation'.[11] The moral management approach represented a significant break from the past which had emphasised custodial care rather than engagement with each patient as an individual. In more recent decades, the moral management approach might well be compared with 'milieu therapy' involving a group-based approach to recovery and establishment of therapeutic communities,[12] or occupational therapy.

Although its precise meaning was, at times, rather vague, moral management had the key benefit of representing a significant (although by no means complete) move away from traditional treatments such as bloodletting, routine confinement and restraint. Elsewhere in Ireland, mechanical restraint was an especially disturbing feature of asylums, initially involving manacles, hoops, chains and body-straps, with the emphasis moving to straitjackets in the early 1800s.[13] Physical or bodily restraint was also used, as was chemical restraint, involving bromides, paraldehyde and chloral, among other substances. The moral management approach sought to reduce or end such practices, and strongly emphasised having a good diet, exercise and occupation, as well as reason and human interaction.[14]

The moral approach significantly influenced asylum design during this period[15] and, to emphasise its commitment to the new model, the Richmond was run chiefly by moral governors during the first half of the nineteenth century; these included Richard Grace (1815–30) and Samuel Wrigley (1831–57), separated by a brief interlude during which Dr William Heisse (1830–1) ran the asylum. Heisse was removed from his post rather dramatically in June 1831, apparently owing to the poor condition of the institution.[16]

Notwithstanding the emergence, growth and relatively enlightened approach of the Richmond in the early 1800s, however, it was soon apparent that further, systematic provision was needed across Ireland for the care of the destitute mentally ill. In what would become a recurring paradigm in Irish mental health care, a committee was established to produce a report about the problem and, presumably, try to advance provision.

Select Committee on the Lunatic Poor in Ireland (1817): 'Totally Inadequate for the Reception of the Lunatic Poor'

In March 1817, the indefatigable Robert Peel, Chief Secretary, persuaded the House of Commons to set up a select committee to look into the need for greater provision for 'the lunatic poor in Ireland'.[17] This followed on from the work of Sir John Newport (1756–1843) examining the plight of the 'aged and infirm poor of Ireland', including the mentally ill,[18] but the 1817 initiative focused more specifically and emphatically on the 'lunatic poor'. The committee heard a broad range of evidence, relating to many institutions, and the evidence that Mr James Cleghorn presented to the committee regarding St Patrick's Hospital has already been explored in Chapter 1. The first paragraph of its final report stated the committee's central finding bluntly:

> Your Committee have enquired, as to the extent of the accommodation which may be afforded by the present establishments in the several counties of Ireland, and are of opinion, that those establishments are totally inadequate for the reception of the lunatic poor. An hospital attached to the House of Industry in Dublin, was originally the only receptacle in that city for persons of the lower class, who were afflicted with mental derangement; and the cells attached to the infirmaries or poor houses in some of the counties were by no means calculated for the restoration to sanity, or even for the safe custody and care of the unhappy persons who were suffering under so dreadful a malady.[19]

The committee noted that, in 1815, 170 persons with mental disorder were moved from the Dublin House of Industry into the newly established Richmond Asylum which, like the asylum established by Hallaran in Cork, appeared to be generally well run. The Richmond, however, was already full 'and as the majority of patients are sent from the remoter parts of the country, it is in vain to hope to diminish it, unless by the establishment of other asylums':

> Your Committee beg leave to call the attention of the House to the detailed opinion expressed by the governors of the Richmond Asylum, that the only mode of effectual

relief will be found in the formation of district asylums, exclusively appropriated to the reception of the insane. They can have no doubt that the successful treatment of patients depends more on the adoption of a regular system of moral treatment, than upon casual medical prescription ... there should be four or five district asylums capable of containing each from one hundred and twenty to one hundred and fifty lunatics.[20]

The evidence presented to the committee about the desperate plight of the mentally ill outside asylums, which led to their call for more asylums, was, by any standards, compelling.[21] John Leslie Foster, one of the governors of the Richmond, told the committee about conditions in the Dublin House of Industry which were, for many, 'as defective as can possibly be imagined'.[22] The committee asked if he thought 'the accommodation in the House of Industry for lunatic patients is so defective that upon the whole it is a less evil to exclude them than to admit them?' Foster responded:

> I have seen three, I think, certainly two lunatics in one bed in the House of Industry. I have seen, I think, not fewer than fifty or sixty persons in one room, of which I believe the majority were insane, and the rest mere paupers not afflicted with insanity. I have seen in the same room a lunatic chained to a bed, the other half of which was occupied by a sane pauper, and the room so occupied by beds there was scarcely space to move in it ...[23]

In other parts of the country, provision for the destitute mentally ill was simply non-existent: James Daly, another witness, was asked 'what provision exists in the county of Galway for lunatic paupers?' He responded: 'None; any patients that I have known, it was necessary for them to be sent to Dublin'.[24] The committee also heard there was no accommodation for 'pauper lunatics' in Cavan or Kerry, and that accommodation in Clare comprised 'seven cells, adjoining to the House of Industry, together with a room for convalescent patients, which I deem totally inadequate'.

In a similar vein, Colonel Crosbie confirmed that there was a county infirmary in Kerry but when asked if there was 'any separate accommodation for pauper lunatics', he responded: 'None that I am aware of'.[25] Asked 'would there be any difficulty in attaching a separate asylum to the present infirmary for lunatics', Colonel Crosbie was emphatic: 'None whatever; there is a large yard in which it could be erected'.

The 1817 committee also heard at some length from the illustrious Thomas Spring Rice (1790– 1866), 'life-governor, and member of the regulating committee for [Limerick] Lunatic Asylum for the last three years', who, in 1815, 'visited the asylums of Cork, Waterford, Clonmel and Limerick'.[26] The asylum in Cork was 'the best managed, not only that I had ever seen, but ever considered or heard of'.[27] But Rice warned that the Cork establishment 'derives everything, that can be derived from humanity and skill, from the physician who is at the head of it'[28] (Hallaran, Chapter 1). The Cork arrangement was not, in Rice's view, a solid basis for establishing a broader system of asylums; dedicated, systematic, legislative reform was needed at national level.

The situation in Cork contrasted sharply with that in Waterford, where Rice reported there were 'a few miserable cells attached to the House of Industry, resembling an ill-constructed gaol rather than a retreat for lunatics'.[29] In Clonmel, 'so little understood was the management of the insane that they were unable even to keep them clothed, and some were lying in the yard upon straw in a state of nakedness'.[30]

Matters were worse again at the 'Lunatic Asylum of Limerick, in which the accommodation afforded to the insane' was 'such as we should not appropriate for our dog-kennels'. There was no heating or ventilation, and the mentally ill were 'exposed during the whole of the winter to the extremities of the weather', resulting in amputations (owing to 'that mortification in the extremities, to which the insane are peculiarly liable') and deaths (owing 'to the extreme coldness of the situation'):

> ... two, and sometimes, I believe, three of the insane have been condemned to lie together in one of those cells, the dimensions of which are six feet by ten feet seven inches; some of them in a state of furious insanity. In order to protect them from the obvious results, the usual mode of restraint was by passing their hands under their knees, fastening them with manacles, fastening bolts about their ankles, and passing a chain over all, and then fastening them to a bed. I can assure the Committee, from my own knowledge, they have continued for years, and the result has been (and I believe an honourable friend of mine may also have witnessed the fact) that they have so far lost the use of their limbs, that they are utterly incapable of rising.[31]

Other parts of the Limerick establishment were designated for the physically 'sick, as well as for such insane as may be trusted at large without actual danger':

> In one of these rooms I found four-and-twenty individuals lying, some old, some infirm, one or two dying, some insane, and in the centre of the room was left a corpse of one who died a few hours before. Another instance was still stronger: in the adjoining room I found a woman with the corpse of her child, left upon her knees for two days; it was almost in a state of putridity. I need not say the woman was almost in a state of distraction; another was so ill that she could not leave her bed; and in this establishment, with governors ex officio, and with all the parade of inspection and control, there was not to be found one attendant who would perform the common duties of humanity.[32]

To compound matters, Rice reported that during a period of 'fever', 'all medical attendance had been discontinued' and prescriptions were issued from 'a mile and quarter distance'. In addition to poor conditions and neglect, there was also evidence of active abuse, as 'the keeper of the lunatics claimed an exclusive dominion over the females confided to his charge, and which he exercised in the most abominable manner; I decline going into the instances, the character of which are most atrocious'. While Rice reported that, since these events, there had been changes in personal and practice at the Limerick establishment (on the advice of 'Dr Hallaran in Cork'), the committee was clearly still deeply impressed by Rice's compelling evidence.

Against this background, the committee, in its conclusions, had no doubt but that a properly governed network of district asylums was needed in order to remedy the plight of the destitute mentally ill, an issue which was, they noted, 'so materially importing the character of the country, and so deeply interesting to humanity':

> Your Committee have observed with satisfaction, the disinterested labours of those who have superintended the Asylums in the cities of Dublin and Cork; and if they were to go into any detail of the principles on which the establishments which they propose might be best administered, they would earnestly recommend an entire conformity to the system laid down and acted on in the Richmond Lunatic Asylum, as that system appears to have been considered with great anxiety and acted on with signal success.[33]

John Leslie Foster, one of the governors of the Richmond Lunatic Asylum, gave evidence to the committee about the background to the Richmond's approach and Foster's evidence, like that of Rice outlining abuses in Limerick, shaped the committee's thinking substantially. Foster reported:

> Until within these very few years a much greater degree of coercion has been generally applied in the treatment of lunatics, than is now found to be necessary; a few years ago Mr Pinel, a French physician [Chapter 1], who had the charge of the principal receptacles for the insane at Paris proposed and published a more gentle mode of treatment. It appears in his hands to have been attended with great success; this mode was introduced into this country, I believe, in the first instance in the Quakers Asylum near York; the good effects of which are illustrated in a publication of a Mr Took [sic],[34] the manager of that asylum; and this system appearing to the governors of the Richmond Lunatic Asylum to be founded in good sense, they determined on trying the experiment in their new institution. I beg to add as a proof of this, that there is not in the Richmond Lunatic Asylum, to the best of my belief, a chain, a fetter, or a handcuff. I do not believe there is one patient out of twenty confined to his cell, and that of those who are confined to their cells, in the greater number it is owing to derangement in their bodily health, rather than to the violence of mania.[35]

The stirring endorsement of the Richmond's approach in the 1817 report led to the passage of the Asylums for Lunatic Poor (Ireland) Act 1817 which was amended by the Lunatic Asylums (Ireland) Act 1820, and both of which were then repealed by the Lunacy (Ireland) Act 1821,[36] which aimed 'to make more effectual provision for the establishment of asylums for the lunatic poor, and for the custody of insane persons charged with offences in Ireland'. More specifically, the 1821 Act stated that 'it shall and may be lawful for the lord lieutenant by and with the advice and consent of his Majesty's privy council in Ireland, to direct and order that any number of asylums for the lunatic poor in Ireland shall be erected and established in and for such districts in Ireland, as to the said lord lieutenant and privy council shall seem expedient'.[37]

On the heels of this provision, a mere four years after the hard-hitting 1817 report, the creation of Ireland's district asylums commenced in earnest: four district asylums were rapidly completed during the remainder of the 1820s (Armagh,[38] Belfast,[39] Derry and Limerick) and five more by 1835 (Ballinasloe, Carlow, Waterford, Maryborough (Portlaoise) and Clonmel).[40] Together, these establishments had the capacity to accommodate 1,062 patients in all. This development was consistent (although not continuous) with the emergence of various medical hospitals supported by the professional and merchant classes in the 1700s, the establishment of further 'voluntary' medical hospitals in the 1830s, and widespread provision of 'fever hospitals', along with increased organisation of the medical profession, especially dispensary doctors, during this period.[41]

All of these developments represented significant changes for the poor, the ill and the excluded in nineteenth-century Ireland: social problems were pressing; institutions were the answer; and the mentally ill were among those most desperately in need of care. The era of the asylum had well and truly arrived.

Treatment in Asylums: 'Education and Training form the Basis of the Moral Treatment'

The establishment of Ireland's asylums was accompanied by a significant consolidation and expansion of the roles of doctors in the treatment of the mentally ill and management of the new institutions. At the Richmond, Dr John Mollan (a native of Newry, educated in Edinburgh) was appointed as 'physician extraordinary' in January 1836 owing to his medical experience across various Dublin hospitals and a particular interest in the insane.[42] Two years later, Mollan presented a detailed 'statistical report on the Richmond Lunatic Asylum' at the Evening Meeting of the Royal College of Physicians on 26 March 1838.[43]

Mollan commenced his overview by emphasising that the Richmond was intended not just for the safekeeping of the insane, but for their rational treatment and cure. The Richmond was, he said, the first institution in Ireland *specifically constructed* for the classification of the insane, with a view to the provision of better, more appropriate care. Mollan was a strong proponent of laborious employment and, in 1838, 60 men were involved in cultivating the Richmond asylum grounds; 15 were employed in various trades (e.g. tailors, shoemakers, carpenters); and others were engaged in activities such as making mats and domestic work. Female patients were occupied with spinning, knitting, needlework, washing and other domestic tasks.

Mollan, who was instrumental in establishing a patients' library in 1844, became senior physician at the asylum in 1848, following the death of Dr Alexander Jackson.[44] Mollan was a remarkable figure who had previously assisted with the fever epidemic in Galway (1822) and went on to serve as president of the King and Queen's College of Physicians in Ireland (1855–6).[45] He took an active part in the formation of the Royal Medical Benevolent Fund and was noted for his charitable works. In 1852, Mollan was also involved in efforts to establish a school at the Richmond, an initiative which was taken up with enthusiasm by Dr Joseph Lalor, RMS from 1857 to 1886,[46] who wrote:

> I consider that education and training are most valuable agents in the treatment ... and that it expresses in name and substance what has been long known in reference to lunatics in general as to their moral treatment ... starting with the proposition that education and training form the basis of the moral treatment of all classes of the insane.[47]

Under Lalor, the school at the Richmond taught a broad range of subjects including reading, writing, arithmetic, algebra, geometry, geography, drawing, needlework and various arts and crafts:[48]

> In reference to the education or training of the insane, no matter of what class or age, I wish to state that I try to have the patients engaged in the same pursuit for not more than from one to one hour and a half consecutively. Monotony, whether of work, education, or recreation, appears to me to be injurious to the insane of all classes and ages. I consider the alternation of literary, aesthetical, moral and physical education, with industrial employment and recreation (so as to produce variety of occupation), to be of great advantage in the treatment of the insane, whether the particular form of the insanity be mania, melancholia, monomania, dementia, idiotcy, or imbecility.[49]

Professional teachers were employed and the National Board of Education recognised the classes in 1862. Lalor was extremely proud of the school:

> Summarizing what I consider some very important items of our system here, I note that out of 479 male patients in the house on the 17th May [1878], 400 were employed either at school or industrially, or both combined, and only 79 were wholly unemployed; 45 of the unemployed were so in consequence of being under medical treatment, leaving only 34 men unemployed purely owing to their state of mind. Of 553 female patients in the house on the same day, 448 were employed either at school or industrially, or both combined, and 105 were wholly unemployed; 89 of the unemployed were so in consequence of being under medical treatment, leaving only 50 unemployed purely from the state of their mind.[50]

Lalor was a major figure in the Irish asylums,[51] as evidenced by his influence on other doctors such as Dr Joseph Petit, who was appointed as Lalor's assistant in 1874 and went on to serve as RMS in Letterkenny and Sligo.[52] Throughout this period, however, Lalor had an extraordinarily complex relationship with the governors at Grangegorman (who had excluded him from meetings since 1871) and a deeply conflictual one with the Inspector, Dr John Nugent, who was continually involved in asylum management; all of which led to an enquiry in 1883, clearly vindicating Lalor.[53]

In 1861, Lalor became the eighth president, and first Irish president, of the Medico-Psychological Association (MPA), which held its annual meeting in Dublin, providing a significant opportunity for Lalor to promote the importance of resident medical superintendents (rather than 'visiting physicians') in the Irish asylums.[54] This was one of many themes that exercised the energetic

Lalor; another was – inevitably – the self-reportedly progressive approach to management that he recounted from the Richmond:

> The total disuse of restraint, and the very infrequent use of seclusion – the freedom allowed to all our patients to exercise and have various sorts of games on the open grounds, in place of enclosed yards – are very gratifying features. The number and cost of our staff, estimated per head on the daily average number of patients, is less in this than in the other district lunatic asylums of Ireland, and this fact, taken in connection with our large teaching and training power, shows that education and industrial employment carried out, as they are here, systematically, by skilled hands, do not necessarily increase expense. [...] The amount of quietude and good order, of literary and industrial occupation, and of contentment, cheerfulness, and amusement here is very satisfactory.[55]

Dr Daniel Hack Tuke (1827–1895) wrote approvingly of the Richmond schools in the influential *Journal of Mental Science*:

> To myself, the schools which are in active operation there under Dr Lalor were of deep interest, and I venture to think that some useful hints may be gathered from what we witnessed on the occasion. Indeed so valuable did the system pursued appear to me to be, that I stayed another day in Dublin in order to see more of the working of the schools [...]. The pupils are divided into three classes on both sides of the house, there being three male and three female trained teachers [...]. The patients stood in circles marked out by a chalk line, presenting a very orderly appearance, while the teacher asked them questions on geography, &c., or gave them an object lesson. While of course there was a great difference in the expression of those who were being taught, and in their responsiveness to the questions put to them, there was a general air not only of propriety but of interestedness which was very striking. Some, in fact, were extremely bright and lively ...[56]

Following Lalor's death, his obituary in the *Journal of Mental Science* described him as 'excellent and kind-hearted' and highlighted his achievements with the school at the Richmond:

> It is stated on good authority that [prior to Lalor's appointment to the Richmond] refractory patients were confined in cells for most of the day as well as the night, receiving their food in such a way as best suited the convenience of the attendants. Open-air exercise was rarely permitted, and then only in the dark confined yards or sheds surrounded by stone walls. All this was changed by Dr Lalor; better grounds were prepared, games were introduced, and the general comfort of the patients was attended to. Dr Lalor, as is well known, enthusiastically carried out the school system [...].

It should be stated that for two years before he became Superintendent a school had been in operation on the female side under an excellent school mistress. It was Dr Lalor who introduced the same system for the male patients, and he obtained additional teachers, trained under the National Board, for the female school. Singing and music were much cultivated, while object and picture lessons were given, as well as others in natural history and geography. At the Exhibition held some years ago in Dublin, drawings, paintings, and industrial work, all executed by the patients, attracted considerable attention. Along with the schools, concerts were given every fortnight, or even weekly ...[57]

Similar sentiments were expressed in the *Irish Times*, which paid generous and deserved tribute to Lalor's foresight and perseverance.[58] Throughout this period, the educational approach advanced by Lalor was not, however, the only therapeutic paradigm in evidence at the Richmond or elsewhere. As Cox notes, the use of moral management did not exclude the employment of various additional medicinal treatments such as purgatives, bloodletting and emetics, which continued until the late 1870s.[59]

Notwithstanding this persistence of older medicinal paradigms in the asylums, Lalor was by no means alone in trying to improve matters for the mentally ill in a fashion that was as enlightened as the institutional framework of the times permitted, even if Lalor and others clearly failed to challenge that framework sufficiently at the time. Such initiatives were heavily influenced by developments in England and elsewhere, and were duly reflected in the literature of the time, including Sir Alexander Halliday's *General View of the Present State of Lunatic Asylums in Great Britain and Ireland and in Some Other Kingdoms*, which stated confidently that a new era of enlightenment and rational treatment had now finally arrived.[60] It hadn't, but there were increasing signs of progress in that direction as evidenced by, for example, the careful, thoughtful writings of John Cheyne.

Cheyne (1777–1836), another leading British physician, worked in Dublin and is best remembered for his description of a breathing pattern seen in conditions such as chronic heart failure, now known as Cheyne-Stokes breathing.[61] Cheyne suffered from depression and in 1843 wrote a striking book titled *Essays on Partial Derangement of the Mind, in Supposed Connexion with Religion*.[62] Cheyne's monograph was notable for his detailed engagement with the signs and symptoms of insanity, based largely on his conversations with persons who were mentally ill[63] but also drawn from his personal experience of depression, which he attributed to a life of overwork.[64]

More specifically, Cheyne rooted his reflections in what he had 'learned from observation; from having long witnessed the passions and affections in unrestrained action; from having long viewed the drama of life from behind the scenes, and attended to the manifestation of character in health and disease; from his having been for some years in superintendence of considerable number of insane persons, nearly one hundred; and, lastly, from introspection, especially while suffering from lowness of spirits, arising from dyspeptic nervousness, aggravated by the wear and tear of a life of continued over-exertion'.[65]

Based on his affecting phenomenological descriptions of various disturbed states of mind, Cheyne concluded that 'mental derangement' could arise:

First - From a disordered condition of the organs of sense.

Secondly - From a disorder of one or more of the intellectual faculties.

Thirdly - From a disorder of one or more of the natural affections and desires.

Fourthly - From a disorder of one or more of the moral affections.

Fifthly - From groups of faculties and affections being disordered, thereby involving derangement of the whole mind.[66]

Cheyne presented four overall conclusions, based on his clinical work and the observations outlined in his book, generally linking mental illness with physical disorders:

I.   That mental derangements are invariably connected with bodily disorder.
II.   That such derangements of the understanding, as are attended with insane speculations on the subject of religion, are generally, in the first instance, perversions of only one power of the mind.
III. That clergymen, to whom these essays are particularly addressed, have little to hope for in placing divine truth before a melancholic or hypochondriacal patient, until the bodily disease, with which the mental delusion is connected, is cured or relieved.
IV.   That many of the doubts and fears of truly religious persons of sane mind depend either upon ignorance of the constitution and operations of the mind, or upon disease of the body.[67]

Cheyne's work is notable for the careful attention he devoted to the signs and symptoms of mental disorder,[68] the links he drew between mental symptoms and physical illness, and his identification of the role of alcohol in precipitating mental disturbance, leading him to advocate abstinence for those with alcohol problems.[69]

Despite the relatively (if selectively) progressive approaches of Cheyne, Lalor, Mollan and various others, however, it remains the case that the number of mentally ill persons in institutions continued to rise alarmingly during the nineteenth century and conditions of detention were very, very poor. In November 1844, the inspector, Dr Francis White, found that conditions in Wexford were filthy and patients half starved.[70] By1892, the Richmond's problems had increased greatly too, owing chiefly to overcrowding. The inspector was beside himself:

During the year no relief has been obtained as regards the overcrowding of this asylum. The number of patients now almost reaches 1,500, whereas the asylum only accommodates about 1,100. It is therefore not to be wondered at that the general health of the institution is far from satisfactory, and that the death-rate, as compared with other Irish asylums, is high, amounting to 12.5%, the average death-rate in a similar institution in this country being 8.3%. Constant outbreaks of zymotic disease [acute infectious diseases] have occurred. Dysentery has for many years past been almost endemic in this institution – 73 cases with 14 deaths occurred last year, and it may be mentioned that in no less than three of these cases secondary abscesses were found in the liver.[71]

Clearly, further, systemic reform was needed at national level to provide appropriate care to the mentally disturbed and minimise the ill effects of Ireland's large scale institutions. One of the key mechanisms used to pursue this goal throughout the 1800s was revision of mental health legislation. This constant, restless process of legislative change[72] was ultimately carried to a point that managed to be industrious, obsessional and almost certainly counterproductive, and was continually accompanied by a rhetoric of care and compassion that rested uneasily with the gargantuan institutions it created and sustained. These matters are considered next.

Mental Health Legislation in the 1800s:
The 'Dangerous Lunatic Act' (1838)

Among all of the many pieces of mental health legislation passed in nineteenth-century Ireland, the best known and most notorious was the Dangerous Lunatic Act of 11 June 1838, formally titled 'An Act to make more Effectual Provision for the Prevention of Offences by Insane Persons in Ireland'. The 1838 Act, as Parry notes, 'formed the basis of the judicial committal procedure which became the most important mode of admission to Irish asylums':

> In essence, this Act was to a large degree similar to its English predecessor, being introduced following the murder of a citizen by a man who had been earlier refused entry to the Richmond Lunatic asylum. The Act provided for the detention of persons denoting 'a Derangement of Mind, and a purpose of committing some Crime', or indeed the detention of persons who were believed, on the basis of other proof, to be insane and hence dangerous. From the beginning committal was notoriously easy to obtain, and for relatives there were considerable advantages in using the Act for it did not require a commitment to take the lunatic back following treatment.[73]

The Act, which followed from the murder in July 1833 of Nathaniel Sneyd, bank director with the House of Sneyd, French and Barton, by John Mason, and the subsequent newspaper publicity, was passed without parliamentary debate.[74] The primary purpose of the Act was to protect the public from the dangers allegedly posed by the mentally ill; its terms of confinement were extremely broad and vague; and, since it permitted the confinement in district asylums of prisoners who appeared mentally ill, people were initially confined to county prisons or bridewells, and then transferred to asylums (often after long delays, sometimes of several years duration).

During the committal process, medical evidence could be heard (and generally was) but was not mandatory, and certificates were signed by two magistrates. The 1838 Act soon became the admission pathway of choice for families seeking institutional care for relatives and a habit grew of encouraging a mentally ill person to commit a minor offence in order to facilitate committal under the Act.[75]

Discharge from the asylum was only possible when the patient's sanity was medically certified to the Lord Lieutenant.

Once the Act was passed, transfers from prisons to asylums commenced at once: in the first fortnight of July 1838, 13 people were referred from jails to the Richmond.[76] This caused immediate problems because the Richmond was already full but, in January 1839, the Chief Secretary, Lord Morpeth, stated that such transfers were to be accepted anyway, regardless of the number of patients already in the asylum. The asylums further objected that some of the transfers were not suitable for asylums and that inpatient numbers kept on rising, especially since discharge required the authority of the Lord Lieutenant. These very real problems, robustly highlighted by Mollan and others at the Richmond, were largely ignored by the government. Objections in the House of Commons and an 1843 amendment requiring at least one credible witness in each case made little difference either: the 1838 Act quickly became the main mechanism for asylum admission and a key contributor to the intractable overcrowding that blighted Irish asylums throughout the 1800s.[77]

As Finnane points out, between 1854 and 1856, committals of 'dangerous lunatics' accounted for 41.8 per cent of male and 31.8 per cent of female admissions to district lunatic asylums; by 1890–2, these proportions had risen to 75.7 per cent for men and 67.3 per cent for women, with some regional variation.[78] To make matters worse, approximately 17.1 per cent of all male patients and 18.2 per cent of female patients were discharged from district lunatic asylums in 1851, and these annual proportions fell steadily to 7.7 per cent for men and 7.4 per cent for women in 1911.[79] In that year, readmissions accounted for 21.9 per cent of male and 21.0 per cent of female admissions, while 5.9 per cent of male and 6.2 per cent of female patients died in the asylums (down slightly since 1851, when the proportions dying were 7.6 per cent for men and 6.4 per cent for women).[80] By 1914, Ireland's population had declined by a third since the Great Irish Famine (1845–52, Chapter 3) but the number of 'insane' persons in public asylums had increased sevenfold.[81]

If there was one single, standout event among the many factors that set Ireland on a course towards mass institutionalisation of the mentally ill, it was the 1838 Act.[82] Asylum doctors, including Woods in Killarney and Garner in Clonmel, objected vociferously, to little avail.[83] The legislation was ill conceived, poorly implemented and grossly unjust,[84] and, even after it was revised later in the 1800s, its echoes reverberated through the asylum system for much longer, setting the tone for the dominance of asylum care for the mentally ill and intellectually disabled well into the twentieth century.

Lord Naas attempted to enact reforms with the Lunacy Law Amendment Bill 1859, following the commissions of enquiry of 1858. He was, however, unsuccessful at that point, so it was not until 1867 that the 1838 Act was finally amended, with the effect of ending confinement in gaols prior to asylums and requiring magistrates to call a dispensary medical officer to examine the patient and sign the certificate.[85] Many decades later, when introducing the 1944 Mental Treatment Bill for a second reading in Dáil Éireann (part of the Irish parliament), the Parliamentary Secretary to the Minister for Local Government and Public Health, Dr Conn Ward, summarised the revised process, post-1867:

> The committal order was made by two peace commissioners or a district justice after the person concerned had been certified as a dangerous lunatic by a dispensary medical

officer. The expenses connected with the committal, including the payment to the medical officer for his services, were defrayed by the local public assistance authority [...]. The procedure under the Act of 1867 is that the Gárda apprehend the person and bring him before two peace commissioners before whom evidence is given that the person is dangerous and likely to commit an indictable crime. When it is proved to the satisfaction of the peace commissioners that the person was discovered and apprehended under circumstances denoting derangement of mind and a purpose of committing an indictable offence the peace commissioners call to their assistance the dispensary medical officer and if he certifies that the person is a dangerous lunatic or a dangerous idiot the peace commissioners, by warrant, direct the person to be taken to the district mental hospital for the district in which he was apprehended. This procedure has much in common with that followed in a criminal case. The patient is dealt with as if he were suspected of being guilty of a crime.[86]

While the 1867 amendment excluded doctors in private practice, it meant that local dispensary medical officers were required to sign certificates, even if asylum staff had provided evidence during petty session hearings. These measures, along with further amendments in the Lunatic Asylums (Ireland) Act 1875, improved the certification process but certainly did not eliminate errors or misuse. The fundamentally flawed and deeply unjust Dangerous Lunatic Act remained in place until the advent of the Mental Treatment Act 1945. Therefore, while the 1838 Act did not represent the only admission pathway during this period – and Cox devotes much needed attention to the 'ordinary' certification procedure and its increased medicalisation in 1862 – it was the Dangerous Lunatic Act that firmly set the tone for asylum care in nineteenth-century Ireland and accounted for the majority of admission in the early twentieth century.[87]

Against this distinctly dispiriting legislative background, there were three identifiable waves of asylum building in Ireland. The first wave saw, in addition to the Richmond, the construction of four district asylums during the 1820s and five more by 1835.[88] Legislation in 1845 made provision for the Central Criminal Lunatic Asylum in Dundrum, Dublin[89] and a large, 500 bed establishment in Cork, the Eglinton Asylum, which opened in the early 1850s. Originally in three blocks, which were later joined together, the Eglinton Asylum formed the longest façade of any building in Ireland.[90] Various other asylums were also opened during this, the second phase of asylum building, including establishments in Mullingar (1855) as well as Letterkenny (1866) and Castlebar (1866), both of which were designed by George Wilkinson (1814–1890), known for designing workhouses. There was considerable controversy about various aspects of the asylum building process in the 1850s, resulting in a highly critical report by London architect T.L Donaldson and James Wilkes, medical officer at Stafford Lunatic Asylum, supporting local concerns about how the building work was being directed from Dublin.[91] Problems persisted, and delays with progressing the asylum in Castlebar, for example, were publicly reported and lamented.[92] The Castlebar asylum was predated by 'the Chatterhouse', a bridewell on Station Road ('Mad House Hill') where patients were held before the Royal Irish Constabulary (RIC) transported them to Ballinasloe for admission.[93] Eventually, 'the

Chatterhouse' was replaced by the Castlebar asylum proper, which opened on 5 March 1866, at a cost of £34,906.

The growth of the asylums was unstoppable. The third phase of asylum building involved a range of individual architects and included the asylum in Ennis (with its Florentine palazzo, in 1868), the Monaghan asylum (the first to adopt a villa or pavilion format, in 1869) and the auxiliary asylum to the Richmond, in Portrane, County Dublin.[94] In 1900, the *Building News and Engineering Journal* reported that Portrane was 'constructed to accommodate 1,200 patients which [*sic*] are divided up into four classes – viz., chronics, melancholic and suicidal, recent and acute, the epileptic and infirm [...]. The total cost, when completed, will probably be about £250,000'.[95] The building contract for Portrane was the largest ever awarded to a single contractor in Ireland (the Collen brothers of Portadown). A further asylum was opened in Antrim in 1899, and, as Walsh and Daly point out, by 1900 approximately 21,000 people, 0.5 per cent of the population of the 32 counties of Ireland, were accommodated in the district asylums, with a small number of the mentally ill still in workhouses.[96]

Private Asylums in Ireland:
'Sent by an All-Bounteous Providence'?

In parallel with the steady and genuinely alarming expansion of Ireland's public asylum system, a limited, although by no means insignificant, network of private asylums also emerged and carved out a role for itself in Irish medicine and society. In 1799, Hallaran opened a private establishment, Citadella, near Cork, and further private asylums were established in Carlow, Downpatrick and Portobello in Dublin (Dr Boate's asylum).

One of the more dramatic episodes in the history of private asylums in Ireland concerns Dr Philip Parry Price Middleton who blew up Carlow Castle in 1814, when attempting to remodel the imposing, historic thirteenth-century building near the River Barrow. Middleton had earlier cofounded 'Hanover Park Asylum for the Recovery of Persons labouring under Mental Derangement' in Carlow town, with two surgeons, Dr Clay and Charles Delahoyd.[97] An 1815 pamphlet about the establishment emphasised that the 'humane means' used at Hanover Park had the '*safe and positive powers*' of readily tranquilising the most furious maniac':[98]

> The unequivocal results arising from the humane means employed by the Conductors
> of this Institution, for regenerating Reason and Health, in that once wretched portion
> of our fellow-creatures, *who had long been deemed incurable;* and consequently doomed
> to rigid confinement, constant coercion, and hopeless misery, in this life as though
> Insanity were a Crime, instead of a Calamity, naturally excited the most lively Interest
> in the minds of all ranks of the Community in the Metropolis of the British Empire: it
> was there hailed as a celestial meteor, sent by an all-bounteous Providence, to illumine
> the dark and dreary destiny of the unhappy sufferers, by restoring them to the long-lost
> faculty of Reason, and the wonted energies of the Soul.[99]

The vision underpinning Hanover Park was, it seems, enlightened to the point of utopian:

> This institution, emanating from the one at Iver, near London, under the direction of A. Hutchinson, M.D. F.R.C.S. &c.; is established here, for the accommodation of this part of Ireland; combining, at once, all the domestic comforts of a private family, and well-regulated society; formed into select classes, according to the progressive stages of convalescence. By the new mode of treatment adopted in this Institution, *every kind of coercion is entirely laid aside, as no longer necessary*; while innocent amusements, with the salutary agremens of a carriage, are employed to renovate general Health.
>
> The situation also, in point of salubrity, cannot be excelled by any in the United Kingdom; and independently of the Principal edifices, the park will be studded with detached Pavilions and flower Gardens, for Patients of both sexes, in spacious and separate walled enclosures, for Pedestrian recreation; under the immediate superintendence of Dr Myddelton, and an experienced resident Surgeon.[100]

Middleton was well established as principal medical superintendent at Hanover Park before turning his entrepreneurial eye on Carlow Castle. His injudicious use of blasting powder, however, resulted in an explosion early on the morning of 13 February 1814: the castle's two eastern towers collapsed, as well as part of the adjoining walls.[101] Middleton's subsequent career was marked by further controversy and litigation, although he did publish, in 1827, a noted 'essay on gout'.[102]

By 1825, there were at least five private asylums in Ireland, in addition to charitable asylums in Dublin.[103] As well as Hallaran's Citadella in Cork, there were three private asylums in Finglas, County Dublin (including asylums managed by Dr William Harty and Mr Gregory) and one in Downpatrick (Mr Reed). From 1826, it was necessary for the Inspector-General of Prisons to visit and report on asylums kept for profit every two years.[104]

The situation for private asylums changed significantly in 1842 when the Private Lunatic Asylums (Ireland) Act made it unlawful for anyone to keep a house for two or more insane persons unless that house was licensed.[105] Patients could only be detained on foot if a certificate signed by two doctors and medical input was required at the establishment. Harty, in Finglas, objected strenuously against official interference in private asylums, penning a pamphlet addressed to Sir Robert Peel arguing that private asylums were well conducted and under the control of doctors.[106] Ironically, Harty's own establishment was subject to court proceedings in 1842, when the Lord Chancellor directed Harty to release a woman patient after Harty had refused to allow visits by her brother and her doctor. Further controversy followed and Harty's establishment soon vanished from the list of private asylums.

In addition to the private asylums, paying patients were accepted into the Carlow, Maryborough and Richmond asylums during the 1840s.[107] Other asylums were less enthusiastic: the first paying patients were admitted to Cork in the 1870s and, even then, initially on a small scale.[108] By the end of 1862, there were some 21 private asylums in Ireland and the inspectors (Drs John Nugent and George Hatchell) found that the quality of care varied considerably between them. Mauger, in a superb study of private asylums in Ireland, notes that the number of such establishments generally increased from 1820 onwards, in notable contrast to England and Wales, reflecting differing legislative provisions.[109] The increasing importance of this sector in Ireland was highlighted by the 1842 Act, the first legislative measure exclusively devoted to private asylums, which for the first time provided for the licensing and regulation of these establishments. While they catered chiefly for the Irish upper classes, this did not mean restraint was not used or that the private asylums were free from allegations of poor conditions, although, for the most part, conditions were generally reported as acceptable.[110]

Private asylums continued to operate throughout the latter part of the 1800s and early 1900s. By 31 December 1929 there were 841 patients (333 males, 508 females) in private establishments, of which eight were 'licensed in pursuance of the provisions of the Private Lunatic Asylums (Ireland) Act, 1842. The remaining four (Bloomfield Institution, St Patrick's Hospital, St Vincent's Institution, and Stewart Institution) being "charitable, institutions supported wholly or in part by voluntary contributions and not kept for profit by any private individual" [were] exempt from licensing. Licences were granted in 1929 for the reception of 553 patients, an increase of 20 compared with the previous year'.[111]

Private asylums played important roles in both providing care and developing the profession of psychiatry during this period. Prominent establishments included Dr Osborne's Lindville Private Lunatic Asylum on Blackrock Road in Cork[112] and Verville Retreat in Clontarf, Dublin. By 1930, Lindville, then under the stewardship of Mrs Elizabeth E. S. Osborne, received a generally positive report from the Inspector of Mental Hospitals:

> The demeanour of the patients, as well as their neat appearance, reflects credit on the management of this institution. Concerts, dances and card parties are held. One patient required restraint. Catholic and Church of Ireland clergy visit the house frequently. A number of patients are allowed out on parole and some occupy themselves at gardening and fancywork.[113]

At Verville, Dr Patrick Daniel Sullivan was elected to the Irish Division of the MPA in 1922.[114] In 1929, the Inspector reported that Verville was 'well kept' and the 'general health' of the patients 'remarkably good';[115] by 1933 a veranda had been erected, 'restraint or seclusion was not necessary in any case', and 'some of the patients attend cinema performances';[116] and in 1934 it was noted that 'several patients go for walks and motor drives in the country'.[117] In April 1949, the Irish Division of the RMPA held its Spring Quarterly Meeting in Verville, at the invitation of Dr Mary Sullivan.[118] Thirty-six members and two guests attended. Dr M. O'Connor Drury read his 'Report on a Series of Cases Treated by the ECT-Pentothal-Curare Technique' and Dr Gilmartin gave a clinical demonstration of the use of curare and pysostigmine to produce a modified seizure in ECT (Chapter 5).

In that year, Verville had 30 patients, all female, including 7 women detained under the Mental Treatment Act 1945.[119] The Inspector provided a positive report with particular emphasis on the use of 'modern treatment':

This home was well maintained. Re-decoration of some rooms had been carried out. Patients appeared to receive excellent nursing and many took part in outdoor recreation. All forms of modem treatment were applied with very good results.[120]

By 1949, Lindville had forty-one patients (including eight men), of whom eight were detained.[121] Both Lindville and Verville would later close as mental hospitals, but back in the mid-nineteenth century, these kinds of private asylums were a key part of Ireland's complicated, emergent 'system' of care, which was becoming noticeably more medical in nature with each passing year.[122] A general lack of enthusiasm among governors for attending board meetings was another factor in shaping the evolving asylums:[123] many governors never visited the institutions or attended any meetings, seeing their appointments simply as expected recognition of their positions in the local ascendancy.[124]

But, as Parry notes, it was, above all else, the advent, in 1843, of the *General Rules for the Government of All the District Lunatic Asylums of Ireland*[125] that was pivotal in setting developments on their distinctively medical trajectory:

> A major advance in the medical take-over of Irish asylums was the passing into law of the General Rules for the Government of all the District Lunatic Asylums in Ireland on March 27th 1843 ... the 1843 rules gave the visiting physician complete authority in Irish district asylums. Describing the duties of the various offices on the district asylums, the Rules state that the manager should 'under the direction of the Board, and subject to the directions of the Physician as to the treatment of the Patients, superintend and regulate the whole of the Establishment'[126] [...]. The physician henceforth was 'to direct the course of Moral and Medical treatment of the patients'.[127] The first victory of the Irish medical profession regarding madness was complete.[128]

The 1843 rules indeed placed very many responsibilities on the physician, who was 'to attend on three days (to be named by the Board) at least in each week, and on every day at such Asylums in which the number of Patients shall exceed 250':

- He shall also visit on particular occasions, when called on by the Manager, and shall prescribe for all Patients and Servants who may require Medical aid, and for the Resident Officers who may request Medical assistance. [...]
- He shall attend daily on cases of Fever and on any other cases of an urgent nature.
- He is authorized to order such Diet as he may think necessary for any particular case, having, however, due regard for economy in each Article.[129]
- He should always visit every Patient under restraint, and, when he deems it safe, require such Patients to be temporarily relieved from restraint, and examine them so as to ascertain that they are not cramped or injured; and he should frequently go round the Asylum so as to see the state and condition of every Inmate.[130]

The asylum 'manager' was also accorded a broad range of roles under the 1843 rules, including oversight of the use of 'restraint':

> He [the manager] is to take charge of the instruments of restraint, and is not under any pretence to allow the unauthorized use of them to any person within the Establishment; all cases placed under restraint, seclusion, or other deviation from the ordinary treatment, are to be carefully recorded by him in the daily report, with the particular nature of the restraint or deviation resorted to. But in no case shall the Shower Bath [Chapter 1] be used without the authority of the Physician.[131]

Other rules related to the asylum governors, matron, apothecary, clerk and storekeeper, servants, gardener, gatekeeper, hall porter, keepers, nurses, assistant nurses, cook and laundress.[132] An addition to the rules in 1853 concerned chaplains, who were 'to afford Religious Instruction and Consolation to all patients, except such as shall be declared by the Physician to be unfit and incapable of understanding the nature of the Service, and of appreciating the effects of Religion'.[133] In addition, 'controversial subjects shall be scrupulously avoided, both in public service and in private visitations'.

The 1843 rules also laid out regulations governing admissions, placing strong emphasis on the signing of 'a bond for the removal of the Patient' in due course:

> Every Patient to be admitted upon a special direction by the Board, unless in cases of urgency, when the Physician may admit upon his own authority, stating on the face of his order the grounds upon which he acts. In every case a bond for the removal of the Patient, when required by the Board, to be signed by some responsible person, before the admission of the Patient, unless the Board upon any ground, or the Physician in cases of urgency, shall dispense with the same, or postpone the time for the execution of such Bond.[134]

And who was to be admitted?

> Idiots, as well as Lunatics properly so called, are to be admissible to every Asylum, and so also are Epileptic persons, where the fits produce imbecility of mind as well as of body.[135]

Clearly, then, admission criteria were broad and the 1843 rules clearly set the scene for the continued growth of Ireland's increasingly medicalised asylum system throughout the 1800s.

James Foulis Duncan: 'The Spirit of Innovation is Abroad'

Among the medical professionals and asylum doctors of the mid to late 1800s, the figure of James Foulis Duncan (1812–1895) looms large among his peers.[136] While the Richmond was being built in 1813, Dr Alexander Jackson, with the Reverend James Horner, opened a small private asylum in Finglas, County Dublin and, after the Richmond opened with Jackson as physician, Jackson sold Farnham House to James Duncan, a Scottish doctor, in 1815.[137] James Duncan, a keen hunter, athlete and traveller (he visited Syria and Algiers), died in March 1868, aged 82 years. His son, James Foulis Duncan, born in 1812, spent much of his childhood at the Finglas asylum.[138] Many decades later, in his presidential address to the MPA in 1875, Duncan reminisced about his unusual upbringing:

> It is now exactly sixty years since I was first brought – a child of only a few years old – to the asylum then recently placed under my father's management. My mother was dead, and owing to the circumstance that my father never kept a separate table for his family, I was thrown into closer contact with the inmates of the establishment than usually falls to the lot of children similarly circumstanced; and although there are drawbacks and dangers inseparably connected with such a life, I am here to say that it is not all gloom nor all disadvantage. It has its bright side as well as its dark. In almost all similar institutions of any size there are to be found some of the best and noblest of our race – men of gifted intellect, of high attainments, and of blameless lives. We know not why it should be so, but in the mysterious providence of God the shadow of this cloud is occasionally permitted to darken the path of some eminent for their virtues and their piety. It was my privilege to be indebted to some of these for many acts of kindness, and for much pleasant companionship. My earliest lessons in the Latin language were imparted by one during the short period of his residence at Farnham House, whom I shall ever remember with affection and esteem. Another instructed me, at a later period, in mathematics and the higher branches of science. Many others shared with me all the pleasures of my boyhood. These things have made an impression on me which I can never forget ...[139]

Building on this unusual but effective educational foundation, Duncan was awarded an MD (*Medicinae Doctor*; Doctor of Medicine) by Trinity in 1837 and became first physician to the staff of the reopened Adelaide Hospital in Dublin in 1858. Throughout his career, Duncan displayed several interesting qualities: he was acutely socially aware, especially of the effects of poverty on health; he supported the use of scientific comparisons to test treatments (in language that prefigured later ideas about clinical trials in medicine);[140] and he was highly religious in his views on many matters, including mental ill health, as evidenced in his 1852 publication, *God in Disease, or, The Manifestations of Design in Morbid Phenomena*.[141] From a clinical perspective, Duncan championed both medical and moral treatments for insanity, and Farnham House remained in the Duncan family for over 50 years, providing just such treatment.

Duncan himself achieved considerable prominence in his profession and became president of the MPA in 1875.[142] In his presidential address, delivered on 11 August 1875 at the Royal College of Physicians in Dublin, Duncan emphasised the changes occurring in Irish asylum medicine:

The time is not so very long gone by since everything connected with the management – I cannot say treatment – of the insane was a matter of general reproach, and everyone who devoted himself to the pursuit was avoided as much as possible. They were looked on as left-handed neighbours, very useful in their way, because their assistance could not always be dispensed with, but whose acquaintance no respectable person was expected to acknowledge. Too often they were men of inferior social position, low-minded in their taste, imperfectly educated, and with nothing in their character to command respect, even from those who employed them. Sordid in disposition, their only object was to make money out of those entrusted to their charge, and that at the least expense and trouble to themselves. In the present day all this is changed. [...]

Insanity in its various forms is now universally admitted to be a disease – differing, indeed, from ordinary disease as to its nature and phenomena – but a disease notwithstanding, and therefore to be viewed in the same light and treated on the same principles as those which regulate medical practice in other branches. [...]

Hence the propriety, rather, I should say, the absolute necessity of these cases being handed over to the care of members of the medical profession, who by the nature of their everyday duties are the best fitted to unravel the mysteries of their phenomena – to investigate the intricate chain of circumstances connected with their origin – to discriminate the relative importance of their various symptoms – to estimate the effect of remedies – and above all, to keep steadily before them in despite of every discouragement and disappointment the recovery of the patient as the one great object to be continually aimed at.[143]

Duncan was nonetheless concerned about the state of Irish asylum medicine, lamenting 'that the Irish contingent of this Association [the MPA] has hitherto done so little for the practical advancement of the science', a deficit he linked with the fact that 'only four out of our twenty-two district asylums are provided with a second resident medical officer', which greatly hampered the publication of clinical observations and research,[144] as well as attendance at MPA meetings.[145]

In his 1875 address, Duncan emphasised the importance of education for doctors involved in the committal process[146] and devoted considerable attention to the role of prevailing social circumstances ('an artificial state of living')[147] in causing mental disorder:

A striking feature of the present age is that it is one of incessant mental activity. All is hurry, bustle, and excitement. Men have become restless, and are ever seeking some new stimulus in the way of enjoyment, or some new discovery in the path of science. Formerly they were satisfied to jog on quietly in the easy way their fathers did before them; they lived in the same houses, cultivated the same farms, and followed the same fashions they were accustomed to from childhood. They had no real ambition; none of that feeling of discontent with present things which lies at the basis of all improvements. They did not hatch eggs by steam, or make calculations by a machine. They had implements, but no machines. They disliked new-fangled ways, and when they were told of improvements they were reluctant to adopt them. Now all is reversed. The spirit of innovation is abroad. New inventions are continually chronicled, and everyone is anxious to secure the advantage for himself before his neighbour gets a chance. Is it necessary to prove that the greater the activity of the brain the greater must be its liability to disease, and therefore to insanity?[148]

Continuing in this vein at quite remarkable length, Duncan vehemently denounced a great many features of nineteenth-century life, ranging from 'the substitution of machinery for handicraft labour'[149] to 'the employment of children in factories',[150] and the consequent 'loosening of the family bond' and 'perversion of the natural feelings and affections' which 'indicates a state of mind very favourable to the development of insanity, when circumstances arise calculated to produce it. It lies at the very root of Socialism':[151]

> I think I am warranted in concluding that there is an amount of brain work going on in the present age far different in kind from, and far greater in degree than, any that was ever known before, and which must play a very important part in predisposing the subjects of it to attacks of insanity. And when we come to ask ourselves the question, What can we do to counteract the evil? I fear the answer to be given is, that, practically, we can do very little. The whole is the result of forces far beyond our power of alteration or control. We can no more change the mechanical and commercial character of the age than we can arrest the sun in his course, or put back the hands upon the dial plate of time. Nor, even if it were possible for the world to return to the condition it was in a century ago, would any of us be willing to give up the advantages of our present state to secure such a result. It must not be forgotten that the evil complained of arises, not from mechanical contrivances in the abstract, but from the abuses connected with their working and incidental to their introduction.[152]

Duncan was not, however, a man to be easily defeated, not even by the great, unstoppable forces of history. The solutions he proposed centred on various forms of education: medical education,[153] public education,[154] and a particular form of moral education of the young which he felt held the greatest hope for preventing mental disorder:

> Sickness and disease often come in spite of all the precautions that may be taken against them; so completely are the causes producing them beyond the cognisance and control even of those who suffer from their ravages. And if this is so as regards the ordinary ills that flesh is heir to, it is still more remarkably the case as regards the various forms of insanity. Legislative interference here is altogether powerless in providing any prophylactic. Whatever steps are to be taken with a view of securing this end must be the result of individual effort in the education of the young – by which I do not mean merely the kind and amount of information crammed into the head of the pupil, but the whole system of training required to produce a well-

adjusted balance between all the intellectual and moral faculties of which man's higher nature is composed and that physical development of the entire system which reason and observation have shewn to be the best safeguard against the occurrence of such a calamity in after life.[155]

Duncan's presidency of the MPA was a significant achievement: the MPA was an important organisation in the development of the profession of psychiatry in Ireland and elsewhere, introducing the Certificate in Psychological Medicine in 1885 and adding general legitimacy to the doctors' search for professional recognition and prestige during the latter part of the nineteenth century.[156] Duncan was a good example of these developments, as he served not only as president of the MPA, but also as president of the King and Queen's College of Physicians in Ireland (1873–5), and generally typified a certain model of nineteenth-century asylum doctor: enterprising, powerful, prolific and keen to promote asylum medicine in the eyes of other doctors and the public. Duncan died on 2 April 1895 at the age of 83, many years after retiring from active medical practice. His obituaries in the *British Medical Journal* and *Medical Press* noted the professional esteem in which he was held, as well as his devotion to the promotion of religion and reputation as a man of charity.[157]

Ultimately, Duncan embodied a disquieting paradox that lay at the very heart of Irish asylum medicine throughout the 1800s. While his heartfelt, fluent and humane rhetoric was both scientific and compassionate, it coexisted with the growth of an increasingly large, custodial system of asylums ranged across the country. And while Duncan explicitly promoted efforts to prevent mental disorders (in apparent conflict with the interests of those who ran asylums), he lived during a time when the number of asylum beds – and thus inpatients – rose at a genuinely alarming rate, to a level that was as unjustifiable as it was unsustainable.

This yawning chasm between rhetoric and reality was demonstrated vividly in 1843, when a select committee of the House of Lords provided another chilling report on the 'state of the lunatic poor in Ireland'. Despite the best intentions of Duncan and colleagues, things just kept on getting worse for the mentally ill.

The State of the Lunatic Poor in Ireland (1843): 'I Could Not Describe the Horror'

The 1840s were an important and formative decade for the Irish asylum system. In 1843 a select committee of the House of Lords provided yet another incisive, disturbing report on 'the state of the lunatic poor in Ireland'. The Committee noted the recommendations of its predecessor, the select committee of 1817:

> On the 4th March 1817 a Select Committee of the House of Commons was appointed to consider the expediency of making further provision for the lunatic poor of Ireland. It was then stated that, with the Exception of one institution in Dublin, one in Cork, and one in Tipperary, there was not a provision made for more than 100 lunatics throughout all Ireland. This Select Committee reported (25th June 1817), 'that the

only mode of effectual relief would be found in the formation of District Asylums exclusively appropriated for the reception of the insane; that, in addition to the asylums in Dublin and in Cork, there should be built four or five additional asylums, capable of containing each from 120 to 150 lunatics'. It further recommended that powers should be given to the government to divide Ireland into districts, and to select the site for an asylum in each, and that the whole expense of the new establishments should be borne by the counties included within the several districts.[158]

While the 1843 select committee found that significant action had been taken based on the 1817 report, substantial challenges remained:

> It has been unfortunately found, that although the accommodation provided in the ten District Asylums very considerably exceeds that which was contemplated by the Committee of 1817, it is very far from meeting the necessity of the case. The asylums were originally intended but for 1,220 patients; they now contain 2,028; various additions have been made to them [providing] for the reception of 264 patients; but the increased and rapidly increasing number of incurable cases have lamentably diminished the efficacy of these asylums as hospitals for the cure of insanity.[159]

The select committee noted that, for the most part, the 'system of management adopted in the District Asylums' was 'very satisfactory and successful', involving 'a humane and gentle system of treatment', with 'cases requiring restraint and coercion not exceeding two per cent on the whole'.[160] The select committee was, however, at pains to point out that the apparent success of Ireland's District Asylums provided no reason for complacency, as there were various other institutions that presented cause for concern:

> The House must not, however, imagine that the District Lunatic Asylums are the only establishments in which pauper lunatics are confined in Ireland. Besides Swift's Hospital, which is supported by the private endowment of the eminent Dean of St Patrick's, there are other public establishments provided for the custody if not for the cure of insanity, and which are supported by local taxation. Connected with some of the old Houses of Industry in Ireland, cells or rooms were provided for the insane. Local asylums still subsist at Kilkenny, Lifford, Limerick, Island Bridge, and the House of Industry in Dublin. With the exception of the last two, these miserable and most inadequate places of confinement are under the general authority of the Grand Juries, the funds for their support being raised by presentment or county rate. The description given of these latter most wretched establishments not only proves the necessity of discontinuing them as speedily as accommodation of a different kind can be provided, but also exemplifies the utter hopelessness, or rather the total impossibility, of providing

for the due treatment of insanity in small local asylums. No adequate provision is made or is likely to be made, in such establishments, for the medical or moral treatment of the unfortunate patients; no classification; no employment; no sufficient grounds for air or exercise. Hence the necessity of a coercive and severe system of treatment. The chances of recovery, if not altogether extinguished, are at least reduced to their very lowest term.[161]

The select committee went on to demonstrate its point by citing specific evidence it received relating to conditions in Kilkenny, Wexford and Lifford. In the case of Wexford, the committee drew attention to the evidence of Dr Francis White, Inspector General of Prisons, who reported that 'the state of the Wexford lunatics in the local asylum is most disgraceful; nothing could equal the state in which I found that asylum; it is part of the old House of Industry':

> The number amounted to fourteen males and seventeen females; the place was quite dilapidated; the yards gloomy; the dinner rooms equally so; the cells were the worst I ever saw. There were two patients under restraint, one of whom was chained to a wall. When I went to his cell, with the keeper and the medical officer, I asked to go in. The keeper said it would be dangerous and frightful to go in. However we went in. He was naked, with a parcel of loose straw around him. He darted forward at me, and were it not that he was checked by a chain which went round his leg, and was fastened by a hook to the wall, he would have caught hold of me, and probably used violence. I asked how it was possible they could allow a man to remain in such a state; they said they were obliged to do so, as the funds were so limited that they had not money to buy clothes for him, and that if they had clothes they would have let him out. Now, the consequence of this treatment was, that the man became so violent that his case was made tenfold worse. I went to another cell, and though the individual there was not chained, he was nearly in as bad circumstances as the other. One of the two was once a respectable person. Altogether, those two cases were the most frightful I ever witnessed; I could not describe the horror which seized me when I saw them.[162]

When asked if there was 'any moral superintendence' at the Wexford establishment, White was blunt: 'There was both a male and female keeper, but they appeared to me totally unfit for the discharge of their duties'. There were similar problems with staffing at other locations. An appendix to the select committee report recounted that in Clonmel District Lunatic Asylum[163] efforts to recruit appropriate staff were 'a sad calamity', and Dr James Flynn, manager, reported that 'the majority of attendants had to be removed, after my appointment, for drunkenness, cruelty to and neglect of patients, and a total disregard for order and discipline'.[164]

To illustrate the difficulties faced, Flynn presented three examples of objectionable behaviour in Clonmel:

I visited the Female Refractory Ward, as usual, on 13th September 1841, and found a patient crying bitterly. I had before asked the reason, and received an indefinite reply; however, I examined on this day the cause, and found her arm had been broken for a period of four days, and no report whatever made by the nurse in charge.

I visited the Male Refractory [Ward] on the night of the 6th of October 1841, and found all the keepers of the House, save one, playing cards; the one not so occupied was stupidly drunk in an adjoining bath room.

I visited the Female Tranquil Ward on the night of the 19th December 1841, at 10 o'clock, and found the assistant nurse perfectly intoxicated.

Having considered evidence relating to all places of confinement of the 'lunatic poor' in Ireland, ranging from District Asylums to prisons, the 1843 select committee made a series of recommendations:

1. The necessity of discontinuing, as soon as practicable, the committals of lunatics of gaols and bridewells.
2. The necessity of amending the Act of the 1 Vict. Cap. 27. [Dangerous Lunatic Act 1838], which appears, on the Authority of the Lord Chancellor of Ireland, to have led to the most serious abuse.[165]
3. The inexpedience of appropriating the Union Workhouses as places either for the custody or the treatment of the insane, for both which purposes they appear wholly unsuited.
4. The necessity of providing one central establishment for criminal lunatics, under the immediate control and direction of the government of Ireland, to be supported from the same funds and under the system adopted in respect to criminal lunatics in England.
5. The necessity of increasing the accommodation for pauper lunatics in Ireland, and of providing for the cases of epilepsy, idiocy and chronic disease, by an increased number of the District Asylums, by an enlargement of those asylums, or by the erection of separate establishments specially appropriated for these classes of patients.[166]

Following its completion, Lord Eliot, the Chief Secretary, sent the select committee's report to the governors of the District Asylums, seeking their comments. The report was discussed by the governors of the Richmond District Asylum, Dublin on 3 January 1844 and, while they supported the call for asylums for criminal lunacy, epilepsy, idiocy and chronic insanity, the Richmond governors suggested that, since these measure would take time, District Asylums should be offered some measure of relief by permitting the admission of harmless and chronic patients into workhouses.[167]

Overall, however, the 1843 select committee saw expanding the public asylum system as the key solution to the problems presented by the mentally ill, recommending more public asylums, larger asylums and specialist asylums for certain groups of patients.[168] This was a familiar response to the problems presented by the mentally ill and it defined public mental health services in Ireland for almost a century after the 1843 report. The 'criminally insane' were one of the groups most affected by this trend and these are considered next.

Central Criminal Lunatic Asylum (Ireland) Act 1845:
Insanity and Criminal Responsibility

The idea of reduced criminal responsibility among the mentally ill and intellectually disabled has a long history in most societies for which there is recorded history, stretching from ancient Greece and Rome to contemporary Europe and the US.[169] This idea was also reflected in early Irish law which specified that responsibility for an offence committed by a person of unsound mind devolved to their guardian, and injuries caused by missiles thrown by a *drúth* (person with intellectual disability) did not require compensation: it was the responsibility of the passer-by to keep out of the way.[170]

In more recent centuries, defences based on insanity were presented in the Irish courts with varying degrees of success.[171] One of the most celebrated was that of Captain William Stewart, whose ship, the *Mary Russell*, sailed into Cork Harbour from the West Indies on 25 June 1828. On board, seven crew members had been brutally killed by the Captain, who appeared insane.[172] The Reverend William Scoresby, a fellow of the Royal Societies of London and Edinburgh and Member of the Institute of France, was one of the first eyewitnesses on the vessel, and described it as 'a scene of carnage so appalling ... as to render, by sympathy, association and memory combined, the impression indelible'.[173]

At Captain Stewart's trial, medical evidence of insanity was compelling and the jury returned a guilty verdict but added that they believed Stewart to have been insane at the time.[174] The Chief Baron at the trial rejected this verdict; it was argued that the law did not recognise this as guilt because the act was committed while the person did not know right from wrong. The jury promptly altered its verdict to 'not guilty' owing to Stewart's insanity. This change of verdict in the early 1800s prefigured the verdict of 'not guilty by reason of insanity' outlined much later in Ireland's Criminal Law (Insanity) Act 2006 (Chapter 7).[175]

Internationally, the field of forensic psychiatry took significant steps forward in the mid-1800s with the publication of Dr Isaac Ray's 'Treatise on the Medical Jurisprudence of Insanity' in 1838[176] and the emergence of the McNaughton Rules which proved hugely influential as the insanity defence became more widely used in the courtrooms of Great Britain, Ireland, the US and elsewhere in the latter part of the 1800s.[177] Against this background, the Central Criminal Lunatic Asylum (Ireland) Act 1845[178] was introduced to establish 'a central asylum for insane persons charged with offences in Ireland'. More specifically:

> Whenever and as soon as the said central asylum shall be erected, and fit for the reception of criminal lunatics, it shall be lawful for the lord lieutenant [chief administrator of government in Ireland] to order and direct that all criminal lunatics then in custody in any lunatic asylum or gaol, or who shall thereafter be in custody, shall be removed without delay to such central asylum, and shall be kept therein so long as such criminal lunatics respectively shall be detained in custody.[179]

The 1845 Act also permitted the Lord Lieutenant to direct 'that any person who might be detained in custody in any gaol by virtue of any such warrant as aforesaid should be removed to the [local] lunatic asylum [and] remain under confinement ... until it should be duly certified to the said lord lieutenant, by two physicians or surgeons, or a surgeon and physician, that such person had become of sound mind'.[180] Convicts who were certified insane could also be removed to the new asylum and then returned to prison or discharged (as appropriate) if medically certified as now being of sound mind.[181]

The 1845 Act was also notable for making provision for one or two suitably qualified persons to act as Inspectors of Lunatics in Ireland, to take over relevant duties from the Inspectors General of Prisons.[182] In 1846, the first person appointed to this position was Dr Francis White (1787–1859), a remarkable physician who had opened a hospital and anatomical school on Ormond Quay earlier in his career and had been an Inspector General of Prisons since 1841.[183] A second inspector, Dr John Nugent, was appointed in 1846, having previously served as travelling physician to Daniel O'Connell (1775–1847), an Irish political leader.[184] Nugent had no experience managing the mentally ill and there were various complaints about his performance.[185] The inspectors' first report appeared in July 1846 and Nugent was later knighted by the Lord Lieutenant.[186]

The other historic outcome from the 1845 Act was the establishment of the Central Criminal Lunatic Asylum in Dundrum, Dublin, which was erected relatively swiftly at a cost of £19,547.[187] Individuals were admitted if they were charged with an offence in court and deemed insane at trial or developed symptoms of mental illness while in prison. The asylum opened for admissions in 1850 and by 1853 there were 69 male and 40 female inpatients.

Patients admitted to the Central Criminal Lunatic Asylum generally presented complex combinations of psychiatric, medical and social need, often including poverty.[188] For example, 70 women were admitted between 1868 and 1908, most of whom were Roman Catholic and single, with an average age of 33 years.[189] Over half were charged with or convicted of killing, mostly child killing.[190] Almost one woman in 10 was declared 'sane' on admission, but might have seemed mentally ill at the time of offence or trial. Among the others, 'mania' and 'melancholia' were the most common diagnoses. Approximately 15 per cent of these women died at the asylum; almost 50 per cent were eventually transferred to local asylums; 12 per cent were transferred to prison; and others were released to family or friends.

Between 1910 and 1948, a further 42 women were admitted, a majority of whom were detained 'at the Lord Lieutenant's pleasure' (i.e. indefinitely).[191] The most common diagnoses were 'mania' or 'delusional insanity' (38 per cent) and 'melancholia' (24 per cent); 7 per cent were 'sane'. The average duration of detention was almost six years, after which 28 per cent were transferred to district asylums and the remainder released under various different circumstances.[192] Overall, the average length of stay for women charged with infanticide or the murder of their child between 1850 and 2000 was 9.3 years, although it ranged from three months to 38 years.[193]

There was a complex mix of social, psychiatric and medical problems in evidence among both male and female patients, including mental disorders ranging from 'mania' to *folie à plusieurs* (when several people share delusions or fixed, false beliefs),[194] various issues relating to intellectual disability,[195] and physical illnesses such as syphilis[196] and tuberculosis.[197] Given this complicated combination of factors, it is unsurprising that there were substantial changes in admission practices over time as rates of admission fluctuated, and the use of 'fitness to plead' procedures in the courts varied significantly, peaking during the period from 1910 to 1920.[198]

St Patrick's Hospital in Dublin was founded in 1746 following the bequest of Jonathan Swift (1667–1745), author, poet and cleric. (St Patrick's Mental Health Services. Used with permission.)

St Patrick's University Hospital, Dublin. (St Patrick's Mental Health Services. Used with permission. Photograph by the author, 2015.)

Dr John Cheyne (1777–1836). Engraving by John Cochran (after a portrait by William Deey, 1804–74). (Reproduced by kind permission of the Royal College of Physicians of Ireland.)

The remains of Carlow Castle in 1792, prior to the intervention of Dr Philip Parry Price Middleton, an asylum doctor who blew it up in 1814. (This image is reproduced courtesy of the National Library of Ireland, PD 1976 TX 21.)

Carlow Asylum, Co. Carlow. (The Lawrence Photograph Collection. Image by Robert French (1841–1917), photographer. This image is reproduced courtesy of the National Library of Ireland, L_ROY_07511.)

Asylum, Ballinasloe, Co. Galway (1900–20). (Eason Photographic Collection. This image is reproduced courtesy of the National Library of Ireland, Eas 2159.)

Mullingar Lunatic Asylum, Co. Westmeath. (The Lawrence Photograph Collection. Image by Robert French (1841–1917), photographer. This image is reproduced courtesy of the National Library of Ireland, L_CAB_01593.)

Enniscorthy Lunatic Asylum, Co. Wexford. (The Lawrence Photograph Collection. Image by Robert French (1841–1917), photographer. This image is reproduced courtesy of the National Library of Ireland, L_CAB_04437.)

Omagh Asylum, Co. Tyrone. (The Lawrence Photograph Collection. Image by Robert French (1841–1917), photographer. This image is reproduced courtesy of the National Library of Ireland, L_CAB_01980.)

James Foulis Duncan was the last of the Duncan Family to own Farnham House, a private asylum in Finglas, Co. Dublin. (Reproduced by kind permission of the Royal College of Physicians of Ireland.)

Lunatic Asylum, Co. Armagh. (The Lawrence Photograph Collection. Image by Robert French (1841–1917), photographer. This image is reproduced courtesy of the National Library of Ireland, L_CAB_03638.)

Lunatic Asylum, Ennis, Co. Clare. (The Lawrence Photograph Collection. Image by Robert French (1841–1917), photographer. This image is reproduced courtesy of the National Library of Ireland, L_CAB_06258.)

Dr Conolly Norman (1853–1908), a notably progressive-minded asylum doctor (mounted photograph by Alfred Werner, photographer, c.1890s). (Reproduced by kind permission of the Royal College of Physicians of Ireland.)

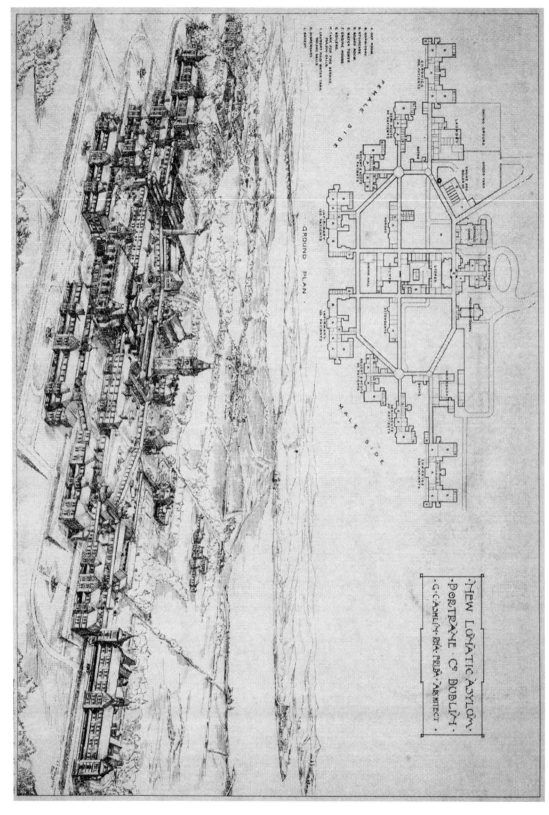

A 'bird's-eye view' of the 'new lunatic asylum' buildings in Portrane, Co. Dublin, 1900. (*Building News and Engineering Journal* 78, 2364, 27 April 1900, pp. 572–3. Courtesy of the Irish Architectural Archive.)

Recurring issues at the Central Criminal Lunatic Asylum included the overcrowding that was so widespread throughout the asylum system during the 1800s and early 1900s;[199] the tangled relationship between gender and the insanity defence;[200] and the troubling matter of persons who were committed to the asylum but appeared sane by the time they actually arrived there.[201] These issues – and many others – were readily apparent throughout the asylum system in general as early as the mid-1850s, when they elicited a by now familiar response from the authorities: the establishment of yet another commission of inquiry and the production of yet another report. But first, however, in 1854, the 1851 Census of Ireland led to the emergence of a fascinating *Report on the Status of Disease* which presented important, formative information about the mentally ill and intellectually disabled in Ireland.

The 1851 Census of Ireland and a 'Report on the Status of Disease'

The Census of Ireland performed in 1851 provided a wealth of fascinating data and reasons for continued concern regarding mental disorder in Ireland. A *Report on the Status of Disease*, based on the census and co-authored by Dr William Wilde, who was knighted in 1864 owing in large part to his work on the census, was published in 1854.[202] Wilde's biographer, Dr T.G. Wilson, wrote that he was especially fascinated by the statistical side of the census, which complemented Wilde's work with individual patients and gave him a broader view of population health.[203]

The *Report* concluded that there were 5,074 'Lunatics' and 4,906 'Idiots' in Ireland, and that 'many individuals in both these classes were also affected with epilepsy'.[204] This meant that 'there was 1 Lunatic in every 1,201 inhabitants, and 1 Idiot in every 1,336 of the population of the entire country':

> In the provinces, the proportions of both classes to the general mass of the community are least in Connaught, being but 1 in 1,022, and greatest in Leinster, where they amount to as many as 1 in 484. The returns of the province of Connaught exhibits a remarkable immunity from both Lunacy and Idiocy. In Ulster we find a proportion of 1 in 679, and in Munster 1 in 729. It would appear that Lunatics prevail most in the cities, but this arises in part from Asylums being located therein, many of the inmates belonging to which could not, from want of proper information on the subject, be distributed according to their native places. Among the counties, the greatest number of Lunatics, in proportion to their populations, were to be found in Dublin, Wexford, Carlow, Westmeath, and Kildare. Idiocy was found to prevail most in Louth, Kildare, Wexford, Monaghan, and Cavan. Both classes taken together prevailed most in the counties of Wexford, Dublin, Kildare, Westmeath, Louth, Queen's [Laois] and Longford. With respect to the sexes, we find among the Lunatics 100 males to 102.72 females, and of the Idiotic class 100 males to 84.02 females.[205]

The report went on to analyse '2,164 cases in which the cause of disease has been investigated, and an opinion offered thereon'.[206] Proposed causes were grouped into three categories: 'physical causes' (44 per cent, with males outnumbering females), 'moral causes' (39 per cent, with females outnumbering males) and 'hereditary taint or family predisposition' (17 per cent, with females again outnumbering males). 'Physical causes' included 'congenital disease' ('specified as malformation of head, and composed chiefly of Idiots'), 'intemperance', 'epilepsy', 'disease of the brain', 'paralysis', 'fever', 'injuries of head', 'puerperal mania', 'the effects of climate, including sunstrokes', 'disease of the brain' (owing to 'cerebral affection'), 'mercury', 'uterine derangement', 'venereal excess', 'dyspepsia', 'rape and seduction', and 'violent hysteria'. 'Moral causes' included 'grief', 'reverse of fortune', 'love and jealousy', 'terror', 'religious excitement', 'study', 'anger or excessive passion', 'ill-treatment', 'anxiety', 'pride and ambition', 'political excitement', 'music', and 'remorse'.

In some cases, information was provided on specific diagnoses:

> Among the insane, Mania was the form of disease manifested in about four-fifths of the whole: of these 669 instances were induced by moral, and 400 by physical causes, while 222 were attributed to hereditary taint. In 44 cases the Mania was of a suicidal character, grief and reverse of fortune being the chief causes which conduced to this phase of disease. Out of 417 persons affected with Dementia, in 73 cases the disease was attributed to moral, and in 69 to physical causes; while in 32 it was traced to hereditary disposition.[207]

This diversity of cause and diagnosis was reflected in asylum case books for many decades to follow.[208] The 1854 report also provided a brief, fascinating account of the 'origin and history of public Asylums for Lunatics and Idiots in Ireland'[209] and a valuable summary of 'popular and Gaelic terms for Insanity and Idiocy':

> Insanity is known under the synonymes and popular terms of mania, monomania, dementia, puerperal mania, madness, lunacy, melancholy, dejection, derangement, out of the mind; and among the Irish-speaking population, as *Gealtaigheacht*, when the madness is believed to result from lunar influence; when the insanity is of a violent and furious character, *Dasaht*; but *Buile* or *Baile* are the terms applied to madness generally.
>
> The number of wandering Idiots in Ireland have frequently been remarked upon; and the fact of this class being regarded by the lower orders with somewhat of a superstitious veneration, has rather encouraged their exposure than the contrary. The analogous terms for Idiocy are fatuous, foolish, simple, silly, an innocent, an idiot, &c. In Irish, the term *Baosradh*, or silliness, is frequently employed, but the terms in more general use are *Amadanacht* and *Oinsigheacht*, the former expressive of Idiocy in the male, and the latter in the female sex.[210]

Commission of Inquiry on the State of Lunatic Asylums in Ireland (1858): 'Places Merely for the Secure Detention of Lunatics'

Against the background of the consolidating asylum system, and the alarming information provided by Wilde and colleagues in their vivid 1854 report, there were, throughout the 1850s, continual complaints about asylum conditions in Ireland, so in 1856 a fresh commission of inquiry was established by the government to look into the matter yet again, for the umpteenth time.[211] The commission assembled in Dublin on 16 October 1856 and comprised five persons: Sir Thomas Nicholas Reddington, who had been Irish Under-Secretary from 1846 to 1852; Robert Andrews (counsel), Robert Wilfred Skeffington Lutwidge (barrister), Dr James Wilkes (medical officer to Stafford County Lunatic Asylum) and Dr Dominic John Corrigan (physician to the Dublin House of Industry Hospitals).

Following an extensive process of investigation and inquiry, two years of work and three extensions of its deadline,[212] the commission finally presented its conclusions in 1858 in the *Report of the Commissioners of Inquiry into the State of the Lunatic Asylums and Other Institutions for the Custody and Treatment of the Insane in Ireland: with Minutes of Evidence and Appendices.*[213] The commission commenced by sketching out the magnitude of the problem, concluding that 'the insane poor of Ireland, maintained at public cost, or at large' numbered 9,286 on 1 January 1857, distributed as follows:

In district asylums	3,824
In workhouses	1,707
In House of Industry (Hardwicke Cells),[214] and at Lifford	108
In the Central Criminal Asylum	127
In gaols and government prisons	168
'At large and unprovided for'	3,352[215]

The commission went on to discuss 'public institutions for the insane' in some detail, examining the position of the mentally ill in district asylums, workhouses, gaols and the Central Criminal Asylum in turn. The commission devoted particular attention to the establishment of the district asylums and was sharply critical of the process:

> It thus resulted that, without any communication with the Grand Juries of the several counties, or any other parties representing the ratepayers, and without any specific statement of the probable cost, to the Privy Council, who directed the establishment of these institutions in the several districts, large and expensive asylums have been erected, and the first public intimation of the charge, thereby imposed upon the district, was the warrant for the repayment of the outlay forwarded to the Grand Juries, on whom such repayment was imperative. This has naturally led to very general discontent, more especially as just cause for complaint also existed of the imperfect manner in which the works had been executed, in the asylums recently erected [...].
>
> [...] We cannot think it right that the ratepayers, or those who represent them, should be excluded from all voice in the determination of questions in which they are so deeply concerned; and although stringent enactments may be required to secure proper provision being made for the lunatic poor, yet it seems to us that it is only when the local authorities obstinately refuse to discharge their duty, in this respect,

that power should be given to the Executive to supersede their action, in order that the benevolent object of the legislature may not remain unfulfilled. We shall be prepared therefore to recommend an alteration of the law in this particular, as well as in the constitution of the Central Authority, which is to superintend and direct the erection, establishment and regulation of lunatic asylums.[216]

The commission also recommended changes with regard to inspections. Despite the 'zealous anxiety of the Inspectors', the commission recommended that inspections should be annual rather than biennial, and should 'report specifically on each institution', rather than reporting generally.[217] In addition:

> The Inspectors of Lunatics were, in 1852, appointed governors, *ex officio*, of all the district asylums, and, as such take part in proceedings, in every respect, as ordinary governors. We consider this position quite inconsistent with that of an Inspector, whose duty it is to report on the state and condition of institutions in the government of which he thus personally shares the responsibility.[218]

The commission noted the existence of regulations permitting the formation of 'rules and regulations for the good conduct and management of district asylums in general, or any asylum in particular' but 'this most important measure for securing the good government of these institutions appears to have been imperfectly carried out for several years':[219]

> The principal defect in the rules, as regards the existing state of things in the asylums, is that the 'duties' assigned to the manager have been drawn up in contemplation of that officer not being a member of the medical profession. Fully concurring in the propriety of the asylums being in charge of professional persons, as our subsequent suggestions for their improvement will indicate, we regard a total alternation of that portion of the rules which affects the manager and physician as absolutely requisite.[220]

More specifically, the commission was unanimously 'of opinion that the resident physician should have charge of the asylum, and be responsible for the treatment of the inmates as regards their insanity':[221]

> We think the resident physician should be relieved from all duties of a civil character connected with the management of the institution, which might interfere with the devotion of his time to his more proper duty, the care and treatment of the inmates. Leaving him the chief officer of the asylum, with authority over all the other officers, except the consulting physician, we propose that his civil duties should be transferred to the officer to be called the clerk.[222]

The commission also made several other recommendations, including better record keeping,[223] changes relating to the appointment and conduct of governors,[224] and review of the wages paid to asylum workers:

Another point, to which we desire to draw attention, is the small amount of wages given to the attendants in some of the asylums. The duty of the persons so employed is at all times disagreeable and irksome – frequently dangerous and disgusting. It requires intelligence, temper, and kindness, on the part of those discharging it, or the conduct of the attendant may undo all the judicious treatment of the manager. A higher class of servants, therefore, should be sought, and care should be taken, in their selection, not alone that they are possessed of the qualities above described, but that they are sufficiently educated to be enabled to contribute to the recreation of the patients by reading for their amusement. Such occupations will beguile the wearisomeness of their watching in the wards, and, helping to cheer and tranquilize the patients, will render their attendance a more grateful task.[225]

The commission lamented variations in admission practices across asylums and recommended that 'there should be one rule, rigidly enforced, for regulating admissions' and that 'idiots, as well as epileptics, where the fits produce imbecility of mind as well as of body, should be admissible'.[226] The commission felt that the 'Resident Medical Manager' should have authority to admit patients between meeting of the Board because 'it is of the utmost importance that cases of insanity should as speedily as possible be removed to an asylum'.[227]

As regards 'paying patients', the commission noted that 'there is no fixed rule in district asylums' as 'some boards decline to receive them; others receive them at a charge equal to the cost of maintenance; and in others the annual payment demanded is regulated at the discretion of the Board of Governors'.[228]

> We are of the opinion that the admission of paying patients should be distinctly recognised, but that it should be subject to such restrictions as the Central Board, which we shall propose to establish, may lay down, both as to the class of patients and the proportion of such cases to be admitted into the asylums, so as at the same time to protect the ratepayers from undue taxation, and the lunatic poor of the lowest class from unfair encroachment upon the accommodation intended more especially for them.
>
> The class of patients to be admitted ought not to comprise those who, from the means which they possess, should be maintained in a private asylum.[229]

After considering the various laws and regulations governing asylums, the commission then turned its attention to the 'general condition of the asylums', and found plenty of causes for concern including, *inter alia*, 'cold and cheerless' airing courts;[230] 'imperfect or ill-planned' sewage arrangements; 'defective' water supplies; 'inattention to cleanliness'; 'privies ... so offensive as to be absolutely injurious to the health of the inmates'; 'improper occupation of inmates'; poor heating and ventilation; bedsteads 'of bad and objectionable construction';[231] 'neglect of school instruction';[232] misuse of restraint in certain asylums;[233] and a 'general want of' recreation and amusement for patients:

At present, whatever attempts have been made in a few instances, and especially at Richmond and Sligo, in the way of evening entertainments, & c.,[234] nothing has been done to mitigate the bare and cheerless character of the apartments usually occupied by the inmates. In corridor or day-room, the lunatic sees nothing but the one undiversified white wall – giving to these hospitals, intended for the restoration of the alienated mind, an air of blankness and desolation more calculated to fix than to remove the awful disease under which it labours.

It cannot be denied, notwithstanding the care and attention which appear generally to be given by the managers and visiting physicians to the patients under their charge, that, on the whole, the lunatic asylums of Ireland wear more the aspect of places merely for the secure detention of lunatics than of curative hospitals for the insane.[235]

After this rather damning consideration of district asylums, the commission next examined the position of the mentally ill in workhouses, and concluded that 'there can be no more unsuitable place for the detention of insane persons than the ordinary lunatic wards of the union workhouses'.[236] On this basis, the commission outlined a proposal 'to appropriate unused workhouse accommodation for certain classes of insane':

It should be competent to the Board of Governors of any asylum to direct the admission of any lunatic of the above class[237] belonging to the district into the workhouse asylum; and, on the recommendation of the resident physician of the asylum, to admit directly to such workhouse asylum any such lunatic then in gaol or workhouse, or for whom admission to the district asylum may be sought. The governors should also have power to transfer patients, when necessary, from these auxiliaries to the district asylums.[238]

Notwithstanding its approval of 'workhouse asylums', the commission did not approve of the idea of 'provincial asylums', recommending instead that 'as far as possible, all cases should be treated in the district asylum'.[239] The commission advised clarity on the role of the Central Criminal Asylum and, specifically, that 'a law should explicitly define who is to be detained in the criminal asylum; and as cure is not the only object with which such an institution has been founded by the state, the incurable inmate should not, because his case is hopeless, and he may himself be harmless, be again remitted to association with lunatics who are not criminal'.[240] Other recommendations included establishment of a 'central board' to control and direct asylums;[241] various changes to the establishment and conduct of 'private asylums'[242] and the role of chaplains;[243] and the 'desirableness of benevolent institutions for the insane';[244] and various other suggestions.[245]

Many of the commission's conclusions were not new: it recommended expansion of the asylum system (e.g. through 'workhouse asylums') and strongly endorsed the idea of permanent segregation as a key element in management.[246] More progressively, however, it drew attention to the importance of the asylums 'as educational establishments, for the purpose of extending a knowledge of the nature and treatment of insanity':[247]

We feel confident that, if the lunatic asylums of Ireland were made places of instruction, medical science would be improved and humanity benefited; and that the benefit would not be limited to Ireland, but that the blessing of a humane and enlightened treatment of the insane would be extended through other countries [...].

We cannot doubt that, if proper exertion were made, students in medicine, or graduates who had just completed their course, would seek for appointments as residents in asylums, as the knowledge thus acquired, and the certificates they would obtain of such residence, would be esteemed recommendations in many positions in which they might afterwards be placed. We would recommend that, in the first instance, the experiment of such appointments should be made in the asylums of Dublin (St Patrick's and the Richmond), of Cork, and of Belfast, in which towns there are large medical schools [...].

Such resident pupils might be appointed by the Board of Governors, on the recommendation of the resident physician, and should be subject to his direction. Their duties would consist in keeping notes of the cases admitted, and their treatment, in seeing to the due administration of medicines, baths, & c., and in a general care of the inmates and patients in the intervals of the visits of the resident or visiting physician; in short, in discharging towards the inmates of the asylum such duties as are now performed by resident pupils towards the sick in general hospitals.[248]

This was an innovative, progressive proposal, aimed at improving standards of care in the longer term, and clearly in line with the commission's other recommendations for greater medical involvement in the asylums and improved education of staff. Overall, however, the commission's recommendations were strongly in the direction of an expanded asylum system and permanent institutionalisation for certain patients. Scant attention was paid to the possible merits of other possibilities (e.g. treatment at home),[249] as the commission emphatically endorsed the fundamental tenet that 'it is of the utmost importance that cases of insanity should as speedily as possible be removed to an asylum'.[250]

Case Studies: Restraint, Neglect and Cruelty

The 1858 commission's strong endorsement of asylums as the central element of care for the mentally ill was all the more remarkable in light of the disturbing low standards and gross abuses revealed in their report. This was most evident in relation to the use of restraint, a topic to which the commission devoted particular attention:

We feel it is our duty also to notice the culpable disregard with which the 23rd Rule of the Privy Council has in many instances been treated. This rule requires that 'The manager is to take charge of the instruments of restraint, and is not, under any pretence, to allow the unauthorized use of them to any person within the establishment; all cases placed under restraint, seclusion, or other deviation from the ordinary treatment, are to be carefully recorded by him in the daily report, with the particular nature of the restraint or deviation resorted to; but in no case shall the shower-bath be used without the authority of the physician'.[251] And, by rule 4, he is to enter in the Morning Statement Book 'the names of those under restraint or seclusion, and the causes thereof'. In some instances, the managers informed us that they were not even aware of the rule, although a printed copy of the Privy Council regulations was furnished to every asylum; in others, that they deemed it a sufficient compliance with the rules to leave the instruments of restraint in charge of the keepers, trusting to their integrity to report the cases in which they were used.[252]

The commission was especially disturbed by specific examples of restraint in Armagh Asylum, examples which some readers might find disturbing. One 'patient, on the female side, was strapped down in bed, with body-straps of hard leather, three inches wide, and twisted under the body, with wrist-locks, strapped and locked, and with wrists frayed from want of lining to straps; this patient was seriously ill. There was no record of her being under restraint in the Morning Statement Book, as required by the order of the Privy Council. Another female was in the day room, without shoes or stockings, with strait waistcoat and wrist-locks; she had been two years in the house, and almost continually kept in that state day and night'.[253]

The most egregious abuse, however, was seen in the case of a male patient in Armagh, whose situation was outlined in detail by the commission and which, again, some readers might find disturbing:

> A male patient, in Ward No. 2, was found at our visit, strapped down in bed; in addition, he was confined in a strait waistcoat, with the sleeves knotted behind him; and as he could only lie on his back, from a contrivance we shall presently describe, his sufferings must have been great; his arms were, moreover, confined with wrist-locks of hard leather, and his legs with leg-locks of similar kind; the strapping was so tight that he could not turn on either side; and any change of position was still more effectually prevented by a cylindrical stuffed bolster of ticken,[254] of about ten inches thick, which ran round the sides, and top, and bottom of the bed, leaving a narrow hollow in the centre in which the lunatic was retained, as in a box, without power to turn or move. On liberating the patient, and raising him, he was very feeble, unable to stand, with pulse scarcely perceptible, and feet dark red and cold; the man had been under confinement in this state for four days and nights, being merely raised for purposes of cleanliness.[255]

The commission was deeply affected by this case and all the more alarmed to discover that 'the manager stated he was aware of the man being in bed, but not of his having all these instruments of restraint upon him. No record of the case of restraint appeared in the Morning Statement Book'. They concluded that 'neither the manager nor physician had seen or visited this patient while under confinement, or even been aware of his state'. The manager in Armagh was Thomas Jackson, who, some thirty years earlier, had worked to improve conditions in the old Dublin House of Industry; clearly, decades spent working in institutional conditions had greatly limited the effectiveness of his reformist zeal.[256]

Unsurprisingly, the commission found similar problems elsewhere:

> We may here mention that in Omagh Asylum we found a bed in use for refractory patients, thus described by the resident physician: 'It is a wooden bed in the sides, and there is an iron cover which goes over both rails; it is sufficiently high to allow a patient to turn and twist, but he cannot get up ... the bars are from twelve to fourteen inches above the patient's head'.[257]

Faced with these damning examples of the use, overuse, misuse and abuse of restraint, the commission felt it was 'scarcely necessary to say that we recommend that the most strict observance of the rule should be enforced; that all instruments of restraint should be kept solely in the custody of the manager or resident physician; that their unauthorised use shall never be permitted, and that all cases of restraint should be daily visited and recorded'.[258]

These violations of standards regarding restraint were especially disappointing given the emergence of a strong 'non-restraint' movement in the late 1830s, some twenty years prior to the commission's report. Progress in certain English asylums had been significant, if incomplete: the use of mechanical restraints was abolished at the Lincoln County Asylum in 1838; Northampton Asylum (now St Andrew's Hospital) was the first institution to advocate non-restraint *as a philosophy* from the time it opened, in 1838; and non-restraint was introduced in Hanwell Asylum by Dr John Conolly (1794–1866) in the summer of 1839.[259] Interestingly, the position was very different in the US, where asylum managers were explicitly hostile towards the English 'non-restraint' movement.[260] In Ireland, however, the *Report from the Select Committee of the House of Lords Appointed to Consider the State of the Lunatic Poor in Ireland* noted, in 1843, that, for the most part, the 'system of management adopted in the District Asylums' in Ireland involved 'a humane and gentle system of treatment', with 'cases requiring restraint and coercion not exceeding two per cent on the whole'.[261]

Given the stark contrast between, on the one hand, the non-restraint movement in England in the 1830s and apparently low rates of seclusion in Ireland in 1843, and, on the other, the commission's damning report of 1858, it is unsurprising that the commission's findings regarding restraint were highlighted in the *Journal of Mental Science* in January 1859, by Dr John Charles Bucknill (1817–1897), founder of the journal (as the *Asylum Journal*) in 1853 and editor until 1862.[262] In an incisive commentary, Bucknill also drew attention to various other aspects of the 1858 report and the publicly expressed view of Dr Nugent, Inspector of Lunatic Asylums, that the commission's report was excessively negative and one sided.

Overall, however, despite the objections of Nugent and others,[263] and despite the apparently caring attitudes of certain asylum managers, doctors and governors, the picture painted by the commission was undeniably horrific. As the asylums had grown, grotesque institutional apathy had commonly replaced the relatively enlightened ideals of moral management. A bill aimed at remedying matters by implementing the commission's recommendations was introduced by Lord Naas, the

Chief Secretary, in 1859 but did not progress owing to the fall of the government. In 1860, Lord Naas's successor, Edward Cardwell, made some progress on the matter by having an order in council made by the Lord Lieutenant, establishing a new Board of Correspondence and Control, made up of the two inspectors of lunatic asylums, the chairman and a commissioner of the Board of Works. Real, systematic reform of the asylums would, however, take much longer to achieve.

Life and Death in the Nineteenth-Century Asylum

A significant step forward was taken on 16 January 1862, when new Privy Council rules were issued, designed to improve the running of district asylums in Ireland and to pacify both visiting and resident physicians.[264] These *General Rules and Regulations for the Management of District Lunatic Asylums in Ireland* covered a broad range of areas, including the role of the Board of Governors; procedures for admission, treatment and discharge of patients; the posts of Resident Medical Superintendent (RMS) and 'consulting and visiting physician'; and the astonishing range of other posts in the asylums, including chaplains, matrons, apothecaries, clerks, storekeepers, servants, attendants, cooks, laundresses, porters, land stewards, gardeners and gatekeepers.

Particular attention was paid to the precise roles of the RMS and visiting physician, the latter of whom had to visit the asylum three days each week, and every day if the number of patients exceeded 200. Either the RMS or visiting physician had to examine the mental state of each patient at least once every fortnight. Discharge, for the most part, required an order from the board on a certificate signed by both medical officers, but discharge of a 'dangerous lunatic' required a joint certificate from the medical officers that the patient was no longer dangerous. The 1862 rules, which strongly favoured the RMS ('he shall superintend and regulate the whole establishment'),[265] were warmly welcomed in the *Journal of Mental Science*, which noted that the previous rules (1843) were contradictory and generally unsatisfactory.[266]

The rules were revised again in 1874 and admission procedures laid out clearly:

> Persons labouring under mental disease, for whom papers of application are filled up in the prescribed forms, to the satisfaction of the Board, and who shall be duly certified as insane by a registered physician or surgeon, who shall state on the grounds on which he forms his opinion, shall be admissible into District Asylums, after having been examined by the Resident Medical Superintendent or, in his absence, by the visiting physician or surgeon.[267]
>
> [...] No patient, other than a 'dangerous Lunatic' shall be admitted without the sanction of the Board, except by order of the Lord Lieutenant, or of the Inspectors of Lunatics or one of them, or in case of urgency, when any three Governors or the Resident Medical Superintendent, or in his absence, the Consulting and Visiting Physician of the Asylum, may admit upon their or his own authority, stating on the face of the order the ground thereof, provided always that when a patient has been admitted under this rule, the Resident Medical Superintendent, or in his absence the

Visiting Physician, shall submit that case to the *special* consideration of the Board at its next meeting for the decision of the Governors thereon.[268]

Various other regulations governed conditions and procedures within the asylums, and provide a valuable insight into the recommended patterns of asylum life:

- 'The patients shall, on admission, be carefully bathed and cleansed, unless the Resident Medical Superintendent shall otherwise direct. They shall be treated with all the gentleness compatible with their condition; and restraint, when necessary, shall be as moderate, both in extent and duration, as is consistent with the safety and advantage of the patient.'[269]
- 'Patients, except when special reasons to the contrary may exist, are to be clad in the dress of the institution, and their own clothes are carefully to be laid by, to be returned to them on their discharge.'[270]
- 'Strict regularity shall be observed with respect to the hours for rising in the morning and retiring for the night; that for rising being fixed at six o'clock from the 1st of April to the 30th of September, called the Summer six months, and for retiring at an hour not earlier than half-past eight o'clock nor later than nine for the same period. During the Winter six months the patients shall rise at seven, and retire not earlier than seven nor later than eight o'clock.'[271]
- 'The like regularity must be observed with respect to meals; in no case shall the ordinary number of meals be less than three, and they shall be supplied during the Summer six months at the following hours, viz: breakfast at eight o'clock; dinner at one o'clock; and supper at six o'clock; – and during the Winter six months at the following hours, viz: breakfast at nine o'clock; dinner at two o'clock; and supper at six o'clock; but patients actively employed in or out of doors may have an additional allowance of food between the usual meals by direction of the Resident Medical Superintendent.'[272]
- 'On the admission of a patient the Resident Medical Superintendent, or if he shall be absent on leave, the Consulting and Visiting Physician, shall make himself acquainted as far as possible with the history of the case, and note the same down in the General Registry; he shall also examine into the bodily condition of the patient, who is to be placed in an appropriate division, and carefully attended to both medical and personally.'[273]
- 'Patients may be visited from time to time by their friends, with the permission of the Resident Medical Superintendent, and as a general rule between the hours of noon and 4 o'clock, P.M..'[274]

These revised rules were certainly much needed as there was, during the 1860s and 1870s, a compelling and recognised need for better regulation of the asylums. John A. Blake (1826–1887), MP for Waterford and a governor of Waterford Asylum, was especially outspoken about asylum conditions, which, he claimed, had not improved despite the stark findings of the 1858 commission. In the early 1860s, Blake drew particular attention to the low quality of asylum staff, arguing that both staff selection and working conditions were deeply unsatisfactory.[275] He also highlighted the lack of recreation or employment for patients, which impacted greatly on their wellbeing. Other problems included violence towards staff and between patients, sometimes resulting in death by, for example, choking (in Ballinasloe, 1873).[276] A chamber pot was a common weapon: one female patient killed another with a chamber pot in the Richmond in July 1889,[277] while five years later, in the Cork asylum, a male patient died owing to a combination of 'shock' and being hit on the head by another patient with a delf chamber utensil.[278]

There were many other problems in the asylums too, not least of which were various illnesses and the relatively high risk of death as an inpatient.[279] In the Richmond, for example, numerous patients were affected by a mysterious illness in the summer of 1894, and several died of the disorder which appeared to involve inflammation of the nerves. The RMS, Conolly Norman, consulted various experts, including Dr Walter G. Smith (president of the Royal College of Physicians of Ireland) and Sir Thornley Stoker[280] (president of the Royal College of Surgeons in Ireland and brother of Bram, author of *Dracula*),[281] among others. Though the condition was initially deeply puzzling for the physicians it ultimately proved likely that the asylum diet (low in fruit and vegetables and high in white bread) had led to beri beri,[282] stemming primarily from a nutritional deficit in vitamin B1 (thiamine). While this mysterious episode remains the subject of scholarly study,[283] it did, at least, draw considerable attention to the importance of diet in the asylum and highlighted the need for good physical healthcare for patients.[284]

Tuberculosis, too, presented significant challenges to physical health in nineteenth and early twentieth-century Ireland, both inside and outside the asylums. By 1904, tuberculosis accounted for almost 16 per cent of all deaths in the Irish general population.[285] Staff and patients in asylums were at particular risk and in 1901 tuberculosis accounted for 25 per cent of deaths in Irish asylums, with an average age of death of between 37 and 39 years.[286] This problem was by no means exclusive to the Irish asylums: tuberculosis was also the leading cause of death in South Carolina Lunatic Asylum at the turn of the century.[287] In Ireland, progress with tuberculosis was slow, but the start of the twentieth century saw renewed public health initiatives,[288] dedicated legislative measures, such as the Tuberculosis Prevention (Ireland) Act of 1908,[289] and changes in sociopolitical circumstances that helped alleviate matters somewhat.[290]

Even so, death rates in Irish asylums still presented a substantial cause for concern throughout this period. In 1893, the Inspector of Lunatics reported a national death rate of 8.3 per cent in the asylums; this figure was derived by dividing the number of deaths in Irish district asylums in 1892 (995 deaths) by the daily average number of asylum residents; on 1 January 1893, that number stood at 12,133.[291] Of those who died in district asylums, 198 (19.9 per cent) underwent post-mortem examinations which were, in the Inspector's opinion, 'of so much importance for the protection of the insane and for the furtherance of the scientific study of insanity'.[292]

Death rates varied between asylums, with, for example, the Richmond in Dublin reporting a death rate (12.5 per cent) higher than the national average (8.3 per cent), possibly related to particular problems with overcrowding and infective illnesses at the Richmond.[293] Comparable rates were, however, reported in other jurisdictions, with a 14 per cent death rate in South Carolina Lunatic Asylum between 1890 and 1915.[294] Similarly, one third of men and 21 per cent of women admitted to the Toronto Asylum between 1851 and 1891 died there.[295] At the Central Criminal

Lunatic Asylum in Dublin, 42 per cent of individuals committed following a court finding of mental disorder between 1850 and 1995 died there,[296] and 27 per cent of women committed following infanticide or child murder between 1850 and 2000 died there.[297]

Walsh and Daly studied admissions to Sligo District Lunatic Asylum between 2 February 1892 and 6 May 1901, during which period there were 454 admissions with sufficient details for analysis.[298] Of these, 75 per cent were male, 64 per cent single and 86 per cent Roman Catholic. Among those for whom family history was recorded, some 87 per cent had a family history of mental disorder. The most common recorded causes were heredity, alcohol, and domestic issues or financial worries. The most common diagnoses were mania (40 per cent) and melancholia (28 per cent). The most frequent recorded causes of death were tuberculosis and phthisis (probably pulmonary tuberculosis; 23 per cent), exhaustion (16 per cent) and dementia (9 per cent).

Serious challenges with physical health continued into the 1900s, with the influenza epidemic of 1918[299] hitting the asylums especially hard: a fifth of all patients in Belfast asylum died of it, and one patient in every seven in the asylums in Kilkenny, Castlebar, Maryborough and Armagh fell victim.[300] Against this rather bleak background, there were, nonetheless, continued efforts to ameliorate the problems in the asylums, with Norman at the Richmond, for example, doggedly (if unsuccessfully) promoting 'boarding out' in the late 1800s and early 1900s.[301] In addition, outpatient clinics were promoted in the early 1900s and the Society of St Vincent de Paul was later approached to set up an after care committee.[302]

Notwithstanding these efforts, conditions in Irish asylums remained very difficult throughout the late 1800s and early 1900s, owing to toxic combinations of mental disorder, physical illness, overcrowding, suicide, and violence – the latter involving both patients and staff, and often resulting in physical or chemical restraint.[303] In the early 1900s, a night nurse in Castlebar was violent towards a patient with a poker and was found guilty of burning the patient, resulting in a sentence of 18 months hard labour.[304]

From the outset, medical conflicts were common in the asylums, especially between visiting physicians and resident medical superintendents: in 1862, the latter was accorded superiority[305] and in 1892 the post of visiting physician was abolished in new rules drafted by the Inspectors of Lunatics (then including Dr E.M. Courtenay); this was a defining moment in the emergence of the profession of psychiatry in Ireland.[306] The new specialists, increasingly trained in the asylums themselves,[307] were immediately confronted with complex tangles of psychiatric, medical, social and legal challenges in many individual cases, with no immediate solutions to hand, apart from further institutional care. These challenges are well illustrated by some interesting cases of *folie à plusieurs*, a rare but fascinating psychiatric syndrome, drawn from the archives of the Central Criminal Lunatic Asylum in the 1890s.

Case Studies: Folie à Plusieurs

Folie à deux is a rare psychiatric syndrome in which two individuals share symptoms of mental disorder, most commonly paranoid delusions. While there were several clinical descriptions of the syndrome throughout the seventeenth and eighteenth centuries,[308] the term *folie à deux* was coined in the 1870s[309] and translated as 'communicated insanity' by William Wetherspoon Ireland, a Scottish polymath, in the 1880s.[310]

The term *folie à plusieurs* refers to cases of 'communicated insanity' in which symptoms are shared by three or more individuals. There tends to be one 'primary' patient, whose symptoms are 'transmitted' to 'secondary' patients. The majority of cases of induced psychotic disorder occur within families and involve, most commonly, mother and child, wife and husband, or woman and sibling.[311] Treatment involves identifying the primary patient[312] and treating their mental illness and physical disorder (if present); the secondary patient may not require specific treatment following separation from the primary patient. The concept of *Capgras à plusieurs* (a shared delusional belief that a person has been replaced by a double) has been invoked in relation to the celebrated case of Bridget Cleary, burned to death in 1895.[313]

From the outset, there were reports of forensic or criminal complications of 'communicated insanity',[314] including theft, violence,[315] attempted murder[316] and murder.[317] One Irish case from the late 1800s involved two brothers admitted to the Central Criminal Lunatic Asylum on the same day in 1896. Both were single farmers who lived on a family farm. They were charged with the murder of another brother and detained in the Central Criminal Lunatic Asylum 'at the Lord Lieutenant's pleasure' (i.e. indefinitely).[318] Patrick, the elder, was 36 years of age and admission notes described him as 'industrious, honest ... timid and nervous'. At the time of admission, Patrick had 'two brothers and a sister in an asylum' because 'all the family became insane at the same time'. Patrick himself was 'timorous and sleepless, watching an insane brother for about 12 days'. He was diagnosed with 'acute delusional mania, convalescent'. The cause was 'hereditary'.

While physical examination on admission to the Central Criminal Lunatic Asylum was normal, the Prison Surgeon's Report from four months earlier (when the brothers were in prison awaiting trial), noted that they were 'wild and haggard-looking'. Patrick's temperature was 100° Fahrenheit (38° Celsius) with a pulse rate of 116 beats per minute (i.e. raised). At night time, the brothers' conditions worsened: Patrick became 'wildly delirious, believed there were devils in his cell, sprinkling bed and cell with water, praying constantly, pupils dilated, voice hoarse, spitting frequently ... hallucinations of sight and hearing, refused food, slept none that night, were placed in muffs ...'

Over the following days, Patrick began to recover, although 'he remained in a state of the most extreme collapse for some weeks, tongue white and furred, complained of headache and giddiness. Prisoner was kept quiet in hospital and given plenty of milk beef tea and two bottles of stout daily'. Apparently, 'delirium occurred at night in the different police barracks where [the brothers] were confined previous to committal to prison'.

When Patrick was 'charged with the murder of his brother' he said that his (now deceased) 'brother was insane for ten days previous'. At his trial, Patrick was charged with murder and detained indefinitely at the Central Criminal Lunatic Asylum. Clinical notes record that he 'recovered from the attack of acute mania from which he suffered while in [prison] and for some days previously; he accounts for the insanity in his family (which occurred almost suddenly) being brought on by "something" they all partook of while at meals, but is unable to say what the nature of this "something" was. He recognises perfectly the crime that both he and his brothers committed and is fully aware that he was at the time "out of his mind". He has a somewhat down-cast appearance, a slow slouching gait and is depressed in manner and appearance'. He 'never presented any symptoms of insanity'.

Patrick's younger brother, John, was admitted on the same day in 1896 with a very similar history. John was diagnosed with 'acute delusional mania, convalescent' and he, like Patrick, soon 'recovered from the attack of acute mania from which he suffered at the time of committing the murder of his brother and afterwards while in [prison]. Patient is very quiet and well-conducted, is in fair health, takes his food well and sleeps soundly. Has been sent with his brother [Patrick] to work on the land and they are both satisfied and pleased to do so'.

Later in 1896, a third brother, Brendan, was also charged with the murder of his brother and detained 'at the Lord Lieutenant's pleasure'. Admission notes describe Brendan as 'very quiet, well-spoken and most respectful; both in manner and appearance he much resembles his brothers ... He presents no symptoms of insanity. I consider him perfectly sane; but like his brothers he suffered from an attack of acute mania while in [prison] ... He is quite unable to in any way account for the insanity which occurred in his family, he feels deeply the great misfortune which has befallen them and is depressed when speaking of his brother ... who was the unfortunate victim of their insanity'.

On admission, Brendan had a history of 'phthisis' (tuberculosis) which worsened in the hospital. In 1897, the medical officers wrote to the Inspector of Lunatics stating that Brendan was 'suffering from effects of detention and presents symptoms of incipient phthisis. We strongly recommend his discharge on the grounds that his disease will be aggravated by his detention'. Despite treatment with cod liver oil, medical notes recorded that 'phthisis makes itself more evident each day'. The medical officers again wrote to the Inspector of Lunatics stating that Brendan's 'condition has become critical and that if he is to be discharged, he should be released at once, as in our opinion, he will soon become too ill to be removed. His temperature at night has reached 102 [° Fahrenheit (39° Celsius); i.e. raised] and in our opinion he will not survive this winter'. After two more weeks, Brendan was discharged to the care of his sister, but died three months later, in late 1897.

Neither Patrick nor John showed any convincing signs of mental disorder during their time at the Central Criminal Lunatic Asylum. In 1898, the medical officer sent a report to the Inspector of Lunatics stating that both brothers were 'suitable for discharge. They both have been industrious and extremely well behaved since admission here. The only distinction I wish to make is that detention is having a bad effect on John's health and he may become ill in the same manner as his brother Brendan, who died soon after his being released from here'. Four months later, the medical officer sent an additional report stating that John was now 'in very delicate health and threatened with phthisis and we consider that he will die from this disease if not discharged soon. We also certify that he may be discharged with safety to himself and others'. Later that year, John was 'discharged in care of sister' and three years later Patrick, too, was discharged 'in care of his sister', after more than five years in the asylum.

Overall, these cases demonstrate clear forensic complications of *folie à plusieurs*, involving, in this case, the killing of a family member. These cases occurred in the 1890s, just a decade after the clinical syndrome of *folie à plusieurs* had been described in detail by Ireland in his collection of clinical vignettes illustrating both clinical and forensic aspects of the syndrome.[319] Three years after Ireland's publication, Dr Daniel Hack Tuke, formerly of the York Retreat,[320] also published a detailed account of *folie à deux* or 'double insanity' in the respected journal *Brain*.[321]

These cases of the three brothers are particularly interesting in light of indications that they suffered from an acute physical illness with delirium, which accounted for their delusions and other psychiatric symptoms. Their treatment in hospital was described as 'moral supervision and dietetic', an approach which involved regular exercise, gainful employment and an emphasis on healthy diet,[322] all of which were consistent with the principles of 'moral management'.[323] Other activities the Central Criminal Lunatic Asylum during this period included were ball games, dancing, music, evening parties and reading books and newspapers (although many patients were unable to read).[324]

These cases also demonstrate the problems with tuberculosis ('phthisis') in the Irish asylums in the late 1800s and early 1900s:[325] at least one of the three brothers, Brendan, died of the disease. Interestingly, one of the other brothers, Patrick, contended that their illness was 'brought on by "something" they all partook of while at meals, but is unable to say what the nature of this "something" was'. This is consistent with evidence from another case of *folie à plusieurs* described by the remarkable Dr Oscar T. Woods, medical superintendent of the Killarney Asylum, in 1889 and, later, president of the MPA,[326] in which bad food was also seen as a contributory cause.[327]

Overall, the cases of the three brothers demonstrate many of the challenges that 'communicated insanity' presented to mental health and judicial services in nineteenth-century Ireland and which remain relevant in the 2000s. Over a century after these cases, the optimal balance between punishment and treatment still continues to be difficult to achieve in contemporary mental health services,[328] and both treatment[329] and community reintegration present ongoing challenges, especially in cases with substantial forensic dimensions.

Women and Mental Illness in Nineteenth-Century Ireland

Women with mental disorder were treated differently than men throughout the nineteenth and twentieth centuries by the Irish criminal justice and psychiatric systems.[330] Following committal to the Central Criminal Lunatic Asylum in Dundrum, for example, women generally experienced shorter periods of detention and were more likely to be discharged than men.[331] This might be attributable to the nature of offences committed by women: 54 per cent of women detained at the Central Criminal Lunatic Asylum between 1868 and 1908 (a total of 70) were charged with or convicted of killing, of which a majority (70 per cent) involved child killing.[332]

Issues related to menstruation, pregnancy and childbirth were significant factors in determining how these women were viewed in many jurisdictions, including Ireland.[333] Parry writes that Hallaran's 'emphasis [in 1810] on childbirth and menopause as factors which led to insanity in women was the beginning of what would become medical orthodoxy – the link between female biology and insanity. The work of Thomas More Madden, at the end of the century, shows how this opinion of the causes of insanity had gained wide acceptance. Madden, who was physician to St Joseph's Hospital, Dublin, argued forcefully that insanity in women was caused by their reproductive capacity'.[334]

In a similar vein, Dr Fleetwood Churchill wrote, in the *Dublin Quarterly Journal of Medical Science* in 1850, that cyclic changes in bodily health affected women more than men, with consequent effects on mental activities, and that menstruation, conception, pregnancy and childbirth could all produce disturbances which could amount to insanity.[335] In Great Britain, Dr Henry Maudsley (1835–1918) agreed, pinpointing irregularities of menstruation as known causes of mental disorder which could generate suicidal or homicidal impulses.[336]

Similar emphasis was placed on menstruation as a cause of mental disorder or disturbed behaviour in the US.[337] In 1865, one female defendant was found insane at the time of a particular shooting owing to apparent insanity resulting from a combination of romantic problems and dysmenorrhea.[338] Dr Isaac Ray (1807–1881), founding father of forensic psychiatry in the US, in his *Treatise on the Medical Jurisprudence of Insanity*, described an apparent association between menstruation and fire setting, citing several cases 'in which the incendiary propensity was excited by disordered menstruation, accompanied in some of them by other pathological conditions.'[339]

One particular case involved a 22-year-old woman who 'committed three incendiary acts' but 'had had a disease two years before, that was accompanied by violent pains in the head, disordered circulation, insensibility, and epileptic fits; and that since then menstruation had ceased':

> That the evolution of the sexual functions is very often attended by more or less constitutional disturbance, especially in the female sex, is now a well-established psychological truth [...]. Any irregularity whatsoever of the menstrual discharge, is a fact of the greatest importance in determining the mental condition of incendiary girls.

Ray also described a link between 'the propensity to steal' and 'certain physiological changes' in women, including pregnancy. He outlined the case of one 'pregnant woman who, otherwise perfectly honest and respectable, suddenly conceived a violent longing for some apples from a particular orchard ... and was detected by the owner in the act of stealing apples'. The woman was 'convicted of theft' but a 'medical commission was appointed' to review the matter:

> Their enquiries resulted in the opinion that she was not morally free, and consequently not legally responsible while under the influence of those desires peculiar to pregnancy; adding that if Eve had been in the condition of the accused, when she plucked the forbidden fruit from the tree, the curse of original sin would never have fallen on the race.

Medical and judicial views on menstruation, pregnancy and childbirth were to remain highly relevant to issues of criminal responsibility in women throughout the remainder of the nineteenth century, especially in relation to infanticide. This emphasis was not, however, limited to the field of forensic psychiatry. Parry notes that the very idea of 'moral insanity' had particular implications for women in the Irish asylum system:

> The concept of moral insanity, in essence denotes the re-conceptualisation of madness as deviance from socially-accepted behaviour, that is to say, traditional society was defined as normal, and violations of it labelled deviant. For women, this meant the risk of being labelled mad if one stepped outside the bounds of a very narrow definition

of femininity [...]. Moral management was designed to re-educate the mad into the conforming to society, in the case of the female, into conforming to the notion of the 'ideal woman'.[340]

This situation had clear implications for treatment, as 'moral management aimed to re-educate deviant women to conform to Victorian society. Of necessity, this meant educating women to conform to the ideals of the prevailing ideology of femininity. As a result of this, the treatment women received in Irish asylums, being orientated to this end, was essentially gendered'.[341]

The issue of gender was raised explicitly in 1891 by the Inspectors of Lunatics who reported that in Ireland 54 per cent of 'pauper patients' were male, compared to just 49 per cent in Scotland and 45 per cent in England:[342]

> That the number of males admitted should exceed the females cannot be explained by any difference in the form of disease occurring in Ireland. On the contrary, we find that General Paralysis [neuropsychiatric disorder resulting from late stage syphilis] – a disease to which the male sex is particularly prone – occurs with much greater frequency in England and Scotland. [...] The explanation of this relative excess of male patients would appear to us to be found in the cumbrous and difficult procedures necessary to obtain admission to public asylums in Ireland; so that the women, more easily controlled in their homes or contributing less to family support, remain at home or gravitate to the workhouses.[343]

The links between gender and women's asylum experiences and, indeed, risk of committal, was by no means limited to Ireland, as interpretations of psychological distress in women differed systematically from those in men in many countries, especially as the profession of psychiatry emerged and established itself within the medical firmament during the 1800s and 1900s.[344] This persisted beyond the 1800s: Hanniffy, for example, notes a diagnosis of 'climacteric insanity melancholia' in the records of St Fintan's, Portlaoise in June 1924, apparently the first occurrence of a diagnosis linked to the menopause in the asylum's books.[345]

More broadly, writing in the context of Enniscorthy Lunatic Asylum between 1916 and 1925, McCarthy notes that admissions of women were commonly related to menstruation, childbirth or miscarriage, and that single women often ended up drifting into the asylum in a lost, purposeless and generally unwanted state.[346] In all, 56 per cent of women admitted to Enniscorthy between 1916 and 1925 were single and, like others so committed, they often struggled with impossible combinations of family misfortune, strict behavioural codes and expectations, economic uncertainty and social powerlessness.

Indeed, Parry argues that, from a gender perspective, the asylums 'replicated the social structure of wider society':

> The administration of the system was predominately in the hands of men. Each asylum had a Board of Governors, made up of prominent men from the surrounding county.

Rarely, if indeed ever, did a woman feature on these Boards – the prevailing ideology of femininity held women to be mentally and physically unsuited to public life, and hence to holding public posts. Except for the position of Matron, all top staff positions (Medical Superintendent, Clerk, Storekeeper) were all held by men. In the early days of moral management, when asylums were run by a Moral Governor, women had a certain amount of power in the asylum system in that the Governor's wife usually superintended over the female wards. However, lay managers of asylums were gradually replaced by doctors as the century progressed, and simultaneously the role of matron declined in status. Medical superintendents believed they held their posts based on specific expertise, and hence could not justify their wives, in the absence of any expertise, holding any sort of managerial position in the asylum system.[347]

The fate of women in Irish asylums and the ways in which gender affected the development of the asylum system are fascinating themes that merit greater consideration.[348] Particular attention could usefully be paid to specific, albeit difficult to research aspects of these themes such as the fate of babies born *in* the asylums[349] and the experiences of children admitted to them.[350] These are stories that need to be told.

3

PSYCHIATRY AND SOCIETY IN THE 1800S

Every Physician holding or accepting of an appointment [in a District Lunatic Asylum in Ireland], is requested to bear in mind that the object of the Government is not simply to have the bodily ailments of the Patients attended to, but to assist their recovery by moral or medical means, and to advance Medical Science in cases of Lunacy through the great range of experience which the Public Asylums afford.

> Lord Lieutenant and Council of Ireland, *General Rules for the Government of All the District Lunatic Asylums of Ireland, Made, Framed and Established by the Lord Lieutenant and Council of Ireland* (1843)[1]

The avowedly humanitarian approach to the mentally ill adopted by Hallaran in Cork in the late eighteenth century,[2] consistent with Pinel in France[3] and Tuke in England,[4] was much needed in nineteenth-century Ireland owing not only to under provision for the mentally ill, but also the Great Irish Famine (1845–52). The Famine was one of the most devastating natural disasters in the history of modern Europe: between 1841 and 1851, the population of Ireland fell by approximately 20 per cent.[5] Over a million Irish people died as a result of the Famine and one million more emigrated in its immediate aftermath. Given the Famine's seismic impact on nineteenth-century Ireland, its effects on psychiatry are considered next.

The Great Irish Famine (1845–52): 'Weak Minded from the Start'

Interestingly, the Great Irish Famine is generally under-represented in the historiography of mental disorder in Ireland. This is likely attributable, at least in part, to the broader literature's strong focus on the building of asylums which occurred around the same time. There is, however, little doubt that the Famine increased reliance on various forms of social support among the Irish population in general,[6] including those with mental disorder,[7] as was duly noted by asylum doctors at the time.[8] But did the Famine itself actually increase the rates of occurrence of mental disorder?

Evidence from other countries suggests that this is certainly possible: certain cohorts of people, who were in gestation during the Dutch Winter Hunger of 1944 and born shortly afterwards, were found to have twice the risk of schizophrenia in later life compared to those not exposed to famine conditions during pre-birth development.[9] This is likely attributable to the effects of hunger and stress on the developing brain prior to birth, leading to altered patterns of brain development in childhood and adolescence and increased risk of schizophrenia in young adulthood.[10] Did something similar occur in Ireland during the Famine?

Walsh used data derived chiefly from the Annual Reports of the Irish Inspectors of Lunacy on the District, Criminal and Private Lunatic Asylums, adjusting nineteenth-century diagnostic labels to elucidate, as best as feasible, if the Famine increased rates of schizophrenia in Ireland.[11] He found that while there was indeed an increase of 86 per cent in first admission rates for apparent schizophrenia between 1860 and 1875 (when those in gestation during the Famine reached the high risk age for developing schizophrenia), admissions with other diagnoses (chiefly 'melancholia') also increased, and similar increases were evident in other jurisdictions over the same period. These results are, therefore, inconclusive.

The absence of any dramatic trend in Walsh's work is consistent with the views of Torrey and Miller, who suggest that the effect of the Famine on committal rates was minimal, as admissions simply continued to rise steadily during this period anyway.[12] Given the devastation wrought by the Famine and the fact that the asylum system had been firmly established by the late 1830s,[13] the continued rise in admissions is unsurprising: in times of unprecedented difficulty and distress the asylum offered, at the very least, food and shelter for those in need. In 1844 there were 2,136 'mentally ill' persons resident in public asylums on the island of Ireland and by 1855 this had risen to 3,522.[14] This trend, however, continued long after the Famine: by 1900, the number had reached 16,404.

Given these generally increasing admission rates over the course of the 1800s, is there any other way of looking at existing data so as to elucidate further any possible links between the Famine and admission patterns? First, it is useful to note that, although no part of Ireland fully escaped the effects of the Famine, not all counties were affected equally. Counties in the west of Ireland, such as Galway, Mayo and Roscommon, were particularly badly hit: the death rate in County Mayo between 1846 and 1851 was approximately 60 per 1,000, while the death rate in Kildare and Wexford was under 5 per 1,000.[15] Western counties had a particular reliance on potato crops, so when the crops failed from 1845 to 1849, western subsistence farmers and their families were especially vulnerable.

Grimsley-Smith, in a fascinating analysis of admission rates over the decades following the Famine, notes a significant and sustained increase in admissions of 20- to-30-year-olds between 1857 and 1868 in Connaught (the area worst affected by the Famine) but not in Ulster, Leinster and Munster.[16] She also points to the 1914 report of the Inspectors of Lunatics who examined statistics from this period and concluded, subject to certain caveats, that there seemed to be 'an exceptional number of insane and idiots derived from the population born during the decade 1841-51':

> It seems probable that children born and partially reared amidst the horrors of the famine and the epidemics of disease that followed it were so handicapped in their nervous equipment as to be weak minded from the start or to fall victims to mental disease later.[17]

This supports the idea that, in the areas worst affected, the Famine altered early human development in such a fashion as to increase risk of mental disorder later on, in young adulthood. There are, of course, many challenges associated with reaching such a conclusion, not least of which are the potentially confounding effects of concurrent changes in committal practices, rates of co-occurring physical illnesses, patterns of migration, changes in population structure, declining rates of marriage, and various other demographic factors. There are, in addition, great challenges associated with interpreting diagnostic categories from the past and translating them into contemporary diagnostic categories, even on an approximate basis.[18]

Even in light of these issues, however, it still appears reasonable to conclude that the Great Irish Famine, like the Dutch Winter Hunger, increased risk of mental disorder among persons who were in gestation during the Famine and born during it or shortly afterwards. Other, variously related factors, such as family structure, family conflict and emigration, were also relevant to committal practices in post-Famine Ireland.[19] There may also have been transgenerational effects which affected patterns of illness many decades later, and this possibility richly merits, and is the subject of, further study.[20]

Finally, it is readily apparent that, at the time of the Famine, both starvation and prevailing deprivation acutely increased *social* need among the mentally ill[21] and also likely led to a worsening of psychiatric symptoms among people with pre-existing mental disorder, both of which increased pressure on asylums to admit people with starvation related distress and intensified mental disorder.[22]

Analogous evidence for the latter is available from studies of the 'famine' which occurred in French psychiatric hospitals between 1940 and 1944, when France was under Nazi rule and rations to French asylums were reduced to levels incompatible with life.[23] This resulted in increased mortality in French asylums and a sharp intensification of all forms of mental disorder. The philosopher Simone Weil (1909–1943), herself in an English hospital at the time, died of starvation, possibly in solidarity with the conditions endured by her compatriots in France.[24]

The famine in French asylums was a specific, demarcated phenomenon which only affected individuals *already in* asylums, at a particular moment in France's history. Nonetheless, the deterioration in mental health produced by the lack of food in French asylums provides strong evidence that famine conditions have adverse effects on mental health, at least amongst the mentally ill. This was also the case in Ireland, where persons with worsening mental disorder and starvation related distress sought not only to enter the asylums but also the workhouses, which, despite their drawbacks, at least provided a certain level of care for those with nowhere else to go.

Workhouses and the Mentally Ill:
'Little More Than a Dungeon'

Even prior to the Famine, destitute persons with mental disorder or intellectual disability had commonly been admitted to workhouses and various charitable establishments, especially during times of social or economic difficulty.[25] In 1708, the Dublin workhouse built six cells for persons with apparent mental disorder, intellectual disability or epilepsy.[26] The number of places increased to approximately 40 by 1729, but conditions were dreadful: the inmates were chained in foul, unglazed, underground cells with little light or freedom.[27]

In 1787, the Prisons Act empowered Grand Juries (county administrative and judicial bodies) systematically to establish lunatic wards in houses of industry, and dictated that such wards would be subject to inspection by the Inspector General of prisons.[28] The wards were to house insane persons or 'idiots' who had to be certified by at least two magistrates.[29] The initial response to the 1787 legislation was relatively modest, however, and lunatic wards were only established in Dublin, Cork, Waterford and Limerick.[30]

As a result, Dublin House of Industry became a major centre for admission of 'lunatics' from all over Ireland: between 1811 and 1815, some 754 of its 1,179 admissions came from outside Dublin.[31] The investigation ordered by Robert Peel in 1816 recommended that more extensive provision be provided in Cork and Belfast.[32] Several decades later, the *Commission of Inquiry in the State of Lunatic Asylums in Ireland* (1858)[33] looked into the matter again and found that the 'wretched inmates' in the Hardwicke Cells, connected with the Dublin House of Industry, were 'in a most unsatisfactory state'. In 1857, these inmates were removed from this 'disgracefully conducted' establishment to a 'new establishment at Lucan' which was 'commodious, airy, and cheerful, and every care and attention appeared to be paid to the wants of the inmates, of whom there were ninety-eight at the period of our visit'.

As the 1800s progressed, the Poor Law Act (1838) was introduced to relieve the distress of 'deserving' poor in Ireland.[34] The system initially consisted of 130 Poor Law Unions, aimed at providing accommodation, food and medical care to the poor of the area. Despite the establishment of several new asylums for the mentally ill during this period,[35] many persons with mental disorder or intellectual disability still had to enter the workhouses,[36] which generated even greater fear than the asylums did.[37] The food was reportedly better in the asylums, compared to workhouses.[38]

By 1844, there were 957 'mentally ill' persons in workhouses or poorhouses on the island of Ireland and by 1851, towards the end of the Famine, this had increased to 2,393.[39] The number continued to rise throughout the remainder of the 1800s, reaching a peak in 1892, when there were 4,198 'mentally ill' persons in workhouses. The previous year, there were some 1,170 'idiots' in workhouses.[40] Interestingly, while males tended to outnumber females in public asylums throughout the 1800s,[41] 'mentally ill' females outnumbered 'mentally ill' males in workhouses.[42]

It is difficult to gain a systematic picture of the specific experiences of the mentally ill in workhouses throughout the 1800s, although conditions were generally very poor and designed to repel,[43] as was vividly outlined in the 1817 *Report from the Select Committee on the Lunatic Poor in Ireland*.[44] Efforts were, however, made to improve matters in at least some establishments, albeit with limited success. Ballinrobe Poor Law Union in County Mayo, for example, was located in one of the areas worst affected by the Famine and commonly received persons with mental disorder. In August 1846, a man 'who was confined to the workhouse as a cured patient from the Castlebar Lunatic Asylum took his discharge and went to his home'; there is no record of his mental state on departure or any attempt at follow up.[45] In October 1896, the Ballinrobe workhouse employed 'a woman at a shilling a day to mind ... a woman who is insane'.

Conditions in workhouses were very difficult, not least owing to illnesses such as cholera, typhus and dysentery.[46] As a result, there was significant public and official concern about the plight of the mentally ill in the workhouses,[47] and it is notable that, unlike the English commissioners in lunacy,

Irish inspectors did not approve particular workhouses as suitable for the mentally ill.[48] Nonetheless, workhouses rapidly became *de facto* elements of the system of 'care' for the mentally ill during the 1800s,[49] as patients were routinely admitted from workhouses to asylums[50] and discharged from asylums back to workhouses.[51] Relations between the institutions were commonly strained: in 1881, there were 148 persons with intellectual disability or mental illness huddled together in grossly unhealthy conditions in Cork workhouse, and they suffered further during a bitter dispute between the workhouse and the asylum over who was responsible for them.[52]

Against the background of this close, conflicted relationship between asylums and workhouses, the problem of the mentally ill in workhouses persisted well after the Famine had eased. In 1895, at a meeting of the Irish Division of the MPA in the Royal College of Physicians, Kildare Street, Dr Oscar Woods (secretary of the division) 'introduced the question of dealing with lunatics in workhouses, and after some discussion, in which the following – Drs Drapes, Finegan, Lawless, John Eustace and the president – joined, the following resolution was unanimously adopted: "That the time has arrived when provision should be made for the large number of lunatics in the workhouses of the country at present uncertified for, not properly cared for, and treated not as lunatics, but merely as paupers, and that a copy of this resolution be sent to the Inspectors of Lunatics".'[53]

The concerns of the MPA were strongly supported by admission statistics: Walsh, in an especially valuable study of the Ennis District Lunatic Asylum, County Clare, and the Clare Workhouse Lunatic Asylums in 1901, notes that there were eight workhouse asylums in Clare, housing a total of 263 residents.[54] From a diagnostic perspective, 41 per cent had 'dementia'; 30 per cent were 'idiots' or 'imbeciles'; 20 per cent had 'mania'; 6 per cent had 'melancholia'; and 2 per cent suffered from epilepsy. There is also evidence that persons with other conditions, such as delirium tremens (from alcohol withdrawal), were admitted during the 1890s.[55]

In 1907, at a meeting of the Richmond District Asylum Joint Committee (in Grangegorman, Dublin), the chairman highlighted the magnitude of the issue at the Richmond:

> A large number of our admissions come here direct from workhouses. I have looked up the exact numbers and find they average about 30% of total admissions. During the last four financial years 709 patients came from workhouses. I do not think I would be very much in error in estimating that 50% of these 709 admissions would come under the head of Chronic and Harmless Lunatics, and probably at the present time there are not far short of 700 or 800 cases in the whole institution who could be so classified. The 76th section of the Local Government Act of 1898 provides for the establishment of auxiliary asylums for such cases.[56]

The Richmond Joint Committee dutifully appointed a 'special committee' to look into the matter, and the committee visited asylums at Youghal,[57] Cork and Downpatrick, and inspected Union Workhouses in North and South Dublin.[58] The committee examined patient numbers, clinical conditions and financial arrangements and reported back to the Richmond Joint Committee on 19 December 1907.

Downpatrick Asylum was of particular interest because 'Down County Council in 1901, after the fullest examination into the fiscal aspect of the question, decided to enlarge the Downpatrick Asylum for the reception of the insane then located in the workhouses'.[59] The committee presented details of the accommodation provided at Downpatrick and agreed with the Inspector of Lunatics who, on 16 November 1906, concluded that 'this county is amongst the few in Ireland which has made full provision for all the insane chargeable to it [...]. Nowhere are the insane better housed in bright, cheerful, well-furnished and well-heated wards, where they are properly cared for, well fed, and well clothed'.[60]

The committee also visited North Dublin workhouse, where they found 'that the provision for the inmates of the lunatic departments is truly deplorable. The overcrowding is very marked, and calls for prompt relief'.[61] The female ward for 'healthy lunatics' is 'little more than a dungeon, ventilation is inadequate, and the beds are laid upon wooden trestles. The patients are obliged to take their meals in this repellent place'.[62] The male wards 'are much overcrowded [...]. Forty-two of the patients are confined to bed, 20 of them being of the dirty class. Ten patients have to be spoonfed'. The committee concluded that 'all buildings occupied by the lunatic patients are deficient in light and air' and 'all lunatic inmates of the North Dublin Union Workhouse ought to be removed as speedily as possible'.[63] Dr Fottrell at the workhouse 'supplied us with a list of 60 patients, 20 males and 40 females, with an urgent request that these be provided for without delay'.[64] The committee also visited South Dublin Union Workhouse where their 'experiences were much more agreeable'.[65]

In the end, the committee made four recommendations to the Richmond District Asylum Joint Committee. First, they urged the Joint Committee 'to assume the full responsibility imposed upon them by the Local Government Act of 1898 with respect to pauper lunatics within the district'.[66] Second, they recommended 'that provision for the 600 patients should be made by the erection of suitable buildings at Portrane, where ample space for that purpose is available'.[67] Third, they concluded that 'a thorough classification and segregation of our existing inmates at Richmond and Portrane would secure an immediate reduction in our cost of maintenance'. Finally, 'inasmuch as the condition of things in the North Dublin Union Workhouse requires prompt remedy', they suggested 'that the Portrane Committee be instructed to make immediate provision in the temporary buildings at their disposal for the patients whose removal is applied for by Dr Fottrell'. The Joint Committee adapted all four recommendations on 19 December 1907.

Notwithstanding these measures, the problem of the mentally ill in Irish workhouses remained a concern well into the 1900s. In 1913, for example, despite the transfer of 58 patients from the South Dublin Union to the Richmond Asylum, the number in the Union continued to increase, to 202.[68] There were similar problems at the North Dublin Union. Clearly the workhouses presented a persistent problem, regardless of how large the asylums themselves became.

Ultimately, the number of 'mentally ill' persons in workhouses finally began to decrease from the highs of the 1890s down to 1,821 in 1919, and generally declined further (in analogous establishments) throughout the 1920s, 1930s and 1940s.[69] Notwithstanding this reduction, however, a range of challenges remained, not least of which was the plight of the intellectually disabled in the asylums and various other establishments in the early 1900s. These are considered next.

The Intellectually Disabled in the Nineteenth Century: 'Verily We Are Guilty in This Matter'

The fate of the intellectually disabled in early-nineteenth-century Ireland was similar in many respects to that of the mentally ill. There was minimal dedicated provision, with the result that intellectually disabled persons were cared for at home, admitted to workhouses or, increasingly, committed to the growing number of asylums for the mentally ill.[70]

The 1843 rules for the operation of asylums provided specifically for the admission of the intellectually disabled and it was estimated that there was a total of 6,127 intellectually disabled persons in Ireland at that time.[71] Precise numbers varied, but the Inspectors of Lunatics calculated that, in 1851, there were 3,562 'idiots' 'at large'; 202 in asylums; 13 in prisons; and 1,129 in workhouses, yielding a total of 4,906.[72] By 1861, the number in asylums had doubled (to 403) and the total number risen to 7,033.

During the 1860s, Cheyne Brady, a member of the Royal Irish Academy, governor of the Meath Hospital,[73] and prolific author on social matters, was notably exercised by this issue and wrote a pamphlet on *The Training of Idiotic and Feeble-Minded Children*, grimly outlining the position of the intellectually disabled in nineteenth-century Ireland and elsewhere (using contemporaneous terminology that some readers might find disturbing):

> It is not very long since we used to see boys and girls, and sometimes stunted men and women, running wild in our streets and villages in a state of idiocy [...]. They were carefully avoided, as the continual worrying of the village urchins had soured their tempers and rendered them in some cases dangerous.
>
> Then, again, on visiting the poor, we have from time to time seen a bundle of rags in a corner, and, on inquiry, have ascertained that it contained an idiot child, living in dirt and degradation, worse than one would permit his dog or pig to live in.
>
> Prejudice and popular ignorance respecting them have led to strange treatment of this afflicted class. By the Hindoo [*sic*] they are superstitiously venerated, while by many Europeans these helpless creatures have been regarded as human beings without souls. Some poor parents fancy that, as their children cannot remember what they hear, their brain must be soft, and apply poultices of oak-bark in order to tan or harden the fibres; others, finding it impossible to make any impression on the mind, conclude that the brain is too hard, and they torture their unhappy offspring with hot poultices of bread and milk, or plaster the skull with tar, keeping it on for a long time. Others, again, give mercury to act as a solder to close up the supposed crevices in the brain [...]. The utmost stretch of humanity has hitherto thrust them out of sight in our workhouses, where they are suffered to exist uncared for and untaught.[74]

Brady presented a call to action, suggesting the opening of asylums for the intellectually disabled, as had already occurred in Bath (1846), Highgate (1848) and elsewhere:[75]

And if it cannot be gainsayed that the condition of the idiot and imbecile can be thus improved, is not our duty plain?

But what shall we answer for our past neglect? Verily we are guilty in this matter.

The future, however, is before us. Shall we not redeem the time, and gird up our loins to make up for past deficiency by a strenuous effort on behalf of this neglected class?

There are three courses open for adoption:-

I.   The foundation of a general institution for the reception of all degrees of idiocy, from the hopeless to the most improvable.

II. The opening of an asylum for the pure idiots, who are not susceptible of much improvement, but who can be housed, cared for, and cured of bad habits.

III. The establishment of a training school for the improvable cases, where, as in the asylums of which I have attempted a description, they may be trained to habits of usefulness, rendered able to earn a livelihood, and be taught the way of salvation.[76]

Brady's words inspired immediate activism on the part of George Hugh Kidd, an obstetric surgeon in Dublin,[77] who penned *An Appeal on Behalf of the Idiotic and Imbecile Children of Ireland*, seeking the building of an asylum for intellectually disabled children, in line with Brady's suggestion.[78]

One of the key supporters of Kidd's proposal was a certain Henry Hutchinson Stewart (1798–1879), second son of Reverend Abraham Augustus Stewart, Rector of Donabate, County Dublin.[79] Stewart, a key figure in the history of the intellectually disabled in Ireland, was born on 23 June 1798 and, shortly after the Duke of Richmond came to Ireland as Lord Lieutenant in 1807, was appointed as a page to the Duchess. Stewart later studied medicine, taking his MD in Edinburgh in 1829 and obtaining the Licentiate of the Royal College of Surgeons in Ireland.

Stewart worked in Killucan Dispensary District in County Westmeath before taking Fellowship of the Royal College of Surgeons in Ireland in 1840 and being appointed Governor of the Hospital of the Houses of Industry in North Brunswick Street in Dublin. He was medical attendant to the School for the Sons of the Irish Clergy at the original Spa Hotel in Lucan, County Dublin.

In the mid-1850s, when the *Commission of Inquiry in the State of Lunatic Asylums in Ireland*[80] found that the 'wretched inmates' in the 'Hardwicke Cells', connected with the Dublin House of Industry, were 'in a most unsatisfactory state', it was Stewart's suggestion in 1857 that they be moved to a 'new establishment at Lucan', where he established an asylum at Lucan Spa House.[81]

Against this backdrop, Stewart was a predictable supporter of Kidd's calls for an asylum for children with intellectual disability and of the work of the related committee set up by Lord Charlemont. Stewart went on to propose giving his asylum at Lucan for this purpose, together with a donation of £4,000, provided the asylum's work was continued and its profits used for the maintenance of an institution for the intellectually disabled.[82] Premises were duly acquired in Lucan, on the same plot of ground as Stewart's Asylum at the Crescent, and made ready to receive 12 pupils in 1869.

Two separate institutions were established: the Stewart Institution for Idiots, based on Protestant principles, and the Stewart Asylum for Lunatic Patients of the Middle Classes, with no religious distinctions.[83] Dr Frederick Pim became medical director and, despite complexities involving the Catholic primate, Cardinal Cullen, by 1870 the premises were quickly oversubscribed and overcrowded. Later in the 1870s, the establishment, now termed the Stewart Institution for Idiotic and Imbecile Children and Middle Class Lunatic Asylum, moved to the mansion and 40 acre demesne of the late Lord Donoughmore in nearby Palmerstown.[84]

In parallel with this dedicated but isolated development, persons with intellectual disability continued steadily to be admitted to workhouses and asylums throughout the rest of Ireland.[85] By 1908, the Royal Commission on the Care and Control of the Feeble-Minded estimated that, based on the 1901 census, 'there were 5,216 idiots in Ireland, of whom 3,272 were at large, 1,181 were in workhouses, and 763 in asylums':

> As regards the existing accommodation in Ireland, we have shown that the accommodation for these cases in workhouses is absolutely unsuitable; that the provision for those in asylums, although more suitable is by no means ideal, and is unnecessarily expensive; while of the cases 'at large' although a minority may be suitably provided for at home, there is ample evidence to show that in the majority of cases the unfortunate patient at home is even in a worse plight than the patient in the workhouse.
>
> With the exception of the Stewart Institution for Imbeciles at Palmerstown, which is entirely supported by charitable donations, and only provides for 103 inmates, there is absolutely no special provision in Ireland at the present time for probably 64 per cent of the uncertified idiots, imbeciles and feeble-minded, or for the majority of the 763 certified idiots in asylums as returned in the Census, 1901.[86]

Overall, it is likely that the institutional experiences of the intellectually disabled in late nineteenth-century Ireland were similar, in at least some respects, to those of individuals without intellectual disability who were similarly institutionalised and who tended to experience lengthy periods of detention in poorly therapeutic facilities, poor mental and physical health, and a high risk of dying in the asylum: once a person had been detained in an Irish asylum for more than five years, it was almost inevitable that he or she would die there.[87]

The institutional experiences of the intellectually disabled in Ireland were similar to those in other jurisdictions.[88] In Great Britain, the late 1800s saw the management of the intellectually disabled move increasingly out of the private, family sphere and into the public sphere, thus becoming a 'social problem', presumed to necessitate the development of institutional provisions.[89] This period also saw the emergence of the principle of 'segregation' of the intellectually disabled from the rest of society, and a particular commitment to *permanent* 'segregation', deemed to be in the best interests of both the individual and society.[90]

These public and professional attitudes resulted in widespread institutionalisation of the intellectual disabled throughout the 1800s,[91] focused, in Ireland, on the workhouses and emerging asylum system. It is worth noting, however, that the precise nature of the psychiatric institutions across Ireland varied considerably, and there were significant pockets of enlightened practice scattered across the country, where staff sought to humanise conditions and improve outcomes for their patients. The asylum in Enniscorthy, under the punctilious superintendence of the prolific Dr Thomas Drapes, is a good example.

Dr Thomas Drapes:
Asylum Doctor Extraordinaire

Dr Thomas Drapes (1847–1919) was RMS of the Enniscorthy District Asylum in County Wexford from 1883 to 1919, and one of the leading figures in Irish asylum medicine for several decades.[92] Drapes's career was as complex as it was noteworthy, and his legacy was to help shape Irish psychiatry for several decades to follow.[93]

Drapes was born in Lakeview, Cavan on 17 January 1847, the third son of Dr Thomas Drapes who died shortly after Drapes's birth.[94] His mother moved the family to Kingstown (Dún Laoghaire), County Dublin, and Drapes spent time at a preparatory establishment in Derbyshire before completing his early education at Mr Wall's private school. In 1864, he went to Trinity College Dublin, from which he graduated in Arts in 1867. He then studied medicine at the Trinity College Medical School and the City of Dublin Hospital. Drapes took the first Medical Scholarship at Trinity College Medical School in 1869, as well as the Purser Studentship and Clinical Medal at the City of Dublin Hospital, before attaining the degree of MB (Bachelor of Medicine; *Medicinae Baccalaureus*) in 1871. In the same year, Drapes took the Licence of the Royal College of Surgeons in Ireland and the Licence in Midwifery of the Rotunda Hospital.

After completing his training, Drapes was appointed as visiting and consulting physician to Enniscorthy District Lunatic Asylum in County Wexford. Enniscorthy Asylum had opened in 1869, one of 21 such institutions built during this wave of asylum building.[95] In 1883, following the death of Dr Joseph Edmundson, Drapes became RMS, a position he held until his retirement on 15 May 1919. As with all asylums during this period, admission rates increased at Enniscorthy, from 4 per 100,000 population in 1871, to 6 in 1911.

The positon of RMS was an extraordinary and, in many senses, impossible one. In 1874, revised *General Rules and Regulations for the Management of District Lunatic Asylums in Ireland* specified that the RMS was to 'superintend and regulate the whole establishment, and is to be intrusted with the moral and general medical treatment of its inmates, for whose well-being and safe custody he [*sic*] shall be responsible; and he shall at all times devote his best exertions to the efficient management of the institution'.[96]

> He shall, before one o'clock, P.M., and also occasionally at other times, inspect the whole establishment, daily – dormitories, – dining-rooms, – kitchen, – laundry, – stores, and other places. He shall go through all the divisions, and see that they are orderly, clean, well ventilated, and of a proper temperature. He shall carefully examine each patient who may seem to require his advice, or to whom his attention may be directed. When going round the female division he shall be accompanied by the Matron or Head Nurse of the division, who shall direct his attention to any matter worthy of attention.[97]

[...] He shall also visit the male divisions after the patients have retired to rest, and satisfy himself that they are safely and comfortably located for the night.[98]

Other regulations related to communication with the 'Consulting and Visiting Physician' in 'complicated or difficult cases of mental disease, or any case requiring particular treatment';[99] the RMS being absent from the asylum for a night, which required 'special leave from a Board of Governors or the Inspectors';[100] the keeping of books[101] and minutes;[102] 'disbursement of money';[103] and various other matters. The role of RMS was clearly an extensive and responsible one, both in local asylums and in the criminal asylum at Dundrum.[104]

During his time as RMS in Enniscorthy, Drapes, in addition to his daily duties, introduced improvements to the establishment including the addition of two new wings, a laundry, kitchen, new drainage system, new water supply, a general heating plant and a mill to supply electricity at an economical rate. Drapes remained, however, primarily a physician, noted for his kindness to patients,[105] albeit within the context of the times when institutional practices such as withholding patients' letters were routine elements of asylum life in Enniscorthy as elsewhere.[106]

Once he became RMS, Drapes joined the MPA and became an exceptionally active member and enthusiastic contributor to the MPA's *Journal of Mental Science*.[107] Drapes was elected president of the MPA for the term 1911–12 but declined on health grounds. In 1912, he was unanimously elected as co-editor of the *Journal of Mental Science*, to which he devoted his considerable energies and intellect: in 1917, the *Journal* published Drapes's translation of a paper by Yves Delage, titled 'Psychoanalysis, a new psychosis' ('*Une psychose nouvelle: la psychoanalyse*').[108] Both the breadth of Drapes's learning and his myriad intellectual gifts were clear in his deft rendering of Delage's coruscating critique of psychoanalysis.

In addition to his duties with the MPA and *Journal of Mental Science*, Drapes took a keen interest in many other matters relating to mental disorder and its treatment. These ranged from the 'alleged increase in insanity in Ireland'[109] to the role of trauma in producing 'hallucinatory insanity'.[110] Throughout his contributions to these debates, Drapes was unafraid to challenge theories he believed to be unhelpful or wrong. This was most apparent in his views on emergent classification systems for mental disorder, systems which he felt should not proceed until there was better definition and use of key terms, such as 'hallucinations' and 'illusions'.[111]

Drapes was especially unimpressed by Kraepelin's proposed division of 'functional' psychosis into manic-depressive illness (bipolar affective disorder) and dementia praecox (schizophrenia);[112] Drapes, like a number of significant others,[113] preferred the idea of a 'unitary' psychosis.[114] This stood in contrast to those who supported the German approach,[115] including the influential Norman (RMS at the Richmond), who read a paper titled 'variations in form of mental affections in relation to the classification of insanity' before the Medical Section of the Academy of Medicine in Ireland on 28 January 1887.[116] In his engaging paper, Norman described previous diagnostic systems as metaphysical and fanciful, rather than clinically meaningful, and welcomed the new, emerging systems.

Unafraid of controversy, Drapes published a paper in the *Journal of Mental Science* addressing the use of 'punitive measures' in asylums[117] and, while punishment was used in many asylums in order to maintain order during this period, the Inspectors of Lunatics, following their inspection of

Enniscorthy on 4 July 1913, reported a notably low rate of restraint there.[118] Even in 1916, by which point the Enniscorthy asylum was 'considerably overcrowded', the institution was still maintained 'in very good order'.[119]

The following year, at the spring 1917 meeting of the Irish Division of the MPA, Drapes, as chairman, heard a detailed account of the Richmond War Hospital (1916–19), and went on to reflect on the folly of 'psychophysical parallelism', or the spurious division between mental and physical symptoms in medicine.[120] Given Drapes's prominence in Irish and British medicine at the time, his emphasis on the continuity between physical and mental symptoms was both influential and prescient, and prefigured many of the developments in psychiatry following the end of the First World War.

Indeed, this issue, the spurious division between mental and physical phenomena, was to remain a theme in clinical practice for many decades to follow and was a key element in the false dichotomies in psychiatry identified by Andreasen, editor-in-chief of the *American Journal of Psychiatry*, almost a century later.[121] Drapes's insight remains highly relevant to clinical practice today.[122]

Despite his general independence of judgment, Drapes was not immune to passing trends in medical thought. At the 1910 Spring meeting of the Irish Division of the MPA, in response to a paper by Dr H.M. Eustace on the 'prophylaxis of insanity', Drapes spoke about measures proposed elsewhere to prevent the occurrence of mental disorder:

> Dr Drapes said that [Dr Eustace's] paper was highly suggestive. The nineteenth century had been eminent in preventive medicine and hygiene, but mental hygiene had been omitted – Hamlet without the Prince. Medical examination before marriage was good in theory, but stopping marriage would not stop procreation. The public must be educated, and the teaching of the structure and function of the body should commence from infancy. Sterilisation would be even more necessary in improvable cases, those which were discharged quasi-recovered, and these should be given the choice of sterilisation or perpetual detention. He also alluded to the necessity for better teaching of medical men in psychology and psychiatry.[123]

Like many others who proposed measures such as sterilisation of the mentally ill, Drapes was chiefly motivated by the size of the asylum system and the perceived increase in rates of insanity that underpinned it. Similar measures had been proposed and even adopted elsewhere (e.g. certain parts of the US) at this time.[124] Even so, Drapes's endorsement of sterilisation was a rare and regrettable misstep for one of the leading independent thinkers in asylum medicine in Ireland and Great Britain. Despite advocacy from certain asylum doctors in Ireland, such as Dr William Dawson, eugenics did not gain widespread support in Ireland and the movement did not generally progress.[125]

In his personal life, Drapes was active in the Church of Ireland and sought to combine adherence to scientific medical principles with commitment to the tenets of Christianity.[126] He was on the Synod of his diocese, took a keen interest in temperance activities, and was secretary of the local choir union for some 30 years. The emphasis that Drapes placed on religion was duly reflected in the Enniscorthy asylum, as the Inspectors of Lunatics noted following their 1913 inspection:

Religious ministration receives careful attention. One hundred and forty-one men and 127 women [49% of the patient population] were able to be present at Divine Service on last Sunday. A Roman Catholic and a Protestant Chaplain visit the institution at least twice in the week.[127]

Drapes's other interests included chess, croquet and golf. Drapes retired from the Enniscorthy Asylum on 15 May 1919, and though he appeared active and in good health, he died of double pneumonia on 5 October 1919. In his obituary in the *Journal of Mental Science*, Dawson deeply mourned the loss of an outstanding figure in Irish and British asylum medicine.[128] Dawson was, himself, a remarkable figure in Irish psychiatric history, appointed by the War Office in 1915 as a specialist in nerve disease for the British army in Ireland, having previously served in many other prominent roles, including Inspector of Lunatic Asylums in Ireland and president of the MPA (1911).[129]

Overall, Drapes represented a broadly progressive strand within Irish asylum medicine, focused on patient care and recovery, albeit still within the confines of the custodial Irish asylum system and with the caveat that he was not opposed to considering sterilisation as one way of addressing the apparent increase in insanity that troubled him so much.[130] Like many leading figures of his day, Drapes's thought was dominated by the size of the asylum system and the perception that rates of insanity were increasing uncontrollably.[131] This perception, and the debates it stimulated, were a defining feature of this phase in the history of psychiatry in Ireland.

'The Increase of Insanity in Ireland' (1894)

Even in the early 1700s there was clear recognition that the needs of increasing numbers of mentally ill persons were not being met by existing provisions in workhouses, prisons or hospitals.[132] Concern about the apparent increase in insanity in Ireland grew steadily throughout the 1700s and 1800s, despite efforts to increase provision through the opening of St Patrick's Hospital, Dublin, in the mid-1700s and various developments and initiatives at workhouses, such as that in Cork, at the turn of the nineteenth century.

By 1810, elucidating the 'cause of the extraordinary increase of insanity in Ireland' was a key concern for Hallaran in Cork. In his celebrated textbook, *An Enquiry into the Causes Producing the Extraordinary Addition to the Number of Insane together with Extended Observations on the Cure of Insanity with Hints as to the Better Management of Public Asylums for Insane Persons*, he wrote:

> It has been for some few years back a subject of deep regret, as well as of speculative research, with several humane and intelligent persons of this vicinity, who have had frequent occasions to remark the progressive increase of insane persons, as returned at each Assizes to the Grand Juries, and claiming support from the public purse. To me it has been at times a source of extreme difficulty to contrive the means of accommodation for this hurried weight of human calamity![133]

Hallaran believed that the reasons for this apparent increase in insanity related to both 'corporeal' (physical or bodily) and 'mental excitement' (in the mind),[134] as well as 'the unrestrained use and abuse of ardent spirits' (i.e. alcohol):

> So frequently do instances of furious madness present themselves to me, and arising from long continued inebriety, that I seldom have occasion to enquire the cause, from the habit which repeated opportunities have given me at first sight, of detecting its well-known ravages.[135]

When an individual had developed 'the habit of daily intoxication', Hallaran noted that 'the countenance now bespeaks a dreary waste of mind and body; all is confusion and wild extravagance. The temper which previously partook of the grateful endearments of social intercourse, becomes dark, irritable and suspicious'.[136] The challenges of treatment were only too apparent: 'Perhaps there is not in nature a greater difficulty than that of restoring a professed drunkard to a permanent abhorrence of such a habit'.[137]

In Hallaran's view, the solution to the problems presented by alcohol lay in reforming revenue laws, limiting availability and optimising the *quality* of alcohol consumed:

> As I have every reason to suppose that the revenue laws, so far at least as they relate to this part of the Empire, give ample opportunity of regulating and inspecting the *quantum* of this valuable commodity, *at its first shot*, I would also consider of the possibility of officers in this department laying such restraint upon it, as must effectually prevent its making further progress in society [...]. I would therefore, at the fountain head, commence the measures of reform, by enforcing the necessary limitations to its unreserved dispensation [...]. If then we must admit the expediency of indulging the lower orders with a free admission to the *bewitching* charms of our native whiskey, let it be, in the name of pity, in the name of decency and good order, under such stipulations, as that it may at least be dealt out to them in its purity, free from those vicious frauds which not only constitute the immediate cause of the most inveterate maladies in the general sense, but also render them particularly liable to the horrors of continued insanity.[138]

Hallaran identified 'terror from religious enthusiasm' as another cause contributing to apparently increasing rates of 'mental derangement':

> On the whole, I am much inclined to indulge the hope, that however well-disposed my fellow countrymen may be, to cherish and hold fast the full impression of a pure and rational religion, still, that possessing a strong and lively discriminating faculty, they will continue to resist all charlatanical efforts to dissuade them from the substantial blessings which they now enjoy: either by submitting themselves to the distorted

doctrines of the libertine, any more than to the circumscribed dogmas of our modern declaimers.[139]

Hallaran was by no means alone in his concerns: the apparent increase in insanity became *the* leading concern among asylum doctors in Ireland and Great Britain throughout the 1800s. In 1829 there were 2,097 'mentally ill' persons in institutions in Ireland and by 1894 this had increased to 17,665.[140]

In 1887 the Inspectors, John Nugent and G.W. Hatchell, maintained that this increase in numbers was, at least in part, attributable to 'better and more generous treatment of the insane' in the asylums.[141] They reported that, in 1887, the 'lunatic population of this country under Governmental supervision' stood at 14,702, comprising 10,077 in district lunatic asylums, 602 in private lunatic asylums, 3,841 in poorhouses, 172 in the Central Lunatic Asylum, 9 in Palmerston Private Asylum and 1 in gaol.[142] This was an increase from a total of 14,419 the previous year and the Inspectors linked the increase with the quality of care provided:

> With regard to the condition of the 10,077 patients in district asylums on the 1st of January in the present year [1887], the probably curable, or perhaps, more cautiously speaking, those who admit of hope of recovery, were estimated at 2,228, and the incurable at 7,779, each class, it may be added, needing an equal professional care and domestic supervision; for it should be remembered, that though alike innocuous and tranquil when properly attended to, if neglected they may become dangerous and unmanageable; perhaps, too, of all others, those whose insanity is less varied, and those whose reasoning powers, save on special subjects, are scarcely impaired.
>
> Such being the case, it cannot be a matter of surprise, if for its own protection, and that of the public, a continued deprivation of personal freedom is entailed on an innocent community, and, at the same time, if owing to a better and more generous treatment of the insane, their longevity is notably increased, that additional provision should be made to meet growing requirements.
>
> Hence the progressive enlargement of public asylums has become a necessity. Twelve years ago the accommodation in them was limited to 7,000 beds; it has been since increased by over 2,600 and even now there exists a marked deficiency.
>
> The same process which has obtained here is strongly evidenced in England, particularly in its most populous and manufacturing districts.'[143]

Drapes,[144] writing in the *Journal of Mental Science* in 1894, noted that between 1859 and 1889 the *rate* of increase in certified 'lunatics' in England had decreased, but in Ireland had *increased*, a difference that Drapes found difficult to explain:

> If we take the 30 years from 1859 to 1889 we find that in England the ratio of total lunatics to population increased in the first decade by 526 per million, in the second by 361, and in the last by 211, denoting a very large diminution in the rate of increase. On the other hand, if we take a similar, though not exactly corresponding, period in

the case of Ireland, viz., 1861 to 1891, we find that the ratio of lunatics increased in the first decade by 600 per million, in the second by 510, and in the last by 940. So that while in England the rate of increase during the period mentioned fell continuously from 526 to 211 per million, or to considerably less than one-half, in Ireland it rose from 600 to 940, an advance of over 50 per cent – a truly remarkable difference.[145]

In the same year, Dr Daniel Hack Tuke (1827–1895),[146] also in the *Journal of Mental Science*, noted that both the numbers certified as 'insane' and the numbers admitted to asylums had risen in Great Britain, a situation apparently attributable to increases in the causes of insanity, new forms of mental disorder, and premature discharge from asylums at the request of families.[147] Having considered a range of arguments and positions on the topic, Tuke concluded that (a) there had been a large increase in the number of patients in asylums and workhouses, especially the former, since 1870; and (b) there had been a considerable, but not as great, rise in admissions to asylums; but (c) this did *not* indicate increased susceptibility to insanity in the population because the increased numbers were attributable, at least in part, to increased appreciation of the value of asylums, movement of patients from workhouses to asylums, and increased registration of persons with mental disorder who had not previously been so registered.

With regard to Ireland in particular, Tuke, in a separate *Journal of Mental Science* paper devoted to the 'alleged increase of insanity in Ireland', noted the emphasis that RMS Norman at the Richmond in Dublin placed on social attitudes in increasing rates of presentation to asylums:

> Although the number of persons under treatment in the Dublin Asylum has risen from 1,055 in 1883 to 1,467 at the end of 1892 (or 412 more) the medical Reporter, Dr Conolly Norman [below], observes: 'At the same time, as the result of much consideration, it is not thought that the facts warrant the conclusion that there has been during the period any very marked increase in the tendency to insanity among the inhabitants of the district'. So far as there is an apparent increase, Dr Norman attributes it to: (1) Decreased prejudice against asylums; (2) The friends of patients being less tolerant of having insane persons in their midst; (3) Poor-Law Authorities being more sensible of the unsuitability of most workhouses to provide for the insane; (4) The fact that the increase is almost confined to Dublin itself, where the population is increasing. The death-rate and the recovery-rate have also decreased, and will largely account for the accumulation of cases, though, as I have already said, not for the rise in admissions.[148]

Tuke himself explored a range of possible contributory factors including selective emigration of the mentally healthy, which, he concluded, could result in an increase in the *proportion* of the population that was mentally ill, but not an increase in the *absolute number*. He did, however, draw attention to the possibilities that the emigration of mentally healthy persons placed increased pressure on those left behind; evictions could have a negative effect on mental health; political tumult could increase rates of insanity; and abuse of alcohol or tea might also be relevant. Considering all these factors together, Tuke concluded that there was indeed an actual as well as apparent increase in insanity in Ireland, even after taking account of the accumulation of mentally ill in the asylums over time.

Tuke's specific concerns were shared, to varying degrees, by asylum doctors throughout Ireland. In Castlebar District Asylum, Dr G.W. Hatchell complained in 1893 that the habit of drinking tea was being encouraged by travelling salesmen driving in carts throughout the countryside, and the addictive qualities of tea were also noted by Dr William Graham of Armagh and Dr E.E. Moore of Letterkenny, who believed that heredity was the predisposing cause of insanity in 70 per cent of admissions.[149] Tea was, however, also implicated.

Ireland and Great Britain were by no means alone in experiencing these problems with increased rates of committal. There were similar trends apparent in other countries, including France, England and the US,[150] but Ireland's rates were especially high at their peak, and especially slow to decline.[151] Doctors and commentators elsewhere considered proposed contributory factors similar to those considered by Hallaran, Drapes, Tuke and Norman in Ireland, and many, like F.B. Sanborn, previous Inspector with the Massachusetts State Board of Health, Lunacy and Charity, concluded that there was a real increase in incident cases of insanity in their areas too, even after various other factors were taken into consideration.[152]

The extent of alarm produced by this apparent trend in Ireland is evident in the broad range of solutions proposed (ranging from increased institutional provision to sterilisation), and the publication, in 1894, of the *Special Report from the Inspectors of Lunatics to the Chief Secretary: Alleged Increasing Prevalence of Insanity in Ireland*.[153] Even relatively enlightened figures, such as Drapes, were sufficiently alarmed that their generally humane approach was regrettably affected by the prevailing sense of panic about the key unresolved question that dominated, and still dominates, the history of Irish psychiatry: was there really an increase in mental disorder in nineteenth-century Ireland?[154]

Why did the Asylums Grow so Large?

In considering whether or not there was a true increase in the incidence of mental disorder in nineteenth-century Ireland, it is useful first to examine other, relatively clearer reasons why the Irish asylums grew so large in the 1800s and early 1900s.[155] Was this development really due to increased rates of mental disorder or were these other factors more relevant?

Taking a bird's eye view, it appears highly likely that a variety of related and mutually reinforcing circumstances contributed to the growth of the Irish asylums, including (1) increased societal recognition of, and diminished tolerance for, the problems presented by mental disorder; (2) mutually reinforcing patterns of asylum building and psychiatric committal, underpinned by continual, almost obsessional legislative change;[156] (3) changes in diagnostic and clinical practices (including the search for professional prestige among clinical staff); and (4) possible epidemiological change, owing to sociodemographic changes in Irish society and/or unidentified biological factors leading to altered patterns (although not increased incidence) of mental disorder.[157]

In the first instance, the end of the eighteenth century saw substantial changes in societal attitudes to mental disorder throughout Europe. The growing humanitarian approach of the early-nineteenth-century greatly increased efforts to provide care to persons with mental disorder, resulting in an apparent increase in incidence owing to increased diagnosis,[158] as suggested by Tuke in 1894.[159] This change in attitude was evident not just in Ireland but throughout Great Britain and Europe, and led to considerable systematic governmental reform in many countries, including Great Britain.[160] In Ireland, the 1804 Select Committee of the House of Commons recommended the establishment of four provincial asylums dedicated to the treatment of the mentally ill[161] and in 1814 one such establishment, the Richmond Asylum, finally opened in Dublin.[162] While it is difficult to quantify the precise role of changes in professional and public attitudes in these developments, it is inevitable that, at the very least, they contributed to increased recognition and diagnosis of mental disorder and, in turn, increased rates of presentation to the newly established asylums.

The latter part of the nineteenth century was also a time of industrialisation, resulting in significant reconfigurations at family, community and societal levels in many European countries, albeit somewhat limited in Ireland. Nonetheless, structural community changes associated with this era of history increased the visibility of individuals with mental disorder in Irish communities, resulting in increased presentations to asylums and an apparent (although not actual) increase in rates of mental disorder for this reason.[163]

This is consistent with Tuke's observation that Norman, at the Richmond Asylum, emphasised the centrality of social attitudes, such as decreased prejudice against asylums and reduced tolerance for mental disorder in communities, in increasing presentations.[164] These changes in social attitudes, community structures and patterns of presentation, as well as changes in diagnostic practices, represented significant modifications in the interpretation and experience of mental disorder at both individual and societal levels, contributing to increased presentations to asylums. Various complexities relating to land, marriage, family relations, inheritances and emigration were also likely relevant in different ways in specific cases.[165]

The second key factor that contributed to increased rates of presentation was the elaborate process of legislative reform and asylum building that commenced in the early 1800s and gathered extraordinary pace as the nineteenth century progressed. The Lunatic Asylums (Ireland) Act 1821 authorised the establishment of a network of district asylums throughout the country and within fifteen years there were large public asylums established in Armagh, Limerick, Belfast, Derry, Carlow, Portlaoise, Clonmel and Waterford.[166] The reports of the Inspectors of Lunatics for this period demonstrate that these asylums were rapidly filled to capacity soon after opening.[167] As Finnane demonstrates in his brilliant, path-finding book, *Insanity and the Insane in Post-Famine Ireland*, this process was much more centralised in Ireland compared to England,[168] resulting in greater institutionalisation.[169]

In any case, there can be little doubt that the sudden availability of hundreds of asylum beds led to increased rates of presentation by mentally ill individuals who had previously lived with families, lodged in workhouses, languished in prisons, or been homeless. The Great Irish Famine also played a role in increasing social need and pressure for accommodation and food (as well as potentially affecting future mental health needs). It remains unclear, however, precisely what proportion of asylum admissions was truly suffering from mental disorder, what proportion was admitted for other reasons (e.g. intellectual disability or social problems), and what proportion was admitted owing to misuse of the 'dangerous lunatic' procedures which offered several practical advantages to families seeking to have family members committed (e.g. the asylum could not refuse to admit a 'dangerous lunatic').[170]

It is clear, however, that the rapid overcrowding of asylums was related not only to increased rates of presentation, but also prolonged length of stay and accumulation by non-discharge. Between the years 1850 and 1890, the excess of admissions over discharges was approximately 200 annually; i.e. there were, potentially, 200 new long stay patients created in district asylums each year,[171] which further increased occupancy and pressure on beds.

Changes in diagnostic and clinical practices are the third factor that contributed to increased rates of psychiatric hospitalisation in the 1800s, in addition to increased recognition of the problems presented by mental disorder and mutually reinforcing patterns of asylum building and psychiatric committal, underpinned by a constant churn of legislative activity (Chapter 2).

Diagnostic practices are constantly changing in psychiatry with the result that there are significant difficulties establishing the contemporary equivalents of diagnoses made in the nineteenth century, especially when retrospective diagnostic endeavours are based on inconsistent, incomplete medical records.[172] There were likely at least four nineteenth-century terms that correlated with diagnoses that are now known as 'functional psychoses' (i.e. schizophrenia and bipolar affective disorder): mania, melancholia, monomania and dementia.[173] The confusion and conflation of these terms in the literature adds greatly to the difficulties of interpreting statistics from the 1800s and early 1900s. Some of these diagnostic challenges, along with the difficulties separating mental disorder from socioeconomic concerns, are demonstrated by the case of Mary, outlined here based on her original case records from the Central Criminal Lunatic Asylum, Dublin.[174]

Mary was a 40-year-old 'housekeeper' with seven children who was charged with the manslaughter of her 4-year-old child in the mid-1890s. She was 'acquitted on the grounds of insanity' and detained at the Central Criminal Lunatic Asylum 'at Her Majesty's Pleasure' (i.e. indefinitely). Mary's admission diagnosis was 'chronic melancholia', attributed to 'heredity'; admission notes record that she had a sister in a district asylum.

Medical records note that Mary's 'expression of face, attitude and gestures are characteristic of melancholia; she is emotional at times. [She] does not exhibit any delusion'. Her notes also, however, record that 'she takes an interest in her surroundings and associates with the other patients; readily enters conversation. Appetite good, sleeps well, clean and tidy in dress and person. [She] is bad tempered and inclined to sulk if corrected. [She] does needlework and house cleaning'.

Subsequent entries confirm that Mary was 'well-behaved, quiet and respectable', and 'an excellent worker'. Much of this is not consistent with the diagnosis of 'chronic melancholia'. Notes from almost two years after her admission specify that Mary 'will cry when meditating on her misfortunes'; this reaction appears understandable, given Mary's situation, following the loss of her child and her indefinite detention at the hospital.

Clinical notes from six years after Mary's admission record that 'this patient is perfectly sane and is most anxious for her discharge but there is some difficulty as her husband is in a workhouse and she has no friends sufficiently well off to provide for her'. Two years later, however, Mary, then described as 'perfectly harmless', was 'discharged ... in care of her daughter'. In this case, the diagnosis of 'chronic melancholia' appears, by today's diagnostic criteria, largely unsupported by the clinical details recorded in the sparse notes documenting Mary's stay in the Central Criminal Lunatic Asylum.

Despite these difficulties with the interpretation of clinical records, some general conclusions can still be drawn about changes in diagnostic practices throughout the nineteenth century. There is, for example, strong evidence of a diagnostic shift from intellectual disability ('idiots') towards mental disorder ('lunatics') during the latter part of the 1800s. In 1893, the Inspectors of Lunatics presented findings from the General Report of the Census Commissioners demonstrating a fall in the number of 'idiots' (from 7,033 in 1861 to 6,243 in 1891) and a rise in the number of 'lunatics' (from 7,065 in 1861 to 14,945 in 1891).[175] There are many possible reasons for these changes, the most significant of which is the sudden availability of hundreds of asylum beds for individuals with mental disorder, which may have prompted a reclassification of certain intellectually disabled individuals as 'lunatics' in order to secure easier access to long term asylum accommodation.

Another contributor to the rising inpatient numbers was the search for professional prestige among asylum doctors, who were very keen to enhance their status, income and control over asylums.[176] The 1874 *General Rules and Regulations for the Management of District Lunatic Asylums in Ireland* articulated a direct link between patient numbers and pay:

> The annual sums and allowances to be paid and made to the several Resident Medical Superintendents, whose salaries and allowances have not been equivalently fixed by order of the Lord Lieutenant in Council, and to all persons hereafter to be appointed as such Resident Medical Superintendents, shall be as follows: -
>
> When the accommodation for patients in the Institution shall be under 250, the salary of the Resident Medical Superintendent shall be at the rate of £340 per annum.
>
> When the accommodation for patients shall be 250 and under 350, such salary shall be at the rate of £400 per annum.
>
> When the accommodation for patients shall be 350 and under 500, such salary shall be at the rate of £450 per annum.
>
> When the accommodation for patients shall be 500 and under 600, such salary shall be at the rate of £500 per annum.
>
> When the accommodation for patients shall be 600 and under 800, such salary shall be at the rate of £550 per annum.
>
> It shall, however, be lawful for the Lord Lieutenant in Council to increase the salary of any Resident Medical Superintendent who may have served eight years in any Asylum to the satisfaction of the Board of Governors, upon the recommendation of such Board and of the Inspectors; such increase not exceeding in any case £100 per annum.
>
> And the allowances to be made to all such Resident Medical Superintendents shall be apartments, fuel, light, washing, vegetables, bread, and milk.[177]

Any RMS appointed after that date (23 February 1874) was not 'allowed any furniture for the apartments occupied by them, save and except the following fixtures: chimney pieces, grates, presses, fixed shelves, locks, bells, gas fittings and gasaliers, blinds. Carpets or matting may, with the sanction of the Board of Governors or of the Inspectors, be allowed in corridors or on stairs in the Resident Medical Superintendent's apartments, if such corridors or stairs are used by officers, patients, or attendants.'

These arrangements were revised on the '28th day of April, 1885', when the 'Lords Justices-General and General Governors of Ireland, by and with the advice of the Privy Council of Ireland' declared that the RMS's basic salary was to be determined by the institution in which he [*sic*] worked, as follows: Richmond and Cork: £600; Ballinasloe, Belfast, Limerick and Omagh: £500; Castlebar, Clonmel, Downpatrick, Kilkenny and Killarney: £450; Letterkenny, Maryborough, Monaghan, Mullingar and Sligo: £450; Armagh, Carlow, Ennis, Enniscorthy, Londonderry and Waterford: £400. Various other payments and allowances were also mandated, including a £100 'increase in salary' after serving 'eight years to the satisfaction of the Board of Governors'.[178] While it is difficult to determine the precise magnitude of the effect of these arrangements on asylum admission rates, they clearly linked higher pay with asylum size, presumably with predictable consequences.

Possible epidemiological change is the fourth factor that contributed to increased rates of psychiatric hospitalisation, in addition to (1) increased societal recognition of the problems presented by mental disorder; (2) mutually reinforcing patterns of asylum building and psychiatric committal, underpinned by continual legislative change; and (3) changes in diagnostic practices and the emergence of a distinct profession of psychiatry hungry for recognition and respectability.[179]

The possibility of true epidemiological change in the incidence of mental disorder in nineteenth century Ireland is, however, difficult to resolve definitively, owing to the absence of reliable data about both the incidence of mental disorder and the precise population of Ireland. Even at the time, it was recognised that epidemiological analysis was significantly hampered by the absence of reliable data about the population in general, a point made with particular clarity by Dr Richard Powell, in a paper read to the Royal College of Physicians in London in 1810.[180] If the baseline population is not accurately known, how can a possible increase in rates of insanity be identified?

Notwithstanding these statistical challenges, it remains reasonable to conclude that certain demographic factors and changes in population structure might have played a role in producing, at the very least, an apparent increase in the rate of mental disorder in nineteenth-century Ireland. There were, for example, substantial increases in life expectancy around 1800 and these increased the survival of individuals prone to develop schizophrenia.[181] This increased the *prevalence* of mental disorder (i.e. number of cases extant at any given moment) and, therefore, burden of care, but not necessarily the *incidence* (i.e. number of new cases per year). This was one of the factors emphasised by the Inspectors of Lunatics in their 1906 *Special Report on the Alleged Increase of Insanity*, along with fewer discharges and deaths than in English asylums, greater accessibility to asylums, less sick patients being admitted, transfers from workhouses, reduced stigma and the alleged return of emigrants who had become insane[182] (which undoubtedly occurred).[183] In addition, increased preoccupation with quality of life, rather than mere survival, may have further increased rates of presentation to asylums, thus increasing burden of care without truly increasing incidence.

Torrey and Miller note that many medical directors in the nineteenth century believed that there was a true increase in rates of mental disorder and cast doubt on arguments suggesting this phenomenon were entirely attributable to accumulation of patients in asylums, decreased stigma, incarceration of individuals with alcohol problems, transfers from workhouses, heredity, the return of unwell emigrants, or various other factors.[184] Torrey and Miller argue that there has been an epidemic of mental disorder over the past three centuries and that while this has gone largely unnoticed owing to its gradual onset, it represents an important but neglected force in world history.

It remains exceedingly difficult to determine, with any degree of accuracy, how much of the pressure on asylums in nineteenth-century Ireland was due to true epidemiological change and how much was due to other factors, such as changes in diagnostic practices and societal circumstances.[185] The matter is further complicated by the fact that certain societal circumstances (e.g. conflict, famine) tend to produce a true increase in rates of certain mental disorders, and not just an apparent increase due to increased rates of presentation. Broadly, however, I agree with Brennan that institutionalisation during this period was primarily driven by social factors rather than a biomedical increase in insanity.[186]

All told, it is my conclusion that the growth of the Irish asylums in the 1800s and 1900s was attributable to a combination of increased societal recognition of mental disorder (owing to changes in society rather than changes in the nature or occurrence of mental disorder); continual legislative change, asylum building and psychiatric committal throughout the 1800s (with each of these three processes reinforcing the other two); evolving changes in diagnostic and clinical practices (underpinned by asylum doctors' search for professional status and respectability); and – possibly most importantly – sociodemographic changes, especially increased survival, leading to altered patterns and prevalence of mental disorder (although not a proven rise in core rates of occurrence).

While some of these matters will likely continue to be the subject of debate, it is beyond dispute that the *perception* of an increase in insanity, and rising rates of presentation to asylums, had a decisive influence on mental health policy and legislation in Ireland in the 1800s and early 1900s. This perception was strongly linked with the remarkable asylum building programme of the 1800s and the steady increase in asylum populations over the course of the nineteenth and early twentieth-centuries. The asylums in Carlow and Kilkenny demonstrate many of the key trends during this period, especially in terms of diagnostic practices, ranging from the mundane and repetitive to the quixotic and unexpected.

Psychiatric Diagnoses in the Nineteenth Century: Mania, Melancholia and 'Insane Ears'

The asylum in Carlow (later St Dympna's Hospital) opened in 1832 to care for the mentally ill of Carlow, Kildare, Kilkenny and Wexford.[187] A review of the diagnoses in its clinical archives offers a valuable window into diagnostic practices and some of the clinical outcomes in the late 1800s.

The Register of Patients admitted between 1848 and 1896 ('Admission Book') demonstrates a wide range of diagnoses in use during this period, along with suggestions about the 'supposed cause of insanity' in each case.[188] Among men, common diagnoses included 'mania', 'melancholia'[189] (with or without delusions), 'paranoia', 'epilepsy', 'post-febrile' illness (i.e. mental illness following a fever), 'idiot', 'imbecile', 'homicidal and suicidal', and 'dementia' (diagnosed in young people, this was likely similar to 'mania'). 'Senile mania', 'senile melancholia' and 'senile dementia' were reported in the elderly, and 'mania *a potú*' also featured, referring to 'mania' owing to 'intemperance' or 'alcohol'.

'Mania' itself could be 'acute', 'chronic' or 'religious'. The term 'monomania' was used when a single pathological feature (e.g. delusion) was the central feature of the disorder. The 'supposed causes' of 'mania' in men ranged from 'poverty and drinking excess of porter' to 'sunstroke', from 'mental annoyance' to 'heredity', from 'unknown' to 'can't say'. More specific causes included psychological traumas ('loss of money', 'matrimonial disappointment', 'death of wife'), physical traumas ('a beating received', 'fell from a horse') and hypothesised disorders of the brain ('effusion of blood on brain', 'affection of the brain', 'disease of brain, fits', 'probably an attack of meningitis when a child').

One man was admitted with 'acute mania' owing to 'shock on his brother being sent to asylum', his brother having been admitted two months earlier with 'mania' due to 'religious excitement'. Another man was admitted in the mid-1890s with a four day history of 'mania', the 'supposed cause' of which was his 'wife's insanity', his wife having been admitted with 'mania'.

The range of diagnoses recorded in women was similarly broad and included 'mania', 'melancholia' (with or without delusions), 'delusional insanity', 'dementia', 'paranoia', 'senile mania', 'senile melancholia' and 'monomania'. 'Mania' in women could be 'recurrent', 'acute', 'chronic', 'partial', 'suicidal', 'religious' or 'puerperal' (i.e. occurring during or immediately following childbirth). Causes of mania in women included 'heredity', 'drink', 'intemperance', 'domestic troubles', 'adverse circumstances', 'mental anxiety and worry', 'grief', 'loss of employment', 'desire to leave workhouse', 'injury to spine', 'childbirth' and 'religious excitement'.

Causes of melancholia among women included 'fright', 'mental anxiety', 'sudden death of a friend', 'sudden death of husband', and 'domestic troubles'. Other entries for women under 'diagnosis' included 'insanity doubtful' or simply a blank space; in one such case, an additional note was added to the page, presumably in order to explain the admission: 'statements against character'.

The cases linked with childbirth are especially involving. One woman in her 30s, the 'wife of a carpenter', was admitted in the mid-1890s with a one month history of 'puerperal melancholia' which was ascribed to 'heredity and puerperium' (i.e. occurring in the first six weeks after giving birth). Noted to be anaemic on admission (pale, likely owing to blood loss), this woman spent just over six months in the asylum before she 'was removed at request of husband'. She was described as 'relieved' (as opposed to 'recovered') on the day of discharge and was readmitted just a week later, with a recurrence of 'puerperal melancholia', now simply ascribed to 'heredity'. Related diagnoses in other women included 'recurrent mania' 'following pregnancy'; 'puerperal mania' after 'childbirth'; 'dementia' 'in childbirth' or 'following parturition'; and 'mania' owing to 'amenorrhoea' or 'loss of child'.

Other causes of 'insanity' among women included 'poverty and hardship' (linked with 'senile melancholia'); 'sunstroke', 'worry and hardship' ('paranoia'); 'fright' ('melancholia with delusions'); 'pecuniary disappointment' ('monomania'); 'cerebral changes' ('religious mania'); 'sunstroke' and 'loss of situation' ('dementia'); and 'heredity', linked with 'delusional insanity', 'senile mania' and 'dementia' (also associated with 'paralysis agitans' or Parkinson's disease).

Readmission was not uncommon. A school teacher in her early 60s was admitted in the mid-1890s with a 'relapse' of 'monomania', having had a previous episode four years earlier. She was discharged 'recovered' after a year but readmitted after a further year, this time with 'recurrent melancholia' due to 'heredity'. On this occasion, she spent five months in the asylum before being discharged, 'recovered'. At around the same time, a 'labourer' in his 50s was admitted with a one week history of 'mania', having 'inflicted a wound on his throat'. Just over two years later, he was 'allowed out on approval as "relieved"', at the request of his friends', but readmitted just six days later.

Another 'labourer' and 'ex-soldier' in his early 20s experienced several admissions, initially spending two months in the asylum with 'melancholia' due to 'heredity'. On readmission 10 months later, he was diagnosed with 'mania *a potú*' owing to 'alcohol' (rather than melancholia) and spent three months in the asylum. 'Melancholia' was linked with a broad range of 'causes' among men at this time, including syphilis, 'heredity', 'family troubles', 'domestic troubles', 'love affairs', 'pecuniary loss', 'betting on race horses', 'religion', 'fright', 'influenza', 'phthisis [tuberculosis] and exhaustion'.

Some patients were presented to the asylum through the criminal justice system. In the early 1890s, one man in his early 20s was 'transferred from Kilmainham jail' (Dublin) by the authority of the 'Lord Lieutenant', with a one week history of 'mania' owing to 'religious delusions'. He spent almost two years in the Carlow asylum before being discharged, 'recovered', 'by order' of the Lord Lieutenant. A man in his 40s of no fixed abode was admitted from Kilkenny jail at around the same time, with diagnoses of 'imbecility and mania'; he died in the asylum five months later. A woman with 'partial mania' was admitted from Grangegorman Prison (Dublin) and a man in his 40s transferred from the Central Criminal Lunatic Asylum (Dundrum, Dublin), as his sentence had expired. He had previously been in 'Kilkenny prison' and spent three months in the Carlow asylum with 'melancholia' due to 'domestic troubles'.

A woman in her 50s also developed 'melancholia' due to 'domestic trouble' during this period, but her record is notable because it records that she had 'left insane ear'. 'Insane ear' referred to 'haematoma auris', a swelling of the ear lobe owing to effusion of blood. Throughout the 1800s, this was thought to be connected with certain forms of insanity including GPI (late stage syphilis, affecting the brain) and epilepsy (especially when associated with mania).[190] 'Insane ear' was, however, also linked with the use of physical restraint or coercion,[191] and this seems a more likely explanation for its reported frequency in asylums.

Various physical causes were commonly cited as reasons for insanity. In the mid-1890s, a 'housekeeper' in her late 50s was admitted for two months with a two week history of 'epileptic mania', and was also physically 'debilitated'. A 'labourer's wife' in her 50s was admitted with 'melancholia' attributed to 'sequelae of influenza'; she too was physically 'debilitated'. One man's 'dementia' was attributed to 'injury to head', another's 'paranoia' was linked with 'possible injury to cranium', and another man was 'homicidal and suicidal' owing to 'injury of head'. In the late 1890s, a woman was admitted with 'acute melancholia with delusions' owing to 'domestic troubles' but was also 'much emaciated' from 'tuberculosis'.

Life circumstances were commonly cited as reasons for admission. A case of 'senile melancholia' in a 'servant' in his 70s admitted from 'Carlow Union, Carlow' was attributed to 'poverty and hardship'; his 'bodily condition' was only 'fair' and he died six months later. Another man in his 70s had 'senile mania' owing to 'want and age'. A 'coachman' in his 40s developed 'acute mania' owing to 'business troubles and loss of sleep'; he had previously been 'a patient in Mullingar Asylum on two occasions' and spent three months in the Carlow asylum. A man in his late 20s was admitted with 'acute mania' due to a 'love affair', while a farmer in his 30s developed 'melancholia' also owing to 'love affairs'.

Some diagnoses appear somewhat curious. In the mid-1890s a 'servant' in her late 20s was admitted with 'mania' due to 'overwork'. Around the same time, a 'well educated' man in his early 40s spent three months in the asylum with 'diagnosis' of 'insanity doubtful'. The same description was applied to a woman admitted in her 60s during the same period, although she was also 'debilitated from old age'.

Perhaps the most moving cases relate to women who lost or missed their children. One woman was admitted with 'mania' owing to 'loss of a child', while a 'housekeeper' in her 40s was 'fretting for a daughter left the country', and had 'palpitation of the heart'. Most affecting, however, was the case of a woman in her 50s who was admitted in the mid-1880s with a three month history of 'acute mania' owing to 'her two sons going to America'. This woman was never discharged: she died in the asylum 10 years later.

In 1848, 16 years after the asylum opened in Carlow, building began for 'Kilkenny District Lunatic Asylum' (later St Canice's Hospital), which was formally opened on 1 September 1852.[192] Dr Joseph Lalor was the first Resident Physician and manager. The first patient was a 70-year-old woman who had been committed at the age of 30 owing to a nervous breakdown following childbirth. She and 53 other Kilkenny patients were admitted to the new asylum from 'Carlow District Hospital for the Insane'. They were joined by 47 patients from 'Kilkenny Local Lunatic Asylum' (a small local establishment), 24 from the county Kilkenny Prison, and 10 directly from the district.[193]

Patient numbers in Kilkenny increased rapidly, to 295 in 1880, 440 in 1902, and peaking at 550 in 1939. By the early 2000s, however, numbers had decreased to approximately 100, in line with national psychiatric deinstitutionalisation. In March 2003 a new purpose built acute psychiatric admission unit opened on the site of Kilkenny General Hospital resulting in significant improvements in care and a sharp contrast with the district asylums of the 1800s and 1900s.[194]

From an historical perspective, the litany of diagnosis from Carlow in the 1880s and 1890s shows the diversity of cases that presented to the asylums during that period and the inventiveness of some of the diagnoses applied. Similar diagnoses were described in Portlaoise,[195] Sligo[196] and elsewhere.[197] The records of discharges are also interesting, and, even if some discharges were followed by readmission, they still provide evidence of a desire to minimise asylum stays and avoid the institutionalisation that so concerned asylum staff and broader society at this time.

Asylums, Friends and Religious Involvement in Mental Health Care

One of the outstanding features of the history of psychiatry in Ireland, and the emergence of the asylum system in particular, is the limited role played by the Roman Catholic Church in developing services for the mentally ill.[198] While there was some accommodation for the mentally ill in the early Irish monasteries, this was always very limited in scope and the dissolution of the monasteries in the mid-1500s diminished it even further.[199] Following this, the Roman Catholic Church remained generally uninvolved in formal mental health care, apart from providing chaplains to the asylums – and even this was not without controversy in, for example, Belfast.[200] This was the position up until the late-1800s and mid-1900s when certain organisations (e.g. Daughters of Charity, Brothers of Charity, Brothers of St John of God, Sisters of La Sagesse and Sisters of Jesus and Mary) became central to the provision of services to the intellectually disabled, building on the histories many of these organisations had in this field.[201]

The late 1800s and early 1900s also saw increased involvement of locally powerful Catholic figures on asylum boards in certain locations, such as Carlow[202] and Cork,[203] but, notwithstanding these local developments, the Roman Catholic Church never attained, or sought, a dominant, national position in mental health care similar to that it assumed in general healthcare and education.

There were, nonetheless, specific initiatives, chiefly relating to specific religious orders. In 1882, the Brothers of St John of God established a private psychiatric hospital in Stillorgan, County Dublin (Chapter 6).[204] St Vincent's Hospital in Fairview, Dublin is another one of the relatively few examples of a Roman Catholic organisation, the Daughters of Charity of St Vincent de Paul, becoming involved in mental health care in Ireland.[205] St Vincent's was founded in 1857 following the bequest of Francis Magan, a barrister and member of the United Irishmen (an Irish republican organisation) whose fortune had resulted from his informing on the leader of the 1798 rebellion, Lord Edward Fitzgerald (1763–1798).[206] When Magan's sister died, the fortune was used to found a hospital in Fairview for mentally ill Catholic women and men, although only the female side progressed. In 1857 the hospital had seven patients; by 1862 there were 30.[207] The first physician was Sir Dominic Corrigan (1802–1880), who was also the first Catholic president of the Royal College of Physicians of Ireland (1859). The French Daughters of Charity of St Vincent de Paul came to Ireland to run St Vincent's and remained until 1998.

St Vincent's expanded substantially throughout the 1800s, and underwent further developments in 1932, 1978 and 1993. By 1997, St Vincent's had 97 inpatients and there were 1,074 admissions and 1,073 discharges (and two deaths) over the previous twelve months.[208] There were also 14 patients in St Aloysius Ward, which opened in October 1994 in the Mater Misericordiae University Hospital, one of Dublin's major general hospitals founded in 1861 by the Sisters of Mercy.[209] Both of these developments in mental health care, at St Vincent's and the Mater, found their backgrounds in the Catholic organisations that operated the establishments.

Overall, however, while certain Catholic organisations became involved in specific initiatives within mental health care (e.g. a Child Guidance Clinic was opened at the Mater in 1962),[210] it remains the case that the official Roman Catholic Church is notable by its general absence from the history of the systematic provision of psychiatric services in Ireland. While certain people with psychological problems undoubtedly sought individual guidance from the Church and from priests or other religious, the Church itself did not become systematically involved in *formal* mental health services. As a result, the Irish asylums were very much State institutions rather than Church ones.

This is intriguing: the Roman Catholic Church was deeply involved in Irish politics, general (i.e. physical) healthcare and education, but did not develop formal, systematic initiatives in *mental* health care. The reasons for this are complex (and in need of further study) but likely relate, at least in part, to the Church's attention to other areas (e.g. medical care, schools) rather than mental health care, and the prominent involvement of figures from other religious traditions in early Irish mental health care, most notably Jonathan Swift, an ordained priest in the Established Church of Ireland who bequeathed his entire estate to establish the hospital for 'idiots and lunaticks' that later became St Patrick's Hospital, the first formal asylum in Ireland.[211]

The Religious Society of Friends ('Quakers') was another religious group that developed a strong association with early mental health care, exemplified by the establishment of The Retreat at York in England in the 1790s.[212] In Ireland, representatives of the Yearly Meeting of Friends in Ireland, along with some other Friends, met on 29 April 1807 to consider providing accommodation for the mentally ill.[213] Three years later they bought Bloomfield in Donnybrook, Dublin, a house formerly occupied by Dr Robert Emmett, State Physician and physician to St Patrick's Hospital.[214] On 16 March 1812, the first patient was admitted to Bloomfield.[215] Among the sources of funding were the proceeds from the sales in Ireland of the works of Henry Tuke (1755–1814), eldest son of William of The Retreat. There was also Quaker involvement in other early initiatives in Cork.[216]

On 15 May 1815, John Eustace (1791–1867) arrived at Bloomfield as lay superintendent and, two months later, received permission to continue medical studies in Trinity.[217] Eustace served as physician to the Cork Street Fever Hospital and, in 1825, opened up an Asylum and House of Recovery for Persons Afflicted with Disorders of the Mind at Hampstead in Glasnevin, Dublin.[218] Accommodation at Hampstead was relatively luxurious and surrounded by 1,200 acres of land. Treatments focused on therapy in the garden and farm, among other interventions. Eustace departed definitively from Bloomfield in 1831.

Moral treatment continued to the fore at Bloomfield, actively informed by the ongoing development of practices at The Retreat.[219] A second wing was built in 1830[220] and, between 1863 and 1912, some 537 patients were admitted.[221] The 1900s saw various further developments at Bloomfield and by 1997 the accommodation comprised 60 beds, albeit with just eight admissions over the previous year.[222] At that point, 49 patients at Bloomfield were voluntary and 11 were Wards of Court. Standards of hygiene, decor and 'patient care were of a very high order', according to the Inspector of Mental Hospitals. Medical services were provided by two general practitioners and there were psychiatric consultations by two old age psychiatrists.[223]

In 2005, Bloomfield moved from Donnybrook to Rathfarnham, Dublin. Ten years later, this 114 bed hospital was offering a range of specialist services including mental health treatment and care for older adults; services for persons with acute, serious and enduring mental health disorders; complex mental health issues associated with neuropsychiatric disorders and dementia; and a memory clinic.

In parallel with the evolution of Bloomfield, Eustace's Hampstead Hospital developed and expanded throughout the 1800s, based on the idea that care should be offered in a comfortable, family setting. Highfield Hospital was opened for female patients and in 1888 the remarkable Dr Richard Leeper gained his introduction to psychiatry there when he was appointed Resident Physician at Hampstead and Highfield.[224] Leeper held this positon for three years before going on to a long and distinguished career, including becoming Medical Superintendent at St Patrick's Hospital in 1899 (Chapter 5).[225] The services at Hampstead and Highfield evolved further throughout the 1900s and by 1997 there were 42 female patients in Highfield (including two Wards of Court) and

41 patients at Hampstead (including two Wards of Court), and, the Inspector noted, the 'standard of care, hygiene and décor were high'.[226]

By the early 2000s the Eustace family had been providing mental health care at Hampstead and Highfield for six generations over almost two centuries, becoming such a part of the fabric of Dublin that they were mentioned in James Joyce's *Ulysses* in 1922.[227] In 2015, 'Highfield Healthcare' was providing specialist care to the elderly across four facilities, with a total of 313 beds. An adult acute psychiatry unit had also been developed. Throughout its fascinating history, the organisation maintained a core commitment 'to providing the highest standard of care and support to all our residents' in 'an environment appropriate to their needs, where the priority is to preserve their dignity and promote their independence'.

Overall, in terms of the role of the Roman Catholic Church in Irish mental health care, it is clear that while certain Catholic groups became involved with specific developments (e.g. St Vincent's in Fairview, the Mater Hospital services, St John of God Hospital and various services for the intellectually disabled), the Roman Catholic Church itself did not develop a systematic, formal or dominating involvement in the field as it did in relation to general hospitals and schools. For many decades, then, the key role of the Roman Catholic Church in Irish mental health care lay chiefly in the provision of chaplains to the state run asylums that emerged in the 1800s and early 1900s.

That is not to say that the Church was entirely without influence: the specific initiatives described above were both substantive and innovative, and priests were often significant figures in shaping and informing care.[228] But it is worthy of note that the field of mental health care in Ireland, unlike the fields of general healthcare and education, was *not* dominated by the Roman Catholic Church and that the asylums were, for the most part, *not* religious institutions. As a result, there was plenty of room for developments and innovations by others within the asylum system, including other religious traditions, such as the Society of Friends, and individual clinicians, such as the singular Dr Conolly Norman of the Richmond Asylum in Dublin.

Dr Conolly Norman:
Reforming Doctor

Conolly Norman (1853–1908), the leading psychiatrist of his generation, was born on 12 March 1853 at All Saints' Glebe, Newtown Cunningham, County Donegal. He was the fifth of six sons of Hugh Norman, rector of All Saints Church, and Anne Norman (née Ball). Norman was educated at Trinity College Dublin, the Carmichael School of Medicine (North Brunswick Street) and the Richmond Hospital. He received the licences of the Royal College of Surgeons in Ireland, King and Queen's College of Physicians in Ireland, and Rotunda Hospital in 1874. He was elected fellow of the Royal College of Surgeons in Ireland in 1878 and member of the King and Queen's College of Physicians in Ireland in 1879; he became a fellow of the latter in 1890.

Norman was interested in psychiatry from the outset and worked as assistant medical officer at Monaghan District Asylum from 1874 to 1881, before a period at Bethlem Royal Hospital in London, after which he served as medical superintendent at Castlebar (1882–5)[229] and Monaghan District Asylums (1885–6).

Throughout his career, Norman was an inveterate innovator and a freethinker. In Monaghan, he experimented with hypnone (phenyl-methyl-acetone) and, in a case series published in the *Journal of Mental Science* in 1887, concluded that it was a useful sleep inducing agent, especially in cases characterised by excitement.[230]

In 1886, Norman was appointed as RMS in Richmond District Asylum in Dublin, a notably powerful and prominent position in Irish medicine. The energetic, enthusiastic doctor had a profound effect on the vast institution: restraints were relaxed, buildings renovated, staff numbers increased and a laboratory built, placed under the direction of Dr Daniel Rambaut.[231]

As the *Irish Times* later noted, Norman's appointment had immediate positive effects both in the Richmond and beyond:

> When he became Superintendent he immediately started a campaign with a view to improving the condition of the patients, and it is mainly owing to his efforts that the dietary and clothing of the inmates have undergone a vast improvement. The reforms he effected in the management of the institution are almost innumerable. To him must also be attributed the initiation of a campaign against the use of instruments of restraint in asylums. On his advice the 'straight jacket' was abolished in the institution, and his influence in this respect penetrated into all the asylums in Ireland and very many institutions in England and Scotland. He established the principle of allowing the patients with violent tendencies to walk in the grounds instead of confining them in irons indoors [...]. The nursing and attendant staff also engaged his close attention, and he did much in securing for them better accommodation, better clothing, better pay and shorter hours of duty. Dr Norman's name will be associated with almost all asylum reforms in this country, and it is impossible to estimate his efforts in this respect. His services have brought about a wonderful change in the treatment of lunatics, and many lives have been brightened by his zealous devotion to their welfare.[232]

While this effusive praise is well deserved and based in fact, Norman was by no means alone in seeking to reduce the use of restraint in the Irish asylums; Dr John Jacob of Maryborough (Portlaoise), for example, was another pioneer in the removal of restraints, in the 1840s.[233] Jacob belonged to a distinguished Quaker family and also operated a private asylum in the area. Jacob's initiative was strongly consistent with the broader 'non-restraint' movement in England in the late 1830s,[234] as were Norman's fruitful efforts at the Richmond in the latter part of the century.

Like other reformers, Norman encountered stern opposition to certain of his efforts, including his attempt to develop a model of 'boarding out' similar to those in Scotland[235] and Belgium.[236] The colony at Gheel in Belgium had been founded in the tradition of St Dymphna, an Irish girl who, in the early seventh century, fled there from her father when he sought to marry her in replacement of his deceased wife.[237] She went to Gheel with her priest, but her father followed and killed them both. St Dymphna's remains at Gheel became a focus of pilgrimage for the mentally ill, and Gheel later evolved into a colony for their care.

In 1904, Norman wrote in the *Journal of Mental Science* about the need for similar 'family care of persons of unsound mind in Ireland', noting that there were many objections to be made against asylum life, not least of which was its separation of patients from the ordinary interests of life.[238] Norman was deeply opposed to prolonged institutionalisation[239] and there was already long standing evidence that care outside of institutions could be effective in Ireland. One such case (and there were likely many) concerned the 16-year-old Charles Stock, son of Bishop Joseph Stock of Killala, who suffered from likely schizophrenia a full century earlier, between 1806 and 1813, but was treated chiefly at home, under the supervision of Dr William Harvey, physician at Steevens Hospital and a governor of the Richmond Asylum.[240] Notwithstanding such cases and the many clear objections to asylum life, Norman's enlightened suggestions about 'boarding out' and 'family care' did not find favour with governmental authorities and so did not prosper at that time.

Notwithstanding these setbacks, Norman remained extremely active, enthusiastic and highly productive both in his clinical work and in the broader context of the emerging profession of psychiatry. He was deeply involved with the MPA, becoming a member in 1880, secretary to the Irish division in 1887 (until 1904), and president in 1894. In his presidential address, Norman touched on many of the themes that defined his career and contribution to psychiatry: education in asylums, research in pathology and physiology, asylum management and models of family care.[241]

More broadly, Norman's vivid, incisive and plentiful writings covered such themes as aphasia, brain tumours, dementia, medication trials, hallucinations, delusional insanity, beri beri (based on his controversial experiences at the Richmond from 1894 onward),[242] diagnostic systems[243] and dysentery.[244] Norman spoke out strongly about mental health law (bemoaning disproportionate force and incarceration)[245] and made robust contributions to Allbutt's *System of Medicine*[246] and Tuke's *Dictionary of Psychological Medicine*.[247] In his personal life, Norman maintained strong interests in book collecting, literature, botany, archaeology, architecture, music and languages, and was a keen student of German, French and Italian. His library, presented to the Royal College of Physicians of Ireland following his death, reveals the depth and breadth of his reading across classic and lesser known texts in English, French and German.[248]

In addition to his participation in the MPA, Norman was a member of the British Medical Association, joint editor of the MPA's *Journal of Mental Science*,[249] and vice president of the Royal College of Physicians of Ireland,[250] among other positions.[251] In 1907, he received a richly merited honorary doctorate (MD) from Trinity College, Dublin.

The following year, however, Norman died unexpectedly just outside his home on the North Circular Road, as reported in the *Irish Times*:

> With deep regret we announce the death of Dr Conolly Norman, Resident Medical Superintendent, Richmond Lunatic Asylum, Dublin, which occurred with painful suddenness on Sunday afternoon. About four o'clock in the afternoon Dr Norman left his residence, St Dympna's, North Circular Road, Dublin for a short walk, but after going a few hundred yards he became ill, and collapsed on the pavement. Mr Neill, Head Attendant at the Asylum, who lived near, was informed, and had Dr Norman conveyed to his home. Sir Thornley Stoker, Dr Finny, and Dr Cullinan were quickly

in attendance, but Dr Norman had already died. For some months past he was unwell, suffering from a severe attack of influenza, followed by bronchitis, and moreover, he suffered from a cardiac affection.[252] In December last he was obliged to relinquish his duties with a view to recuperating his health. Last week he resumed duty and appeared to have greatly benefited by his rest.[253]

The *Irish Times* noted that Norman's sudden death on 23 February 1908 would 'be received with sincere regret by every section of the community. His loss is a public one for Dr Norman devoted his life to the care of afflicted humanity, and how nobly he fulfilled his trust is recognised on all sides.'[254] Norman was buried in Mount Jerome Cemetery on 26 February 1908[255] and fulsome tributes were paid at a special meeting of the Joint Committee of the Richmond District Asylum the following day.[256]

Norman was a well-known figure, widely respected and duly mentioned in the opening pages of Joyce's *Ulysses*.[257] A memorial by Joseph M.S. Carré was erected by public subscription in St Patrick's Cathedral, Dublin and unveiled on 18 October 1910 by the Lord Lieutenant, the Earl of Aberdeen, who spoke highly of Norman's life and work.[258] An after-care programme was established in Norman's honour and a portrait presented to the Royal College of Physicians, of which he had been vice president.[259] The Conolly Norman medal was also initiated, to be presented to the best student in psychiatry at Trinity College Dublin annually.

As the *British Medical Journal* noted, Norman's career combined intellectual brilliance with pragmatic devotion to developing new models for better treatment of mental disorder.[260] While Norman's campaign in favour of alternatives to large institutions met with distinctly mixed success at the time, it still paved the way for many future reforms, as did his efforts to provide specialist treatment for the intellectually disabled and persons with alcohol problems. Fittingly, Norman's own house at Grangegorman was later named 'St Dymphna's' and devoted to the treatment of alcohol problems. Later again, it was renamed 'Conolly Norman House' and housed a mental health service; it is now a mental health service management centre.

In terms of his overall contribution, it is clear that Norman continued and deepened the progressive tradition of certain of his predecessors, such as Hallaran in Cork who, a century earlier, had similarly combined intellectual enquiry with energetic innovation and pragmatic efforts to improve care of the mentally ill.[261] Norman is, however, remembered not just for his reforms of asylum care and his writings, but also his contributions to the development of psychiatry as a profession. These contributions include, not least, Norman's strong promotion of the career of Dr Eleonora Fleury and the historic change that her professional progression brought to the emerging discipline of psychiatry in Ireland and Great Britain.

Dr Eleonora Fleury: Republican Doctor

As the 1800s drew to a close, there were, finally, emerging signs of significant change in the Irish asylums. The increase in inpatient numbers might have shown no signs of abating, but this apparently unstoppable trend was now accompanied by subtle but definite signs of reform. These changes were, in the first instance, most visible within the profession of psychiatry itself, and their complexity is well demonstrated by the life and career of Dr Eleonora Fleury (1867–1960),[262] the first female psychiatrist in Ireland or Great Britain.

Eleonora (Norah) Lilian Fleury was born in Manchester in 1867.[263] Fleury studied medicine at the London School of Medicine for Women and the Royal Free Hospital. She received first class honours and in 1890 became the first female medical graduate of the Royal University of Ireland.[264] In 1893, Fleury was awarded an MD from the Royal University of Ireland and won a gold medal.[265] She then went on to work at Homerton Fever Hospital in London, the Richmond Asylum in Grangegorman and its sister asylum in Portrane (later St Ita's Hospital).[266]

The Richmond Asylum had opened in 1814 in response to growing evidence of unmet medical and social need amongst the mentally ill.[267] As the 1800s progressed, however, the Richmond, like the other asylums, expanded at an alarming rate.[268] As a result, official attention shifted from the humane treatment of individual patients to the management of the increasingly complex institutions, which were beset by problems relating to overcrowding, staff shortages, poor funding, and lack of activity for patients.[269] Nationally, this led to significant disillusionment with the asylum project itself.[270] By the early 1890s, when Fleury arrived to work there, the Richmond Asylum had almost 1,500 patients resident in accommodation designed for 1,100.[271]

Notwithstanding these problems, as the 1800s drew to a close psychiatry had clearly emerged as a profession within Irish medicine. In Great Britain, this process took a significant step forward in 1841 with the foundation of the Association of Medical Officers of Asylums and Hospitals for the Insane, later known as the Medico-Psychological Association (MPA).[272] The purpose of the organisation was to facilitate communication between doctors working in asylums and thus improve patient care. An Irish division was formed in 1872, although Irish members had participated in the organisation long before that,[273] and the organisation consistently urged Dublin Castle to appoint medical doctors as managers of asylums.[274] The MPA (as it was known from 1865 onward) was central to the emergence of psychiatry as a profession in Ireland and was indelibly linked with the asylums. From its foundation, however, the organisation admitted only men until, in 1893, Fleury's name was put forward for membership by the ever forward-looking Norman.[275]

A discussion ensued at the MPA and, in 1894, its rules were duly altered:[276] Fleury became the first woman member and, thus, the first female psychiatrist in Ireland or Great Britain. The following year, Fleury's paper on 'Agitated Melancholia in Women' was read at the meeting of the MPA's Irish Division, held at the College of Physicians, Kildare Street, Dublin. Fleury herself was unavoidably absent but her paper outlined specific cases of 'agitated melancholia' in younger and older women. These case histories are remarkable not only for their astute clinical descriptions, but also the extent to which Fleury linked psychiatric problems with social and life events such as examinations, marital difficulties, separations and bereavements.[277]

Also in 1895, the *British Medical Journal* announced that Fleury had been appointed to the post of assistant medical officer at the Richmond.[278] Fleury's work at the Richmond involved not only treating patients but also teaching nurses and attendants studying for the newly established certificate of proficiency in mental nursing.[279] Interestingly, the *Medical Directory* for 1905 records both Fleury and Dr Ada English (1875–1944; see Chapter 4) at the Richmond that year, with English there as a clinical assistant, shortly after graduating.[280] The lives and careers of Fleury and English were to bear significant similarities to each other in the decades to follow.[281]

Following the death of Norman in 1908, Fleury was made medical officer in charge of the female house at the Richmond.[282] In 1912, when there was a vacancy for a new head of the asylum in Portrane, Fleury was passed over, as the committee felt it would be inadvisable to place a woman in such a position. Fleury later became deputy medical superintendent in Portrane.[283]

Like English, Fleury's medical concerns extended to population health and wellbeing, and, like Dr Kathleen Lynn (1874–1955), a contemporary doctor and political activist, Fleury was very concerned about the spread of venereal disease in the early 1900s.[284] Also, like English, Fleury was deeply involved in the nationalist movement, often using the Richmond and Portrane asylums to conceal and assist wounded republican fugitives.[285] As was the case with English, Fleury's activism landed her in trouble with the authorities and she was arrested and imprisoned in 1923.[286] (This period in Fleury's life is discussed in greater detail in Chapter 4.) During her imprisonment, Fleury was especially concerned with the medical welfare of republican women prisoners – a concern which persisted following her release – as she highlighted the prisoners' plight and appealed for better conditions.

Following her release from prison, Fleury returned to work at the asylum in Portrane and continued her medical career. After her retirement, she lived at Upper Rathmines Road in Dublin and, like Lynn, remained exceptionally physically active all her life. Fleury died in 1960 and is, like Norman, buried in Mount Jerome Cemetery in Harold's Cross, Dublin.[287]

Over the course of her life, Fleury, like English, combined academic ability with progressive medical practice and persistent republican activism. In these regards, Fleury had much in common not only with English but also with Lynn,[288] Dr Dorothy Stopford Price (1890–1954), a republican doctor remembered for her work on tuberculosis,[289] and Dr Brigid Lyons Thornton (1898–1987), a politically active public health doctor.[290] All combined progressive medical practice with acute social conscience and political activism. They made remarkable contributions at a time when Ireland was undergoing a period of exceptionally rapid political change and when there appeared to be genuine opportunities to effect political, social and medical reform, for the betterment of all.

Emily Winifred Dickson (1866–1944) was another comparable figure who worked in asylums and shared Fleury's concern with public health, although Dickson worked in the English asylum system and for shorter periods than Fleury. Dickson had graduated with first class honours from the Royal College of Surgeons in Ireland in 1893 and later worked at Rainhill Mental Hospital in northern England.[291] Like English, Dickson lectured extensively, was involved in the Irish Women's National Health Association,[292] and was deeply concerned with public health, especially among the socially excluded (e.g. women and children in workhouses).[293]

While Fleury, English and Dickson focused their medical work on the mentally ill, both Fleury and English, like Lynn, Price and Thornton, were deeply concerned about the medical and social wellbeing of the disadvantaged, and consistently linked this concern with the need for political and social change. The decision of these women to enter medicine in the first instance was likely linked, at least in part, to their personal awareness of health and social problems during their childhoods. Their continued awareness of the social context of medicine was likely deepened by their medical training, growing political awareness, experiences in the practice of their profession, and contacts with other woman practitioners.

To this extent, these women were living embodiments of the views of Rudolf Virchow (1821–1902), the German pathologist and politician, who declared that 'medicine is a social science, and politics nothing but medicine on a large scale'.[294] The lives and contributions of Fleury, Lynn, Price, Thornton and English certainly supported the truth of Virchow's statement, and their pioneering work demonstrated the power of combining medicine with revolutionary politics at a time of exceptional challenge and opportunity in Irish history.[295]

Psychiatry and Society in the 1800s: 'A Distant, Deviant Other'

Throughout the 1800s, the development of psychiatry in Ireland, as elsewhere, was largely shaped by the society in which the discipline evolved and came of age. From this perspective, the Famine was undoubtedly one of the defining events of the century, as people with worsening mental disorder and starvation-related distress sought to enter workhouses and asylums in unprecedented numbers.

The Famine may have also shaped the epidemiology of mental disorder in Ireland for several further generations if, as seems likely, it both increased risk of mental disorder in persons who were in gestation at the time (and born during or shortly after the Famine) and had transgenerational effects on patterns of illness many decades later, possibly through epigenetic change (i.e. changes in the ways genes are expressed, rather than changes in genes themselves).[296] This possible impact of the Famine on mental disorder both requires and merits further study, just as the Famine's possible (although likely quite different) impact on the epidemiology of cardiovascular disease has been similarly raised in recent years.[297] These areas merit closer study.[298]

It is already clear, however, that the presence of large numbers of mentally ill persons in workhouses presented very real problems during the 1800s. The Irish workhouses were chronically overcrowded, deeply unsanitary and grossly unsuited to the needs of the destitute mentally ill or intellectually disabled. Nonetheless, the nineteenth century saw workhouses become *de facto* elements of the system of 'care' for the mentally ill,[299] as patients were commonly admitted from workhouses to asylums,[300] and discharged from asylums back to workhouses.[301]

The intellectually disabled, much neglected in most historical studies, were also much neglected during this period, with the result that their fate was often similar to that of the mentally ill: there was minimal dedicated provision for their needs, and they either lived at home, became homeless or were admitted to workhouses or, increasingly, the growing number of asylums for the mentally ill.[302] As a result, the experiences of the intellectually disabled were in many cases similar to those of the mentally ill who tended to experience lengthy periods of detention in poorly therapeutic facilities, poor mental and physical health, and a high risk of dying in asylums.[303]

Certain practitioners, such as RMS Drapes of the Enniscorthy District Asylum, sought to improve matters though relatively enlightened asylum management,[304] but these efforts were continually hampered by the seemingly inexorable 'increase of insanity in Ireland',[305] as the number of 'mentally ill' persons in Irish institutions increased from 2,097 in 1829 to an astonishing 17,665 in 1894.[306] As Walsh notes, 'between 1880 and 1900 the number of asylum beds in Ireland doubled and between 1860 and 1900 the numbers of admissions, whether first admissions or not first admissions, increased four-fold'.[307] Why?

It is, in summary, clear that a number of different factors contributed to the growth of the Irish asylums, including increased recognition of mental disorder; the search for professional prestige among asylum staff; mutually reinforcing patterns of asylum building and committal, underpinned by continual, restless legislative change; changes in diagnostic practices throughout the 1800s; and possible epidemiological change, although there is insufficient evidence to conclude that there was any true increase in the occurrence of new cases of mental disorder to justify the increase in admissions.[308]

Ultimately, the Irish asylums were primarily social rather than medical creations, expanding to meet societal and community requirements, rather than demonstrated medical needs. They were, however, constantly accompanied by a certain rhetoric about psychiatric and social care,[309] care that was deeply needed (and, often, provided) for many patients; was clearly excessive for others; and was utterly inappropriate for some other unfortunate individuals who were simply fed into the system by a society that saw few alternative, non-institutional options for them. The asylums were, to an extent, necessary at the time, but they were also excessively large, commonly misused and ultimately counterproductive for both the mentally ill and society in general. They were an unmitigated disaster for the profession of psychiatry in Ireland, which was to be haunted and defined by the idea of custodial asylum care for several generations to follow.

Nonetheless, the asylums contributed significantly to the emergence of psychiatry as a profession, a process that took a significant step forward when the annual meeting of the Association of Medical Officers of Asylums of Great Britain and Ireland took place in Dublin on 22 August 1861, with Lalor as president.[310] The asylums were also intriguing reflections of a complex, conflicted society, and, in this light, one of the most remarkable features of their history is, as already discussed, the virtual absence of the Roman Catholic Church from the story. Apart from its involvement in specific initiatives, the Church and its associated organisations simply did not concern themselves with systematic or large scale provision of mental health care in nineteenth- or twentieth-century Ireland. This contrasted sharply with the Church's dominant involvement in general healthcare and education, and means that Ireland's asylums for the mentally ill were, for the most part, State institutions rather than religious ones.

Against this background, throughout the 1800s there was plenty of room for development and innovation in this field by actors other than the Church, including other religious groups such as the Society of Friends and various individual clinicians, such as Norman of the Richmond, who championed 'family care of persons of unsound mind'.[311] Like many reform-minded doctors, however, Norman found that his enlightened initiative did not find favour with governmental authorities. Many of Norman's other ideas did, however, bear significant fruit, including his nomination of Fleury for membership of the MPA in 1893.[312]

Other professional developments during the 1800s included increased emphasis on the treatment of mental disorder in professional medical circles. In June 1844, for example, the College of Physicians was notified that Sir Edward Sugden (1781–1875), later Lord St Leonards, Lord Chancellor of Ireland, had decided to give 10 guineas annually as a prize for the best essay on the treatment of mental disorder,[313] having also sought to establish a school for the treatment of mental diseases at St Patrick's.[314] The prize was to be awarded for the following 10 years alternately by the College of Physicians and the College of Surgeons, and it duly stimulated much needed interest in the subject.

Throughout this eventful period in the history of Irish psychiatry, it is unsurprising that the asylums and issues related to mental disorder were a staple feature in the popular press, and subjects of much public discussion.[315] O'Neill, in a fascinating study of the 'portrayal of madness in the Limerick press' from 1772 to 1845, notes that newspaper accounts of mental disorder and its treatment were influenced by a relatively broad range of factors and not simply a desire to convey information in an impartial and informative fashion:

> For newspapers in Limerick, accounts of madness – even accounts with an explicit moral or educational intent – were subsidiary to another consideration, the capacity of the account to attract the reader. Selling newspapers was a business, far more than was mad medicine. Output was driven by an overriding need to gain and sustain readers' attention and information was a raw product that could be processed into a form to be used to achieve this end. Therefore, stories were re-packaged into forms that were already familiar and were perceived as interesting to the printers and proprietors themselves and to the target audience.[316]

Other factors were also relevant to coverage of mental disorder in the media, including political concerns, commercial considerations, and a perceived requirement for drama:

> The tendency towards sensationalism also worked against the local press discussing changes in the attitude to the insane and their care. Madness was often presented in the newspaper as a way of sensationalising deviant behaviour, all in the interest of generating sales. In reports of suicides, and less frequently of murders, the madness of the perpetrator was used to explain the action or as a mitigating circumstance. Both social class and the location of the incident determined the press attitude. Few details were given regarding local suicides or murders, especially those involving individuals of high social status.[317]

Ultimately, the position of the mentally ill in nineteenth-century Ireland, both in reality and in the eyes of the press, was rather bleakly defined by institutional care followed by either death in the asylum or a life of social exclusion:

> What is certain is that once labelled as mad, an individual was not permitted to maintain any public identity of which the press approved. Therefore, though by the

end of the period under discussion insanity was described in the Limerick press as misunderstood, the old stereotypes remained and even after discharge from an asylum the label of lunatic followed individuals into their everyday life and social dealings. Geographic, economic and class issues had clouded opportunities for balanced representations of the mad and madness, and the lunatic was still constructed and portrayed as a distant, deviant other.[318]

4

☧

EARLY-TWENTIETH-CENTURY PSYCHIATRY

Good lunacy laws should make it possible to obtain care and treatment in asylums with ease, but they should make unnecessary detention difficult.

Committee on Lunacy
Administration (Ireland), *Second Report*
of the Committee Appointed by the
Lord Lieutenant of Ireland on Lunacy
Administration (Ireland) (1891)[1]

The early twentieth century was a time of extraordinary change in Ireland with the advents of the Easter Rising (1916), War of Independence (1919–21) and Civil War (1922–3), and establishment of the Irish Free State (Saorstát Éireann; 1922–37). This was also a time of considerable change in Irish psychiatry, as determined efforts were made to move from the asylum based system of the 1800s to a better, more humane model of service provision for the mentally ill.

The problems presented by the mentally ill were clearly acute: by 1900, the 11 pre-existing district asylums had increased to 22, housing a total of 16,404 patients.[2] There were, in addition, 709 patients in 12 private asylums and 4 charitable hospitals; 162 patients in the Central Criminal Lunatic Asylum; 89 patients looked after as single patients in private residences; and some 3,805 patients in workhouses. That came to a total of 21,169 patients in these locations in 1900; the number outside these settings was unknown.

Nine years earlier, in 1891, the issue of patient numbers was considered (yet again) by the Committee on Lunacy Administration (Ireland), which comprised Sir Arthur Mitchell (Lunacy Commissioner for Scotland), R.W.A. Holmes (Treasury Remembrancer for Ireland) and Dr F.X.F. MacCabe (medical inspector with the Local Government Board).[3] The Committee noted that many factors, other than mental disorder itself, contributed to rates of certification, especially among the poor:

> It has been said that 'human power cannot multiply the lunatics of a country,' but this opinion is here treated as entirely erroneous, if by lunatics are meant those persons whom the State registers and treats as such; and it must be erroneous, unless the views here expressed are wrong. In point of fact, the lunacy of a country is far from being

a fixed amount, which can neither be increased nor diminished. There is no uniform standard of mental soundness or unsoundness which is accepted by all medical men when considering whether a certificate of insanity shall or shall not be granted, nor indeed by any one medical man in all circumstances. The ease or difficulty of getting certificates of insanity may depend, and does often depend, on the object in view, or the results which will follow certification. Circumstances apart altogether from the mental condition necessarily influence the granting of these certificates – the source, for instance, from which any expenditure consequent on the granting of the certificates is to be obtained, cannot fail to have an influence.

If all this is true of lunacy generally, it is of necessity still truer of pauper lunacy, because, in addition to the lunacy, there is then the pauperism, about the determination of which it is clear there may be uncertainty. A lunatic, for example, will become a pauper lunatic in one locality who will almost certainly remain a private lunatic in another. A rich parish will admit a lunatic as a pauper, whom a poor parish would refuse to admit, and of course, a poor parish will admit him, if the consequent expenditure by the parish is to be small more readily than it will if the consequent expenditure is to be considerable.[4]

One of the key variables in this context was the parlous state of Ireland's lunacy legislation. By the end of the 1800s mental health law had become impossibly complex, frequently contradictory and ultimately impenetrable. In 1886, a definitive tome on the topic was published, impressively titled *The Law and Practice of Lunacy in Ireland as Administered by the Lord Chancellor under the Sign Manual Together with a Compendium of the Law Relating to Establishments for the Care of the Insane*.[5] Written by George Whitley Abraham, Barrister-at-Law and Registrar in Lunacy, the book ran to a total of 752 densely written, convoluted pages, and the indefatigable author did not even live to see his masterwork published: he died when it was with the printer. Nonetheless, Abraham's impressive book presented useful, if lengthy, accounts of topics ranging from the 'general policy of laws concerning the insane' to 'management of the lunatic's estate', from 'civil contracts' to 'varieties of incapacity attaching upon lunacy', and included a 'compendium of the law relating to establishments for the care of the insane'. Ultimately, however, there was no hiding the fact that the legal position of the mentally ill was a desperate mess, albeit an exhaustively documented one.

The matter was stated even more directly in 1891 by the Committee on Lunacy Administration (Ireland) which concluded, with admirable brevity, that 'fresh Lunacy legislation for Ireland is beyond question necessary':

In regard to many matters it is extremely difficult, if not impossible, to know what is, or is not, statutory. For this reason alone, the codification or consolidation of the Statutes relating to Lunacy appears to us to have become necessary. But, apart from this, the provisions of the Statutes are in many respects of an undesirable character. They do not sufficiently guarantee the proper treatment of the insane, nor do they adequately safeguard the public against unnecessary detention in Asylums.[6]

In terms of service provision, the Committee suggested 'that it be considered whether some of the empty Workhouses could not be acquired and converted into' provincial asylums:

> If this were done, the buildings would cease altogether to be Workhouses, and would be as unconnected with the Poor Law Authorities as District Asylums. In this way increased Asylum accommodation might be cheaply obtained in those cases in which extensive structural changes would not be necessary for the conversion of the Workhouse accommodation into Asylum accommodation, and in which the acquisition of additional land would not be needed. Sometimes the necessary structural changes are very extensive and costly [...]. But there may be other unoccupied Workhouses which could be altered at small cost so as to afford suitable accommodation for incurable and easily-managed Lunatics, and our suggestion is that the possibility of utilising some of the disused Workhouses in this way should be carefully considered.[7]

The Committee suggested 'the creation of a General Board of Lunacy for Ireland'[8] and various changes to administration[9] and admission procedures.[10] It also supported the idea of lunatics 'boarding out' of workhouses, in private homes:

> It would not be difficult, in our opinion, by co-operation between the Lunacy Inspectors and the Local Government Board, to make such rules and arrangements as would afford a reasonable security that the money given for the relief of lunatics so boarded out of Workhouses, whether with relatives or with strangers, was spent for their benefit. If this reasonable security were obtained in such a way as to enable the Inspectors of Lunatics to certify that they believed the boarded-out pauper lunatics to be properly cared for, it seems to us only right that there should be participation on their account in the Grant from Imperial Sources towards the maintenance of the insane poor.[11]

Sadly, the Committee's relatively enlightened and compassionate stances on many matters were generally not reflected in policy changes,[12] although the early years of the 1900s did see continued discussion about possible reform along these and other lines. Issues relating to overcrowding inevitably dominated the Conference of the Irish Asylums Committee at the Richmond Asylum in 1903;[13] the Richmond itself organised a special enquiry 'into the question of provision for workhouse lunatics' and a diagnostic 'segregation' of all asylum patients in 1907;[14] and, in 1927, the Irish Free State published its seminal *Report of the Commission on the Relief of the Sick and Destitute Poor, Including the Insane Poor*.[15]

The 1927 Report noted that the Commission, appointed in 1925, was instructed 'to inquire into the existing provision in public institutions for the care and treatment of mentally defective persons and to advise as to whether more efficient methods can be introduced especially as regards the care and training of mentally defective children, due regard being had to the expense involved'.[16] The Commission interpreted the term 'mentally defective' to 'include mentally disordered as well as mentally deficient persons'.

The Commission provided a mercifully brisk, useful summary of legislation underpinning the asylum system from the 1700s up to the early 1900s, with particular emphasis on changes occurring around the turn of the century:

> The system of administration which we have outlined underwent radical alteration when the Local Government Act, 1898, came into operation. From 1821 to 1899 the asylums were in the general control of the Lord Lieutenant. The administration was divided amongst three bodies whom he appointed, namely, the Board of Control, the Boards of Governors and the Inspectors of Lunatics. The Board of Control was entrusted with the provision of accommodation, the local Boards of Governors managed the asylums in accordance with prescribed uniform rules called the Privy Council Rules, and the Inspectors had not only the duty of visiting the asylums and inquiring into their condition, but had administrative functions, such as the framing of estimates, the approval of pensions, the regulation of dietary scales, the fixing of hours of meals and of rising and retiring, and also certain duties in connection with the audit of accounts.
>
> Under the Act of 1898 a new administrative system was set up and it became the duty of the County Councils created by the Act to provide sufficient accommodation for the lunatic poor, and manage the asylum for the county. The Board of Control was abolished and the powers of the Lord Lieutenant and the Inspectors as to the appointment and removal of officers and the regulation of expenditure were transferred to the Councils. The County Council's powers were to be exercised through a Committee appointed by them, one-fourth of which might be composed of persons not members of the Council [...].
>
> The Committees of Management were given power to make regulations respecting the government and management of the asylums; the admission, detention and discharge of patients; and the conditions as to payment and accommodation for private patients. The Privy Council Rules were to continue in operation until these regulations were made and approved. All the Committees of Management except those for the asylums at Carlow, Castlebar, and Mullingar [had by 1927] made regulations under the Act.[17]

The Commission also noted that the Local Government Act 1898 made provision for the establishment of 'auxiliary asylums for chronic and harmless lunatics',[18] and that the Lunacy Act 1901 introduced various additional reforms:

> The Lunacy Act of 1901 provided for the conditional discharge of criminal lunatics and extended to Ireland certain provisions of the English Lunacy Act of 1890 designed to protect lunatics from ill-treatment. It provided for the expenses connected with the maintenance of criminal lunatics in district asylums being defrayed out of government funds. The central asylum at Dundum could not accommodate all persons classed as

criminal lunatics, and it had become the practice to send persons who had committed only trivial offences, or were serving short sentences, to the district asylums, reserving the Central Asylum largely for those who had committed serious offences. The Act of 1901 gave the same power of recovering the cost of maintenance of dangerous lunatics as existed in the case of ordinary patients, and it also permitted Committees of Management to unite for the purposes of promoting pathological research.[19]

Against this background, the early twentieth century was, clearly, a time of considerable discussion and, to a certain extent at least, change in mental health services owing not only to the reforming Acts of 1898 and 1901, but also to growing unrest about the state of Irish asylums and the fate of the destitute mentally ill. Before considering asylum reforms of the early 1900s any further, however, it is worth exploring briefly what is known about the fate of the mentally ill *outside* the asylums in the early years of the new century.

Outside the Walls: The Mentally Ill Outside the Asylums (1901)

The historiography of Irish psychiatry demonstrates a strong focus on the history of institutions, echoing the emphasis government traditionally placed on institutional provision as a key element in resolving the social problems presented by people with apparent mental disorder or intellectual disability.

Throughout the nineteenth century, these developments were largely shaped by a strong belief that rates of mental disorder were increasing rapidly, especially toward the end of the 1800s.[20] As explored in Chapter 3, the subsequent expansion of the Irish asylum system was a complex sociomedical phenomenon,[21] as was the admission of increasing numbers of the mentally ill to the Irish workhouse system.[22]

Notwithstanding these developments, there was still a large number of people with mental disorder who were not in asylums, workhouses or other institutions in Ireland at the start of the twentieth century. One study, based on Ireland's 1901 national census,[23] found that there were 482 persons described as 'lunatics' and not resident in psychiatric hospitals, workhouses or other institutions in Ireland on census night (31 March) in 1901, yielding a point prevalence of 11 per 100,000 population (i.e. approximately one in every 10,000 persons outside an institution was recorded in the census as a 'lunatic').[24]

This overall prevalence seems quite low, presumably as a result of specific aspects of census methodology.[25] The very lowest prevalence of 'lunatics' outside of institutions (8 per 100,000 population) was recorded in Leinster (possibly owing to enhanced provision of workhouses and asylums); the highest was in Connaught (18 per 100,000 population). A majority of these 'lunatics' were female (60 per cent) with an average age of 46 years. Two thirds were single (i.e. never married), while one third of females were married, compared to 14 per cent of males. The most common relationship to the 'head of household' (as recorded in the census) was child (33 per cent) although some were boarders or lodgers. Majorities were Roman Catholic (82 per cent) and could 'read and

TABLE 1
Geographical distribution of persons described as 'lunatics' and not resident in psychiatric hospitals, workhouses or other institutions in Ireland on census night (31 March) in 1901.

Province	County	Population	Number of 'lunatics' outside institutions	Number of 'lunatics' outside institutions per 100,000 population
Connaught	Galway	192,845	31	16
	Leitrim	69,460	12	17
	Mayo	198,098	33	17
	Roscommon	100,563	23	23
	Sligo	80,555	13	16
	Connaught Total	**641,521**	**112**	**18**
Munster	Clare	112,309	21	19
	Cork	402,388	48	12
	Kerry	165,940	34	21
	Limerick	147,154	9	6
	Tipperary	155,517	11	7
	Waterford	87,205	12	14
	Munster Total	**1,070,513**	**135**	**13**
Leinster	Carlow	37,228	7	19
	Dublin	439,915	21	5
	Kildare	61,312	4	7
	Kilkenny	75,447	8	11
	Laois	57,171	8	14
	Longford	46,720	8	17
	Louth	65,107	1	2
	Meath	70,304	10	14
	Offaly	60,341	9	15
	Westmeath	61,998	3	5
	Wexford	104,028	8	8
	Wicklow	59,906	11	18
	Leinster Total	**1,256,989**	**98**	**8**

	Antrim	457,983	20	4
	Armagh	124,803	12	10
	Cavan	97,437	7	7
	Donegal	173,121	26	15
	Down	290,061	14	5
Ulster	Fermanagh	65,015	17	26
	Derry	144,823	15	10
	Monaghan	74,425	8	11
	Tyrone	150,687	18	12
	Ulster Total	**1,578,355**	**137**	**9**
Ireland Total		**4,547,378**	**482**	**11**

write' (65 per cent). Among those for whom the ability to speak Irish was recorded, 74 per cent spoke *both* Irish and English.

These results, although interesting, need to be interpreted with an awareness of various limitations of the census methodology, not least of which is the (likely) inconsistent use of the terms 'imbecile', 'idiot' and 'lunatic', despite definitions being provided. A 'lunatic', for example, was 'a mentally ill person with periods of lucidity'. This definition is similar, although not identical, to the definition of a person of 'unsound mind' in the Fourth Census of Canada in 1901, which stated that 'it is not necessary that the degree of infirmity should be absolute or total, but that it should be so sufficiently marked in any one of the classes as to have reached the stage of incapacity'.[26] The Irish definition is quite similar, at least to the extent that it defines lunacy as involving a lesser degree of impairment than 'imbecile' or 'idiot'.

It is difficult, if not impossible, to clarify just how conscientiously these definitions were used by various enumerators in 1901. It seems likely that, at the very least, the terms 'imbecile' and 'idiot' were used interchangeably. The Mental Deficiency Act of 1913 later defined an 'imbecile' as an individual unable to take care of himself or herself, and an 'idiot' as a person unable to protect himself or herself from common dangers.[27] The 1901 census, however, preceded the Mental Deficiency Act of 1913 by more than a decade, and the 1913 Act was not, in any case, applied in Ireland. As a result, the terms 'imbecile' and 'idiot' were likely used interchangeably in the 1901 census. In this context, it also appears likely that the low prevalence of 'lunatics' in the census is explained, at least in part, by the way in which the definition of 'lunatic' was used.

Notwithstanding these complexities, it is interesting that a majority (60 per cent) of 'lunatics' outside the institutions in 1901 were female and the average age of females (47 years) was higher than that of males (44 years). By way of comparison, there were, on 1 January 1901, 21,169 mentally ill people in Irish institutions, of whom 48 per cent were female.[28] This difference in gender distribution inside and outside the institutions might reflect an increased likelihood for women, possibly especially slightly older women, to remain in the home, despite showing signs of mental disorder. This is consistent with the fact that women generally tended to be admitted to asylums at a later stage in their illness than men, and were more likely to be discharged.[29]

From the 1901 census, the most common relationship outside the institutions between a 'lunatic' and the 'head of household' was child (33 per cent), suggesting that children with mental disorder may have remained in the home in order to be cared for by their families, or, alternatively, in order to care for their parents, attend to household tasks or work on farms.

It is interesting that certain counties with large asylums (e.g. Kerry) had a relatively high prevalence of 'lunatics' outside the asylums and workhouses. This might reflect the fact that many Irish asylums demonstrated significant rates of both admission and discharge,[30] possibly resulting in relatively larger numbers of persons with *diagnosed* mental disorder living in counties with asylums. Local geography was also important, as people living near asylums were more likely to be admitted than those living far distances away, at least in the 1800s.[31]

On the other hand, the prevalence in Dublin was relatively low, despite the presence of a number of asylums, suggesting that this explanation was not universal, or that other factors were at play, especially in Dublin. It is also notable that some of the 'lunatics' outside the institutions who were 'boarders' were unrelated to the 'head of household' suggesting the possibility that these households may have represented early or informal *de facto* 'boarding out' initiatives, as championed tirelessly by Norman at the Richmond.[32]

While no 'occupation' was provided for 38 per cent of 'lunatics' in the 1901 census, farming was the most common occupation recorded (41 per cent).[33] Also consistent with the broader population, majorities were Roman Catholic (82 per cent); could 'read and write' (65 per cent); and, among those for whom ability to speak Irish was recorded, 74 per cent spoke both Irish and English. This, too, is consistent with broader trends in Ireland, as illiteracy had fallen rapidly in preceding decades from 53 per cent in 1841 to 18 per cent in 1891.[34]

In these important respects (occupation, religion, literacy), 'lunatics' living outside the Irish institutions in 1901 bore significant similarities to the broader population, although it remained the case that the lives they led differed significantly from the lives of those who were not labelled as 'lunatics'. This situation was largely attributable to the twin processes of continual legislative change and inexorable expansion of institutions for the mentally ill during the late nineteenth and early twentieth centuries. These matters were of enormous concern to asylum doctors in the early 1900s and predictably dominated the Conference of the Irish Asylum Committees in 1903.

Conference of the Irish Asylum Committees (1903): Degeneration, Politics and Tea

Issues relating to overcrowding were strongly to the fore of the agenda at the Conference of the Irish Asylums Committee convened at the Richmond Asylum in 1903.[35] By that time, it was felt that the increase in admissions was related in large part to 'heredity' rather than poverty, adversity, religion or mental anxiety – a conclusion which contrasted in certain respects with that of Hallaran a century earlier, who had emphasised physical illness, alcohol, political disturbance and 'terror from religious enthusiasm' as causes of mental disorder.[36] This was not a universally agreed position, however, with some commentators, such as Dr M.J. Nolan, then RMS in Downpatrick (having previously worked in Dublin and Limerick), citing 'stress' as a key contributor, and appealing passionately that the needs of the mentally ill should not be ignored.[37]

With palpable alarm, the 1903 conference noted that there were 22,139 'registered lunatics' in Ireland and this number was increasing.[38] Dr Edward D. O'Neill, medical superintendent of Limerick District Lunatic Asylum, read a paper titled *Increase of Lunacy and Special Reasons Applicable to Ireland* and noted, at the outset, the difficulties with accurate data collection:

> In approaching the subject of the increase of insanity in Ireland the writer realises the difficulties that have to be encountered in obtaining satisfactory information as to the causes of the increase, owing (1) to the meagre and unsatisfactory returns afforded by Asylum Records, and (2) the insufficient description derivable from the admission forms.[39]

Notwithstanding these challenges, O'Neill believed the number of *first* admissions presented a reliable estimate of the overall trend:

> It is conceded that the only true criterion of the increase or decrease of insanity is to be found in the number of first admissions, which in 1880 amounted to 1,925, as against 3,173 during last year [1902], or an increase of 65 per cent, notwithstanding the great decrease in the population.
>
> I do not think I am far wrong in fixing the date and initial cause of the increase of insanity to the darkest period in the History of Ireland – the famine years of 1816–7 [and] the deplorable condition to which the people were reduced. Is it to be wondered at that the stamina of the peasantry was affected, with the inevitable result of mental and physical degeneration?[40]

O'Neill then sought to explore why the rate of 'increase of insanity' was so apparently high *in Ireland* in particular:

> Having thus briefly referred to the increase of insanity, I desire briefly to touch on the causes that are specially applicable to Ireland, and to deal with them in the following order. (1) Accumulation. (2) Emigration and Agricultural depression. (3) Intemperance and Dietary. (4) Masturbation, and (5) Heredity, the commonest cause of insanity, though perhaps not more specially applicable to Ireland than to any other country from which statistics are available.
>
> Accumulation must be regarded as primarily responsible for the increase in the number of insane under treatment; this is explained by the preponderance of each year's admissions over the discharges and deaths, consequent on low discharge and

death rates. The admission for the twenty years ending 31st December, 1902, amount to 63,311, the discharges 34,872, and the deaths 19,976, showing an actual increase of 9,463 [*sic*] patients.

It is not easy to account for the low recovery rate unless it is due to the change in the form of insanity which has taken place in recent years. Formerly the greater number of the admissions were suffering from Acute Mania, characterised by the suddenness of the attack with delirium, violence, and usually, rapid recovery. Now the attack comes on slowly, the lunatic is melancholic, silent, depressed, and the recovery is either very slow or doubtful. Besides, the physical condition is generally very much impaired, and this greatly retards recovery.[41]

O'Neill highlighted the 'political atmosphere',[42] 'excessive tea drinking' and the 'cigarette craze that has caught on to the children of to-day', among other contributory factors:[43]

Masturbation – I regret to say – is another fruitful source of insanity. Of late years, this baneful habit has become very common, and amongst its victims are the young, middle-aged and elderly. By some it is held to be only an effect, but I hold that in a large number of cases it is the cause of insanity. On this point I must not be mistaken, as the habit is a complication in nearly all forms of insanity. It is a prevalent custom with boys at school – the result of example – and with adults, perhaps owing to the fact that our agricultural population do not marry at as early an age as the same class in England and other countries. Unfortunately, our marriage rate seems to be decreasing each year, and is by far the lowest in Europe, being 518 per 1,000, or less than one-third the English rate.[44]

There were, in addition to O'Neill, myriad other spirited participants at the 1903 conference, including Drapes from Enniscorthy and Dr William Graham of Belfast Asylum, as well as religious leaders and various others.[45] The meeting concluded with resolutions calling for a pathological laboratory for further research, legislation permitting family care for patients, and enhanced government funding of asylums. Notwithstanding the possible benefits of these proposed measures, there was still clear alarm, bordering on hysteria, about rising admission rates.

Interestingly, within a few short years of the 1903 conference, Norman, RMS at the Richmond Asylum and one of the secretaries of the 1903 conference (along with Drapes),[46] expressed cautious optimism that the numbers presenting with mental disorder were finally in decline. In 1907, he reported the apparent good news to the Richmond Asylum Joint Committee:

The number of patients in the asylum has actually undergone a slight decrease since this time last year. It is, therefore, perhaps, possible, without being unduly optimistic, to indulge the expectation that the rate of increase may have reached its summit, and that the difficulty of dealing with the question may not progressively be augmented.[47]

Norman's optimism was misplaced: Ireland's asylum population continued to rise throughout the first half of the twentieth century, with just two short lived declines during the two world wars; by 1945 there were 17,708 individuals resident in Irish asylums.[48] The extent of official concern about these trends was reflected by the establishment of three separate inquiries that dealt, to greater or lesser extents, with issues related to mental disorder, within the first decade of the new century: the Viceregal Commission on Poor Law Reform in Ireland (1906), the Royal Commission on the Care and Control of the Feeble-Minded (1908) and the Royal Commission on the Poor Laws and Relief of Distress (1909).

Notwithstanding these reports,[49] there was little real change in the management or conditions of district asylums in the opening decades of the twentieth century. E. Boyd Barrett SJ (Society of Jesus; i.e. a Jesuit priest), writing in *Studies: An Irish Quarterly Review* in 1924, made this point emphatically:

> One would suppose that it should be the first aim of asylum staff to apply the best methods of treatment that science has evolved, and to keep *au courant* with psycho-therapeutic investigations. But there is little sign of this. The Medical Superintendent finds himself so engrossed in administrative duties (which should be done by a manager or steward) that he has little time to attend to patients. The zeal which, as a doctor, he should have for a generous outlay of money on medical requirements, is chilled by his anxiety as an administrator to cut down expenses [...]. There should be strong public demand for immediate reform of the asylum system, and the complete segregation and scientific treatment of curable cases should be insisted upon. Suitable asylums should be built – healthy, bright, beautiful homes, where patients would be enticed by every art to renew their interests in things. Nerve clinics should be opened in every populous district, where advice and treatment should be available for ordinary cases of nerve trouble and incipient insanity.[50]

Three years later, the Commission on the Relief of the Sick and Destitute Poor, Including the Insane Poor, was appointed and duly highlighted serious problems with overcrowding and lack of treatment in Irish asylums, proposing the development of outpatient services and short term admission facilities in general hospitals, among other changes.[51] Reform of the asylum system was, however, excruciatingly slow and another two decades were to elapse before the Mental Treatment Act of 1945 was introduced. Voluntary admission processes had been already implemented many years earlier in several other jurisdictions, including Switzerland[52] and France (in 1876).[53]

The Mental Treatment Act of 1945 was to reenergise the overall process of reform in Ireland not only through the introduction of new admission procedures but also through the establishment of a range of measures designed to improve practices and standards in mental health care more broadly.[54] Reducing the ever rising tide of admissions, however, was to prove a more complex and challenging task that would occupy doctors, legislators and policy makers throughout most of the remainder of the twentieth century.

The Richmond Asylum, Dublin in 1907:
'A Grave and Alarming Crisis'

Reducing admissions was to prove a particular challenge at the Richmond in Dublin, site of the 1903 Conference. Minutes of the Richmond Asylum Joint Committee meetings in 1907 are of particular interest because in that year the Richmond District Asylum Joint Committee appointed a 'Special Committee' to 'enquire into the question of provision for workhouse lunatics' and RMS Norman was directed to perform a diagnostic 'segregation' of all asylum patients, with a view to resolving the overcrowding.[55] Both of these projects demonstrate the distinctly dispiriting starting point for reforms of the asylum system during the remainder of the 1900s.

Throughout 1907, the Richmond District Asylum Joint Committee was regularly provided with a census of inpatients in the Richmond and its sister asylum at Portrane. At the meeting of 17 January, the Committee heard that there were 2,924 patients (1,505 male, 1,419 female) in the asylums, of whom 1,321 (728 male, 593 female) were at Portrane.[56] Over the course of the year, this figure did not change significantly, although there were many admissions and discharges: at the meeting of 18 December 1907, for example, Norman reported that over the previous month 'twenty-two men and twenty-two women have been admitted, making a total of forty-four [...]. Fourteen were admitted from the various workhouses within the district, and eleven were cases of readmission.'[57]

From a diagnostic perspective, Dr J.M. Redington, assistant medical officer, and Dr P.J. Dwyer, clinical assistant, performed an analysis of 292 male admissions to the Richmond in 1907,[58] paying special attention to the occurrence of 'maniacal-depressive insanity' as described by Kraepelin.[59] They came across just one patient who fitted Kraepelin's description of the disorder, apparently consistent with Drapes's doubts about the applicability and usefulness of Kraepelin's paradigm (Chapter 3).[60]

On 31 January 1907, the Chairman left the Richmond Committee in no doubt about the pressure the asylum was under, noting that 'for the year 1898, preceding the date on which we took office, the daily average number of patients on our books was 1,958, as compared with 2,878, the daily average number resident during 1906. In a period of eight years, therefore, there has been an increase of no less than 920 patients [...]. I say it with all deliberation and intense regret, and with experience of the last ten years, that we have already reached a grave and alarming crisis.'[61]

The Chairman noted that 'a large number of our admissions come here direct from workhouses.'[62] A 'special committee' from the Richmond duly visited various establishments around Ireland, including the nearby North Dublin workhouse, where they concluded 'that the provision for the inmates of the lunatic departments is truly deplorable. The overcrowding is very marked, and calls for prompt relief'.[63] Notwithstanding subsequent initiatives, the problem of the mentally ill in Irish workhouses remained deeply concerning well into the 1900s,[64] apparently regardless of how large the asylums themselves became (Chapter 3).

Another problem at the Richmond and elsewhere lay in establishing clear and meaningful diagnoses for patients. On 26 September 1907, the law adviser at the Richmond pointed out that 'the legal definition of the term "lunatic" is very wide and would seem to include any feeble-minded person'.[65] Certainly, official figures indicate that workhouses contained large numbers of both 'lunatics' and 'idiots' in the latter half of the nineteenth century,[66] so it is unsurprising that diagnostic issues, in both asylums and workhouses, generated considerable anxiety in the early 1900s.

On 31 January 1907, the Chairman noted that the Richmond asylum population was increasing rapidly and suggested obtaining 'an exhaustive report from our Medical Superintendent on the segregation of patients at present in the asylum, and I propose that we request Dr Norman to-day to prepare such a report for our information'.[67] Norman duly reported back to the Committee:

> There are now [24 September 1907] in the Richmond Asylums (Dublin and Portrane) 2,894 patients and, according to the latest official statistics at my disposal, there are in the various workhouses in the district 618 persons of unsound mind of various classes. Thus a total of 3,512 persons have to be considered [...]. I hope I shall not be deemed anxious to minimize the very serious state of things thus revealed, if I point out that there are some indications that the increase in the number of cases of mental disease coming under official cognisance, which has been so alarming of recent years, may be drawing to a close ... the great increase in the asylum population in this district of late years was rather among the old and those past middle age than among the young [...]. This appears to show that the increase of total numbers was not due to racial degeneration, but to altered social and other conditions, together with accumulation.[68]

Given that the census returns for 1901 showed the population for the district to be 574,850, Norman concluded 'that the proportion of the insane to the general population is very high – 1 to 163.6. This is no doubt partly accounted for by the large floating [i.e. homeless] population in Dublin'.[69]

Norman had clear proposals for reforming the management of patients who were 'fairly orderly and capable of work' through 'the establishment of a proper system of family care' which 'is cheaper than institutional treatment, not only through the saving in capital cost, but also because maintenance charges are less':

> This has been found everywhere, but I may exemplify Scotland [...]. If 20 per cent of the chargeable insane in this district were thus provided for the necessity for accommodating in asylums no less than 700 patients would be removed [...]. The attempt was made in the Department of the Seine in France, where 82 patients were placed in family care in 1892. Within fourteen years the number in family care had risen to 1,500. This shows how rapidly the system can, with energy and determination, be adapted to a country where it is perfectly new.[70]

Not all patients, however, were 'fairly orderly and capable of work' and appropriate attention needed to be paid to 'the old, the feeble, the demented':[71]

> Experience, however, has taught that the most hopeless class are also those that really require most careful nursing, and this means expense. The classes that are most neglected in workhouses are the senile, the bedridden, the unclean, the utterly demented, and

the paralytic, and they cause us the most anxiety in an asylum [...]. From what I hear, and from the Inspectors' reports, it is evident that many of the workhouse cases belong to this category. I fear it will be impossible ever to accommodate them cheaply and yet with that humanity which I know every member of the Committee would be anxious to extend to this most pitiable class.[72]

Norman opposed the idea of segregating these patients into an 'auxiliary asylum', noting that 'attempts have been made in several countries, notably in Germany and in the State of New York, to establish "chronic" or "incurable" asylums as distinct from acute asylums, but the system has failed, and has in both instances been given up. It was found that the notion of incurability attached to an asylum demoralised patients and staff, and led to all kinds of abuses'.[73]

Instead of establishing an 'auxiliary asylum', Norman pointed towards developments in the Down District, where 'this question was considered very carefully, and the Committee eventually decided that it would in the end be cheaper to put up additional buildings of a very economical structure on the asylum property. This was done, and the result seems very satisfactory'.[74] In the event, the following years saw many workhouse patients admitted to both the Richmond and Portrane, both of which duly experienced the full range of problems associated with such vast, complex, institutions catering for disparate groups of patients: overcrowding, physical illness, accidents, staff demoralisation and general institutional apathy.

In an effort to cope with this situation, the Richmond had a notably extensive staff including doctors, nurses, porters, 'attendants', 'keepers' and, from 1855, teaching staff.[75] Various tradesmen were employed, including carpenters, engineers, tailors and shoemakers. The relevant management committees regularly discussed matters related to employment,[76] salaries,[77] and discipline,[78] as well as foodstuffs,[79] water,[80] straw,[81] hay,[82] and structural supplies for ongoing developments.[83]

Specific issues relating to staff included the consumption of excessive quantities of alcohol by certain employees. At the meeting of the Richmond Visiting Committee on 13 June 1907, for example, Norman reported that two weeks earlier one of the attendants 'was noticed at the patients' breakfast to be under the influence of drink. I saw him shortly before 9am when he was under the influence of drink. I ordered him to leave the wards and go to his bedroom and stay there. I saw him again about 2pm. He was still under the influence of drink. He boasted that he had not carried out my orders and he disputed my authority. I then suspended him'.[84] The Committee was 'of opinion that he should be dismissed from the services of the Asylum'. Similar cases were reported elsewhere (e.g. Portlaoise).[85]

Alcohol was also a problem among patients at the Richmond: on 12 December 1907, Norman reported that 'since the last meeting of this Committee, eighteen male and twenty-four female patients have been admitted, making a total of forty-two. In at least nine of the male and seven of the female admissions, drink was a main factor in producing insanity'.[86] On the previous Christmas morning (1906), Norman found one male patient 'extremely drunk'[87] and, on investigating the matter further, was concerned about the role of one particular male attendant whose 'conduct in the matter is very suspicious'.[88] Later that day another patient was 'under the influence of drink. The patient got a fit when he was being removed from the dining room, and was subsequently highly excited. Next day he said he had taken some of the attendants' beer (apparently heel taps left in the tumblers)'.[89] Norman noted that 'it is a very serious matter giving a patient drink, or allowing him to get drink'.[90] There was 'only one way to prevent such lamentable occurrences, and that is to have a staff on whose good feeling and sense of duty one can depend'.[91]

One of the central problems that confronted the asylum was the provision of adequate medical care to increasing numbers of inpatients. On 11 April 1907, Norman reported that 'the London County Council Asylums spend a good deal more than we do on the junior medical staff'.[92] He noted 'that there should be one Medical Officer for every hundred patients [...]. In Ireland the proportion is generally low, often dangerously so'.[93] The numbers of patients and assistant medical officers in Irish asylums (1906) and asylums in the London County Council area (1904) are shown in Table 2, supporting Norman's concerns that levels of staffing in many asylums, including the Richmond, were well below the standards he outlined.

Asylum Life: Medical Problems, Accidents and Sports

The challenges faced by asylum doctors in the early 1900s were varied and substantial. In addition to mental illness and alcohol problems, asylum patients presented a range of medical and surgical problems including infective diseases and self-injury. On 10 January 1907, Norman reported that one male patient 'suffered from an extensive incised wound of the throat, self-inflicted'; 'a case of dysentery has occurred in the female house'; and 'an old patient, a deaf mute ... died on December 30 somewhat suddenly and unexpectedly. There was time to summon medical assistance before he expired. On post-mortem examination extensive fatty disease of the heart was found to have existed. The Coroner was notified, but did not consider an inquest necessary'.[94]

On the same date, Norman reported that a female patient 'admitted on January 3, was delivered of a female infant on January 6. Her husband removed the child home from the asylum at once'.[95] One month later, a 'female patient ... an unmarried woman, who was pregnant when admitted on February 1, and suffered from uraemia [a complication of kidney disease] died on February 10, having given birth to a still-born child'.[96]

It was not only the patients who suffered in asylums, illness and injury to staff were also common. On 9 May 1907 the Richmond Visiting Committee heard that a nurse 'who has recently been appointed, has contracted very serious and acute lung trouble'; despite medical intervention, this nurse 'died of acute tubercular consumption on May 26th'.[97] At this time, consumption (pulmonary tuberculosis) was a common cause of death in Ireland in general and in the asylums in particular.[98] Other illnesses in the Richmond and Portrane (and elsewhere) included general paralysis (tertiary syphilis),[99] maniacal chorea (a movement disorder in the context of mental disorder), dysentery (an infection of the intestines),[100] acute rheumatism,[101] extensive fatty disease of the heart',[102] 'extensive valvular disease of the heart',[103] uraemia,[104] epilepsy,[105] and erysipelas (a skin infection).[106]

Similar challenges were reported in other locations, with the mental hospital in Castlebar, for example, reporting fatal cases of paralysis, asthma, bronchitis, wasting disease, epilepsy, chronic

TABLE 2
Numbers of patients and assistant medical officers in Irish asylums (1906) and asylums in the London County Council area (1904).[107]

Location	Asylum	Number of patients	Number of assistant medical officers
Ireland	Antrim	567	1
	Armagh	522	1
	Ballinasloe	1,340	2
	Belfast	1,108	2
	Carlow	441	1
	Castlebar	676	1
	Clonmel	785	1
	Cork	1,570	4
	Downpatrick	723	2
	Ennis	409	1
	Enniscorthy	500	1
	Kilkenny	465	1
	Killarney	577	1
	Letterkenny	704	1
	Limerick	642	1
	Londonderry	519	1
	Maryborough	536	1
	Monaghan	848	2
	Mullingar	925	1
	Omagh	739	1
	Richmond	1,498	5
	Portrane	1332	2
	Sligo	687	1
	Waterford	548	1
London County Council Area	Banstead	2,451	5
	Bexley	2,087	6
	Cave Hill	2,109	5
	Claybury	2394	6
	Colney Hatch	2,153	5
	Hanwell	2,559	6
	Horton	1,964	5

diarrhoea, tuberculosis and liver disease, as well as maniacal exhaustion.[108] The annual death rate in the Castlebar establishment was 8 per cent in 1869, which compared well with other asylums, but was still shockingly high: all of the overcrowded, unhygienic asylums were subject to repeated outbreaks of various fevers and epidemics, which were commonly fatal and attributable in no small part to defective water supply and sewerage arrangements.[109]

On 14 March 1907, Norman reported 'a lamentable casualty to one of the female employees' who 'accidentally set fire to her clothes' and was 'sent to the Mater Misericordiae Hospital, where she died the next day. It is to be observed that this poor woman's petticoats and undergarments were made of that very dangerous material, flannelette'.[110] The following week, the Joint Committee noted receipt of a 'letter on behalf of the attendants and nurses ... making an appeal on behalf of the four orphan children' of the nurse 'who was accidentally burned on the 3rd inst. A sum of money had been collected which would be applied to the relief of the orphans if the Committee would be so kind as to defray the funeral expenses, which amounted to £6 6s 6d' (six pounds, six shillings and sixpence).[111] The Committee agreed to this proposal.

Patients also suffered injuries as a result of being put to work in asylums: on 4 December 1907, the Portrane Visiting Committee heard that one male patient 'who was assisting in repairing the roof of the boot-shop' had 'overbalanced himself, and fell through one of the glass lights to the floor, a distance of perhaps some seventeen feet. He was stunned, but happily seems to have received no serious injury. Dr Donelan rightly points out the danger of putting patients to work on roofs, a practice which certainly must be discontinued'.[112] Another male patient 'was thrown down by another patient ... and sustained a fracture of the right thigh bone. As he is a feeble old man, and this is a serious injury, he will probably die'.

Notwithstanding the difficulties and dangers faced by staff and patients, there were various initiatives to improve safety and working conditions, including improvements to fire alarms[113] and the introduction of electric lights,[114] as well as ongoing amendments to insurance and compensation schemes.[115] Norman was habitually seized of the need for better living conditions for patients and, on 4 December 1907, wondered if the Portrane Committee would 'take into consideration the question of painting the wards generally? The walls are now in a condition in which this could be done properly [...]. May I suggest to the Committee to make a small grant for cheap pictures to decorate the wards? Such objects have a very beneficial effect upon the patients, and tend to bring about the spirit of contentment and tranquility'.[116]

While the Committee deferred this particular decision, there is evidence that some consideration was indeed given to the experiences of patients: a meeting of Richmond District Asylum Joint Committee on 19 September 1907, for example, records a letter from a patient in Portrane 'suggesting that the substitution of a dinner of corned beef instead of curry dinner on Mondays would prove a most acceptable change to the patients'.[117]

Significant emphasis was placed on games and sporting activities for both patients and staff in most asylums, including the Richmond, especially from the mid-nineteenth century onwards.[118] On 14 March 1907, Norman lamented the departure of 'Dr Samuels, who has been about a year and nine months clinical assistant', and was just 'appointed third Assistant Medical Officer to the Warwick Asylum [...]. Dr Samuels will be really a loss to the Institution, as he was not only an excellent medical worker, but was most enthusiastic in promoting games and sports and entertainments among the patients and staff, with whom he was universally and deservedly popular'.[119]

Sport was a recurring theme among the Richmond doctors, including most notably the illustrious and accomplished Daniel Frederick Rambaut (1865–1937).[120] Rambaut was born in Waterford in 1865 and graduated from Trinity with first place in the final medical examination. He spent nine years as Assistant Medical Officer and Pathologist in the Richmond before becoming Medical Superintendent at the County Mental Hospital in Shrewsbury (1902) and at St Andrew's Hospital, Northampton (1913). He became registrar of the MPA in 1924 and RMPA president in 1934. At the Richmond, Rambaut was a strong proponent of occupational therapy, promoting hand-loom weaving and other crafts. He was a keen sportsman and played rugby internationally for Ireland in 1887 and 1888: in February 1887, when Ireland beat England at rugby for the first time, Rambaut converted two tries, both of which he was instrumental in scoring and which decided the historic outcome in Ireland's favour.

Overall, however, despite the benefits of sports and other activities for patients, and despite the efforts of staff, managing a large asylum such as the Richmond or Portrane in the early twentieth century was a complex and arguably impossible task. The exertion took its toll on the hardworking Norman who, on 6 March 1907, was labouring under 'a rather severe cold and lumbago',[121] and died early the following year, apparently of heart disease (Chapter 3).[122] Despite this loss, the Richmond, of course, carried on its business into the turbulent twentieth century, witnessing first hand many tumultuous events in this dramatic period in Irish history including, not least, the Easter Rising of 1916.

The Dublin Asylums during the 1916 Easter Rising: 'Confusional Insanity due to Shock'

The Easter Rising began on 24 April 1916 and lasted for just under a week. The Rising which had been apparently scheduled for Easter Sunday did not commence until Easter Monday, leading to considerable confusion. Some potential participants, including members of Cumann na mBan (a women's paramilitary republican organisation), had expected manoeuvres rather than an uprising.[123] When military activity finally commenced, public confusion about unfolding events meant there was insufficient support for the rebels among the population. The rebels were, in any case, no match for the British forces, and the Rising was crushed relatively quickly. Padraig Pearse (1879–1916) and fourteen other leaders, including Pearse's brother Willie (1881–1916), were court martialled and executed by firing squad. Roger Casement (1864–1916), an Irish nationalist and poet, was later hanged at Pentonville Prison in England for his activities.[124]

Notwithstanding the lack of coordination, confusion and disappointment surrounding the Rising, military activity was not confined to Dublin. In Ashbourne, County Meath, there was an attack on a Royal Irish Constabulary (RIC) Barracks. In Cork, 1,200 volunteers assembled, under the command of Tomás Mac Curtain (1884–1920), although they did not engage in action owing to confusion about orders. In Wexford, one hundred volunteers took over the town of Enniscorthy for three days, before British reinforcements were dispatched and rebel leaders escorted to Arbour

Hill Prison in Dublin. There was also significant military action in Country Galway, where Dr Ada English was active in Cumann na mBan.[125] Military activity in Galway was led by Liam Mellows (1892–1922), a nationalist and Sinn Féin politician.[126]

In Dublin, the Rising had an interesting effect on admission patterns to the asylums. Collins, in his ground breaking work on effects of the Rising on the Richmond, notes, in the first instance, the generally disturbing effect that the Rising had on residents of central Dublin, where the Richmond was located and where 'there was an initial horror by many ... at the outbreak of violence and the destruction of parts of the city'.[127]

In terms of medical care, a Red Cross Hospital with 250 beds had already been established in Dublin Castle to care for soldiers wounded abroad, and the King George V military hospital (now St Bricin's Hospital) provided a further 462 beds. Despite these measures, various other Dublin hospitals, including the psychiatric establishments, were soon to become involved in the conflict, both in terms of providing care and simply getting caught in the crossfire. At St Patrick's Hospital, just south of the river Liffey and near South Dublin Union, the RMS Dr Richard Leeper reported to the Board of Governors that 'we have been in the centre of a battlefield for 10 days surrounded by the armies and this experience is one that few have experienced':

> On my arrival here from Lucan on Easter Monday firing commenced all round this district and continued more or less constantly for 10 days. At many times the rattle of machine gun fire was often continuous for hours and the bullets came into the wards in several places [...]. Bullets entered the New Wing and raked the top ward on the ladies side. When this began I personally placed barricades and padding material such as mattresses in the windows. It seems most wonderful that none of the patients or nurses were killed as the fire lasted for several hours. A guard of 40 soldiers were at the front gate and I and my wife fed these men as well as we could during the rebellion. My greatest anxiety at first was that the Hospital would be occupied by the Rebels [...].[128]

Across the river at the Richmond, the RMS Dr John O'Conor Donelan[129] described Easter week as 'a rather anxious period' and reported 'belligerents' firing into the asylum grounds:

> A rebellion has come and gone, and now that we are able to review the situation it is gratifying to find that our institution has not suffered by the incident [...]. It is a matter of satisfaction at being able to state that neither amongst the patients or staff was there a single casualty, nor did the buildings suffer in any way, although the belligerents on both sides were constantly firing through the grounds. Immediately we found we were in the danger zone we removed the patients from exposed positions; at night their mattresses were placed on the floor, and, of course, they were confined to the house during the disturbance. The gate lodge at Brunswick Street and the grounds in the neighbourhood were occupied by the insurgents for a day and a half, but further than constructing a barricade they did no damage.[130]

While admission rates at the Richmond fell during the Rising itself, the weeks following the Rising produced an interesting change in admission patterns. On 1 May, a woman was admitted with a diagnosis of 'melancholia due to shock' which, as Collins points out, 'may be the first occasion that the word "shock" appears in the admission books of Grangegorman'.[131] The diagnosis of 'shock' then appeared some 10 times at the Richmond during the month of May 1916, immediately following the Rising, with presentations varying from 'melancholia due to shock' to 'mania secondary to shock' to 'confusional insanity due to shock'.[132]

At St Patrick's Hospital, too, Leeper reported to the Governors that two admissions during 'the height of the rebellion' were attributable to 'shock and terror caused by the insurrection'; in one case, the army ambulance 'was fired on whilst conveying the patient to the Hospital'.[133] Leeper's phraseology, especially his use of the word 'terror', has echoes of the terminology used by Hallaran in Cork more than a century earlier, when Hallaran speculated on the possible 'cause of the extraordinary increase of insanity in Ireland' and concluded that the 'terror' of the Irish Rebellion of 1798 and its aftermath played significant roles in the apparent increase in insanity in Cork:

> To account therefore correctly for this unlooked for pressure of a public and private calamity, it appears to be indispensably requisite to take into account the high degree of corporeal as well as of mental excitement, which may be supposed a consequence of continued warfare in the general sense [...]. In some it was evident that terror merely had its sole influence, producing in most instances an incurable melancholia. In others where disappointed ambition had been prevalent, the patients were of an opposite cast, and were in general cheerful, gay and fanciful; but extremely treacherous and vindictive.[134]

Over a hundred years after Hallaran, the relationship between the diagnosis of 'shock', as used at the Richmond in May 1916 (as well as the 'shock and terror' described at St Patrick's Hospital), and the diagnosis of 'shell shock', as it related to soldiers in the First World War at the Richmond War Hospital, is fascinating (below).[135]

There is also evidence that the 1916 Rising itself produced psychiatric symptoms in at least some of the combatants. One witness statement provided by Mr James Coughlan, a member of the Irish Volunteers ('C' Company, 4th Battalion, Dublin Brigade 1914–16), recounted one such story, highlighting the extraordinary leadership and consideration of Éamonn Ceannt (1881–1916; one of the leaders of the Rising, later executed), even after his group of rebels, following surrender, were brought by the British to Richmond Barracks, in Inchicore, Dublin:

> Next we had a visit from about twenty 'G' men (detectives from Dublin Castle) who also carefully scrutinised us. On sight (without any questioning as to name) they picked out our leaders and other prominent republicans and ordered them to the opposite side of the room. I recognised a good number of those on the opposite side of the room as men who were subsequently court-martialled.
>
> When E. Ceannt was picked out, he called the attention of the senior British officer present to one of our garrison, a volunteer named Fogarty, who had become

mentally deranged. (Fogarty, I learned from my comrades on Tuesday, was in the same room with Frank Burke when the latter was killed on that morning.) Fogarty, I was told, lighted his pipe when near a window. F. Burke leaned across from the other side of the window to light his cigarette from Fogarty's lighted match, and presented an easy target to a British soldier in the hospital across the roadway. As F. Burke fell, with a bullet through the left side of the neck, an officer, Lieutenant 'Wilsie' Byrne, I think, entered the room and, sizing up the situation, exclaimed to Fogarty: 'You are responsible for that man's death'.

Shortly after this incident – when I was told of it – I visited the room and saw F. Burke's body lying in the pool of blood where he died. From the instant of F. Burke's death until some weeks later Fogarty was mentally deranged, and during the remainder of Easter week with us he was kept disarmed, and a volunteer – Jim Kenny – was detailed to keep him company and out of harm's way. It was distressing at times to watch Fogarty's reactions. On one occasion during a meal in the kitchen W.T. Cosgrave [another Irish Volunteer who went on to serve as first President of the Executive Council of the Irish Free State from 1922 to 1932] was relating an incident that happened at a Dublin Corporation meeting, at which one member called another 'Traitor'. Fogarty muttered that W.T. Cosgrave was referring to him (Fogarty), and Jim Kenny subsequently had trouble trying to convince him to the contrary.

Thus E. Ceannt's thoughts on being separated from us to face court-martial were in consideration of one of the humblest of those who had served under him.[136]

Given Ceannt's consideration for his mentally ill colleague under very difficult circumstances in Richmond Barracks, it is noteworthy that the renovated barracks now houses a Health Service Executive (HSE; public healthcare provider in Ireland) community mental health service and primary care centre, among other facilities.

In light of these events, and especially the traumatic nature of the 1916 conflict, it is clear that the Easter Rising produced a significant change in admission patterns at the Richmond Asylum in Dublin, and that the word 'shock' came into prominent diagnostic use in the month following the Rising. This was also the month just prior to the opening of the Richmond War Hospital at the Richmond Asylum, an interesting establishment which explicitly aimed to care for shell shocked and traumatised soldiers returning from the First World War.

The Richmond War Hospital (1916–19): Visions, Insomnia and 'Noises in his Head'

The First World War (1914–18) was a significant event in the development of psychiatry in Ireland and Great Britain. Over the course of the war, almost nine million soldiers served in the British army, of whom approximately one million were killed. Over 200,000 Irish soldiers fought, of whom up to 35,000 died.[137] Many more received physical injuries or had to return home owing to mental troubles which occurred during the conflict and which, for many, seemed attributable to it.

The Richmond War Hospital was a 32 bed establishment on the grounds of the larger Richmond Asylum in Dublin which, from 16 June 1916 until 23 December 1919, treated soldiers with shell shock and other mental disorders that necessitated their return from the battlefield.[138] Over this three and a half year period, 362 soldiers were admitted and more than half of these were treated and enabled to return home without ever being certified insane, much to the satisfaction of RMS Donelan.[139]

The hospital was established following a request from the military authorities for a facility specifically for soldiers with nervous and mental troubles.[140] This need had become apparent over the previous two years as soldiers complained of both physical injuries *and* psychological symptoms such as loss of memory, dizziness, tremor, headache, poor concentration, tinnitus and hypersensitivity to noise.[141] The term 'shell shock' evolved to describe such cases which developed following exposure to shell fire but were not associated with identifiable physical injury.[142] Over time, a series of psychiatric facilities throughout Great Britain and Ireland was made available to assess and treat such soldiers when they were sent back from the Front.

While the Richmond War Hospital was located on the grounds of the main Richmond Asylum and was an administrative element within the larger institution, the War Hospital was, in many important respects, separate from the main establishment. In the first instance, a new and separate block was put at the disposal of the army for the War Hospital, and its patients did not appear on the main asylum's record books.[143] Moreover, the army agreed to pay twenty-one shillings a week per occupied bed – a rate that was distinctly advantageous for the asylum managers: the weekly cost per patient was under fourteen shillings – and the army provided clothing for its own patients, making the arrangement an especially lucrative one for the broader asylum.[144]

The War Hospital was staffed by Richmond Asylum staff, and while this arrangement was not without complexity,[145] there was little time for hesitation because immediately following its opening, soldiers began to arrive at the Richmond War Hospital with all of the signs and symptoms of shell shock and various other mental and physical disorders. The case of Private VW is a good example.[146]

Private VW was a 23-year-old Presbyterian private admitted from King George V Hospital (a war hospital dealing with physical injuries, in Dublin). On admission, Private VW's 'tongue [was] tremulous. Speech stammering and hesitating'. Mentally, he 'has headache every now and again and suffers from noises in his head at times', and he also complained of 'visions' and 'insomnia'. Private VW had joined the army in 1911 and 'was out in India at the outbreak of the war. He states he was blown out of a trench at Arras [a city in northern France, associated with the Battle of Arras, 1917] and since then his speech has been affected'.

One week after admission, Private VW was 'quiet and well-conducted and gives no trouble. He states he had no voices in his head since he came here and that he is feeling much better'. This improvement was sustained and one month after admission Private VW continued 'to improve. He states he is now feeling all right in every way except that he is not physically strong. Sleeps and eats well'. Two months after admission, Private VW was 'discharged and sent to his home'.

Private VW clearly demonstrated many of the symptoms commonly associated with psychological problems among soldiers at this time: tremulousness, speech problems, headache, 'visions' and 'insomnia', all following exposure to shell fire in France. Overall, soldiers admitted to the Richmond War Hospital presented with a wide variety of symptoms, many, but not all, of which accorded with contemporary clinical descriptions of shell shock, commonly combined with depression.[147]

As the diagnosis of shell shock became increasingly common, a broad range of treatments were proposed across Great Britain and Ireland. Some of the initial treatments were essentially disciplinary in nature, highlighting an apparent conflict between private intentions of the soldier and a sense of public duty, leading to the use of isolation, restricted diet and electric shocks to alter soldiers' behaviour.[148] Other treatments were more psychological in tone, regarding war neurosis as attributable, at least in part, to unconscious psychological conflict in the soldier's mind. This idea led to treatments such as hypnosis and abreaction, which involved soldiers re-experiencing or reliving traumatic memories in an effort to purge them of their emotional impact.

In all cases, there was a strong emphasis on prompt treatment, cognitive restructuring of traumatic experiences (i.e. thinking differently about the past and present),[149] and collaboration with the therapist in the search for a cure. Many of these therapies have certain similarities with current cognitive and behavioural approaches to post-traumatic stress disorder.[150] There were, however, other approaches to the management of shell shock which certain authorities viewed as equally if not more effective including, most notably, approaches based primarily on rest and less intrusive forms of therapy.[151]

This approach, based primarily on rest and recuperation, was in plentiful evidence at the Richmond War Hospital, where soldiers were taken out on trips, and singers and dramatic groups visited the hospital.[152] Additional treatments were also given, including hot and cold baths, bromides, antipyrin and citrate of caffeine.[153]

The use of baths was a continuation of the longstanding practice of hydrotherapy (e.g. regular showers) in asylums (Chapter 1),[154] and would later be explicitly recommended for shell shock in the 1922 *Report of the War Office Committee of Enquiry into 'Shell-Shock'*.[155] Antipyrin, also known as phenazone, was an analgesic, nonsteroidal anti-inflammatory medication which reduced pain and body temperature, and was thus very useful for returning soldiers.[156] Caffeine, too, was commonly used to promote wellbeing during this period.[157]

Bromides, also used at the War Hospital, have a distinctly chequered history in psychiatry, having been used to induce sleep towards the end of the 1800s, but then abandoned, possibly owing to toxicity.[158] Fletcher's hydrobromate syrup was nonetheless still in use for the treatment of various nervous ailments and other disorders in the early 1900s, and was used at the Richmond War Hospital.[159]

As well as shell shock and other mental illness, physical illnesses such as epilepsy and malaria were apparent among soldiers at the Richmond War Hospital, as they were at other war hospitals, including Lord Derby Hospital in Warrington which, like the Richmond, also recorded significant rates of discharge and recovery.[160] Over the three and a half year period it operated, the Richmond War Hospital treated 362 soldiers, of whom more than half were enabled to return home, although a few returned to battle and a small number were transferred to the main asylum system.[161] In addition, some 790 soldiers and sailors (of whom 576 served overseas) were admitted to general asylums between 1915 and 1919, apparently owing to the war.[162]

Overall, the Richmond War Hospital provided a significant contrast to the general asylum system owing to its brief inpatient stays, generally positive treatment outcomes, emphasis on non-medical interventions (e.g. trips, drama), and facilitation of voluntary admission status for its patients, thus avoiding the stigma of involuntary detention; this was a reform that was to gain a strong foothold in the Irish asylum system more generally only with the rather belated introduction of the Mental Treatment Act 1945.[163]

Experiences at the Richmond and other war hospitals also brought doctors and others to realise that even 'normal' people could break down in situations of sufficient trauma and stress,[164] and this was in stark contrast to the pre-existing theory of degeneration; i.e. the idea that mental illness was largely biological and genetic in origin, and worsened with each generational cycle.[165] In addition, the experience of shell shock generated new scope for the practice of psychotherapy, much of which appears more aligned with later movements into cognitive therapy rather than the Freudian approaches which had been so evident in many places (but not, interestingly, Ireland) up until then.[166] Moreover, the First World War, with the psychological *and* physical symptoms its soldiers experienced, provided further evidence that there often was no identifiable physical cause for psychological symptoms, but rather a unity between psychological and physical phenomena,[167] supporting Drapes's comments about the folly of 'psychophysical parallelism', or the spurious division between mental and physical symptoms (Chapter 3).[168]

Finally, the Richmond War Hospital plays a significant part in Ireland's memory and commemoration of the First World War and, in particular, historical recognition of the contribution made by the Irish to the war effort. While the psychological problems associated with the war were certainly somewhat recognised at the time (e.g. through the establishment of the War Hospital)[169] and, to a certain extent, in the early aftermath of the war (e.g. in Liam O'Flaherty's novel, *Return of the Brute*),[170] there was limited further remembrance of the psychological suffering of soldiers until the centenary of the commencement of the war, in 2014.[171] The Richmond War Hospital is an important part of that forgotten story.

Case Study: Michael, 'Insane on Arraignment'

While soldiers were being treated for shell shock at the Richmond War Hospital and elsewhere, the rest of Ireland's asylum system continued to experience apparently inexorable problems of increasing rates of admission and chronic overcrowding. The Central Criminal Lunatic Asylum faced particular problems with rising committal rates, increased use of 'fitness to plead' procedures in the courts (peaking between 1910 and 1920),[172] and ongoing challenges relating to the complex mix of social, psychiatric and medical problems among patients, including mental illnesses such as 'mania' and *folie à plusieurs*,[173] physical illnesses such as syphilis[174] and tuberculosis,[175] and various issues relating to intellectual disability.[176]

The latter concern, stemming from apparent intellectual disability, is well demonstrated by the case of Michael, a 35-year-old 'messenger' who was, according to archival case records, committed to the Central Criminal Lunatic Asylum in the 1890s having been charged with 'assault' and declared 'insane on arraignment'.[177] Michael was sent to the Central Criminal Lunatic Asylum, to remain there 'at the Lord Lieutenant's pleasure'; i.e. indefinitely, at the discretion of the chief administrator of government in Ireland.

Admission notes record a diagnosis of 'congenital imbecile' and that Michael's 'expression of face is characteristic, especially while laughing. His gait is slouching; [he] manages his legs badly [...]. He has slight nystagmus. Teeth are decayed, irregular and somewhat crowded together. The hard palate is much arched. His speech is indistinct, halting and stammering, and becomes much worse if patient is excited'. Michael was 'quick-tempered, pettish and requires to be humoured. His memory is bad'. Michael's 'appetite is large' and he was 'subject to attacks of vomiting after meals due to over-eating'.

Four days after admission, Michael was adjusting quickly to institutional life and 'much improved. His expression of face is brighter and more intelligent-looking. [He] is a very good house-cleaner'. Eight months later, Michael was 'much brighter and tidier, and is useful and trustworthy. He presents the usual physical characteristics of imbecility and no improvement in mental power is possible'.

Three years after admission, Michael was 'very childish in his ways' but 'very quiet and well conducted'. He took 'part in the cricket and has a very exaggerated opinion of himself on that subject'. Eight years after admission, Michael was playing cricket and football and 'enjoys life well'.

After fourteen years at the hospital, Michael developed 'pneumonia of the right lung' and was treated with milk, beef tea, eggs, digitalis and blisters. As his condition worsened, he received 'strychnine, digitalis and morphia'. Some days later Michael died, having spent the final fourteen years of his life in the hospital.

Michael's case history is interesting because it demonstrates clearly the emphasis placed on gainful occupation ('a very good house-cleaner') and sporting activity ('cricket, football, etc.') in asylums in the late nineteenth and early twentieth centuries, consistent with the principles of 'moral management'.[178] Michael's eventual, fatal respiratory illness also demonstrates the broader problem with physical ill health (especially infective illnesses) in the overcrowded, unsanitary institutions.

These challenges were compounded by the absence of effective treatments for illnesses such as pneumonia, which commonly proved fatal. Michael's treatments included strychnine, which was used throughout the nineteenth century for 'shock', poor muscle tone, reduced appetite and 'weak bladder'; digitalis, used for 'shock', 'weak heart' and irregular heartbeat; and morphine, used for diarrhea, cough, asthma, pain, gall stones and kidney colic.[179]

In addition to developing physical illnesses, individuals with intellectual disability who engaged in offending behaviour and were committed to asylums presented a range of other challenges to physicians and asylum managers. In 1907, Norman, at the Richmond, reported that there were 'in the Asylum about 200 idiots' and 'an ordinary asylum is not a suitable place for them in any way'.[180] Notwithstanding Norman's concern, however, there is still a remarkable dearth of systematic information about the institutional experiences of individuals with intellectual disability in the asylums of nineteenth- and early-twentieth-century Ireland.[181]

Overall, it is likely that the institutional experiences of this group were similar, in at least some respects, to those of individuals without intellectual disability who were similarly institutionalised, and who tended to experience lengthy periods of detention, poor physical and mental health, and a relatively high risk of dying in the asylum.[182] It is also likely that the institutional experiences of individuals with intellectual disability in Ireland were similar, in at least some respects, to those of individuals with intellectual disability in other jurisdictions during this period;[183] there is, however, a similar paucity of systematic information about the historical experiences of this group in most jurisdictions (not just Ireland).

This is especially regrettable because the problems presented by individuals with intellectual disability who offend were to prove remarkably persistent: even in the early 2000s there were substantial problems with service provision for this group, and particular concern about the accumulation of individuals with intellectual disability in prisons. In the United Kingdom, for example, up to one in five young offenders had an intellectual disability in the early 2000s.[184] The fact that these individuals so often end up in prisons appears attributable, at least in part, to a general paucity of support and accommodation facilities in the community appropriate to their needs.

In the early 2000s, the Irish College of Psychiatrists re-emphasised the need for dedicated service provision for this population, recommending that Ireland's health service should 'make the development of a national forensic learning disability service a strategic priority'.[185] The College proposals, along with the recommendations in *A Vision for Change*,[186] provided a set of clear, reasonable and achievable measures, and progress was duly made in recent years, although much still remains to be done.[187]

In the early 1900s, these kinds of policy solutions were in especially short supply and the asylums continued to grow, year on year. There were, however, nascent signs of change and the resilient, if occasionally ineffectual, progressive tradition in Irish psychiatry was to find new champions, not least of whom was Dr Adeline English, a patriot and asylum doctor who spent almost four decades working to improve the plight of the mentally ill in Ireland – and attain Irish freedom.

Dr Ada English: Patriot and Psychiatrist

The early twentieth century saw considerable discussion about reform of mental health services in Ireland, even as admission rates continued to rise precipitously. The paradox of progressive, reform-minded individuals working in institutions which continued grimly to expand is clearly demonstrated by the life and work of Dr Ada (Adeline) English (1875–1944).[188]

As one of the first generation of female medical graduates in Ireland and Great Britain, and an asylum doctor who championed novel treatments for mental illness (occupational therapy, convulsive therapy), English occupies an important position in Irish medical history. Like her close contemporaries, Lynn,[189] Dr Dorothy Stopford Price,[190] Dr Brigid Lyons Thornton[191] and Fleury (Chapter 3),[192] English was active in both medical and political affairs.

English was born on 10 January 1875 in Cahersiveen, County Kerry. When she was a young child the family moved to Mullingar, County Westmeath, where her father was a pharmacist and member of Mullingar Town Commissioners. English's grandfather, Richard, was master of the nearby Old Castle Workhouse and the destitution that English witnessed in others suffering affected her deeply.[193]

English received her secondary education at the Loreto Convent in Mullingar and graduated from the Royal University as a doctor in 1903, after attending the Catholic University School of Medicine in Cecilia Street, Dublin.[194] English was tutored in Irish by Pádraig Pearse[195] and became a medical officer to the Irish Volunteers (Óglaigh na hÉireann) and an executive member of Cumann na mBan.[196] She was a friend of Liam Mellows, who led the 1916 Easter Rising in Galway,[197] and it is reported that English served as medical officer for the wounded rebels in Galway.[198]

On 20 January 1921, during the War of Independence, English was arrested in Ballinasloe[199] and tried by court martial in Galway for possession of illegal nationalist documents.[200] English served just part of her nine month sentence in Galway gaol, before it was commuted on 15 May 1921[201] and she was released early owing to food poisoning.[202]

While in prison, English was elected unopposed to Dáil Eireann (Irish parliament), as a Sinn Féin candidate for the National University of Ireland constituency.[203] She was an active participant in Dáil debates and on 26 August 1921 supported Sean MacEoin's nomination of Éamon de Valera (1882–1975) as President of the Irish Republic:

> I have very great pleasure in supporting the resolution put before you by Commandant MacEoin. There is no necessity for me to praise Éamonn de Valera to the men and women of the Dáil or to the men and women of Ireland. He has been tested in times of the greatest stress both as a soldier and statesman. We all know how he has come out of it – and the enemy knows it. The fact that for the past forty years the enemy has refused Home Rule and now are offering most cheerfully what they called 'Dominion Status,' shows what has been done by him. As a new member of the Dáil, I should like to say how much we appreciate him and how much we are impressed by him. His desire for the fullest criticism, and his openness to any suggestions and readiness to accept them if they are any good; his courage and manifest honesty in placing before us everything which he is recommending to us, leaves us, even the dullest of us, under no delusion as to what we are asked to do. I have very much pleasure in supporting the motion.[204]

De Valera was duly elected President of the Irish Republic and the Dáil nominated 'envoys plenipotentiary' for negotiations with Great Britain. On 4 January 1922, English spoke in the Dáil debate on the resultant Anglo-Irish Treaty, which proposed the establishment of an 'Irish Free State' with dominion status: 'We repudiate the Republic if this Treaty is passed; we repudiate it absolutely. It is a complete surrender and we don't get peace by it, but we get the certainty of a bitter split and division in this country'.[205] Unlike most of her female colleagues in the Dáil, English had not personally experienced family bereavement, and emphasised that her opposition to the Treaty was not based solely on personal loss:[206]

> There is a point I want to make. I think that it was a most brave thing today to listen to the speech by the deputy from Sligo [Alexander McCabe] in reference to the women members of An Dáil, claiming that they only have the opinions they have because they

have a grievance against England, or because their men folk were killed and murdered by England's representatives in this country. It was a most unworthy thing for any man to say here. I can say this more freely because, I thank my God, I have no dead men to throw in my teeth as a reason for holding the opinions I hold. I should like to say that I think it most unfair to the women Teachtaí because Miss MacSwiney had suffered at England's hands. That, a Chinn Chomhairle, is really all I want to say. I am against the Treaty, and I am very sorry to be in opposition to *(nodding towards Mr [Arthur] Griffith [Irish writer, politician and, later, President of Dáil Éireann] and Mr [Michael] Collins [Irish revolutionary leader and politician]). (Cheers).*[207]

At the next election, on 16 June 1922, pro-Treaty candidates won a majority of votes and English was one of the anti-Treaty candidates not re-elected.[208] Predictably, English supported the anti-Treaty side in the Civil War and it is reported that she served with Cathal Brugha (1874–1922), an Irish revolutionary, at the Hammam Hotel on Sackville Street (later O'Connell Street) in Dublin's city centre in June 1922.[209] The Civil War ended in May 1923 and English played little further part in public life,[210] although she supported Mary MacSwiney's alternative, republican 'Dáil Éireann' in 1929.[211]

Throughout these events English worked steadily at Connaught District Lunatic Asylum (later St Bridgid's Hospital) in Ballinasloe and, while her political involvements were substantial, English's greatest contribution was through her medical career.[212]

English's political interests were immediately apparent after she started in Ballinasloe in September 1904: she campaigned to have the Galway Arms emblazoned on the buttons of the staff uniforms, instead of Queen Victoria,[213] and promoted the use of Irish manufactured products.[214] English befriended powerful local figures, including Dr John Dignan, who became Bishop of the Diocese of Clonfert in 1924. Happily for English, her nationalist views and activities were entirely in tune with the highly politicised positions assumed by the Committee of Management of Ballinasloe District Asylum, which was also pointedly nationalist in outlook (below).

During English's decades in Ballinasloe, many new treatments were introduced[215] and English developed occupational therapy to a high degree,[216] being especially concerned that patients were gainfully occupied.[217] The early introduction of convulsive therapy in Ballinasloe, in 1939, is discussed in Chapter 5 and occurred during English's time there. In addition to novel treatments, however, English also recognised the importance of appropriate amusement for patients (e.g. sports, attending the cinema) and pursued these vigorously.[218]

Other entertainments in mental hospitals at this time included dances and music.[219] The asylum in Cork, for example, had an excellent orchestra in the 1860s and attendants were often recruited chiefly for their musical skills: the position of tailor remained vacant for some time at the Cork asylum because none of the applicants had musical qualifications.[220] In the late 1800s, the indefatigable RMS, Dr James A. Eames, organised a performance of Gilbert and Sullivan's operetta 'Patience' at the asylum, despite the customary opposition from the governors. In the end, the operetta was performed on two consecutive evenings; 1,500 people attended, including 500 patients; and the production received a glowing review in the *Cork Constitution*.[221] The remarkable

Eames was a member of the *Société Médicale Mentale de Belgique* and became president of the MPA in 1885,[222] but was also the first MPA president to die in office, as he succumbed unexpectedly to a carbuncle on the neck on 17 July 1886, at the age of 53 years; a fund was established to provide for his family.[223]

Back in Ballinalsoe in the early 1900s, English was, in addition to attending to her medical duties and political interests, involved in a range of other activities in and around Ballinasloe. In 1913, for example, she applied (unsuccessfully) for the post of 'Tuberculosis Officer for Roscommon'[224] and, during the two World Wars, she organised Red Cross lectures.[225] In 1914 she became the first statutory lecturer in 'mental diseases' at University College Galway.[226] This was not the first university teaching psychiatry in Ireland, however, as lectures were provided in Cork from the mid-1870s (at the instigation of the determined Eames);[227] the Royal University in Dublin was examining in mental diseases in 1885;[228] and Trinity introduced the undergraduate study of mental diseases in 1893.[229]

In 1921, English was offered the position of RMS of Sligo Mental Hospital, but declined, refusing to be separated from her patients in Ballinasloe.[230] In 1940, following an enquiry in Ballinasloe, English took over as acting RMS, by which time the number of inpatients had increased to 1,887. In 1941, English was finally substantively appointed as RMS,[231] in her late 60s. She occupied the post of RMS for fourteen months before, on 11 August 1942, she submitted her letter of resignation.[232] English died in January 1944, at the Private Nursing Home, Mount Pleasant, Ballinasloe. At her own request, she was buried alongside her patients at Creagh Cemetry, adjacent to Ballinasloe Mental Hospital (now St Brigid's Hospital).

Overall, English belonged to a remarkable group of Irish women doctors, each of whom made substantial contributions to the development of Irish medical services and improvement of social conditions, especially for the poor and socially excluded. In April 2016, as part of the 1916 commemorations, a plaque commemorating English was unveiled on Pearse Street in Mullingar, site of English's Medical Hall.[233] In May 2016, a plaque and bench in her memory were unveiled at the Loreto College in Mullingar, which English had attended more than a century earlier.

There are particular parallels between the life and career of English and those of Dr Kathleen Lynn: like English, Lynn was a TD (Teachta Dála; member of Irish parliament) in the 1920s but was also vice-president of Sinn Féin (1923–27); in 1919, Lynn co-founded St Ultan's Hospital for Infants in Dublin and, throughout her career, worked tirelessly to improve the medical and social wellbeing of Dublin's poor.[234] Like English and Lynn, Dr Dorothy Stopford Price also combined political involvement with committed, progressive medical practice and played a key role in the eradication of tuberculosis.[235] There are also similarities between English's life and work and those of Dr Brigid Lyons Thornton[236] and – of course – Fleury (Chapter 3 and below).[237]

Like her contemporaries, English remained deeply concerned with the plight of the poor throughout her medical career and consistently linked this concern with the need for political activism: in 1921, she participated in the Irish Catholic Truth Society's Conference at the Mansion House and emphasised the importance of social and political engagement.[238]

English also advocated strongly for reform of Ireland's mental health legislation. In August 1939, when English was Acting RMS, the Committee of Management at Ballinasloe Lunatic Asylum issued a strong resolution 'calling for a revision of the existing lunacy laws dealing with both the reception and after treatment of mental cases'.[239] When the revised law was finally passing through Seanad Éireann (the upper house of the Irish legislature) on 19 April 1945 (Chapter 5), Senator Helena Concannon paid heartfelt tribute to English:

> One melancholy note resounded in my heart when I read in the newspapers last November the report of the Second Reading in the Dáil of the measure we are now considering. It was that the late Dr Ada English had not been spared to be present when the Parliamentary Secretary was introducing it. He knows – because he, too, had the privilege of knowing well that great-hearted woman – all that I have in mind when I speak thus. All her life, since she entered the mental hospital service as a brilliant and beautiful girl until she was laid to rest, as she herself desired, in the little God's Acre near Ballinasloe, where many of her poor patients await the Resurrection – she worked for the principles embodied in this Bill. The things that make it memorable and worthwhile are things for which she tirelessly pleaded. Some of them were accepted, in principle at least, when in 1925 the term 'mental hospital' replaced the old, depressing designation of 'lunatic asylum'. Implicit in the new designation was the acceptance of the thesis that mental disease is not a crime, but a disease, like any other disease, capable of being cured if proper curative measures can be applied in time. A mental hospital is, therefore, first of all, a place for such curative treatment and not merely a place of detention for unfortunates thus afflicted. She always felt that conditions should be such that the physicians in charge should not be so overburdened with administrative detail that they could not spare the time needed for their own proper job – time to study their patients and to give them the undivided care their condition calls for. Another necessity she tirelessly stressed was that of establishing mental clinics, such as are contemplated in the Bill, where incipient mental disorders might be detected, and their progress stayed by expert treatment to which patients might voluntarily submit themselves. This aim is recognised, too, in important provisions of the present Bill.[240]

Throughout her career, English's trademark combination of republican activism and progressive medical work was made possible by the fact that English's political position accorded closely with that of the asylum management in Ballinasloe. Interestingly, the Ballinasloe asylum was by no means unique in this regard, as similar nationalist sentiment held sway in asylums elsewhere too, including Carlow, the Richmond and Portrane asylums among others.

Nationalism in the Asylum System: 'The Division of Ireland We Will Not Have'

English's nationalist outlook was widely shared among staff in Ireland's public asylums during the early 1900s, owing, as Finnane points out, to specific reforms of local government and the Local

Government Act 1898, which ended landlord control of local government,[241] as administration of asylums moved from Boards of Governors to County Councils.[242] But English was especially fortunate to work in Ballinasloe District Asylum because the Ballinasloe Committee of Management appears to have been particularly outspoken on this topic. Minutes from the Committee meeting of 12 June 1916, for example, record the following resolution passed by the Ballinasloe Committee:

> That we the members of the Committee of Management of the Ballinasloe Asylum, representing both the counties of Galway and Roscommon, determinedly protest against the exclusion of any portion of Ulster from the scheme of national government now about to be established in this country, and we call upon Mr John Redmond and the Irish party to oppose anything that would bring about an accentuation of the religious bitterness that apparently exists between the north and the rest of Ireland. We are willing to concede anything in justice to the bona-fide fears of our northern fellow countrymen, but the division of Ireland we will not have.[243]

The Committee agreed that copies of this resolution would 'be sent to Prime Minister, Mr David Lloyd George, and Mr John Redmond'. This strongly nationalist tone persisted into the 1920s: at the meeting of 11 July 1921, for example, the Committee resolved that 'henceforth no communication of any kind be forwarded to any department of the British Government in Ireland'.[244] When English was arrested in 1921, the minutes of the Committee merely record Dr Mills, RMS, drily informing them that 'Dr English is under detention in a government institution, consequently I engaged the services of Dr Ward as *locum tenens*'.[245] There was no further comment on the matter.

English continued in this vein throughout her time in Ballinalsoe. For example, she used offers of jobs in the Ballinasloe asylum to persuade men to resign from the RIC and thus undermine it; recruited hospital staff based, at least in part, on their ability to play hurling, as part of a careful build-up of nationalist sentiment in the institution; and might also have helped de Valera and others to hide out at the Ballinalsoe asylum during times of trouble.[246] While these kinds of nationalist gestures were occasionally lampooned (e.g. in the MPA's *Journal of Mental Science*),[247] they were important indicators of the growth of nationalist feeling in the asylums. Similarly in Cork, the Committee of Management declared that utensils, delph and crockery stamped with the crown were no longer acceptable; the asylum was now to be known as *Tig na nGeailt i gCrocaigh* (Cork Mental Hospital, in Irish), a title which became official under the Local Government Act 1925.[248]

In Dublin, Fleury was also deeply involved in the nationalist movement, often using the Richmond and Portrane asylums to conceal and assist wounded Republican fugitives. In a Witness Statement supplied to the Bureau of Military History (1913–21), Eilís Bean Uí Chonaill of Clontarf (a member of the Cumann na mBan Executive) recounted the 'removal' of several injured Irish Volunteers to safe houses during the War of Independence, including the injured 'Mr Peter Hunt of Sligo', 'one of the most "hunted" men of the time'. She reported that 'a cab brought the patient from a house in Prussia Street to the house of Dr Fleury in the Richmond Asylum',[249] and thus to safety and medical care.

Mrs Mary Flannery Woods of Rathfarnham, another member of Cumman na mBan, confirms Fleury's role at the Portrane Asylum:

> Dr Fleury of Portrane Asylum was wonderful. She took a lot of men from me who were suffering from various ailments. She took James Brogan when he was suffering from bronchitis and again when he was burnt on the railway. Tormey was also burnt on this occasion and was treated by Dr Fleury. How she cared for them these men told me afterwards. She would first look after her mental patients, then the men I had committed to her care and last she would take her own breakfast. She spent her money on cigarettes and comforts for our men [...]. When Free State troops would swoop on the 'Home' the men 'on the run' used go about the grounds and were mistaken, as intended, of course, for mental patients. Mr Cosgrave's Government found out this and took measures to put an end to it – so I was informed but not by Dr Fleury.[250]

More generally, Woods commented that 'the doctors of Dublin were wonderful. I may have forgotten Dr Lynn and others whose names I cannot remember at the moment. Yes, another – Dr Stopford Price'.[251]

In another fascinating witness statement throwing dramatic light on republicanism within the asylum system, Mr William P. Corrigan, legal advisor to the Joint Committee at Grangegorman, recounts that, in late 1920, the Joint Committee declined to supply its 'books for audit' by the British Local Government Board 'having previously sworn allegiance to Dáil Éireann', with the consequence that funding was cut off.[252] The chairperson, Mrs Jennie Wyse Power (feminist, nationalist and founder member of Sinn Féin), stated that the asylum had food for the patients for a day or two only, but the bank reportedly still declined to supply money on the deeds of the asylum without the consent of the Local Government Board.

The standoff led Corrigan to consult with an old acquaintance, Mr W.E. Wylie, K.C. (King's Counsel; later Judge Wylie),[253] who usually advised the Joint Committee, at his residence:

> In the course of the discussion I [Corrigan] pointed out that if the Committee could not raise the money without the consent of the Local Government Board the Committee would have no alternative but to open the gates and release some 400 inmates. Mr Wylie stated 'this will be a nice town to live in with Black and Tans [Royal Irish Constabulary Special Reserve], I.R.A. [Irish Republican Army] and lunatics abroad'. He then asked me 'what are you fellows fighting for' and following a discussion about this he then said it was a pity that something could not be done to bring the two sides together. He asked me would Arthur Griffith and Michael Collins meet a British Representative. He suggested Sir John Anderson, the General Permanent Under-Secretary in Dublin Castle, as the British Representative and I agreed to make some enquiries and let Mr Wylie know the result of same. I interviewed Arthur Griffith in the Bailey Restaurant and told him of my conversation

with Mr Wylie. He stated that he would not be in favour of Michael Collins meeting any representative as his appearance was not known to the British but he thought if Collins was agreeable, he, Griffith, who was well known to the Authorities would be agreeable to meet the British Representative. After Griffith had consulted Collins he informed me that he was willing to meet a British Representative and I got in touch with Mr Wylie and informed him and it was agreed that the meeting should take place in my office on the following Sunday (from my recollection this was the Sunday after the shooting of Lynch in the Exchequer Hotel).[254] I undertook to guarantee the safe conduct of Sir John Anderson and Mr Wylie gave a similar undertaking with regard to Griffith. The two men came to my office on the Sunday as arranged.[255] One took the front office and the other the back office and Mr Wylie and myself acted as intermediaries between them. I do not think the two men actually met during the course of the proceedings, but I think these were the first steps towards peace negotiations.[256]

Back at Portrane, Fleury's activism landed her in trouble with the authorities. On 10 April 1923, Fleury was arrested for treating wounded Republicans at the Portrane asylum.[257] While in Kilmainham Gaol, Fleury's medical skills proved invaluable, as medical specialists were denied entry to the gaol, despite a clear and demonstrated need.[258] Fleury was also interned at the North Dublin Union building, which had been requisitioned by the British Military in 1918 as a barracks and transferred to the Irish Free State Army in 1922.[259] In the North Dublin Union internment camp, Fleury joined a group of militant female prisoners who, in May 1923, formed a Prisoners' Council, with Una Gordon as chairperson. Fleury took responsibility (from the prisoners' perspective) for the hospital ward, although there already was an official prison medical officer, Dr Laverty.

Fleury's medical skills were in high demand among the internees. Albinia Lucy Brodrick, for example, was arrested on 1 May 1923 in Kerry, having acquired a gunshot wound to her leg while tending to wounded Republicans in Listowel.[260] On arrival in the North Dublin Union, Brodrick promptly went on hunger strike and refused medical care from Dr Laverty, but permitted Fleury to tend to her, as a fellow internee.

The prisoners at the North Dublin Union were extremely vocal and active, protesting strongly against their conditions. Some escaped over the walls into the neighbouring Broadstone railway station. In May 1923, a second Prisoners' Council was elected, with Fleury staying on as medical officer with responsibility for the hospital ward.[261] By this time, the hospital ward had accommodation for 20 patients, who presented a broad range of medical problems, including epilepsy, scarlet fever, scabies and lice.[262] Hygiene was a constant problem and Fleury worked with the prison medical officer to maintain hygiene among the internees.

In June 1923, however, the governor of the internment camp refused to sanction the carrying of coal to the hospital ward and Fleury withdrew her services in protest.[263] Some of the prisoners went on hunger strike. Early the following month, on 7 July 1923, Fleury was released and promptly denounced conditions in the North Dublin Union in a strongly worded article in *Irish Nation*

(Éire), a Republican paper. Fleury wrote that the internment camp was filthy, 'scabies and lice were a problem' and 'illnesses like scarlet fever, chicken-pox and smallpox were a cause for concern'.[264] Fleury's article resulted in a formal inspection of the North Dublin Union, which strongly supported Fleury's concerns.

Given this level of republican activism among medical staff such as English and Fleury, as well as the various asylum committees throughout Ireland, it is unsurprising that many public asylums were focuses of republican sentiment during this period. This was apparent not only in Ballinasloe, the Richmond and Portrane, but also in other public asylums throughout Ireland (e.g. Carlow,[265] Clonmel[266]), and was consistent with the generally democratised and nationalist nature of Irish local government at this time. As ever, the asylums were primarily social creations, reflecting social and political change far more than they ever reflected changes in the practice of medicine and psychiatry.

Staff photograph at the Richmond Asylum, Grangegorman, Dublin, April 1897. Dr Conolly Norman is seated at the centre of the front row. (St Brendan's Hospital Museum and Dr Aidan Collins. Used with permission.)

Dr Eleonora Fleury (1867–1960), centre, second row from front, worked in the Richmond and Portrane Asylums, Dublin. (St Brendan's Hospital Museum and Dr Aidan Collins. Used with permission.)

Interior of an unnamed asylum, 1901–54. (The Poole Photographic Collection, A.H. Poole, studio photographer. This image is reproduced courtesy of the National Library of Ireland, POOLEWP 0131.)

St Edmundsbury House, Lucan. (St Patrick's Mental Health Services. Used with permission.)

Dr Richard Robert Leeper (1864–1942) was appointed Medical Superintendent at St Patrick's in 1899 (portrait by Leo Whelan). (Davison and Associates, Ltd., Dublin, Ireland. Used with permission.)

Downpatrick Asylum, Co. Down. (The Lawrence Photograph Collection. Image by Robert French (1841–1917), photographer. This image is reproduced courtesy of the National Library of Ireland, L_CAB_05084.)

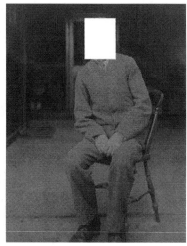

Photographs of patients (1906–8) from the archives of Carlow Asylum (later St Dympna's Hospital), which opened in 1832. The faces have been obscured for the purposes of confidentiality. (Archive of St Dympna's Hospital, Delany Archive, Carlow. Images reproduced by permission of the Health Service Executive.)

William R. Dawson, Inspector of Lunatic Asylums in Ireland, president of the Medico-Psychological Association (1911) and specialist in nerve disease for the British army in Ireland, 1915. (Reproduced by kind permission of the Royal College of Physicians of Ireland.)

Dr Thomas Percy Claude Kirkpatrick (1869–1954), physician, historian and author, 1931. (Reproduced by kind permission of the Royal College of Physicians of Ireland.)

Lunatic Asylum, Belfast, Co. Antrim. (The Lawrence Photograph Collection. Image by Robert French (1841–1917), photographer. This image is reproduced courtesy of the National Library of Ireland, L_CAB_00048.)

TELEPHONE: 5013 (THREE LINES)

RICHMOND DISTRICT ASYLUM,
DUBLIN.

May 21st, 1921.

Dear Sir,

I enclose herewith, for the information of the Committee of your Asylum, some printed copies of the report of the proceedings of the Conference of representatives of Irish District Asylums, which was held in this Asylum on the 5th inst.

The following recommendations were made by the Conference:-

1. That payment of the full 1920 Conference standard scale of wages be made to all attendants and nurses on the basis of their service, irrespective of medal qualifications, but that, as regards attendants and nurses entering the service after 1st June, 1921, their appointments on the permanent staff be postponed until they shall have obtained the certificate of proficiency in mental nursing, conditional on their probationary service being then included in their pensionable service.

2. That the Irish County Councils' General Council be urged to establish an Irish Medico-Psychological Assn.

3. That the Medico-Psychological Association of Great Britain and Ireland be classed as a recognised Association.

4. That the long service payments to attendants and nurses be recognised in principle, and that the minimum additions to scale pay should be £5 after 10 years' service, £10 after 15 years, and £20 after 20 years. Such payments to be made as soon as local financial conditions permit.

5. That the title "District Lunatic Asylum" be changed to "District Mental Hospital".

The revaluation of allowances was discussed, but, not being included in the agenda of Conference, no resolution was adopted.

The desirability of further conferences at stated intervals was accepted, for the discussion of matters affecting the asylum service generally.

Yours faithfully,
JAMES J. DOYLE.
Hon. Secretary of Conference.

To the Resident Medical Superintendent
of each District Lunatic Asylum.

There were significant industrial relations problems at many asylums in the early twentieth century. (Archive of St Dympna's Hospital, Delany Archive, Carlow. Image reproduced by permission of the Health Service Executive.)

Dr Ada English (1875–1944), patriot and psychiatrist, in Gaelic costume. (F.O.C. Meenan, *Cecilia Street: The Catholic University School of Medicine, 1855–1931*, Dublin: Gill and Macmillan, 1987. Used with permission.)

Letterkenny Asylum, Co. Donegal (1880–1900). (The Lawrence Photograph Collection. Image by Robert French (1841–1917), photographer. This image is reproduced courtesy of the National Library of Ireland, L_ROY_05892.)

CLERY'S VAN.
BALLADS OF TO-DAY.

The news of the rescue of Jack Keogh from Dundrum was received with delight by his old comrades in Maryboro' Jail. It will be recalled that the rescue was effected by armed men, who seized a van, the property of Messrs. Clery and Co., Ltd., O'Connell Street, and used it as a means of securing entry into the ground. These lines were written on the occasion by Mr. Kavanagh, who was then in jail:

O, comrades, come and listen,
　Till I tell you, one and all,
The news the birds are singing
　From Cork to Donegal;
From Dublin to the Wicklow Hills
　They have it to a man,
How a daring Galway rebel
　Escaped in Clery's van.

His comrades sat in council
　Throughout one long May night,
And swore they'd give him liberty
　Or wage a bloody fight.
Said the leader, giving orders,
　"Let each man bring a gun;
We'll take him from the tyrants' grasp
　And send him on the run."

On a Dublin street they meet next day
　All present to a man,
And motor cars being rather scarce,
　They held up Clery's van,
And driving to the massive gates,
　The entrance to Dundrum,
They told the gate official
　From Clery's they had come.

The gate-man bade them welcome,
　Saying, "I'll open wide the door,
But Clery's men with Webleys
　I've never seen before."
They drove up to the building
　In a free and easy way,
Wishing to all the warders
　A pleasant time of day.

One man said the grounds were nice,
　And blooming were the flowers;
Another says: "I do believe
　Those men are some of ours."

Then, rising up, he holloaed out:
　"I say, is that Jack Keogh?
Come on my man, get in the van;
　Be quick and let us go."

"'Tis I," says Keogh, "and well
　you know;
I'll reach you when I can;
Three days I have been waiting
　For the boys with Clery's van,
But now you have arrived at last—
　A mhic, I do feel glad,
And some shall know a rebel fights
　Although they've drove him mad."

The gate-man let them out again,
　With a brokenhearted grin:
Says he, "I'm bloody sorry
　That I ever let them in."
The doctor sat and cried for hours;
　Says he: "What would I care,
But to break that Galway rebel's heart
　O'Higgins made me swear."

But the good old rebels now, my boys,
　Are well upon the run,
Each man with ammunition
　And a tried and trusty gun.
The bloodhounds they may follow,
　But one or two will fall,
For the rebels on the mountains
　Are good 'uns, one and all.

Some received this news with joy—
　Their names you all know well;
Those who received it otherwise,
　Their names I need not tell.
This completes my story,
　I've done the best I can.
So God bless Irish rebels and
　The boys of Clery's van.

'Clery's Van' is a ballad describing Jack (John) Keogh's escape from the Central Lunatic Asylum, Dundrum, in 1926. (This image is reproduced courtesy of the National Library of Ireland, EPH B437.)

5

X

REFORMATION AND RENEWAL
IN THE 1900S

*Thanks to this indifference of the public, our asylums are in a bad way. They are over-
crowded. They are both understaffed and inefficiently staffed. Curable and incurable cases
are herded together. There is practically no treatment. The percentage of cures remains at
a very low figure. Public money is wasted. The asylums are unsuitable for their purpose in
almost every respect.*

E. Boyd Barrett, 'Modern psycho-therapy
and our asylums', *Studies* (1924)[1]

As the twentieth century progressed, the case for reform of the mental health system became
increasingly unanswerable. In 1924, Boyd Barrett laid out the problem in stark terms in
Studies:

The rate of committals to asylums goes on increasing, and there exists no means of
treating cases of incipient insanity. Curable nerve cases are allowed to develop into
incurable cases. The public, ignorant and indifferent as regards mental disease, gives no
encouragement to the setting up of nerve clinics or to the practice of the new methods
of psychotherapy. [...]

The most lamentable feature of the present asylum system is the absence of
treatment. Apart from the many hardships that the unfortunate patients have to put
up with – the poor and monotonous diet, the repulsive prison-like surroundings, the
dreary exercise yards, the hideous clothing, the punishments for refractory patients,
the uncongenial associates, the nerve-racking cries, the dirt and general gloom, the
almost total absence of amusement and recreation – there is this appalling difference
between the mental hospital (as an asylum should be) and the ordinary hospital, that
in the latter each kind of disease is carefully treated by the best modern methods,
whereas in the former no type of mental disease is fully treated. [...] To put it bluntly,
the patients committed to asylums are condemned to a degrading and miserable
imprisonment for life.[2]

In 1927, the Commission on the Relief of the Sick and Destitute Poor, Including the Insane Poor made several observations about the underpinnings of the problems, which they attributed largely to issues of administration:

> Many of the mental hospitals are in buildings that present, both externally and internally the appearance of places of detention rather than hospitals. We do not wish to minimise the difficulty of adapting these old structures so as to conform to present-day ideas of a hospital. In a few, notably in Carlow,[3] we found that considerable advances had been made towards the standard to be found in a good general hospital or convalescent home, the surroundings of the patients were bright and cheerful and a good deal of thought and labour had evidently been expended in trying to provide those amenities which distinguish a hospital from a prison. But in most of the institutions the impression was not so favourable; in some it was disappointing. The difference between the worst and the best seemed to be largely though not altogether a matter of administration. The drab and cheerless appearance of the wards, the neglect to remedy small defects, the untidy state of the grounds, the large number of idle patients which was noticeable in some establishments were in some degree indicative of a failure of administration. Some of the arrangements we saw left us under the impression that the routine of institutional life would need to be re-surveyed from the point of view of the patients' comfort.[4]

Mental health law also remained impenetrably complex and generally suboptimal, to say the very least.[5] With wearisome inevitability, the number of mentally ill people resident in institutions continued to rise during the opening decades of the twentieth century, increasing from 19,398 in 1924 to 20,066 in 1929, and 21,125 in 1939.[6] The true numbers were probably higher, as the Inspector of Mental Hospitals, Daniel L. Kelly, highlighted in his 1929 report:

> The number of insane persons under care on the 31st December, 1929, in public and private establishments was 20,050. This number does not include insane persons maintained at home by relatives or other guardians, with the exception of such as are under the control of the Chief Justice or are in unlicensed houses and have been notified to the Department, in pursuance of Section 37 of the Private Lunatic Asylums (Ireland) Act, 1842. Voluntary Boarders residing in Private Mental Hospitals are also excluded from the total number. [...]
>
> Of the total number, 86.7 per cent were in the District and Auxiliary Mental Hospitals [16,951 and 428 patients respectively]; 5 per cent were in Private Mental Hospitals [841 patients] or in Single Care [164 patients]; 7.7 per cent were in Poor Law Institutions [1,551 patients]; and 0.6 per cent in the State Criminal Lunatic Asylum [115 patients].
>
> The distribution of the sexes was 52.2 per cent males, and 47.8 per cent females.
>
> The changes which took place in 1929 may be summarised as follows:- The number in the District and Auxiliary Mental Hospitals increased by 292; the number

in Poor Law Institutions decreased by 12; the number in Private Mental Hospitals increased by 18; the number in Single Care in unlicensed houses remained unchanged; the number in the State Criminal Lunatic Asylum decreased by 1.[7]

The Inspector drew attention to several concerning aspects of mental hospitals, including the increasing death rate:

> The total number of deaths was 1,116 which is 64 more than occurred in 1928. Of the total number 14 or 1.3 per cent were returned as due to General Paralysis of the Insane;[8] 198 or 17.7 per cent to Pulmonary Tuberculosis; 41 or 3.7 per cent to Epilepsy, and 53 or 4.7 per cent to Malignant Disease and other Tumours, except of the Brain. The highest death rate was in Kilkenny Mental Hospital, where it was 9.6 per cent of the daily average number resident. The lowest was 4.4 per cent, the rate in Monaghan. The general death rate was 6.5 per cent, as compared with 6.2 in 1928.[9]

Elevated death rates were a long standing problem in asylums in Ireland and elsewhere,[10] but it was the variation in rates between hospitals that was especially disturbing now. Consistent with this, various specific hospitals attracted additional comments from the Inspector in 1929. In Ballinasloe, 'overcrowding' was a constant feature, but 'the wards, dormitories and dayrooms [were] kept in good condition'.[11] In Carlow, there was 'congestion in dormitory accommodation', although the rooms were generally 'maintained in excellent condition' and 'restraint or seclusion had not been used in any case'.

Castlebar was 'seriously overcrowded' but 'the dayrooms were nicely decorated' and the hospitals 'particularly well kept'.[12] Overcrowding was reported in Cork, Youghal, Ennis, Mullingar and Waterford.[13] Enniscorthy was 'occupied to its fullest capacity' and Portrane 'fully occupied but not overcrowded'.[14] Grangegorman was 'well maintained' and in Kilkenny 'the health of the patients [was] extraordinarily good' (despite the high death rate, oddly).[15] Portlaoise, Sligo and Letterkenny were 'in good order', although the women's boots were 'too heavy' in Letterkenny and Killarney.[16] Limerick was 'well managed' and Monaghan 'well kept but the congestion [was] serious'.[17]

The beleaguered mental hospital in Clonmel received a particularly bad report: a portion of the building was 'in a bad state and beyond repair'; the 'old male building' was 'quite unsuitable for accommodating patients'; the 'method of heating the water [was] wasteful, dangerous and generally unsatisfactory'; 'no attempt [was] made to provide amusements or entertainments for the patients'; the discharge rate was 'rather low'; and 'the continuous seclusion of two patients called for adverse comment. With a sufficient staff this could be obviated'.[18]

Staffing the mental hospitals was a constant challenge, especially in Clonmel. On Christmas Eve, 1934, Dr J.F. O'Dea recalled arriving at Clonmel Mental Hospital to attend an interview for the post of temporary assistant medical officer.[19] As the only applicant, O'Dea was appointed immediately, at a salary of £250 per year. O'Dea's only medical colleague was the RMS so they were on duty alternate nights and alternate weekends, looking after approximately 750 patients. The hospital was damp, gloomy and very large: a full ward round involved walking one and a half miles. Notwithstanding the challenges, O'Dea spent over 37 years working there and, looking back on his career, considered himself lucky to have witnessed substantial changes in Irish mental health services over this period.

Certainly, the opening decades of the 1900s saw increased awareness of the need for such changes, a point emphasised by an anonymous psychiatrist writing in *The Bell*, an Irish literary periodical, in 1944.[20] The psychiatrist bemoaned past attitudes to mental illness in Ireland but contended that there was now increased public and governmental interest in reforming the mental hospitals. The mysterious psychiatrist set out the apparent causes of mental illness, which were listed as heredity, physical diseases, alcoholism, worry and unemployment. Change was clearly needed, but the psychiatrist recommended a careful and deliberate, rather than hasty, approach to reform.

The psychiatrist need not have worried about excess speed or an exuberance of reformist zeal. Mental health care remained a low priority for the Irish government in the early decades of the twentieth century. Even the Irish Hospital Sweepstakes (a national lottery established in 1930 to finance hospitals) did little to improve the lot of the mentally ill; of the £35 million disbursed to hospitals from the Sweepstakes, less than £1.5 million was allocated to mental hospitals.[21]

Interestingly, however, the anonymous psychiatrist in *The Bell* addressed specifically the question of whether or not Ireland had a higher rate of insanity compared to other countries (Chapter 3). The psychiatrist noted that a large number of persons with intellectual disability were housed in Irish mental hospitals, classed as 'insane'. If these people were removed from the statistics, the psychiatrist contended, there was no reason to believe rates of insanity were higher in Ireland than anywhere else. But, of course, regardless of statistical manoeuvres, it was a fact that there were large numbers of persons with intellectual disability resident in Irish asylums at the start of the 1900s and this was yet another aspect of the system that called for urgent remedy.

The Intellectually Disabled in the Twentieth Century: 'It is Neither Wise nor Humane to Neglect this Class'

The inappropriate admission of people with intellectual disability to Irish asylums was a key issue in early twentieth-century psychiatry.[22] At the Richmond in 1907, Norman was clear that more needed to be done for this group:

> An institution specially equipped for teaching the teachable and improving the improvable is essential. It is neither wise nor humane to neglect this class as they are neglected in this country. Many are improvable under proper training undertaken early, and some are even capable of being made self-supporting. An ordinary asylum is not a suitable place for them in any way [...]. It is estimated that there are now in the Asylum about 200 idiots, and this is probably an underestimate. There are stated to be in the workhouses, 143. In the whole island there are said to be between five and six thousand idiots.[23]

This long standing issue had already been highlighted by others, including Eyre E.C. Kenny, superintendent of the asylum in Islandbridge, Dublin, in his *Short Hints and Observations on the*

Arrangement and Management of Lunatic Asylums, in 1848.[24] But Norman felt especially strongly 'every effort should be made to force this matter upon the attention of Government'[25] and hoped 'that the forthcoming Report of the Commission on Imbeciles will contain some proposal for dealing comprehensively with the idiots of the country'.[26]

In March of the previous year, 1906, the Royal Commission on the Care and Control of the Feeble-Minded, to which Norman referred, had visited Dublin and Belfast,[27] and in 1908 the commission published its report, estimating (based on the 1901 census) that 'there were 5,216 idiots in Ireland, of whom 3,272 were at large, 1,181 were in workhouses, and 763 in asylums':[28]

> In the case of Ireland, the evidence given before us and the opinions expressed during our visit, no less than our own personal observation and that of our medical investigators, convinced us that the case for the removal of all mentally defective persons in Ireland from the care and control of the Poor Law Authorities is absolutely overwhelming. We would refer, also, to the recent Report of the Vice-Regal Commission on Poor Law reform in Ireland issued in October, 1906, which recommended:
> (1) That all lunatics, idiots and other cases of mental disease in Irish workhouses, should be removed therefrom; and
> (2) That the Auxiliary Lunatic Asylum system ought to be extended for the reception of all chronic and harmless lunatics who are now in workhouses.[29]
> With these recommendations we concur, although we are of opinion that certain patients might be allowed by the county council or county borough council, as the local authority responsible for the care and control of mentally defective persons, to remain with the guardians, temporarily at any rate.[30]

The commission went on to recommend 'the three methods of oversight, certification, and detention':

> According to the different classes, for some oversight will suffice, for others certification, and for others certification with an order for detention. The aim of the scheme is the application of particular methods suitable for the cases of different persons, not the general adoption of any one method exclusively.[31]

The 1908 commission presented 74 detailed recommendations, including that there should be 'one central authority for the general protection and supervision of mentally defective persons and for the regulation of the provision made for their accommodation and maintenance, care, treatment, education, training and control'[32] and 'that the Council of each County and the Council of each County Borough be the local authority under the proposed Act, and be required by Statute to make suitable and sufficient provision for the care and control of the mentally defective'.[33] There were also recommendations relating to 'guardianship and supervision';[34] the 'procedure in regard to mentally defective persons' to ascertain their numbers; admission and discharge procedures; provision of receiving houses or reception wards, and related legislative changes;[35] education and training (to be the responsibility of the councils);[36] 'criminal mentally defective persons';[37] and various miscellaneous matters.[38]

Five years later, the Mental Deficiency Act 1913 attempted to add clarity to diagnostic issues within intellectual disability, defining an 'imbecile' as a person unable to take care of himself or herself, and an 'idiot' as a person unable to protect himself or herself from common dangers.[39] The 1913 Act was not, however, applied in Ireland.

As a result, and notwithstanding the 1908 commission, the care of the intellectually disabled in Ireland continued to be substantially linked with that of the mentally ill for much of the 1900s. The 1927 Commission on the Relief of the Sick and Destitute Poor, Including the Insane Poor reported that there 16,079 'patients in the district mental hospitals' who 'have been medically certified as either dangerous lunatics or idiots or as of unsound mind and proper persons to be taken charge of under care and treatment'.[40] There were, in addition, 425 residents in the Auxiliary Mental Hospital in Youghal and yet more in County Homes, District Hospitals and the Dublin Workhouse:

> The number of lunatics, idiots and imbeciles in County Homes, District Hospitals, and the Dublin Workhouse on the 31st December, 1925, was 1872 [...]. About two-thirds of the insane inmates of the County Homes are cases of congenital mental deficiency, the remaining third being composed largely, though not altogether, of cases that are fairly tranquil and easily managed.[41]

The commission concluded that 'accommodation for the insane poor in the district mental hospitals (including the auxiliary mental hospital) is either fully occupied or insufficient or unsuitable in all but three institutions (Kilkenny, Letterkenny, and Portlaoise Mental Hospitals'.[42] The commission, however, recommended the establishment of 'auxiliary mental hospitals' rather than expanding existing district mental hospitals, and made a range of other recommendations relating to outpatient care, 'boarding-out of the insane', inspections, voluntary admissions and changes to legislation.[43]

With regard to the intellectually disabled in particular, the commission heard that there were now '124 idiots and imbeciles in Stewart Institution' in Palmerstown, Dublin:[44]

> From the evidence we received from Dr G.H. Keene, the Medical Superintendent of Stewart Institution, it appears that by reason of the high percentage of idiots and low grade imbeciles as compared with improvable cases that have been received it has become increasingly difficult to attain the object for which the Institution was established, that is, the training and education of defectives. The original idea of training has, in the words of this witness, 'entirely disappeared during the last twenty years, and Stewart Institution is an asylum for the most hopeless cases'. Patients received as children are retained as adults, and we find that out of 126 cases in residence on 31st December, 1926, only 54 are under 19 years of age (including 27 under 14 years).[45]

Alarmed by this trend, the commission drew particular attention to another initiative that was clearly focused on 'the training and education of mentally defective children':

In 1926 the Sisters of Charity of St Vincent de Paul undertook, in consultation with the Commissioners for Dublin Union, the establishment of a School and Home for Catholic children. For the purpose, they rented the old workhouse school buildings at Cabra, County Dublin, and opened St Vincent's Home.

There were in the Home on the 31st December, 1926, 118 inmates (72 from Dublin Union, 20 maintained by County Boards of Health, and 26 private cases). It will be seen that at present the Home caters principally for children from Dublin Union. There were on the same date 51 idiot and imbecile children in the county homes.[46]

The commission recommended that the 'Boards of Health should be encouraged to avail of the accommodation for mentally defective children that now exists'; children sent to such places should be certified as 'likely to derive benefit from training'; 'approved institutions for defectives should be visited and reported on by the Inspector of Mental Hospitals'; and 'the Minister should be empowered to make regulations as to the good management of such institutions'.

While the commission did not propose that children be kept indefinitely at these institutions, the longer term solution they outlined was lamentably custodial: sending them to auxiliary mental hospitals:

> We do not propose that children sent by the local authority to a special institution shall be retained indefinitely in the institution. The training side of the work must be kept uppermost, and, we think, that no child should be retained in a training establishment at the public expense beyond the time when improvement in his or her condition cannot be effected. The boy or girl should then be either returned home or transferred to the auxiliary mental hospital of the district from which he or she was sent. Where the numbers would justify it the auxiliary mental hospital should have a department for cases of congenital mental deficiency.[47]

Despite this distinctly institutional approach, there were some significant steps forward in the care of the intellectually disabled in the early to mid-1900s. Some monies were allocated from the Irish Hospital Sweepstakes and specific services were developed by Catholic religious bodies, including the Daughters of Charity, Brothers of Charity, Brothers of St John of God, Sisters of La Sagesse and Sisters of Jesus and Mary.[48] These orders often had histories of working with the intellectually disabled, provided substantial support for the new developments, and continued to expand their services during the 1950s and beyond. A 1943 report by Dr Louis Clifford for the Hospitals Commission stimulated development of further facilities, with a growing emphasis on non-residential services emerging in the late 1950s.

In February 1961, the Minister for Health, Mr Sean McEntee, appointed a Commission of Inquiry on Mental Handicap in order to report on current services for the intellectually disabled and possible improvements.[49] The commission's report, published in 1965, sought to herald a new era for the intellectually disabled:

Mental handicap is one of our gravest problems in the fields of health and education. For many individuals and families it causes considerable strain, frustration, pain and misery which, in turn, may lead to stress, maladjustment and mental illness. It results in great loss to the nation through lack of productivity, through underproductivity of the mentally handicapped and through the dependency of the mentally handicapped on others. In probably every country, the amount of money and effort heretofore expended on prevention, care and treatment has been out of proportion to the impact of mental handicap on the individual, the family and the community.

Too often it was accepted that little, if anything, could be done, but a marked change in attitude has occurred in recent years. Experience has shown that the potential ability of the mentally handicapped is far greater than was previously believed and that, given suitable care and treatment, particularly when they are young, a large number will be able to lead an independent existence; of the remainder, many will be capable of making a contribution towards their maintenance and the dependency of the vast majority will be greatly reduced.

The appreciation of the benefits of care and treatment and the wider awakening of the public conscience have led to a greatly increased interest in the problems presented by mental handicap.[50]

The key shift in this official report, compared to previous ones, was a movement away from the primacy previously attached to residential care, with increased emphasis placed on non-residential elements of care and early intervention:

There should be a clear obligation on each health authority to make available for its area a diagnostic, assessment and advisory service, so that mental handicap can be diagnosed and assessed and that help and advice for the mentally handicapped and their families can be provided from the earliest possible date. To provide a diagnostic, assessment and advisory service (i) school teams should be formed comprising the School Medical Officer, a school psychologist and a social worker; (ii) general teams should be formed, comprising a psychiatrist, a psychologist and a social worker.[51]

There were detailed recommendations relating to preschool and school care, including suggestions that 'the maximum size of classes for mildly mentally handicapped pupils should be sixteen'[52] and 'for the moderately mentally handicapped should be 12 pupils'.[53] There was strong emphasis on 'vocational assessment and placement'[54] and 'an integrated form of aftercare should be provided for mentally handicapped adults living in the community'.[55]

The commission recommended that, 'in addition to the provision already made or planned, 200 places for severely handicapped children, 200 places for moderately handicapped children and 500 places for mildly handicapped children should be provided in residential centres':[56]

The accommodation in district mental hospitals of mentally handicapped children should be discontinued. County homes should not be used for the accommodation of the mentally handicapped, with the exception of some elderly patients who have been in such homes for a long time and whose removal at this stage would cause undue upset. The suitability of district mental hospitals for the care of the adult mentally handicapped should be considered when the future role of these hospitals has been determined. Even if district mental hospitals are found suitable for the care of the adult mentally handicapped, part of the provision for adults should be based on voluntary agencies and their present accommodation should be increased by approximately 1,200 places. (To a great extent these places would be in lieu of accommodation at present provided in county homes and district mental hospitals.)[57]

Other recommendations related to temporary admission facilities for times of illness or stress; 'schemes of prevention and research';[58] dissemination of information; education of relevant professionals; 'a system of family care, properly organised and well supervised';[59] and establishment of an 'Institute of Mental Handicap' to provide advice, make recommendations, coordinate and standardise services, collect information and 'suggest schemes of prevention and research from time to time and, where appropriate, to initiate, carry out, or supervise schemes of prevention and research.'[60]

Overall, the 1965 report represented a welcome rhetorical shift away from institutional care and towards a service model more focused on education, training and improvement of quality of life. In October 1966, Professor Ivor Browne submitted specific proposals regarding the intellectually disabled who numbered approximately 350 in St Ita's in Portrane and 150 in St Brendan's in Grangegorman.[61] Coordinated, organised care was recommended and a director of mental handicap duly appointed.

The 1970s saw growing recognition of the inappropriateness of admitting the intellectually disabled to psychiatric hospitals and in 1981 the 'Mental Handicap Committee' of the Eastern Health Board published a report titled 'Planning Mental Handicap Services', with a notably strong community orientation:

> Underlying all our recommendations is the conviction that the Board's policy should
> be to maintain mentally handicapped persons in the community as long as possible,
> and that the services should be developed with this objective in mind.[62]

The committee recommended that 'a wide range of services to help the mentally handicapped and support their relatives should be developed in the community' including 'community education programmes'; an 'index of the mentally handicapped'; 'genetic counselling'; 'pre-school, school-going and adolescent services'; 'adult fostering'; 'crisis day centres'; 'hostels'; and facility for 'recreation and sports'. The committee also articulated 'a need for an additional 858 residential places for the mentally handicapped now, and a further 787 places' by 1991, and made additional recommendations regarding inpatient care for mental disorder, neuropsychiatric services, 'disturbed mentally handicapped patients' and research. In particular, 'in future a mentally handicapped person should not be admitted to a psychiatric hospital unless in need of psychiatric treatment'.

At this time (1981), there were 22,979 persons with some degree of 'mental handicap' in Ireland, yielding a population prevalence of 6.7 per 1,000 total population.[63] Of these, four in every

10 were classified as 'borderline' or 'mild', and numbers in the 'moderate' category had increased since 1974, possibly owing to changes in classification methods, earlier intervention or reduced numbers in more severe categories. Dedicated provision of appropriate services remained a challenge, however, as Walsh pointed out in 1992:

> The basic problem here is the lack of appropriate services for the mentally handicapped and so the psychiatric service, as often in other instances, has been called into the breach and has been only too willing to respond no matter how inappropriate that response has been.[64]

The following years saw some significant developments in service provision, community-based residences[65] and policy development for this group.[66] But even in 2008, more than a quarter of a century after the 1981 Eastern Health Board report, Dr Susan Finnerty, Acting Inspector of Mental Health Services, reported 'no meaningful response to the lack of care and treatment of people with intellectual disability and mental illness. The Inspectorate remains concerned about the number of people with an intellectual disability inappropriately placed in psychiatric hospitals':[67]

> There are no specialist multidisciplinary teams, and consultant psychiatrists are working in isolation. Practices such as seclusion and restraint are carried out in residences without protection of legislation or monitoring, and access to specialist in-patient care for those with severe mental illness and mental disorder is almost completely absent. There are only two specialist approved centres for treatment of mental illness in people with intellectual disability: St Joseph's Service in Portrane with 177 beds and Stewart's Hospital in Palmerstown with six beds. Neither service had an adequate specialist multidisciplinary team, but endeavoured to provide a comprehensive service with minimal resources. Generic intellectual disability services provide a high level of support to people with mental illness and intellectual disability but, for the most part, staff are not trained in the management of mental illness. There are no forensic services at all for people with intellectual disability. Mental health services for children with intellectual disability are only very minimally available in a few catchment areas.
>
> The mental health needs of this very vulnerable group of people are not being addressed. This has been stated in the past, in report after report, and there was no indication from the inspections of 2007 that there had been any significant moves to even begin to remedy this situation.[68]

Clearly, more than a century after Norman pointed out, in 1907, that 'it is neither wise nor humane to neglect this class as they are neglected in this country',[69] and despite significant advances in the latter decades of the twentieth century (including progress in the area of forensic mental health care),[70] there is still substantial work to be done to promote the rights, interests and independence of persons with disabilities,[71] especially those with comorbid intellectual disability and mental disorder, and many of those still resident in 'congregated settings'.[72]

Industrial Unrest in the Asylums:
The Red Flag Rises

The plight of the intellectually disabled in the Irish asylums was just one of a range of challenges that faced Irish asylum doctors and managers in the opening decades of the twentieth century. Working conditions in these large, unsanitary institutions were poor and commonly frankly dangerous. Injuries, such as burning, were frequent and sometimes fatal.[73] So were infectious illnesses: in 1929, for example, the Committee of Management in Ballinasloe Mental Hospital received a letter from the Department of Local Government and Public Health enquiring in some detail about steps taken following the death of a nurse who suffered from diphtheria.[74]

In the same year, the Ballinasloe RMS, Dr John Mills, reported that Dr Ada English was absent from the January meeting of the Committee of Management because she 'has been laid up with an attack of illness. I will require a substitute for her'.[75] In 1930, English's colleague 'Dr Delaney sustained a severe sprain of the leg by being knocked down on the stairs ... by a patient who was trying to escape'.[76] There were escapes from all mental hospitals, including Dundrum, from time to time, generally resulting in recapture and re-committal.[77]

Management of disturbed patients presented real challenges. In 1929, Mills in Ballinasloe reported to the Committee of Management that 'a patient in No. 9 suicidal division damaged a padded cell and I hold the attendants in charge responsible. The house is very much overcrowded'.[78] This particular patient had damaged the padded cell using a small religious medal. Mills was away at the time and English informed the Committee 'that it would be almost impossible to find out where the patient got the medal. The night men assured her that he had not got the medal at night and suggested that someone might have dropped it at breakfast time'.[79] The attendants involved were each fined £1.

During this period there were, unsurprisingly, significant industrial relations problems at many mental hospitals. In 1918, attendants at Monaghan Asylum went on strike to demand union recognition and improved pay, and achieved moderate concessions from management as a result.[80] In early January 1919, however, the dispute intensified and staff occupied the Monaghan asylum. The red flag was raised over the building and the Monaghan Asylum Soviet came into being. These assertive actions secured improvements in both hours and pay, and, perhaps more importantly, set a rather dramatic example for similar institutions throughout Ireland and Great Britain.[81]

In Ireland, at least some of these industrial relations problems found their roots in various trade-offs between contesting priorities in the new Irish state as the 1900s progressed.[82] In effect, the early phases of national autonomy in Ireland led to sacrifices as part of the progressive realisation of self-governance, and one of these sacrifices was timely improvement in conditions and training for asylum workers. Initially, the native Irish were not appreciably more generous to asylum workers or patients than the British government in Ireland had been.[83]

Industrial action was by no means limited to Monaghan.[84] In September 1919, the mayor of Clonmel, Mr Daniel F. O'Meara, had to step in to facilitate a resolution to a three month strike by attendants at St Luke's.[85] In 1924 all but seven staff members caring for 616 patients in Letterkenny District Mental Hospital went on strike when certain allowances were abolished; the Committee, encouraged by the Minister for Local Government and Public Health, recruited replacement staff.[86] In the Eglinton Asylum in Cork, the Eglinton Society of Attendants, sought (but did not receive) official recognition from the Board of Management as early as July 1899.[87] In February 1916, however, the Eglinton Asylum Attendants Association was re-formed and remained active until a Cork branch of the Irish Asylum Workers Union first met in January 1918.[88] Considerable industrial unrest – and progress – followed at the Cork establishment.[89]

Overall, however, there were recurring industrial relations problems at asylums right across Ireland during this period with few signs of agreed settlement. In July 1923, staff in Ballinasloe presented an ultimatum to the Committee of Management there, threatening to strike if certain demands were not favourably considered.[90] The Committee was not convinced by all of the claims, with, for example the Most Rev. Dr O'Doherty, Bishop of Clonfert, presiding over the meeting, describing as preposterous the claim for fires at 5pm during warm weather. This particular claim was turned down but others seemed reasonable and were considered favourably.

Sustained industrial peace proved elusive.[91] By September 1924, staff in Ballinasloe were out on strike and approximately 50 Civic Guards requisitioned for night duty at the hospital.[92] In this case, the problem related to the appointment of a gate porter who was not a member of the Mental Hospital Attendants' Union.[93] As a result, the attendants went out on strike, taking the keys of the patients' accommodation with them. RMS Mills stated that the strikers ill-treated attendants who did not strike with them. Some attendants reportedly opened the doors of patients' rooms and let them out into the corridors. Some patients escaped. Mills and English, assisted by Mills' wife and family, and the remaining staff, tried to manage the situation as best they could, but found that the telephone wires had been cut in two places, with the result that they could not phone for assistance. General chaos ensued and Mills, fearing for the safety of the patients, sent the offending gate porter away and requested that the strikers return, which they did.[94]

Industrial relations continued to present challenges throughout the 1930s[95] and in 1938 employees in mental hospitals, at their conference in Mullingar, demanded the general establishment of a 48 hour week, three weeks' annual leave, and a salary increase of 20 per cent.[96] One delegate from Ballinasloe, Mr M. Kelly, drew attention to retirement arrangements, stating that retirement after 25 years' service should be made compulsory, asking how many people at the age of 60 or 65 years could deal with violent patients or do duty in a tuberculosis ward? These kinds of issues persisted for several more decades, although eventually there was significant progress, most notably in Cork in the mid-1950s, resulting in improved recognition of staff demands by management.[97]

Concerns about the mental hospitals, with their many, interlinked problems, ranging from industrial relations to overcrowding, led to renewed and increased pressure to address the apparently increasing number of persons with mental illness presenting for admission. A 1934 committee enquiring into the matter visited establishments in Scotland, England, Holland and Belgium, and reported to the joint committee at Grangegorman that greater occupational therapy and granting patients more freedom were features of similar establishments elsewhere, and might well improve matters here too.[98] The committee recommended setting up more outpatient clinics, developing a voluntary admission status, establishing a new hospital instead of Grangegorman and a colony system (smaller houses, near the main institution), as well as greater research and public education about mental illness. The committee also concluded that facilities for persons with intellectual disability and persons with epilepsy should be provided, in addition to after care for those discharged from mental hospitals.

Future decades were to see many of these recommendations introduced either through gradual changes in service provision or following the Mental Treatment Act 1945. In the meantime, however, Grangegorman itself was to see considerable change and renewal, much of it attributable to the arrival in September 1937 of a new and formidable Chief RMS who went on to become one of the key, iconic figures in twentieth-century Irish psychiatry: Dr John Dunne.[99]

Professor John Dunne:
Physical Sciences and Psychological Medicine

John Dunne was born in Wicklow and educated at Mount St Joseph's Abbey, Roscrea.[100] He qualified as a doctor from the National University of Ireland, Dublin, in 1922 and later that year was appointed assistant medical officer in Grangegorman. In 1925, Dunne introduced malarial treatment for general paralysis of the insane (GPI) to Ireland.[101] Commonly fatal, GPI is a neuropsychiatric disorder caused by late stage syphilis and was a substantial problem in asylums internationally at this time.[102] In 1917, Dr Julius Wagner-Jauregg (1857–1940), an Austrian physician, introduced a 'malarial fever cure' for GPI based on the observation that infections appeared to alleviate mental illness.[103] This involved deliberately giving people malaria in order to treat their mental illness. In an era desperate for ways to empty asylums, the treatment was widely used for GPI and Wagner-Jauregg won a Nobel Prize in 1927.

In 1925, at the Spring meeting of the Irish Division of the MPA, Dunne heard a paper about malarial treatment read by Dr Norman Graham of Purdysburn Villa Colony, Belfast and decided to try the treatment at Grangegorman. Dunne detailed his methods and findings the following year in a paper in the MPA's *Journal of Mental Science*.[104] By then, Dunne had tried the treatment on 35 cases and presented results for 25, as the other 10 had just been recently inoculated. The majority of Dunne's 25 cases had been in the institution for a long time and were in an advanced state of paralysis. Diagnoses of GPI had been confirmed by serological tests. Dunne initially collected mosquitos from customs men in Dublin but, when the mosquitos wouldn't bite in Ireland's chilly climate, switched to using malarial serum from London.

Outcomes were mixed. All patients who developed fever following inoculation also developed anaemia (low blood count); four became jaundiced; and one contracted pneumonia. All of the improvements that occurred emerged gradually after quinine was introduced to treat the malaria. Of Dunne's 25 initial cases, eight improved greatly (of whom two were discharged); seven improved slightly; five were unchanged; and five died (one from pneumonia, two from seizures, and two from GPI itself). Dunne concluded that malarial treatment, if administered early, offered reasonable hope of a cure in GPI. By 1929, the death rate from GPI at Grangegorman had been reduced to 5 per year, having been around 35 per year prior to malarial treatment.[105] The treatment was also used extensively by Leeper in St Patrick's.[106]

Dunne's therapeutic optimism marked a significant shift in mood at Grangegorman. In 1928, there were some 1,897 patients in the enormous establishment (970 male, 927 female), and a further

1,653 in Portrane (843 male, 810 female).[107] Conscious of the pressing need for treatment and eager to learn more about novel therapies, Dunne, in 1928, applied for six months study leave with pay but this was declined by the Department of Local Government and Public Health, much to the chagrin of the Grangegorman Joint Committee, which supported Dunne's application.[108] Notwithstanding this setback, Dunne was eventually granted three months leave in June 1929[109] and acquired a diploma from the University of Vienna after attending a special course of lectures there on the study and treatment of insanity and nervous diseases.[110]

Like Dunne, RMS Donelan in Grangegorman was strongly in favour of trying various new treatments as they appeared but, in 1930, Dunne resigned from Grangegorman, having been appointed medical superintendent in Sligo Mental Hospital.[111] In July 1935, Dunne hosted the Summer quarterly meeting of the Irish Division of the RMPA in Sligo,[112] at which attendees noted with great interest his plans for extensive additions to the hospital where, in 1936, he instigated an open door policy for rehabilitated patients.[113]

In May 1937 Dunne was notified that the Appointments Commission had recommended him for the position of Chief Medical Superintendent of Grangegorman, arguably the most powerful and influential position in Irish psychiatry. Despite some rather heated discussion of the matter by the Joint Committee of the Grangegorman and Portrane Mental Hospitals in June,[114] Dunne duly took up his post on the 10 September 1937.[115] Early the following year, in February 1938, Dunne reported to the Committee that patient numbers had again increased, and now stood at 2,037 in Grangegorman and 1,586 in Portrane.[116] Clearly, steps needed to be taken to manage the institutions better and in March 1938 Dunne recommended introducing a 'colony system' as had been implemented elsewhere (e.g. Belfast).[117]

In addition to his efforts at reforming the asylums, Dunne devoted considerable energies to teaching and was appointed professor of psychiatry at UCD in 1950. In 1954 the Senate of the National University of Ireland awarded him an MD based on published work.[118] In an invaluable interview with Dr (later Professor) David Healy (a leading psychiatrist and historian), Professor Thomas Lynch later (1992) recalled being taught by Dunne at Grangegorman in the 1940s:

> When I was doing psychiatry, teaching consisted of about 10 lectures in Grangegorman Hospital at some stage between April and June. You attended there at about 4.30 p.m. and met all your colleagues from the three medical schools. We went into an enormous ward unit and sat around a dais. John Dunne stood on the podium and presented the cases. Even in my ignorance I was often very embarrassed for the patient. I remember one patient who was quite theatrical being made to demonstrate that with the stethoscope he could listen to Tokyo. It was comic stage stuff rather than teaching. You got your attendance sheets signed, paid your fees, and the exam was a formality'.[119]

Throughout his various endeavours, Dunne was always chiefly concerned with treating mental illness and, broadly, believed that there was no form of mental illness that was not treatable.[120] His therapeutic interests lay not only in physical treatments, such as malarial therapy and various others, but also in psychological therapies, which he emphasised strongly in his presidential address to the 114th annual meeting of the RMPA in Dublin in July 1955.[121] Again, towards the end of his life, Dunne, reflecting on over 65 years of psychiatric experience, clearly recognised the benefits of psychotropic medication, but also emphasised that pharmacology cannot replace psychological or human means of treatment[122] – a view that resonated strongly with contemporary practitioners.[123]

Dunne was a highly influential figure in Irish psychiatry over many decades,[124] from the 1920s to the early 1990s, and worked not only in the mental hospitals but also as consultant psychiatrist to Mercer's Hospital, Sir Patrick Dun's, Dr Steevens and Our Lady of Lourdes Hospital in Drogheda.[125] He advised the Department of Health on the framing of the Mental Treatment Act 1945; served on the National Health Council;[126] and was a friend of Seán Lemass (1899–1971), who was Taoiseach from 1959 to 1966.[127] Throughout his time at Grangegorman (or St Brendan's, as it was known from 1958 onwards), Dunne encountered a multitude of challenges, many of which were discussed at committee and board meetings, as well as in the public media, including overcrowding,[128] challenges with recruitment,[129] tuberculosis[130] and escapes.[131]

Dunne oversaw numerous developments at Grangegorman and Portrane including the opening of new units[132] and, in 1958, a cinema in Grangegorman.[133] He represented Grangegorman at various meetings, such as the 1954 International Congress on Mental Health in Toronto,[134] and toured hospitals in Scandinavia, America and Russia, where he was especially impressed by the treatments provided.[135] Dunne gave evidence in many high profile legal cases[136] including, in 1961, a case involving writer Brendan Behan (1923–1964) charged with assault and malicious damage.[137] Dunne said that Behan had an intolerance of alcohol which would make him more easily unbalanced by alcohol than the average person. Otherwise, Behan was perfectly normal and must have taken sufficient alcohol to suffer a temporary aberration of his reason. Behan was fined £30 and ordered to pay compensation of £19 and 5 shillings. The District Justice endorsed the advice of the Garda Sergeant in the case who concluded that Behan was a man who should never drink.

By the time Dunne retired from St Brendan's, on 31 December 1965, inpatient numbers at the hospital had decreased to approximately 700, with a further 17,000 outpatients attending its services. Following his retirement from the hospital, Dunne continued to practice psychiatry and, in 1971, published an account of two years of outpatient clinic work in Mercer's Hospital.[138] Depression and anxiety were the most common diagnoses among the patients there, and Dunne warned against undue haste in the outpatient setting, emphasising the need for good rapport and a personal relationship with the patient. A keen golfer and sportsman, Dunne died on 1 January 1991 at the age of 92.

Over the course of Dunne's career much had changed in Irish psychiatry, and Dunne was a key figure in the evolving system of care.[139] While some staff found the hospital frustrating and foreboding during Dunne's time there[140] (somewhat contrasting with St Loman's, under Dr Vincent Crotty),[141] and Dunne arguably underestimated the harmfulness of institutional life,[142] he also undeniably brought many positive changes to the establishment, including a large reduction in patient numbers; improvements in patients' bedding and living conditions; establishment of a medical library;[143] promoting the appointment of social workers;[144] campaigning tirelessly for appropriate medical staffing;[145] leading the formation of an after care committee;[146] and promoting rehabilitation.[147]

Most of all, though, Dunne brought unprecedented critical rigour to the evaluation of the extraordinary range of novel therapies that were transforming psychiatry in Ireland elsewhere during this period, such as insulin coma therapy, convulsive therapy and lobotomy.[148] These are considered next, along with Dunne's contributions to establishing their precise roles in twentieth-century psychiatry in Ireland.

Insulin Therapy:
Coma, Convulsions

In the early twentieth century, the preeminent intellectual movement of the day, psychoanalysis, conspicuously failed to grab the imagination of psychiatrists in Ireland as much as it did elsewhere, despite some limited acceptance (e.g. in Belfast).[149] Although the Irish Psycho-Analytical Association was founded in 1942, by poet, writer and psychoanalyst Jonathan Hanaghan (1887–1967),[150] who began psychoanalytical practice in Ireland in 1920,[151] psychoanalysis still did not have an enormous impact on Irish psychiatry, possibly owing to Ireland's peripheral location, the absence of a preeminent *medical* professional willing to take the lead in the early days,[152] or the Catholic Church's disapproval of psychoanalysis:[153] in 1963, the Most Reverend John C. McQuaid, Archbishop of Dublin, stated that Freud had not discovered reality but attempted to *construct* it.[154] In that year, the Irish Psycho-Analytical Association had just five practicing psychoanalysts in Ireland.[155]

Notwithstanding this muted medical enthusiasm for psychoanalysis, however, other novel therapeutic approaches came into widespread use relatively quickly in Ireland during the early 1900s. At St Patrick's in the 1920s and 1930s, these included short-wave diathermy (using electricity to produce heat in deeper body tissues) for schizophrenia and general paralysis; violet rays (electrotherapy) for schizophrenia and melancholia; hydrotherapy and massage for alcohol and drug addiction; and continuous baths for mania.[156] More broadly used, however, it was insulin coma therapy, convulsive therapy and lobotomy that came to dominate the re-emergent field of physical therapies for mental disorder.

Insulin therapy was developed in the early 1930s by Austrian psychiatrist and neurophysiologist Manfred Sakel (1900–1957), and initially involved administering insulin (a hormone normally produced in the human pancreas) to individuals with mental disorder in order to increase weight and inhibit excitement.[157] Sakel noted, however, that the unintentional comas occasionally induced by insulin appeared to produce remission in schizophrenia. As a result, inducing coma was soon regarded as the key therapeutic mechanism of insulin among the mentally ill.

Insulin coma therapy generally involved inducing comas five or six mornings per week until such time as either a satisfactory therapeutic response was produced or 50 to 60 comas had been induced.[158] The patient spent up to 15 minutes in deep coma on each occasion, although some patients were liable to develop convulsions. Each coma was terminated by the administration of glucose intravenously or via a nasal tube. Most patients became obese during the course of treatment; possible complications included permanent brain damage; and there was a mortality rate somewhere between 2 and 5 per cent.[159]

The fact that insulin coma therapy came to be widely used despite these drawbacks reflects the therapeutic enthusiasm (bordering on desperation) that emerged for novel physical treatments in the early twentieth century, fuelled chiefly by an awareness of the size of asylums in many countries and the paucity of alternative therapies. By 1937 there were favourable reports about insulin coma therapy from some 22 countries worldwide.[160] There was particular enthusiasm among British hospital psychiatrists, who endorsed the new treatment excitedly.[161]

In Ireland, insulin coma therapy was introduced at Grangegorman Mental Hospital in Dublin in 1938.[162] Both Dunne and Dr Eveleen O'Brien (1901–1981), assistant medical officer,[163] were involved in this initiative and the first patient to receive the new treatment, a 25-year-old woman, reportedly recovered sufficiently to return home. Close monitoring was, however, required as the procedure was complex and could present a danger to the life of the patient. In November 1938, Dunne and O'Brien presented a series of cases treated with insulin therapy at the meeting of the Irish Division of the RMPA and concluded that, despite the expense, challenges and risks involved, insulin coma therapy was still a valuable treatment, once used with due care.[164]

Insulin coma was used extensively throughout the Irish asylum system, with reportedly good results. It was introduced in St Davnet's in Monaghan in the 1940s, and positive outcomes were recorded. One patient, for example, underwent 15 insulin comas and reportedly made a good recovery, with improvements in mood, appetite and sleep, resulting in discharge.[165] In Cork, modified insulin therapy (a sub-coma treatment) was introduced at Our Lady's Hospital in November 1945 and administered up until 1960.[166] Patients fasted overnight and were then given 20 units of soluble insulin, increasing daily by 5–10 units until the patient was soporic. Some patients required 100 units. At 11am, those who were still alert ate breakfast while the others received glucose via a nasal tube. A nurse supervised the times of sweating, sopor and coma. Protein, tonics and vitamins were given, and there was frequent sponging, bathing and changing of bed linen (up to three times within the hour).

Despite reports of positive outcomes in Cork and elsewhere, it remained unclear just how systematically useful or dangerous insulin coma really was for the broad generality of patients. In 1950, Dunne published a relatively detailed analysis of insulin treatment in Grangegorman, reporting that 405 out of 605 patients treated with insulin recovered.[167] On the basis of this and similar reports from elsewhere, insulin coma continued to be used quite widely during the 1940s and 1950s, although it was increasingly recognised that the risks and adverse effects were such that it could only be performed in fully equipped centres with specialised staff.[168] And while there were some suggestions that insulin therapy might be useful in depression, it was used mostly in schizophrenia.[169]

Insulin treatment went into decline in the late 1950s and early 1960s owing to the emergence of safer and more effective treatments for schizophrenia (chiefly antipsychotic medication)[170] as well as growing disillusionment with the therapy within the medical profession.[171] Professor Thomas Lynch later (1992) noted that, at St Patrick's in Dublin, 'we had given up insulin coma before they gave it up elsewhere. Once they discovered another less dangerous way of treating schizophrenic patients, they took that on board very fast and were quick to use the neuroleptics and the antidepressants'.[172] There was also a view that insulin coma represented a form of psychiatric oppression and was thus undesirable, according to critics within the profession of psychiatry.[173]

Despite these criticisms, insulin coma therapy was slow to disappear entirely.[174] In Ireland, the 1966 Commission of Inquiry on Mental Illness tellingly included insulin coma therapy (and even malaria treatment) in a list of apparent advances in psychiatric treatment, under the heading 'Further change in attitudes':

Gradually, however, a change in attitude again occurred. The first major change probably followed the discovery, in 1917, of malaria therapy for general paralysis of the insane, a prevalent and debilitating form of mental illness which affected an appreciable number of all patients admitted to asylums. The fact that it was possible to treat with success a large number of seriously ill patients renewed interest in positive treatment. Several countries made provision for the voluntary admission of patients, an acknowledgment that mental hospitals were places of treatment – and not merely places in which to segregate the mentally ill. The discovery of insulin treatment in 1933 and electro-convulsive therapy in 1937 further maintained the impetus. [...]

Still further emphasis was added to active treatment by the introduction of the tranquillising drugs in 1954. Since then, other drugs are being added continually to the therapeutic equipment of the physician. These drugs have greatly facilitated the early discharge of patients, and many who formerly could have been treated only as inpatients are now treated in the community. The position arrived at to-day is unique in the history of psychiatry. Modern treatments frequently reduce the duration of the illness and a good measure of social recovery can be achieved in many cases where complete cure is not possible. An era of considerable hope has arrived. Old ideas are being discarded or challenged. Doctors, nurses and public alike display a greater interest than ever before. Mental health has taken a leading part on world stage. Emphasis has changed completely from custody to treatment.[175]

This passage is interesting for two reasons. First, it clearly reflects a rather bright eyed therapeutic enthusiasm as a key driver of the development of psychiatry in early twentieth-century Ireland. Second, it presents the history of psychiatry during this period as a linear, onward march of progress, and places insulin coma and various other treatments firmly in a line of apparently progressive developments over this period.

The truth about these treatments is far more complex and interesting to unravel. There can be no doubt that therapeutic enthusiasms in psychiatry were frequently excessive and led to adverse outcomes as well as real successes.[176] The motivations behind these enthusiasms were, however, a convoluted mix of therapeutic zeal (based on concern at the size and conditions of asylums, and social conditions of the mentally ill), genuine desire to relieve the suffering of people with mental illness and their families,[177] and, on at least some occasions, a complex and sometimes distorted relationship with the idea of therapeutic power and psychiatric professionalisation.[178]

Despite the complexity of these motivations, however, or, perhaps, because of them, new physical and biological treatments continued to be introduced and tried throughout the early 1900s. Just a year after Sakel announced his new insulin based therapy, yet another dramatic innovation in treatment made its historic appearance, this time based on the idea that schizophrenia and epilepsy tended not to coexist. This interesting view led to psychiatry's most iconic and misunderstood treatment to date: electroconvulsive therapy (ECT).[179]

Convulsive Therapy:
Shock Treatment

ECT refers to the use of electricity, applied across the brain, to produce epileptic-type seizures (convulsions). Convulsive therapy was based on the idea that seizures were therapeutic in individuals with mental disorder and built on the more general enthusiasm for biological treatments, such as insulin coma, in the early twentieth century.[180] Programmes of convulsive therapy were introduced by Ladislas Joseph Meduna (1896–1964), a Hungarian neurologist who, in 1938, went on to develop *electro*convulsive therapy, with Ugo Cerletti (1877–1963), an Italian neurologist at the Rome University Psychiatric Clinic.[181]

Convulsive therapy, and especially ECT, has proven a complex, controversial[182] but notably enduring treatment. A definitive, independent assessment of its usefulness emerged in 2010, when, following an extensive, systematic review of evidence, the UK's National Institute for Clinical Excellence (NICE) recommended ECT for rapid, short term improvement of severe symptoms after a trial of other treatments has been ineffective and/or when the condition is potentially life threatening, in persons with severe depressive illness, catatonia, or a severe or prolonged episode of mania.[183] There is also now increased public recognition of the (rare) necessity for, and benefits of, involuntary ECT.[184] The path to this point in the history of ECT was, however, anything but smooth.

Early convulsive therapy found roots in the idea that producing convulsions, rather than coma, was therapeutic.[185] In the initial years of convulsive therapy, seizures were induced using chemicals rather than electricity. More specifically, Cardiazol (Metrazol) was the European trade name of pentamethylenetetrazol, a camphor-like compound, used initially by Meduna for convulsive treatment of schizophrenia.[186] In 1935, Meduna reported positive results in 10 out of the first 26 of his patients to receive Cardiazol treatment.[187] As a result, convulsive treatment soon spread to other psychiatric centres throughout Europe and beyond. The first recorded use of Cardiazol in England was at Moorcroft House, a private institution in Middlesex, in 1937. As the 1930s progressed, Cardiazol treatment became the most widely used physical treatment in public mental hospitals in Great Britain.

In Ireland, the earliest recorded uses of convulsive therapy appear to have been in Cork in July 1939 (Cardiazol and Triazol)[188] and Ballinasloe District Mental Hospital (Cardiazol) in December of that year.[189] Opened in 1833, the Ballinasloe establishment was to the forefront of introducing novel medical treatments throughout the early decades of the twentieth century, as well as introducing occupational therapy for patients. In 1939, Dr Bernard Lyons, who became RMS in 1937, reported to the Committee of Management in Ballinasloe that:

> Dr James Clyne, who acted as locum here before, and who is after having six months special training in modern treatments of mental patients in Cardiff Mental Hospital, is acting as locum. I am availing of this opportunity of trying some of the new treatments in this hospital.[190]

Dr Ada English was working in the hospital throughout this period (Chapter 4),[191] and, following her death in 1944, her obituary in the *East Galway Democrat* recorded that, during English's time there, Ballinasloe was to the forefront of convulsive therapy in Ireland.[192] This is confirmed by a communication received by the Ballinasloe Committee of Management in December 1939 from the 'Local Government Department ... stating that the Minister has no objection to the proposal to carry out Cardiazol treatment on certain patients provided the RMS accepts responsibility'.[193]

Notwithstanding this finding, there is still insufficient primary historical evidence to determine precisely when the focus of physical treatments in the Irish asylums moved from insulin coma to convulsive therapy. It is clear, however, that both Cork and Ballinasloe were to the forefront of novel therapies during this period.

Convulsive therapy soon moved on from Cardiozol and in April 1942 Dunne introduced ECT at Grangegorman in Dublin.[194] This was consistent with Dunne's general therapeutic enthusiasm and constant search for clinical improvements in the large numbers of institutionalised patients in Grangegorman. ECT was introduced in Our Lady's in Cork in 1943, shortly after electrification of the asylum buildings, and was given without anaesthesia up until 1952.[195]

In 1950, Dunne duly reported significant rates of recovery with ECT in Grangegorman, as 209 out of 327 patients with 'involutional melancholia' (depression) 'recovered' following ECT.[196] The treatment was used widely throughout the Irish asylum system: in Castlebar, for example, the RMS, Dr Sheridan, recommended to the board in December 1942 that ECT should be introduced.[197] In St Davnet's in Monaghan, ECT was introduced in the mid-1940s and some patients received combinations of coma therapy and ECT (e.g. one patient had eight comas and six ECT seizures, after which he was discharged, 'recovered').[198] Interestingly, the Mental Treatment Act 1945 did not provide specific guidance regarding consent or any other issues surrounding ECT.[199]

Professor Thomas Lynch, who returned to work in St Patrick's in Dublin in 1956, later (1992) recalled that 'the only therapy was ECT for the psychotic depressed patients and insulin coma for the schizophrenic patients. I ran the insulin unit for nine months. We had 18 to 20 patients every morning for insulin coma and also an enormous number of patients for ECT every day of the week; of course, it was straight ECT [i.e. without anaesthetic]. I was there when Scoline [a short term muscle relaxant][200] first came on stream'.[201] Over the decades following its introduction in the 1940s, there were various changes in the use and administration of ECT in Ireland, with, most notably, 'straight' ECT being replaced by modified ECT (i.e. with anaesthetic).

ECT use declined in Ireland and elsewhere over the course of the 1970s, although rates of use in Ireland still tended to be higher than in Great Britain, possibly owing to larger numbers of patients presenting for treatment in Ireland; a paucity of community services that might reduce need for ECT; or particular use of ECT for schizophrenia in Ireland.[202] These matters were explored in depth in a major 1982 survey of ECT in Ireland from the University Department of Psychiatry in Galway, which showed that Irish psychiatrists' attitudes towards ECT were broadly similar to those in Great Britain; there was less emphasis on complex issues of informed and valid consent in Ireland; and premises and equipment varied considerably across the country.[203] The report presented various recommendations to the Irish Division of the Royal College of Psychiatrists relating to both training and clinical practice, with particular emphasis on the need for informed consent.

Consistent with this, a 'critical appraisal' of ECT by Dr Petr Skrabanek (1940–1994) at Trinity College, Dublin, published in the *Irish Medical Journal* in 1986, concluded that the use of ECT should be regulated by law,[204] and the issue of ECT without consent was duly addressed in detail in the Mental Health Act 2001 and Mental Health (Amendment) Act 2015 (Chapters 7 and 8).[205] By 2008, ECT was in use in 24 of 64 'approved centres' (registered psychiatric inpatient facilities) in Ireland, and a total of 407 people received the treatment.[206] This rate of ECT use (9.6 people per 100,000 population per year) was comparable to those in other countries, such as Scotland and Canada.

Despite this standard level of use in 2008, and clear, independent endorsement of ECT by NICE in 2010, ECT remained the subject of debate in Ireland, especially when administered without consent.[207] The Mental Health Act 2001 stated that ECT could be administered to an involuntary patient only if he or she consented in writing, or, if the patient was 'unable or unwilling' to consent, it was approved by the treating consultant psychiatrist and another psychiatrist.[208] In 2015, the Expert Group on the Review of the Mental Health Act 2001 recommended deleting the word 'unwilling' from this section, so that any patient who had mental capacity to decide about ECT and declined to have it, would have that decision respected.[209] Psychiatrists had long campaigned for this change[210] which occurred in February 2016 following implementation of the Mental Health (Amendment) Act 2015 (which also deleted 'unwilling' in relation to medication without consent for more than three months for detained patients; Chapter 8).

While the deletion of 'unwilling' in relation to ECT was a significant step towards greater patient autonomy, it was historically very interesting that, by the time this change was made in 2016, it only affected a tiny number of patients, if any. In 2012, there were 1,921 involuntary admissions in Ireland and the 'unwilling' criterion in the ECT provisions was relevant to just four of these, three of whom were also documented as lacking mental capacity to decide about treatment.[211] As a result, ECT without consent was administered to just one patient solely on the basis of the 'unwilling' criterion in 2012.[212]

Three years later, by the time the Expert Group report recommending the deletion of 'unwilling' was published, the numbers receiving ECT on this basis had dwindled to the point that the relevant government minister informed Dáil Éireann (Irish parliament) that the Mental Health Commission could no longer publish the figures as they were now so low as to permit individual patients to be identified.[213] Despite these extremely low numbers affected by the proposed change in ECT legislation, and the fact that many of the Expert Group's other 164 recommendations in 2015 would affect far greater numbers of patients, this ECT recommendation dominated media coverage of the Expert Group report, even though it had been flagged long in advance.[214]

This disproportionate focus on ECT may be attributable to the strong, negative public image of ECT both historically and in classic films such as *One Flew Over the Cuckoo's Nest* (United Artists, 1975), as well as more local Irish films, such as *Patrick's Day* (Ignition Film Productions, 2015). *Patrick's Day* is an interesting film that tells the story of a young man with schizophrenia and demonstrates that, despite the misunderstandings associated with the illness, people with schizophrenia retain the abilities to live and love, hope and dream, just like everyone else.[215] However, the film also shows Patrick receiving ECT in a scene that is more reminiscent of the 1960s than 2015: the setting is dramatically institutional; the treatment itself highly traumatic; and clinical staff leave the room while Patrick is having a seizure, all of which would be clearly inconsistent with the Mental Health Commission rules governing the use of ECT.[216]

Evidently, ECT, despite clear endorsement by NICE and substantial changes in practice since the 1960s, retains its extraordinary power to command public attention and so to shape the public image of psychiatry in powerful, disproportionate and often inaccurate ways.

Lobotomy: Therapy, Tragedy

Alongside insulin coma therapy and ECT, lobotomy was a third key, novel physical treatment that sought – controversially – to transform psychiatry during the mid-twentieth century.

While brain surgery has a very long history in medicine, frontal lobotomy or leucotomy (which involves surgery on the frontal part of the brain) for mental disorder was developed in the early 1930s by Dr António Egas Moniz (1874–1955), a Portuguese neurologist who shared a Nobel Prize for his work in 1949.[217] The practice was adopted enthusiastically in the US by Dr Walter Freeman (1895–1972) who performed up to 3,500 lobotomies over the course of his career.[218] Along with James W. Watts (1904–1994), Freeman's patients included Rosemary Kennedy (1918–2005), sister of US president John F. Kennedy; she underwent lobotomy at age 23, with tragic consequences.[219]

Lobotomy was a controversial, contested treatment from the outset and involved cutting nerve connections to and from the prefrontal part of the brain. According to some experts, lobotomy reduced feelings of anxiety and introspection, as well as emotional tension and catatonia (severe mental disorder).[220] As a result, patients appeared to become more placid and tranquil,[221] with significant reductions in symptom expression.[222] On this basis, the treatment was used quite widely, even among soldiers during the Second World War in certain centres.[223] Critics disagreed vocally and early, pointing to negative effects on personality, among other matters,[224] but they were generally overridden in the rush of enthusiasm for the new technique in both the US and Europe.[225]

In Ireland, lobotomy was introduced to patients of Grangegorman Mental Hospital in April 1946 when Mr Adams Andrew McConnell (1884–1972) was engaged to perform the procedure at the nearby Richmond Surgical Hospital.[226] McConnell had graduated first in his class in Trinity College Dublin in 1909 and then trained in Sir Patrick Dun's Hospital before working at the Richmond Hospital from 1911 onward.[227] McConnell had a long and distinguished career in clinical and academic surgery, serving as Professor of Surgery at RCSI (1926–9), president of RCSI (1936–8), Regius Professor of Surgery at Trinity College Dublin (1946–61) and president of the Royal Academy of Medicine in Ireland (1946–7).

Pioneering and rigorous, McConnell was the undisputed 'father of Irish neurosurgery' and lobotomies took place at the Richmond Hospital under his direction.[228] While it appears that some hundreds of lobotomies were performed, Dunne, at nearby Grangegorman, was keenly aware of the seriousness of the operation and limited the surgery to patients with schizophrenia who had not improved with insulin therapy or ECT and had ongoing symptoms of a very impulsive, negative, suicidal or homicidal nature, or presented a constant worry or threat to self, staff or others.[229]

By June 1947, 23 lobotomies had been performed on patients in Grangegorman with decidedly mixed results: while three patients became well enough to be discharged, others, who were less disturbed following the surgery, still had to be cared for within the hospital.[230] In 1950, Dunne reported more extensive and detailed outcome data: out of 63 patients with schizophrenia and poor prognosis who underwent lobotomy, 19 recovered sufficiently to be discharged; 19 showed considerable improvements in behaviour; 18 showed no change; 4 disimproved markedly; and 3 died.[231] Even among those who were discharged, however, problems remained, according to Dunne, who was clearly very interested in the possibilities of lobotomy but by no means blindly enthusiastic about it.

In 1952, Dr David Stafford-Clark (1916–1999), a leading English psychiatrist, wrote at some length about the controversial procedure, which he saw as a peculiar combination of crudity and brilliance, and, while he advised great care with its use, Stafford-Clark still felt lobotomy had a role in certain cases.[232] Despite this lingering enthusiasm, lobotomy went into decline during the 1950s, owing chiefly to its adverse effects and lack of efficacy, as well as the arrival of safer alternative treatments (i.e. antipsychotic medications).[233] As a result, the standard lobotomy operation became less popular and the surgery, when performed, was frequently of a less traumatic variety.[234] Systematically, the effects of lobotomy were overwhelmingly negative with many patients, like Rosemary Kennedy, ending up institutionalised for decades, if not for life, following the procedure.

From today's perspective, the story of lobotomy is one of therapeutic enthusiasm that went unchecked for too long.[235] It found its roots in a deep desire to discharge people from large, unsuitable mental hospitals and alleviate suffering, but it is now clear that the procedure was taken to an unacceptable extreme, used too widely and for too long, often with tragic results. It is a sobering, humbling, haunting episode in the history of psychiatry, demonstrating the profound dangers of therapeutic enthusiasm that transitions into therapeutic desperation,[236] underpinned, arguably, by the psychiatric profession's search for professional legitimacy during this period,[237] as well as a deep desire to empty asylums. It was a big mistake, possibly the biggest single mistake in the history of psychiatry.

The long-neglected history of lobotomy in Ireland was recently explored in 'A Flick of the Wrist', a penetrating radio documentary by Jonathan McCrea on Newstalk radio on 30 May 2015,[238] and in 'Anatomy of a Lobotomy' at Smock Alley Theatre, Dublin, as part of The Festival of Curiosity on 23 July 2015. Lobotomy was not, however, entirely without success in Ireland, at least in certain cases. Dr Maurice Guéret, after publishing a fascinating essay on lobotomy in Ireland,[239] records that he received a letter from an elderly man in the North West of Ireland who had a lobotomy as a young man for an obsessional condition and 'never looked back'. Guéret also received a letter from a retired physician who wrote that a 'female civil servant patient' of his had also done well following lobotomy. While lobotomy was rightly abandoned as a routine procedure several decades ago, it is still extremely interesting to hear these reports.[240] However, these reports are provided by survivors: those who died, or were irreparably damaged by the procedure, cannot tell their tales.

In more recent times, Ireland's Mental Health Act 2001 introduced new regulations governing all forms of psychosurgery (including lobotomy, if it were to be suggested) for patients detained in Irish psychiatric facilities. The 2001 Act defined psychosurgery as 'any surgical operation that destroys brain tissue or the functioning of brain tissue and which is performed for the purposes of ameliorating a mental disorder'.[241] Such surgery cannot be performed on a detained patient 'unless (a) the patient gives his or her consent in writing to the psycho-surgery and (b) the psycho-surgery is authorised by a [mental health] tribunal'.[242]

The 2001 Act further specifies that 'where it is proposed to perform psycho-surgery on a [detained] patient and the consent of the patient has been obtained, the consultant psychiatrist responsible for the care and treatment of the patient shall notify in writing the [Mental Health] Commission of the proposal and the Commission shall refer the matter to a tribunal'.[243] The tribunal shall only authorise the surgery 'if it is satisfied that it is in the best interests of the health of the patient concerned'.[244]

In practice, psychosurgery for mental disorder had become a very uncommon treatment by the end of the twentieth century and by the early twenty-first century surgical interest focused chiefly on 'deep brain stimulation' (DBS), which involves implanting electrodes to deliver controlled electrical pulses to targeted parts of the brain.[245] This adjustable, reversible technique holds significant promise for treatment-resistant obsessive-compulsive disorder and, possibly, treatment-resistant depression, addiction and Tourette syndrome (a neuropsychiatric disorder characterised by motor and vocal tics).

Even with the emergence of DBS, however, psychosurgical intervention of any description is now a very rare occurrence in psychiatry, and radical psychosurgery for mental disorder is an exclusively historical phenomenon in Ireland. In the mid-1900s, however, lobotomy belonged firmly alongside insulin coma and ECT in a long line of novel biological treatments which were introduced with enormous drama, followed by growing realisations that apparent benefits were not as great as initially thought and that, in certain cases, serious, irreparable harm resulted.[246]

Interestingly, at the same time that these dramatic waves of biological treatments were transforming psychiatry every few years, the old idea of 'moral management' was quietly evolving in many psychiatric hospitals and asylums. Indeed, by the mid-1950s Ireland was to lead the world with the development of 'occupational therapy' as a key therapeutic element of psychiatric hospital care.[247]

Occupational Therapy:
The New 'Moral Management'?

The idea that occupation and activity were important elements of treatment and asylum life was a long standing one in Irish mental hospitals. In 1810, Hallaran suggested that patients in the asylum 'might on convalescence, be conveyed in covered carriages to the farms, each of which, holding an intimate communication with, and depending on the original foundation, should make daily returns of their proceedings to the principal master, for the weekly inspection of the board of trustees, according to the present invariable custom in this city'.[248] Occupation had already been used as therapy for some time elsewhere, including Pennsylvania Hospital in the US where it was introduced by Benjamin Rush as early as 1796.[249]

Gainful activity, such as working on a farm, duly became an important element of 'moral management' approaches of the nineteenth century.[250] In Castlebar, for example, patients were making mats for the asylum in 1866, and working in various other roles around the institution.[251] As the 1800s and early 1900s progressed, however, the relatively enlightened principles of moral management became less apparent, so that the overcrowded twentieth-century Irish asylums bore little resemblance to the idealised moral management institutions that were dreamed up in the 1800s.[252] At the Central Criminal Lunatic Asylum in Dundrum, for example, the decline in moral management resulted in diminished opportunity for patients to engage in leisure occupations in the late nineteenth and early twentieth centuries, although certain activities managed to survive, including sports (e.g. cricket), religion, music, concerts and reading (with the medical superintendents frequently requesting funds and donations for the libraries).[253]

There were several reasons for the decline of moral management. Ireland's asylums continually grew in size and were quickly overcrowded, with the result that attention was diverted away from the relatively enlightened moral management approach and towards the management of the increasingly large institutions themselves.[254] Key issues included regulation of large numbers of patients within enclosed spaces, the spread of infectious diseases throughout asylum buildings, and an ever increasing pressure on beds. In addition, a renewed emphasis on biological treatments soon emerged, especially at the start of the 1900s, contributing further to the decline of moral management.[255]

The spirit of moral management was not, however, completely extinguished. Throughout the first half of the 1900s, many of its central ideas, especially its focus on exercise and gainful occupation, reappeared in a new form in many asylums, often under the new title 'occupational therapy'. While the emergent model of occupational therapy was by no means identical to moral management, echoes of moral management were immediately recognisable in these renewed practices as they percolated once again through the asylum system.

In Ireland, the institution leading the way in this field was Killarney Mental Hospital where, in 1933, Dr Eamonn O'Sullivan established an occupational therapy department, following visits to several European hospitals that already had programmes of occupational therapy in place.[256] O'Sullivan ensured that 85–90 per cent of all patients, including the acutely ill, were involved in occupational therapy. There were special craft centres, re-education therapy classes and recreational treatment centres. Sports, dances and films were encouraged, as were visits from groups outside the hospital.

O'Sullivan went on to write an influential book on occupational therapy in psychiatry, said to be the first dedicated text in the world, the *Textbook of Occupational Therapy with Chief Reference to Psychological Medicine*.[257] Begun in the 1930s, O'Sullivan's book was published in 1955 and the first thousand copies sold out immediately. O'Sullivan's textbook outlined his views on occupational therapy in considerable detail, and included chapters on the definition and history of occupational therapy; its principles, rules and advantages; personnel requirements; recreation and re-education as forms of therapy; and the commercial side of such undertakings (i.e. purchases, sales, records). Willowcraft, canecraft, woodcraft and weaving were discussed in detail. Weaving assumed particular significance during the Second World War as clothing was in short supply and in, for example, Castlebar, weaving provided the mental hospital with much needed blankets.[258]

The introduction to O'Sullivan's ground breaking book, written by William Rush Dunton, Jr (1868–1966) of Catonsville, Maryland, a founder and president of the American Occupational Therapy Association, noted O'Sullivan's strong emphasis on the importance of considering each patient as an individual when prescribing occupational therapy. In the text itself, O'Sullivan emphasised that occupational therapy is a form of *treatment* and should occur under expert medical direction; be applied methodically; take account of the patient's competence and interests; exhibit diversity and novelty; and be judged by its effect on the patient rather than the quality of workmanship.

In addition, the occupational therapist should have knowledge, aptitude, temperament and manner suited to the task.

The emergent practice of occupational therapy in the asylums was by no means confined to Killarney. In Cork, there was a long history of engaging male patients in agricultural work, tailoring, carpentry and cleaning; and female patients in spinning, needlework, knitting, fancy work, laundry and cleaning.[259] The establishment was criticised in its early years for involving patients in inappropriate, non-therapeutic work (such as clearing rubble), but by the 1930s attention was shifting to more therapeutic art and crafts. In the 1940s, 90 per cent of patients in Cork were engaged in suitable employment in the wards, occupational therapy department, sewing rooms, laundry and kitchen, or assisting trades' staff and on the farm.

In 1934, a committee from Dublin was sent to examine mental hospitals in Scotland, England, Holland and Belgium and reported back to the Grangegorman Joint Committee that occupational therapy was developed to a much greater extent elsewhere compared to Ireland.[260] The committee was especially impressed with Santpoort Mental Hospital in the Netherlands which housed a population of some 1,517 patients, of whom 97 per cent of the physically fit patients were engaged in useful work each day under the supervision of trained occupational therapists. The committee duly recommended that 90 per cent of Grangegorman patients should be in daily active employment supervised by trained, experienced staff. The following year, nurses were seconded to Cardiff Mental Hospital for training and by December 1935 approximately 30 patients in Grangegorman were making rugs and baskets or engaged in embroidery and knitting.

Efforts to implement occupational therapy more widely were, however, frustrated by the sheer size of the hospital in Grangegorman and continual congestion in its wards. In 1935, the Inspector of Mental Hospitals, D.L. Kelly, noted that there were 'far too many women patients idle who might be usefully employed. Steps are being taken to remedy this by organising arts and crafts in the hospital'.[261] The challenges were, however, very great as the Inspector noted that not only was Grangegorman overcrowded but portions of the buildings needed to be replaced.

There were similar initiatives – and problems – in Portrane:

> Occupational therapy has been started and it is hoped this will be taken up seriously. All the tweed used is made in the institution. Large numbers of dresses and other garments are turned out annually. The number of men employed on the farm should be much increased. The number employed within the tradesmen is fairly satisfactory. The grounds and playing fields are maintained in splendid order. The woods and shrubberies, however, are in a very bad state, and the cleaning up of these places would provide suitable employment for a large number of patients.[262]

Over a decade later, in 1949, the Inspector still saw room for improvement. At Grangegorman, 'occupational therapy departments were provided but there was need for extension of this work in all wards. [...] Many indoor and outdoor recreations were provided but recreational therapy needs to be re-organised. The recreation grounds should be extended'.[263] There was still room for improvement in Portrane too:

Excellent care was given to the patients but there was some overcrowding generally in the Institution. The farm supplied milk, meat, potatoes, cereals and vegetables. Patients found useful employment on the farm, at household duties and in the occupational therapy workshops, laundry, and kitchen. Occupational and recreational therapy could be much further extended.

There were similar initiatives at various other mental hospitals during this period. In Ballinasloe, Dr Ada English oversaw substantial advances in occupational therapy during her time there from 1904 to 1942.[264] English was most especially concerned that asylum patients should be gainfully occupied and, as a result, activities on the asylum farms included 'sowing potatoes, mangolds and turnips. They were also employed making fences ...'[265] The asylum farm at Ballinasloe was the subject of particular attention in July 1917 when the Summer Meeting of the Irish Division of the MPA was held in Ballinasloe and the extensive farm and increased food production were deemed especially impressive.[266]

The emphasis on gainful activity for patients in Ballinasloe persisted throughout the 1920s and 1930s. By 1937, female patients were engaged in making rugs, flowers, cardigans, and tapestry, and sewing and crochet work. In addition to working on the farm, the men played football and tennis, and there were billiard tables, cards and musical instruments for amusement.[267] In 1939, the Inspector of Mental Hospitals made particular reference to the 'occupational therapy department' in Ballinasloe, noting that 'a total of 996 patients are engaged in various occupations, as many as 250 being employed on the farm; others are engaged at various trades and handicrafts [...]. The amusements – both indoor and outdoor – of the patients are well catered for; dances are held weekly during the winter months'.[268]

But how much of this activity was truly therapeutic, and, setting aside recreational activity, how much of it reflected unpaid and possibly exploitative labour? Large mental hospitals needed a great deal of work in order to continue functioning and there was continual difficulty ensuring that patient work was genuinely 'therapeutic', and not just cheap labour for the institution. In 1961, a statutory instrument with new 'Mental Treatment Regulations' specified – clearly but belatedly – that work assigned to patients needed to serve a clear 'therapeutic' purpose:

> The assignment of work to a patient in a mental institution shall be in accordance with therapeutic principles and not in accordance with the considerations which would apply if he were employed as a servant, or under a contract of service.[269]

Subsequent years saw considerable change, as the psychiatric institutions became smaller and certain kinds of work were seen as being of little therapeutic value. Space was made for 'industrial therapy', chiefly aimed at rehabilitating patients by involving them in work under simulated factory conditions.[270] The 1961 Regulations did not rule out 'payments to patients for work done', but neither did they make payment mandatory:

> (1) A mental hospital authority may make payments to patients in respect of work done where the authority, acting on the advice of the resident medical superintendent, consider that it is in the interests of the patients that such payments shall be made.

(2) The amount of any payment shall not exceed such sum as may, from time to time, be approved by the Minister.

(3) Payments shall be made only to such patients as, in the opinion of the resident medical superintendent, are likely to use the amount received for their benefit.

(4) Payments may be made in cash or by means of a voucher entitling the patient to purchase from the hospital goods to the value of the amount stated therein.[271]

Other regulations issued in 1961 related to keeping a 'register of patients', seclusion, bodily restraint, 'correspondence of patients', visiting committees, the role of 'chief medical officer', and various other matters. A series of 'prescribed forms' were provided for use with the Mental Treatment Act 1945.

Back in the earlier 1900s, English (a keen golfer) at Ballinasloe was an especially strong promoter of sports. In most asylums, both staff and patients participated in sport, which could act as an important leveller of relations between staff and patients.[272] Ballinasloe had especially strong teams in camogie, hockey and tug-of-war, all of which competed nationally.[273] In 1915, English was largely responsible for the introduction of camogie and the hospital team duly became one of the best in the country.[274] In 1921, a cinder track was laid for the purpose of cycling competitions and National Cycling Championships were duly held there.

These innovations were consistent with the importance many mental hospitals in Ireland and elsewhere attached to sport as both an important activity for patients and staff, and as a form of therapy.[275] Dr Patrick Heffernan, appointed as Assistant Medical Officer at Clonmel Lunatic Asylum in 1902, recalls the centrality of rugby, rowing and cricket in Clonmel in the early 1900s,[276] while in 1932, Dr Patrick O'Callaghan (1905–1991), Assistant Medical Officer at Clonmel, retained, at the Los Angeles Olympic Games, the gold medal he had won at the 1928 Amsterdam Olympics for the hammer throw.[277]

In 1930, 'mental hospital sports' in Carlow included running, hurdles, running high jump, running broad jump, putting shot, cycling and pole vaulting.[278] In Castlebar, the hospital sports were a focus for many local societies and the hospital sports field was used by the Gaelic League Committee and Castlebar Committee for Horse Jumping and Trotting.[279] In September 1912, an aeroplane exhibition was held in the hospital grounds, to the great enjoyment of patients and others.

In 1935, the Inspector of Mental Hospitals noted with approval that football, hurling, cricket, croquet, indoor billiards and other games were played at Grangegorman in Dublin, and that the annual sports were 'an enjoyable feature'.[280] Clearly, sport served as an important way for patients to engage with each other and with staff, and could even create a valuable bridge to the world outside the asylum walls.[281] In Portlaoise mental hospital, sports included ball playing, hand ball, football, cricket[282] and rugby.[283] (Also in Portlaoise, in an apparently minor but fascinating development, staff reported the first use of a 'biro' (a kind of ballpoint pen) in the hospital in 1945: the fact that the 'biro', first used by Dr Grace, did not need to be refilled with ink was immediately the topic of conversation.)[284]

Notwithstanding these activities and developments, it remained a stubborn, undeniable fact that patients in Irish mental hospitals were still resident in overcrowded, unhygienic institutions. Efforts to improve their quality of life through sports or occupational therapy or any other means *within the hospitals* were grossly hampered by the institutional settings themselves, and, more profoundly, by the lack of liberty and hope that these patients commonly experienced.

Clearly, local initiatives, however well intentioned, were proving insufficient to provide the systemic reforms necessary to enhance patient dignity and genuinely transform Ireland's mental hospitals. More profound change, at national level, was needed.

Mental Treatment Act 1945: Reforming the Law

By the mid-1900s, it had been apparent for several decades that Irish mental health legislation was in urgent need of reform. Interestingly, the Mental Treatment Bill 1944 was ultimately tabled without particularly broad consultation,[285] although some of the reforms discussed at the Conference of the Irish Asylums Committee in 1903 (especially those related to community care) were advanced by the new Bill,[286] and Dunne at Grangegorman advised the Department of Health on the final legislation.[287]

Introducing the 1944 Bill for a second reading in the Dáil on 29 November 1944, the Parliamentary Secretary to the Minister for Local Government and Public Health, Dr Conn Ward, was unsparing about the need for change. He noted that some of the legislation governing mental illness dated 'back as far as the year 1821. The general consensus of opinion with persons engaged in administration favours the replacement of those Acts by one complete measure'. Ward went on to note that:

> The Commission on the Relief of the Sick and Destitute Poor, Including the Insane Poor, in their report, which was published in 1927, said:
> 'The law governing lunacy [administration] is, as we have shown, to be found in numerous statutes passed in the course of a century. These statutes do not form one consistent whole; they are in some respects obsolete, defective, and even contradictory. We, therefore, recommend that all the existing lunacy Acts be repealed and that new legislation take the form of an amending and consolidating Act'.[288]
> That commission made other suggestions for the amendment of the law, particularly in regard to the procedure by which admission to mental institutions was obtained and to the question of provision for early treatment of incipient mental disease. Their views in these matters are endorsed by medical practitioners engaged in the treatment of mental disease. They support the opinion that the law on the subject requires radical reform. There is no provision in the law to enable a poor person to submit himself voluntarily for mental treatment, nor is it possible for a patient to be admitted to an institution for treatment for temporary mental disorder. Furthermore, very little latitude is given as to the nature and kind of mental institutions which may be provided by mental hospital authorities.
> In the Bill before the House it is proposed to remedy these defects and to make other amendments in the law to secure for mental patients the benefits of the advances

made in medical science and treatment in the present century. It is proposed in the Bill to substitute for the law at present in force relating to the prevention and treatment of mental disorders a new code in harmony with modern views on the treatment of mental illness.[289]

The 1945 Act, which came into force on 1 January 1947, presented several important reforms.[290] These included, most notably, the introduction of a voluntary admission status,[291] a reform which had already been implemented in Great Britain (1930) and Northern Ireland (1932).[292] Ireland's 1945 Act also introduced two new procedures for involuntary admission, one for 'persons of unsound mind' and the other for 'temporary chargeable patients'. Both procedures required that a family member, relative or other person make an 'application' for involuntary admission,[293] and that an 'authorised medical officer' (e.g. general practitioner) examine the individual, who was then transported to the psychiatric hospital (by the Gardaí, if necessary) where a detention order could be completed by a doctor, following psychiatric examination.[294]

The key difference between the 'person of unsound mind' and 'temporary chargeable patient' procedures was that the former resulted in detention and involuntary treatment for an indefinite period, while the latter resulted in detention and involuntary treatment for up to six months (although it could be extended if clinically indicated). Neither form of detention involved automatic review by tribunal or a court, although any detention order could be revoked at any time by the treating psychiatrist. If the patient wished to challenge his or her detention, he or she could write privately to the 'Inspector of Mental Hospitals' who could look into the matter and report to the Minister for Health, who could then order the discharge of the patient.[295]

The patient also had the right to have a letter forwarded, unopened, to the Minister for Health, President of the High Court, Registrar of Wards of Court or 'mental hospital authority'.[296] Alternatively, the patient could instigate legal action in the courts under the Constitution of Ireland.[297] As a result, the 'person of unsound mind' procedure resulted in indefinite, potentially life long detention, without automatic external review, especially for individuals who lacked the mental capacity or financial resources to access the courts.[298]

Moreover, even if a detained patient accessed legal representation in order to challenge their detention in the High Court, the 1945 Act, as amended by Section 2(3) of the Public Authorities Judicial Proceedings Act 1954, stated:

> No civil proceedings shall be instituted in respect of an act purporting to have been done in pursuance of this Act save by leave of the High Court and such leave shall not be granted unless the High Court is satisfied that there are substantial grounds for contending that the person against whom the proceedings are to be brought acted in bad faith or without reasonable care.[299]

In 2008, after the Mental Treatment Act 1945 had been replaced by the Mental Health Act 2001, the Irish Supreme Court found that this section of the 1945 Act had been unconstitutional, as it restricted grounds for challenging detention to two specific grounds (acting in 'bad faith' or proceeding 'without reasonable care').[300] The Supreme Court stated that this was a disproportionate restriction on the detained patient's right to access the courts where a fundamental right, liberty, had been restricted, and was, thus, contrary to the Constitution of Ireland.

As well as its changes in relation to voluntary and involuntary admission, the 1945 Act introduced many changes to Ireland's network of psychiatric hospitals, with provisions relating to the Inspector of Mental Hospitals, Mental Hospital Districts and Mental Hospital Authorities, and superannuation, in addition to matters relating to officers of Mental Hospital Authorities, private institutions, private charitable institutions, authorised institutions, approved institutions and various other matters.

O'Brien, in 1967, described the legislation as enlightened,[301] and more recently Brown noted that the purpose of the 1945 Act was *treatment* of persons with mental disorder and that it provided psychiatry with complete control over detention of the mentally ill.[302] It certainly represented a significant shift in the balance between medicalism and legalism, although it was extremely difficult then (as it is today) to disentangle these two concepts in the setting of involuntary psychiatric care. In any case, in 1947, the first year of operation of the new legislation, 941 psychiatric admissions were voluntary, which amounted to 23 per cent of all admissions, and in 1959 this had increased dramatically to 6,871 voluntary admissions in that year, accounting for 59 per cent of admissions.

The overtly paternal nature of the 1945 Act was, however, strongly reinforced by the Supreme Court in 1949, which concluded that the legislation was clearly intended for the custody and care of persons who were mentally ill and for the safety and wellbeing of the public.[303] Thus it was the legal establishment, rather than the medical one, that espoused paternalism with particular enthusiasm. The Court concluded that the 1945 Act was designed for the protection of the citizen and the public good, and could not be considered as an attack on the personal rights of the citizen. Indeed, when Ward presented the Bill for a second reading in the Dáil in 1944, he emphasised the Bill's intention to *reduce* the numbers in hospitals, particularly those denied their liberty for lengthy periods:

> It is the considered opinion of specialists engaged in the treatment of mental disease that to reduce the numbers in the mental institutions attention should be focused on the treatment of early cases of mental disorder and that failure to make provision for the treatment of such cases must result in an increase of the numbers suffering from mental afflictions and requiring prolonged or permanent treatment in mental institutions.
>
> The arguments already put forward in favour of the establishment of consulting rooms and clinics apply with equal force to the provision of facilities for the treatment of voluntary patients. Persons suspecting symptoms of mental or nervous disease should be encouraged to seek advice and treatment in the early stages before the disease is too far developed. It is essential, therefore, to remove all formalities such as certification and formal committal to mental institutions which are likely to deter or discourage patients from seeking treatment of their own accord.[304]

If the purpose of the Mental Treatment Act 1945 was to stem the ever rising tide of committals to Irish asylums, however, as well as reducing stigma, it did not succeed immediately. The number of inpatients continued to rise following the new legislation, reaching a peak in the late 1950s, when there were approximately 21,000 people in Irish psychiatric hospitals and units, representing 0.7 per cent of the Republic's entire population.[305] This was attributed, at least in part, to the increase in voluntary patients following the new legislation.[306] In some towns, the asylum continued to dominate the local economy: in 1951 the town of Ballinasloe had a population of 5,596, of whom 2,078 were patients in the asylum.[307]

Change was, however, starting to occur. In 1966, Dunne, recently retired from St Brendan's, reported that the annual number of admissions to Dublin psychiatric hospitals had increased from 400 in 1945 to 2,989 in 1965, a trend that Dunne attributed largely to a change in attitudes towards mental illness since the 1945 Act was passed.[308] Critically, however, the number of discharges had also increased, from 400 in 1945 to 3,000 in 1965. Consequently, on balance, inpatient numbers were now firmly in decline, and, nationally, reached 16,802 in 1969, 7,897 in 1989 and 4,469 in 1999.[309]

As a result, the 1945 Act certainly, at the very least, preceded the resolution of Ireland's high rates of psychiatric detention. As regards the mechanism of that resolution, it is now clear that the legislation's increased medicalisation of involuntary admissions *both* predated *and* facilitated the decline in numbers. This, in turn, set the scene for the most influential report on Irish mental health services in the twentieth century: the seminal '1966 Report' of the Commission of Inquiry on Mental Illness.[310]

Commission of Inquiry on Mental Illness (1966): 'A Health Problem of the First Magnitude'

The process of mental health reform took a substantial step forward in the mid-1960s with the publication of the '1966 Report' of the Commission of Inquiry on Mental Illness (Coimisiún Fiosrúcháin um Easláinte Meabhrach). The commission was appointed in 1961 by Seán MacEntee, Minister for Health, to report on the services available to the mentally ill and propose improvements.[311] MacEntee had previously addressed a meeting of resident medical superintendents of district mental hospitals and criticised the services on offer to the mentally ill both within and outside mental hospitals, as well as the high numbers of inpatients.[312] The resultant commission was chaired by Mr Justice Seamus Henchy and presented its findings to Seán Flanagan, Minister for Health, on 11 November 1966. The '1966 Report' was published on 29 March 1967.[313]

The commission was an important, interesting body, which comprised a broad range of persons, including psychiatrists; received 'memoranda of evidence' for its consideration; and heard from witnesses including representatives of the Irish Division of the RMPA and Dr Dermot Walsh of St Loman's Hospital, Ballyowen, Dublin. The composition of the commission changed over the course of its work: Mr Michael Viney, a journalist, was appointed on 16 July 1965.

The eventual cost of the 1966 report was approximately £14,760 of which £1,600 was the 'estimated cost of printing and publication'.[314] The report was 'unanimous' and unsparing in its opening assessment of the magnitude of the problems it sought to address:

> Mental illness constitutes one of the major health problems of modern society. It has
> been estimated in other countries that, at present, about one of every three people

seeking medical treatment at general practitioner level has a psychiatric aspect to his illness and that about one person in twelve, at some stage of life, is likely to need in-patient psychiatric care. In many countries, 30 per cent to 40 per cent of the hospital beds are assigned to the mentally ill.

In Ireland, approximately 7.3 psychiatric beds were provided in 1961 per 1,000 of the population; this rate appears to be the highest in the world and compared with 4.5 in Northern Ireland, 4.6 in England and Wales, 4.3 in Scotland, 2.1 in France and 4.3 in U.S.A. At any given time, about one in every seventy of our people above the age of 24 years is in a mental hospital. When it is remembered that every mentally ill person brings stress into the lives of people around him, it will be clear that in Ireland mental illness poses a health problem of the first magnitude.[315]

The commission recommended 'radical and widespread changes'[316] to mental health services, including a move away from 'barrack-like structures characterised by large wards, gloomy corridors and stone stairways':[317]

> The capacity of modern psychiatry to give good results with intensive and comprehensive in-patient treatment in a great number of cases, together with the desirability of providing such treatment within the ambit of general medicine, has led the Commission to recommend the setting up of short-term residential units in, or in association with, general hospitals. Such units would require to be adequately staffed and equipped, to be associated with the community services of a particular area, to be ready to treat all types of mental illness requiring short-term in-patient care, and to work in close conjunction with the other psychiatric services and with the general hospital [...].
>
> For the patient requiring long-term treatment, the Commission recommends the development of long-term hospitals fulfilling a positive and creative role. The aim will be to provide active treatment as well as residential care, to rehabilitate and restore to the community as many patients as possible, and to provide for all patients lives as full and happy as their disabilities permit.[318]

Overall, the commission aimed 'to reduce the present estimated total of 10,000 long-stay places to approximately 5,000 over the next 15 years. The commission is satisfied that, with increased emphasis on community care and on active treatment and early discharge of patients, there will be a considerable reduction in the number requiring long-term residential care'.[319] The commission acknowledged that 'the general medical practitioner will have a particularly important part to play' in the new system[320] and recommended that 'provision should be made for a system of family care, properly organised and supervised and closely linked with the general scheme of psychiatric services.'[321]

In addition to these overarching measures and policy shifts towards community based services, the commission presented specific recommendations relating to private psychiatric facilities; children and adolescents; older persons; persons with problems related to alcohol and drugs; persons with epilepsy; persons in custody; 'homicidal and very violent patients';[322] people appearing before the courts; and 'sexual deviates' ('sexual deviates are not necessarily mentally ill, but they are a vulnerable group who may be in need of help. At present the main form of treatment is proper counselling')[323] (Chapter 6). The commission expressed the view that 'all treatment services have a preventive aspect. Concentration on these aspects and the institution of specific preventive measures are necessary to reduce the enormous impact of mental illness'.[324]

The commission placed strong emphasis on research, recommending that 'the Minister for Health should provide funds for research':[325]

> Despite the enormous impact of mental illness, research into treatment, into the efficacy of different forms of care and into causes and possible methods of prevention are practically non-existent in this country. The Commission considers it essential that such research be carried out. In many other countries an appreciable part of mental health expenditure is devoted to research.[326]

The commission was similarly emphatic on the theme of 'education and training' and made specific recommendations relating to medical education ('a wholetime Chair in Psychiatry should be established in each of the medical schools'),[327] psychologists, psychiatric nurses, social workers, occupational therapists and chaplains:

> The quality of a mental health service ultimately depends on the availability of adequate and well-trained staff to operate it effectively. In the development of psychiatric services, therefore, it is essential that priority should be given to the education and training of professional staff and that a considerable part of available resources should be devoted to this work. In addition to professional staff, there are many members of the general public, such as clergy and teachers, who can make a major contribution to the psychiatric services, provided they have an adequate appreciation of the needs of psychiatric patients.[328]

The commission recommended further 'education of the public' because 'full support from the community is essential if psychiatric services are to be fully developed';[329] various changes to the 'organisation of services', including establishment of a 'National Advisory Council' and 'national voluntary body' to 'help advance the cause of the mentally ill';[330] and revisions to legislation, including 'a system of compulsory admission' to 'provide for detention for an observation and examination period not exceeding 14 days', which, if necessary, 'could be extended for a further period not exceeding six weeks from the date of admission', followed, if necessary, by further periods of 3 and 6 months from the date of admission, and then periods of not more than 12 months.[331]

The 1966 report was an important and generally progressive document,[332] albeit that many of its recommendations were not new: Norman at the Richmond, for example, had recommended 'domestic treatment of the insane' in 1896 [333] and 'family care of the insane' in 1905.[334] In 1957, the Royal Commission on the Law Relating to Mental Illness and Mental Deficiency in Great Britain had declared that when any hospital inpatient was at a point where he or she could be discharged if he or she had a reasonably good home to go to, provision of residential care became the responsibility of the local authority.[335] The 1957 commission also recommended that psychiatric treatment should be provided with the minimum curtailment of liberty and as little legal formality as possible.

In Ireland, the 1966 report was generally praised for its sensible proposals and community orientation, with particular attention drawn to the role of the general practitioner.[336] The 'national voluntary body' that it recommended to 'help advance the cause of the mentally ill'[337] had already been set up as the Mental Health Association of Ireland and held its inaugural meeting on 24 February 1967.[338]

Notwithstanding these signs of progress, however, full implementation of the 1966 report was clearly going to be challenging, as commentators soon highlighted a range of ongoing issues relating to, *inter alia*, facilities for children with autism,[339] forensic mental health care,[340] and the need for epidemiological research into Ireland's high rates of psychiatric hospitalisation.[341]

The tasks set out in the 1966 report were clearly large, important ones, and changing attitudes towards mental disorder was to prove complex and slow. Less than two weeks after the 1966 Report was published, for example, one judge stated, in the context of a specific case, that a priest 'is the best psychiatrist in the world'.[342] This was rapidly and hotly disputed by Dr Noël Browne (1915–1997)[343] and served to highlight the real need for 'education of the public' which the 1966 report regarded as 'essential if psychiatric services are to be fully developed'.[344] One of the areas within psychiatric services that was already being actively developed over this period, even prior to the 1966 report, was the independent sector, and these developments are reflected well in the ongoing story of the historic St Patrick's Hospital in Dublin.

St Patrick's Hospital: 'Dedication, Understanding and Trust'

By the end of the nineteenth century, St Patrick's Hospital was in a state of decline. Inspection reports were poor, conditions in the hospital were far from optimal, and finances were in disarray.[345] The first clear signs of reform became apparent in the 1890s. In 1897, Dr John Moloney (medical superintendent from 1884 to 1899) became the first university examiner in mental diseases in Trinity (teaching in mental diseases having been introduced in 1893),[346] and in 1899 a new, reforming medical superintendent was appointed: Dr Richard Robert Leeper (1864–1942).

Leeper was born in Tinahely, County Wicklow on 6 December 1864.[347] His father, Richard John Leeper, who was in medical practice in Wicklow, died when Leeper was three weeks old, so Leeper spent much of his boyhood at the home of his uncle, the Reverend Canon Leeper, Rector of St Audeon's Church, Dublin, close to St Patrick's Hospital.[348] Leeper attended Dr Benson's School in Rathmines, alongside Daniel Rambaut, who, like Leeper, would also go on to a distinguished career in psychiatry (Chapter 4).

Leeper commenced medical studies at the age of 16 years in the Royal College of Surgeons and obtained the Licentiate of the College four years later. In 1886 he obtained the Licentiate of the Royal College of Physicians and, in 1890, Fellowship of the Irish Royal College of Surgeons. Leeper first worked in psychiatry at Hampstead and Highfield Private Mental Hospitals in Dublin, for three years from 1888, and then went into private practice in Wicklow. In 1899 Leeper was appointed Medical Superintendent at St Patrick's, having been encouraged to accept the post by, among other governors, the prominent surgeon Sir Thornley Stoker.[349]

Leeper's impact on St Patrick's was rapid, positive and profound, characterised by his energetic approach to administration and practical approach to psychiatric care.[350] He focused especially on expanding the hospital, according to his obituarist, Thompson, in the *Journal of Mental Science*:

> Many of the additions which Leeper made to the hospital showed vision and courage of a high order. About the year 1907 he built a spacious Villa for gentlemen patients in the lovely old demesne of the Branch Hospital at Lucan [now St Edmundsbury Hospital]. The investment, made when funds could not have been too liberal, amply repaid the outlay. In 1916 he added male and female wings to the main hospital, and from then onwards, for the next twenty years, he carried out continuous improvements. Further male and female wings of a new architectural design, a dental and electro-therapeutic block, cinema theatre, extensions to the visiting rooms and pharmacy, remodelling of the offices and kitchens, re-roofing of farm buildings, installation of power plants, etc., were only the main items in a continuous programme.[351]

Professor Thomas Lynch later (1992) noted that Leeper 'was in charge of St Patrick's from 1906 to about 1942. He was credited for having changed the cells to rooms. He took out the straw and he put in beds and mattresses. He built a cinema and recreation centre for patients and was instrumental in purchasing St Edmundsbury as a convalescent hospital'.[352]

Leeper persuaded the board of the hospital to pursue a more rigorous admission policy, with the result that admission numbers rose and the proportion of 'free' patients fell from 28 per cent in 1899 to 7 per cent in 1933, by which time the proportion of patients maintained 'at or over cost' had increased to 50 per cent.[353] Leeper also worked incessantly for better conditions for patients and placed strong emphases on careful history taking and examination, rest, restoration of physical health, recreation and occupational therapy:

> Perhaps, however, Leeper's greatest claim to fame as a psychiatrist lay in his use of suggestion. His buoyant personality and fund of anecdote and story were in themselves suggestion of a powerful order. In his wide reading and manifold interests he had grounds in common with almost every patient, but he constantly added touches which were of a purely personal nature. A Sunday morning round, for example, might end up in his own house, where for several hours he would show a selected group of patients the various treasures of Swift he had collected, or his sets of duelling pistols, or curios of old Dublin. Throughout the spring and summer months it was a common sight to see his car 'filled to capacity' with convalescent patients on a visit to the Branch Hospital at Lucan. Here he would display the gardens, or give the history of the old manor house, or perhaps fix up a rod and let them see his skill on the river. The party

might arrive back at any hour up to near midnight, and those who had been on similar excursions never refused the invitation.[354]

Leeper also found time to write academic papers and engage in research: at a meeting of the Irish Division of the MPA in the College of Physicians, Kildare Street on 23 May 1902, Leeper read a paper titled 'Observations on the neuroglia cell and its processes'.[355] He also showed a series of microscopic preparations of neuroglia fibres from the brain of a patient with epilepsy.[356] Other speakers on that occasion included Rambaut, who read a paper on 'case-taking in large asylums',[357] and Norman, who read a paper on 'obsessions'.

Leeper went on to serve as secretary of the Irish Division of the MPA from 1911 to 1929 ('RMPA' from 1926 onward), before becoming first chairman of the Division in 1929, two years prior to assuming overall presidency in 1931.[358] Leeper's hobbies included shooting, fencing, armoury, period furniture and natural history. After an eventful life which saw him lead a remarkable revival of fortunes at St Patrick's, Leeper died of cardiac failure on 25 March 1942.

Leeper's enthusiastic work at St Patrick's was carried on by Dr (later Professor) J.N.P. Moore (1911–1996) who served as junior assistant medical officer from 1938 to 1941, and medical superintendent from 1946 to 1977.[359] Moore was born in Beragh, County Tyrone in 1911 and, following a stellar medical undergraduate career at Trinity, applied successfully for the post of medical officer at St Patrick's in the late 1930s.[360] After two years at St Patrick's, he went on for further training in psychiatry at the Crichton Royal in Dumfries, where he was strongly influenced by Professor Wilhelm Mayer-Gross, a charismatic, gifted teacher.[361]

Moore returned to Ireland and became medical superintendent of St Patrick's in 1946. He was a leading, much admired figure in Irish psychiatry for several decades.[362] Clare, in a moving obituary, highlighted Moore's therapeutic enthusiasm:

> He exuded optimism: for him psychiatric illness was, for the most part, eminently treatable. What was needed was appropriate knowledge, a healing atmosphere, an optimistic therapist, and time. He fostered training, developed out-patient care, built up the staff. He could be stern, even intimidating – yet the only thing he could not forgive was indifference. The hospital under his influence, supported by a wise Board of Governors, gave him his head and he repaid their confidence by making St Patrick's a byword for dedication, understanding and trust. Patient turnover soared, length of stay fell and the hospital embarked on a major programme of redevelopment which continued throughout his time in office.[363]

Moore held the position of Clinical Professor of Psychiatry at Trinity College Dublin. He attracted Peter Beckett (1922–1974) back to Ireland and Beckett was appointed first professor of psychiatry and head of the recently established department at Trinity in 1969.[364] Beckett made invaluable contributions to academic and clinical psychiatry, as well as postgraduate training programmes. He served as Professor of Psychiatry (1969–74) and Dean of the Faculty at Trinity (1972–4), and a prize in his memory is now awarded annually to the Trinity medical student showing the greatest potential in psychiatry.

A strong public advocate for psychiatry, Moore was a member of the influential Commission of Inquiry on Mental Illness in the mid-1960s, which was to shape psychiatric care in Ireland for decades to follow.[365] Moore also, along with Dr Maurice O'Connor 'Con' Drury, deputy director of St Patrick's, had contact with the philosopher Ludwig Wittgenstein (1889–1951) in Dublin in the late 1940s.[366] The relationship between Drury and Wittgenstein is especially fascinating and of considerable significance in the history of Wittgenstein's life and thought.[367] Drury himself was a remarkable figure, with deep interests in psychiatry, philosophy, religion, hypnosis, Freud, Jung and many other areas.[368]

Professor Thomas Lynch later (1992) described Moore as 'very articulate, intelligent, and influential', as well as 'easy to work with':[369]

> Norman [Moore] was keen on fishing and shooting and St Edmondsbury was a lovely place with over 300 acres. He used to go shooting and fishing with us, in our single days. The hospital had an old Austin 1929 car with a luggage grid in the back which you could stand on. I was usually the lad without the gun and I was selected to drive the car at night with the headlights on, while Maurice Pillsworth and Denis Doorley stood on the luggage carrier shooting rabbits. It was a different life at that period.[370]

At the end of his tenure as medical director St Patrick's (1946–77),[371] Moore was succeeded as medical director by a succession of prominent medical figures who reformed and expanded the hospital in various different ways: P.J. Meehan (medical director from 1978 to 1983),[372] Karl O'Sullivan (1983–8),[373] Anthony Clare (1989–2001),[374] Patrick McKeon (2002–7)[375] and James Lucey (2008–the present).[376] Over this period, St Patrick's continued to develop and expand in highly progressive ways, and was renamed St Patrick's University Hospital owing to its strong academic history and connections.

By the early 2000s, St Patrick's had become Ireland's largest, independent, not-for-profit mental health service, and a recognised leader in the provision of quality mental health care and promotion of mental health awareness.[377] St Patrick's Mental Health Services now offer a broad array of inpatient and outpatient treatment programmes, including dedicated mental health services for adolescents (aged 14 to 18 years) and young adults (aged 18 to 25 years), and an eating disorders service.[378]

In 2014, the Inspector of Mental Health Services reported that 'St Patrick's University Hospital was compliant with all Regulations, Rules and Codes of Practice. There was a wide range of therapeutic programmes and excellent multidisciplinary input with good individual care planning'.[379] This was a far cry from the highly critical inspection reports of St Patrick's Hospital in the distant past,[380] and more in keeping with the far-seeing intentions of the hospital's illustrious founder, Jonathan Swift.[381]

6

Ж

THE TWENTIETH CENTURY:
DECLINE OF THE INSTITUTIONS

In short, although doubts were being expressed about the reliance on psychiatric hospitals for the care of the mentally ill at the end of the last [nineteenth] century, no alternative was proposed until the 1940s and little provision made before the late 1950s. Where alternatives have been provided they are often unequally distributed and while some areas are well supplied with community facilities, in other areas there are considerable inadequacies.

Study Group on the Development of the
Psychiatric Services, *The Psychiatric
Services – Planning for the Future*
(1984)[1]

By the mid-1960s, the number of patients in Ireland's psychiatric institutions was in firm decline. Deinstitutionalisation in Ireland was steady rather than sudden, attributable chiefly to gradual changes in Irish society and psychiatric practice, in contrast with the more dramatic mental health reforms in, for example, Italy.[2] In Ireland, inpatient numbers decreased slowly but steadily from 19,801 in 1963, to 16,661 in 1971, 13,984 in 1981, 8,207 in 1991 and 4,256 in 2001.[3]

In parallel with this decrease in the number of people who were inpatients at any given time, the annual number of *admissions* (a more dynamic measure of activity) increased from 15,440 in 1965 to 19,697 in 1969 – an increase of some 27.6 per cent – reflecting shorter lengths of stay and greater likelihood of discharge.[4] This increase in admissions had commenced some decades earlier and continued into the 1960s and well beyond.[5] By 31 December 2014, the number of inpatients stood at 2,228, a decrease of 173 since 2013 and an 89 per cent reduction since 1963.[6] There were also, in 2014, 71 children and adolescents (under the age of 18 years) in specialist child and adolescent units. During the course of 2014, there was a total of 17,797 admissions, a decrease since 2013, when there were 18,457 admissions.[7]

This chapter explores various aspects of this fundamental change in Irish mental health services during the latter part of the 1900s and the early 2000s, and also discusses a series of prominent figures in Irish psychiatry who were involved with these changes. These figures are, for the most part, either recently retired or recently deceased, so it is too soon to present a historically informed critical appraisal of their contributions. As a result, this chapter chiefly sets out key facts about their careers and accomplishments (with some brief comments), without engaging in premature attempts at a critical evaluation of their work. These accounts and comments should not, therefore, be read as historical analyses. It is, however, hoped that they will assist future historians in evaluating critically the contributions made by these pivotal figures during this period of rapid change in Irish psychiatry.

One of the undeniable drivers of this change, although by no means the only or even most important one, was the discovery and introduction of antipsychotic medication.[8] The most significant of these agents, chlorpromazine, came to prominence in the 1950s, when Jean Delay and Pierre Deniker in Paris published data indicating the agent's usefulness for the treatment of psychosis, thus introducing the first effective medication for schizophrenia.[9] Initially regarded as an anaesthetic, the value of chlorpromazine as an antipsychotic medication soon had far-reaching effects, especially in reducing the use of physical restraints in psychiatric hospitals.[10]

Chlorpromazine was described as a 'major tranquilizer'[11] and appeared to reduce the intensity of emotional states without substantial reduction of intellectual function.[12] Some 1960s commentators were exceptionally enthusiastic about the new discovery and saw chlorpromazine and related medications (known as 'phenothiazines') as more than simply tranquilizers and as potentially reversing the very pathology of schizophrenia.[13]

In Ireland, Dunne gave a generally positive account of the new medications to the monthly meeting of the Grangegorman Mental Hospital Board in November 1956, reporting significant benefits from their use, although these benefits were not, he said, quite as substantial as he had been led to expect.[14] By 1961, Dunne noted that there was now a new spirit of hope in mental hospitals,[15] but also (wisely) continued to emphasise the importance of non-medication aspects of care, such as rehabilitation.[16] Hill states that the effect of the new medications (both antipsychotics and antidepressants), combined with structural and other improvements at the mental hospital in Portlaoise in the 1950s, were such as to finally merit the term 'hospital' rather than 'institution'.[17] McDermott, writing in the context of Castlebar, also notes the improvements that these medications brought to the old mental hospitals;[18] Henry reports the same in Cork;[19] and there were similar benefits reported from, for example, Portrane.[20] In Carlow, RMS Bertram Blake, supported by the management committee, had the asylum walls reduced to three feet and topped with flowers.[21]

The introduction of the new antipsychotic medications, also known as 'neuroleptics', in the form of long-acting injections meant that they could be administered just once every few weeks, without necessarily requiring daily tablets. This facilitated discharge and care at home for many long stay patients right across Ireland.[22] In 1992, Professor Thomas Lynch recalled the effect of these tablets and injections when first introduced:

> Regarding neuroleptics, my first dramatic experience was with an out-patient in County Waterford, a young boy who was prescribed a small dose of chlorpromazine – he had paranoid symptoms and while he was on the drug he was symptom free but when he omitted to take it he would relapse within weeks. This was very dramatic,

so much so that I became convinced that it wasn't just purely damping down the psychotic symptoms, until they naturally abated of their accord. This, to my mind, provided proof of an anti-psychotic effect.

The depot [long-acting, injected] neuroleptics appeared in the late 1960s. There are a plethora of these available now. In those days nobody knew how they worked. It was clear that they were effective and in some patients dramatically so.[23]

While these new medications, including lithium in the 1970s,[24] undoubtedly helped alleviate severe mental disorder for many patients in Irish mental hospitals, dismantling institutional structures that were as socially embedded as the asylums was to require much more than just medication. Societal change and media pressure, especially in the late 1960s, made vital contributions to the eventual decline in inpatient numbers. In the late 1960s, the report of the Commission of Inquiry on Mental Illness also strongly underlined the need to move away from institutional care and towards care in the community,[25] as Irish society in general finally moved to become somewhat less custodial in character.[26]

In October 1963, the *Irish Times* published an especially affecting series of articles by Michael Viney highlighting the broad range of problems related to mental health care and, in particular, the disproportionate numbers still resident in Irish psychiatric hospitals.[27] Viney drew much needed attention to persistent issues of overcrowding, gloomy facilities, the roles of psychotherapy and rehabilitation, and various misunderstandings about mental disorder.[28] Similar themes emerged in a hard hitting 1980 report in *Magill* magazine written by Helen Connolly, with searing, unforgettable photographs by Derek Speirs.[29] The *Magill* report also noted the difficulty in getting families involved in care, with some hospitals reporting that just 25 per cent of patients received at least an occasional visit.

In 1981, when inpatient numbers still stood at 13,984,[30] the *Irish Times* carried another very useful analysis of Ireland's psychiatric services, noting that Ireland had 377 inpatients in public psychiatric hospitals per 100,000 population, compared to 334 in Scotland and approximately 164 in England.[31] The number of psychiatrists (consultant and non-consultant doctors) working in Ireland's public psychiatric services was relatively low, at 4.9 per 100,000 population, compared to 9.5 in Scotland and 6.8 in England. The article explored various specific challenges in Irish mental health but also noted one of the few examples of community care at St Lawrence's Road in Clontarf, Dublin, run by Dr Brian McCaffrey, a strong, effective and highly progressive advocate for improved mental health services.[32]

Against this background of a declining system of mental hospitals,[33] and scattered but definite signs of change, this chapter examines specific aspects of this period of critical transition in Irish psychiatry, exploring evolving views on allegedly high rates of mental disorder in Ireland, the role of psychiatry in relation to homosexuality, leaders of change in mental health services, the ill-fated Health (Mental Services) Act 1981, the development of mental health nursing and policy, and emerging recognition of the importance of human rights in the context of mental disorder.

First, however, this chapter turns its attention to two rare but valuable examples of patients in Irish mental hospitals finding clear and public voice to recount their experiences, one from Monaghan

Mental Hospital in the mid-1930s and the other from St Loman's Hospital, Mullingar, spanning a period from the 1940s to the early 1960s. These are vital, compelling chronicles that deserve wider audiences.

Case Studies: Reverend Clarence Duffy and Hanna Greally

Patients' accounts of psychiatric institutions provide important records of life in mental hospitals and offer perspectives which merit particular attention and study.[34]

In 1838, John Thomas Perceval (1803–1876), son of Spencer Perceval (1762–1812; prime minister of the UK, 1809–12), published his account of his 17 month stay at Dr Edward Fox's Lunatic Asylum in Brislington, near Bristol,[35] titled *A Narrative of the Treatment Experienced by a Gentleman During a State of Mental Derangement Designed to Explain the Causes and Nature of Insanity, and to Expose the Injudicious Conduct Pursued Towards Many Unfortunate Sufferers under that Calamity*.[36] In 1908, in the US, Clifford Whittingham Beers (1876–1943) published his account of psychiatric hospitalisation, titled *A Mind that Found Itself: An Autobiography*[37] and went on, in 1909, to co-found the National Committee for Mental Hygiene.[38]

Both of these accounts were highly critical of the asylum systems of England and the US, respectively, and both generated considerable publicity. Ireland, however, had to wait until the mid-1900s for similarly personalised accounts of psychiatric institutionalisation to generate significant impact, with the appearances of *It Happened in Ireland* by Reverend Clarence Duffy in 1944[39] and Hanna Greally's fascinating memoir, *Bird's Nest Soup*, in 1971.[40]

It Happened in Ireland, by Reverend Clarence Duffy, was published in New York in 1944 by the Christian Press and presented an account of Duffy's six month admission to Monaghan Mental Hospital in the mid-1930s. Before he was committed, Duffy had been staying on his parents' farm when his Bishop concluded that Duffy was suffering from a 'nervous breakdown' and communicated this to Duffy's parents.[41]

According to his own account, Duffy had developed the belief that a Communist cell had been established near his parents' home; his brother was somehow linked with the Communists; and various strangers were acting in a suspicious fashion, providing further evidence of conspiracy. Duffy's fascinating 1944 text provides a detailed discussion of Communism around the world before recounting the arrival of three Gardaí (police officers) in the kitchen of his home in early May 1937,[42] after an argument with his brother. This was followed by an examination by the local dispensary doctor at the barracks and, after a conversation with the local curate, Duffy was brought to Monaghan Mental Hospital, accompanied by two Gardaí and his brother, Patrick.

Duffy was assessed by the medical officer on arrival, at 1.45am on 2 May 1937. He was placed in a cell and seen by the RMS at 11am. Duffy objected vociferously to various elements of the hospital regime including bathing in the presence of others, wearing institutional clothes and eating hospital food. He described his room as like a cell, dark, poorly ventilated and with an unpleasant odour. Duffy agitated for relief of these conditions for himself (with some success) and for the other patients.

Duffy wrote that the treatment of patients was brutal and rough, and outlined a physical altercation with an attendant following which Duffy was placed in a solitary cell and threatened with an injection. Duffy wrote that he was refused access to a lawyer and, in any case, his brother told him that his lawyer declined to have anything to do with the case. Duffy was permitted to write to the US Consul General in Dublin (Duffy was a US citizen), but even though at least one letter was forwarded by the hospital to the Consul, this had little effect; the RMS later told Duffy that the Consul no longer wished to hear from him. Duffy wrote various other letters but most were undelivered.

Throughout this period, Duffy saw the doctor for around five minutes each day, so the asylum attendants had the greatest influence on day-to-day life. Duffy describes many of them as untrained, poorly educated men who treated the patients like animals or slaves and, on occasion, beat them. Some of the attendants were more compassionate than others, but, while kind in manner and seemingly aware of the injustices endured by patients, even these attendants appeared powerless to remedy matters in the overall scheme of the asylum.

Duffy provides an especially interesting account of his fellow patients, stating that most were there owing to diseases of the brain or mind, poor diet, lack of self-restraint or in order to avoid prison. Others, he felt, were lazy and sly, and knew how to get into and stay in the asylum; he recommended that compulsory work would quickly cure these patients of their apparent insanity. Finally, there were people who appeared to be possessed, deaf-mutes, and individuals with epilepsy, whom Duffy describes with particular sympathy and insight.

Duffy was eventually discharged from Monaghan Mental Hospital in November 1937 whereupon he proceeded to Dublin and took the first boat to England. Later, he wrote his invaluable account of these events, *It Happened in Ireland*, in order to both raise awareness of the threat allegedly presented by Communism and appeal for more humane conditions in asylums in Ireland and elsewhere. His account is a very compelling one, emphasising the objectionable living conditions for patients and the difficulties they faced in appealing their detentions from within the asylum system.

Similar issues were brought to the fore again almost three decades later in 1971, in another valuable account of the Irish psychiatric inpatient experience, this time written by Hanna Greally (1925–1987) and titled *Bird's Nest Soup*.[43] Greally was born in Athlone in 1925 and had a generally happy childhood.[44] She wrote poetry that was published in the *Westmeath Independent*. After completing her secondary schooling at the Bower Convent in Athlone, she went to London to train as a nurse but soon returned home. In 1943 she was admitted to St Loman's Hospital, Mullingar, ostensibly for a rest, based on a civil committal signed by her mother, who died six months later. Greally was to remain in St Loman's until 1962, when a newly appointed doctor approved her discharge.

St Loman's had been established almost a century earlier when the Lord Lieutenant and Council of Ireland made an order in 1847 to establish an asylum near Mullingar.[45] Twenty-five acres of land were purchased in 1848 at a cost of £829 and the main building was completed in 1855. The asylum was intended to house 300 patients and opened on 23 August 1855, with Dr Henry Berkeley as RMS. In 1881, Dr Berkeley was succeeded by Dr G.W. Hatchell, son of Dr George Hatchell who had served as inspector. Electricity was introduced to the asylum in the early 1890s. As with Ireland's other asylums, St Loman's expanded steadily: in 1932 patient numbers exceeded 1,150 and by 1959, when Greally was a patient, the number had reached 1,296.

In *Bird's Nest Soup*, Greally provided a thinly veiled, compelling and disturbing account of her 19 years in St Loman's between 1943 and 1962. She described her tearful parting from her mother following her arrival in 1943 and painted a picture of grey walls, bad food and profound lack of privacy. She wrote about treatments provided to patients including sedatives, liquid paraffin, ECT (which Greally received) and insulin therapy, which was explained to her as being part of the hospital's research efforts.

Most of all, however, Greally conveyed the profound disempowerment she felt in St Loman's, especially as she understood that there were 3,000 patients in the hospital with only 10 reportedly discharged each month. Following a period of six months in the admission ward, Greally spent approximately six years moving between other wards, apparently based on efforts at behavioural modification (punishment, reward, etc.); seven years working in the hospital laundry; and a final six years in Prospect House, which was characterised by less supervision and a certain degree of autonomy. Over all of this time, there were periods of great despair during which Greally wished she was dead and tried, on occasion, to escape.

Ultimately, a change in medical staffing was accompanied by the opening of a new rehabilitation centre, to which Greally was discharged in 1962. Greally went on to work in Ireland and later travelled to England. She wrote poetry, short stories and three full length manuscripts.[46] Her account of her hospitalisation in St Loman's, *Bird's Nest Soup*, appeared in 1971 and was followed by a memorable appearance on the *Late, Late Show*, a long running television chat show on Raidió Teilifís Éireann (RTÉ; Ireland's national broadcaster). Greally died in Roscommon in 1987 but left behind a considerable body of work, not least of which is her searing account of her years in St Loman's, which, even several decades after publication, retains its power to evoke, shock and, hopefully, educate.

Homosexuality and Irish Psychiatry

If Greally's story is important as a unique educational lesson for Irish psychiatry, then the story of the relationship between psychiatry and homosexuality holds similar value, albeit in a different way, in that the latter demonstrates especially clearly the changeability of psychiatric practices over time and the extent to which certain psychiatric diagnoses are subject to social, political and various other influences.[47]

Homosexuality was listed as a mental disorder (sexual deviation) in the American Psychiatric Association's iconic classification systems DSM-I (1952)[48] and DSM-II (1968).[49] This situation led to significant opposition and activism including demonstrations by gay rights groups at the annual meeting of the American Psychiatric Association in San Francisco in 1970.[50] In 1973, the DSM-III task force decided to delete homosexuality from the classification system and that decision was confirmed by a referendum of members in 1974.[51]

Prior to this point, however, there was a long history of psychological, psychoanalytic and psychiatric engagement with homosexuality. And, as is invariably the case, these engagements reflected broader social judgements about homosexuality: homosexuality was often judged negatively, both medically and morally,[52] and discrimination was widespread.[53]

Psychiatrists were not, however, the most judgemental group and Keith Simpson, Emeritus Professor of Forensic Medicine to the University of London at Guy's Hospital, lamented the relatively tolerant attitudes of psychiatrists towards homosexuality in the 1979 edition of his textbook of forensic medicine:

> 'Homo' and 'queer' have become almost playful epithets, and the psychiatrist has done little but excuse or condone such practices. They are rotting the fabric of the arts as well as the more solid principles of family life, and the law properly regards such unnatural sex practices with a stern eye.[54]

There was particularly long standing and persistent interest in homosexuality in the field of psychoanalysis,[55] and while psychoanalytic 'treatment' of homosexuality was provided, it was later reported as unhelpful and even more alienating for an already stigmatised, alienated group.[56] Even more disturbingly, from 1933 onward homosexuality became a criterion for incarceration in psychiatric hospitals in Germany.[57]

This development formed part of a broader and, from today's perspective, deeply disturbing societal (and, thus, psychiatric) effort to reorient homosexual persons to heterosexual preferences.[58] Specific treatments in various countries included aversion therapies delivering painful electric shocks to homosexual men at the wrists, calves, feet[59] or genitals,[60] as they fantasised or viewed images of undressed males; administering emetic medication (such as apomorphine) to produce vomiting while such materials were viewed; administration of testosterone followed by showing films of nude or semi-nude women; playing tape recordings every two hours outlining the alleged adverse effects of homosexual behaviour (in association with emetic medication); and, later, repeatedly playing tape recordings outlining the alleged positive consequences of no longer being homosexual.[61]

These 'treatments' for homosexuality have been clearly described as occurring in various countries around the world, but even though specialist clinics were established in London, Manchester, Birmingham, Glasgow and Belfast, such treatments never became mainstream in British psychiatry.[62] Did they occur in Ireland?

Recent decades have seen increased exploration of the history of sexuality in general,[63] and homosexuality in particular, in Ireland.[64] For much of the twentieth century, Ireland was a very difficult place to be gay: same-sex sexual acts were criminal up until 1993, and between 1962 and 1972 there were some 455 convictions of men for crimes such as 'indecency with males' and 'gross indecency'.[65] There were also, however, mixed attitudes to homosexual activity during this period. Some Gardaí assumed a humane and sympathetic approach[66] and in 1973 one letter writer to the *Irish Times* advised against incarceration, albeit out of sympathy rather than a sense of justice:

> It must be rather sad to be homosexual, sad and pathetic. Not for these people (as a rule) the joys of family life as we know them. If, on occasion, they find solace and

pleasure in each other, then let us be charitable and understanding. It will do no good at all just to lock them up.[67]

From a mental health perspective, one 1963 volume, *The Priest and Mental Health*, considered the matter of homosexuality from several angles, with Reverend E.F. O'Doherty, Professor of Logic and Psychology at University College Dublin, stating that while being homosexual was not a sin, homosexual acts were sins, and while sexual deviations were not themselves illnesses, they were very often symptomatic of deeper pathological processes.[68]

Professor John Dunne of UCD and St Brendan's Hospital (Grangegorman), expressed the view that many 'sexual deviations' (a category in which he included homosexuality) had a compulsive obsessional component,[69] while another contributor to *The Priest and Mental Health* associated homosexual acts in the intellectually disabled with inadequacy and inability to engage in adult relationships.[70]

As regards 'treatment' for homosexuality, there was awareness in Ireland in the early 1960s that aversion therapies were being used in Great Britain,[71] but neither homosexuality nor aversion therapy were explicitly mentioned by Ireland's Commission of Inquiry on Mental Illness in the late 1960s. There was, however, a section devoted to 'sexual deviates' (a category which, at that time, included persons who engaged in homosexual acts, according to the American Psychiatric Association and WHO):

> Sexual deviates are not necessarily mentally ill, but they are a vulnerable group who may be in need of help. In the past, the only measures adopted by society were punitive. In recent years, there has been a considerable change for the better in public attitudes as more insight is gained into the causes of, and the possibility of altering, deviant behaviour. It would be, however, an exaggeration to claim that the causation of such behaviour is fully understood or that much progress has been made in its treatment. Although this is so, the sexual deviate needs whatever help he can obtain from medical science. Apart from the fact that it may be contrary to the law of the land, deviant behaviour can result in considerable unhappiness. The deviate is usually aware that he or she is different and this often causes considerable stress and worry; deviant behaviour frequently results in the break-up of families, with resultant stress to children and other dependants.[72]

Treatment was to consist 'largely of counselling aimed at acquainting the patient with the social consequences of his deviation and helping him voluntarily to abandon his deviant behaviour. Counselling of this nature can be very effective, particularly at the adolescent stage'. Ultimately, the Commission recommended that:

- 'Parents, teachers, general practitioners and other persons who may be aware of individual cases which would warrant psychiatric intervention should try to ensure that the persons concerned attend at the local psychiatric clinics';

- 'Psychological and psychiatric reports should be available to the Courts when dealing with sexual deviates'.[73]

Progress with 'counselling' services was slow. In 1971, the *Irish Times* reported that 'in the secondary schools, students with problems like homosexuality did not know to whom to turn, but with the development of psychological services in the psychiatric clinics more treatment would be available'.[74] Three years later, Professor Thomas Lynch, Professor of Psychiatry at the Royal College of Surgeons in Ireland, noted that homosexuality was a constant feature in all societies over the course of history:

> For the genuine exclusive homosexual the only realistic 'treatment' Professor Lynch points out, is 'to make him a better adapted homosexual', to help him to accept himself and to adjust to his role in society. Trying to 'reform' them is pretty pointless. Homosexuals themselves, not unnaturally, object strongly to references to 'treatment' or 'reform' or being regarded as problems or, worse again, 'patients'. They feel that as homosexuality is a natural state, it should be accepted as such and that we should stop thinking of them as medical cases who need treatment. What they need, they say, is a more understanding and accommodating society which will stop regarding them as freaks and criminals and allow them to live normal lives.[75]

The following year, 1975, Dr Noël Browne made similar points in Seanad Éireann (the Irish upper house), stating that homosexuality was 'perfectly normal, but in our society it is a very crippling disability':

> Homosexuality is simply a kind of sexuality completely normal for the homosexual. There is nothing abnormal in being homosexual if you happen to be born that way or become a homosexual. It is no more credit to me to be a heterosexual or no more wrong for me to be a heterosexual than it is for the homosexual to be a homosexual. Unfortunately it is not looked on in that way and it is still a crime in our society [...]. In psychiatric practice I find it to be a very common presenting problem by people, presenting in different ways in the form of depression and alcoholism, people who are simply misfits in life and drop out in all sorts of ways. But they all conceal this kind of homosexuality of one kind or another – the appalling sense that they are outcasts and not wanted in society, which they are not, and the whole Irish society is very unkind to them and very unchristian if I might use that much abused word. Because of that, suicide is another very common sequel to the unfortunate homosexual's attempt to live with this disability, which should not be a disability. It is not a disability. It is perfectly normal, but in our society it is a very crippling disability. Therefore I would ask the Attorney General that we do something about at least having a debate on this subject [...].[76]

Even following the American Psychiatric Association's delisting of homosexuality as a mental disorder in 1973, psychiatrists in Ireland and elsewhere were still involved in court proceedings linked with homosexual acts. Some defendants were fined, given suspended sentences or ordered to see psychiatrists.[77] In other cases which did not relate directly to homosexual acts, expert psychiatric evidence was given regarding homosexuality in the context of, for example, circumstances connected with manslaughter.[78]

In 1975, Nell McCafferty reported, in the *Irish Times*, the cases of two men brought before Dublin District Court having been apprehended together in a public location. The prosecuting Garda stopped both accused and while 'at that time, they denied everything', later 'they admitted all':[79]

> A psychiatrist for the younger man, aged 25, was called to testify. The dependent had been referred to him by a priest.
>
> 'He has been attending me regularly, five days a week, since this happened', the doctor said. 'The conclusion I came to is that first he is very sincere [...]. I am very slow to come to conclusions about cases which are pending in court. But in this case I am convinced of his sincerity. He did not think in fact, that he could be treated, and was wrongly advised to this effect by a psychiatric nurse. Depending on his desire, he can be treated ... with psychotherapy ... no medication is being used'.
>
> Was it fair to suggest that he was sexually immature, the solicitor asked. He was, the doctor agreed. [...]
>
> The other solicitor went into the case history of the married man. He has married two years ago, and unfortunately his job entailed his being away from home very often. 'The only conclusion I can come to,' said the solicitor, 'is that he was suffering from depression. He'd taken a few drinks that evening [...].'

The judge described homosexual behaviour as 'a completely unnatural performance' but the men were not jailed:

> 'Well,' said the Justice firmly, 'It's against the law here. The law's the law and they broke the law. One answer is prison obviously. If they had been dealt with before a jury they could have gotten penal servitude, strange as it seems to say. In the interests of justice, I will bind them in their own bonds to keep the peace for a year. It goes without saying that their association must break up and there must be no repetition of this.'

Psychiatric 'Treatments' for Homosexuality in Ireland

In the 1975 case reported by McCafferty, 'psychotherapy' was the only reported psychiatric 'treatment' for the younger man's homosexuality. Just two years later, however, David Norris, chairman of the Irish Gay Rights Movement and later Senator, suggested at a Rotary Club luncheon in Dublin that aversion therapy was also being used by Irish psychiatrists. The *Irish Times* reported his remarks:

> Mr Norris said that it was also necessary to call publicly for an urgent enquiry into the extent in Ireland of the practice of Aversion Therapy, saying that he knew of at least one psychiatrist who was seemingly quite proud of having used electric shock treatment in an attempt to alter homosexual orientation, and he invited comments from the medical profession in Ireland on the ethics of such treatment.
>
> The psychiatric profession had largely abandoned the notion that homosexuality was a disease, Mr Norris said, pointing to the American Psychiatric Association's decision to remove it from classification as a nervous disorder. There were, however, some vested interests in the 'sickness theory', such as a manufacturer of psycho-pharmacologic drugs who distributed free to the psychiatric profession a pamphlet containing the statement that psychiatrists agree unanimously that the homosexual is a sick person.[80]

Senator Norris recalls the case of one gay man in the east of Ireland whose family sent him for treatment when he revealed his homosexuality and who reportedly received ECT in Ireland for this in the 1970s.[81] Later in life, the same man was badly harassed owing to his sexual orientation and saw a psychiatrist who reportedly taught him to 'walk butch' (i.e. in a stereotypically masculine fashion) in order to minimise harassment.

It is difficult to establish to what extent aversion therapies for homosexuality were *systematically* provided in Irish psychiatry, or whether homosexuality played a role in certain admissions to psychiatric hospitals. There are references to aversion therapy in the Irish popular press[82] and history texts,[83] and to lectures on the topic being given to Irish psychiatrists,[84] but there is a paucity of primary evidence about the extent to which various therapies other than psychotherapy were provided specifically for homosexuality in Irish psychiatric hospitals or clinics during the 1900s. For this book, I canvassed the opinions and memories of 10 prominent psychiatrists and clinical directors who practiced during the 1950s up to the 2000s, and none recalled hearing of ECT being used for the 'treatment' of homosexuality in Ireland, although psychological and aversion therapies were provided.[85] This is an area in need of further study,[86] from the perspectives of both patients and professionals,[87] to clarify these matters further.

There is also a need for further original research into the historical evolution of public, professional and legal views of homosexuality in Ireland and Great Britain, including Irish responses to the *Report of the Committee on Homosexual Offences and Prostitution* of September 1957 ('Wolfenden Report'), which included one psychiatrist (Dr Desmond Curran of St George's Hospital, London); recommended that 'homosexual behaviour between consenting adults in private should no longer be a criminal offence' (despite various contrary views);[88] and led to the emergence of the Sexual Offences Act of 1967. There is a need for systematic research into the effects of these developments in Ireland and how, precisely, psychiatry, through its nosologies, has regarded and ultimately changed views on the issue from early ideas about 'treatment' of homosexuality as a 'disorder'. In addition, the evolution of professional attitudes on this theme in Irish psychiatry is worthy of particular exploration, including the influence, if any, of the Royal College of Psychiatrists on professional views and practices.

What is already clear, however, is that medical, psychiatric and general attitudes towards homosexuality evolved, albeit slowly, throughout the 1970s, 1980s and 1990s. In November 1977, Norris began legal proceedings against the Attorney General in relation to the Offences Against the Person Act 1861 and also in connection with the Criminal Law (Amendment) Act 1885.[89] In the course of proceedings, Norris himself recounted seeing a psychiatrist owing to stress and anxiety. He states that the psychiatrist gave him 'fatherly advice'[90] about the legal situation in Ireland and suggested that Norris's anxiety would not occur if he lived in a country with different legal arrangements, such as England or France.[91] Norris regarded that 1966 psychiatric report as the most important advantage he had in taking his case, which opened in June 1980 in the High Court.[92]

During the proceedings, John P. Spiegel, an American psychiatrist and professor, gave evidence that decriminalising homosexual acts would relieve the stress on homosexual people that led to mental illness.[93] Ivor Browne, Professor of Psychiatry at University College Dublin, also gave evidence and warned against treatment that tried to 'change the homosexual into a heterosexual' because this 'was not the true nature of the problem'; such efforts, he said, 'could cause harm'.[94]

The government did not produce expert psychiatric evidence in the case because, according to Norris, no psychiatrist was willing to risk his or her reputation.[95] Norris's case was, nonetheless, defeated in the first instance but, following further protracted and ultimately ground breaking legal action, Norris finally prevailed in 1988, when the European Court of Human Rights ruled that Ireland's law criminalising same sex activities violated Article 8 of the European Convention on Human Rights concerning the 'right to respect for private and family life'.[96]

Clearly, the fact that the American Psychiatric Association's DSM-III task force had deleted homosexuality from the classification system in 1973 had been an important development, but it had not immediately dispelled the association between homosexuality and psychiatry.[97] In Ireland in the late 1970s, for example, one gay man who experienced difficulties coming out consulted both a psychiatrist and a GP, as reported in the *Irish Times*:

> So, being almost suicidal – gay people have very high rates of alcoholism, psychiatric admissions and suicides – he went to a psychiatrist. 'He asked me about my relationship with my parents and with my religion and if I played sports and concluded from the answers that there was no way I could be gay; that I should try to think positively'.
>
> Earlier [he] had been to a GP but that was only worse. 'When I told him the kernel of my, inverted commas, problem he nearly fell off the chair, said he knew nothing about the subject and told me to ring St Brendan's [Psychiatric] Hospital for an appointment'.[98]

Attitudes were, however, steadily changing in many areas of Irish life. In 1979, Fr Ralph Gallagher, a Redemptorist priest in Dublin, wrote at some length about homosexuality in *The Furrow*, an

Irish Roman Catholic theological periodical, arguing that no person should undergo behaviour modification or aversion therapy unless it was his or her free and conscious decision to do so.[99] He noted that many within the medical profession had turned away from such treatments and highlighted the need for self-acceptance and reasonable adjustment to society.

The issue of self-image was further explored in a 1984 research study of androgyny, depression and self-esteem in 49 homosexual men, 23 heterosexual men, 23 homosexual women and 17 heterosexual women in Ireland.[100] The researchers concluded that it was not one's homosexuality or heterosexuality that affected psychological health, but how one perceived one's own psychological masculinity or femininity. Another 1984 study, by researchers in Northern Ireland, found that the degree of homosexual men's integration into the homosexual community was significantly related to scores on relevant anxiety scales.[101] Clearly, community acceptance and integration were critical to wellbeing.

Acceptance and integration were still difficult to achieve, however, not least because it was not until 1990 that the WHO finally removed homosexuality from its list of mental disorders,[102] some 17 years after the American Psychiatric Association had done so. Despite these developments, finding psychological support in Ireland was still sometimes difficult: in 1990, one Leaving Certificate student, struggling to come to terms with his homosexuality, went to see his GP but couldn't bring himself to tell the doctor the problem, even though the doctor was generally easy to talk to.[103] The GP concluded that the young man was depressed and sent him to a psychiatrist. Later, the young man took an overdose owing to homophobic bullying and was admitted to psychiatric hospital for six weeks, where he reported receiving little by way of meaningful assistance.

Others, however, reported much more positive experiences with psychiatrists[104] and in January 1990 Professor Anthony Clare offered clear evidence of evolving attitudes within Irish psychiatry, stating publicly that the primary purpose of psychiatric treatment was to assist homosexual persons in accepting their orientation and coping with a generally hostile society.[105] The following month, February 1990, Clare revisited the theme in the letters column of the *Irish Times*:

> In practice, the great majority of clinical psychiatrists do not regard homosexuality as a psychiatric disorder and do not regard it as warranting treatment. [...] I take consolation from the fact that wherever repressive and intolerant regimes seize power and set about persecuting and intimidating minority and opposition groups they invariably include amongst those groups – homosexuals *and* psychiatrists. We must be doing something right.[106]

Over the course of the following two decades, there was growing awareness of the mental health needs of lesbian, gay, bisexual and transgender (LGBT) people in Ireland. In 2007, Mary McAleese, President of Ireland, made particular reference to the psychological effects of bias and hostility towards gay people.[107] In 2009, an online survey of some 1,110 LGBT people showed that 86 per cent had experienced feelings of depression at some point in their lives and 60 per cent of those interviewed attributed this directly to social and/or personal challenges associated with LGBT identity.[108] Twenty-five per cent of online participants had taken prescribed medication for depression or anxiety and 27 per cent had self-harmed.

Another study of the mental health experiences and needs of LGBT people over the age of 55 years in Ireland confirmed that a significant number had mental health problems over the course of their lives and recommended that the mental health needs of older LGBT people be addressed in future strategic directives, supporting the principles of inclusion, equality and respect for diversity.[109]

In 2011, the College of Psychiatry of Ireland and the Gay and Lesbian Equality Network (GLEN) published guidelines 'to inform psychiatrists of what they need to know when providing a mental health service to a lesbian, gay or bisexual (LGB) person'.[110] They advised 'psychiatrists to challenge any anti-gay bias they may have' so as to avoid behaviour such as 'presuming patients are heterosexual'; 'failing to appreciate any non-heterosexual form of behaviour, identity, relationship, family or community'; or 'attempts to change a patient's sexual orientation'.[111] Psychiatrists were also advised to:

- Be aware of LGB mental health issues and gay-specific stressors.
- Respond supportively when patients disclose they are LGB.
- Take a gay-affirmative approach.
- Demonstrate that their practice is inclusive of LGB people.[112]

In May 2015, Ireland became the first country to decide to legalise same sex marriage on a national level by popular vote.[113] Despite this development, significant challenges remain, especially in the area of mental health. In 2014, a research study of 125 LGBT people in Ireland found that 64 per cent believe that mental health professionals still lack knowledge about LGBT issues and 43 per cent believe practitioners are unresponsive to their needs.[114]

In 2016, a *National Study of the Mental Health and Wellbeing of Lesbian, Gay, Bisexual, Transgender and Intersex People in Ireland* reported that between 12 per cent and 35 per cent of participants showed evidence of severe or extremely severe depression, anxiety, and stress, with the youngest age group (14–18 years) showing the most psychopathology and notably low scores on satisfaction, happiness and self-esteem. A lifetime history of self-harm was reported by a third (34 per cent) of participants, which represents an increase on the 27 per cent previously reported in the LGBT population in Ireland.[115] While there is little doubt that matters have improved considerably in recent decades, there is still, clearly, work to be done.

The Mad Irish? No

The troubled, evolving relationship between psychiatry and homosexuality was just one of the many psychiatric narratives unfolding in mid- and late-twentieth-century Ireland. As we have seen, there was, throughout the 1800s and early 1900s, a persistent belief that rates of mental disorder in Ireland were both high and rising,[116] and, notwithstanding the distinctly limited evidence to support this belief, it persisted well into the mid-1900s. But this narrative, too, was to take an unexpected turn in the late 1900s, when this long standing article of faith in Irish psychiatry was finally and definitively upturned.

Striking a tone that was remarkably similar to its predecessors, the '1966 Report' of the Commission of Inquiry on Mental Illness pointed out, as we have seen, that 'in Ireland, approximately 7.3 psychiatric beds were provided in 1961 per 1,000 of the population; this rate appears to be the highest in the world and compared with 4.5 in Northern Ireland, 4.6 in England and Wales, 4.3 in Scotland, 2.1 in France and 4.3 in U.S.A'.[117] Against this background, 'one of the first tasks to which the Commission addressed itself was to consider the exceptional rates of residence in the psychiatric hospitals in Ireland':

> No clear explanation has emerged. There are indications that mental illness may be more prevalent in Ireland than in other countries; however, there are many factors involved, and in the absence of more detailed research, the evidence to this effect cannot be said to be conclusive. Special demographic features, such as the high emigration rate, the low marriage rate and problems of employment, may be relevant to the unusually high rate of hospitalisation. In a largely rural country with few large centres of population, social and geographic isolations may affect both the mental health of individuals and the effectiveness of the mental health services. The public attitude towards mental illness may not be helpful to the discharge of patients and their reintegration in the community. On all these points, the Commission could do little more than ask questions. To provide answers would demand years of scientific inquiry for which neither the personnel of the Commission nor the time at its disposal would have been adequate. The Commission considers that a greatly expanded programme of research, not only into these social and epidemiological problems, but into other aspects of mental illness in Ireland, is urgently necessary.[118]

The Commission recommended 'radical and widespread changes'[119] to mental health services, as well as further research into the epidemiology of Ireland's apparently high rates of mental disorder. The call for epidemiological research was especially important and timely. Papers by Dermot and Brendan Walsh[120] in the later 1960s duly provided important, rigorous and credible insights into hospitalised psychiatric morbidity in Ireland,[121] as well as variations in admission rates.[122] The need for this kind of research was readily apparent[123] and, in 1984, Torrey and colleagues published an influential paper titled 'endemic psychosis in western Ireland' in the *American Journal of Psychiatry*.[124]

Torrey and colleagues noted that earlier studies had shown higher rates of psychiatric hospitalisation in Ireland compared to other countries.[125] They conducted their study in a small area within County Roscommon, in which a relatively high prevalence of schizophrenia had been reported previously. Their findings indicated that some 4 per cent of the population over the age of 40 years were actively psychotic in this area, and that the six-month prevalence of schizophrenia, schizoaffective and atypical psychosis was 12.6 per 1,000 population, compared to 3.6 in parts of the US (for broadly defined schizophrenia) and 9.1 in a comparable area of northern Sweden. The authors also pointed to possible sources of error in their work, including selective migration of mentally healthy persons leading to an accumulation of mentally ill persons who either never emigrated or were sent home.[126]

This apparently high prevalence of schizophrenia in one rural area appeared consistent with a 1975 study of psychiatric admissions in Cork, which associated admission owing to schizophrenia with being reared in rural areas, at least for men.[127] In 1988, however, a separate study of admissions in one rural and one urban area between 1978 and 1980 showed that readmission rates for schizophrenia were equivalent in urban and rural areas, but that people with schizophrenia in rural areas were admitted at a later age.[128] Keatinge also showed that while incidence rates did not differ between rural counties, treated prevalence and readmission rates did, indicating that social and community variables significantly influenced psychiatric hospital utilisation.[129]

In 1993, a paper from the Roscommon Family Study demonstrated that, in the west of Ireland, schizophrenia was a strongly familial disorder, and that diminished reproductive rates had a large impact on pattern of risk in relatives.[130] That study also reached an ancillary conclusion that its results were *not* consistent with previous claims that the prevalence of schizophrenia was elevated either in Ireland as a whole or in western Ireland. Torrey, in response, pointed out, *inter alia*, that earlier work had indicated increased rates of schizophrenia in persons born prior to 1940, and that the 1993 study looked at those born from 1930 onward; i.e. a significantly different population.[131] Walsh and Kendler, in response, pointed out that studies looking at 'first admissions' might result in overestimates, as certain hospitals used the term 'first admission' to refer to first admission *to that hospital*, rather than lifetime first admission.[132] There were also concerns about the reliability of the application of diagnostic categories in unsupervised hospital data.

Waddington and colleagues, the following year, brought significant clarity to the overall picture by pointing out that a systematic catchment area study of the incidence and prevalence of schizophrenia in rural Ireland indicated entirely unremarkable rates that were well within the mid-range of values recorded worldwide (e.g. lifetime risk of 0.7 per cent).[133] This finding did not rule out the possibility of variations in rates between geographical regions within Ireland or over different time periods, but it provided convincing evidence that the overall rate of schizophrenia in Ireland in recent times is no higher than the worldwide average.[134]

As a result, after many decades of theorising about possible causes for apparently increased rates of mental disorder in Ireland, it finally appeared that Ireland does not, in fact, have a notably high rate at all.[135] While incidence rates of schizophrenia may well differ somewhat between different geographical locations within or between various countries,[136] or over time, Ireland's unremarkable rate of psychosis is entirely consistent with a 1986 WHO multi-centre study which included Ireland and demonstrated little systematic or overall difference across countries.[137] Notwithstanding this conclusion, the accumulated literature on this topic remains complex and intriguing.[138] The matter is discussed in some detail and placed in a certain anthropological context by Scheper-Hughes in the twentieth anniversary edition of *Saints, Scholars and Schizophrenics*, an anthropological study based in rural Ireland first published in 1977,[139] which led to interesting exchanges in the *Irish Times*[140] and elsewhere.[141] Anthropological work in Irish psychiatry continues in the twenty-first century.[142]

Overall, however, the epidemiological evidence is now clear: despite a high rate of psychiatric hospitalisation, there is insufficient evidence to conclude that Ireland ever had a higher rate of mental disorder than elsewhere, and the reasons for variations in hospital admissions appear significantly related to social and nosocomial (i.e. hospital related) factors rather than true variations in incidence.[143] Ultimately, Ireland's epidemic of psychiatric institutionalisation cannot be explained by any single factor (including any postulated increased rate of mental disorder) but, as Brennan wisely points out, was part of a social process driven by broader structures and systems, combined with the actions of various individuals and groups.[144]

It is certainly true that there were increased rates of *admission* to psychiatric institutions throughout the 1800s in various countries, including Ireland, England, France and the US, and that Ireland's rates were especially high at their peak, and especially slow to decline.[145] Ireland's increase in committals was, however, influenced by such a broad range of social, political, legal, economic, demographic and clinical practice factors, that an explanation based on a true increase in the incidence of mental disorder is neither necessary nor supported by the balance of historical and epidemiological evidence. So what, then, *is* the explanation for the apparently inexorable rise of the Irish asylum during the 1800s and early 1900s?

It is my conclusion, based on the accumulated literature on this topic and the story told in this book, that Ireland's high rate of psychiatric institutionalisation was linked with a range of diverse contributory factors, including increased recognition of the problems presented by mental disorder throughout the nineteenth and twentieth centuries, combined with the growing philanthropic impulses of the times; mutually reinforcing patterns of asylum building and psychiatric committal, underpinned by continual, almost obsessional, legislative change; the inevitable evolution and revision of diagnostic practices with limited basis in biological medicine; and possible epidemiological change owing to sociodemographic changes in Irish society, such as selective migration and increased longevity, producing an increase in the prevalence but not incidence of mental disorder (i.e. the mentally ill stayed in Ireland and lived longer, thus producing an increase in the numbers of mentally ill but not an increase in *incidence* of new cases).[146]

Other factors included increased recognition of the mentally ill in communities and society in general, leading to multiple waves of systemic, governmental reforms, including the apparently endless expansion of asylums and workhouse asylums; changes in professional and public attitudes leading to increased recognition and diagnosis of mental disorder and, in turn, increased rates of presentation to the emerging institutions; the search for professional prestige among doctors and nurses in the new fields of asylum medicine and psychiatry, especially when pay was linked with asylum size and patient numbers; poverty and other socioeconomic pressures on family resources, especially during the 1800s; and significant reconfigurations of family, community and societal structures throughout the 1800s and 1900s, resulting in decreased community tolerance of the mentally ill, the intellectually disabled and various other persons who stood out within their communities (Chapter 3).

Taken together, these factors fuelled the growth of an asylum system that soon became far too large, grossly unhygienic, profoundly anti-therapeutic and deeply stigmatising for patients, families and staff. By the late 1950s, as inpatient numbers reached 20,063,[147] the situation in Irish mental hospitals was both unsustainable and indefensible. One particularly moving account of an Irish psychiatric hospital in the 1970s records the persistence of highly institutional conditions which the Chief Medical Officer tried very hard to get funding to improve over many years, but with limited success.[148] Urgent, systematic change was needed.

Leading Change:
Browne, Walsh, McGrath

Against this background, the decline of Ireland's psychiatric institutions in the latter part of the 1900s was a complex, protracted process, fuelled by an emerging awareness that Ireland's rates of mental disorder were not irretrievably high, subsequent changes in the tone of mental health policy, broader changes in Irish society as a whole, and the work of particular psychiatrists and reformers who stepped forward to embrace and shape the much needed reforms. It is still too early to present valid, historical evaluations of the contributions made by such recent figures, so this section focuses on recording their careers and activities (along with some brief comments), rather than historical critical appraisals, which would be premature. It is hoped that these accounts will assist future historians with mature and measured evaluations of the enduring contributions of these reforming figures.

One of the best known of these leading figures was Professor Ivor Browne,[149] who has provided invaluable reflections on psychiatry, as well as his own career and work, in two books, *Music and Madness* (2008, which contains a rare first-hand account of lobotomy in Ireland)[150] and *The Writings of Ivor Browne – Steps Along the Road: The Evolution of a Slow Learner* (2013), a collection of writings.[151]

Born in March 1929 in Sandycove, Dublin, Browne graduated from the Royal College of Surgeons in Ireland in 1954 and worked in both the UK (where therapeutic tools included lysergic acid diethylamide (LSD)) and US, being awarded a fellowship to study public and community mental health from Harvard in the early 1960s. He returned to Ireland as Senior Administrative Medical Officer at Grangegorman in July 1962, and went on to serve as Chief Psychiatrist of the Eastern Health Board (1965–94) and Professor of Psychiatry at UCD (1967–94).

Browne's career was as remarkable as it was influential: he pioneered novel and, at times, unorthodox forms of psychological therapy at Grangegorman,[152] while also systematically dismantling the old institution and seeking to replace it with community based facilities.[153] Novelist Colm Tóibín provides a fascinating account of psychological therapy with Browne, involving ketamine and music among other elements, at the disused Protestant church at St Brendan's in May 1992.[154] Writer John Waters has written another vivid, affecting account of this therapy in his 2010 book, *Beyond Consolation*.[155]

Throughout this career, Browne published extensively on various topics relating to psychiatry, psychotherapy and social change, including psychiatric night hospitals, therapeutic communities, psychosocial problems, community mental health care, living system theory, and how psychotherapy works.[156] These papers are notable for both their breadth and depth, and their continuous empathic awareness of individual suffering.

Browne was a very practical *social* reformer too: he conceived, established and was director of the Irish Foundation for Human Development (1968–79) and out of this grew the North West Centre for Learning and Development and the Inner City Trust which transformed the city of Derry, making it a model for the Prince of Wales' urban village development project and other urban renewal developments around the world. In 1983, Browne was appointed chairman of the group of European experts set up by the European Economic Community for the reform of Greek psychiatry.[157] Following his retirement from the Eastern Health Board and UCD in 1994, Browne continued clinical work and pursued interests in stress management, how the brain processes traumatic experience, and living system theory, as well as the Sahag Marg system of meditation, which he had practiced since 1978.[158]

Over the course of his career, Browne was a public figure who occasionally attracted controversy but always acted in the interests of his patients.[159] Most of all, Browne was strongly and rightly associated with expediting the end of the era of the large mental hospital in Grangegorman, a gargantuan task which he and others (such as Dr Angela Mohan) worked hard to achieve over a sustained period of time. The establishment of an assessment unit in St Brendan's in April 1979 is just one example of the reforms implemented to achieve this goal: this initiative alone reduced the annual admission rate at St Brendan's from 2,676 in 1978 to 1,558 in 1980, simply by diverting less ill patients to community based sector mental health services.[160] This was just one aspect of a protracted, successful programme to accord greater dignity to the mentally ill and, ultimately, close the old mental hospital at Grangegorman.

Another psychiatrist with whom Browne worked,[161] and who played a pivotal part in psychiatric deinstitutionalisation, was Dr Dermot Walsh. Among his many roles, Walsh was clinical director of St Loman's Hospital (Dublin), Principal Investigator at the Mental Health Division of the Health Research Board, and Inspector of Mental Hospitals from 1987 to 2003. In 1965 and 1966, Walsh acted as Regional Officer for Mental Health at the European regional office of WHO based in Copenhagen, and, over many subsequent years, as consultant to the office, being member of a number of relevant committees.

In Ireland, Walsh gave evidence to the 1966 Commission of Inquiry on Mental Illness[162] and participated in the development of both *Planning for the Future* (1984)[163] and *A Vision for Change* (2006).[164] As Clinical Director he was involved pivotally in opening the Lakeview Unit in Naas, County Kildare in 1992 and remained clinical director there until 1996. Also as Clinical Director, he led the move of psychiatric services from St Loman's Hospital (Ballyowen, Dublin) to the Adelaide and Meath Hospital, Incorporating the National Children's Hospital (later renamed Tallaght Hospital) in 1999.

From a research perspective, Walsh was involved in developing a depression rating scale in Leeds and was a key figure in the Roscommon Family Study, an epidemiological study of psychosis,[165] conducted jointly with Ken Kendler (Department of Psychiatry, Medical College of Virginia), as were later studies of the genetic epidemiology of schizophrenia and alcoholism, as parts of a collaboration extending over nearly a quarter century. Walsh also established the National Psychiatric In-patient Reporting System (NPIRS) in what was then the Medico-Social Research Board (amalgamated with the Medical Research Council of Ireland to form the Health Research Board in 1986) and the contemporary three county case register initiative, reproduced in the St Loman's catchment area.

Walsh has, in addition, written numerous original contributions on the history of psychiatry in Ireland,[166] including an outstandingly lucid history of schizophrenia in Ireland[167] and an insightful account of mental health services from 1959 to 2010.[168] He also co-authored, with Antoinette Daly, a data rich account of the rise and fall of Ireland's psychiatric institutions, titled *Mental Illness in Ireland 1750–2002: Reflections on the Rise and Fall of Institutional Care.*[169]

From 1982, Walsh edited the *Irish Journal of Psychiatry*, published by the Irish Institute of Psychiatry, and devoted editorials to signs of emergent change in Irish psychiatry[170] and the extent of psychiatric illness in populations,[171] among other topics. A key leader of deinstitutionalisation,[172] Walsh made a vast and unique contribution to enlightened mental health policy, law and practice through his clinical work, medical leadership, involvement with governmental reviews and policy, and the Health Research Board.

An erudite and prolific communicator, Walsh has written for public,[173] academic[174] and professional audiences,[175] commenting on, *inter alia*, the need for, and evolution of, an independent college of psychiatrists for Ireland.[176] This has been a long standing theme: in 1992, Professor Thomas Lynch recalled Walsh's early suggestions that Ireland should have its own college, rather than a division of the London based Royal College of Psychiatrists:

> This has been mooted many times. It would be very expensive to have an Irish College. We have tried to look at the situation, and point out that the Royal College of Psychiatrists headquarters just happens to be in London. We are the Irish Branch of the Royal College of Psychiatrists. Actually psychiatry, rugby and hockey are the only truly joint ventures between North and South. We have never had any problem. In fact, I took over as Chairman of the Irish Division from John Fennelly and was succeeded by Gordon McCallam of Belfast. At least one meeting in the year is held in Belfast.
>
> At one stage the Irish Division felt if our Chairman had been from the North, it wouldn't be appropriate for him to negotiate with our Department of Health for conditions for either patients or staff in the South. So we decided, on the advice of Professor Ken Rawnsley who said there were some similar problems in Wales, to change our hats and just call ourselves the Irish Psychiatric Association when arguing in the Department of Health over conditions or such things. But in essence we were the same body of men as the Irish Division of the Royal College.
>
> Dermot Walsh was always keen to have an Irish College of Psychiatry but that requires a lot of funding and I don't think it is practical. Norman Moore in his day was very anxious that the Postgraduate Training Committee would be a faculty of Royal College of Physicians of Ireland.[177]

In the event, the Irish organisation of psychiatrists was to undergo many transformations and changes of name, before the College of Psychiatry of Ireland (retitled College of Psychiatrists of Ireland in 2013) finally emerged as a single organisation in 2009, when three former bodies merged: the Irish College of Psychiatrists (a division of the Royal College of Psychiatrists in the UK), the Irish Psychiatric Association, and the then training body for psychiatry, the Irish Psychiatric Training Committee.

By this time, much of the deinstitutionalisation of Irish psychiatry had already occurred, as inpatient numbers fell from 19,801 in 1963 to 4,256 in 2001.[178] Various other changes had also taken place, as the independent sector developed considerably in the mid- and late-1900s. In 1882, the Brothers of St John of God had established a private psychiatric hospital in Stillorgan, County Dublin,[179] which was recognised by the RMPA in 1926;[180] hosted a prestigious three day Psychiatric Congress (including an official RMPA meeting) in 1950;[181] and became the first psychiatric hospital in Ireland to introduce 'the open door system' in 1956.[182] This involved according greater liberty to patients, expanding occupational and recreational therapies, and increased group activities; the new system met with notable success.[183]

A true pioneer in teaching and developing psychiatry in Ireland, St John of God Hospital had just 132 admissions per year in 1955 when Dr Desmond McGrath, an outstanding clinician, trainer and service developer,[184] took up a post there, and approximately 1,750 per year by the time he retired in the 1990s. In 1997 there were 210 beds at the hospital, including inpatient provision for the innovative Cluain Mhuire community mental health service.[185] The Inspector of Mental Hospitals noted that 'the quality of inpatient accommodation at St John of God was very high and continuous improvements were being made'. The hospital went on to develop speciality services in addictions, adolescent mental health, eating disorders, psychiatry of later life, psychosis, stress management, wellness and recovery programmes, and programmes for mindfulness and relaxation.

Other changes were also afoot, as Irish psychiatry in the late 1900s developed in new and sometimes unexpected ways. The psychiatric service in the Defence Forces, for example, developed significantly during this period, and the first full time military psychiatrist in the modern era in Ireland was Dr Fionnuala O'Loughlin.[186] Prior to that, services were provided through a weekly clinic by psychiatrists who also worked with the public services, such as Dr James Wilson (Carlow RMS) in the Curragh, Dr David Dunne (of Sarsfield Court, Cork) and, in Dublin, Dr Gabriel Byrne and Dr Dick Whitty, who also pioneered old age psychiatry[187] and development of community based facilities. Dr John Tobin served as Director of Mental Health Services in the Irish Defence Forces from 1 February 1997 until 30 June 2011, at the rank of Lieutenant Colonel, and, following this, provided a clinic for the Irish Defence Forces two days per week, as well as developing further his expertise in mental health and human rights.[188]

Psychiatric Units:
Alternatives to Mental Hospitals

From the outset, it was clear that systematic, nationwide reform of Irish mental health services in the twentieth century would need to see a shift away from the large mental hospitals of the early 1900s, towards a new, less institutional model of care. To this end, the 1966 Commission recommended 'the setting up of short-term residential units in, or in association with, general hospitals [...]. The Commission considers that the siting of these units at, or their association with, general hospitals would benefit both the unit and the general hospital and would be a valuable step towards creating a link between psychiatry and other forms of medicine'.[189]

A psychiatric unit was established at the general hospital in Waterford in 1965[190] and by the time a new mental health policy, *Planning for the Future*, was developed in 1984[191] there were already acute psychiatry admission units at 10 general hospitals.[192] The 1984 policy reaffirmed this direction for reform, noting that 'the benefits which follow the implementation of this policy are compelling':

1. It brings to an end the isolation which has been so damaging to the concept and the practice of modern psychiatry.
2. It recognises psychiatry as a medical specialty to the advantage of both psychiatry and other areas of medical practice – in particular, it improves the treatment facilities in the many cases in which mental illness has a physical as well as a psychiatric basis.
3. It makes psychiatric treatment more acceptable to those who need it.
4. It increases the attractiveness of a career in psychiatry with consequential benefits in the recruitment of staff of a high calibre.
5. It brings psychiatric nurses into a closer working relationship with general nurses to their mutual advantage.
6. It enhances the development of specialist psychiatric out-patient care by linking it to the out-patient facilities which are already available for other specialties at the general hospital;
7. It makes long-term economic sense by enabling the psychiatric inpatient unit to share services and facilities at the general hospital.[193]

The 1984 policy also noted various challenges with the plan, including a need for capital investment, possible effects on morale in psychiatric hospitals, and anxieties on the part of staff in general hospitals. Progress in the early 1980s was slow: in 1981, 2.7 per cent of psychiatric inpatients were in psychiatric units at general hospitals as opposed to psychiatric hospitals, and 10 years later, in 1991, this had risen to a mere 4.4 per cent.[194] By 1992, however, more units had been established at general hospitals, ranging in size from 51 beds (St James's Hospital, Dublin) to 22 beds (James Connolly Memorial Hospital, Blanchardstown and St Vincent's Hospital, Elm Park, Dublin).[195]

The following decades saw emerging evidence that the move to acute psychiatry units resulted in many benefits in terms of length of stay, levels of medication prescription, levels of aggression and rates of involuntary admission. In 1987, 11 years after the establishment of a new psychiatric unit at Galway Regional Hospital, length of stay had become very brief, averaging one month, and the new unit was associated with increased extramural activities (such as day hospital care) and expansion of community facilities (such as day centres, hostels and outpatient clinics).[196]

Outpatient clinics had developed in many areas over previous decades. The first psychiatric outpatient clinic at a general hospital was established in the private sector by Dr H. Jocelyn Eustace of the Adelaide Hospital in the mid-1930s.[197] At the Richmond, outpatient clinics had been suggested in 1931 and in August 1935 RMS Donelan tried to further the initiative, but was comprehensively stymied by various administrative issues.[198] Eventually, an outpatient service was developed from the Richmond[199] and grew quickly: in the first nine months of 1963 some 7,600 people attended.[200] The first outpatient clinics in County Cork opened in 1948, and clinics were held twice monthly in Cork (North Infirmary) and monthly in Bantry and Kanturk.[201] A twice weekly clinic was established at Our Lady's Hospital, Cork in 1958 and in 1960 there were 1,168 attendances.

This pattern was replicated across the country: the first outpatient clinic in Belmullet, County Mayo took place on 7 March 1950, when a visiting doctor saw seven patients, including a boy aged seven years, a girl aged two, and adults with neurosis, sleeplessness and hypochondria.[202] The aim was to intervene early and hopefully obviate the need for admission or facilitate earlier discharge.

In Tipperary, outpatient clinics were opened in towns throughout the county during the 1950s.[203] Other areas, such as that served by St Fintan's in Portlaoise, also saw day centres, sheltered workshops and community residential facilities offer further support in the community.[204] In 1960, the Health Authorities Act dissolved mental hospital boards and health authorities became responsible for mental health care.[205] By 1961, more patients were being treated in outpatient clinics than in hospitals and by 1962, 60 per cent of inpatient admissions were voluntary.[206] The number of mentally ill persons in inpatient settings was also – finally – in steady decline,[207] firmly setting the scene for the development of psychiatric inpatient units in general hospitals.

Against this background, reduced length of stay was the most visible change that accompanied the establishment of the new inpatient units: by 1988, 76 per cent of patients discharged from general hospital units had stayed for less than one month and only 3 per cent had stayed for more than three months; less than a quarter of 1 per cent had remained as inpatients for more than one year, compared to 7 per cent of those discharged from old psychiatric hospitals.[208] There was, however, a significant difference between Dublin and the rest of the country: in 1990, only 14 per cent of psychiatric admissions in Dublin were to general hospital units, compared to 35 per cent for the rest of the country.[209] Nevertheless, a survey of the medical directors of all 12 psychiatric units in general hospitals in 1991 confirmed that the overall picture was very encouraging, the chief challenges being identified as the management of disturbed patients and the growing demands of liaison psychiatry.[210]

More recently, in March 2003 a new, purpose built, acute psychiatric unit opened on the site of Kilkenny General Hospital as the admission wards of the two local standalone psychiatric hospitals closed. Research by Dr Larkin Feeney and colleagues demonstrated that this move resulted in reduced levels of aggression, reduced levels of benzodiazepine prescription, and reduced numbers of patients leaving hospital against medical advice.[211] There were also trends towards reduced antipsychotic prescribing, and reduced rates of involuntary admission, admission of intoxicated individuals and abuse of intoxicants by inpatients. Overall, the establishment of acute psychiatric units in general hospitals generated significant changes from the 1960s onwards, in a generally positive direction, with 22 such units operational by 2006.[212]

Health (Mental Services) Act 1981:
Seeking 'Further and Better Provision'

Throughout the late 1960s and 1970s there was a gradual but unmistakable downward trend in the number of inpatients in Irish psychiatric hospitals and units. In 1963 the number stood at 19,801; by 1971 it had fallen to 16,661; and by 1981 it was 13,984.[213] While the direction of this trend was welcome, there was still a clear need for further reform, most notably in relation to mental health legislation. A new act, the Health (Mental Services) Act 1981 was duly passed but – intriguingly – was never brought into force. Notwithstanding its curious fate – or, perhaps, because of it – the 1981 Act is worthy of consideration, not least as an indicator of the direction of proposed (if failed) reform during this period.

According to its preamble, the 1981 Act aimed 'to make further and better provision for the regulation of the care and treatment of persons suffering from mental disorders and to provide for related matters'.[214] In relation to 'admission and discharge procedures', the Act specified that an application for involuntary admission could be made by certain relatives, a member of the Garda Síochána, an 'authorised officer'[215] or 'any other person'.[216] The Gardaí were accorded powers to take a person into custody if a Garda was 'of opinion or is informed by an authorised officer that he is of opinion that a person is suffering from mental disorder of such a degree that he should, in the interest of his own health or safety or for the protection of other persons or property, be placed forthwith under care and control'.[217]

Following such an 'application', 'a recommendation for the reception of a person in a psychiatric centre shall require the written recommendation in the prescribed form of two registered medical practitioners', with the second application occurring within seven days of the first (or within 24 hours in the case of a patient in Garda custody).[218] The doctors would have to set out reasons for their opinions and certify:

> (i) That the person is suffering from mental disorder of such a degree that detention and treatment in a psychiatric centre are necessary in the interest of the person's health or safety or for the protection of other persons or property, and (ii) that the person is not prepared to accept or is not suitable for treatment otherwise than as a detained patient.[219]

Following the recommendations, the patient could be escorted to the psychiatric centre, with the assistance of Gardaí if required,[220] within seven days.[221] The patient was to 'be received in the psychiatric centre by a medical officer of the centre who shall examine the person as soon as may be after the arrival of the person';[222] the patient could be detained for up to 48 hours for this purpose.[223]

During that period, the 'authorised medical practitioner of the approved centre'[224] had to 'either (a) make an order in the prescribed form (in this Part referred to as a reception order) that the person shall be received, detained and treated in the centre, or (b) discharge the person'.[225] The Act also specified, however, that 'nothing in this Part shall be read as preventing or discouraging a person from being admitted voluntarily for care and treatment in a psychiatric centre'.[226] These measures, if implemented, would have represented a considerable tightening up of existing procedures under the Mental Treatment Act 1945, albeit that the requirement for recommendations from two medical practitioners would have been a logistical challenge.

Once completed, a 'reception order' would permit detention and treatment for up to 28 days but could be extended by an 'extension order' (for three months from date of admission in the first instance, and for 12 month periods thereafter) which had to be 'signed by two authorised medical practitioners each of whom has separately examined the person'.[227] Both the recommending doctor[228] and the certifying doctor at the psychiatric centre had to inform the patient of their actions and, in the case of the certifying doctor, of the right to review.[229]

The Act also outlined provisions for 'boarding out',[230] 'return of person absent without leave',[231] 'permitted absence',[232] 'transfers',[233] 'transfer to special psychiatric centre' (e.g. Central Mental Hospital)[234] at the direction of a 'review board',[235] and 'discharge', when criteria for detention were no longer met.[236] In addition:

A person who is under care in a psychiatric centre otherwise than as a detained patient may give written notice to the medical officer in charge of the centre that he wishes to leave the centre not earlier than twenty-four hours after giving the notice and he shall be entitled and shall be allowed to leave the centre at any time after the expiration of the said twenty-four hours.[237]

One of the most progressive parts of the 1981 Act concerned 'safeguards for patients'[238] including provision of 'information as to persons detained',[239] 'furnishing of documents to detained and discharged persons' (including 'a statement in writing of his rights and entitlements under this Act')[240] and 'inspection of centres and homes'.[241] In addition, 'psychiatric review boards' were to be established, comprising 'three persons to be appointed by the Minister [for Health] one of whom shall be a person who is or has been a barrister or solicitor who has practised his profession for at least 7 years, one an authorised medical practitioner and one a person who is not a member of the legal or medical profession'.[242]

An application to a Review Board would be granted if made by the detained person or his or her parent, guardian, spouse, sibling or child,[243] or 'the Minister [for Health], the President of the High Court or the Registrar of Wards of Court'.[244] Others could also apply but the application might not be granted.[245] If the application was granted, the Review Board 'examination' had to occur within one month,[246] and 'the manner of making applications and the procedure of a review board, including the making of arrangements by it for an independent medical examination of the patient, may be prescribed'.[247]

When the Review Board carried out the 'examination' it would have to '(a) decide that the person should not be discharged, or (b) direct the discharge of the person either unconditionally or subject to conditions in regard to his continuing care or supervision'.[248] If the patient remained detained, another 'examination' could not occur for a further six months[249] but the applicant could, 'within one month of being informed of the decision of the board, appeal to the Minister [for Health] against the decision';[250] the Minister, following medical examination, could 'refuse the appeal or direct the discharge of the person conditionally or unconditionally'.[251]

For a patient who had been discharged conditionally, the Review Board could '(a) confirm the conditions applying to him, (b) vary or cancel the conditions, or (c) cancel the direction for his discharge and make an order in the prescribed form directing that he be received and detained for treatment in a psychiatric centre'.[252] If a patient was detained for two years and his or her case was not examined by the Review Board within the previous six months, the 'medical officer in charge of the centre' would be obliged to furnish a report to the Review Board within one month and the Review Board would then review the matter.[253] A Review Board decision to confirm such a detention could be appealed to the Minister for Health by certain parties within one month of being informed of the Review Board decision.[254]

The 1981 Act made various specific provisions regarding Review Board examinations including that 'the person whose detention is being examined shall have a right to be represented by another person during the board's examination'[255] and 'a review board may determine an application without an oral hearing where such a hearing is not requested by the applicant or where it appears to the board that such a hearing might be harmful to the health of the person concerned.'[256]

In relation to 'consent for certain therapeutic procedures', the Act specified that 'the Medical Council may, with the consent of the Minister [for Health], make rules in accordance with accepted medical practice (a) in regard to the application to any person of any specified therapeutic procedure for the treatment of mental illness, and (b) specifying the conditions to be complied with and the precautions to be taken to safeguard the rights and well-being of patients to whom the procedure is applied.'[257]

Most interestingly, the 1981 Act specified that 'it shall not be lawful to apply or cause to be applied any procedure so specified unless the person has given his consent in the manner provided for in the rules or, notwithstanding the provisions of Section 4 of the Health Act 1953,[258] where the person has not the mental capacity to give his consent, consent is given by a person specified in the rules.'[259]

With regard to civil proceedings, the Act stated that no such proceedings 'shall be instituted in respect of an act purporting to have been done in pursuance of this Act save by leave of the High Court and such leave shall not be granted unless the High Court is satisfied that there are substantial grounds for contending that the person against whom the proceedings are to be brought acted in bad faith or without reasonable care.'[260] The Act also dealt with 'registration and supervision of psychiatric institutions'[261] including 'registered psychiatric homes',[262] and 'report of certain matters to Minister [for Health]' (e.g. serious injury, death or assault of a patient).[263]

Despite the fact that it was never implemented, the 1981 Act was very interesting and progressive in many ways. Positive provisions included abolishing the distinction between private and chargeable (public) patients; requiring that the patient be informed of doctors' intentions to proceed to involuntary admission;[264] and enhanced rights following detention, especially the establishment of Review Boards. Unsurprisingly, the failure to bring the 1981 Act into force provoked considerable comment.[265] On 23 April 1985, the Minister for Health, Mr Desmond, explained to the Dáil why it had not been implemented:

> I have always considered the provisions of the Health (Mental Services) Act, 1981 to be not only inoperable in practice in certain respects but not fulfilling the objective of producing a legislative base upon which the mental health services could be developed. When I became Minister I had a detailed review of the Act undertaken and I will, in the course of the next few months, be drafting new legislation which will take into account any changes required by the recommendations in the planning framework report. This report is now being studied by the interested bodies and I hope to have their views without undue delay.[266]

Pressed further, the Minister repeated the word 'inoperable' several times:

> The Bill is being drafted. It will be a comprehensive piece of legislation dealing with the provision of psychiatric services at health board level with the registration of

institutions, admission and discharge procedures and safeguards for patients in such hospitals. It will deal also with the role of review boards. It is essential that we have new legislation in that area. Soon after the 1981 regulations were drafted it was apparent that they were inoperable. The provision in regard to doctors and the system relating to review tribunals were regarded generally as inadequate and inoperable [...]. Undoubtedly there is a need for a new review board procedure. The procedure dealt with in the 1981 Act was regarded as cumbersome and inoperable.[267]

Four years later, in 1989, the issue was still provoking comment and criticism.[268] In 1991 the Irish Association of Civil Liberty again highlighted the failure to implement the 1981 Act.[269] In 1992, Liz Keating in the *Irish Times* drew particular attention to the human rights implications of detention under the Mental Treatment Act 1945 which lacked adequate safeguards or review.[270] She noted the view of some doctors that the 1981 Act's requirement for certification by two doctors seemed unworkable for all patients; that there was an alleged lack of consultation during the development of the 1981 Act; and that the 1981 Act would not have resolved many of the problems with the 1945 Act anyway.

In response, Dr Niall Griffin, Chairman of the National Committee of RMSs, Chief Psychiatrists and Clinical Directors, wrote that he was thankful the 1981 Act had not been brought into force because it was, he said, a much weaker Act and would not have been in the interests of patients or their relatives.[271] Dr James J. Wilson, consultant psychiatrist, stated that the views of most senior psychiatrists had been dismissed during the development of the Act and that the resulting legislation was absurd.[272] Ms Nuala Fennell, TD (1935–2009), in response, alleged that abuses under the 1945 Act had occurred particularly (but not exclusively) when marital relationships had broken down, and that the 1981 Act had offered important safeguards including an appeal procedure.[273] Deputy Fennell's own private members' Bill, the Mental Treatment (Amendment) Bill 1992, was defeated on 6 May 1992, despite general agreement on the importance of the issue and the need for such reform.[274]

The following month, the Department of Health published a Green Paper on mental health policy and law, noting that the current legislation (still the Mental Treatment Act 1945) lacked a mechanism for independent review of detention orders, as had been proposed in the 1981 Act.[275] This led, in due course, to a 1995 White Paper proposing a 'new Mental Health Act', openly acknowledging that the current legislation did 'not fully comply with this country's obligations under international law'.[276] This, in turn, led to the Mental Health Act 2001 which incorporated some but not all of the measures presented in the ill-fated 1981 Act.

Overall, the Health (Mental Services) Act 1981 was an interesting, if failed, effort at reform of a historically important area of mental health practice: involuntary admission and treatment. As a result of the failure to implement the 1981 Act, legitimate and well deserved concern about the Mental Treatment Act 1945 persisted well into the 1990s,[277] and it was not until the advent of the Mental Health Act 2001 that Irish mental health legislation saw any real reform.[278] By that time, legislative change was long overdue: since the Mental Treatment Act 1945 was introduced, the international human rights environment had evolved beyond recognition and the practice of psychiatry had also changed in profound and lasting ways, necessitating a complete overhaul of mental health legislation and, indeed, policy. Mental health nursing was one of the key areas in which such progressive changes were becoming more and more evident with each passing decade, and this is considered next.

Mental Health Nursing: 'Helping to Build a Free, Independent and Self-Reliant Person'

There is a growing literature on the history of mental health nursing in Ireland, especially during the late nineteenth and early twentieth centuries.[279] In broad terms, Nolan and Sheridan note that Irish asylum staff tended to come from rural areas; possess agricultural skills; and be able to communicate with patients in either Irish or English.[280] One of their key roles was to impart various skills to patients to assist them in finding employment or contributing to the upkeep of the asylum.

Despite the attractions of steady employment in the asylums, life as an attendant or nurse was difficult[281] and recruitment was a recurrent challenge in Ireland, as it was in England.[282] The reasons were partly financial: in mid-1800s Ireland, a male attendant's wages were between £7 and £10 per annum and a female attendant received £4 to £6.[283] This was considerably less than their counterparts in England and Scotland, and also less than farm labourers in Ireland, who received £8 to £12 per annum. Wages were slightly higher at the Central Criminal Lunatic Asylum in Dundrum.[284] Nonetheless, the hours were long, averaging at 83 hours per week in most asylums, and the social standing of attendants was extremely low.[285]

In terms of training, the first known set of lectures given to mental health nurses was delivered by Sir Alexander Morison at Surrey Asylum, later Springfield Hospital, in 1843–4.[286] The MPA later introduced a handbook for 'attendants' in 1885 and examinations some years later. The first Irish asylum to enter candidates for the MPA examination was the District Asylum in Londonderry in May 1894, when 13 nurses gained the MPA certificate.[287] In 1895, 9 staff members in Cork asylum presented for the examination.[288] There were also significant developments in Mullingar, where Dr Arthur Finegan pioneered the training of attendants; promoted the idea of patients 'boarding out';[289] instituted the 'Finegan Prize' (awarded annually in Mullingar from the late 1890s to the early 1960s); and was buried, at his own request, in the patients' graveyard[290] – just like Dr Ada English in Ballinasloe (Chapter 4).

Doheny has studied the history of psychiatric nurse training in one Irish asylum, Clonmel, where the first staff members to take the 'Certificate of Proficiency in Mental Nursing' did so in 1896.[291] Following lectures from Dr Harvey, Assistant Medical Officer, 14 Clonmel staff members presented for the examination, and 5 successfully attained the certificate: Terence Kelly, Michael Norris, Kate Walshe, Bridget Lonergan and Mary Alward. They received certificates, badges and a £2 increase in annual salary. By 1908, 27 of the asylum's 71 staff members had MPA certificates, reflecting a significant advance in training standards. In Maryborough District Lunatic Asylum in Portlaoise, the first person to attain the certificate was Edward Dunne who took training from August 1898 and gained the certificate in 1901.[292]

These were times of considerable change in other respects too: in 1896, attendants at the Richmond in Dublin attempted to form a union, the National Union of Asylum Attendants in

Ireland, and while this was not recognised by the Board of Governors[293] it was a clear signal of further industrial unrest to follow and the strikes that duly characterised the 1920s and 1930s (Chapter 5).[294] Some changes did occur in the early 1900s, however, as the working week was reduced from an average of 80 hours to 56, and staff/patient ratios fell somewhat; e.g. to 1:12 in Mullingar in 1901.[295]

The regulatory situation also evolved when the General Nursing Council (GNC) of Ireland was established under the Nurses' Registration (Ireland) Act 1919[296] and, from 1 June 1936, only mental hospital nurses who passed the examination of the Council could be registered. By this time, increased numbers of nurses in Irish mental hospitals were passing the examination of the RMPA: in May 1933, 32 male and 47 female nurses in Irish mental hospitals were successful.[297]

These two systems – the Irish GNC examination and the RMPA certificate – continued to operate in parallel for many years, but from 1935 onward numbers on the RMPA register began to decline.[298] Predictably, the numbers registering with the GNC increased, but the overall number training as psychiatric nurses fell. In addition, nursing shortages in Great Britain during the 1940s were such that Irish staff there were asked if relatives in Ireland would like to apply for posts, and nursing superintendents and matrons went on recruiting missions to Ireland, to replace staff who had been called up for military service.[299]

In 1950, the GNC was replaced by An Bord Altranais (Irish Nursing Board) and in 1955 the Psychiatric Nurse Training Syllabus was revised.[300] This renewed commitment to training was much needed: in 1951, Dr Joseph Kearney, Inspector of Mental Hospitals (and also a member of An Bord Altranais), reported that half of the staff at Kilkenny Mental Hospital did not have any nursing qualifications.[301]

Despite these challenges, there were emergent signs of positive change. In 1958, Nurse Thomas Farrell became the first community psychiatric nurse in Ireland, based at St Luke's in Clonmel.[302] In the late 1960s, the *Report of the Commission of Inquiry on Mental Illness* articulated a strong community orientation and devoted considerable attention to psychiatric nursing:

> An Bord Altranais controls the registration, training and certification of nurses within the State. At present the training of psychiatric nurses is separate from that of general nurses. There is a noticeable international trend towards the introduction of a common basic training for all nurses, followed by specialisation in particular fields. There appears to be no immediate prospect of introducing such a system in Ireland, but steps towards a closer integration of general and psychiatric nurse training are possible.[303]

The Commission made a series of specific recommendations in relation to nurses, many of which concerned education and training:

- Joint training schemes [for nurses], in neighbouring approved psychiatric and general hospitals, should be established on an experimental basis.
- The training period for qualification should be reduced to 18 months in the case of general trained nurses undertaking psychiatric training and of psychiatric nurses undertaking general training.

- All nurses undergoing general training should spend a period of at least three months full-time training and instruction in accordance with an approved syllabus in a psychiatric hospital.
- All nurses undergoing psychiatric training should spend a period of at least three months full-time training and instruction in accordance with an approved syllabus in a general hospital, preferably a hospital incorporating a training school.
- The minimum age of entry for student psychiatric nurses should be reduced to 17 years. While it is hoped that, ultimately, the Secondary Schools' Leaving Certificate will be specified as the minimum educational qualification the Intermediate Certificate (or its equivalent) should be stipulated as the minimum educational level for the present.
- Because of the increasing emphasis on domiciliary care, instruction about the social services and out-patient and domiciliary work should be included in the curriculum of the student nurse.
- Refresher courses should be organised regularly for both senior and junior qualified psychiatric nurses.
- Suitable library facilities should be provided in every psychiatric hospital.
- Courses to provide training and experience in group leadership and activation should be organised at local centres.[304]

The 1966 Report had a strong influence on subsequent policy throughout the 1970s, including the report of a Department of Health Working Party in 1972, which noted the transformation that was clearly occurring in Irish mental health care and nursing:

> With the development of modern treatments, together with the involvement of other trained personnel to complement the work of the doctors and nurses, a complete transformation has come about in the whole concept of psychiatric care. For many people there is no longer any need to enter hospital to be treated effectively; for those who have to enter hospital, the length of stay has been shortened and there has been a quickening of the tempo and the activity within the hospitals. The way has been cleared for these custodial care institutions to become active treatment and rehabilitation centres even for those patients who of necessity have to remain in hospital.[305]

The Working Party recognised that, for some staff, these changes were 'bewildering':

> The transformation which has been taking place in the psychiatric services has been somewhat bewildering for many of those working in the service. This has applied to all classes of staff and not to the nurses alone. The old concept of nurses protecting and caring for the patient, attending to his every need, is, in many cases, now seen to be damaging to the patient and detrimental to his chances of recovery. The nurse's job is now seen in the context of his helping to build a free, independent and self-reliant

person by permitting and encouraging the patient to do things for himself, thereby maintaining and, if necessary, restoring his independence and self-respect. Patients are now to be found often outside the hospital wards, in their own homes, at clinics, in workshops, and the nurse has also to move out of the hospital wards to where the patients are.[306]

Consistent with this, the 1972 Working Party made a series of recommendations relating to the role of the psychiatric nurse, recruitment and selection, student training, post-registration training, organisational structure, system of promotion, auxiliary nursing and other support personnel, research, duty rosters and various other matters:

> In considering these matters it became apparent to the Working Party that there is much uneasiness on the part of nurses which it was felt mainly arose from the ill-defined role of the psychiatric nurse. This, in turn, has led to feelings of insecurity and fears that the traditional role of the nurse was being encroached upon and eroded by new disciplines. Unfavourable working conditions in some areas do not help and the nett result is a general lack of job satisfaction. [...] The Working Party would like to make it clear at this stage that it is not concerned with apportioning blame for the deficiencies in the present situation. It is clear that nursing staff attitudes have often been inflexible in the past and have not been helpful to progressive development. There has also been, however, evidence of the absence of the kind of dynamic leadership, which nurses could reasonably expect from management at administrative, medical and senior nursing levels.[307]

The Working Party's report appeared during a time of significant industrial unrest in Irish psychiatric nursing, a fact that the Working Party laid out in no uncertain terms:

> The unsatisfactory features mentioned and other factors, referred to later in this report, have contributed to the unrest and dissatisfaction which have been so obvious within the psychiatric nursing profession in recent years and reached a climax with the withdrawal of their services by many nurses in November 1971. Action such as this must seriously retard the development of progressive nursing care in mental health, must impede programmes of care, and must gravely undermine public confidence in the service as a whole. The patient is inevitably the most vulnerable and the greatest loser. The Working Party recognises that some element of conflict is to be expected in a situation where patients' needs are required to be balanced against staff expectations. That the situation should have been reached where nurses caring for the mentally ill take strike action is, however, an index of a gravity which is outside the average cut and thrust of professional negotiation.[308]

The Working Party called for a 'wholehearted effort' to improve matters, but the task was 'daunting':

Mention of the strike by psychiatric nurses forces the Working Party to express its surprise at the inadequacy of the efforts made by management to publicise the reasons for the dispute. In the opinion of the Working Party this highlights the need, where there can be great public concern, for public authorities to have access to the means of putting the issues fully before the public. [...] If the nurses are to play their full and proper role in looking after the mental health and welfare of the people a wholehearted effort on the part of all concerned will be required. Given the necessary goodwill and co-operation the task is still daunting.

Ultimately, the 1972 report appeared to be an effort to both resolve the industrial unrest pertaining at the time and move forward the recommendations of the 1966 Commission.[309] By this point, the Psychiatric Nurses Association had also been founded with an initial membership of 500 in 1970, rising to over 2,000 a decade later.[310]

There was continued change throughout the 1980s as the role of psychiatric nurses evolved further, generally moving towards a more community based model of care.[311] In 1992, Professor Thomas Lynch pointed to real progress in the development of community mental health facilities in Ireland, with particular emphasis on the role of community based nursing staff:

Workshops, day hospitals, day centres and hostel places are very well provided throughout Ireland. Our nursing staff are better trained in Ireland. I also think that the concept of psychiatric nurses in the community is more advanced in Ireland. We have some excellent community services developed by these nursing staff.[312]

Much of this change was attributable to the continued orientation of mental health policy toward community care, as was duly reflected in the 1984 policy document, *The Psychiatric Services: Planning for the Future*.[313]

Mental Health Policy:
Planning for the Future (1984)

In the early 1980s, the need for continued mental health services reform was apparent right across Ireland. In February 1980, the South Eastern Health Board appointed a subcommittee 'to examine the Board's psychiatric services in hospitals and in the community and to make recommendations to the Board as to how best these services might be developed and improved'.[314] The subcommittee's first three recommendations signalled a continued shift, at least in theory, away from hospital based care:

1. The Board should develop a policy for the prevention, early detection and treatment of psychiatric illness.
2. The primary service for the mentally ill, as with other illnesses, should be the family doctor, supported as appropriate by the psychiatric services.

3. Admission to a psychiatric hospital or a psychiatric unit in a general hospital, should be regarded as a final treatment resource and to this end treatment facilities outside hospital should be developed so as to maintain as much as possible the patient's links with his community and to minimise his stay in hospital when this is necessary.[315]

In October 1981, Mrs Eileen Desmond TD, Minister for Health, appointed a national 'Study Group on the Development of the Psychiatric Services' with broad terms of reference:

> To examine the main components, both institutional and community, of the psychiatric services; to assess the existing services, to clarify their objectives and to draw up planning guidelines for future development of the service with due regard to cost implications; to carry out such studies and to take part in such consultations as are necessary to assist this examination.[316]

The resultant study group included the Inspector of Mental Hospitals (Dr Fergus Campbell) as well as five psychiatrists, a Chief Nursing Officer, various officials from the Department of Health and the Chief Executive Officer of the South Eastern Health Board. The Group was later criticised for not including other allied health professionals, such as occupational therapists, social workers and psychologists.[317]

The study group's report, titled *The Psychiatric Services: Planning for the Future* and dated December 1984, was published on 5 March 1985.[318] At the outset, the authors, in what was already a rather repetitive mantra, were clear about the need for a shift from institutional to community care:

> At present, the psychiatric hospital is the focal point of the psychiatric service in most parts of the country. Large numbers of patients reside permanently in these hospitals. Many of them have lived there for years in conditions which in many cases are less than adequate because of overcrowding and capital underfunding. In addition, staff and public attitudes have tended to concentrate effort on hospital care as a result of which community facilities are relatively underdeveloped. [...]
>
> Every person who needs it should have access to a comprehensive psychiatric service. A comprehensive service is one which caters for the varying needs of people with psychiatric illness. The components of such a service include:
>
> - Prevention and early identification
> - Assessment, diagnostic and treatment services
> - In-patient care (see above)
> - Day care
> - Out-patient care
> - Community-based residences

This range of services should be available locally. The different services should be co-ordinated so that a patient can transfer easily from one to another. The psychiatric team should be responsible for ensuring that the services provided by them are integrated with general practitioner, community care and voluntary services. The contribution of general practitioners and other professionals to the primary care of the mentally ill should be supported by the psychiatric teams through the formation of effective working links with them.[319]

Overall, the report directed that psychiatric services should be comprehensive and community oriented, aimed at delivering care that is continuous, coordinated and multidisciplinary. The population was to be divided into sectors, each comprising 25,000 to 30,000 individuals. Psychiatric care was to be delivered by consultant-led multidisciplinary teams in each sector. The authors recommended that a dedicated crisis service be developed in each sector and additional specialised services be developed to cover more than one sector. Day hospitals were directed to provide intensive treatment equivalent to that available in an inpatient setting for acutely ill patients.

More specifically, the authors recommended the provision of 0.75 day places per 1,000 population; 0.5 inpatient beds per 1,000 population for short stay (up to three months) and medium stay (up to one year) patients; 0.5 beds per 1,000 population for 'new long-stay' patients; and 60 places in community residential accommodation per 100,000 population (increasing to 100 places per 100,000 population in areas with a backlog of existing long stay patients). The policy also addressed a number of specialised areas within psychiatry, including the provision of liaison services, rehabilitation programmes, services for elderly people and mental health research.

The authors recommended the establishment of one child guidance team per 200,000 population, and the development of community based interventions for alcohol related problems, aimed at prevention rather than just treatment. The report also included appendices dealing with the epidemiology of mental illness; psychiatric services for the adult deaf (prepared by Dr Jim O'Boyle, a consultant psychiatrist and member of the study group, Chapter 7);[320] statistics on psychiatric services and staffing; estimating the future long term bed needs for St Ita's Hospital, Portrane; and provision of child psychiatric services.

Throughout its text, the report placed particular emphasis on the role of primary care in providing psychiatric services, noting that 'the results of various studies show that general practitioners are presented with and treat the largest proportion of psychiatric morbidity among the population, leaving only a small and atypical proportion to the specialised psychiatric services'.[321] This welcome recognition of the central role of general practitioners and primary healthcare professionals was long overdue and remains relevant several decades after *Planning for the Future* was published, as primary care remains the location for most mental health care today.

The publication of *Planning for the Future* in 1985 was duly noted in the national press[322] and elicited a range of responses from professional groups, voluntary organisations, political parties and various commentators.[323] Just four months after the policy was launched, the *Irish Times* carried an optimistic two part series noting that reform was already in process at certain psychiatric hospitals, including St Brendan's at Grangegorman.[324]

Criticisms of the policy included suggestions that its recommendations would inappropriately medicalise psychological problems,[325] it did not face up to the role of stigma,[326] failed to distinguish sufficiently between different kinds of mental disorder and psychological problems,[327] and might increase stress on families.[328] There were also concerns about implementation,[329] with the Simon Community pointing out that communities might not yet be ready for community care.[330]

In a most unusual turn of events, in October 1985 a High Court injunction was granted to two members and one officer of the Eastern Health Board to restrain the Board and its committees from discussing or adopting *Planning for the Future*, on the basis that more time for consultation and preparation was needed before the report was adopted.[331] The chief concern in this instance was that inpatient facilities might be closed before adequate community facilities were put into place and Professor Ivor Browne pointed out that there would be only one opportunity to make community psychiatry work in Ireland. The importance of adequate community support was further emphasised by Dr E. Fuller Torrey, a world expert on schizophrenia and mental health systems,[332] at the fourth biennial conference of the Schizophrenia Association of Ireland in June 1986.[333]

Concerns about the quality of mental health services persisted during this period. In 1985, the Simon Community organised a lecture series as a tribute to the work of Dr Ian Hart, a psychologist and social researcher with the Economic and Social Research Institute, centred on the theme of 'poverty in Ireland and the role of four institutions: finance, law, psychiatry and the Church'.[334] Dr Michael Corry, a psychiatrist, issued a convincing, prescient warning against medicalising social problems;[335] Peig Murphy, a social worker, highlighted the importance of appropriate housing, an issue which would persist;[336] and Peter McLoone, of the Local Government and Public Services Union (Health and Welfare Services), emphasised the need for a properly resourced programme of community care.[337]

In April 1986, the Minister for Health, Mr Desmond, strongly reaffirmed his commitment to *Planning for the Future*[338] and steps towards implementation went ahead in due course.[339] The following years saw consistent concerns expressed that patients were being discharged too early owing to financial cutbacks in psychiatric hospitals[340] and that reductions in bed numbers resulted in increased numbers of mentally ill persons entering the criminal justice system.[341] There remained, nonetheless, considerable support for the general thrust of the policy in most professional groups.[342]

Overall, *Planning for the Future* set out both a community based philosophy of mental health care and a series of recommendations in relation to levels of service provision.[343] As Walsh notes, the policy essentially endorsed and extended the recommendations of the 1966 Commission of Inquiry on Mental Illness but also dealt in greater detail with implementation and suggested appropriate management structures for each service.[344] Did the 1984 policy succeed in its goals?

It is difficult to perform direct comparisons between the planning guidelines outlined in *Planning for the Future* in 1984 and the levels of service provision some decades later, owing to the confounding effects of changing diagnostic practices, evolving therapeutic approaches and changes in the broader structure of Irish health services over that time. Almost 20 years after its publication, however, the Mental Health Commission, in its 2002 Annual Report, pointed out that the principles outlined in *Planning for the Future* were still relevant to psychiatric care in Ireland, and that while all of its recommendations had not yet been implemented, *Planning for the Future* had succeeded in bringing significant improvements to Irish psychiatric services, particularly in relation to deinstitutionalisation,[345] although that process was well underway prior to the new policy.

In addition, considerable challenges remained in relation to particular areas (e.g. the elderly with mental illness),[346] and the overall picture was decidedly mixed: for example, while *Planning for the Future* recommended the provision of 0.75 psychiatric day places per 1,000 population, there were, by 2001, 0.42 day hospital places per 1,000 population, plus 0.93 day centre places.[347] There was also considerable variation in the provision of both day hospital and day centre places across Ireland, with some health boards providing service levels well below the average figures. Implementation was, to say the least, uneven.

Planning for the Future also recommended the provision of 100 places in community residential accommodation per 100,000 population in areas with an existing backlog of long stay patients. By 2001, there were 114.2 places per 100,000 population in low, medium and high support community residences.[348] There was, however, again considerable variation in provision across different health board areas, with the highest rate of places recorded in the North Western Health Board at 199.2 per 100,000 population, in marked contrast with the South Western Area Health Board at 58.6 per 100,000.[349]

These comparisons between planning recommendations in 1984 and service provision in 2001 are interesting but, as cautioned above, the possible effects of multiple confounders are difficult to estimate and must be borne in mind. Overall, since *Planning for the Future* was published the continued reduction in psychiatric inpatient numbers was indeed notable (from 12,484 in 1984 to 4,256 in 2001),[350] but it was equally notable that the adequacy of community based alternatives remained a cause of concern for many, including the Mental Health Commission.[351] Various other, specific concerns were also expressed in the two decades following *Planning for the Future*,[352] especially in relation to services for adolescents with mental illness,[353] the elderly,[354] the forensic population,[355] migrants with mental illness,[356] and the homeless mentally ill.[357]

Research in the area of forensic psychiatry, for example, showed strong evidence that general psychiatric services were under resourced in the areas of greatest predicted need and that this, in turn, was associated with increased use of forensic psychiatry services.[358] In addition, there was strong evidence of gross over representation of Irish Travellers among forensic psychiatric admissions.[359] Clearly, the provisions outlined in *Planning for the Future* would require significant updating to address forensic mental health need in Ireland, especially in terms of *community* forensic psychiatry services.

In summary, then, the two decades following the publication of *Planning for the Future* saw significant progress in the development of Irish mental health services and especially the reduction in inpatient numbers, but many challenges remained. While the process of deinstitutionalisation progressed considerably, there was still substantial concern about the adequacy of community based services for adults with mental disorder and development of specialist services to meet the needs of particular groups such as children, adolescents, elderly people, the learning disabled and the forensic population.

These challenges were not unexpected. In his foreword to *Planning for the Future*, Barry Desmond TD, Minister for Health, struck a hopeful but cautious note, pointing out that the policy's proposals would be implemented within certain budgetary parameters:

This Report, prepared by a specially appointed study group, contains a detailed analysis of our psychiatric service and provides guidelines for its future development as a community-based service meeting, in the most effective way, the psychiatric needs of the population. It is in accordance with a major objective of health policy which has been identified in the Government's National Plan 'Building on Reality' which is the shifting of resources from institutional services to community services.

I am pleased to introduce the Report and to invite comments on its contents. Subject to any changes arising from these comments and from subsequent consultations, it is the Government's intention to implement the recommendations contained in the Report. While this must take place within the framework of the allocations for health services which are contained in the National Plan, I am confident that considerable progress can be made towards a realisation of the service described in the Report in the years immediately ahead.[360]

There can be little doubt that while the recommendations in *Planning for the Future* were generally positive and forward looking, the timing of the report was challenging as regards the funding required for community facilities: in 1980s Ireland it was certainly seen as necessary, as Minister Desmond pointed out, to keep 'within the framework of the allocations for health services'. To compound matters, the reports of the Inspector of Mental Hospitals were not even published during the 1980s (as they had been up until 1977), significantly reducing grounds for strong public advocacy to develop the community facilities recommended in *Planning for the Future*.[361]

Despite these challenges, *Planning for the Future* certainly played an important role in renewing commitment to the principles of community mental health care which had been outlined almost two decades earlier by the 1966 Commission of Inquiry on Mental Illness and would be rehearsed yet again just over two decades later in 2006 in the next iteration of mental health policy, *A Vision for Change*.[362]

Notwithstanding the various delays and difficulties in implementing *Planning for the Future*, however, there were signs of significant change in Irish psychiatry during this period, not only in terms of reducing inpatient numbers and developing community services, but also in relation to the profession of psychiatry itself, which gained new voice and greater public understanding in Ireland and elsewhere. One of the leaders of this change was one of the most remarkable and historically noteworthy psychiatrists of his generation, Professor Anthony Clare.

Professor Anthony Clare:
Psychiatrist and Broadcaster

Anthony Ward Clare (1942–2007), who went on to become the best known psychiatrist in Ireland and Great Britain,[363] was born in Dublin on 24 December 1942 and brought up in Ranelagh on Dublin's Southside. Clare attended the Jesuit Gonzaga College, where he helped edit the school's newspaper, before studying medicine at UCD.[364] Clare had become interested in medicine when recovering from an accident in his teens and graduated as a doctor in 1966.[365] During his years at university, Clare excelled at the debates of the famed Literary and Historical Society, of which he became auditor.[366] In 1964, Clare and his debating colleague, Patrick Cosgrave, won the highly prestigious Observer Mace Trophy in the universities debating competition.

After graduation, Clare completed a family practice rotating internship at St Joseph's Hospital in Syracuse, New York.[367] He then trained in psychiatry at St Patrick's Hospital, Dublin, for over two years, followed by five years as registrar and senior registrar at the Maudsley Hospital, London. Clare's first scientific publication, a case report concerning 'diazepam, alcohol, and barbiturate abuse', appeared in the *British Medical Journal* on 6 November 1971;[368] many more were to follow over the subsequent decades, accompanied by books, broadcasts and newspaper articles.

Professor Sir Robin Murray remembers Clare as a dominant figure in the Maudsley in the 1970s, an impressive speaker, dressed in a velvet suit.[369] During this period, Clare fought strongly for better conditions for trainees in psychiatry, with considerable success.[370]

In 1976, just 10 years after graduating, Clare published an extraordinary book titled *Psychiatry in Dissent: Controversial Issues in Thought and Practice*.[371] Originally conceived as part of a textbook, Clare's text, lucid, incisive and endlessly compassionate, has become a classic of twentieth-century psychiatry. In it, Clare explored the concept of psychiatric diagnosis in considerable depth and pointed out, *inter alia*, the importance of classification systems in protecting people from being labelled as mentally ill for purposes of political or societal convenience. Clare also provided clear headed, pragmatic discussions of schizophrenia, ECT and psychosurgery, as well as a fascinating chapter on responsibility and involuntary psychiatric admission.

In his measured, persuasive tones, Clare argued that it was unhelpful to conceptualise normality and madness as dichotomous, and better to see them as points on a continuum. Clare warned against too crisp a dichotomy between 'organic' and 'functional' mental disorders, a warning that remains as relevant in the twenty-first century as it was in 1976.[372] Most of all, Clare's iconic text provided psychiatry with a clear, logical and persuasive response to the critics of psychiatry throughout the 1960s and 1970s. Several decades later, *Psychiatry in Dissent* is still routinely cited as one of the most influential texts in twentieth-century psychiatry and beyond.[373]

Also in 1976, Clare commenced a six year period in the General Practice Research Unit at the Institute of Psychiatry in London, working with Professor Michael Shepherd. Clare wrote his doctoral (MD) thesis on premenstrual tension and gained a Master's degree in philosophy (MPhil) from the University of London for a dissertation concerning psychiatric illness in an Irish immigrant population.[374]

Clare became Vice-Dean of the Institute of Psychiatry in 1982. In 1983, he was appointed Professor and Head of Psychological Medicine at St Bartholomew's Hospital, London.[375] He continued to write, co-write and edit publications on a range of themes including mental illness in general practice, social work, primary health care and various aspects of psychiatry.[376]

Over this period, Clare's engagement with media deepened considerably. Most notably, Clare was a regular contributor to BBC Radio 4's 'Stop the Week' programme and this, in turn, led to his best known media work, 'In the Psychiatrist's Chair'. For this series, which ran between 1982 and 2001, Clare interviewed a broad range of guests with an engaged, inquisitive charm that elicited fascinating insights from Bob Monkhouse, Anthony Hopkins, Eartha Kitt, Arthur Ashe, P.D. James, Derek Jarman and R.D. Laing, among others.[377]

Clare was also involved in an innovative series of programmes about various psychotherapies, and held considered views on many of them, including psychoanalysis.[378] He later worked with both the *Sunday Independent* and Channel 4, among other media organisations. Other radio programmes included 'All in the Mind' and 'Father Figures', and Clare also contributed to various television programmes (e.g. 'Nationwide', 'QED' and 'After Dark', among others).

In 1989, Clare returned to Dublin and became Medical Director of St Patrick's Hospital and Clinical Professor at the Department of Psychiatry in Trinity College Dublin. Clare introduced many changes at St Patrick's: new facilities were built; a new intensive care unit was opened; and Clare persuaded the governors of St Patrick's to fund research posts in psychiatry.[379] Clare made particular contributions to reorganising and strengthening postgraduate training and attracted world leaders in psychiatry to speak at the annual 'Founder's Day' meeting in St Patrick's.[380]

Alongside his clinical work, Clare continued to teach, research, write and engage with media to discuss issues relating to psychiatry, always with a view to advancing public education and debate about mental illness and psychological wellbeing.[381] Clare was deeply charitable, serving on the board of Plan Ireland, for example, a charity that promotes child rights in order to end child poverty.[382] He was chairperson of the Prince of Wales's advisory group on disability from 1989 to 1997.[383] In his personal life, Clare was deeply devoted to his family, and enjoyed tennis, opera and cinema.[384]

Following two terms as medical director of St Patrick's, Clare worked in St Edmundsbury Hospital, Lucan, and largely withdrew from media and public life.[385] He was due to retire in December 2007 but died suddenly in Paris on 28 October. Clare, who had by then attained Honorary Fellowship of the Royal College of Psychiatrists among other honours, was widely mourned.[386] Most notably, a broad range of colleagues immediately acknowledged his undoubted intellectual brilliance, deep sense of compassion and profound supportiveness towards colleagues.[387]

In 2005, when I contacted Clare about an upcoming paper reappraising *Psychiatry in Dissent*,[388] Clare reflected that, some thirty years after his iconic book first appeared, 'some of the debates of the 1960s do indeed take on a different perspective':

> When I was defending the emphasis on classification, for example, I never anticipated a situation whereby a preoccupation with classification bordering on the obsessional would develop and that arguments of a religious intensity would surround such dubious concepts as borderline personality or that concepts such as rapid cycling [bipolar disorder] and ADHD [attention deficit hyperactivity disorder] would grow so elastically [...]. I had forgotten that I had favoured the continuum notion of mental health/mental illness but relieved that I did! [...] Now I feel there are new controversial issues that have taken over from such concerns as the existence of mental illness and the efficacy of ECT. I think of the remorseless psychiatrization of so much of human experience [...]. I remain concerned about the seemingly irresistible tendency on the part of human beings to dichotomize – in psychiatry this leads to an incorrigible desire to assign primacy to this or that cause – biological over psychological – when the evidence such as it is suggests a more systems-appreciation might well be more defensible [...]. Other issues of dissent? Many, but I must stop or you will never get this letter![389]

Following the appearance of our positive reappraisal of *Psychiatry in Dissent*, Clare wrote that he 'was often tempted to write a follow-up' but 'never got round to it':

> Of the issues raised in the book some thirty years ago the one that perhaps worries me most now concerns the issue of 'dichotomies'. I know that theoretically there is so much emphasis on multi-axial approaches and you rightly draw attention to the evidence [in] support of a more dimensional way of thinking, but I am afraid what I never foresaw back in the 1970s was the massive swing in the United States away from the dogma of psychoanalysis to the dogma of DSM [Diagnostic and Statistical Manual of Mental Disorders]! It may well be that in years to come people will look back at the age of the American empire and one of the manifestations of it will be the domination of international classification by the American way of thinking.[390]

Clare was a truly outstanding figure in the history of Irish psychiatry, who made a unique and vital contribution to the demystification of psychiatry both in Ireland and internationally. He was, in the words of Murray, 'a better ambassador to the general public than psychiatry could have wished, or even hoped for'.[391] He was, as Murray concludes, 'arguably the most brilliant and multi-talented psychiatrist of his generation'.

Human Rights and Mental Health in Ireland

Clare was living and working during a period of significant change in attitudes towards mental disorder and psychiatry in many countries, including Ireland. Walsh, in 1992, noted that much of the impetus for change during this time emanated from the Department of Health rather than any professional grouping of psychiatrists:

> The Irish division of the Royal College of Psychiatrists has been a singularly inactive body and it has had little impact on pointing the future direction of psychiatry in this country. Instead the initiative in all these fields has been taken by the Department of Health. This has led to a devaluation of professional input from psychiatrists in the future direction of our psychiatric services, in their planning, organisation and administration.[392]

There were, however, important international influences, most notably in the area of human rights. The early 1990s saw the emergence of the first comprehensive statement of the rights of the mentally ill, with the UN's *Principles for the Protection of Persons with Mental Illness and the Improvement of Mental Health Care* in 1991.[393] The UN emphasised that all people are entitled to receive the best mental health care available and be treated with humanity and respect, and that there should be no discrimination on the grounds of mental disorder. This was notably consistent with Clare's broad, intensely humane vision of psychiatry.

The UN also stated that all people with mental disorder have the same rights to medical and social care as others. In addition:

- Everyone with mental disorder has the right to live, work and receive treatment in the community, as far as possible;
- Mental health care should be based on internationally accepted ethical standards, and not on political, religious or cultural factors;
- Each patient's treatment plan should be reviewed regularly with the patient;
- There shall be no misuse of mental health skills and knowledge;
- Medication should meet the health needs of the patient and should not be administered for the convenience of others or as a punishment;
- For involuntary patients, every effort should be made to inform the patient about treatment;
- Physical restraint or involuntary seclusion should be used only in accordance with official guidelines;
- Mental health facilities should be appropriately structured and resourced;
- An impartial review body should, in consultation with mental health practitioners, review the cases of involuntary patients.

At that time (1991), Ireland was in clear violation of the requirement for impartial reviews of psychiatric detention, and was, at best, poorly compliant with several of the other standards. The 1991 UN statement was important not only for its specific provisions, however, but also for its acknowledgement of a particular need to protect the rights of the mentally ill, especially those with enduring mental disorder whose rights had been significantly violated in the past.[394] An understanding of these international developments is critical for an understanding of subsequent mental health reform in Ireland.

Five years after the 1991 UN statement, the WHO, as the directing and coordinating authority for health within the UN system, developed this rights-based approach further by publishing 10 basic principles of mental health law, based on a comparative analysis of relevant laws in 45 countries, as well as the 1991 UN principles.[395] The WHO stated that:

- All persons should benefit from the best possible measures to promote mental well-being and *prevent* mental disorders;
- All persons in need should have access to basic mental health care;
- Mental health assessments should be performed in accordance with internationally accepted medical principles and instruments;
- All persons with mental disorders should be provided with health care which is the least restrictive possible;
- Consent is needed before any type of interference with a person can occur;
- If a patient experiences difficulties appreciating the implications of a decision, although not unable to decide, the patient shall benefit from the assistance of an appropriate third party of his or her choice;

- There should be a review procedure for any decision made by official, surrogate or representative decision-makers and health care providers;
- For decisions affecting integrity or liberty, with a long-lasting impact, there should be automatic periodical review mechanisms;
- All decision-makers acting in official or surrogate capacity should be qualified to do so;
- All decisions should be made in keeping with the body of law in force in the jurisdiction involved and not on any other basis, or an arbitrary basis.

These principles were underscored by the WHO's 1996 *Guidelines for the Promotion of Human Rights of Persons with Mental Disorders*, which noted that international instruments supporting the human rights of the mentally ill had been very slow to develop, and provided much needed detail on the implementation of the WHO's 10 basic principles of mental health law at national level.[396] At global policy level, these rights-based considerations were further underscored in 2001 when the WHO devoted its World Health Report to *Mental Health: New Understanding, New Hope*.[397]

Throughout these rights-based publications from the UN and WHO, the division between law and policy was not always apparent, and the extent to which legislation, as opposed to policy, should govern some of these matters was not always clear. Other issues for discussion related to the WHO's acceptance of involuntary committal in the first instance, something to which the World Network of Survivors and Users of Psychiatry objected on principle.[398] Some of these issues were clarified somewhat in 2005 in the WHO *Resource Book on Mental Health, Human Rights and Legislation* which presented a detailed statement of human rights issues which, according to the WHO, need to be addressed at national level (Chapter 8).[399]

The idea of deprivation of liberty based on mental ill health was, however, clearly endorsed in 1950 by the Council of Europe when it drafted the *Convention for the Protection of Human Rights and Fundamental Freedoms*, also known as the *European Convention on Human Rights* (ECHR), which aimed to protect human rights and the fundamental freedoms 'which are the foundation of justice and peace in the world and are best maintained on the one hand by an effective political democracy and on the other by a common understanding and observance of the human rights upon which they depend'.[400]

With regard to mental disorder, the ECHR states that 'everyone has the right to liberty and security of person. No one shall be deprived of his liberty save in the following cases and in accordance with a procedure prescribed by law', including 'the lawful detention of persons for the prevention of the spreading of infectious diseases, of persons of unsound mind, alcoholics or drug addicts or vagrants'.[401] In addition:

> Everyone who is deprived of his liberty by arrest or detention shall be entitled to take proceedings by which the lawfulness of his detention shall be decided speedily by a court and his release ordered if the detention is not lawful.[402]

These ECHR provisions led to a relatively large number of relevant cases in the European Court of Human Rights over the following decades,[403] many of which related to the nature and conditions of psychiatric detention.[404] The European Court of Human Rights delivered its first significant decision in this area in 1979 and between 2000 and 2004 delivered forty judgments in this area.[405] As a result, there is now a significant body of ECHR jurisprudence in relation to mental disorder.[406] These cases and concerns contributed significantly to shaping mental health legislation in both Ireland and England, as well as contributing positively to overall attitudes towards involuntary psychiatric care.

More specifically, the Irish Law Society relied explicitly on both the ECHR and 1991 UN principles in its influential recommendations for reform of Ireland's mental health legislation in 1999.[407] The Irish government, too, openly acknowledged in 1995 that the Mental Treatment Act 1945 did 'not fully comply with this country's obligations under international law',[408] and that 'changes in Irish law [were] required to ensure full compliance with our obligations under the European Convention'.[409] Matters came to a head in 2000 when the lack of automatic review of psychiatric detention in Ireland formed the focus of a landmark case in the European Court of Human Rights.[410]

It was the ECHR and UN principles, then, rather than the EU (which Ireland joined in 1973), that led to increased emphasis on human rights in Irish mental health legislation, ultimately resulting in the Mental Health Act 2001. The EU did eventually become involved in mental health care, most notably in 2005, when the Health and Consumer Protectorate Director-General of the European Commission published a Green Paper on mental health and launched a consultation process.[411] This led to the establishment of an EU 'Consultative Platform'[412] and, in 2008, the *European Pact for Mental Health and Well-being*, published by the EU with the WHO.[413]

The issue of human rights emerged as an especially important concern throughout this process, consistent with the EU's involvement in other areas of legislation, including health law, and the EU *Charter of Fundamental Rights* (2000). Against this background, the EU's *European Pact for Mental Health and Well-being* placed strong emphases on improving social inclusion of the mentally ill and protecting human rights, including economic and social, as well as civil and political, rights.

From an historical perspective, however, assertive recognition of the rights of the mentally ill in Irish legislation is more attributable to the ECHR and UN than the EU. At service level, the shift towards improved protection of human rights and patient dignity is also attributable to a remarkable generation of psychiatrists who worked in Ireland during the closing decades of the twentieth century and the opening decades of the twenty-first. Like Clare, many of these figures combined progressive clinical care with academic work and teaching, seeking to transform Irish psychiatry and deliver better, more informed, more empowering services to the mentally ill.

Change and Development
in Irish Psychiatry

The latter decades of the twentieth century saw the emergence of several significant reforming figures in Irish psychiatry. While it is too early to present an historically informed, critical appraisal of the work of each, it is important to record key facts about their careers and accomplishments, in order to both elucidate the story of Irish psychiatry during this period and assist historians in future critical analyses of these developments. Some comments are added but these do not represent informed historical analyses at this time.

Thomas Lynch (1922–2005) was one of these influential figures whose career touched on many key themes in this history of psychiatry in Ireland. Lynch qualified from the RCSI in 1946 with first class honours and, following intern year, accepted an invitation from Professor Norman Moore to become assistant physician at St Patrick's Hospital, Dublin.[414] He gained membership of the Royal College of Physicians of Ireland in 1948 and passed the Diploma in Psychological Medicine (DPM). Lynch spent 1952 at the Maudsley Hospital in London and returned in 1956 as staff physician at St Patrick's and visiting consultant to the Meath Hospital. Five years later, Lynch became Resident Medical Superintendent at St Otteran's Hospital in Waterford and went on to set up a psychiatric unit in the general hospital in Waterford:

> The one big achievement came when the opportunity arose to start a psychiatric unit in a general hospital, Ardkeen. It was possible in Waterford only because the district general hospital had been a sanatorium with numerous units. These were changed into medical, surgical and obstetric units, and also a gynaecological unit, orthopaedic unit and eye unit. There were spare chest units half empty, and with the co-operation of the RMS of Ardkeen Hospital, Dr Fintan Corrigan, and my own medical and nursing staff we developed a psychiatric unit which opened in 1965. It was the first psychiatric unit developed in a general hospital in Southern Ireland.[415]

In 1968, Lynch returned to Dublin as Foundation Professor of Psychiatry at RCSI and Clinical Director with his base at St Brendan's Hospital. Lynch also opened a general hospital unit at James Connolly Memorial Hospital in Blanchardstown, Dublin. He was a strong supporter of the Royal College of Psychiatrists, which duly transformed psychiatric training in Ireland.[416] Lynch was elected a Foundation Fellow in 1971 and later served as Senior Vice-President (1981–83) and on the Court of Electors. He was also involved in forming the Irish National Psychiatric Postgraduate Training Committee and served on the National Drugs Advisory Board, National Rehabilitation Board, Central Remedial Clinic and Eastern Health Board.

Lynch came from a staunchly republican family, a fact that was not lost upon his colleagues, including Professor Thomas Fahy of University College Galway (later National University of Ireland, Galway) who referred to Lynch's father's illustrious history at a 1990 meeting of Irish professors of psychiatry in Drimcong, County Galway. Lynch later recalled:

> My father [Fionán Lynch] took part in the [Easter] Rising in 1916. He was captain of the company in North King Street and he was eventually arrested and taken prisoner in the Four Courts. He was one of four sentenced to death and not executed (de Valera, Countess Markiewicz and Tom Ashe were the other three). He was subsequently transferred to prison in England, 'Strangeways' (where he spent two years).
>
> While in prison he was elected to the first Dáil as a TD (MP). He was not aware he was a candidate but he was a good friend of Michael Collins, who was inclined

to do this sort of thing – put one's name down and tell one afterwards. When he was released about 1917 in a general amnesty from prison, he took part in the Treaty Negotiations in London. He and Erskine Childers, father of the Erskine [Hamilton] Childers who later became Minister for Health[417] and President of Ireland,[418] were two secretaries to the Treaty negotiations in Hans Square.

It all makes a good story. When we had the Spring Quarterly Meeting of the College in Galway in 1990, Tom Fahy organised a professors' dinner out in Drimcong. He wanted to get each of us Irish professors to say a few words and got up to introduce us. Starting with me, he said, 'Of course you're not anything in Irish psychiatry, unless your father's been stood up in front of a British firing squad' – which was a typical Tom Fahy way to start things off.[419]

Like Lynch, Professor Thomas Fahy in Galway made enormous contributions to the development of psychiatry in Ireland during this period in relation to clinical practice, undergraduate teaching, postgraduate training and academic research.[420] Fahy qualified in medicine at UCD in 1959 and, following training in England, returned as Clinical Director at St Loman's Hospital, Dublin in 1968. He received his MD in 1969 for his ground breaking work on the 'Phenomenology of Depression in Hospital and in the Community'.[421] Fahy spent a sabbatical year as Assistant Professor and Unit Director at White Plains Hospital, New York in 1971, after which he was offered Associate Professorship with a guaranteed Chair of Psychiatry at Cornell University within two years. Instead, he took up the Chair of Psychiatry at Galway in 1975.[422]

A Foundation Fellow of the Royal College of Psychiatrists, Fahy was deeply involved in College activities; was Founder Chairman of the Irish Psychiatric Training Committee; and served as a member of the Medical Council and Medical Research Council, among other bodies. A particularly gifted speaker, Fahy brought extraordinary creative and critical rigour to academic psychiatry in Ireland and was responsible in no small part for the high academic standards in Irish psychiatry at the start of the twenty-first century. In September 2001, Fahy retired as Clinical Director of the West Galway Psychiatric Service and from the Chair of Psychiatry in Galway.

Also in Galway, Dr Tony Carney served as Dean of Medicine & Health Sciences, Head of the Academic Department of Psychiatry, and Clinical Director. In 2005, Professor Colm McDonald took up in the Chair of Psychiatry. In 2012, he was joined by Dr Brian Hallahan as Senior Lecturer. The department has particular expertise in psychosis research and has established a laboratory for the analysis of brain imaging data acquired using magnetic resonance imaging.[423]

In Cork, Dr Robert McCarthy played a leading role in reforming institutional psychiatric care and creating the context for the evolution of modern psychiatric services. McCarthy graduated from University College Cork (UCC) in 1938, first in his class, with first class honours and winning the Blayney Scholar prize.[424] He received his MD and became a member of the Royal College of Physicians of Ireland in 1940. McCarthy went on to work as a medical officer in Our Lady's Hospital, Cork (1944–54) and senior assistant medical officer in Grangegorman (1954–61), after which he returned to Our Lady's as RMS.[425]

At that time, Our Lady's had over 2,000 patients, and McCarthy led the abolition of padded cells and straitjackets, and developed programmes of rehabilitation and community re-socialisation. Following the polio epidemic in Cork in the 1950s, McCarthy assisted in establishing the Cork Poliomyelitis and General Aftercare Association ('Cope Foundation') in 1959, and served as its medical director from 1972 to 1992. With others, in 1962 McCarthy also helped establish the Cork Mental Health Association and served as lecturer in psychiatry at UCC from 1962 to 1972. His work and tireless advocacy led to the establishment of the Mental Health Association of Ireland in 1966[426] and greatly advanced psychiatric deinstitutionalisation in Cork and elsewhere.[427]

Also in Cork, Professor Robert Daly was another prominent figure who had substantial impact on the practice and perception of psychiatry in Ireland, and his was the first chair of psychiatry outside Dublin. A graduate of Trinity College, Dublin, Daly completed a residency and served as Instructor at the University of North Carolina, where, in 1966, he received a first place science award for a thesis titled *An Empirical Investigation of the Values of Various Affective Disorders*.[428] Daly went on to become an expert on post-traumatic stress disorder[429] (publishing the first European paper on that subject)[430] and human rights (with particular interest in the psychological effects of interrogation techniques in Northern Ireland),[431] and served on the Irish Government team in the case against Great Britain at the European Commission on Human Rights in the 1970s.[432]

Daly opposed the involvement of medical doctors in capital punishment[433] and urged doctors to provide greater assistance with the examination of torture victims, documentation of effects,[434] research and rehabilitation.[435] He also contributed significantly to public education about various other issues in psychiatry such as postnatal depression,[436] psychiatric nursing[437] and development of services.[438] In his work in the US, Daly wrote seminal articles on the addictive qualities of benzodiazepines[439] and the mood effects of the oral contraceptive pill.[440] His time working with the Royal Air Force (while a lecturer at the University of Edinburgh) led to developing the first effective treatment of (aircrew with) flying phobia, which had hitherto been deemed a result of lack of moral fibre.[441]

Daly was a member of the Amnesty International Medical Advisory Board awarded the European Peace Prize in 1986, the European Committee for the Prevention of Torture,[442] and the Medical Research Council; and served as Commissioner on Ireland's first Human Rights Commission. He worked with many other organisations including the World Psychiatric Association, Royal College of Psychiatrists, and American Civil Liberties Union; assisted the Bosnian authorities in establishing a medical and psychiatric programme for war victims;[443] and worked for victims of abuse in many other countries, including Latin American states. He was Dean of Medicine and head of the Department of Psychiatry at UCC[444] as well as Clinical Director in the Southern Health Board.

Dr Brian O'Shea, another leading figure, qualified from UCD in 1974 and was a consultant psychiatrist at St Brendan's Hospital for two years before moving to County Wicklow in 1985. There, he served as consultant psychiatrist and clinical director at Newcastle Hospital, Greystones until December 2006. In 1985 he co-wrote, with Dr Jane Falvey, *A Textbook of Psychological Medicine for the Irish Student*.[445] Two further editions were published by the Eastern Health Board (1988, 1993) and O'Shea edited the fourth[446] and fifth[447] editions in 2002 and 2010 respectively; the latter was published by the College of Psychiatry of Ireland. O'Shea also published more than 400 articles over the course of his career. A dedicated clinician, researcher and educator, O'Shea served as editor of *Irish Psychiatrist* (2000–11) and *Psychiatry Professional* (2011–12), published by MedMedia Group (Dún Laoghaire, County Dublin).

In Dublin, Professor John P. (Seán) Malone became Professor of Psychiatry at UCD in 1973, where he was noted as a dedicated clinician and teacher. In his undergraduate days, Malone was a star of the UCD soccer team, playing alongside his brother Michael and colleague Kevin O'Flanagan, an Irish international. Malone scored two goals in every round of the 1945 Intermediate Cup and a hat trick in the final to win the cup for UCD for just the second time in the university's history. Malone trained in neurology at Queen's Square London and returned to the Mater Misericordiae Hospital in 1951 as a consultant neurologist. He developed a lifelong interest in psychiatry and in 1962 the Mater Hospital Child Guidance Clinic was opened, with Malone as the first medical director.[448] In 1973, Malone became Professor of Psychiatry at UCD and the Seán Malone Medal in Psychiatry is now awarded annually to the undergraduate student who attains first place in psychiatry at UCD.

Malone was instrumental in forging and establishing the close links between the Mater Hospital and St Vincent's Hospital Fairview by suggesting that Professor Freeman and subsequently Professors Bryan Alton and David Powell would serve as Chairman of their hospital board.[449] He was also consultant psychiatrist and neurologist to the National Maternity Hospital in Holles Street for 40 years, as well as clinically serving, for several decades, the Coombe Lying-In Hospital, St Luke's Hospital (Rathgar), Cherry Orchard Hospital, the Richmond Hospital and the Bons Secours Hospital (Glasnevin). He was a biological psychiatrist first and foremost, and his teaching of how to conduct an examination of the central nervous system was legendary throughout Dublin medicine.

Professor Noel Walsh also worked at UCD[450] and, for a number of years, with Penang Medical College in Malaysia. Walsh was one of the founders of the School of Psychotherapy at St Vincent's University Hospital, Dublin, with Cormac Gallagher and Professor Michael Fitzgerald. He was also, among other roles, a member of the Health Education Bureau, established in 1975 by the Minister for Health, Mr Brendan Corish, to assume responsibility for health education in Ireland.[451]

Walsh researched, wrote and spoke about many topical issues including the need for better understanding of addiction,[452] depression and non-organic pain,[453] and issues relating to abortion.[454] In April 1976, Professor David Goldberg from Manchester University spoke at a seminar titled 'The Doctor and Psychiatric Illness' at St Vincent's, to mark the completion of the new 27 bed psychiatric unit there.[455] One of the highlights was a paper by Walsh, director of the unit, and Dr Mary Darby, on the nature and importance of empathy in the doctor-patient interaction.

In March 1977, Walsh presented a paper on psychiatry in the People's Republic of China, at the World Psychiatric Association's symposium in Dublin on 'Current Problems in Psychiatry',[456] and a paper on psychosomatic pain at the 31st World Medical Assembly in Dublin in September of that year.[457] In September 1988, Walsh placed particular emphasis on the need for greater interdisciplinary working in mental health at a one day conference at St Vincent's, titled 'Millennium Dialogue with Psychiatry'.[458]

Walsh's extensive research outputs, with various collaborators, included papers on anorexia nervosa,[459] binge eating and bulimia,[460] joint medical and psychiatric care,[461] social networks in affective disorders,[462] the effect of paracetamol regulations on overdosing,[463] and attitudes toward psychiatry among Irish final year medical students.[464] Walsh also co-authored papers on the cost of chronic pain,[465] cholesterol and parasuicide,[466] cortisol and breast cancer,[467] stress hormones,[468] and the use of psychotropic medication in patients referred to a psycho-oncology service.[469]

Professor Eadbhard O'Callaghan (1957–2011) of UCD was another outstanding figure in Irish academic psychiatry towards the end of the 1900s and start of the 2000s. A graduate of RCSI (1982), O'Callaghan trained on the St John of God rotational training scheme in Dublin and took up a Research Fellow post under the supervision of Dr Conall Larkin and Professor John Waddington.[470] He published highly cited papers on neurodevelopmental theories of schizophrenia[471] and completed a fellowship with Professor Robin Murray at the Institute of Psychiatry, King's College, London. There, O'Callaghan developed an interest in epidemiology and published a seminal paper in the *Lancet* on prenatal influenza and risk of schizophrenia.[472]

O'Callaghan returned to Dublin in 1991, working clinically with the Cluain Mhuire/St John of God mental health service[473] and continuing to publish widely in prestigious journals with Dr Abbie Lane, Dr (later Professor) Mary Clarke, Dr Larkin Feeney, Dr Niall Crumlish, Dr Peter Whitty, Dr (later Professor) Brendan Kelly and others,[474] including Dr Siobhan Barry, clinical director of the Cluain Mhuire service and one of the most progressive, forward looking and dedicated psychiatrists of her generation.[475]

O'Callaghan was duly appointed to a personal chair as Newman Professor of Mental Health Research at UCD and awarded an International Gold Medal by the Italian Cognitive Neuroscience Research Society in 2001.[476] He also spent six months in Malawi, helping to establish mental health services, and was visiting lecturer at the Department of Epidemiology and Genetics at Johns Hopkins University, Baltimore in 1994. In February 2006, O'Callaghan, along with colleagues, set up Ireland's first dedicated early intervention programme for psychosis, the Dublin and East Treatment and Early Care Team (DETECT), which has subsequently flourished with the involvement of colleagues including Professor Mary Clarke.[477]

Above all, O'Callaghan brought searing intelligence, deep compassion and endless humanity to his clinical, research and academic work. He inspired a generation of clinicians and academic psychiatrists in Ireland, and his contribution to the development of mental health services in Ireland and beyond cannot be overstated. Plato said that 'the greatest mistake in the treatment of diseases is that there are physicians for the body and physicians for the soul, although the two cannot be separated'. O'Callaghan was both kinds of physician, and much more besides.

At Trinity, the tradition of academic psychiatry has already been expertly chronicled by Professor Marcus Webb[478] and notable figures included Dr Maurice O'Connor Drury (1907–1976), philosopher and psychiatrist (Chapter 5);[479] Dr H. Jocelyn Eustace (1908–1996), a member of the fourth generation of the Eustace medical family; Professor Norman Moore (Chapter 5); Dr Patrick Melia, appointed lecturer in mental health in 1966; Professor Peter Beckett (1922–1974), who became first professor of psychiatry and head of the recently established department at Trinity in 1969;[480] Dr Mary Martin (1929–2008) at the Rotunda Hospital;[481] Dr Ronald Draper, who was appointed as a lecturer in Trinity in 1975 and as professor at the University of Ottawa in 1992; and Dr George Mullett, consultant psychiatrist at St James's and St Patrick's Hospitals, remembered as an outstanding clinician and teacher (and in whose memory an annual prize is awarded to the undergraduate students who perform best in the clinical aspects of their course work in Trinity).[482]

In 1977, Beckett was replaced in Trinity by Professor Marcus Webb, who, in addition to his clinical and research activities, chaired the Irish Psychiatric Training Committee and was visiting professor to the University of Pennsylvania.[483] In 2001 Professor Michael Gill took over as professor and head of a department which also includes Professors Veronica O'Keane, Aiden Corvin, Brendan Kelly, Louise Gallagher, Brian Lawlor, Declan McLoughlin, James Lucey, Harry Kennedy, Paul Fearon, Gregory Swanwick, Simon McCarthy-Jones and Anne-Marie O'Dwyer, among others.

The Trinity Discipline of Psychiatry, now headed by Professor Aiden Corvin, has world leading expertise in a number of areas including the genetics of neuropsychiatric disorders.[484] Clinical and molecular neuroscience is a strategic research cluster within the Discipline of Psychiatry, the School of Medicine and its partner hospitals, St James's Hospital, Tallaght Hospital, St Patrick's University Hospital and linked HSE community mental health clinics. The Discipline also has close associations with the Trinity College Institute of Neuroscience and Molecular Medicine Ireland.

In 2015, Professor Brendan Kelly took up the Chair of Psychiatry at Trinity College Dublin and Tallaght Hospital, replacing Professor Harold Hampel, who had been appointed in 2007 but left to take up the Chair of Psychiatry at the Johann Wolfgang Goethe University in Frankfurt am Main in 2010.[485]

While recent decades have clearly seen significant change and developments in academic psychiatry in Ireland, however, it was notable that at the end of the 1900s, despite the previous prominence of Dr Eleonora Fleury and Dr Ada English in the early 1900s, the figures of greatest prominence in Irish academic psychiatry were predominantly male.[486] This began to change towards the very end of the twentieth century, however, as Professor Patricia Casey of UCD became the first female Professor of Psychiatry in Ireland in 1991. Casey continued to publish widely in the fields of personality disorder, adjustment disorder and myriad other areas; served as editor of *The Psychiatrist* (published by the Royal College of Psychiatrists); and currently (2016) edits *Advances in Psychiatric Treatment*. Several other women followed her to positions of prominence in Irish academic psychiatry over the subsequent decades. Many of these advances occurred in parallel with innovative developments in service provision with, for example, Casey initiating the appointment of Dr (later Professor) John Sheehan as a full time liaison psychiatrist at the Mater Misericordiae University Hospital in 1995.

In 1998, Professor Carol Fitzpatrick of UCD became the first female Professor of Child Psychiatry in Ireland, a position she held until 2011. A second, Professor Fiona McNicholas, was appointed as Professor of Child and Adolescent Psychiatry at UCD in 2001, and Professor Louise Gallagher was later appointed to the Chair in Child and Adolescent Psychiatry at Trinity.

At RCSI, Professor Kieran Murphy became head of the Department of Psychiatry in January 2002 and oversaw considerable departmental expansion, with the addition of Professors Mary Cannon and David Cotter, among others, to the staff. Specific research themes that were developed included structural and functional neuroimaging of genetic and neuropsychiatric disorders, cellular cytoarchitectural and protein signature of major psychiatric disorders, the developmental epidemiology of psychosis, the neuropsychiatry of epilepsy, behavioural phenotypes of genetic disorders and a PhD programme in Mental Health Services research.[487]

In Cork, Professor Ted Dinan, a medical graduate of UCC, is Professor of Psychiatry, having previously been Chair of Clinical Neurosciences and Professor of Psychological Medicine at St Bartholomew's Hospital, London. In 1995 he was awarded the Melvin Ramsey Prize for his research into the biology of stress. Dinan's main current research is focused on how gut microbes influence brain development and function, and his team has over 40 people in the laboratory, which is partly funded by Science Foundation Ireland, Ireland's principle science and engineering research funding agency.

Overall, the opening decades of the twenty-first century saw academic psychiatry in Ireland in a state of expansion and development, closely linked with innovations in service delivery and provision of mental health care, as well as improvements in research, teaching and public engagement. The Section of Psychiatry in the Royal Academy of Medicine in Ireland played an important role in this process, most notably through its academic meetings and research prizes. Despite this progress, however, deep challenges remained across mental health services and services for people with intellectual disabilities.[488] These difficulties stemmed not least from continued difficulties in finally moving from an institutional model of care to a community based model.

Therefore, while the 1900s had seen much progress in mental health services in many respects, especially with the closure of beds in institutional settings and the development of academic psychiatry, there was still, clearly, much to be done to improve matters and better promote the human rights of the mentally ill both in inpatient settings and in the community.

Carlow Asylum, Co. Carlow. (The Lawrence Photograph Collection. Image by Robert French (1841–1917), photographer. This image is reproduced courtesy of the National Library of Ireland, L_ROY_07510.)

Auxiliary Asylum, Youghal, Co. Cork. (The Lawrence Photograph Collection. Image by Robert French (1841–1917), photographer. This image is reproduced courtesy of the National Library of Ireland, L_ROY_09609.)

Sligo Lunatic Asylum, Co. Sligo. (The Lawrence Photograph Collection. Image by Robert French (1841–1917), photographer. This image is reproduced courtesy of the National Library of Ireland, L_CAB_02946.)

Carlow Mental Hospital Sports

UNDER N.A. AND C.A. RULES.

:o:

JUNE 19th, 1930

:o:

ENTRY FORM

1.—100 Yards. Open. Handicap.
2.—220 Yards. Open. Handicap.
3.—440 Yards. Open. Handicap.
4.—880 Yards. Open. Handicap.
5.—1 Mile. Open. Handicap.
6.—120 Yards. Hurdles.
7.—Running High Jump.
8.—Running Broad Jump.
9.—56 lbs. For Height. Over Bar.
10.—Putting Shot. Open. Handicap.
11.—100 Yards. Girls' Race (under 14).
12.—220 Yards. Boys' Race (under 14).
13.—1 Mile Cycle. Open. Scratch.
14.—3 Miles Cycle. Open. Handicap.
15.—5 Miles Cycle. Open. Handicap.
16.—2 Miles Cycle. Novice.
17.—Half Mile Cycle, short limit, handicap. Open.
18.—Pole Vault. Open. Handicap.

:o:

Entries Close on 5th June, 1930.

Handicapper and Starter—Capt. D. Harkins.

Entry Forms can be had from the Hon. Secs.:—

WILLIAM ELLIS.

WILLIAM HAYDEN.

"Nationalist and Leinster Times," Carlow.

Sport was an important way for patients to engage with each other, with staff, and, on occasion, with the community outside the walls. (Archive of St Dympna's Hospital, Delany Archive, Carlow. Image reproduced by permission of the Health Service Executive.)

Medico-Psychological Association, Irish branch, outside St Patrick's Hospital, Dublin, April 1933. (Reproduced by kind permission the Royal College of Physicians of Ireland.)

Meeting of the Irish Division of the Royal Medico-Psychological Association, Kilkenny Mental Hospital, 24 July 1937. (Dr Maurice Guéret. Used with permission.)

County Asylum, Kilkenny. (The Lawrence Photograph Collection. Image by Robert French (1841–1917), photographer. This image is reproduced courtesy of the National Library of Ireland, L_ROY_10051.)

Professor J.N. Moore (1911–96). (St Patrick's Mental Health Services. Used with permission. Portrait by Derek Hill.)

St John of God Hospital, Stillorgan, Dublin (1900–39). (Eason Photographic Collection. This image is reproduced courtesy of the National Library of Ireland, EAS_2027.)

Left to right: Sammy Lyons, Dave McIlvenna, Harry Bradshaw, Seán Lemass and Professor John Dunne, 1955. (J. Horgan, *Séan Lemass: The Enigmatic Patriot*, Dublin: Gill and Macmillan, 1999. Image by Bobby Hopkins. Used with permission.)

Left to right: Dr Maxwell Jones, Mr Justice Séamus Henchy and Dr Ivor Browne, in Maynooth, circa early 1970s. (Professor Ivor Browne. Used with permission.)

President Erskine Hamilton Childers (right) and Dr Desmond McGrath at the first annual dinner of the Irish Division of the Royal College of Psychiatrists in the Royal College of Physicians, Kildare Street, Dublin, 16 November 1974. This is the last photograph of President Childers before suffering a heart attack after his speech at the event, and dying some hours later. (*Irish Times*; photograph: Eddie Kelly. Copyright: *Irish Times*. Used with permission.)

Professor Anthony Clare (1942–2007), the best-known psychiatrist in Ireland and Great Britain. (Copyright: *Irish Times*. Used with permission.)

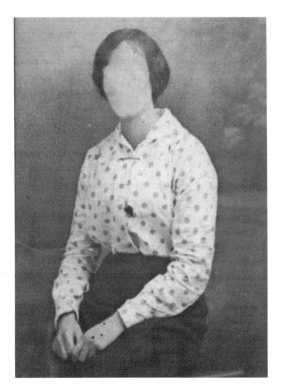

Image from 'Personal Effects: A History of Possession' by artist Alan Counihan, exhibited at Grangegorman in 2014. (Alan Counihan/www.alancounihan.net. Reproduced with permission. © Alan Counihan. Image is copyright of the artist and may not be reproduced in any format without permission. The author is grateful to the Health Service Executive, CHO9, Dublin North City.)

Figs 43 and 44 by artist Úna Spain explore remnants of Connaught District Lunatic Asylum (later St Brigid's Hospital). (Úna Spain/www.unaspain.com. Reproduced with permission of Ms Spain and the Health Service Executive. © Úna Spain (for each image). All images are the copyright of the artist and may not be reproduced in any format without permission.)

7

⅍

The Twenty-First Century:
New Policy, New Law

At the very least, and despite all of the horrors of the old hospitals, despite the nearly anomic loss of faith by mainstream Irish society in institutions of care, particularly those historically associated with the Catholic Church, I want to leave a space for Ray's perspective on the social good of the total institution. I also want to acknowledge that Dr Lynch and his colleagues, despite their trepidation in the face of the spectre of institutionalization, were able to hear Ray, after a fashion, and honour his request for community and perhaps for containment, if only for a little while. I want to be able to reject the terms of Ray's final question for me – am I a holy man, or am I crazy? – and answer 'why not both?'

M. D'Arcy, 'The Hospital and the Holy
Spirit: Psychotic Subjectivity and
Institutional Returns in Dublin', paper delivered at the *Society
for Psychological Anthropology*, Boston,
MA (10 April 2015)[1]

The history of psychiatry in Ireland up to the twenty-first century presents an interesting if frustrating story. It is interesting owing to the prominence that mental disorder assumed in public and professional minds throughout the nineteenth and twentieth century, resulting in the emergence of Ireland's remarkable asylum system and its subsequent demise. It is frustrating because the history shows the severe limitations and paradoxical effects of a series of initiatives which were invariably based on good intentions but generally failed to produce sufficient benefit (if any) for the mentally ill and intellectually disabled. There were failures of provision, compassion and, perhaps most of all, understanding.

As a result, and notwithstanding the pioneering work the generation of psychiatrists discussed toward the end of the previous chapter, the closing decades of the twentieth century saw Irish mental health services still fail to achieve the optimal mix of inpatient and outpatient care, as institutions duly closed but the community services offered in their place were commonly insufficient, inappropriate or inaccessible to those who needed them most. Observance of the right to liberty might have improved, but the right to treatment suffered.

Too often the history of medicine, especially (although not exclusively) as written by doctors, is presented as the linear march of progress and enlightenment, as scientific insights lead, apparently inexorably, to improvements in services and care, culminating in a high point of achievement in the present day.[2] Presumably, anyone who came to this volume expecting such a relentlessly uplifting account has realised by now that the history of psychiatry in Ireland is anything but linear, logical or uplifting. The same ideas emerge repeatedly (e.g. institution based care, community care); similar patterns recur (e.g. new legislation modifies but does not fundamentally reform existing law; the mentally ill become even more socially excluded); and chillingly familiar problems beset every generation of doctors, policymakers and patients, chiefly related to the enormous chasms between official rhetoric and the lived experience of mental disorder in Ireland.

It comes as little surprise, then, that at the start of the twenty-first century, it was again apparent (as it had been at the start of most previous centuries) that change was needed in Ireland's mental health policy and legislation.[3] Governmental policy and national law had both palpably failed to keep pace with developments in clinical practice, psychiatric research, human rights discourse, and broader developments in Irish and European society. The world was changing rapidly and psychiatry needed to change too.

The problem with mental law was especially pressing this time round. In 1999, the Irish Law Society highlighted a range of fundamental problems with the Mental Treatment Act 1945 in a remarkably hard hitting report titled *Mental Health: The Case for Reform*.[4] In this report, the Law Society reviewed case law and international human rights legislation, and suggested that criteria for involuntary committal should be more clearly defined; a 'least restrictive alternative' principle applied; a right to a minimum level of psychiatric service introduced by statute; formal safeguards extended to voluntary patients; and measures introduced to enable the proposed 'Mental Health Review Board' to review detention orders and order 'planned discharge'. None of these matters had been satisfactorily addressed in the Mental Treatment Act 1945 and all were needed in order to modernise Irish mental health legislation to meet international human rights standards.[5]

Many of these proposals were consistent with the Irish government's 1995 White Paper which proposed a 'new Mental Health Act' and, in a triumph of understatement, blithely acknowledged that the Mental Treatment Act 1945 did 'not fully comply with this country's obligations under international law':[6]

> The changes in Irish law that are required to ensure full compliance with our obligations under the European Convention[7] ... include a redefinition of the criteria for detention of mentally disordered persons, the introduction of procedures to review the decision to detain a person in a psychiatric hospital by a body independent of both the person who took the decision to detain and of the executive, an automatic review of long-term detention, and the introduction of greater safeguards for the protection of detained persons.[8]

Thus, in the years leading up to the Mental Health Act 2001 the drive towards legislative reform was largely driven by European and international influences, as evidenced by the Irish government's concern to 'ensure full compliance with our obligations under the European Convention,'[9] and the Law Society's explicit reliance on the European Convention on Human Rights and UN *Principles for the Protection of Persons with Mental Illness and the Improvement of Mental Health Care*[10] in their 1999 recommendations.[11] In 2000, this European dimension came even more urgently into focus when the lack of automatic review of detention under the Mental Treatment Act 1945 formed the focus of a landmark case in the European Court of Human Rights.[12]

In this case, a detained patient pointed to the lack of an automatic, independent review of psychiatric detention in Ireland and when the Irish Supreme Court stated this was not unconstitutional the applicant took the case to the European Court of Human Rights, to argue that this breached his rights under the European Convention on Human Rights. A 'friendly settlement' was reached in 2000, under which the Irish state noted its obligations under the Convention and undertook to pay an agreed compensatory sum to the applicant. Most importantly, the Irish state noted that the applicant was the first individual to bring this important issue in front of the European Court of Human Rights and that the applicant's claim had been initiated prior to the publication of the Mental Health Bill 1999, which formed a key part of Ireland's defence.

The process of reform reflected in the Mental Health Bill 1999 was pursued with considerably greater urgency after this case was instigated in the Irish courts in 1994 and later in the European Court of Human Rights.[13] As a result, this case reinforced the European Convention on Human Rights as the key driver of reform of mental health law in Ireland, and the Mental Health Bill 1999 led, in due course, to the Mental Health Act 2001. Human rights standards, as reflected in the Convention, continued to dominate this reform process to the very end, as concerns about the human rights of detained patients persisted even after the 2001 Act had passed through the Oireachtas (Irish parliament) on 8 July 2001, and full implementation was awaited.[14] The Mental Health Act 2001 was finally, fully implemented on 1 November 2006.

Before exploring the Mental Health Act 2001 itself, however, it is worth noting that the issue of public safety was virtually absent from the debate leading to the new legislation in Ireland.[15] This contrasts with the situation in England, where public safety was a key driver of the reform process.[16] Interestingly, issues of human dignity and capabilities did not play an appreciable role in the reform process in either jurisdiction, possibly because both reform processes largely predated the UN Convention on the Rights of Persons with Disabilities, which places particular emphasis on dignity,[17] an increasingly important concept in this field.[18]

Mental Health Act 2001:
Involuntary Detention and Assuring Standards of Care

The Mental Health Act 2001, which replaced the Mental Treatment Act 1945, is chiefly concerned with two aspects of psychiatric services: involuntary detention and mechanisms for assuring standards of care, including inspection processes.[19]

The introduction of the 2001 legislation was historically significant for many reasons, not least of which is the fact that it provided a definition of 'mental illness', as a 'state of mind of a person which affects the person's thinking, perceiving, emotion or judgment and which seriously impairs the mental function of the person to the extent that he or she requires care or medical treatment in his or her own interest or in the interest of other persons'.[20]

The term 'mental disorder' was also defined in the Act, as 'mental illness, severe dementia or significant intellectual disability' where 'there is a serious likelihood of the person concerned causing immediate and serious harm to himself or herself or to other persons' or 'the judgment of the person concerned is so impaired that failure to admit the person to an approved centre would be likely to lead to a serious deterioration in his or her condition or would prevent the administration of appropriate treatment that could be given only by such admission'.[21] For involuntary admission under the second criterion, the 2001 Act also made it necessary that the relevant measures 'would be likely to benefit or alleviate the condition of that person to a material extent'.[22]

Overall, the definitions in the 2001 Act were closer to those in England's Mental Health Act 1983 than its Mental Health Act 2007: England's Mental Health Act 1983 defined 'mental disorder' as 'mental illness, arrested or incomplete development of mind, psychopathic disorder and any other disorder or disability of mind',[23] which is quite similar to Ireland's 2001 Act (apart from the inclusion of 'psychopathic disorder' in England and not Ireland). England's Mental Health Act 2007, however, removed these four categories and redefined 'mental disorder' as 'any disorder or disability of the mind'.[24] While this change was in line with the recommendations of the Richardson Committee[25] and Mental Health Act Commission,[26] it contrasted with developments in Ireland, where the Mental Health Act 2001 introduced subtypes of mental disorder as well as detailed definitions of mental illness and various other terms for the first time. As Walsh noted in 1992:

> Irish legislation for the mentally ill has always been modelled on, and lagged behind, that of England and Wales. For example the Lunacy Laws (England and Wales) of 1890 were followed by the Lunacy Laws (Ireland) of 1903. The Mental Treatment Act (England and Wales) 1930 was followed by the Irish equivalent of 1945 [...].[27]

Under Ireland's 2001 Act, a person can be involuntarily admitted to an 'approved centre' (i.e. registered psychiatric inpatient facility) on the grounds that the person is suffering from a 'mental disorder'; a person *cannot* be so admitted solely on the grounds that the person '(a) is suffering from a personality disorder, (b) is socially deviant, or (c) is addicted to drugs or intoxicants'.[28]

An application for involuntary admission can be made by a spouse, relative, 'authorised officer',[29] member of the Garda Síochána (police force) or, in circumstances where no one in these categories can be found, anyone else, subject to certain conditions.[30] In all cases, the applicant must have observed the person within 48 hours of making the application.[31]

The next step involves examination by a registered medical practitioner (e.g. general practitioner).[32] Following this recommendation, the person can be conveyed 'to the approved centre' (inpatient psychiatric unit or hospital),[33] with the assistance of 'staff of the approved centre', if needed.[34] If 'there is a serious likelihood of the person concerned causing immediate and serious harm to himself or herself or to other persons', the Garda Síochána can enter the person's dwelling by force and ensure removal of the person.[35]

At the approved centre, a consultant psychiatrist 'shall, as soon as may be, carry out an examination of the person' and shall either (a) complete an 'admission order' if 'he or she is satisfied that the person is suffering from a mental disorder' or (b) refuse to make such an order.[36] The patient cannot be detained for more than 24 hours without such an examination taking place and such an order being made or refused. If an admission order is made it is authorises 'the reception, detention and treatment of the patient concerned and shall remain in force for a period of 21 days';[37] this period may be extended by a 'renewal order' for a period of up to three months;[38] this may be further extended by a period of up to six months; and each further extension can be for a period of up to 12 months.[39]

Following the completion of an involuntary admission order, the consultant psychiatrist must inform the Mental Health Commission of the order and the Mental Health Commission shall then (a) refer the matter to a mental health tribunal; (b) assign a legal representative to the patient, 'unless he or she proposes to engage one'; and (c) direct that an independent psychiatrist examine the patient, interview the patient's consultant psychiatrist and review the patient's records.[40] Within 21 days of an involuntary admission, a mental health tribunal shall review the detention of the patient. There are also provisions for detaining voluntary inpatients, based on a second opinion from another psychiatrist.[41]

The Mental Health Act 2001 also made provision for the appointment of a 'Mental Health Commission', one of the principal functions of which is to appoint mental health tribunals 'to determine such matter or matters as may be referred to it by the Commission'.[42] One of the chief functions of tribunals is to review involuntary detention orders. Each tribunal comprises three members, including one consultant psychiatrist, one barrister or solicitor (of not less than seven years' experience) and one other person.[43] Decisions are made by majority voting.[44] This innovation was an extraordinarily important and historic element of the 2001 Act, ensuring independent reviews of all detention orders for the very first time in the history of psychiatry in Ireland. Hannah Greally (Chapter 6), for example, would undoubtedly have benefitted from mental health tribunals during her decades in Mullingar, as would have the Reverend Clarence Duffy in Monaghan in the mid-1930s.

Under the 2001 Act, a mental health tribunal reviews each involuntary admission within 21 days, and, 'if satisfied that the patient is suffering from a mental disorder' and that the appropriate procedure has been followed, shall affirm the order; if the tribunal is not so satisfied, the tribunal shall 'revoke the order and direct that the patient be discharged from the approved centre concerned'.[45] These changes are strongly protective of the patient's right to liberty and support patient dignity by facilitating exercise of specific capabilities in appealing detention orders. As such, the tribunal process helps set to rest two centuries of custodial care without adequate reviews for psychiatric patients.

Grounds for appeal of tribunal decisions are, however, limited: the patient 'may appeal to the Circuit Court against a decision of a tribunal to affirm an order made in respect of him or her on the grounds that he or she is not suffering from a mental disorder';[46] i.e. there is no possibility of appeal to the Circuit Court on other grounds (e.g. procedural aberrations). The patient may appeal to the High Court solely 'on a point of law'.[47]

Regarding consent to treatment, the 2001 Act specifies that 'the consent of a [detained] patient shall be required for treatment' except where the patient is incapable of providing consent and the treating psychiatrist believes it 'is necessary to safeguard the life of the patient, to restore his or her health, to alleviate his or her condition, or to relieve his or her suffering'.[48] There are specific provisions and additional safeguards for psychosurgery[49] as well as ECT[50] and administration of medication for three months,[51] both of which were modified in 2016 (Chapter 8).

Prior to implementation of the 2001 Act, a range of concerns were expressed about the Irish psychiatric service's apparent unreadiness for the legislation, including issues related to an apparent lack of resources,[52] potential effects of tribunals on therapeutic relationships,[53] legal representation at tribunals for psychiatrists,[54] staffing of tribunals,[55] disagreements about indemnity[56] and rates of payment for psychiatrists at tribunals,[57] and unclearness about responsibility for harm to patients resulting from lack of resources for implementing the new legislation.[58] Psychiatrists expressed particular concern about the potential effects of adversarial tribunals on the therapeutic alliance, increased administrative activity, and potential for the legislation disproportionately to divert resources from voluntary to involuntary patient services.[59]

In 2005, prior to full implementation of the Act, the Irish College of Psychiatrists stated that the absence of funding to implement the legislation in a timely fashion had serious implications in terms of human rights, for both future *and* current patients, whose mental health services might be curtailed in order to divert resources towards the implementation of the Act.[60] Following considerable discussion, some additional resources were made available for mental health services, including extra consultant psychiatrist posts and additional funds,[61] and the final elements of the legislation (relating chiefly to tribunals) were implemented on 1 November 2006. In the first 11 months following full implementation, approximately 12 per cent of involuntary admission and renewal orders examined by tribunals were revoked.[62]

Overall, the Mental Health Act 2001 introduced several historic changes to Irish mental health law, with significant implications for human rights.[63] Key improvements include removing detention orders of indefinite duration; new involuntary admission procedures; automatic review of detention orders by tribunals; free legal representation and independent psychiatric opinions for detained patients; and establishment of the Mental Health Commission to oversee standards. These measures hold strong potential to protect specific rights (e.g. right to liberty), enhance patient dignity, and promote the exercise of specific capabilities (especially in relation to reviews of involuntary detention).

These potential benefits are, however, accompanied by significant caveats, often indicating strong paternalistic or welfare based considerations, which have been such a prominent feature of the history of psychiatry in Ireland. Specific human rights concerns about the 2001 Act relate to lack of clarity regarding the extent to which procedural aberrations are overlooked by tribunals; the absence of (possibly anonymised) cumulative tribunal case law for patients or lawyers to consult; restrictions on grounds for civil proceedings in Circuit and High Courts; the fact that the burden of proof lies with the patient in the Circuit Court; and the notably paternalistic definition of voluntary patient, which does not require an individual to possess capacity in order to become or remain a voluntary patient.[64] Critically, there is also evidence of arguably excessive emphasis on paternalism and welfare based concern in the interpretation of the Mental Health Act 2001 in the Irish courts, and it remains unclear whether or not this is proportionate to the strong welfare based obligations outlined in the Irish Constitution.[65]

Despite any alleged, lingering paternalism, however, it is undeniable that the Mental Health Act 2001 was and is a significant milestone in the evolution of mental health legislation in Ireland.[66] Just two years after implementation, it was already apparent that the 2001 Act, despite various hiccups, had brought both challenges and benefits to Irish mental health services.[67] Happily, and notwithstanding reported problems (such as increased legalisation of psychiatric practice), 73 per cent of psychiatrists reported that the legislation resulted in greater protection of the rights of involuntary patients.[68]

This is important: the history of psychiatry in Ireland shows that legislation plays a key role in determining the extent to which the rights of the mentally ill are protected and promoted, and the extent to which mental health services are delivered effectively. While patient satisfaction with the new system was soon generally high,[69] however, it was also apparent that legislative reform alone was not enough: to address the real needs of the mentally ill, a new policy was needed too.

Mental Health Policy:
A Vision for Change (2006)

In 2006, the Irish government published *A Vision for Change: Report of the Expert Group on Mental Health Policy*,[70] the most extensive review of mental health policy since *The Psychiatric Services: Planning for the Future* (1984).[71] The process behind *A Vision for Change* began in August 2003 when the Minister of State at the Department of Health and Children with Special Responsibility for Mental Health established the Expert Group on Mental Health Policy to develop a blueprint for comprehensive, modern, high quality mental health services.[72]

Over two decades earlier, *Planning for the Future* had already suggested that mental health services should be comprehensive and community-oriented, aimed at delivering continuous, coordinated, multidisciplinary care. The policy recommended that the population be divided into sectors, each comprising 25,000 to 30,000 people; psychiatric care should be delivered by consultant-led multidisciplinary teams; dedicated crisis teams should be developed; and additional specialised services should be developed to cover more than one sector. Day hospitals were to provide intensive treatment essentially equivalent to inpatient care.

While the two decades following the publication of *Planning for the Future* saw considerable changes in the delivery of mental health care in Ireland, not all of the report's recommendations were implemented.[73] There was, in particular, evidence of variations in the levels of service provision across different geographical areas.[74]

There was also evidence of suboptimal use of resources. One study of the Eastern region, published in 1999, identified inpatient psychiatry bed occupancy of 98 per cent, with 7 of the 11 hospitals studied reporting occupancy rates of 100 per cent or more.[75] Almost half of the patients in acute beds (45 per cent) were deemed not to require acute beds, resulting in an estimated 91,500 inappropriate bed-days per year. Length of stay was also a concern, with one fifth of patients staying in an acute bed for a year or longer. There were notable shortages of community based continuing care residential places and community based emergency outreach services, as well as domiciliary and homecare services.

In 2003, Amnesty International published a detailed analysis of mental health services in Ireland and concluded that while progress had been made in recent years, both inpatient and outpatient care were inadequate, inconsistent and severely under resourced.[76] Amnesty expressed concern about the human rights of the mentally ill and urged government to take action in the areas of improving services, research, funding, specialised treatments, education, advocacy and rights-based disability and mental health legislation.

Notwithstanding these unresolved issues, as the Mental Health Commission pointed out in its inaugural Annual Report (2002),[77] the principles outlined in *Planning for the Future* remained highly relevant to psychiatric care throughout this period, and while all its recommendations had not yet been implemented, the policy had brought significant improvements to Irish psychiatric services, particularly in relation to (continued) deinstitutionalisation.

Between 1984 and 2006, however, much had changed in Irish society: unemployment fell significantly and the net outward migration of some 2 per cent of the entire population in 1988/1989 reversed, with the number of immigrants into Ireland between 1995 and 2000 amounting to 7 per cent of the population.[78] There were also significant developments in general health policy with the publications of *Shaping A Healthier Future: A Strategy For Effective Healthcare In The 1990s*[79] and *Quality and Fairness: A Health System for You*,[80] which emphasised the principles of equity, quality, accountability and people-centredness in planning and delivering care.

The period between 1984 and 2006 also saw considerable changes in relation to psychiatry. At the international level, the WHO devoted its 2001 annual report to the topic of *Mental Health: New Understanding, New Hope*.[81] This renewed emphasis on mental health services and policy was accompanied by a similar revival of interest in the principles of evidence based medicine,[82] with organisations such as the Cochrane Collaboration (www.cochrane.org) providing systematic reviews of scientific and clinical evidence to support interventions in all areas of healthcare, including psychiatry.

At the national level, Ireland's Mental Health Act 2001 was formally enacted by the Irish Houses of Oireachtas (parliament) on 8 July 2001 and implemented in a phased fashion, with the Mental Health Commission being established in April 2002 with the aim of advancing high standards and good practice.[83] Dr John Owens served as first chairman. These developments, combined with generally increased public interest in psychological wellbeing and mental health, created the context in which Ireland's new mental health policy was developed and introduced.

A Vision for Change duly aimed to create a framework for promoting positive mental health in all sectors of the community and providing accessible specialist mental health services.[84] The policy was divided into three main sections outlining (a) the vision underlying the policy; (b) the plan for service developments; and (c) the process of implementing various policy measures.

The vision underpinning the policy underlined the need for a population based approach to mental health, involving not only mental health services but also primary care and community supports (e.g. informal sources of assistance). It also emphasised the importance of partnership with service users, carers and broader groups of stakeholders. Links between mental health and education, poverty, unemployment, housing and social exclusion were explored; mental health promotion discussed; and various protective factors and risk factors for mental illness articulated.

The policy then went on to deal in greater detail with its plan for service developments based on this vision. After a brief summary of the current situation, the policy recommended that a comprehensive range of services be available at primary care level for those who do not require specialist services; a consultation/liaison model should ensure formal links between specialist services and primary care, especially in relation to discharge planning; suitably trained staff should be available in primary care settings to meet mental health needs; and relevant education, training and research should be developed.

In terms of adult mental health services, the report recommended that one multidisciplinary community mental health team be provided per 50,000 population, with two consultant psychiatrists per team.[85] It recommended the provision of 50 beds per 300,000 person catchment area, comprising 35 beds for general adult mental health services (including 6 close observation beds), 8 beds for mental health services for older people, 5 beds for persons with intellectual disability and 2 beds for individuals with eating disorders.[86] These modest numbers were a far cry from the enormous asylums of Ireland's past.

The 2006 report also made a series of other recommendations, including provision of one crisis house per 300,000 population (10 places) and, nationally, 4 intensive care rehabilitation units (30 beds each); 8 high support intensive care residences (10 places each); 2 early intervention services; and various other facilities. In terms of rehabilitation psychiatry, the report recommended one multidisciplinary team, 3 community residential units (10 places each) and 1 service user provided support centre per 100,000 population, as well as one to two day centres (with a total of 30 places) per 300,000 population.[87]

In addition to the above, the rather lengthy report addressed services for specific service user groups, including older people, people with intellectual disability, the homeless, people with substance misuse disorders and people with eating disorders, as well as forensic mental health services and liaison mental health services. Attention was paid to special categories of service provision including people with co-morbid severe mental illness and substance abuse problems, people with neuropsychiatric disorders requiring specialist services, and borderline personality disorder. In terms of suicide prevention, the report supported implementation of the recommendations of National Strategy for Action on Suicide Prevention.[88]

As well as making specific recommendations about levels of service provision in these and other areas, the report explored more general principles that should inform mental health care and particular attention was paid to multidisciplinary teamwork, care planning, the process of recovery, and the development of needs based models of service delivery. These were overarching principles, intended to inform implementation of the more specific measures outlined.

The third section of *A Vision for Change* was devoted to implementation and recommended that mental health catchment areas should be established (with populations of 250,000–400,000), to be managed by multidisciplinary Mental Health Catchment Area Management Teams, and the establishment of a National Mental Health Services Directorate.[89] Other recommendations related to different aspects of clinical governance, service user involvement, and integration with other community care area programmes and the work of voluntary groups.

From the outset, it was apparent that implementation of *A Vision for Change* would require substantial extra funding and the report suggested that resources be remodelled so as to increase equity, with special attention paid to areas of socioeconomic disadvantage that have a high prevalence of mental illness.[90] It was also apparent that implementation would have implications for manpower, education and training, and these areas were all explored in the report; in particular, it was suggested that a multi-profession manpower plan be put in place.[91] Finally, *A Vision for Change* emphasised the importance of mental health information systems and research, and recommended that a national mental health minimum data set be prepared, in consultation with stakeholders.[92]

Notwithstanding its remarkable length and the decidedly vague basis of some of its calculations, the preparation and publication of *A Vision for Change* reflected a welcome renewal of emphasis on mental health policy in Ireland.[93] The new policy clearly advanced many of the recommendations outlined by the WHO in *Mental Health: New Understanding, New Hope*, especially in relation to the provision of treatment in primary care settings, increased community involvement, improved educational initiatives, development of national mental health policies and increased research.[94]

A Vision for Change reaffirmed many of the principles outlined some 22 years earlier in *Planning for the Future*.[95] Both documents placed considerable emphasis on developing the community basis of mental health care, with *A Vision for Change* recommending very clearly that a plan should be developed to close down all psychiatric hospitals and invest the resultant resources back into mental health services.[96]

Notwithstanding this continuity with previous policy priorities, specific areas within *A Vision for Change* raised specific issues. For example, the new policy recommended that four community based forensic mental health teams be provided, one in each HSE region.[97] This recommendation, while apparently consistent with the principle of 'equity',[98] did not appear to take adequate account of need, and appeared to presume that there was equal need for forensic mental health services in all geographical areas. In fact, while all areas certainly need some level of forensic mental health service, there was strong evidence that forensic mental health need was inequitably distributed throughout Ireland. One especially compelling study by Dr Conor O'Neill and colleagues in the National Forensic Mental Health Service looked at all admissions to the service from courts and prisons between 1997 and 1999 and found that 63 per cent of admissions were from the East of the country (the area of the former Eastern Regional Health Authority).[99] While service use does not necessarily reflect service need, these findings nonetheless strongly suggested that the presumption of equal need in all geographical areas ('horizontal equity') was not consistent with the efficient distribution of services on the basis of need ('vertical equity').

The redefinition of catchment areas outlined in *A Vision for Change* also raised important operational issues, especially in relation to the redistribution of existing patient populations and development of arrangements for transfers of care. Implementing this element of policy would clearly require a phased approach, taking careful account of existing arrangements and resources, while also advancing the process of change. Implementation would also require the development of specific proposals for specific patient groups, including the homeless, up to one third of whom have mental health problems,[100] and migrants, refugees and asylum seekers, who also tend to have increased mental health need.[101]

The physical and mental health needs of migrants in Ireland had been highlighted well prior to *A Vision for Change*,[102] and the issue was further underlined by a later study of 178 Irish and migrant mental health service users, which found that a high percentage of both Irish (47 per cent) and migrant groups (70 per cent) had experienced two or more traumatic life events.[103] Forced migrants displayed more traumatic life events, post-traumatic symptoms, and higher levels of post-traumatic stress disorder than their voluntary migrant and Irish counterparts, with over 50 per cent experiencing torture prior to arrival in Ireland. Pioneering work by Irish psychiatrist Dr Niall Crumlish and neurologist Dr Killian O'Rourke highlighted evidence to support certain treatments for post-traumatic stress disorder among refugees and asylum seekers (e.g. narrative exposure therapy, cognitive-behavioural therapy) but also concluded that future trials should evaluate interventions developed within refugees' own cultures, based on local understandings of psychological distress and trauma.[104] Clearly, this growing group merited more dedicated attention in Irish mental health policy too,[105] as later reflected in the HSE's *National Intercultural Health Strategy, 2007–2012* in 2008.[106]

Other notable initiatives in *A Vision for Change* included the policy's endorsement of early intervention programmes for psychosis, which was a welcome recognition of the specific needs of this patient group and wholly consistent with international developments in this field.[107] In fact, in February 2006, Ireland's first such dedicated service, the Dublin and East Treatment and Early Care Team (DETECT), came into operation, receiving referrals from a catchment area population of 372,000 people.[108] In 2010, the National Clinical Programme for Mental Health included early intervention for people developing first episode psychosis as one of the key areas for which it aimed to standardise high quality evidence based practice across mental health services.

From the outset, it was plain that the sequencing of implementation of various measures in *A Vision for Change* was likely to be critical. It was imperative, for example, that community mental health services would be substantially strengthened prior to any changes in levels of inpatient care, and pre-existing disparities in levels of service provision across different geographical areas resolved.[109] Linked to this, *A Vision for Change* placed a welcome emphasis on the need for effective health information systems,[110] although there remains much progress to be made in this important area.

Overall, *A Vision for Change* represented a welcome renewal of emphasis on the importance of establishing a clear strategic direction for mental health services and on community based provision of care. One area of early criticism, however, related to the policy's indication that people with drug and alcohol problems would be treated within mental health services only if they had co-morbid mental illness;[111] this was described by a group of experts as a retrograde step for people with drug and alcohol addiction.[112]

Despite this criticism, *A Vision for Change* was largely welcomed as representing an important further shift away from institution based psychiatry and towards community based care.[113] Shortly after the policy was launched, a monitoring group was established to assess implementation and the degree to which specific policy measures truly improved services.[114] One of the key and long neglected areas to be addressed was child and adolescent psychiatry and this is considered next.

Child and Adolescent Psychiatry: Emergence of a New Discipline

In the twentieth century, child and adolescent psychiatry was largely based on the work of Leo Kanner (1894–1981), an Austrian-American psychiatrist who published an influential textbook titled *Child Psychiatry* in 1935.[115] Kanner had previously organised a child guidance clinic in Boston in 1921, aimed chiefly at treating children with delinquent behaviours.[116] Child guidance clinics soon spread to Europe and in 1933 a children's department was opened at the Tavistock Clinic in London. Child psychiatry became an independent speciality in the National Health Service (NHS) in the late 1940s.

In Ireland, too, child and adolescent psychiatry is a relatively recent feature within mental health services, and even today requires additional attention.[117] In the early 1950s, following discussion with the WHO, the Department of Health approached the St John of God Order and in 1955 the Order established the first child guidance clinic in Ireland in Orwell Road in Rathgar, Dublin.[118] The first medical director, Dr John Stack, was appointed in September 1955 when, following a successful interview, he completed further training in child psychiatry, with a psychoanalytic orientation, in Cincinnati.[119] On his return, there were child psychiatry outpatient services operating at Temple Street (Dr Mulvany) and the National Children's Hospital on Harcourt Street (Dr Maureen Walsh).

Despite some scepticism from certain parties within child health services, Stack went on to develop and expand the Orwell Road child psychiatry service and was joined, in October 1955, by Dr John McKenna, a clinical psychologist and member of the Commission on Mental Handicap,[120] who was frequently engaged by the WHO in connection with related matters and later became Professor of Psychology in the Royal College of Surgeons in Ireland.[121] In December 1955, Irene Mulaney, the first social worker, joined the service, and the Irish National Teachers Organisation soon proved a strong ally.[122]

In 1962, the Mater Hospital Child Guidance Clinic was opened, with Dr Seán Malone as the first medical director, Dr Maureen Walsh as child psychiatrist, Sr Jo Kennedy as speech therapist and administrator, Pia Kasteel as clinical psychologist, and Anita Thompson and Sr Margherita Rock as psychiatric social workers.[123] In 1964, Dr Paul McQuaid joined the staff and became medical director. In 1972, Dr Nuala Healy was appointed to the staff and this clinic went on to develop extensive training, educational and therapeutic dimensions.[124] Extensive catchment area services were piloted, to include schools, homes, residential services, etc., and two satellite facilities were opened in 1970: St. Paul's Hospital and special school for children with autism (at Beaumont Woods) and a clinic in Ballymun. The Mater Child Guidance Clinic building was demolished in 2008 to make way for other developments and the service relocated to James Joyce Street.

At Temple Street Children's Hospital, a child guidance clinic operated in the outpatient department from 1962 to 1965, at which time a special unit, St Francis's Clinic, was opened.[125] A training scheme for psychiatric social workers was also established and in 1968 Dr Paul McCarthy joined the Eastern Health Board as clinical director of the child psychiatry service.

In 1966, the *Report of the Commission of Inquiry on Mental Illness* placed considerable emphasis on services for children and adolescents, recommending that there should be 'the equivalent of at least one child guidance team per 100,000 of the population of all ages'; 'district child psychiatric clinics should be developed in conjunction with clinics for adults but should be held at different times'; 'any doctor should have the right to refer a child directly to a district psychiatric clinic'; and 'regional child psychiatric clinics should be developed to deal with cases presenting particular difficulty, or requiring facilities not available at the district clinics. The existing clinics in Dublin should be provided with any additional facilities required to enable them to act as regional clinics. Three additional regional clinics should be provided outside Dublin.'[126]

There were recommendations in relation to 'residential accommodation'; 'a system of foster care and family group homes' (as 'an alternative to residential units'); and specific measures relating to schools, reports for courts and industrial schools.[127] In relation to adolescents, the report noted that 'many adolescents can suitably be catered for by the services for children. Some can suitably be catered for by the services for adults, but there are some for whom special provisions are necessary.'[128]

More specifically, 'specialist staff in the psychiatric services should, where necessary, provide advice and assistance for parents and others concerned with the counselling of adolescents'; 'psychiatric advice for adolescents should be provided at the district or regional child psychiatric clinics, or at adult clinics'; 'development of youth organisations should be encouraged'; 'approximately 150 residential places, located in a few regional centres, should be provided to cater for the special needs of adolescents'; and 'as in the case of children, psychiatric and psychological services should be available in respect of certain adolescents who appear before the Courts and in respect of those detained in reformatories and industrial schools'.

Against this backdrop, services continued to develop across Ireland throughout the 1970s. In Galway, Dr Anthony Carroll took up the position of clinical director of child psychiatric services in the Western Health Board in 1975 and three years later the expanding service moved to St Anne's children's home in Taylor's Hill.[129] Family therapy soon became the favoured treatment modality and influential workshops were held on Inishbofin in June 1980.

Carroll was also a member of the study group that developed the 1984 policy document *Planning for the Future*, which strongly emphasised services for children and adolescents with particular focus on preventive work; 'training of general practitioners and of public health nurses' to 'place a greater emphasis on psychology'; establishment of a Department of Child and Adolescent Psychiatry in 'at least one of the medical schools'; and provision of 'a comprehensive psychological service in primary schools'.[130]

In addition, 'the child guidance team should consist of a child psychiatrist, child psychologists and social workers'; 'each health board should develop one child guidance team per 200,000 population and there should be at least one child and family guidance centre in each health board area'; 'in addition to the existing inpatient units in Dublin, Cork and Galway, small inpatient units should be provided as part of the child guidance service in Limerick, Sligo and Waterford'; 'residential treatment facilities for adolescents should be developed at Dublin, Cork and Galway'; and 'walk-in' centres were recommended. There were specific recommendations relating to homeless teenagers, 'emotionally disturbed adolescents coming before the courts', juvenile offenders, and 'children in whom autism is suspected', who, according to the policy, 'should be referred to a specialised centre where assessment can take place'.

Following developments in the Eastern and Western Health Boards, other areas duly developed their services in line with policy recommendations, either in collaboration with voluntary agencies providing services to children with intellectual disabilities, sharing staff across boundaries, co-working with adult psychiatry services, or sending children to Dublin for opinions.[131] In Cork, the child psychiatry service evolved out of services for boys with intellectual disability provided by the

Brothers of Charity in Lota since 1936. Services developed further during the 1970s and 1980s, and a child psychiatry service was formally established by the Southern Health Board in 1994, with Dr Finbar O'Leary as clinical director.

Similarly in Limerick, the child psychiatry service of the Mid-Western Health Board was formally established in 1993, building on the work of the Brothers of Charity.[132] The service in the South Eastern Health Board also developed out of the work of the Brothers of Charity. In the North Western Health Board, Dr Don McDwyer was appointed consultant child psychiatrist in 1992, whereas the Midland Health Board had a service from at least the early 1970s (with Dr Ellen Cody in Mullingar), which the North Eastern Health Board also used until its own regional service was established in the 1990s.

The services provided by various of these teams included not only psychiatric and psychological inputs, but also social work services (including family therapy),[133] the *Stay Safe* programme (a school based child sexual abuse prevention programme),[134] child care work,[135] and speech and language therapy,[136] among other therapies. In 1996, Michael Fitzgerald, Henry Marsh Professor of Child and Adolescent Psychiatry at Trinity College, Dublin became the first professor of child psychiatry in Ireland and has written extensively about autism, among other subjects.[137]

In 2005, the Irish College of Psychiatrists[138] (later the College of Psychiatrists of Ireland) produced a position statement on psychiatric services for children and adolescents, titled *A Better Future Now*.[139] The College's Faculty of Child and Adolescent Psychiatry noted that child and adolescent psychiatric services accounted for only 5–10 per cent of spending on mental health services, while serving some 23 per cent of the population. The Faculty reported that there were 55 whole-time equivalent consultant child and adolescent psychiatry posts in the Republic of Ireland, yielding a ratio of one consultant for every 16,150 persons under 16 years; in Finland, the ratio was one for every 6,000 persons aged under 19.

The Faculty noted that there were, in 2005, 40 specialist outpatient multidisciplinary teams (the recommended number was 59) and that the majority of teams were significantly below the recommended multidisciplinary staffing levels. Inpatient facilities for people under 16 years were located in two centres with a total of 20 beds, while the recommended number was 156 beds, with the 16- to 17-year age group requiring an additional 80 beds.

The following year, *A Vision for Change* echoed many of these themes, emphasising 'the need to prioritise the full range of mental health care, from primary care to specialist mental health services for children and adolescents'.[140] The policy recommended the provision of two multidisciplinary teams per 100,000 population; completion of inpatient units (20 beds each) in Cork, Limerick, Galway and Dublin; and one liaison team per catchment area of 300,000 people, among other services.

Some progress was made over the following years and in 2014 the Mental Health Commission reported that there were now 82 beds across six child and adolescent units.[141] There were, however, still clear challenges with provision of care:[142] in 2013, there were 91 admissions of children (aged under 18 years) to adult psychiatry units, comprising 22 per cent of all child admissions.[143] While this number fell marginally to 89 in 2014,[144] child and adolescent services continued to be discussed in the media[145] and key opinion leaders, such as Dr Brian Houlihan, continued to advocate strongly for better services.[146] Regrettably, the number of child admissions to adult units rose again in 2015, compared to 2014.[147] Even in 2016 there remains substantial progress to be made,[148] though the proposal by Minister Helen McEntee, Minister of State for Mental Health and Older People, for a taskforce on youth mental health, represents an important commitment to progress in this area.[149]

The Irish Journal of Psychological Medicine (1982) and the College of Psychiatrists of Ireland (2009)

Against the background of these legislative and policy developments, the late twentieth and early twenty-first centuries saw significant, consolidating developments within Irish psychiatry. In 1982, the *Irish Journal of Psychological Medicine* was founded by Dr Mark Hartman (1942–1994), a remarkable figure in the history of psychiatry in Ireland.[150] Hartman was born in Chicago, the son of an eminent forensic psychologist. After high school, he completed a degree in mathematics and physics and came to Ireland in the early 1960s.[151] Hartman studied medicine in Trinity College, Dublin, where he qualified in 1969, following a brilliant undergraduate career which saw him elected a scholar of the university. Hartman studied psychiatry under Professor Peter Beckett, first professor of psychiatry at Trinity,[152] who described Mark as the best student in his class.[153]

Hartman served his internship in Sir Patrick Duns Hospital and then worked in St Patrick's, St Ita's, St Brendan's and St Vincent's, Fairview. He was elected a Member of the Royal College of Psychiatrists in 1973 and worked in St Mary's, Castlebar until permanently appointed at St Brendan's in 1978. In 1983, Hartman took a three year career break to the US, where he was associate professor of psychiatry in Boston University and medical director of Lakeshore Hospital, Manchester, New Hampshire.

Also in 1983, Hartman attained his American Board Examinations in Psychiatry and Neurology in Boston, and was ranked in the top 2 per cent of all candidates who had previously sat the examination. Following his career break in the United States, Hartman returned to Dublin and worked at Vergemount Psychiatric Clinic. He died in 1994, following a year long illness. Hartman was posthumously elected to Fellowship of the Royal College of Psychiatrists.

Throughout his career, Hartman demonstrated an enormous depth of knowledge and passion for psychiatry. He had a particular interest in psychoanalytical psychotherapy, a field which informed his approach to both psychiatric education and clinical care.[154] Hartman was deeply involved in psychiatric training: he was appointed clinical tutor in St Brendan's in 1973, taught at the Royal College of Surgeons in Ireland, and was specialty tutor for the Eastern Region Postgraduate Training Programme from 1979 to 1994.

In addition to his interests in psychiatry and psychotherapy, Hartman had interests in many other fields. He had a particular love of Middle English and held a Master's Degree in English from Trinity.

In the midst of all of these activities and accomplishments, Hartman founded the *Irish Journal of Psychological Medicine*, in 1982. At first, it was an uphill battle to attract submissions, rewrite certain papers, edit the *Journal*, and organise publication. Hartman performed all of these tasks with insight and enthusiasm, at all hours of the day and night. He brought enormous vision and drive to the undertaking, travelling to Northern Ireland and England to seek out submissions and inviting international speakers to Ireland in order to obtain more papers. He oversaw the establishment of a circulation base for the *Journal*, a remarkable growth in circulation (in terms of both numbers and geography), broad based scientific indexing, and the stocking of the *Journal* in libraries around the world.

In 1994, following Hartman's untimely death, Professor Brian Lawlor became editor-in-chief. On appointment, Lawlor explicitly renewed the *Journal's* commitment to its central objectives: disseminating the results of original scientific research to a national and international readership; expressing the unique identity of Irish psychiatry; and underscoring the importance of cross-cultural differences in psychiatry.[155]

Over the following years, the *Journal* continued to publish national and international research papers, as well as editorials, review papers, case reports and book reviews, in partnership with its long-time publisher, MedMedia Group (Dún Laoghaire, County Dublin). The *Irish Journal of Psychological Medicine* also awarded the John Dunne Medal, established in honour of Professor John Dunne (Chapter 5).[156] The Medal is now awarded annually to a trainee from Ireland or the UK who has made a significant contribution to an original paper published by the *Journal* over the previous year. The John Dunne Medal has come to symbolise excellence and originality in the field of psychiatric research.

The *Irish Journal of Psychological Medicine* was not, however, the only journal in Irish psychiatry over this period. Other titles included the *Irish Journal of Psychiatry*, which first appeared in 1982, edited by Dr Dermot Walsh and published by the Irish Institute of Psychiatry (its invaluable articles are quoted many times in this book), *Irish Psychiatrist* (2000–11) and *Psychiatry Professional* (2011–12); the latter two edited by Dr Brian O'Shea and published by MedMedia Group.

In 2010, Professor Brendan Kelly became editor-in-chief of the *Irish Journal of Psychological Medicine*,[157] following periods as trainee editor (2004–8)[158] and deputy editor (2008–10). This was an especially eventful time for the *Journal* and for Irish psychiatry, not least because the College of Psychiatry of Ireland (retitled College of Psychiatrists of Ireland in 2013) emerged as an organisation in 2009 when three former bodies merged: the Irish College of Psychiatrists (a division of the Royal College of Psychiatrists in the UK)[159], the Irish Psychiatric Association, and the then training body for psychiatry, the Irish Psychiatric Training Committee.[160] Dr Kate Ganter was Chair of the Irish Division of the Royal College of Psychiatrists for some years prior to this, from 2003 to 2007.[161] Dr Justin Brophy became first president of the new College of Psychiatry of Ireland, followed by Dr Anthony McCarthy, Dr Ruth Loane and Dr John Hillery (president elect, 2017).

Following its establishment, the College became the sole professional body for psychiatrists in Ireland and the only such body recognised by the Medical Council and HSE for competence assurance and training in psychiatry. The constitution of the College notes that the College 'is the professional body of psychiatrists in Ireland'.[162] 'The main objects for which the College is constituted is the advancement of education in psychiatry through the following':

(a) The formation and training of doctors in psychiatry.
(b) The on-going professional development and education of trained psychiatrists.

(c) The promotion, development and furtherance of the College's engagement and collaboration with others concerned in the development of best practice in mental health services for the benefit of those availing of those services.

(d) To act as a consultative body in relation to matters of public and professional interest concerning psychiatry and the prevention and treatment of mental disorder in all its forms and aspects.

In conjunction with its representative, training and advocacy roles, the College also has a growing role in promoting and encouraging research, with a view to generating an improved evidence base for psychiatric practice. In this respect, the College is assuming at least some of the roles envisioned in long standing calls for a research-oriented Irish Institute of Psychiatry, which has not yet materialised as such.[163] Its role in postgraduate training also remains central, under the direction of Professor Greg Swanwick, Dean of Education. The College's patron, President Michael D. Higgins, addressed its Winter Conference in 2012.[164]

Following the emergence of the College in 2009, and given its manifold roles, it was soon apparent that the College needed a journal in order to strengthen its participation in the international research community and assist the College in shaping and improving standards of mental health care. In 2012, the *Irish Journal of Psychological Medicine* duly became the official research journal of the College.

Following this development, the *Journal* continued to publish high quality original research from around the world. Today, these original data papers still form the central focus of the *Journal*, supplemented by briefer reports of smaller research projects, audit cycles, and various other kinds of papers which reflect different approaches to research, practice and education. The *Journal* also remains committed to publishing case reports and historical papers examining key topics in the histories of psychiatry in Ireland and elsewhere.

The years since 2010 saw substantial changes in the format and distribution of the *Journal*, especially since 2013 with its new publisher, Cambridge University Press. These changes produced a large increase in *Journal* usage and distribution; the majority of the *Journal* archive was made available online in one location, with additional link-out functionality; and author survey feedback was highly positive.

There were also various other advances and innovations at the *Journal* over this period, with a reformulated international editorial board playing a substantial role in *Journal* policy and development. In March 2011, the *Journal* published a special supplement dedicated to 'head shop' drugs[165] and in March 2015 published its first special issue, devoted to youth mental health, edited by Dr John Lyne and Professor Mary Cannon.[166]

In 2016, Professor Brendan Kelly stepped down as editor-in-chief after overseeing the *Journal*'s move to Cambridge University Press and the College of Psychiatrists of Ireland, as well as the various changes and reforms of the previous six years.[167] Kelly was succeeded by Dr John Lyne, who has continued to develop and expand the *Journal*, with the aim of better informing the evidence base for mental health services and deepening the role and remit of the *Journal* in the context of psychiatry in Ireland and well beyond.[168]

Does the Community Care?

Against the backdrop of these complex, significant developments in Irish psychiatric policy, practice and professional organisation, mental health services in Ireland continued to change and evolve. Given the rather uneven history of mental health reform in Ireland over the past two centuries, however, it is reasonable to wonder if all of these changes, especially the expansive vision of community mental health services in *A Vision for Change* (2006), really came to pass over the following decade. In others words, after the rhetoric faded, did the community really care?[169] Or did all of these policy statements and professional developments adhere to the well-worn pattern of pious promises being followed by minimal positive change, resulting in little actual improvement, if any, in the lives of persons with mental disorder? Did anything really change? And, if so, did things get better or worse for the mentally ill?

Long before *A Vision for Change* was published, there were already some well-established programmes of community mental health care in place, based on the ideas in *Planning for the Future* (1984) and even the '1966 Report' which recommended 'radical and widespread changes',[170] moving away from 'barrack-like structures characterised by large wards, gloomy corridors and stone stairways',[171] and towards community care. As a result, well before *A Vision for Change* appeared, there was a strong emphasis on community care in at least certain parts of the country, as reflected in the reduction of the number of 'mentally ill' persons resident in institutions from 18,188 in 1966 to 4,522 in 2000.[172] There were particularly innovative developments in the Clondalkin mental health service in Dublin (led by Dr Ian Daly), which provided home based care for severe mental illness,[173] and in the Cavan/Monaghan mental health service (led by Dr John Owens), developing multidisciplinary, community-based and home-based mental health teams.[174]

Even outside of these pioneering developments, however, Irish psychiatry in general was increasingly characterised by community-oriented teams and many psychiatrists, such as Dr James Maguire (1950–2007) in Ardee and Navan, were leaders of remarkable change as care transitioned from the old mental hospitals to community based clinics, day hospitals and domiciliary teams.[175]

At national level, however, the overall rate of implementation of *A Vision for Change* was commonly criticised as being too slow. In 2008, one study of 32 mental health services reported that just 16 per cent of services had received the resources promised in order to implement the new policy; 32 per cent had not been promised such resources and nor was there tangible evidence of the requisite enhancement of clinical teams; and there was significant concern about low levels of recruitment to multidisciplinary teams.[176] This study, published on behalf of the Faculty of Clinical Directors of the College of Psychiatry of Ireland (as it was then named), emphasised the importance of adequate resourcing in order to implement *A Vision for Change* and noted an increase in admissions in 2007 compared to the previous year:

> Unless the process outlined above is reversed, either by protecting mental health services from cuts, identifying new resource, or redirecting resource internally within mental health services or from other HSE services, *A Vision for Change* will not be realised. With it will perish the hopes and aspirations of a generation of mental health

service-users and providers. A deep sense of betrayal will be consolidated and likely lead to a loss of morale and staff engagement with reform. Standards will decline and recruitment into and development of mental health services will be significantly damaged. Most importantly those who suffer from mental ill health and their carers will have been seriously misled and denied basic services and basic reforms. This is clearly at odds with the expressed will of the Irish people and government not to mention the stakeholders in the services. If this happens it will pose a risk of a verdict of abject failure by those responsible to deliver those reforms.[177]

In September 2009, a report by Indecon International Consultants, submitted to Amnesty International, made some similar points, highlighting that while definite progress had been made, significant deficits remained in relation to the number of community mental health teams and their composition.[178] The report pointed to an over reliance on traditional acute and long stay inpatient facilities and presented a series of recommendations for future developments, including setting new, realistic implementation targets.

Rate of implementation was also a key concern of the Independent Monitoring Group (IMC) established as part of *A Vision for Change* in March 2006. In June 2012, the IMC, in its sixth annual report, concluded that implementation of the policy was still 'slow and inconsistent'.[179] The IMC pointed in particular to the 'continued absence of a National Mental Health Service Directorate with authority and control of resources. Such a body has the potential to give strong corporate leadership and act as a catalyst for change':

> The absence of a comprehensive, time-lined and costed implementation plan has made it difficult to put in place a consistent framework for the development of all mental health specialities and has led to a lack of coherency in the planning and development of community based services. Existing community mental health teams are poorly populated with an estimated 1,500 vacant posts. These are mostly allied health professional posts. Consequently, the service that is delivered through medical and nursing posts is not based on multiple interventions as envisaged in [*A Vision for Change*]. [...] There is an absence of the ethos of recovery and poor development of recovery competencies in service delivery resulting in a reactive rather than proactive approach to the needs of individuals and their families.[180]

On a more positive note, there was 'evidence of many local and regional initiatives being developed in line with [*A Vision for Change*]. These are principally "bottom-up" developments led by local leadership'. The IMC noted that 'the HSE in combination with the Mental Health Commission has driven the continued closure of unfit for purpose facilities in favour of modern community based approaches. In respect of capital developments, progress has and is being made in the area of general adult mental health services, child and adolescent mental health services and forensic mental health services'.

Interestingly, the IMC specifically noted that the closure of outdated hospitals was attributable to 'a combination of policy initiatives by the HSE and the imposition of conditions on registration by the [Mental Health Commission], following inspections'.[181] While executive and regulatory mechanisms appeared to work well together in this regard, there was still much to be done to advance other areas of the policy:

> What is still required to achieve full implementation of [*A Vision for Change*] is an operational framework for the development of recovery competencies for all staff both at entry training level and ongoing in-service development. As a matter of urgency, the specialist mental health services for older people, rehabilitation and recovery, eating disorders, intellectual disability, co-morbid severe mental illness and substance abuse problems and others described in [*A Vision for Change*] need to be fully developed and delivered. Government Departments, other than the Department of Health and the Department of the Environment, Community and Local Government need to focus on their responsibilities for the implementation of [*A Vision for Change*].[182]

There priorities were duly reflected in the IMC's final recommendations, which set out detailed priorities in relation to the HSE; government departments; addressing the biological, psychological and social factors that contribute to mental health problems; the National Mental Health Programme (clinical programmes); recovery; and further monitoring of implementation.[183] More specifically, in relation to the HSE, the IMC recommended, *inter alia*, that:

- A National Mental Health Service Directorate as envisaged by [*A Vision for Change*] must be established.
- Staffing of [community mental health teams] should be continued as described in [*A Vision for Change*].
- A comprehensive, time-lined and costed implementation plan should be developed.
- Cultural issues such as personal attitude, professional policies and attitudes, philosophical biases, historical precedent and practice, should be addressed in any policy implementation process.
- Team working and shared planning should involve the service user and where appropriate family members.
- There should be a consistent national approach to the development and support of service users and family members.[184]

Many of these themes recurred in a further, independent study of implementation by Dr Helen Johnston published in 2014, which identified a significant body of opinion that saw implementation as slow, haphazard and uneven.[185] That study identified a need for authoritative, accountable leadership as a key factor for implementation:[186] in 2013, the HSE appointed a National Director for Mental Health (Mr Stephen Mulvany).

By 2015 the Mental Health Division of the HSE had responsibility for all HSE mental health services, including area based mental health services (approved inpatient residential centres, all community based teams), child and adolescent mental health, general adult psychiatry, psychiatry of old age, the National Forensic Mental Health Service, National Counselling Service and National Office for Suicide Prevention.

The HSE Mental Health Management Team, led by the National Director (Ms Anne O'Connor), comprised a Head of Planning, Performance and Programme Management (Ms Yvonne O'Neill), Head of Operations, Quality and Service Improvement (Mr Jim Ryan), Interim Head of Service User, Family Member and Carer Engagement (Mr Patrick McGowan) and National Clinical Adviser and Clinical Programme Group Lead for Mental Health (Dr Margo Wrigley).[187] Mr Liam Hennessy later became Head of Service User, Family Member and Carer Engagement in the Mental Health Division.

In 2010, there was further progress with the launch of See Change, Ireland's national programme working to change minds about mental health problems. See Change works in partnership with over 80 voluntary organisations, state agencies, universities and youth groups to create a social movement to reduce the stigma and discrimination associated with mental health problems (www.seechange. ie). Further invaluable activity to combat stigma is reflected in the work of First Fortnight, a charity based organisation with the express aim of challenging mental health prejudice through the creative arts (www.firstfortnight.ie).

Also in 2010, the National Clinical Programme for Mental Health was set up as a joint initiative between HSE Clinical Strategy and Programmes Division and the College of Psychiatry of Ireland (as it was then called; now College of Psychiatrists of Ireland). The overarching aim of the national programme was to standardise high quality evidence based practice across mental health services in relation to (a) assessment and management of patients presenting to emergency departments following self-harm; (b) early intervention for people developing first episode psychosis; and (c) management of persons with eating disorders (spanning child and adolescent and adult mental health services). These programmes aimed to address identified areas of high need and provide a programmatic response in which integration with other services was key to successful delivery and reform. While change of this magnitude is invariably complex, significant progress was reported in several areas with, for example, 23 of the 35 posts identified to address self-harm in Emergency Departments in place by March 2015, and the remainder in the recruitment process.[188]

Notwithstanding these developments, substantial challenges remained. In 2014, the Chairman of the Mental Health Commission (Mr John Saunders) pointed to some of the outstanding challenges in relation to *A Vision for Change*:

> The implementation of policy to date is still reliant on innovative and imaginative clinical and administrative leadership at regional and local levels. There is considerable commitment to the policy. Despite these actions the policy is being implemented unevenly and inconsistently across the country and there is a requirement for innovative actions to be supported and reinforced by strong corporate governance at national level.[189]

While acknowledging recent progress in relation to governance and certain other areas, the Chairman stated that 'the [Mental Health] Commission is also concerned regarding a number of specific areas of service provision which impinge on human rights and where, in 2013, standards fell below what is acceptable'.[190] These areas included individualised care plans (implemented appropriately in an estimated 60 per cent of approved centres), unacceptable use of seclusion and restraint, continued admission of children to adult facilities (22 per cent of all child admissions in 2013), the absence of reformed, enacted mental capacity legislation, and various issues relating to staffing.

Clearly, then, while progress was made with *A Vision for Change* in the decade following publication, further work was still very much needed: the process of reform must always be a continuous one. Nowhere does this remain in greater evidence than in one of the most specialised, challenging and progressive areas within Irish mental health services: the National Forensic Mental Health Service.

National Forensic Mental Health Service: Psychiatry and Offending Behaviour

The twentieth century saw significant change in relation to forensic psychiatry in Ireland as the National Forensic Mental Health Service moved from a nineteenth century, asylum based model, in which it was primarily the legal process rather than medical professionals that determined outcomes,[191] to a twenty-first century service with inpatient provision, award-winning prison in-reach programmes, extensive research activities, growing community elements, and advanced plans for a new inpatient facility in Portrane, County Dublin to replace the Central Mental Hospital in Dundrum.

In the early 1900s, however, the asylum at Dundrum still held a large number of inpatients, amounting to 146 men and 24 women in 1902.[192] Many were long stay patients: over the course of the previous year, just 24 patients were admitted; 5 were discharged recovered; and 4 died (2 due to consumption and 2 due to heart disease). Forensic psychiatry remained a topic of considerable public interest during these decades. An especially controversial 'guilty but insane' verdict was returned in 1916 at the court marital of Captain J.C. Bowen-Colthurst, an Irishman in the British Army, who had 6 unarmed civilians, including pacifist Francis Sheehy Skeffington (1878–1916), shot during the 1916 Rising.[193] Bowen-Colthurst was sent to Broadmoor in England and eventually settled in Canada, with a military pension.

Back in Ireland, the 1927 Commission on the Relief of the Sick and Destitute Poor addressed the issue of 'criminal lunatics' in some detail:

> It was apparently at one time intended that all criminal lunatics would be accommodated in the central asylum at Dundrum; but in practice the Dundrum establishment is reserved for those charged with or convicted of grave offences. No complaints arise from the placing of persons legally classed as criminal lunatics in the same institution as other insane persons and we see no objection to the practice.
>
> We consider that new legislation should provide for the periodical review of the cases of persons classed as criminal lunatics. An annual report should be made by the Resident Medical Superintendent on the condition and circumstances of every

criminal lunatic and the Minister for Justice should determine whether he ought be discharged or, if the patient is not considered fit for discharge, whether the history and circumstances of the case would justify steps being taken to have the patient's name removed from the list of criminal lunatics.

On a patient classed as a criminal lunatic ceasing to be so classed, the Minister should have power to direct his transfer to any other mental hospital.[194]

In 1949, Dr William J. Coyne became Resident Physician and Governor, a post he held until 1965.[195] Coyne was a committed, enthusiastic, reforming governor, doubling the hospital's financial allocation within a few years; ensuring that patients no longer shared communal garments; and arranging trips outside the hospital for patients. Coyne even permitted one patient, interested in sailing, to build boats in the hospital grounds.

Coyne was succeeded in 1965 by Dr Michael Reynolds, who had been Assistant Medical Officer since January 1965 and took over from the acting Resident Physician and Governor, Dr Paddy Cassin (previously RMS at St Canice's Mental Hospital, Kilkenny) in October 1965.[196] Reynolds and his family lived firstly in an apartment in the hospital block but then moved to a new, purpose-built governor's house on the grounds. At this time, there was one qualified psychiatric nurse working on the male care staff and one on the female care staff; the remainder were attendants. The majority of patients were there on a long term basis but there was a steady turnover of short term emergency patients too, chiefly from Mountjoy Prison.

By 1967, patient numbers had fallen to 91 men and 19 women, of whom 8 were in regular employment outside the hospital.[197] Attendants occasionally invited patients home for tea and there were four dances in the hospital each year, with girls from the Legion of Mary attending to make up the disparity in numbers of men and women. A visiting committee, established by Dr Noël Browne in 1948, visited regularly and heard any complaints. While there were three medical doctors on the staff in 1967, there was no social worker, qualified occupational therapist or placement officer.

Throughout his tenure as Resident Physician and Governor (1965–8), Reynolds was a civil servant employed directly by the Minister for Health, although the bulk of his responsibilities related to the Minister for Justice.[198] Reynolds was succeeded in 1968 by Dr Eveleen O'Brien (previously of Grangegorman Mental Hospital), who held the post of acting Resident Physician and Governor until Dr Liam Daly was appointed as first Clinical Director under the provisions of the Health Act 1970, as the hospital moved from direct control of the Minister for Health to the Eastern Health Board.[199]

Daly became acting Clinical Director in 1971 and was fully appointed in 1974. In the early 1970s, Daly was involved in the management of hunger strikers in the Curragh Prison and he served as president of the Medico-Legal Society in the late 1970s.[200] Daly took leave of absence in 1985 and Dr Charles Smith became acting Clinical Director.

The hospital continued to evolve and by 1986 the number of medical staff had increased to 7, comprising 3 consultant psychiatrists and 4 non-consultant hospital doctors.[201] By that time, there were 95 inpatients, 51 per cent of whom had schizophrenia; the next most common diagnostic category was personality disorder and neurosis (21 per cent), while some 18 per cent had intellectual disability (without coexisting mental disorder). The death rate at the hospital was generally stable during the 1960s, 1970s and 1980s, averaging at around 12 deaths per 1,000 admissions, with cardiovascular disease the most common cause of natural death, and 5 suicides reported between 1963 and 1982.[202]

Throughout the mid-1980s the most common primary diagnosis among prisoners transferred to the hospital was schizophrenia in men (31 per cent)[203] and personality disorder in women (36 per cent).[204] In 1993, Dr Charles Smith, now fully appointed as Clinical Director, highlighted that up to 5 per cent of prisoners in Ireland were mentally ill, almost double the rate in England.[205] In the late 1990s, further research at the hospital demonstrated that, throughout Ireland, general psychiatric resources were relatively under resourced in areas of greatest predicted need, and that this was associated with increased use of forensic psychiatric services.[206] Clearly, further research and reform were needed.[207]

The broad based research programme based within the forensic service went on to demonstrate that members of the Irish Travellers community were over represented among forensic psychiatric admissions;[208] almost one half of long stay forensic psychiatric patients were inappropriately placed;[209] and there was substantial unmet need for mental health services among various categories of male[210] and female prisoners.[211] Against this background, Professor Harry Kennedy, Clinical Director of the National Forensic Mental Health Service since 2000, highlighted the importance of developing pathways though care that reflected patient need and preference, rather than historical and legal artefacts.[212]

In the early 2000s, various proposed reforms of the service generated considerable discussion in professional[213] and public forums.[214] There was, however, particularly long standing and generally agreed recognition of the need for revised legislation on criminal insanity,[215] as reflected in the 1978 report of the Interdepartmental Committee on Mentally Ill and Maladjusted Persons (chaired by the Honourable Mr Justice Henchy, Judge of the Supreme Court) regarding the *Treatment and Care of Persons Suffering From Mental Disorder Who Appear Before the Courts on Criminal Charges*.[216] The Criminal Law (Insanity) Act 2006 duly introduced significant change in this area, replacing the 'guilty but insane' verdict with 'not guilty by reason of insanity', and providing for the concept of 'diminished responsibility' in murder cases, among other reforms.[217] The legislation was undoubtedly a significant step forward, although further legislative reform was still needed.[218]

In terms of service provision, there were considerable developments at the Central Mental Hospital through the early 2000s, although significant problems remained with the building and various other resources.[219] There were also pressures resulting from the increasing numbers of mentally ill prisoners, especially since Ireland's psychiatric hospitals started to close in the 1960s:[220] between 1963 and 2003 the number of inpatients in Irish psychiatric hospitals decreased from 19,801 to 3,658 (a five-fold decrease, or 82 per cent) while the daily number of prisoners increased from 534 to 3,176 (a five-fold increase, or 495 per cent).[221] This phenomenon is known as 'Penrose's Law', after Professor Lionel Penrose (1898–1972) who studied data from 14 European countries and concluded that the number of persons in mental 'institutions' was inversely correlated with the number in prison.[222] In Ireland, a highly progressive and effective court diversion scheme was developed in the early 2000s by Dr Conor O'Neill and colleagues to help address this issue.[223]

As a result of this and various other reforms, the 1900s and early 2000s saw the National Forensic Mental Health Service develop into a deeply reformed service, highly progressive by national and international standards, with specialised, multidisciplinary inpatient treatment, award winning prison in-reach services,[224] and a comprehensive research programme.[225] Challenges, however, remain. In May 2016, Kennedy pointed out in the *Irish Times* that psychiatric bed numbers in Ireland are significantly lower than in other advanced European countries, with a particular deficit in secure (forensic) beds, resulting in psychotic young men still ending up in prison.[226] Clearly, more needs to be done.

In June 2015, planning permission was granted for a 120 bed national forensic hospital in Portrane, County Dublin, as well as two 10 bed specialist units for persons with intellectual disabilities and children and adolescents.[227] The project included progressing design work for three 30 bed Intensive Care Rehabilitation Units in Cork, Galway and Portrane,[228] and represented the most substantial step forward for Ireland's forensic mental health services in several decades.[229]

Forensic psychiatry is, however, just one specialist area in need of further attention. There are various other groups which require dedicated provision of services, and similar progress is not evident in all of these areas. Mental health services for the deaf is one such area, which has seen significant developments in past decades, but which also requires further thought and attention in the future.

Mental Illness and Deafness

More than one person in every seven has hearing loss. Approximately seven per 10,000 people in the general population have severe to profound deafness with onset before language has been established, amounting to 3,000–3,500 people in the Republic of Ireland. Of these, 50 per cent may experience mental health difficulties at some time in their lives.[230]

Deaf people are a diverse population as regards their deafness, cultural identity and mental health needs.[231] Despite the absence of comprehensive databases or population registers, as well as difficulties relating to the representativeness of studies from specialist centres, it is now clear that deaf people have higher rates of mental health problems than the general population. This is attributable to neurological risk associated with certain causes of deafness; psychological effects of delayed language and other adverse childhood experiences (e.g. institutionalisation, neglect, abuse); and longer duration of untreated mental disorder, owing to the fact that the mental health needs of the deaf are often neither recognised nor appropriately met in many countries, including Ireland.

The 1984 policy document, *Planning for the Future*, presented an appendix acknowledging the importance of 'Psychiatric Services for the Adult Deaf', prepared by Dr Jim O'Boyle, consultant psychiatrist with the Eastern Health Board and member of the study group that prepared the overall policy. O'Boyle noted the need for greater focus on this population:

> During the last 25 years provision of specialised services for deaf adults has been a feature of the development of comprehensive psychiatric services in many countries, particularly in North America. In this country we have not, as yet, developed such a

service. Deaf adults requiring psychiatric treatment are assessed and treated in a setting which is not equipped for those who are suffering from severe hearing impairment. The objective in setting up specialised psychiatric services for the deaf in other countries has been to provide assessment, diagnosis and treatment at a centre where all staff members are skilled in communicating with the deaf.[232]

O'Boyle reviewed the literature relating to mental disorder and deafness, pointing out that 'social isolation is recognised as one of the principal complications of profound or severe hearing impairment'.[233] He also identified misdiagnosis as a significant risk, owing, in part, to communication difficulties:

> There is a high risk of mis-diagnosis in deaf adults suffering from psychiatric illness who are treated in a setting where the staff are not skilled in the use of sign-language. Abnormal behaviour arising from a psychotic illness may erroneously be ascribed to deafness or vice versa i.e. abnormal behaviour resulting from deafness may be considered to be due to a psychosis.[234]

Greater attention was needed to this area, along with better information, training and services. O'Boyle presented six recommendations:

1. There is a need for a survey to be undertaken of all psychiatric hospitals using researchers who are highly proficient in communication skills with the deaf to determine the prevalence of severe hearing impairment and the presence or absence of a formal psychiatric illness in the in-patient population. This survey would give an indication of the number of patients who have been inappropriately placed in our psychiatric hospitals in the absence of suitable alternatives.

2. A separate out-patient service should be available in each health board area to the adult deaf presenting for a psychiatric consultation. All staff working in this service should receive special training in sign-language.

3. There is a need for supervised hostels for the adult deaf. These would be set up on a pilot project basis, when the results of the in-patient deaf survey have been completed. In association with the establishment of such special hostels for the deaf, a supporting rehabilitation programme will be required so that residents may be trained for placement in open employment. An important member of any rehabilitation team will be a teacher for the deaf who will provide classes to improve the communication skills of both the deaf patients and the staff.

4. The staff in the out-patient special service for the deaf should be available to follow-up patients who may be admitted to a psychiatric unit for further assessment and treatment.

5. A social worker from every community care programme should be seconded for special training in sign-language with a view to having the social worker available to liaise between the deaf adults, their employers, and family.

6.   Where a number of deaf patients are resident in a large psychiatric hospital, steps should be taken to ensure that these patients are, wherever possible, brought together in the same unit to reduce the risk of social isolation and to encourage interpersonal communication.[235]

The survey that O'Boyle recommended was not performed, despite clear need,[236] but an outpatient mental health service for the deaf had been developed in 1979 by the Eastern Health Board at the request of the Department of Health, to respond to frequent requests for a specialist psychiatric service for deaf adults.[237] The service continued up until the retirement of the consultant psychiatrist providing the service, O'Boyle, in 2007.

Referrals were mainly from Dublin, the East coast region, Louth, Meath and Wicklow. The service was staffed in the early years by a consultant psychiatrist and social worker from the National Association for the Deaf (now DeafHear, www.deafhear.ie), who was fluent in Irish Sign Language and doubled as an interpreter and co-therapist. In later years, there was also a professional interpreter and community psychiatric nurse. The service was provided through one outpatient session per week in a community mental health facility at 140 St Lawrence's Road in Clontarf, Dublin. In addition, Dr Irene Aherne of Cork Regional Hospital provided a service for adults in Cork during the 1980s.[238]

In Dublin, Dr Paul McQuaid provided a psychiatric service for many years to the schools for deaf children, St Joseph's and St Mary's, on the Navan Road in Dublin, after being approached by the Dominican Sisters in Cabra to participate in a team made up of other professional colleagues from the National Rehabilitation Board and public health paediatric service. They visited Cabra fortnightly and provided a consultation forum, including evaluation of individual girls (following meetings with both teacher and pupil). The service extended to St Joseph's School and, later, Beechpark School for boys in Stillorgan, run by Sisters of Our Lady of Charity of Refuge. This arrangement continued up to the 1990s.[239]

The mental health needs of the deaf population featured again in the 2006 policy, *A Vision for Change*, which noted that 'deaf individuals', among others, 'require specific knowledge and understanding on the part of those delivering mental health services, in terms of their culture and other characteristics. The employment of professionals from a wide variety of backgrounds and cultures in mental health services is a positive step that should be taken to respond to the needs of the diverse population in Ireland':[240]

> Good communication is at the heart of mental health work. Therefore the question of language is extremely important. Good interpreters are vital not just for effective cross-cultural working, but also for ensuring access to mental health services by other individuals in the population, specifically deaf individuals and those for whom Irish is their first language. Mental health work requires interpreters who are able to interpret the 'idiom' of the patient's distress as well as the actual words used. Interpreters must be able to empathise with the patient's position and ethnic and gender conflicts are to be avoided. Children or family members of the individual in question should not be used as interpreters.[241]

Against this background, there has been a pilot Mental Health and Deafness Service in Ireland since 2005, when the National Association for the Deaf People (now DeafHear), submitted a business case proposal to the HSE, with the aim of providing an all-Ireland Mental Health and Deafness Service for profoundly deaf adults to meet their mental health needs on an equivalent basis with the hearing population. The service was commissioned in conjunction with the HSE North East acting on behalf of the former Chief Executive Officers, South East Belfast Health and Social Services Trust, and DeafHear.

The service comprises a part-time psychiatrist and one clinical nurse specialist, with Irish Sign Language interpreting, management and administrative support. By 2016, this service had seen over 400 patients but referral rates were just half the predicted level (owing, presumably, to low recognition of need) and treatment options remained severely limited.

The Mental Health and Deafness Service provides mental health assessment and support to deaf people in psychiatric hospitals and general hospital wards, homeless deaf people and deaf people in prison; newly presenting deaf service users (in outpatient clinics or on home visits); deaf adults with learning disabilities, including those in residential care; and elderly deaf people, including those in nursing homes.[242] The team works in collaboration with local mental health services, general practitioners and social workers, but has no direct access to inpatient or other resources, so effective co-working and care planning with mainstream mental health services and other agencies are vital for the effective delivery of services.

A mental health service for the deaf was also established in the Midlands region by Dr Lorcan Martin, consultant psychiatrist, and Joan O'Toole (social work clinical supervisor, DeafHear). This service is fully integrated with the local mainstream adult mental health team where, in addition to the consultant psychiatrist, the community mental health nurses and occupational therapist have trained in Irish Sign Language.[243]

More needs to be done. Dr Margaret du Feu, psychiatrist with the national Mental Health and Deafness Service and tireless advocate for better services, points out that there continues to be significant gaps in service provision; the Mental Health and Deafness Service needs to be conjoined with mainstream HSE mental health services; and each HSE area needs a part-time consultant psychiatrist with a special interest in deafness as well as other services (including interpretation support and specialist community nursing) in order to correct the historical neglect of the mental health needs of this group.

Review of the Mental Health Act 2001 (2015): Revision, Renewal, Reform

Notwithstanding these challenges in various specific areas within psychiatry, significant steps forward were proposed in March 2015 when a comprehensive review of Ireland's mental health legislation was published. This development, along with many others, benefitted greatly from the dedication and enthusiasm of Minister Kathleen Lynch who held responsibility for mental health during this period and proved to be an exceptionally effective communicator and advocate for better mental health services and legislative reform.[244]

In July 2011, the Irish government announced a review of the Mental Health Act 2001 commencing with the formation of a Steering Group to identify key areas of the 2001 Act to be examined in more detail during the second and more detailed phase of the review. The *Interim Report of the Steering Group on the Review of the Mental Health Act 2001* was published in June 2012,[245] and informed the work of the subsequent Expert Group on the Review of the Mental Health Act 2001.

The *Report of the Expert Group on the Review of the Mental Health Act 2001* was published in March 2015 and presented 165 recommendations relating to virtually all areas of the Act.[246] From an historical perspective, it is notable that this entire review process was, from the outset, to be built on 'human rights',[247] thus marking an explicit and substantial shift from similar processes in the past, which were less concerned with human rights and more concerned with welfare based provision of care.

When the final *Report of the Expert Group* was published in 2015, it duly recommended that 'insofar as practicable, a rights based approach should be adopted throughout any revised mental health legislation',[248] and that the principle of 'best interests' in the 2001 Act[249] should be replaced by 'the following list of guiding principles of equal importance' to 'be specified in the new law':

- The enjoyment of the highest attainable standard of mental health, with the person's own understanding of his or her mental health being given due respect.
- Autonomy and self-determination.
- Dignity (there should be a presumption that the patient is the person best placed to determine what promotes/compromises his or her own dignity).
- Bodily integrity.
- Least restrictive care.

These principles are historically noteworthy for their strong emphasis on autonomy and dignity.[250] The report also recommended that 'mental illness' should be defined as 'a complex and changeable condition where the state of mind of a person affects the person's thinking, perceiving, emotion or judgment and seriously impairs the mental function of the person to the extent that he or she requires treatment'.[251] This is similar, although not identical, to the redefinition of 'mental disorder' in the Mental Health Act 2007 in England and Wales, which removed the four categories in their Mental Health Act 1983 and redefined 'mental disorder' as 'any disorder or disability of the mind'.[252]

In Ireland, the *Report of the Expert Group* made a series of other recommendations including, most notably, new criteria for involuntary admission and treatment, so that for involuntary admission to occur the person would have to fulfil all three of the following criteria:

a. The individual is suffering from mental illness of a nature or degree of severity which makes it necessary for him or her to receive treatment in an approved centre which cannot be given in the community; and

b. It is immediately necessary for the protection of life of the person, for protection from a serious and imminent threat to the health of the person, or for the protection of other persons that he or she should receive such treatment and it cannot be provided unless he or she is detained in an approved centre under the Act; and

  c.   The reception, detention and treatment of the person concerned in an approved centre
       would be likely to benefit the condition of that person to a material extent.[253]

While these criteria mark an incremental change from those outlined in the 2001 Act,[254] they are in
substantial contrast with the legislation of the 1800s and early 1900s, the shift being characterised by
increased emphasis on community treatment and a requirement that detention and treatment 'would
be likely to benefit the condition of that person to a material extent'. These are important emphases,
protective of *both* the right to liberty and the right to treatment – two rights which were commonly
ignored in the past.

The *Report of the Expert Group* recommended a series of other changes including redefinitions
of 'treatment' and 'voluntary patient' (now to require mental capacity); additional protections for
patients who are not detained but lack mental capacity; mandatory multidisciplinary input into
detention decisions; earlier tribunals (to be renamed 'mental health review boards'); shorter detention
orders; various measures relating to children; more inspection of community mental facilities; better
access to information; and provisions to ensure that any detained patient who has mental capacity to
refuse ECT or medication has his or her decision respected.

Most interestingly, the *Report of the Expert Group* recommended that families should no
longer sign forms to apply for the involuntary admission of a family member, but should instead
contact an 'authorised officer' of the health service who would, 'after consultation with family/
carers where possible and appropriate, make the decision on whether or not an application for
involuntary admission of the person should be made'.[255] This change would mark a radical shift from
past practices which generally involved a family member signing a form to instigate the detention
process,[256] leading (understandably) to the impression of people being 'signed in' by their families.

As discussed elsewhere in this book (Introduction, Chapter 8), the involuntary admission
process was always more complex than that, generally involving other people in addition to families,
but this particular proposal from the Expert Group would mean that families would no longer sign
any forms as part of the involuntary admission process, although they could still express concern to
an 'authorised officer' who could then commence the procedure. This would be a shift of historical
proportions in this complex and sometimes contested process.

The *Report of the Expert Group* also presented interesting measures designed to limit the amount
of time a patient can spend in Garda (police) custody, if Gardaí are involved in the involuntary
admission process.[257] It is important that Garda involvement in this process is both permitted and
carefully regulated. A research study of 820 general practitioners in 2013 showed that one of the
key concerns about the 2001 Act centred on difficulties with transport of patients to psychiatric
centres.[258] This is a particular concern because difficulties with transport may, arguably, create an
incentive to invoke Section 12 of the legislation, which involves Gardaí in the involuntary admission
process and, if the detention proceeds, places Gardaí under an obligation to transport the patient to
the psychiatric centre. As a result, invoking Section 12 resolves transport difficulties.

Already in 2011, Gardaí were involved in 24 per cent of involuntary admissions[259] and any
further shift in that direction would repeat the mistakes of the past. More specifically, as discussed in
Chapter 2, the Dangerous Lunatic Act 1838 permitted the transfer of a person to an asylum if they

were considered dangerous and either mentally ill or intellectually disabled. This soon became the admission pathway of choice, partly because it gave the police full responsibility for transporting the individual to the asylum, which was then under an obligation to admit them.[260]

For these reasons, the stigmatising and unnecessarily punitive 'dangerous lunatic' procedure was widely abused throughout the nineteenth century.[261] It would be deeply regrettable if concerns about transporting patients to psychiatric centres under the Mental Health Act 2001 were to generate a similar reliance on involving the Gardaí, especially in an era when destigmatising mental illness is a priority.[262] On this basis, early involvement of authorised officers, rather than Gardaí, in the detention process was recommended in the *Report of the Expert Group,* which also suggested new limits for the maximum period of time that can be spent in Garda custody as part of this procedure.[263]

Despite this and other generally progressive measures in the report, it is a sobering reflection on the history and public image of psychiatry in Ireland that media coverage of the detailed, comprehensive report by the Expert Group focused strongly on the measures it suggested relating to ECT,[264] which were among the least radical and had been signalled well in advance.[265] It is particularly interesting that little attention was devoted to one of the genuinely substantial changes recommended in the report, which was the elimination of the principle of 'best interests' from the legislation,[266] a move which would contrast sharply with developments in neighbouring jurisdictions.[267] In Northern Ireland, for example, the Mental Capacity Bill 2014 (which proposed fusing mental health legislation and capacity legislation into a single bill) included a requirement that every act must be done or decision made 'in the person's best interests'.[268]

The Northern Irish bill provided detailed guidelines to prevent over paternal interpretation of 'best interests', including a legal requirement to 'have special regard to' (a) the patient's (P's) 'past and present wishes and feelings (and, in particular, any relevant written statement made by P when P had capacity); (b) the beliefs and values that would be likely to influence P's decision if P had capacity; and (c) the other factors that P would be likely to consider if able to do so'.[269] There was also a legal requirement to 'consult the relevant people about what would be in P's best interests' and 'take into account the views of those people' (if practicable).[270] This duly led to the Mental Capacity Act (Northern Ireland) 2016, which received Royal Assent on 9 May 2016.

In England and Wales, the Mental Health Act 2007 included 'patient wellbeing and safety' as a principle[271] and the Mental Health (Care and Treatment) (Scotland) Act 2003 included 'the importance of providing the maximum benefit to the patient' in its principles.[272] The McManus Review did not propose changing this in Scotland,[273] and nor did the Mental Health (Scotland) Act 2015.

This is an important issue. The history of psychiatry is replete with examples of various actors (state, private, medical) taking actions which were societally convenient but of questionable benefit to the mentally ill. A clear requirement for benefit to the patient is a critical element in any mental health legislation that genuinely seeks to protect rights and focus public, professional and political attention on the need to provide services that are effective, efficient, beneficial and empowering for the mentally ill.

The lessons of history are stark and disturbing: if the best interests of the person are not at the centre of decision making, then other interests will be served.

8

The Future of Psychiatry
in Ireland

The position arrived at today is unique in the history of psychiatry. Modern treatments frequently reduce the duration of the illness and a good measure of social recovery can be achieved in many cases where complete cure is not possible. An era of considerable hope has arrived. Old ideas are being discarded or challenged. Doctors, nurses and public alike display a greater interest than ever before. Mental health has taken a leading part on the world stage.

Commission of Inquiry on Mental Illness, *Report of the Commission of Inquiry on Mental Illness* (1966)[1]

The early years of the twenty-first century saw considerable governmental and public attention focus on Irish mental health services, most notably in 2006 with the publication of *A Vision for Change*[2] and full implementation of the Mental Health Act 2001 (Chapter 7). These developments were generally positive, placing renewed emphasis on mental health policy and protecting the rights of people involuntarily admitted to psychiatric hospitals and units. This enlightened rhetoric has changed remarkably little since the 1966 *Report of the Commission of Inquiry on Mental Illness* (above) and much good has come of it over the past fifty years, as services steadily evolved along the line suggested, at least to a certain degree.

However, despite these reforms real challenges persist.[3] This was entirely predictable, given that the history of psychiatry in Ireland, as is the case elsewhere, has always been shaped by unstable cycles of therapeutic enthusiasm, disillusionment and reform. Despite minor variations in the rhetoric surrounding such reforms, the end result over past centuries was all too often the same: further embedding of institutional care, essentially regardless of the enlightened motivations underpinning the impulse to reform. Did the most recent wave of reform at the start of the 2000s adhere to that pattern?

Inevitably, at this short remove, this wave of reform seems different to those that preceded it. In the first instance, overall perspectives shifted considerably over preceding decades, especially during the late 1900s. Few of the asylum-promoting reformers of the 1800s could have possibly predicted that clinicians and historians in the late 1900s and early 2000s would look back on the enormous nineteenth-century asylums and find them difficult to understand let alone justify. Even in the late 1900s, the slow demise of the psychiatric institution as an archetypal feature of Irish life continued to raise complex issues both within psychiatry and across society. Put simply, closing psychiatric hospitals generated significant anxiety and ambivalence among staff, patients and local communities, all of whom had become accustomed to these large institutions in their midst.[4] As Walsh points out, 'the psychiatric hospitals, particularly in rural areas, were a fertile source of employment in places where jobs were not easily come by. They were strenuously competed for and often passed down in families'.[5] The demise of the psychiatric hospitals was complex, nuanced and generated many mixed feelings.[6]

Some of these themes were explored in Sebastian Barry's extraordinary novel, *The Secret Scripture*, which also provided a rare, insightful portrayal of a psychiatrist as the era of Ireland's large public asylums finally drew to a close.[7] Another, equally interesting perspective was explored in the Irish feature film, *My Name is Emily* (Newgrange Pictures and Kennedy Films, 2015),[8] which was written and directed by Simon Fitzmaurice,[9] and explored the complex ramifications of one man's period of inpatient psychiatric care. Most interestingly, the film presented a memorable portrayal of a consultant psychiatrist, Dr Golding, played by Barry McGovern: while many psychiatrists might not quote Plato quite as readily as Dr Golding did, the portrayal was nonetheless a subtle one, suffused with empathy and understanding about the impact of psychological suffering and psychiatric hospitalisation on the broader family.

Against this background, it is useful to ponder on which features of early twenty-first century mental health care might puzzle future historians after another century has passed, and the extent to which the period of reform at the start of the 2000s differed from its predecessors, if at all.

First, in terms of psychiatric admissions, Ireland's psychiatric admission rates clearly continued to fall in the early 2000s, as *A Vision for Change* and the Mental Health Act 2001 were introduced: in 2002 there were 23,677 admissions to inpatient psychiatric care and by 2011 this had fallen to 18,992.[10] This trend remained strong despite the economic problems Ireland experienced from 2008 onwards: in 2010 the rate of psychiatric admission was 463 per 100,000 population; in 2011 this fell to 414; and by 2014 it had fallen again to 388.[11]

While this trend is certainly in the right direction from the perspective of the history of psychiatry in Ireland, it is still worth posing the question – as has been posed elsewhere[12] – as to whether the reduction in inpatient numbers in Ireland has finally gone too far. The right to liberty is increasingly respected, but has the right to treatment suffered?[13] Is the balance now swinging too far in the other direction, away from the over assertive, custodial care of the past and towards neglect of the mentally ill, under the guise of 'community care'?

There is evidence that this might well be the case.[14] In April 2016, Dr Martha Finnegan wrote in the *Irish Times* about performing emergency, out-of-hours ('on call') psychiatric assessments as a psychiatry trainee in Ireland:

> Let me tell you what it's like to be the junior doctor on call for psychiatry, in any
> hospital. You assess these four people with their distraught families in the emergency

department and you try to understand their problems so you can make a judgement call on the level of risk they pose. You know they all need admission for treatment, but there are only two free beds on your unit. Even this is stretching your nurse colleagues to the limit, they're short on numbers and you know that by admitting these people you're creating a dangerous situation for patients and staff, but you have no choice, and they support you. You ring around all the other hospitals in your region or beyond, to see if there are any beds in other hospitals, and eventually find a safe place for your third patient. One person has to be sent home with their bewildered family and a referral for an outpatient clinic. You are awake for several nights wondering if they'll make it. [...]

As far as I know, nobody in mental health services around the country was looking for eternity pools or Nespressos for acute psychiatry units. We want to be allowed to continue providing services that save lives. Maybe even build on them so that finally mental health care will be as well-developed as other medical services. We're not looking to reinvent the wheel, just to bring services up to scratch.[15]

Finnegan's powerful article continued a long tradition of Irish psychiatrists advocating for better services for patients (as repeatedly demonstrated in this book) and appeared in the context of a particular public and political discussion about mental health services funding[16] – a discussion that reinforced (yet again) the facts that deinstitutionalisation needs to be accompanied by increases in community services *and* that inpatient care still needs to be available and accessible when required. A 2016 'impact evaluation' of *A Vision for Change*, published by the Psychiatric Nurses Association and the Faculty of Nursing and Midwifery in the Royal College of Surgeons in Ireland, also showed significant deficits in implementing the policy with negative consequences for the quality of mental health care in Ireland.[17] Clearly, there is still much to be done to ensure that the vision outlined in *A Vision for Change* is truly realised[18] and is supported by a widening and deepening of a full range of mental health services, including relatively neglected therapies such as psychoanalysis.[19]

As regards Ireland's *involuntary* admission rate, the 2015 Expert Group on the Review of the Mental Health Act 2001[20] noted that 'there were 2,132 admissions on an involuntary basis [in Ireland in 2013],[21] which is a rate of 46.67 per 100,000 total population in 2013 and this compares favourably with other jurisdictions; e.g. England had a rate of 53.8 per 100,000' in 2013.[22] On this basis, the reforms of the opening decade of the 2000s saw Ireland's psychiatric admission rates continue to fall and rates of involuntary admission remain relatively low too. These features alone would be sufficient to mark out this period of reform as different to its more distant predecessors in at least one important respect: recent reforms have not resulted in an increase in psychiatric admissions or the growth of psychiatric institutions. The start of the 2000s was, then, at least to this extent, a clear continuation of the deinstitutionalisation process that commenced officially in the 1960s with the *Commission of Inquiry on Mental Illness*,[23] but had really started to emerge some years prior to that.

But what about other indices of mental health service activity in the early 2000s? Rates of prescription of psychiatric medication were a topical issue during this period, both internationally and in Ireland, with much criticism focusing on allegedly excessive or inappropriate use of medications such as antidepressants.[24] One study of antidepressant use across the EU, however, found that the proportion of Irish adults who used antidepressants in 2010 was similar to, or slightly lower than, the EU average (7.2 per cent), with the highest use recorded in Portugal (15.7 per cent) and the lowest in Greece (2.7 per cent).[25]

Intriguingly, Ireland's average or low rate of antidepressant use remained evident even during the economic recession that commenced in 2008: in 2006–7 (prior to the recession), 4.4 per cent of Irish adults had used antidepressants over the previous year, and in 2010–11, in the midst of the recession, this figure was not substantially different, at 4.8 per cent.[26] In Northern Ireland (part of the UK) the rate of antidepressant use in 2010–11 was almost three times that in the Republic (12.0 per cent, compared with 4.8 per cent) and the rate of sedative and tranquilliser use almost double (11.0 per cent, compared with 6.5 per cent). The College of Psychiatrists of Ireland has emphasised the importance of appropriate and judicious use of medication, as well as other therapies.[27]

Notwithstanding these figures and developments, controversies about the use of medication in Ireland persist.[28] Ultimately, in a given case, the role of psychiatric medication, if any, will vary considerably from person to person, depending on the features of the person's mental health problems, response to other forms of therapy (psychological therapies, social support, etc.), and the person's own preference. A similarly modulated approach is required in relation to the use of psychiatric diagnostic systems such as the APA's *Diagnostic and Statistical Manual of Mental Disorders (Fifth Edition)*[29] and the WHO's *International Classification of Mental and Behavioural Disorders (Volume 10)*,[30] which also generated continued controversy in Ireland during this period.[31] Much of this ongoing criticism stems from the alleged misuse of these diagnostic systems, despite both the APA[32] and WHO[33] clearly emphasising that these systems are not to be used in a tick-box fashion and that individual patient stories always take precedence. Ultimately, such systems are essential for research purposes and help protect human rights by ensuring clinical accountability in involuntary care; judicious, compassionate use is both necessary and wise.[34]

With regard to population wellbeing, the early 2000s were a time of considerable challenge in Ireland, owing not least to the economic recession of the late 2000s. One study, the European Social Survey, assessed happiness across the Irish population over this period, asking participants to rate their own happiness on a scale from 0 (extremely unhappy) to 10 (extremely happy).[35] In 2005 the mean happiness score was 7.9, but by 2007 this had decreased to 7.7 and it continued to fall thereafter, reaching 7.5 in 2009[36] and 6.8 in 2012, as the effects of the recession were felt most widely.[37] Analysis of more recent European Social Survey data, however, performed for the purpose of this book, showed that, in 2014, mean happiness in Ireland had recovered significantly to 7.2, in line with the country's consolidating economic recovery. By 2016, Ireland was ranked 19th happiest country in the world out of 157 countries assessed in the *World Happiness Report* from the Sustainable Development Solutions Network.[38] The importance of actively maintaining and promoting mental wellness was convincingly underlined in 2015 by Dublin clinical psychologist Dr Keith Gaynor in his book *Protecting Mental Health*.[39]

Even in the face of these developments, however, the greatest controversy in mental health care throughout the early 2000s, and the one that appears most likely to define this period, relates to social exclusion of the mentally ill, especially those with enduring mental illness. Schizophrenia is a good example, as there is long standing evidence that the illness is associated with reduced social interaction, diminished rates of marriage and reproduction, low educational attainment and unemployment.[40] While these outcomes certainly do not occur in every case, and are neither inevitable nor core features of the illness, there is clear evidence of a systematic increase in risk of these and other negative outcomes among many people with schizophrenia.

In addition, people from lower socioeconomic groups tend to present with schizophrenia at an earlier age than those from higher socioeconomic groups, and this is important because early age at first presentation is generally associated with more severe forms of illness. People from lower socioeconomic groups also have a longer duration of untreated illness prior to first presentation and this too is associated with more severe illness and poor treatment outcome. In Ireland, as is the case elsewhere, mental illness is also strongly associated with homelessness,[41] imprisonment[42] and difficulty accessing justice after being a victim of crime,[43] further emphasising the links between mental illness and various forms of social exclusion and discrimination. The killing, in 1997, of two elderly patients of St Brendan's Hospital in sheltered accommodation near the hospital is, perhaps, the most dramatic example of the mentally ill becoming victims of violent crime in Ireland.[44]

These phenomena are not integral elements of mental illnesses such as schizophrenia, but are attributable to the ways in which schizophrenia is patterned, interpreted and treated by society, and the diminished access to health, social services and justice commonly experienced by the mentally ill. These factors, allied with the enduring stigma of mental illness,[45] constitute a form of 'structural violence' which greatly magnifies the effects of mental illness in the lives of patients and their families, resulting in increased disability, denial of rights, erosion of opportunity and broad based social exclusion.[46]

Regrettably, the story outlined in this book demonstrates that these problems are by no means new. Over a century ago, in 1911, Dr William R. Dawson, in his 'presidential address [to the MPA] on the relation between the geographical distribution of insanity and that of certain social and other conditions in Ireland', pointed to a strong association between 'insanity' and 'pauperism', and various other social and economic features of Irish society.[47] The social marginalisation of the mentally ill was an established problem even then, stretching back to well before the emergence of the Irish asylums during the 1800s, and even earlier.

The fact that these problems are long standing and well recognised does not mean that they are inevitable features of severe mental illness, or that there are no solutions. The remedies are, however, complex, and lie not just in better mental and physical health care but also in the generation of political will to address the entrenched social problems faced by the mentally ill. The enhancement of individual agency is a vital element in this process and will of necessity involve continual reform of national mental health legislation (of particular relevance to involuntary patients); improvement of advocacy, empowerment and guardianship processes (of particular relevance to those with diminished mental capacity at certain times); and development of more meaningful governance, accountability and quality procedures across health and social services.[48] Approaches based on enhancing direct political participation are also vital, including development of more effective interest groups to advocate for those with mental illness, and voter registration programmes for the mentally ill, their families, carers and other stakeholders.[49]

Better medical care is also needed. Life expectancy is dramatically reduced in people with schizophrenia compared to the general population: on average, men with schizophrenia die 15 years earlier, and women 12 years earlier, than the rest of the population.[50] The excess mortality is not explained by unnatural deaths: the most common causes are heart disease and cancer. The rise in mortality is worse in those who do not receive antipsychotic medication. This adds to the body of evidence that mental health services require continual development. It is essential that implementation of *A Vision for Change* proceeds and services evolve to reflect developing research bases for specific modalities of care, which can be life-saving.[51]

The resourcing of mental health services required to facilitate these changes was – rightly – the subject of considerable discussion in the early 2000s. In October 2015, the College of Psychiatrists of Ireland laid out the positon in no uncertain terms:

> Mental illness causes both social and financial damage. The cost to the nation of poor mental health (leaving aside the human costs to individuals and society) is over 2% of GNP [gross national product]. As a percentage of overall health spend, the budget for mental health has reduced from 13% in the 1980s to 6.2% in 2015. This is still scandalously low compared to other countries (UK 12%, Canada and New Zealand 11%). This is a human rights issue and should be seen as such by anyone who cares about the health of our nation. The recommendation from *A Vision for Change* was to gradually build up to 8.24% of the health budget[52] but the time frame foreseen for this is past.[53]

The College went on to present 'a list of key points for consideration by Government', including 'the provision of community based mental health teams for patients of all ages on a 24/7 basis nationally' if 'inroads are to be made into the continued morbidity and mortality due to suicide, self-harm, chronic mental illness and alcohol and substance abuse'.

Mental health services remained a feature on the political agenda in December 2015[54] and the general election in February 2016 saw considerable focus on the topic in media[55] and political campaigns.[56] Mental Health Reform organised a campaign titled 'Our State of Mind', urging voters to ask canvassers to prioritise mental health and to request those elected to take specific steps to improve mental health services and promote good mental health, starting in childhood.[57] It is interesting that much of this discussion related to improving services and expanding care, reflecting welcome emphasis on the importance of access to treatment. There was considerably less public discussion about mental health legislation during this period, despite significant and long awaited developments in this field, both in Ireland and internationally. There interesting developments merit consideration next, chiefly from the perspective of human rights.

Human Rights

The international background to human rights in mental health is of direct relevance to recent developments in Ireland. In 1991 the UN published its *Principles for the Protection of Persons with Mental Illness and the Improvement of Mental Health Care*, which articulated the rights to receive the best mental health care available; to be able to live, work and receive treatment in the community; and to have access to mental health facilities which are appropriately structured and resourced (Chapter 6).[58]

Following from this, in 2005 the WHO published a systematic set of human rights standards for national mental health legislation in its *Resource Book on Mental Health, Human Rights and Legislation*, which presented a detailed statement of human rights issues which, according to the WHO, need to be addressed at national level.[59] The following year, full implementation of the Mental Health Act 2001 brought Ireland into much greater (but still incomplete) accordance with these standards.

In its *Resource Book*, the WHO set out a 'Checklist for Mental Health Legislation' detailing specific human rights standards which, according to the WHO, need to be met in each jurisdiction. These standards were clearly based on previous UN and WHO publications and centre on the provision of mental health care that is reasonable, equitable and in accordance with international standards. Inevitably, mental health legislation plays a key role in meeting these standards. In Ireland, civil mental health legislation (chiefly the Mental Health Act 2001) meets 80 (48.2 per cent) of the 166 relevant standards for adults.[60] Areas of relatively high compliance include definitions of mental disorder, procedures for involuntary admission and treatment, and clarity regarding offences and penalties. Areas of medium compliance relate to competence, capacity and consent, and certain aspects of oversight and review (which exclude long term voluntary patients). Areas of low compliance relate to promoting rights, voluntary patients (especially non-protesting, incapacitated patients) and protection of vulnerable groups.

As discussed in Chapter 7, the 2015 *Report of the Expert Group on the Review of the Mental Health Act 2001* presented a series of recommendations for further revisions to Irish mental health legislation.[61] This was followed by the Mental Health (Amendment) Act 2015, which commenced in February 2016 and eliminated the words 'or unwilling' from Sections 59(1)[62] and 60[63] of the 2001 Act that govern ECT and medication (for more than three months) for involuntary patients. As a result, ECT and medication for more than three months can be administered to an involuntary patient only if the patient is 'unable' (i.e. lacks the mental capacity) to provide consent; a capacitous refusal cannot be overridden.

This is a significant change. Under the 2001 Act, a person with 'mental illness, severe dementia or significant intellectual disability' can be detained under either Section 3(1)(a) or 3(1)(b). Section 3(1)(b) focuses on treatment, and requires that 'the reception, detention and treatment of the person concerned in an approved centre would be likely to benefit or alleviate the condition of that person to a material extent'. Therefore, if a detained patient possesses mental capacity and declines medication and/or ECT, the 2015 amendments mean that the patient cannot receive involuntary medication and/or ECT, and might therefore no longer fulfil the 'benefit' criterion of the Section

3(1)(b) detention criteria. As a result, unless nursing and other forms of care (other than medication and ECT) meet the 'benefit' criteria, the detention order will, presumably, have to be revoked and the patient will have the option of leaving the inpatient facility.

The situation is slightly different for someone detained under Section 3(1)(a) because this includes no 'benefit' criterion: a person with 'mental illness, severe dementia or significant intellectual disability' can be detained under Section 3(1)(a) solely because 'the illness, disability or dementia' results in 'a serious likelihood of the person concerned causing immediate and serious harm to himself or herself or to other persons'. There is no legal requirement for treatment to benefit the person in order for such a detention to continue. In this situation, the 2015 amendments mean that if such a person possesses mental capacity and declines treatment, he or she can be detained indefinitely simply by virtue of the fact that he or she is thought to present a risk as a result of mental disorder *but cannot be treated*.

This dilemma would be alleviated, at least in part, if, as recommended by the 2015 Expert Group on the Review of the Mental Health Act 2001, criteria for involuntary admission were revised to require that, in *all* cases, 'reception, detention and treatment of the person concerned in an approved centre would be likely to benefit the condition of that person to a material extent' (Chapter 7).[64]

In practice, these dilemmas are likely to be rare, however, not least because few persons detained under the 2001 Act are likely to possess mental capacity to decide about treatment. Moreover, nursing and other forms of treatment (apart from medication and ECT) might well meet the 'benefit' criterion for some patients detained under Section 3(1)(b). Nonetheless, the 2015 amendments still present a sharp contrast with the position in England and Wales, where the Mental Health Act 2007 explicitly retained the possibility of involuntary treatment for a detained patient with mental capacity based on the idea that such treatment might, on rare occasions, be in the interests of public safety.[65] That is no longer the case in Ireland.

At the international level, the most significant human rights development in the early 2000s was the adoption of the UN Convention on the Rights of Persons with Disabilities (CRPD) by the UN General Assembly.[66] This convention commits signatory countries 'to promote, protect and ensure the full and equal enjoyment of all human rights and fundamental freedoms by all persons with disabilities, and to promote respect for their inherent dignity'.[67] It specifies that 'persons with disabilities include those who have long-term physical, mental, intellectual or sensory impairments which in interaction with various barriers may hinder their full and effective participation in society on an equal basis with others'.

In the context of psychiatry, it seems clear that this definition does not include all people with mental illness, not least because many mental disorders (e.g. adjustment disorder) are not 'long-term'.[68] The CRPD does not, however, present its definition of 'persons with disabilities' as a comprehensive one but states that the term 'persons with disabilities' *includes* people with 'long-term' impairments; others, presumably, might also fit the definition. As a result, it is likely that some people with mental disorder meet the definition at least some of the time (e.g. a person with an intellectual disability or chronic schizophrenia) but others do not (e.g. a person with adjustment disorder).[69] The CRPD also states 'that disability is an evolving concept and that disability results from the interaction between persons with impairments and attitudinal and environmental barriers that hinders their full and effective participation in society on an equal basis with others';[70] this decouples the definition of 'persons with disabilities' from any specific diagnoses and moves it into a social context (a most welcome move).

Ireland signed the CRPD in 2007 but, as of 2016, had not ratified it.[71] From a mental health perspective, the CRPD raises two key issues for Ireland, relating to involuntary admission under the Mental Health Act 2001, and mental capacity legislation.

First, with regard to involuntary admission, the CRPD specifies that 'the existence of a disability shall in no case justify a deprivation of liberty'.[72] If certain persons with mental disorder (e.g. some people with chronic schizophrenia) fit the UN definition of 'persons with disabilities', then Ireland's Mental Health Act 2001 is inconsistent with this provision, given the Act's clear links between mental disorder, risk and involuntary admission. This is also the case for mental health legislation in England, Wales, Scotland, Northern Ireland and most other jurisdictions: all violate this article of the CRPD.

In 2009, the UN High Commissioner for Human Rights objected explicitly to any link between 'preventive detention' and risk to self or others stemming from 'mental illness':

> Legislation authorising the institutionalisation of persons with disabilities on the grounds of their disability without their free and informed consent must be abolished. This must include the repeal of provisions authorising institutionalisation of persons with disabilities for their care and treatment without their free and informed consent, as well as provisions authorising the preventive detention of persons with disabilities on grounds such as the likelihood of them posing a danger to themselves or others, in all cases in which such grounds of care, treatment and public security are linked in legislation to an apparent or diagnosed mental illness.[73]

This UN position stands in remarkable contrast to the history of mental health services in Ireland and most other countries, where a degree of involuntary care has always been based on the presence of mental illness and associated risk. It is not, however, clear that persons with mental illness are 'persons with disabilities' under the CRPD, and acute psychiatric admission is not necessarily 'institutionalisation'. In any case, denial of care (especially to the most distressed) on the basis of the CRPD would appear grossly inconsistent with the fundamental aims and purpose of the Convention: people with disabilities should be entitled to all the levels and modalities of care that are available to the general population, without distinction of any description. On this basis, abolishing involuntary care in order to comply with the CRPD would be a historically radical, counterproductive and, it would seem, unlikely step.

The second key issue that the CRPD raises for Ireland from a mental health perspective relates to capacity legislation, which became the subject of considerable activity and attention in the early 2000s.[74] On 30 December 2015, the Assisted Decision-Making (Capacity) Act 2015 was signed by President Higgins and scheduled for commencement in 2016.[75] The 2015 Act is designed to replace the outdated Ward of Court system by which, under the Lunacy Regulation (Ireland) Act 1871, the wardship court gained jurisdiction over all matters in relation to the 'person and estate' of an individual who is deemed to lack mental capacity. In addition, the ward of court framework did not adequately define 'capacity'; was poorly responsive to changes in capacity; made unwieldy provision for appointing decision makers; and had insufficient provision for review.[76]

The 2015 Act places the 'will and preferences' of persons with impaired mental capacity at the heart of all decision making in relation to 'personal welfare' (including healthcare) and 'property and affairs'.[77] Capacity is to be 'construed functionally' (i.e. it is person-specific, time-specific and decision-specific)[78] and all interventions must be 'in good faith and for the benefit of the relevant person'.[79] The Act outlines three levels of supported decision making: 'decision-making assistant', 'co-decision-maker' (joint decision making) and 'decision-making representative' (substitute decision making).[80] There are procedures relating to 'enduring powers of attorney'[81] and 'advance healthcare directives'; under the latter, a 'refusal of treatment' can be legally binding, while a 'request for a specific treatment' must 'be taken into consideration'.[82] If the person's treatment is regulated under Part 4 of the Mental Health Act 2001 (i.e. the person is detained, or 'is the subject of a conditional discharge order' under Section 13A of the Criminal Law (Insanity) Act 2006), the advance healthcare directive is not legally binding, except 'where a refusal of treatment' relates 'to the treatment of a physical illness not related to the amelioration of a mental disorder', in which case 'the refusal shall be complied with'.[83] The person can appoint 'a designated healthcare representative' to help interpret an advance healthcare directive.

Overall, the 2015 Act reflects a significant advance in placing the 'will and preferences' of the person at the heart of decision making. This development is long overdue and increases Ireland's compliance with the CRPD, although compliance will still be incomplete, even following the 2015 Act.[84] Nonetheless, the 2015 Act is considerably more workable than the 2013 Bill that preceded it.[85] Key challenges include the complex decision making required by patients, healthcare staff, Circuit Court judges and the director of the proposed Decision Support Service, and the implementation of advance healthcare directives. Ideally, these would form part of a broader model of advance care planning that would incorporate the flexibility required for unknowable future circumstances and advances in care.

The issue of logistics is critical. In 2013, there were 503,509 discharges from medical inpatient care in Ireland[86] and studies from other jurisdictions indicate that between 30 per cent[87] and 51 per cent[88] of medical inpatients lack mental capacity to make healthcare decisions. In 2014, there were 17,797 psychiatric admissions in Ireland[89] and studies from other jurisdictions indicate that 29 per cent of psychiatry patients lack mental capacity to make healthcare decisions.[90] In addition, there were approximately 27,000 people in nursing homes in Ireland in 2014,[91] and studies from other jurisdictions indicate that over 60 per cent of these people lack mental capacity to make healthcare decisions.[92] These are large numbers.

In theory, all of these people, as well as patients who lack mental capacity in primary care, will require support under the 2015 Act. While it is likely that a decision making assistant will be sufficient for most, it is not at all clear how many will require greater levels of support or how many Circuit Court hearings will be needed.

The challenges are substantial. Not least of these is the need to balance the principle of autonomy with the principles of beneficence and mutuality, to result in healthcare that is consistent with the person's values and is effective, humane and dignified. Such challenges are, however, inevitable with any development of this magnitude, which seeks to systematise many of the principles that already define good healthcare practice in Ireland but will be placed on a more explicit footing when the 2015 Act is commenced. These are historically important changes, which need to be operationalised in an effective, empowering fashion, especially for particular groups, such as people with intellectual disability and co-morbid mental disorder.

This group merits particular attention in the context of the 2015 Act. In 2006, *A Vision for Change* recommended that 'delivery of mental health services to people with intellectual disability should be similar to that for every other citizen'.[93] Services 'should be provided by a specialist mental health of intellectual disability (MHID) team that is catchment-area based. These services should be distinct and separate from, but closely linked to, the multidisciplinary teams in intellectual disability services who provide a health and social care service for people with intellectual disability'. In 2016, over a century after Norman at the Richmond warned that 'it is neither wise nor humane to neglect this class as they are neglected in this country',[94] it is hoped that the 2015 Act will strengthen the agency of the intellectually disabled and their families, and assist in providing them with mental health care, as well as further protecting and promoting their rights more broadly in a society that has ignored their voices too often in the past.

Voices of Change in Irish Psychiatry

Against the background of this increased emphasis on human rights, the latter part of the twentieth century and early twenty-first century saw the emergence of new and exciting voices of change in Irish psychiatry and mental health care. In particular, several mental health service user groups were either founded or expanded substantially during this period and these organisations continue to provide extensive information and support to persons affected by mental disorder, their families and carers.[95]

The Mental Health Association of Ireland (www.mentalhealthireland.ie) was established in 1966, with Dr Tom Lynch (later Professor of Psychiatry at the Royal College of Surgeons in Ireland) as one of its founders[96] and chairperson.[97] Mental Health Ireland, as it is now called, is a national voluntary organisation comprising a network of 92 mental health associations throughout Ireland, all led by volunteers. Its associations fundraise to organise outings and events for those struggling with mental health problems in their communities. The organisation's core staff includes a chief executive officer and support staff who operate at a national level, as well as a team of area development officers in regional areas of the country. The area development officers support the mental health associations and deliver awareness-raising initiatives and targeted education and training programmes on mental health issues in a variety of settings in local communities.

Shine (formerly 'Schizophrenia Ireland'; www.shine.ie) is another national organisation dedicated to upholding the rights and addressing the needs of those affected by mental ill health. Shine aims to empower people with mental ill health and their families through support, information and education. It advocates for social change, promoting and defending the right of all those affected by mental ill health to equal rights and quality services. The organisation promotes the development of self-help groups for people with mental ill health and their family members and carers; empowers through support, information and education; promotes rights to person-centred services which support recovery; engages in public awareness activities aimed at challenging stigma and discrimination; and seeks to influence positive policy changes in the provision of mental health services.

Another support and advocacy organisation, Aware (www.aware.ie), was founded in 1985 by Dr (later Professor) Patrick McKeon, a psychiatrist, and a dedicated team of volunteers, many of whom had personal experience with depression or bipolar disorder. The organisation developed in response to a clear need for information, understanding and support among persons affected by depression or bipolar disorder and their families. The organisation expanded across Ireland and seeks to create a society where people affected by stress, depression, bipolar and mood disorders are better understood, supported, free from stigma, and encouraged to access appropriate therapies. The organisation's work involves information, education and support and it organises group meetings, a telephone and email support service and a number of programmes based on principles of cognitive behavioural therapy.[98] Aware also works in schools and offers education and training programmes in workplaces nationwide.

Another organisation, Mad Pride Ireland (www.madprideireland.ie), was founded by Mr John McCarthy, a gifted, powerful advocate for the mentally ill who argued for the normality of madness, a theme duly taken up by thousands of supporters at events in Cork, Tullamore and Portlaoise.[99] The Mad Pride approach is based on the idea that the best way to advance understanding of issues surrounding mental health is by engaging the community through active participation in a fun environment. This is achieved by holding family events that are inclusive, fun and suitable for everyone, including children, teenagers, adults and families. The aim of such events is to demonstrate that 'madness' is a feature of everyday life; that it affects everyone in one way or another; and that it can be dealt with lovingly and openly.

The National Service Users Executive (www.nsue.ie), was formed with the aim of informing the National Health Service Directorate and the Mental Health Commission on issues relating to service user involvement and participation in planning, delivering, evaluating and monitoring services, as well as implementing best practice guidelines at the service user and provider interface. GROW (www.grow.ie) is another mental health organisation that helps people who have suffered, or are suffering, from mental health problems. Founded in Australia in 1957, GROW has a national network of over 130 groups in Ireland and its principal strength lies in the support members give each other from their own experience.

The Mental Health Trialogue Network Ireland (www.trialogue.co) is a community development initiative in Irish mental health. Its aim is to empower communities to become proactive in communicating about mental health through an open dialogue and participatory process called 'trialogue'. These groups seek to change the perception that only those who work in the field of mental health are experts in mental health: mental health concerns everyone, regardless of background and experience.

Hearing Voices Ireland (www.voicesireland.com) was founded in Limerick in 2006 by Mr Brian Hartnett, with the aim of fostering acceptance of voice hearing as a valid human experience. By 2015, there were 'hearing voices' groups in Cork, Donegal, Dublin, Kerry, Kildare, Kilkenny, Longford, Tipperary and Belfast. This development is part of a larger international 'hearing voices' movement, with some 29 national networks and over 270 national, regional, and local hearing voices networks, groups, research and training centres, and trainers throughout the world. The movement reflects an exceptionally powerful reinterpretation of the experience of hearing voices, which used to be invariably associated with major mental illness but is now subject to more nuanced interpretations, formulated chiefly by those having such experiences (rather than mental health professionals).[100] This movement reflects the development of psychiatry and mental health care in new and exciting directions.

Also founded in 2006, Mental Health Reform (then named the Irish Mental Health Coalition; www.mentalhealthreform.ie) emerged at a time when there was little public advocacy on behalf of better mental health services, little political will for reform, and little presence of mental health as an issue covered in the media.[101] The coalition was founded in part in response to the recognition in *A Vision for Change* that 'there is no equivalent advocacy for improving mental health services as exists for various other health services'.[102] With a shared objective to campaign for the improvement of mental health services in Ireland, the establishment of the coalition reflected its members' collective desire to ensure the new mental health policy translated into real change for people using mental health services.

Initially established with just five members, Mental Health Reform soon grew to more than 50 member organisations, including most of the national mental health not-for-profit organisations and professional associations – along with many other not-for-profit organisations who have a strong interest in better mental health supports for their clients. The aim of the coalition is to provide a coordinated public voice advocating for reform of the entire mental health system. More than 10,000 people are also connected to the coalition through social media, reflecting a growing movement for better mental health services. In 2014, more than 22,000 individuals signed the coalition's pre-budget petition to Government.

In parallel with these developments, various clinicians and academics have come to the fore in articulating alternative and improved visions for mental health services in Ireland and elsewhere. Dr Pat Bracken, for example, has written extensively and convincingly on the subjects of trauma,[103] moving beyond the current paradigm in psychiatry,[104] critical psychiatry[105] and 'postpsychiatry'.[106] Postpsychiatry finds its roots in the concept that there is diminishing belief in the idea that science and technology can resolve human and social problems, and that psychiatry needs to move beyond its modernist paradigm in order to, among other matters, engage with the growing power of service users.[107] Against this background, postpsychiatry emphasises cultural and social contexts; places ethics before technology; and seeks to minimise medical control of coercive interventions in psychiatry.

As the history presented in this book demonstrates, this issue of culture in mental health care is an especially important one not only within psychiatry but also in broader society and, especially, in shaping the relationship between psychiatry and society. This relationship is, in turn, particularly important in connection with one of the most troubling and widely discussed issues in contemporary psychiatry and mental health care: suicide.

Suicide in Ireland

Suicide is intentional self-killing[108] and it features in every society for which there is recorded history. The history of suicide and self-harm in Ireland merits a separate book in itself both because the topic is an important one and because its early history in Ireland is significantly under researched.[109]

Fahy, in 1991, provided an interesting overview of religious and other dimensions of suicide from Ireland's past, noting the suicide of Deirdre in Irish mythology and the self-sacrificial death of Cú Chulainn.[110] Patient suicide was a recurring feature of asylum life in the 1800s and 1900s, and there have been studies of suicides in Irish asylums,[111] narratives of poverty in suicides between the Famine and First World War,[112] the history of political suicide by hunger strike among the Irish, and various other specific aspects of the topic.[113] Despite these valuable contributions, however, the absence of reliable statistics from earlier periods greatly hampers efforts to establish rates of suicide and trends in Ireland over past centuries. Further research is needed to determine these statistics (as best as possible) and explore evolving societal and medical attitudes since the 1700s and earlier.

In the early 1900s, it was generally thought that Ireland had a low suicide rate,[114] which is said to have increased significantly as the twentieth century progressed, with some fluctuation. Osman and Parnell, for example, demonstrate that suicide rates showed a slow rising trend between 1864 and 1913, but declined in 1914, as rates of suicide were notably reduced during the First World War, especially in men (whose rate declined by 13.6 per cent during the war).[115]

In 1954, the Central Statistics Office reported the annual average number of deaths from suicide in Ireland was 89 between 1921 and 1930 (yielding a rate of 3.0 per 100,000 population per year), 98 between 1931 and 1940 (3.3 per 100,000 population per year), and 77 between 1941 and 1950 (2.6 per 100,000 per year).[116] Suicide was likely under reported during this period and, in 1967, the Central Statistics Office introduced a new form (Form 104) to improve recording accuracy and facilitate study. In 1997, Swanwick and Clare reported that the total suicide rate had increased steadily since 1969, the increase being chiefly attributable to a rise in male suicides.[117] During much of this period, suicide was a felony under Irish law and attempted suicide a misdemeanour; both offences were abolished in 1993 with the Criminal Law (Suicide) Act.[118]

More than three decades earlier, in 1962, the Samaritans (www.samaritans.org; telephone [Ireland and United Kingdom]: 116123; email: jo@samaritans.org) were established in Ireland and their volunteers continue to provide a listening service to anyone who contacts them; many, but not all, of those who contact them are suicidal. By 2016, there were 20 Samaritans branches across Ireland with 2,400 active volunteers doing extraordinarily skilled and selfless work; their contribution to Irish society is quiet, consistent and utterly invaluable.

In 1996, the Irish Association of Suicidology (www.ias.ie) was founded by Dr John Connolly, Dr Michael Kelleher and Mr Dan Neville TD, to work with community, voluntary and statutory bodies to inform, educate and promote positive suicide prevention policies.[119] It is a forum where all organisations can come together and exchange knowledge regarding any aspect of suicidology gained from differing perspectives and experiences.

There are now a number of sources of information and statistics about suicide, including the National Suicide Research Foundation (www.nsrf.ie), an independent, multidisciplinary research unit that investigates the causes of suicide and deliberate self-harm in Ireland. From a policy perspective, the National Office for Suicide Prevention (NOSP; www.nosp.ie) was set up in 2005 within the HSE to oversee the implementation, monitoring and coordination of *Reach Out: National Strategy for Action on Suicide Prevention, 2005–2014*, Ireland's first national suicide prevention strategy.[120] NOSP is now a core part of the HSE National Mental Health Division, strongly aligned with mental health promotion and specialist mental health services.

NOSP's 2014 *Annual Report* analysed trends in suicide and self-harm in Ireland from 2004 to 2014, for which it presented provisional figures.[121] The report noted that the rate of suicide in 2004 was 12.2 per 100,000 population per year, which had fallen to 10 by 2014, following some fluctuation over the course of the decade. While suicide remains a deeply concerning problem, it is notable that provisional figures showed 459 suicide deaths in 2014, down from 487 in 2013 (despite likely growth in population).[122] The 2014 rate in men (16.1 per 100,000 per year) was substantially higher than that in women (3.9). While under-reporting likely remains an issue, it is also noteworthy that the rate of undetermined deaths (which might well include some suicides) also fell during this period, from 2.0 per 100,000 population per year in 2004 to 1.3 in 2014. The rate of self-harm also fluctuated over this time, but by 2014 the rate was again equivalent to that in 2002.

The precise effects of the economic recession of the late 2000s on suicide and deliberate self-harm during that decade remain unclear,[123] but particular and legitimate concern has emerged about suicide and deliberate self-harm in young people, especially young men,[124] and children. Professor Kevin Malone, a leading researcher in this area, has, with colleagues, noted that suicide rates in children rose between 1993 and 2008, especially among boys.[125] Despite the overall decrease in suicide in Ireland in the early years of the twenty-first century, then, rates of youth suicide and deliberate self-harm remain a real source of concern, especially as rates of youth suicide are persistently very high in Ireland compared to other EU countries.[126] This merits greater investigation and coordinated psychological, social and educational intervention and support for young people.

In 2010, the College of Psychiatry of Ireland (as it was then called) noted that 'effective treatment of depression is an important means of reducing suicide rates' and addressed the much-discussed role of antidepressant medication in adults in some detail:

> Untreated depression can have a fatal outcome. Those experiencing moderate to severe depression frequently describe having thoughts of self-harm. Antidepressants are effective in the treatment of depression. The effective treatment of depression is an important means of reducing suicide rates. A huge volume of research in recent years has failed to establish a causal link between antidepressant use and suicide. At an individual level, the period early in treatment may be a time of relatively high risk, as treatment tends to start when the person's depression is severe and treatment takes some weeks to work. As treatment takes effect and energy and motivation return, people who have recently commenced antidepressant treatment may be more able to act on suicidal thoughts that are inherent to their condition. That the early recovery period is potentially a period of increased risk for suicidality is something of which all doctors

should be aware. The College of Psychiatry of Ireland, in unison with the advice of the Irish Medicines Board, recommends close monitoring of all individuals commenced on antidepressant therapy. There is no evidence of a link between antidepressant use and homicide.[127]

In 2015, a new suicide prevention strategy was launched, *Connecting for Life: Ireland's National Strategy to Reduce Suicide, 2015–2020*, involving preventive and awareness-raising work with the population as a whole, supportive work with local communities and targeted approaches for priority groups.[128] The strategy proposed high quality standards of practice across service delivery areas and – most importantly – an underpinning evaluation and research framework. The budget for NOSP was increased from €3.7 million in 2010 to €11.5 million in 2016.[129]

Also in 2015, Derek Beattie, a social researcher, and Dr Patrick Devitt, a psychiatrist, made a substantial contribution to the public conversation about suicide with their book *Suicide: A Modern Obsession*,[130] and the following year Dr Declan Murray, another psychiatrist, noted the profound difficulties with estimating suicide risk and recommended that management of suicidal thoughts, feelings and behaviours should focus on reducing and tolerating emotional pain.[131] Pieta House (www.pieta.ie), a service for the prevention of self-harm or suicide, saw in excess of 5,000 people suffering from suicidal ideation or engaging in self-harm in 2015 alone, and in 2016 its founder, Joan Freeman, was one of three Taoiseach nominees to the Seanad Éireann chosen by Fianna Fáil leader, Micheál Martin.[132]

Despite such increased public and professional discussion and recognition, however, much remains to be done to provide effective, coordinated support to those at risk of suicide and those bereaved. In 2016, it was estimated that there were up to 300 different groups providing support for those at risk.[133] Clearly, a coordinated, effective and compassionate approach is needed, linking community and state resources with each other in order to optimise efforts to address a problem which has been a long standing issue in the history of psychiatry in Ireland, as has been the case elsewhere. Approaches rooted outside of core mental health services will be vital in this process: addressing alcohol problems and other addictions, reducing homelessness and improving access to social care.

The Future of Psychiatry in Ireland

Psychiatry has always been subject to waves of therapeutic enthusiasm and reform, some of which are positive and progressive, and others which are at best questionable and at worst actively harmful. Consistent with this history, the opening decades of the twenty-first century saw not only changes in mental health policy and law, but also a significant shift in therapeutic language, with increased emphasis on the 'recovery model' of mental health services. As I hope this book demonstrates, this enhanced emphasis on recovery is to be greatly welcomed, even if the most recent re-articulation of this idea initially conceptualised 'recovery' as being in direct opposition to what was termed a 'medical model' of treatment, a regrettable rhetorical construct, presented as inconsistent with 'recovery'.

In 2005, the Mental Health Commission published a 'discussion paper' about the 'recovery model',[134] followed in 2007 by a qualitative analysis of submissions on this theme.[135] In 2008, the Commission went on to publish a 'framework for development' of 'a recovery approach within the Irish mental health services', outlining six 'pillars' of recovery: leadership; person-centred and empowering care; hope-inspiring relationships; access and inclusion; education; and research and evaluation.[136] This approach duly facilitated the progressive integration of the *Advancing Recovery in Ireland* movement across certain mental health services over the following years.[137]

The EOLAS project (www.eolasproject.ie) is one especially notable development. Initiated in 2011 by the Kildare West Wicklow mental health team, with Dr Pat Gibbons, consultant psychiatrist, as chairperson of the project group, EOLAS (the Irish word for 'knowledge') was developed through collaboration with users of mental health services, family members, mental health support organisations, clinicians and academia. Its objective is to design, deliver and evaluate two mental health information and support programmes to assist in the recovery journey of those diagnosed with schizophrenia spectrum and bipolar disorders and also their family members and friends. EOLAS programmes are co-facilitated by a peer facilitator and a clinical facilitator: clinicians bring their professional expertise and family members and service users are experts by experience. Following a positive evaluation of the programme by the School of Nursing and Midwifery at Trinity College Dublin (2015), this programme is now being rolled out nationally. Initially funded by Genio (www.genio.ie), EOLAS is today part of the HSE programme for mental health.[138]

Notwithstanding these developments, and similar initiatives elsewhere, mental health care continues to provoke comment from within the services and without, in relation to services in general[139] and certain specific areas, such as child and adolescent mental health care,[140] in particular. One of the key unresolved issues is the precise relationship between the management of substance misuse problems in relation to general mental health services. There is an historical basis to this issue, as, over the 1800s and 1900s, problems with alcohol were commonly linked with Irish asylums and the emergent profession of psychiatry.[141] This persisted despite various other initiatives to address this issue, such as inebriate reformatories.[142]

The link with psychiatry was, however, never without controversy: in December 1907, Norman at the Richmond reported on three particularly challenging admissions of women from Mountjoy Prison, who 'were more or less habitual drunkards [...]. It is a pity that there is not some mode of dealing with people of this class besides sending them to ordinary district asylums. Ordinary asylum care and treatment have little or no permanent effect, and seem to be as inoperative almost as imprisonment with a view to effecting any real cure'.[143] In 1854, over 12 per cent of patients admitted to the asylum in Belfast were 'intemperate'.[144]

More detailed histories of various aspects of the management of alcohol problems are provided by Malcolm,[145] Bretherton,[146] Finnane,[147] and Butler, who chronicles the religious temperance movement and various other aspects of alcohol in Ireland, as well as the emergence of Alcoholics Anonymous, which held its first Irish meeting in November 1946 with the support of St Patrick's Hospital.[148] Given the associations between alcohol and mental disorder, self-harm and suicide,[149] it is unsurprising that psychiatric hospitals remained deeply involved in the management of alcohol problems up to the present day. At St Patricks, Dr John Cooney pioneered a specialist programme for the management of alcohol-related disorders.[150] On a national level, Cooney obtained a grant from the then Minister for Health, Donogh O'Malley, to found the Irish National Council on Alcoholism. With a role in education and research, the organisation's first executive director was Mr Richard Percival, who had held a similar post in the UK's National Council on Alcoholism and in 1946 had attended the first Irish meeting of Alcoholics Anonymous. In 1971, at St John of God Hospital in Stillorgan, Dr Pat Tubridy (1936–2013) was appointed as consultant psychiatrist. There he developed the Richard Pampuri Unit for the treatment of alcohol problems, incorporating extensive and progressive therapeutic, research and educational initiatives.[151]

In more recent years, the balance of emphasis has shifted to outpatient management of alcohol and substance misuse problems, combined with renewed public health measures to reduce the harm caused by alcohol[152] and other substances of abuse, such as cannabis.[153] Nonetheless, the relationship between substance misuse services and mental health services in Ireland remains unclear. In 2006, *A Vision for Change* stated that 'mental health services for both adults and children are responsible for providing a mental health service only to those individuals who have co-morbid substance abuse and mental health problems'.[154] The implication was that services for persons with substance misuse problems alone should not be located within mental health services; this was described by a group of experts as a retrograde step for people with drug and alcohol addiction.[155] While relationships between mental health and substance misuse services do work well in certain areas, this remains an area in need of greater role clarification and cooperation.

Role clarification is also relevant to general adult psychiatry services more broadly. In June 2016, Drs Leonard Douglas and Larkin Feeney published an analysis of 'thirty years of referrals to a community mental health service' in the *Irish Journal of Psychological Medicine* and found that referral rates had increased 20 fold over the period studied (1983–2013), with a significant decrease in the proportion of referrals relating to psychosis and an increase in referrals relating to various other matters.[156] Douglas and Feeney conclude that the work of community mental health teams is increasingly associated with emotional crises rather than severe mental disorder, a trend which reflects a significant shift in the role of psychiatric services and a profound change in societal expectations of psychiatry over the past three decades. They add that services, although now more multidisciplinary than in the past, have not been adequately resourced to meet these changing demands.

Such changing demands are undoubtedly part of a broader international trend for people to medicalise a wide range of psychological problems,[157] many of which would be better addressed outside of medical settings. In this context, the relationship between primary and secondary mental health care is critical and needs to work well in order to ensure appropriate care is delivered to those who really need it when they need it most. There are, however, problems. One 2016 study, performed by Dr Claire Collins and colleagues and published by the Irish College of General Practitioners (www.icgp.ie), studied 104 patients who, over a six month period, had a mental health consultation with an out-of-hours primary care service: among those referred onward to hospital services, some 37.7 per cent did not attend.[158] Most mental health care is delivered in primary care so it is clearly vital that the relationship between primary and secondary care works efficiently and well.

Another significant challenge in the early twenty-first century relates to mental health services for migrants, asylum seekers and refuges. Traditionally, Ireland was more accustomed to outward rather than inward migration but between 1995 and 2000 approximately 250,000 persons migrated into Ireland: the aggregate figure for immigrants over this five year period represented some 7 per cent of Ireland's entire population.[159] Migration is associated with particular challenges to mental health, especially among forced migrants or those who experience torture.[160]

Many countries report increased rates of involuntary psychiatric admission among migrants and persons of minority ethnic groups,[161] but figures from Dublin, interestingly, suggest that rates of involuntary admission among persons not born in Ireland do not differ from those for persons born in Ireland.[162] There is, however, evidence that migrants experience difficulty accessing voluntary mental health care, and this is a real concern. While Spirasi (www.spirasi.ie), an organisation located on Dublin's North Circular Road, provides vital psychological and social support to migrants and survivors of torture,[163] and the HSE published a *National Intercultural Health Strategy, 2007–2012* in 2008,[164] the mental health needs of minority ethnic communities, including the Traveller community,[165] still present a challenge that must be met more inclusively by Irish mental health and social services in the future.[166]

This is an important, growing issue.[167] In May 2016, Drs Molly O'Connell, Richard Duffy and Niall Crumlish noted, in *BJPsych International*, that the number of people seeking asylum in Ireland was increasing, with 3,271 applications for refugee status in 2015, more than double the figure for 2014 and triple that for 2013.[168] They recommended that a national programme of mental health care for refugees and asylum seekers should commence with the establishment of specialist regional teams, focusing on specialised clinical care, training and advocacy.

The mental health needs of Ireland's ageing population is another area in need of further thought and planning.[169] In October 1988, a Working Party on Services for the Elderly produced a 'policy for the elderly' titled *The Years Ahead ... A Policy for the Elderly*,[170] building on a 1968 report *Care of the Aged*, which had concluded that 'it is better and probably much cheaper, to help the aged to live in the community than to provide for them in hospitals or other institutions'.[171] Twenty years later, the 1988 Working Party noted that the 1968 policy had 'recommended improvements in existing services, payments and the provision of new services and allowances where they identified a need. Many of these recommendations have been implemented and, as a result, services for the elderly have been transformed'.[172]

The 1988 policy went on to propose a series of further measures relating to 'comprehensive and coordinated' services for the elderly; maintaining health; housing; 'care at home', in the community and in general hospitals; community hospitals; and the need for partnership.[173] The policy placed particular emphasis on 'care of the elderly mentally ill and infirm' and articulated the importance of specialist services and screening for dementia.[174] Three years later, however, Walsh pointed to a significant divergence between policy and practice:

> Services for the elderly and the mentally handicapped in this country have much in common. For neither is there a comprehensive nationwide, rationally-controlled and operated coherent system of care-delivery despite recent policy documents in both cases. What does exist is a ramshackle ad hoc jumble of poorly-orientated inputs without an overall policy objective or planned programme approach. Unfortunately all this rebounds

on the psychiatric service so that, as a general catchall for fringe medical and social problems, psychiatry has taken up the slack. [...] Apart from refusing admissions there is very little psychiatrists themselves can do. Help must come from without through the development of appropriate services for mentally handicapped and elderly.[175]

A 1998 review raised further issues about both the pace of change and the adequacy of the vision outlined in *The Years Ahead*.[176] Nonetheless, in 2003, O'Neill and O'Keefe reported that, despite a relatively low level of popular advocacy for older people, specialist medical and psychiatric services had indeed developed in Ireland and geriatric medicine had become the largest medical specialty in hospital practice.[177] Ongoing challenges related to policy implementation, funding, staffing, and development of community and long term care.

In 2006, *A Vision for Change* outlined a clear vison of 'mental health services for older people', noting that in 2001 there were 21,500 people over the age of 65 with dementia in Ireland and this was projected to increase to 55,750 in 2036.[178] Similarly, the number of people aged 65 or over with depression was projected to rise from 47,300 in 2001 to 122,540 in 2036. The accuracy or otherwise of these projections remains to be seen, however, it now appears that gains in life expectancy at age 65 years are accompanied by equivalent gains in years free of any cognitive impairment (i.e. free of dementia or early dementia), decreased years with mild or moderate–severe cognitive impairment, and gains in years in excellent or good self-perceived health.[179] There is, nonetheless, still need to devote attention to the needs of ageing persons, and especially those with intellectual disability and their carers.[180]

In April 2013, the government's *National Positive Ageing Strategy* placed considerable emphasis on mental health in later life and included the maintenance of 'physical and mental health and wellbeing' as a 'national goal'.[181] The strategy also noted the broad range of factors relevant to achieving this 'national goal', especially in the context of mental health:

> While dementia and Alzheimer's disease are a significant cause of disability among the older population, depression is the most common mental health problem in those aged 65 years and over. It is of note that recent Irish research found a high prevalence of undiagnosed depression and anxiety in the older population. Consistent with physical health, a range of factors contribute to good or poor mental health, such as environmental, economic and social determinants, including the physical environment, geography, education, occupation, income, social status, social support, culture and gender.[182]

Some months later, in December 2013, the College of Psychiatrists of Ireland published its *Workforce Planning Report 2013–2023*, noting that 'old age psychiatry' is 'an expanding area and requires consideration to be given to the number of specialists in old age psychiatry that will be required to meet the needs' of this population.[183] More specifically, the College stated that only approximately 50 per cent of the required consultant psychiatrist posts needed for old age psychiatry work were currently provided.

Looking more broadly at the future of psychiatry in Ireland, the College, in its lucid, forthright report, concluded that Ireland needs to 'move to a situation where we have 800 consultants, and the number of psychiatric trainees required to meet future manpower planning needs for these 800 consultants':[184]

> Within Europe the number of consultant psychiatrists per head of population varies from 30 per 100,000 population in Switzerland, to 1 per 100,000 in Albania and Turkey. When looking at total numbers of psychiatrists (consultant and NCHD [non-consultant hospital doctors; e.g. trainees]) per 100,000 in OECD [Organisation for Economic Co-operation and Development] countries, Ireland, at 19 per 100,000, ranks below all other northern European countries, with consultant numbers at 8 per 100,000 [...]. We recommend an increase of consultant numbers to 16 per 100,000. We also recommend that the number of NCHDs in psychiatry be matched to the number required to train this number of consultants and to provide training for future general practitioners.[185]

One of the key ways to address the staffing deficit and retain NCHDs and consultants in Ireland is through the further development of academic psychiatry. As outlined in Chapter 6, academic psychiatry expanded considerably in Ireland in the late 1900s and early 2000s, even though a research-oriented Irish Institute of Psychiatry has still not yet materialised as such.[186] There have, however, been other developments and expansions in academic psychiatry in Ireland over this period. A Graduate Entry Medical School was established at the University of Limerick in 2007 and offers a four year medical degree programme open to graduates from any discipline. Professor David Meagher was appointed as foundational professor of psychiatry and has particular expertise in delirium,[187] an interest shared by his colleagues including Dr Maeve Leonard (1968–2015), a particularly gifted researcher and teacher.[188]

And as the 2000s have progressed, Ireland has continued to produce world leading research not only in the area of delirium but also in psychiatric genetics,[189] brain imaging[190] and a range of other domains.[191] Other research has touched on a wide variety of diverse topics (e.g. the psychological effects of being sentenced to capital punishment in Texas)[192] and there have been excellent books by psychiatrists and medical writers such as Dr Stephen McWilliams[193] and Dr Conor Farren,[194] both of whom substantially enrich their chosen fields through their work.

The Future of the History of Psychiatry in Ireland

The early 2000s saw the emergence of renewed emphasis on the academic study of the history of psychiatry in Ireland. In 2006, the Centre for the History of Medicine in Ireland was established in the UCD School of History and Archives and is a partnership with medical historians at the University of Ulster. The UCD Centre seeks to promote the study of the social and cultural history of medicine in Ireland and has established 'psychiatry and mental health' as one of its collaborative research themes, with Dr Catherine Cox as UCD director of the Centre. In parallel with this, there has been an increase in academic and general publications on the history of mental health services in Ireland (see Bibliography), as well as various meetings and seminars devoted to specific themes.

Particular projects by various other groups have focused on particular areas. For example, the 'World Within Walls' project aimed to remember the history of St Davnet's in Monaghan, and explore its evolution from its opening in 1869 up to its present role as a modern community mental health services campus. This project was commissioned by the HSE and delivered by Stair: An Irish History Company Ltd., between February 2014 and February 2015, and was designed as an outreach project to open up the history of the hospital to the community.[195]

The history of mental health services has also featured prominently in several programmes in national media, including the *History Show* on RTÉ Radio 1,[196] and, on television, *The Asylum*, written and directed by Alan Gilsenan for Yellow Asylum Films (RTÉ 1, September 2005);[197] *Behind the Walls*, produced and written by Mary Raftery for Misha Films, with researcher Sheila Ahern (RTÉ 1, September 2011);[198] and *Ár Intinn Eile* ('An Irish State of Mind') directed by Brendan Culleton and Irina Maldea for Blinder Films (TG4, September 2014).[199] A number of memoirs have also explored mental illness and its management, including Kate Millett's *The Loony Bin Trip*,[200] Anthony Scott's *Is That Me? My Life with Schizophrenia*,[201] Mary and Jim Maddock's *Soul Survivor: A Personal Encounter with Psychiatry*,[202] and Vanessa Grattan's *Hidden Grief: Words from a Journey of Hopelessness to a Pathway to Hope and Survival*.[203]

Other books, while not memoirs by patients, touched upon the history of psychiatry and asylums in various different and important ways, including Eibhear Walshe's memoir *Cissie's Abattoir*,[204] Fergus Cleary's memoir *In A World Apart*,[205] and Margaret Hawkins' *Restless Spirit: The Story of Rose Quinn*.[206] The history of Maurice Fitzgerald, sixth Duke of Leinster, admitted to Craighouse Asylum, Edinburgh in 1909, was expertly explored by Terence Dooley in his fascinating volume, *The Decline and Fall of the Dukes of Leinster, 1872–1948: Love, War, Debt and Madness*.[207]

From a broader literary perspective, there has been long standing interest in the relationship between James Joyce and various psychiatric themes,[208] and asylums or mental illness feature (to varying degrees) in the work of John Millington Synge,[209] William Butler Yeats,[210] Samuel Beckett,[211] Seán O'Casey,[212] Kate O'Brien,[213] William Trevor,[214] Liam O'Flaherty,[215] Tom Murphy,[216] and, more recently, Sebastian Barry (in *The Secret Scripture*),[217] among others.[218] Interestingly, asylums and mental illness are comparatively less prominent in earlier Irish literature, with the notable exceptions of *Melmoth the Wanderer* (1820)[219] by Charles Maturin (whose grandfather succeeded Swift as Dean of St Patrick's Cathedral and sat on the original board of St Patrick's Hospital)[220] and the work of Sheridan Le Fanu (1814–1873), especially *The Fortunes of Sir Robert Ardagh* (1838) and *The Rose and the Key* (1871).

Themes relating to psychiatry in Ireland have been explored in a small number of publications focusing on theatre[221] and film,[222] but there is still scope for further work in these areas, and in the fields of poetry, music, song, architecture and visual culture. The power of such work, when mindfully undertaken, was demonstrated by Irish artist Alan Counihan's 'Personal Effects: A History of Possession' at Grangegorman and elsewhere.[223]

From historical, social and architectural perspectives, one of the other undeniable legacies of the Irish asylums is the presence of large mental hospital buildings in numerous towns across Ireland and their gradual reinvention as hotels,[224] educational institutions[225] or healthcare facilities.[226] Reimagining and repurposing these buildings in socially useful fashions is one important way to pay tribute to their complicated, conflicted pasts,[227] especially as the beauty of much of the restoration work draws sharp attention to the neglect of the past.

Other legacies include the archives of these institutions, *all* of which merit careful preservation both in order to remember the lived experiences of patients and staff in these places, and to facilitate systematic academic research and enquiry.[228] The preservation of these legacies is critical if we are to continue to deepen our understanding of this troubled, troubling aspect of Ireland's past.

There are also, however, other, psychological legacies of Ireland's asylum system that present much deeper challenges to Irish society and identity. The key questions centre on the very existence of the asylum system in the first instance: why did it become so large? Why did it persist for so long? What should have been done differently? By whom? When? How? And what does it all mean for Irish mental health services and society today?

As explored throughout this book, the enormity of the Irish asylum system cannot be attributed to high rates of mental illness in Ireland or solely (or even substantially) to the desire of healthcare professionals to enhance their stature; the story is far more complex and interesting than that. The more substantive roots of the disproportionately large Irish asylums, like the roots of other troubled institutions in Irish life (orphanages, industrial schools, laundries, prisons), are fundamentally located in the nature of Irish society itself, as well as in various factors explored earlier in this book, including (1) increased recognition of the problems presented by mental disorder during the 1800s and 1900s; (2) mutually reinforcing patterns of asylum building and psychiatric committal, underpinned by continual, obsessional legislative change; (3) unpredictable shifts in diagnostic and clinical practices during the nineteenth and twentieth centuries; and (4) possible epidemiological change, owing to sociodemographic changes in Irish society and/or unidentified biological factors leading to altered patterns of mental disorder; e.g. increased longevity leading to increased survival of the mentally ill, rather than any true increase in incidence of mental disorder (Chapter 3).

It is both interesting and relevant that the asylums developed more or less independently of other health services in Ireland, owing to the fact that asylums, unlike general hospitals, found their origins in prisons (as well as workhouses) and that the Roman Catholic Church was generally absent from the development of asylums (but not general hospitals). There is, as a result, a complex relationship between the numbers of people in prisons and the numbers in inpatient psychiatric facilities in many countries, including Ireland; broadly, as asylum numbers fall, prison numbers rise, but to a lesser degree.[229] The precise nature of this relationship is not fully clear, however, and other factors are likely involved and possibly even of greater significance.[230]

Nonetheless, it is clear that a certain interchangeability of institutions has been a notable feature in Ireland and elsewhere[231] and might well have varied in nature or magnitude over past centuries: even as the asylums continued to expand in the late 1800s and early 1900s, for example, other institutions were established, including inebriate reformatories[232] and borstals.[233] The emergence of the Irish asylums was part of these broader waves of institutionalisation to a certain degree, but was also separate in other respects, and distinctive in its own way.

From an historiographical perspective, there is a pressing need to examine the effects of these trends and developments at the level of individual patients in the asylums, mental hospitals and, indeed, prisons. The journalist Mary Raftery articulated this need in a May 2005 *Irish Times* article focusing on the ill-fated Health (Mental Services) Act 1981 (Chapter 6):

> The 1981 Act provided a range of safeguards and independent appeals for people locked up against their will in psychiatric hospitals. There had been numerous stories of people wrongly committed to psychiatric hospitals, often locked up there for years, with no rights and no way out. Successive governments had promised reform.
>
> You'd be right to think that all of this sounds familiar. We have recently [2005] heard much about wrongful committal to psychiatric hospitals, particularly around the case of John Manweiler. Earlier this month he was awarded almost €3 million by the High Court for having been unlawfully detained and wrongly prescribed with medication.
>
> Back in 1981, three years before John Manweiler's ordeal at the hands of the psychiatric profession began, the Oireachtas had passed the Health (Mental Services) Act precisely in order to prevent what happened to him and many others like him.
>
> That Act had been voted through in the teeth of opposition from psychiatrists, who regarded the establishment of independent tribunals (with non-medical members) to review their diagnoses and committal orders as an unwarranted interference in their professional expertise. This opposition explains much of what became the ultimate fate of a measure designed to protect patients against the abuse of their rights by the psychiatric profession.
>
> All Acts of the Oireachtas contain a provision whereby they must be enacted (or activated) by the relevant government minister. In the case of the 1981 Act, the minister for health at the time, Fianna Fáil's Michael Woods, simply never signed the section to enact it, and nor did any of his successors. So, while it existed as an Act, in reality it never became law.
>
> It is, apparently, unique in this regard.[234]

While aspects of Raftery's article – rightly – drew reasoned, reasonable and necessary responses from psychiatrists at the time,[235] her comments still highlight the importance of individual patient stories in elucidating the human impact of reform or, indeed, failure to reform Ireland's mental health systems and laws.[236] While the present book has included certain patients' stories insofar as they can be identified over the past two centuries (and I would have liked to uncover many more), there is still a great deal of work to be done in this regard, both in terms of historical research and broader public enquiry. Fundamentally, the stories of most patients' experiences of psychiatric services, both positive and negative,[237] are still largely untold and unexplored, and this needs to change.

With regard to a collective, *public* process of exploration or enquiry to rectify this deficit and further elucidate our psychiatric institutional past, Fintan O'Toole, writer and editor, has called for an 'historical commission' into the state run mental hospitals:

> In truth the major feature distinguishing mental hospitals from the rest of the system of social repression is obvious: they were not run by the Catholic Church. The church is not blameless in that it created the social and moral norms that allowed for this kind of systematic cruelty. But the mental hospital system was overwhelmingly run by the State and local authorities.
>
> In 21st century Ireland it does not offer an outlet for pent-up resentment of church control. It tells us, uncomfortably, about ourselves: our State that sustained the system, our families that used it, our towns that came to regard the asylums as economic assets.
>
> The scale and complexity of the abuse of mental hospitals is such that there is no easy way to address this last part of the system that shaped our society. But there is an obvious way to begin. The State should establish a historical commission to create an official narrative of what happened to so many of its citizens. It is time at least to acknowledge this great wrong and to stop driving on past those grim grey walls.[238]

Back to the Future:
Hearing Voices

The asylums were not hidden institutions. They were large and visible, if foreboding. There were tens of thousands of inpatients; tens of thousands of staff members; tens of thousands of suppliers of goods and services. Despite these numbers, there is still a gap in our social history that can only be filled by the voices of all of those people: patients, families, staff.[239]

Psychiatrists have consistently sought greater openness and public discussion of these matters,[240] often with limited success. In 2004, a study by the Irish Advocacy Network, aiming to inform the development of the new mental health policy (published in 2006 as *A Vision for Change*), presented findings from interviews with 100 mental health service users currently using acute admission wards or long stay facilities.[241] Reported issues included lack of information relating to treatment and rights, overreliance on medication, lack of access to alternative treatments, lack of choice, deficiencies in community based services, lack of meaningful occupation or housing, poverty, and feeling isolated. Unsurprisingly, from an historical perspective, many of these issues relate to broader society as much as they do to psychiatry, to social services as much as to mental health services.

Nonetheless, it remains the case that the voices of patients and families ('experts by experience') have not been sufficiently heard within mental health services.[242] Encouragingly, recent years have seen considerably more public discussion about mental health and illness in Ireland, with key opinion leaders such as Niall Breslin, sports star, musician and author of *Me and My Mate Jeffrey: A Story of Big Dreams, Tough Realities and Facing My Demons Head On*,[243] speaking openly about mental health problems and solutions. Similarly, Lily Bailey, model, journalist and former Trinity student, has written compellingly about recovery from severe obsessive compulsive disorder.[244] There is a need for similar public discussion about a broad range of conditions such as personality disorder, schizophrenia, bipolar disorder and various other psychological problems and mental disorders.[245]

There is also a need for greater exploration of the history of mental health services in Ireland and, especially, the societal impact of the asylums over past decades. The mental hospitals affected not only those admitted to them and their families but also those who provided care, often in difficult circumstances, and those who sought to change the system, with varying degrees of success. Ultimately, the story of the Irish mental hospitals is relevant to everyone who cares about the kind of society we have lived in for the past two centuries, the kind of society we live in today, and the kind of society we want to shape for the future.

There are no grounds for complacency. As psychiatrist Professor Patricia Casey notes, 'our proclivity to institutionalise continued even after other countries were dismantling their asylums':

> More than four decades later in 2011, the late Mary Raftery (*Behind the Walls*, RTÉ 1), identified similar overcrowding but also misdiagnosis. So far none have uncovered systematic physical or sexual abuse. This is not to say that it may not have happened and that other abuses may not also have occurred, such as neglect.
>
> Recently there has been a surge of writing concerning the human rights issues involved in treating those with mental illness (Brendan Kelly, *Irish Journal of Psychological Medicine* 2014),[246] no doubt reflecting the heartfelt concerns of the profession to helping those it treats.
>
> So, let us have an inquiry into the asylums of the past and into current psychiatric practices. I believe that the obvious failings of the past have been rectified. But, no profession must ever be complacent. If there are continuing abuses, either by commission or omission, driven by economics or politicisation, then we must hear about these and correct them.[247]

This book aims to make a contribution to this process of historical exploration. In writing this book, I have inevitably made editorial decisions about which topics to explore in depth and which to mention in passing. I have, for example, focused explicitly on the history of psychiatry *in Ireland* and I do not explore the considerable achievements of Irish mental health professionals in other countries,[248] mental illness among Irish migrants abroad,[249] Irish people currently being detained and treated in UK psychiatric facilities,[250] or the stories of high-profile Irish patients abroad, such as Violet Gibson (1876–1956) who shot Benito Mussolini in Rome on 7 April 1926 and died in psychiatric care in Northampton (on 2 May 1956),[251] as did Lucia Joyce, daughter of writer James Joyce (on 12 December 1982).[252] Nor does this book examine the relationship between civil violence and psychiatry in Northern Ireland,[253] the extent and underpinnings of post-asylum 'trans-institutionalisation' of the mentally ill in other institutional settings,[254] or the detailed histories of the disciplines of clinical psychology, occupational therapy (Chapter 5) and social work, all of which have helped modernise Irish mental health services in recent decades.

The emergence of novel and highly effective models of service provision, such as Social Anxiety Ireland (founded in 1998 by senior clinical psychologist Odhran McCarthy; www.socialanxietyireland.com), also merits further study, as do the internal dynamics of various government departments and bodies concerned with mental health[255] and the evolving mental health policies of political parties (albeit that most are distinctly moveable feasts). The issue of funding also merits deeper, dedicated consideration: in 2016, it was reported that the mental health budget had increased from €711 million in 2012 to €827 million in 2016 (a 16 per cent increase).[256] Walsh and Daly note, however, that in 1960–1 20.8 per cent of Ireland's non-capital health budget was devoted to mental health, yet by 2002 this had fallen to 6.9 per cent,[257] and in 2015, this stood at 6.2 per cent.[258] The dynamics underpinning this fluctuating governmental commitment merit closer examination from the perspectives of both public administration and political studies.

Much as I would have liked to investigate all of these issues in greater depth, the present work is intended as a book of medical history, rather than a work rooted in governmental studies, social history, feminist theory,[259] postmodernism, socialist thought or any of the other possible approaches to a topic as rich as this one. There is, of course, much to be gained from many more retellings of this story from all of these different perspectives with, arguably, an especially compelling case for a doggedly Foucauldian version of the tale, which has been lacking in the Irish literature to date.[260]

There is also a need for deeper analysis of various things that did *not* occur in the history of psychiatry in Ireland including, for example, the general absence of the Roman Catholic Church from the systematic provision of mental health care for so long (Chapter 3). Healy argues – convincingly – that the Catholic Church still had an important influence in various ways, through its opposition to psychoanalysis and behaviourism and its overall influence on health policy and Ireland more generally.[261] But it is still interesting that the Catholic Church did not proactively enter the area of mental health care, as it did physical healthcare and education; this requires further thought. There is also a need for deeper analysis of the failure of psychoanalysis to transform the psychiatric profession in Ireland as it did elsewhere (Chapter 5),[262] and the relative weakness of the anti-psychiatry movement in Ireland in the 1970s and 1980s, although more critical, constructive and forward looking voices have now, thankfully, started to emerge (see above).

Ultimately, it would be most satisfying if this book acted, at least in part, by stimulating counter discourses created by others working in this and related fields, addressing aspects of this history which are not covered in this book, exploring the limits of this book's methodological approaches, and affirming, refining or challenging its conclusions. If this occurs, then this book will have served one of its central purposes: to stimulate broad based discussion about the history of psychiatry in Ireland. There are many ways of telling this story: this book is mine.

There remains, however, ample scope for other stories and there are many more themes in need of deeper consideration. For example, how, precisely, did religion affect the development of mental health services in Ireland, especially the gradual transition from a Protestant ethos to a more Roman Catholic one in the early 1900s?[263] We know this transition was not smooth;[264] further enquiry is needed, especially from the perspective of patients.[265] How did class and gender affect these processes and the patients upon whom they impacted?[266] Was there a language divide between asylum patients and staff and, if so, did language-based subcultures emerge? More recently, have moves towards community care simply replicated asylum-style power relationships or have they resulted in genuine liberation?[267] These themes may be difficult to tease out, but they are all the more important for that.

What is clear, however, is that a simple narrative of victimhood is insufficient to reflect the complexity of the asylums, which brought a mixture of care and custody, treatment and suffering, belonging and isolation, compulsion and negotiation.[268] Nor, as Walsh demonstrates, is it sufficient simply to see the asylums as a straightforward means of social control.[269] Smith makes a similar observation:

> Any interpretation of the lunatic asylum as essentially a monolithic instrument of social control does an injustice to many of its practitioners. Madness was (and is) rather more than a blatant manifestation of deviance. It constituted deep human suffering, likely to be accompanied by risk and danger both to the sufferer and to other people. The twin ideals of 'cure' and 'custody' were not impositions of those empowered to deal with the insane. On the contrary, they were the natural responses to the challenges presented by people who were, by turn, threatening and tormented. Treatment methods, arrangements for managing patients, and the environment within the institution have to be considered in this context.[270]

Smith also notes the roles of communities and families in determining thresholds for admission:

> The early nineteenth-century asylum was not a receptacle for those who were merely deviant, odd, eccentric or socially unacceptable. It catered largely for people who manifested a serious psychological disturbance or major intellectual deficit. Their condition and behaviour would have reached the point where the apparent risk of harm to the sufferer, to other people, or to property meant that their presence within family or community could not be sustained without an unacceptable level of discomfort or stress.[271]

Certification was, as Cox points out, a multi-factorial process subject to many influences, including legal procedures which effectively placed insanity on public display.[272] Discharge, too, was a multi-layered process, often hinging critically on families and, when the family could not or would not be found, the patient might well die in the asylum.[273] And, as Malcolm emphasises, the initial committal often involved many actors and was not always focused on mental disorder: most committals were instigated by hard pressed families, rather than governmental agencies or, indeed, doctors.[274]

All were significant actors in the admission processes and institutional rituals described so vividly in the 1960s by sociologist Erving Goffman, which all too often resulted in lengthy committal and deprivation of liberty.[275] How can the interacting imperatives of patients, families, staff and communities that resulted in the Irish asylums be best described, explored and understood today?[276] Endless questions arise from this complicated tangle of forces and processes, and the experiences of patients caught up in them. The ongoing creation of answers to these questions is commonly surprising, occasionally disturbing and always fascinating.

I hope this book makes a contribution to this process. Many of the key issues are explored at various points throughout the text (and images); some are discussed but not interrogated fully; and others remain untouched, in need of further exploration. This ongoing task of historical exploration is complex, compelling and utterly critical if Ireland is to come to terms with its troubled institutional past and provide a meaningful voice for those who were denied a voice for so very long.

The first and most immediate step in achieving justice and resolution, however, is to address the social exclusion still experienced by the mentally ill today, especially those detained in Irish prisons and homeless on Irish streets.[277] Solutions are to hand: enhancing general psychiatric services (community services and inpatient care) to prevent these problems occurring in the first instance, strengthening forensic mental health services (including secure inpatient care), and creating genuine, functional links between social services and mental health teams to address homelessness and other social problems among the mentally ill and their families.

These goals are readily achievable in partnership with patients, families and community groups. Taking these pragmatic steps is the best way to remember the forgotten multitudes that crowded the Irish asylums of the 1800s and 1900s, and the even greater numbers who languished in prisons and died in squalor prior to the era of the asylum. Addressing these contemporary issues is the most effective, compassionate and transformative way to use the lessons of Ireland's psychiatric past to bring justice and healing to the mentally ill today.

EPILOGUE:
PSYCHIATRY IN HISTORY

Psychiatry has always attracted the interest of film makers.[1] The results are distinctly mixed, with a general tendency to focus on the dramatic rather than the informative, the custodial rather than the compassionate. Occasionally, however, a film demonstrates an important truth about the nature and history of psychiatry, and merits further reflection.

Camille Claudel 1915 (3B Productions, 2013) is one such film. Directed by Bruno Dumont and featuring Juliette Binoche, *Camille Claudel 1915* focuses on the later life of Camille Claudel (1864–1943), a French sculptor and artist, and close associate of Auguste Rodin (1840–1917), a fellow sculptor.[2]

In the early 1900s, following a tempestuous period in her life, Camille began to behave strangely, destroying some of her work and disappearing for periods of time. During this time, Camille's father was her chief support and protector.[3] Just one week after his death in 1913, Camille's family arranged to have her admitted to the psychiatric hospital of Ville-Évrard in Neuilly-sur-Marne, France. Doctors tried to convince her family that Camille did not require institutionalisation, but the family insisted on admission and the doctors acquiesced. Her mother, in particular, believed that Camille had brought intolerable scandal to their lives.[4]

The following year, Camille was transferred the Montdevergues Asylum at Montfavet, near Avignon. There she remained for thirty years until her death in 1943. Camille's mother did not visit her once. Camille was buried in a communal asylum grave in 1943.

Members of the asylum staff were the only people at her funeral.

Towards the end of *Camille Claudel 1915* there is a heartrending scene during Camille's time at the Montdevergues Asylum, when her brother, writer Paul Claudel (1868–1955), speaks with Camille's doctor, who reiterates his view that Camille should be released. Paul strongly disagrees and the asylum doctor again acquiesces, unhappily, to keeping Camille in the asylum.[5]

While this particular scene is located in early twentieth-century France, its content has much broader relevance to the story of psychiatry. Throughout its brief history, psychiatry has all too often acquiesced to the roles pressed upon it by others.[6] Psychiatry and psychiatrists have repeatedly failed to demarcate the limits of the discipline, failed to oppose sufficiently the strong societal pressures to admit ever greater numbers of patients to asylums and hospitals, and failed to press home psychiatry's loud – but insufficiently loud – objections to the growth of large systems of care and control and the use of psychiatry to address awkward societal problems that would be better addressed outside of psychiatric or medical paradigms.[7] This was as true for Ireland over the past two centuries as it was in Camille Claudel's France, if not more so.

Consistent with this, one of the recurring themes in this book is that Irish asylums were a convenient solution for many difficult societal problems, and while there is plentiful evidence that many patients were mentally ill, a significant proportion were not. And, for a great number of those with genuine psychiatric or psychological problems, it is likely that if viable alternatives had been available then these problems could have been resolved without a rush to institutionalisation: outpatient mental health care, better resources for family care, supported accommodation for the homeless, systematic social welfare for the poor, residential facilities for the intellectually disabled, meaningful support for single mothers, and so forth.

In the absence of such provisions, Ireland's asylum beds were routinely oversubscribed as soon as they became available, and the vast, custodial and poorly therapeutic asylum system was chronically overcrowded, unhygienic and, on occasion, fatal. The asylums became all too convenient options for a society with an apparently insatiable hunger for institutions, incarceration and control.

The emergence of clinical professionals, both medical and nursing, was inevitably a factor in this complex mix,[8] but the effects of any search for professional prestige were dwarfed by asylum doctors' clear outrage at what the system had become. Too often, increasingly alarmed doctors lacked sufficient power to scale down the institutions and there were powerful incentives in keeping large local asylums open.[9] As already noted, the town of Ballinasloe had a population of 5,596 in 1951, and of these no fewer than 2,078 were patients in the mental hospital (Introduction).[10] As a result, virtually everyone in the locality was a stakeholder in the mental hospital in one way or other (relative of patient, worker, or supplier), so there were powerful social, not medical, interests in maintaining the hospital's enormous size.

A further incentive is reflected in the fact that communities and families used the mental hospitals in complex and often subtle ways, according to community and family needs:[11] e.g. removing relatives from the asylums in the summer to work at home and then returning them to the asylum for the winter ('wintering in').[12] Medical opinion was not even required for committal for much of the time[13] and Ireland's asylum archives are replete with letters from doctors urging families and governmental authorities[14] to cooperate with the discharge of patients.[15] As occurred with Camille Claudel's doctors in France, Irish doctors' entreaties often fell on deaf ears, or families were genuinely too poor or ill equipped to accept home a person with mental illness or intellectual disability, or doctors failed to make their arguments sufficiently strongly or effectively.

There was strong medical support for alternatives to inpatient care[16] and the reasons why Dr Conolly Norman of the Richmond, for example, did not succeed in his plans for care outside the asylum in the late 1800s and early 1900s lay not within the medical profession but within government, which repeatedly frustrated efforts to deinstitutionalise care. Reformist impulses were further stymied by the stigma of mental illness (as reflected in the Dangerous Lunatic Act 1838) and the fact that Ireland's asylums essentially functioned as a large, unwieldy social welfare system for many patients and staff.[17]

As a result of these observations, it is my contention that Ireland's remarkable asylum system was primarily a social creation rather than a medical one, albeit that asylum doctors were complicit with the growth of the system or, at the very least, their objections were insufficiently effective to control it. For that considerable failing, psychiatry must take responsibility. But that failing was just one part of a broader, more complicated and profoundly disturbing story: the much larger failing lies outside the field of psychiatry entirely, in a society that failed to generate solutions to real human suffering (mental illness, disability, disease, poverty, ill fortune) other than the extraordinary network of institutions that characterised so much of Irish history: orphanages, industrial schools, reformatories, workhouses, laundries, borstals, prisons and – yes – asylums.[18]

Like all histories, the history of Irish psychiatry as told in this book is just one of many possible versions of a rich, complex, disturbing story. All such histories are influenced and shaped by their authors and this one is bound to be no different. As both a practicing psychiatrist and historian, there can be little doubt that my clinical work has influenced my interpretation of the history of Irish psychiatric care, and made me especially seized by the social injustices endured by the mentally ill both today and in the past.

It is, for example, impossible for me to ignore the parallels between the experiences of homeless persons admitted to asylums in the early 1900s and those presenting to psychiatric services in the early 2000s. In 1907, 30 per cent of admissions to the Richmond Asylum at Grangegorman came directly from workhouses.[19] In 2007 – exactly a century later – 35 per cent of emergency psychiatry assessments at the Mater Misericoridae University Hospital (where I worked for a decade, just up the road from Grangegorman) were for homeless persons.[20] How much has really changed?

Porter and Micale provide a fascinating discussion of the peculiar position of the psychiatrist-historian, noting that many influential historical interpreters of psychiatry in the last century were trained as physicians and practiced psychiatry alongside their work as historians.[21] Their comments are highly consistent with the increasing acceptance of disparate voices within the fields of history in general and the history of medicine in particular.

Ultimately, taking both these historical and clinical perspectives into account, one of the clearest features of the history of psychiatry as presented in this book is that the pendulum in Irish psychiatry has now swung strongly away from institution based care, as the number of inpatients has diminished greatly in recent decades and the rate of involuntary admission in Ireland is now comparatively low: in England, there were 54 involuntary admissions per 100,000 population per year in 2012–13,[22] while Ireland's rate was 44.[23] Indeed, it is arguable that his process might now have reached its limit and the pendulum might soon start its swing back towards inpatient care in Ireland. And that might well be a necessary corrective at this time, in order to improve *all* forms of care and support required by the mentally ill and their families at various different stages.[24]

There is also strong evidence of powerful reinterpretations of certain experiences (such as hearing voices) which used to be invariably associated with major mental disorder but are now subject to more nuanced interpretations, formulated chiefly by those having such experiences themselves.[25] This is an especially exciting development which has the potential to combine the need for psychiatric care with real interpretative empowerment by those with specific experiences of hearing voices.

And this is not an isolated development. The 'Open Dialogue' approach, for example, presents another innovative and inclusive approach to mental health, emphasising participation by all stakeholders.[26] The EOLAS project is a further and notably progressive development in Ireland, developed through collaboration with users of mental health services, family members, mental health support organisations, clinicians and academia. There are now myriad voices of change within Irish mental health services and communities (Chapter 8), hopefully balancing any swing back towards inpatient care with progressive developments in community settings. A careful balance is needed: one size does not fit all.

There are also powerful movements to promote the human rights of the mentally ill, as reflected in Ireland's ongoing revisions of mental health legislation.[27] These initiatives need to be matched by continued developments in services themselves and ongoing improvements in social care, in line with national mental health policy.[28] Much has changed, but there is still much to do, especially in the areas of economic and social rights.[29]

If the history recounted in this book has one overarching lesson for today, it is that the rights and voices of people with mental disorder need to be central to the planning and provision of care. All too often in the past, the mentally ill were shamefully neglected by systems of health care and, especially, social care, to the point of the mentally ill dying alone, paradoxically abandoned within a custodial asylum system which, despite considerable effort, could not find a way to persuade broader society to accept them back.

And, as with Camille Claudel, members of asylum staff were often the only ones at the funerals of the forgotten patients of the Irish asylums[30] – a small measure of humanity afforded by a society that has always excluded the mentally ill.

But it was far too little humanity, far, far too late.

We must do better.

CHRONOLOGY: KEY EVENTS IN THE HISTORY OF PSYCHIATRY IN IRELAND

Time	Key events in the history of psychiatry in Ireland
Pre-Christian Ireland	Stories of madness feature in early Irish literature and folklore. Supernatural and religious explanations for 'madness' are given. It is believed that druidic priests, acting for pagan deities, can induce madness by throwing a 'madman's wisp' (a ball of grass or straw) in a person's face.
5th Century	As Christianity arrives in Ireland, beliefs develop that insanity is attributable to possession by the devil or punishment by God and the phrase *duine le Dia* (person of God) comes into common use for persons with intellectual disability. One story claims that St Mochuda cured a man of madness (owing to demonic possession) by interceding with God; another tells how a Norman archer became mad after entering a sacred area surrounding a perpetually burning fire lit by St Brigid in Kildare. Early Irish law seeks to protect the mentally ill from exploitation.
9th to 12th Centuries	The mythic figure of Mad Sweeney (*Suibhne Geilt*) emerges; a chieftain cursed by Ronan the Fair, abbot of Drumiskin, and condemned to a life of madness, flying and wandering through the world. After many years, the curse is fulfilled when he is killed by a spear. A myth develops that at *Gleann na nGealt* (Glenn of the Lunatics), in County Kerry, the mentally ill can be cured by drinking the water and eating watercress from the well, *Tobar na nGealt*, which is said to have cured the madness of Gall, king of Ulster; there is also a 'Mad Stone' and a river crossing known as 'Fool's Crossing'. Overall, there is some, limited monastic provision for the mentally ill, but most live in destitution or imprisonment.
1708	Sir William Fownes, mayor of Dublin, provides six cells for the mentally ill at the workhouse at St James's Gate – the first systematic public provision for the destitute mentally ill in Ireland.
1746	Following the death of Jonathan Swift in 1745 and his bequest to found an asylum, on 8 August 1746 a royal charter is granted to St Patrick's Hospital by King George II. St Patrick's becomes the first psychiatric hospital in Ireland, one of the first in the world, and admits its first patients in 1757.
1787	The Prisons Act empowers Grand Juries (county administrative and judicial bodies) to establish lunatic wards in houses of industry, subject to inspection by the Inspector General of Prisons.

The wards are to house insane persons or 'idiots' who have to be certified by at least two magistrates. The initial response is modest: lunatic wards are only established in Dublin, Cork, Waterford and Limerick.

| 1780s and 1790s | Dr William Saunders Hallaran establishes the Cork Lunatic Asylum and a private asylum, Citadella. In 1810, he publishes the first Irish text book of psychiatry: *An Enquiry into the Causes producing the Extraordinary Addition to the Number of Insane together with Extended Observations on the Cure of Insanity with Hints as to the Better Management of Public Asylums for Insane Persons*. Treatments discussed include the 'circulating chair', emetics, purgatives, hydrotherapy, digitalis, opium, camphor, mercury, diet, exercise and occupational therapies. |

| 1804 | The Houses of Industry contain disturbingly large numbers of people with mental disorder or intellectual disability, including 118 in the Dublin House of Industry, 90 in Cork, and 25 in Waterford. Conditions in the Limerick House of Industry are particularly brutal: the mentally ill are kept naked, chained, handcuffed and exposed to the elements (1806), despite the Inspector General of Prisons having the power (since 1787) to inspect all places where the mentally ill and intellectually disabled are housed. |

| 1812 | In the spirit of the York Retreat in England, the first patient is admitted to Bloomfield Hospital in Donnybrook, Dublin, established by the Religious Society of Friends ('Quakers'). |

| 1814 | The Richmond Asylum at Grangegorman, Dublin, accepts its first admissions; it is intended that the institution will be run along 'moral management' lines, emphasising diet, exercise, occupation and rational thought (rather than restraint and control), although traditional treatments and some restraint are used. The asylum is initially run by moral governors rather than physicians, setting the scene for a protracted power struggle that ultimately results in medical dominance of the asylum system. |

| 1814 | Dr Philip Middleton, co-founder of 'Hanover Park Asylum for the Recovery of Persons labouring under Mental Derangement' in Carlow, demolishes much of Carlow Castle while apparently attempting to remodel it (although it's still not clear exactly what he was trying to do). |

| 1817 | The Select Committee on the Lunatic Poor in Ireland paints a grim picture of public institutions for the mentally ill, concluding that they are 'totally inadequate for the reception of the lunatic poor'; the situation in Limerick is especially disturbing. The committee recommends a properly governed network of asylums, along the lines of the Richmond in Dublin. Four district asylums are rapidly completed by the end of the 1820s (Armagh, Belfast, Derry and Limerick) and five more by 1835 (Ballinasloe, Carlow, Waterford, Maryborough (Portlaoise) and Clonmel); together, these establishments have capacity for 1,062 patients. |

| 1825 | Dr John Eustace opens an 'Asylum and House of Recovery for Persons Afflicted with Disorders of the Mind' at Hampstead in Glasnevin, Dublin. |

| 1828 | In Cork, Captain William Stewart is found 'not guilty' owing to insanity, following the killing of seven crew members aboard the *Mary Russell*, prefiguring the verdict of 'not guilty by reason of insanity' outlined much later in Ireland's Criminal Law (Insanity) Act 2006. |

| 1838 | The Dangerous Lunatic Act permits committal of a 'dangerous lunatic' to prison and then (after possibly spending years in prison) to an asylum, on the basis of alleged risk to the public (even if no offence is actually committed); a medical certificate is not mandatory until 1867. Despite the protests of asylum doctors and the clear injustice of the procedure, this soon becomes the admission pathway of choice for families seeking to have relatives committed. Admission rates soar. |

| 1842 | The Private Lunatic Asylums (Ireland) Act makes it unlawful for anyone to keep a house for two or more insane persons unless that house is licensed; patients can only be detained if a certificate is signed by two doctors, and medical input is required at the establishment. |

| 1843 | Dr John Cheyne writes his influential *Essays on Partial Derangement of the Mind, in Supposed Connexion with Religion*, notable for the careful attention he devotes to signs and symptoms of mental disorder. He draws links between mental symptoms and physical illness and identifies the role of alcohol in precipitating mental disturbance. |

| 1843 | A report on the 'state of the lunatic poor in Ireland' hears of horrific conditions in some asylums, with particular concerns about Wexford ('I could not describe the horror') and Clonmel ('a sad calamity'). The committee recommends removing the mentally ill from gaols, bridewells and workhouses, and expansion of the district asylum system. |

| 1843 | The *General Rules for the Government of All the District Lunatic Asylums of Ireland* set developments on a distinctively medical trajectory and explicitly permit admission of persons with mental illness or intellectual disability to the asylums. |

| 1845–1852 | The Great Irish Famine increases mental health and social need among the mentally ill and intellectually disabled; in 1914, the Inspector of Lunatics reports 'an exceptional number of insane and idiots derived from the population born during the decade 1841–51', and concludes that 'children born and partially reared amidst the horrors of the famine and the epidemics of disease that followed it were so handicapped in their nervous equipment as to be weak minded from the start or to fall victims to mental disease later'. |

| 1840s and 1850s | Legislation in 1845 makes provision for the Central Criminal Lunatic Asylum in Dundrum, Dublin and a large, 500 bed establishment in Cork, the Eglinton Asylum, which opened in the early 1850s. Various other asylums are also opened during this, the second phase of asylum building, including Mullingar (1855), Letterkenny (1866) and Castlebar (1866). Many of these developments prove highly controversial. |

| 1850s | An innovative school is established at the Richmond Asylum in Dublin, led by Drs John Mollan and Joseph Lalor (first Irish president of the Medico-Psychological Association, in 1861). |

| 1850 | In the *Dublin Quarterly Journal of Medical Science*, Dr Fleetwood Churchill writes that cyclic changes in bodily health affect women more than men, with consequent effects on mental activities; this belief is widely shared across the (male) medical and legal establishments and significantly shapes views of insanity and criminal responsibility in women. |

1854	A *Report on the Status of Disease*, based on the 'Census of Ireland for the Year 1851' and co-authored by Dr (later Sir) William Wilde, is published. The report concludes that there are 5,074 'Lunatics' and 4,906 'Idiots' in Ireland. Causes are 'physical', 'moral' or 'hereditary'; 'moral causes' include 'grief', 'love and jealousy', 'terror', 'religious excitement', 'study', 'anger or excessive passion', 'pride and ambition', 'political excitement', 'music' and 'remorse'.
1857	St Vincent's Hospital in Fairview, Dublin is founded, following the bequest of Francis Magan (barrister and member of the United Irishmen) and run by the Daughters of Charity of St Vincent de Paul; the first physician is Sir Dominic Corrigan, who is also the first Catholic president of the Royal College of Physicians of Ireland.
1858	The Commission of Inquiry on the State of Lunatic Asylums in Ireland concludes that the asylums are 'places merely for the secure detention of lunatics' and recommends, *inter alia*, expansion and improvement of the asylum system (despite clear evidence of neglect and cruelty therein): 'it is of the utmost importance that cases of insanity should as speedily as possible be removed to an asylum'.
1862	There are 21 private asylums in Ireland and the inspectors (Drs John Nugent and George Hatchell) find that the quality of care varies, although, for the most part, conditions are generally reported as acceptable.
1862	The *General Rules and Regulations for the Management of District Lunatic Asylums in Ireland* cover a broad range of areas and favour the Resident Medical Superintendent (RMS) – 'he shall superintend and regulate the whole establishment' – rather than the Visiting Physician.
1865	Cheyne Brady, a member of the Royal Irish Academy, governor of the Meath Hospital and prolific author on social matters, writes a pamphlet on *The Training of Idiotic and Feeble-Minded Children*. By 1869, following the work of Dr Henry Hutchinson Stewart and others, an asylum in Lucan is ready to receive children with intellectual disability.
1860s to 1900	The third phase of asylum building includes asylums in Ennis (1868), Monaghan (1869), Antrim (1899) and Portrane, County Dublin (1900); Portrane is the largest ever building contract awarded to a single contractor in Ireland (the Collen brothers of Portadown).
1875	Dr James Foulis Duncan, of Farnham House in Finglas, becomes president of the Medico-Psychological Association and vehemently denounces a great many features of nineteenth-century life; he recommends education as a method of preventing mental disorder.
1882	The Brothers of St John of God establish a private psychiatric hospital in Stillorgan, County Dublin.
1883	Dr Thomas Drapes becomes RMS at Enniscorthy District Lunatic Asylum, and, from 1912, co-editor of the *Journal of Mental Science*; a leading figure in asylum medicine, Drapes opposes Emil Kraepelin's new classification system, preferring the idea of a 'unitary' psychosis.
1886	Dr Conolly Norman is appointed RMS of the Richmond District Asylum at Grangegorman; Norman advocates strongly for 'boarding out' as an alternative to asylum care (although this

is blocked by Dublin Castle) and introduces many reforms at the Richmond. In 1894, he becomes president of the Medico-Psychological Association.

1891   The Committee on Lunacy Administration (Ireland), chaired by Sir Arthur Mitchell, recommends new lunacy legislation, conversion of some unused workhouses into provincial asylums, and 'boarding out' for patients; this generally humane, compassionate report is generally ignored.

1892   Irish asylums are grossly overcrowded, anti-therapeutic and unhygienic, with an annual death rate of 8.3 per cent; infectious diseases are rampant.

1894   Dr Daniel Hack Tuke publishes his paper on the 'increase of insanity in Ireland' in the *Journal of Mental Science*, reflecting wider views that there is a rapid and alarming increase of insanity, especially in Ireland;[1] in 1829 there had been 2,097 'mentally ill' persons in institutions in Ireland and by 1894 there are 17,665.[2]

Dr Eleonora Fleury becomes the first woman member of the Medico-Psychological Association, following nomination by Dr Conolly Norman. She goes on to distinguished careers in both psychiatry and republican activism (resulting in imprisonment in 1923).

In May, the District Asylum in Londonderry becomes the first Irish asylum to enter candidates for the Medico-Psychological Association examination for asylum staff. Thirteen nurses gain the certificate and other asylums follow suit.

1899   Dr Richard Leeper is appointed RMS at St Patrick's Hospital and his impact is rapid, positive and profound, characterised by an energetic approach to administration and a practical approach to psychiatric care; he serves as president of the Medico-Psychological Association in 1931.

1900   Approximately 21,000 people, 0.5 per cent of the population of the 32 counties of Ireland, are accommodated in the district asylums, with a small number of the mentally ill still in workhouses.

1901   The national census reveals that approximately one in every 10,000 persons residing outside an institution is a 'lunatic', yielding a point prevalence of 11 per 100,000 population (likely an underestimate).

1903   Issues relating to overcrowding are strongly to the fore on the agenda of the Conference of the Irish Asylums Committee convened at the Richmond; the meeting calls for a pathological laboratory for further research, legislation permitting family care for patients, and enhanced government funding of asylums. The meeting hears that it is not uncommon for families to remove relatives from the asylums in the summer months to work on the land or at home and then return them to the asylum for the winter ('wintering in').

1906   The number of assistant medical officers in Irish asylums is well below recommended levels and numbers in equivalent London asylums.

1907   The Richmond District Asylum Joint Committee appoints a 'special committee' to look into the issue of the mentally ill in workhouses. The committee reports that the female lunatic ward in the North Dublin Union Workhouse is a 'repellent place', 'little more than a dungeon'. Expansion of asylums is (yet again) seen as the solution, the Richmond itself being already overcrowded to a point of 'grave and alarming crisis'. Dr Conolly Norman highlights the plight of the intellectually disabled: 'It is neither wise nor humane to neglect this class as they are neglected in this country.'

1908
The Royal Commission on the Care and Control of the Feeble-Minded bases its extensive recommendations on 'the three methods of oversight, certification, and detention'.

1916
During the Easter Rising, the Richmond Asylum[3] and St Patrick's Hospital are caught in the crossfire and both receive admissions due to 'shock'.

1916 to 1919
The Richmond War Hospital, a 32 bed establishment, operates at the Richmond District Asylum and treats 362 soldiers with shell shock and other mental disorders resulting from the First World War; treatments include rest, hydrotherapy, analgesia, caffeine, and activities (drama, choirs and trips); more than half of the soldiers are discharged home while a small number are transferred to the main asylum system.

1919
The Monaghan Asylum Soviet comes into being, as industrial unrest spreads throughout Irish asylums.

1921
Dr Adeline (Ada) English is imprisoned in Galway for republican activities and elected to the Second Dáil (Irish parliament); she works in the asylum (later mental hospital) in Ballinasloe for almost four decades from 1904, being finally appointed as RMS in 1941. English's contributions include developing convulsive therapy, occupational therapy and working for improved mental health legislation.

1925
Dr John Dunne introduces malarial treatment for general paralysis of the insane (GPI; a neuropsychiatric disorder caused by late stage syphilis). By 1929, the death rate from GPI at Grangegorman has been reduced to five per year, from around 35 per year prior to malarial treatment.

1927
The Commission on the Relief of the Sick and Destitute Poor, Including the Insane Poor reports that there are 16,079 'patients in the district mental hospitals' who 'have been medically certified as either dangerous lunatics or idiots or as of unsound mind and proper persons to be taken charge of under care and treatment'. It proposes the establishment of 'auxiliary mental hospitals' (rather than expanding existing district mental hospitals) and various measures relating to outpatient care, 'boarding-out of the insane', inspections, voluntary admissions and changes to legislation.

1933
Dr Eamonn O'Sullivan establishes an occupational therapy department at Killarney Mental Hospital.

Mid-1930s
The first private sector psychiatric outpatient clinic at a general hospital in Ireland is established by Dr H. Jocelyn Eustace of the Adelaide Hospital. Public outpatient clinics follow (e.g. Cork in 1948, Belmullet in 1950).

1936
From 1 June, only mental hospital nurses who pass the examination of the General Nursing Council of Ireland can be registered.

1938	Insulin coma therapy is introduced in Grangegorman by Drs John Dunne and Eveleen O'Brien; the use of the treatment declines in the late 1950s and early 1960s owing to the emergence of safer, more effective alternatives (chiefly antipsychotic medication).
1939	Convulsive therapy (using Cardiazol to induce seizures) is introduced in Cork (July) and Ballinasloe District Mental Hospitals (December).
1942	The Irish Psycho-Analytical Association is founded by poet, writer and psychoanalyst, Jonathan Hanaghan, who began psychoanalytical practice in Ireland in 1920. Psychoanalysis does not have an enormous impact on Irish psychiatry, possibly owing to Ireland's peripheral location, the absence of a preeminent medical professional to take the lead, or the Catholic Church's disapproval; in 1963, the Irish Psycho-Analytical Association has just five practicing psychoanalysts.
1942	*Electro*convulsive therapy (ECT; using electricity to induce seizures) is introduced in Grangegorman (April) and, later, Cork (1943), where it is given without anaesthesia up until 1952. In 1950, Professor John Dunne at Grangegorman reports that 209 out of 327 patients with 'involutional melancholia' (depression) 'recovered' following ECT.
1944	*It Happened in Ireland*, by Reverend Clarence Duffy, is published in New York by the Christian Press; it presents an unsparing account of Duffy's six month admission to Monaghan Mental Hospital in the mid-1930s.
1946	Lobotomy is introduced to patients of Grangegorman Mental Hospital in April; the procedure is performed at the nearby Richmond Surgical Hospital. By June 1947, 23 lobotomies have been performed with decidedly mixed results; the use of the procedure goes into decline in the 1950s amid growing evidence of harm. Lobotomy is probably the single greatest mistake in the history of psychiatry. Dr (later Professor) Norman Moore is appointed Medical Superintendent of St Patrick's Hospital and for several decades becomes a leading, much admired figure in Irish psychiatry.
1947	The Mental Treatment Act 1945 comes into force, introducing voluntary admission status, two new processes for involuntary admission, and various other changes. It is a significant, if belated, reform, although its restrictions on grounds for challenging detention are later declared unconstitutional (2008).
1950	Dr John Dunne of Grangegorman is appointed Professor of Psychiatry at University College Dublin.
1950s	Mental hospitals dominate the economies of the towns they are located in: in 1951, the town of Ballinasloe has a population of 5,596, of whom 2,078 are patients in the mental hospital.[4]
1955	Dr Eamonn O'Sullivan of Killarney Mental Hospital, publishes his path-finding *Textbook of Occupational Therapy with Chief Reference to Psychological Medicine*. Dr Desmond McGrath, an outstanding teacher, trainer and service developer, takes up a post at St John of God Hospital in Dublin and in 1956 it becomes the first mental hospital in Ireland to introduce 'the open door system' (affording patients greater liberty).

The St John of God Order establishes the first child guidance clinic in Ireland, at Orwell Road in Rathgar, at the request of the Department of Health and the World Health Organisation.

1956   The number of 'mentally ill' persons in institutions in Ireland reaches 21,720; 20,063 are in public mental hospitals.[5]

In November, Professor John Dunne gives a generally positive account of new medications for schizophrenia (e.g. chlorpromazine) to Grangegorman Mental Hospital Board, reporting significant benefits, although these are not, he says, as substantial as he had been led to expect. Injected forms of these medications later facilitate discharge of many long term patients.

1958   Nurse Thomas Farrell becomes the first community psychiatric nurse in Ireland, based at St Luke's in Clonmel.

1962   Dr (later Professor) Ivor Browne returns to Ireland to work at Grangegorman, pioneering novel therapies and systematically dismantling the old institution, seeking to replace it with community based facilities.

A child guidance clinic is opened at the Mater Misericordiae Hospital, Dublin.

The Samaritans are established in Ireland and by 2016 have 20 branches with 2,400 active volunteers doing extraordinarily skilled and selfless work. Their contribution to Irish society is quiet, consistent and utterly invaluable.

1963   Michael Viney at the *Irish Times* publishes an affecting series of articles highlighting the broad range of problems related to mental health care and, in particular, the disproportionate numbers still resident in Irish psychiatric hospitals.

1965   The Commission of Inquiry on Mental Handicap indicates a movement away from the primacy previously attached to residential care, with increased emphasis on non-residential elements of care and early intervention.

1966   The Commission of Inquiry on Mental Illness notes that 'in Ireland, approximately 7.3 psychiatric beds were provided in 1961 per 1,000 of the population; this rate appears to be the highest in the world and compared with 4.5 in Northern Ireland, 4.6 in England and Wales, 4.3 in Scotland, 2.1 in France and 4.3 in U.S.A.'. The commission describes mental illness as 'a health problem of the first magnitude' and recommends 'radical and widespread changes', moving away from 'barrack-like structures characterised by large wards, gloomy corridors and stone stairways', towards community based care, greater research, more public education and updated legislation.

1969   Professor Peter Beckett becomes Professor of Psychiatry at Trinity College, Dublin and, later, Dean of the Faculty of Medicine (1972–4).

1971   *Bird's Nest Soup*, by Hanna Greally, provides a thinly veiled, compelling and disturbing account of her 19 years in St Loman's Mental Hospital, Mullingar between 1943 and 1962.

1972   The Department of Health publishes *Psychiatric Nursing Services of Health Boards: Report of Working Party*, noting an era of change in mental health services and substantial industrial unrest.

1975	Dr Noël Browne, in Seanad Éireann (the Irish upper house), highlights the negative effects of societal attitudes towards homosexuality, stating that homosexuality is 'perfectly normal, but in our society it is a very crippling disability' owing to stigma, prejudice and the law; same-sex sexual acts remain criminal acts up until 1993.
1978	The report of the Interdepartmental Committee on Mentally Ill and Maladjusted Persons regarding the *Treatment and Care of Persons Suffering From Mental Disorder Who Appear Before the Courts on Criminal Charges* articulates a long standing and generally agreed need for revised legislation on criminal insanity.
1980	In October, *Magill* magazine publishes a hard hitting report, 'The scandal of the mental hospitals', by Helen Connolly with searing, unforgettable photographs by Derek Speirs.
1981	The Health (Mental Services) Act proposes abolishing the distinction between private and chargeable (public) patients; requiring that the patient be informed of doctors' intentions to proceed with involuntary admission; and enhanced rights following detention, especially the establishment of review boards. Despite being passed by the Oireachtas (national parliament), the legislation is never implemented, provoking considerable comment.
1982	The *Irish Journal of Psychiatry* appears, edited by Dr Dermot Walsh and published by the Irish Institute of Psychiatry. In addition, the *Irish Journal of Psychological Medicine* is founded by Dr Mark Hartman and goes on to become research journal of the College of Psychiatrists of Ireland (2012).
1984	A new mental health policy is published, *The Psychiatric Services: Planning for the Future*, proposing further development of community care, development of inpatient units in general hospitals, increased emphasis on primary care, and various other measures; it is largely a re-statement of the report of the Commission of Inquiry on Mental Illness (1966), but contains a welcome commitment to implementation.
1987–2003	Dr Dermot Walsh serves as Inspector of Mental Hospitals; Walsh makes a vast and unique contribution to enlightened mental health policy, law and practice through his clinical work, medical leadership, involvement with governmental reviews and policy, and the Health Research Board.
1989	Professor Anthony Clare becomes Medical Director of St Patrick's Hospital; Clare is the best known psychiatrist in Ireland and Great Britain and makes a vital contribution to the demystification of psychiatry.
1980s to 1990s	After much speculation and research, and many decades of increasingly elaborate theorising, it finally appears that Ireland does not, in fact, have a notably high rate of mental disorder compared to other countries, and while there is evidence of some variation over time and across regions there is insufficient evidence to conclude that Ireland ever had a higher rate of incidence of mental illness, although there was a higher rate of psychiatric hospitalisation for various social, demographic and historical reasons.

Throughout the 1980s and 1990s, clinical psychology, social work and occupational therapy bring substantial changes to mental health services; a separate history of these groups is merited.

1991   Dr (later Professor) Eadbhard O'Callaghan returns to Dublin from the Institute of Psychiatry in London and goes on to develop a world leading psychosis research programme, among other initiatives. He educates and inspires a generation of clinicians and academic psychiatrists in Ireland.

1995   A government White Paper proposes a 'new Mental Health Act', openly acknowledging (in a triumph of understatement) that the Mental Treatment Act 1945 does 'not fully comply with this country's obligations under international law'. In 2000, the lack of automatic review of detention under the Mental Treatment Act 1945 forms the focus of a landmark case in the European Court of Human Rights.[6] This, in turn, leads to the Mental Health Act 2001, which incorporates some but not all of the measures presented in the ill-fated Health (Mental Services) Act 1981.

2001   The Mental Health Act (fully implemented in 2006) establishes a Mental Health Commission, introduces mental health tribunals to review involuntary admission and treatment orders (among other matters) and makes various other changes (e.g. to admission and inspection processes).

2005   The Irish College of Psychiatrists (later College of Psychiatrists of Ireland) produces a position statement on psychiatric services for children and adolescents. The report, *A Better Future Now*, notes that child and adolescent psychiatric services account for only 5–10 per cent of spending on mental health services, while serving 23 per cent of the population.

2006   A new mental health policy, *A Vision for Change*, presents a renewed commitment to community based care. Substantial progress is made, but in June 2012 the Independent Monitoring Group concludes that implementation is 'slow and inconsistent'.[7]

The Criminal Law (Insanity) Act 2006 introduces significant change, replacing the 'guilty but insane' verdict with 'not guilty by reason of insanity' and providing for the concept of 'diminished responsibility' in murder cases, among other reforms.

The United Nations (UN) Convention on the Rights of Persons with Disabilities is adopted by the UN General Assembly, providing a welcome articulation of the rights of persons with disabilities and presenting important challenges to services and legislation.

Hearing Voices Ireland is founded in Limerick by Mr Brian Hartnett with the aim of fostering acceptance of voice hearing as a valid human experience. By 2015, there are 'hearing voices' groups in Cork, Donegal, Dublin, Kerry, Kildare, Kilkenny, Longford, Tipperary and Belfast.

The Centre for the History of Medicine in Ireland is established at University College Dublin, in partnership with medical historians at the University of Ulster. The Centre identifies 'psychiatry and mental health' as one of its collaborative research themes, with Dr Catherine Cox as UCD director.

2008   The Inspector of Mental Health Services expresses concern about the number of people with an intellectual disability still inappropriately placed in psychiatric hospitals; progress is subsequently made (e.g. in specialist forensic mental health services) but more needs to be done.

Sebastian Barry's extraordinary novel, *The Secret Scripture*, provides a rare, insightful portrayal of a psychiatrist as the era of Ireland's large public asylums finally draws to a close.

2009   The College of Psychiatry of Ireland (retitled College of Psychiatrists of Ireland in 2013) emerges from the merger of three former bodies: the Irish College of Psychiatrists (a division of the Royal College of Psychiatrists in the UK), the Irish Psychiatric Association, and the then training body for psychiatry, the Irish Psychiatric Training Committee.

2010   The National Clinical Programme for Mental Health is set up as a joint initiative between the Health Service Executive (HSE; chief provider of public mental health services in Ireland) Clinical Strategy and Programmes Division and the College of Psychiatry of Ireland to standardise high quality evidence based practice in relation to (a) assessment and management of patients presenting to emergency departments following self-harm; (b) early intervention for people developing first episode psychosis; and (c) management of persons with eating disorders.

2011   The College of Psychiatry of Ireland and the Gay and Lesbian Equality Network publish guidelines 'to inform psychiatrists of what they need to know when providing a mental health service to a lesbian, gay or bisexual (LGB) person'.

The EOLAS project is initiated by the Kildare West Wicklow mental health team. Developed in collaboration with users of mental health services, family members, support organisations, clinicians and academia, its objective is to design, deliver and evaluate mental health information and support programmes to assist in the recovery of those diagnosed with schizophrenia and bipolar disorder, and their family and friends.

2013   Ireland's rate of involuntary psychiatric admission is low by international standards, reflecting substantial progress in mental health legislation over the previous two decades. Ireland's rates of antidepressant and sedative use are also relatively low during this period (e.g. in Northern Ireland, rates of antidepressant use are almost three times higher and rates of sedative use almost twice as high, as in the Republic of Ireland).

Nonetheless, there is still much to be done to improve services: in December, for example, the College of Psychiatrists of Ireland notes that 'old age psychiatry' is an expanding area and only 50 per cent of the required consultant psychiatrist posts in this field are currently provided.

2014   Population happiness recovers following the economic recession that commenced in 2008; the mean happiness scores out of 10 (where 0 means extremely unhappy, and 10 means extremely happy) are 7.9 in 2005; 7.7 in 2007; 7.5 in 2009; 6.8 in 2012; and 7.2 in 2014.

Provisional figures from the National Office for Suicide Prevention show that the rate of suicide is 10 per 100,000 population per year, down from 12.2 in 2004, though with some variation during the course of the decade. The rate of undetermined deaths (which might include some suicides) also fell, from 2.0 per 100,000 population per year in 2004 to 1.3 in 2014.[8] The rate of self-harm varied too, but by 2014 it was equivalent to that in 2002. While suicide remains a deeply concerning problem, provisional figures show 459 suicide deaths in 2014, down from 487 in 2013 (despite a likely growth in population).

Nonetheless, in 2015 alone, Pieta House, a service for the prevention of self-harm or suicide, sees in excess of 5,000 people suffering from suicidal ideation or engaging in self-harm. In addition, youth suicide remains very high in Ireland compared to other EU countries, necessitating greater investigation and coordinated psychological, social and educational intervention and support for young people.

On 31 December there are 2,228 patients in Irish psychiatric hospitals and inpatient units – an 89 per cent reduction since 1963.[9]

2015   In March, a detailed review of the Mental Health Act 2001 makes 165 recommendations relating to virtually all areas of the Act, including revised overarching principles and new criteria for involuntary care.

In June, planning permission is granted for a 120 bed national forensic hospital in Portrane, County Dublin, as well as two 10 bed specialist units for persons with intellectual disabilities and children and adolescents; the project includes progressing design work for three 30 bed Intensive Care Rehabilitation Units in Cork, Galway and Portrane.

In October, the College of Psychiatrists of Ireland calls for greater investment in mental health services. The mentally ill continue to experience increased risks of homelessness, imprisonment, physical ill health and social exclusion.

2016   In February, the Mental Health (Amendment) Act 2015 is commenced, with the result that ECT and medication for more than three months can be administered to an involuntary patient only if the patient is 'unable' (i.e. lacks the mental capacity) to provide consent; a capacitous refusal cannot be overridden.

In June, Drs Leonard Douglas and Larkin Feeney note, in the *Irish Journal of Psychological Medicine*, that referral rates to psychiatry increased 20 fold between 1983 and 2013, and that the work of community mental health teams is increasingly associated with emotional crises rather than severe mental disorder; services, although more multidisciplinary than in the past, are not adequately resourced to meet these changing demands.[10]

Despite progress over the past two centuries, there is still much to be done in terms of defining the role of psychiatry, better provision of care, and promoting the economic and social rights of the mentally ill.

ENDNOTES

Prologue

1 B.D. Kelly, 'Syphilis, psychiatry and offending behaviour: clinical cases from nineteenth-century Ireland', *Irish Journal of Medical Science,* 178, 1 (March 2009), pp. 73–7.

2 E. Shorter, *A History of Psychiatry: From the Era of the Asylum to the Age of Prozac* (New York: John Wiley and Sons, 1997) pp. 53–6. See also: I. Ashe, 'Some observations on general paralysis', *Journal of Mental Science*, 22, 97 (April 1876), pp. 82–91.

3 E. Malcolm, '"The house of strident shadows": the asylum, the family and emigration in post-Famine rural Ireland' in G. Jones and E. Malcolm (eds), *Medicine, Disease and the State in Ireland, 1650–1940* (Cork: Cork University Press, 1999), pp. 177–91.

4 S. O'Casey, *Drums Under the Windows. Autobiography: Book 3, 1906–1916* (London: Pan Books Limited, 1972; first published by Macmillan and Company Limited, 1945), pp. 55–6. This extract is reproduced by kind permission of the Estate of Sean O'Casey. See also M. Finnane, *Insanity and the Insane in Post-Famine Ireland* (London: Croom Helm, 1981), p. 129.

5 *The Buffoon Calabacillas,* mistakenly called *The Idiot of Coria,* is a portrait by Diego Velázquez of Don Juan Martín Martín, a jester at the court of Philip IV of Spain. Martín allegedly had mental illness. The painting hangs in the Museo del Prado, Madrid, along with various other 'buffoon' portraits by Velázquez.

Introduction

1 M. Webb, *Trinity's Psychiatrists: From Serenity of the Soul to Neuroscience* (Dublin: Trinity College, 2011), pp. 120–3.

2 A. Clare, 'Psychological medicine', in P. Kumar and M. Clark (eds), *Clinical Medicine: A Textbook for Medical Students and Doctors (Third Edition)* (London: Ballière Tindall, 1994), pp. 957–91; p. 957. [This material was published in *Clinical Medicine: A Textbook for Medical Students and Doctors (Third Edition)* (edited by P. Kumar and M. Clark), by A. Clare, titled 'Psychological medicine', pp. 957–91, Copyright Elsevier 1994. Used with permission.]

3 J. Pearsall and B. Trumble (eds), *The Oxford Reference English Dictionary (Second Edition)* (Oxford and New York: Oxford University Press, 1996), p. 408.

4 World Health Organisation, *International Classification of Mental and Behavioural Disorders (Volume 10)* (Geneva: World Health Organisation, 1992), p. 5.

5 E. Shorter, *A History of Psychiatry: From the Era of the Asylum to the Age of Prozac* (New York: John Wiley and Sons, 1997); M.H. Stone, *Healing the Mind: A History of Psychiatry from Antiquity to the Present* (London: Pimlico, 1998).

6 A. Scull, *Museums of Madness: Social Organization of Insanity in 19th Century England* (New York: St Martin's Press, 1979); A. Scull, *The Most Solitary of Afflictions: Madness and Society in Britain, 1700–1900* (New Haven and London: Yale University Press, 1993); Shorter, *A History of Psychiatry: From the Era of the Asylum to the Age of Prozac*; T. Millon, *Masters of the Mind: Exploring the Story of Mental Illness from Ancient Times to the New Millennium* (Hoboken, New Jersey: John Wiley & Sons, Inc., 2004); R. Porter, *Madmen: A Social History of Mad-houses, Mad-doctors and Lunatics* (Gloucestershire, United Kingdom: Tempus, 2004); M. Foucault, *History of Madness* (Abingdon, Oxon.: Routledge, 2006; first published as *Folie et Déraison: Histoire de la Folie à l'Âge Classique* in Paris by Librarie Plon, 1961) (for a discussion of the 2006 edition of Foucault's book, see: A. Scull, 'Scholarship of fools', *Times Literary Supplement,* 23 March 2007, and letters to the editor on 6, 13 and 20 April, and 8 June 2007; and B.D. Kelly, 'The historical swing of Foucault's pendulum', *Medicine Weekly,* 22 August 2007) (see also: P. Bracken, 'On *Madness and Civilisation: A History of Insanity in the Age of Reason* (1961), by Michel Foucault', *British Journal of Psychiatry,* 207, 5 (November 2015), p. 434); A. Scull, *Madness in Civilization: A Cultural History of Insanity, From the Bible to Freud, From the Madhouse to Modern Medicine* (London: Thames and Hudson Ltd., 2015) (for a useful discussion of Scull's book, see: S. Wise, 'Demon Doctors', *Financial Times,* 21/22 March 2015).

7 A.V. Horowitz, *Creating Mental Illness* (Chicago and London: University of Chicago Press, 2002); E. Watters, *Crazy Like Us: The Globalization of the American Psyche* (New York: Free Press, 2010).

8 For an interesting view on the history of psychiatry, see: J.A. Lieberman with O. Ogas, *Shrinks: The Untold Story of Psychiatry* (London: Weidenfeld and Nicolson, 2015) (for a discussion of this book, see: P. Tyrer, 'Book review: *Shrinks: The Untold Story of Psychiatry*', *British Journal of Psychiatry*, 208, 4 (April 2016), p. 401; for a discussion of this book in an Irish context, see: C. Kelly, 'From quacks to Freud to Quaaludes', *Sunday Independent*, 29 March 2015).

9 J. Reynolds, *Grangegorman: Psychiatric Care in Dublin since 1815* (Dublin: Institute of Public Administration in association with Eastern Health Board, 1992), p. 26.

10 Select Committee on the Lunatic Poor in Ireland, *Report from the Select Committee on the Lunatic Poor in Ireland with Minutes of Evidence Taken Before the Committee and an Appendix* (London: House of Commons, 1817), p. 23. See also: Finnane, *Insanity and the Insane in Post-Famine Ireland*, p. 28; for a perspective on this book, see: C. Mollan, 'Maniacs, melancholics and others', *Irish Times*, 25 July 1981.

11 Finnane, *Insanity and the Insane in Post-Famine Ireland*; J. Robins, *Fools and Mad: A History of the Insane in Ireland* (Dublin: Institute of Public Administration, 1986); E. Malcolm, *Swift's Hospital: A History of St Patrick's Hospital, Dublin, 1746–1989* (Dublin: Gill and Macmillan, 1989) (for a discussion of this book, see: J. Robins, 'A house for fools and mad', *Irish Times*, 3 February 1990); Reynolds, *Grangegorman: Psychiatric Care in Dublin since 1815*; E.F. Torrey and J. Miller, *The Invisible Plague: The Rise of Mental Illness from 1750 to the Present* (New Jersey: Rutgers University Press, 2001); D. Walsh and A. Daly, *Mental Illness in Ireland 1750–2002: Reflections on the Rise and Fall of Institutional Care* (Dublin: Health Research Board, 2004); B.D. Kelly, 'Mental health law in Ireland, 1821 to 1902: building the asylums', *Medico-Legal Journal*, 76, 1 (March 2008), pp. 19–25; B.D. Kelly, 'Mental health law in Ireland, 1821 to 1902: dealing with the "increase of insanity in Ireland"', *Medico-Legal Journal*, 76, 1 (March 2008), pp. 26–33.

12 D. Brennan, *Irish Insanity, 1800–2000* (Abingdon, Oxon.: Routledge, 2014), p. 2; for a discussion of this book, see: B.D. Kelly, 'An important story', *Irish Medical News*, 31 March 2014.

13 US Bureau of the Census, *Historical Statistics of the United States, Colonial Times to 1970, Bicentennial Edition, Part 2* (Washington DC: GPO, 1975); Shorter, *A History of Psychiatry: From the Era of the Asylum to the Age of Prozac*, p. 46; Torrey and Miller, *The Invisible Plague: The Rise of Mental Illness from 1750 to the Present*, pp. 193–214.

14 B.D. Kelly, 'Mental health law in Ireland, 1945 to 2001: reformation and renewal', *Medico-Legal Journal*, 76, 2 (June 2008), pp. 65–72.

15 D. Wright, 'Delusions of gender? Lay identification and clinical diagnosis of insanity in Victorian England', in J. Andrews and A. Digby (eds), *Sex and Seclusion, Class and Custody: Perspectives on Gender and Class in the History of British and Irish Psychiatry* (Amsterdam: Editions Rodopi, 2004), pp. 149–76; p. 170.

16 Scull, *The Most Solitary of Afflictions: Madness and Society in Britain, 1700–1900*, pp. 232–44. This was especially the case when doctors' salaries depended on patient numbers (Chapter 3). See also: A. Scull, *Decarceration: Community Treatment and the Deviant – A Radical View* (Englewood Cliffs, New Jersey: Prentice-Hall, 1977); Scull, *Museums of Madness: Social Organization of Insanity in 19th Century England*; K. Jones, 'Scull's dilemma', *British Journal of Psychiatry*, 141, 3 (September 1982), pp. 221–6.

17 O. Walsh, 'A perfectly ordered establishment: Connaught District Lunatic Asylum (Ballinasloe)', in P.M. Prior (ed.), *Asylums, Mental Health Care and the Irish, 1800–2010* (Dublin: Irish Academic Press, 2012), pp. 246–70; pp. 252–62.

18 D. Walsh, 'Mental illness in Ireland and its management', in D. McCluskey (ed.), *Health Policy and Practice in Ireland* (Dublin: University College Dublin Press, 2006), pp. 29–43; p. 34; B.D. Kelly, 'The Mental Treatment Act 1945 in Ireland: an historical enquiry', *History of Psychiatry*, 19, 73 (1) (March 2008), pp. 47–67.

19 O. Walsh, 'Cure or custody: therapeutic philosophy at the Connaught District Lunatic Asylum', in M.H. Preston and M. Ó hÓgartaigh (eds), *Gender and Medicine in Ireland, 1700–1950* (Syracuse, New York: Syracuse University Press, 2012), pp. 69–85. (For a perspective on this book, see: B.D. Kelly, 'Book review: *Gender and Medicine in Ireland, 1700–1950*', *Irish Journal of Psychological Medicine*, 30, 3 (September 2013), p. 227.) On the theme of families, see also: M. Finnane, 'Asylums, families and the State', *History Workshop Journal*, 20, 1 (Autumn 1985), pp. 134–48; P. Pietikäinen, *Madness: A History* (London and New York: Routledge, 2015), pp. 155–6.

20 E. Malcolm, '"Ireland's crowded madhouses": the institutional confinement of the insane in nineteenth- and twentieth-century Ireland', in R. Porter and D. Wright (eds), *The Confinement of the Insane: International Perspectives, 1800–1965* (Cambridge: Cambridge University Press, 2003), pp. 315–33; p. 330.

21 J. Mills, *Conference of the Irish Asylum Committees* (Dublin: Dollard Printing House, 1904), pp. 55–6; Finnane, *Insanity and the Insane in Post-Famine Ireland*, pp. 175, 213; D. Healy, 'Interview: In conversation with Ivor Browne', *Psychiatric Bulletin*, 16, 1 (January 1992), pp. 1–9; D. Healy, 'Irish psychiatry in the twentieth century', in H. Freeman and G.E. Berrios (eds), *150 Years of British Psychiatry. Volume II: The Aftermath* (London: Athlone Press, 1996), pp. 268–91; p. 173.

22 C. Smith, 'Living with insanity: narratives of poverty, pauperism and sickness in asylum records, 1840–76', in A. Gestrich, E. Hurren and S. King (eds), *Poverty and Sickness in Modern Europe: Narratives of the Sick Poor, 1780–1938* (London and New York: Continuum International Publishing Group, 2012), pp. 117–41; p. 136.

23 Reynolds, *Grangegorman: Psychiatric Care in Dublin since 1815*, p. 78; P. Prior, 'Mad, not bad: crime, mental disorder and gender in nineteenth-century Ireland', in I. O'Donnell and F. McAuley (eds), *Criminal Justice History* (Dublin: Four Courts Press, 2003), pp. 66–82; p. 82; Á. McCarthy, 'Hearths, bodies and minds: gender ideology and women's committal to Enniscorthy Lunatic Asylum, 1916–1925', in A. Hayes and D. Urquhart (eds), *Irish Women's History* (Dublin: Irish Academic Press, 2004), pp. 123–6; B.D. Kelly, 'Clinical and social characteristics of women committed to inpatient forensic psychiatric care in Ireland, 1868–1908', *Journal of Forensic Psychiatry and Psychology*, 19, 2 (June 2008), pp. 261–73; B.D. Kelly, 'Poverty, crime and mental illness', *Social History of Medicine*, 21, 2 (August 2008), pp. 311–28. This was a problem not only in the 1800s and early 1900s, but also into the 1950s; see: M. Guéret, *What the Doctor Saw* (Dublin: IMD, 2013), p. 28.

24 L.M. Geary, *Medicine and Charity in Ireland, 1718–1851* (Dublin: University College Dublin Press, 2004), p. 102; Malcolm, *Swift's Hospital: A History of St Patrick's Hospital, Dublin, 1746–1989*, pp. 94–5.

25 C. Cox, *Negotiating Insanity in the Southeast of Ireland, 1820–1900* (Manchester and New York: Manchester University Press, 2012), pp. 153–61. For perspectives on this invaluable, fascinating book see: S.A. Buckley, 'Certified in the 19th century', *Irish Times*, 9 March 2013; B.D. Kelly, 'Book review: *Negotiating Insanity in the Southeast of Ireland, 1820–1900*', *Irish Journal of Psychological Medicine*, 30, 2 (June 2013), pp. 159–60. In relation to the effects of prolonged institutionalisation, see: Finnane, *Insanity and the Insane in Post-Famine Ireland*, pp. 185–9.

26 Finnane, *Insanity and the Insane in Post-Famine Ireland*, p. 188.

27 Cox, *Negotiating Insanity in the Southeast of Ireland, 1820–1900*, pp. 158–9.

28 B.D. Kelly, '*Folie à plusieurs*: forensic cases from nineteenth-century Ireland', *History of Psychiatry*, 20, 77 (Part 1) (March 2009), pp. 47–60; pp. 51–2.

29 R. Boland, "Isolated from the mainstream': Portrane asylum in the 1950s', *Irish Times*, 10 June 2016.

30 C. Norman, 'Presidential address, delivered at the Royal College of Physicians, Dublin, June 12th, 1894', *Journal of Mental Science*, 40, 171 (1 October 1894), pp. 487–99; C. Norman, 'The domestic treatment of the insane', *Dublin Journal of Medical Science*, 101, 2 (February 1896), pp. 111–21; C. Norman, 'On the need for family care of persons of unsound mind in Ireland', *Journal of Mental Science*, 50, 210 (1 July 1904), pp. 461–73; C. Norman, 'The family care of the insane', *Medical Press and Circular*, 29 November–6 December 1905.

31 Anonymous, 'Psychiatrist who revolutionised care of mentally ill', *Irish Times*, 28 December 2013.

32 I. Browne, *Music and Madness* (Cork: Atrium/Cork University Press, 2008), p. 128.

33 Richmond Asylum Joint Committee. *Richmond Asylum Joint Committee Minutes* (Dublin: Richmond Asylum, 1907), pp. 92–3; B.D. Kelly, 'One hundred years ago', *Irish Journal of Psychological Medicine*, 24, 3 (September 2007), pp. 108–14; p. 112.

34 A. O'Neill, P. Casey and R. Minton, 'The homeless mentally ill: an audit from an inner city hospital', *Irish Journal of Psychological Medicine*, 24, 2 (1 June 2007), pp. 62–6.

35 Walsh and Daly, *Mental Illness in Ireland, 1750–2002: Reflections on the Rise and Fall of Institutional Care*, p. 30.

36 Commission of Inquiry on Mental Illness, *Report of the Commission of Inquiry on Mental Illness* (Dublin: The Stationery Office, 1967); *Irish Times* Reporter, 'Ireland has high mental illness rate', *Irish Times*, 29 March 1967.

37 Study Group on the Development of the Psychiatric Services, *The Psychiatric Services –Planning for the Future* (Dublin: Stationery Office, 1984); Expert Group on Mental Health Policy, *A Vision for Change* (Dublin: The Stationery Office, 2006); S. Guruswamy and B.D. Kelly, 'A change of vision? Mental health policy', *Irish Medical Journal*, 99, 6 (1 June 2006), pp. 164–6.

38 This section of the book contains material adapted by permission from BMJ Publishing Group Limited: 'Searching for the patient's voice in the Irish asylums', *Medical Humanities*, B.D. Kelly, Volume 42, No. 2 (June 2016), pp. 87–91; published Online First: 5 January 2016; doi:10.1136/medhum-2015-010825 © 2016. See also: C. Breathnach and B.D. Kelly, 'Perspectives on patienthood, practitioners and pedagogy' *Medical Humanities*, 42, 2 (June 2016), pp. 73–5.

39 D. Walsh, 'Book review: *Grangegorman: Psychiatric Care in Dublin since 1815*', *Irish Journal of Psychiatry*, 13, 2 (Autumn 1992), p. 17.

40 Reynolds, *Grangegorman: Psychiatric Care in Dublin since 1815*.

41 A.W. Clare, 'St. Patrick's Hospital', *American Journal of Psychiatry*, 155, 11 (November 1998), p. 1599; Malcolm, *Swift's Hospital: A History of St Patrick's Hospital, Dublin, 1746–1989*.

42 A. Collins, *St Vincent's Hospital, Fairview: An Illustrated History, 1857–2007* (Dublin: Albertine Kennedy Publishing with Duke Kennedy Sweetman, 2007). For a perspective on this book, see: B.D. Kelly, 'Book review: *St Vincent's Hospital, Fairview: An Illustrated History, 1857–2007*, *Irish Journal of Psychological Medicine*, 24, 4 (December 2007), p. 163.

43 A. MacLellan, N. Nic Ghabhann and F. Byrne, *World Within Walls* (Monaghan: Health Service Executive and Stair: An Irish Public History Company Ltd., 2015).

44 H.M. Henry, *Our Lady's Psychiatric Hospital Cork* (Cork: Haven Books, 1989).

45 J. McDermott, *St Mary's Hospital Castlebar: Serving Mayo Mental Health from 1866* (Castlebar: Western Health Board, 1999). See also: Mayo Mental Health Services Arts Committee, *St Mary's Hospital, Castlebar:*

'Snapshots in Time' (Castlebar: Galway Mayo Institute of Technology, 2005).

46 M. Mulholland, *To Comfort Always: A History of Holywell Hospital, Antrim, 1898–1998* (Ballymena: Homefirst Community Trust, 1998).

47 D.A. Murphy (ed.), *Tumbling Walls: The Evolution of a Community Institution over 150 Years* (Portlaoise: Midland Health Board, 1983). This volume contains, among other contributions, memoirs by a tailor, Andy Dunne, who started working in the mental hospital in Portlaoise in 1917 (pp. 39–41) and recalls the RIC (Royal Irish Constabulary) tying up patients with ropes to bring to the hospital (p. 63); a nurse, Mabel Byrne, née Gee, who started working there in 1926, discussing the paraldehyde, straitjackets and cold baths (pp. 41–2); a charge nurse, John Reddin, who started in 1932 (pp. 42–7); a matron, Harriett Stanley, who describes significant improvements in the 1950s (pp. 57–62); an administrator, Anne Doogue (pp. 62–8); various head nurses (pp. 68–70); and Dr John P. Hill, a reforming RMS, who notes that the introduction of electroconvulsive therapy (ECT) and voluntary admission status in the 1930s and 1940s *both* improved the public image of psychiatry at the time (pp. 54–7).

48 E. Lonergan (ed.), *St Luke's Hospital, Clonmel, 1834–1984* (Clonmel: South Eastern Health Board, 1984). This volume contains, among other contributions, a history of the hospital (pp. 22–83) and an account of Dr Pat O'Callaghan, Olympic champion, by Eamonn Lonergan (pp. 119–23); and memoirs by Drs Patrick A. Meehan (pp. 85–9), Patrick Heffernan (pp. 91–5) and J.F. O'Dea (pp. 97–103), and Nora Doheny, on psychiatric nurse training (pp. 105–11).

49 G. Douglas, R. Goodbody, A. Mauger and J. Davey, *Bloomfield: Bloomfield: A History, 1812–2012* (Dublin: Ashfield Press, 2012).

50 B.D. Kelly, 'Murder, mercury, mental illness: infanticide in nineteenth-century Ireland', *Irish Journal of Medical Science*, 176, 3 (September 2007), pp. 149–52; B.D. Kelly, 'Clinical and social characteristics of women committed to inpatient forensic psychiatric care in Ireland, 1868–1908', *Journal of Forensic Psychiatry and Psychology*, 19, 2 (June 2008), pp. 261–73; B.D. Kelly, 'Poverty, crime and mental illness', *Social History of Medicine*, 21, 2 (August 2008), pp. 311–28; P.M. Prior, *Madness and Murder: Gender, Crime and Mental Disorder in Nineteenth Century Ireland* (Dublin: Irish Academic Press, 2008) (for a perspective on this book, see: H. Kennedy, 'Book review: *Madness and Murder: Gender, Crime and Mental Disorder in Nineteenth-Century Ireland*', *Journal of Forensic Psychiatry and Psychology*, 20, 4 (2009), pp. 602–4); B.D. Kelly, '*Folie à plusieurs*: forensic cases from nineteenth-century Ireland', *History of Psychiatry*, 20, 77 (Part 1) (March 2009), pp. 47–60; B.D. Kelly, 'Syphilis, psychiatry and offending behaviour: clinical cases from nineteenth-century Ireland', *Irish Journal of Medical Science*, 178, 1 (March 2009), pp. 73–7.

51 F. McAuley, *Insanity, Psychiatry and Criminal Responsibility* (Dublin: Round Hall Press, 1993); T. Cooney and O. O'Neill, *Psychiatric Detention: Civil Commitment in Ireland* (Wicklow: Baikonur, 1996); P. Gibbons, N. Mulryan and A. O'Connor, 'Guilty but insane': the insanity defence in Ireland, 1850–1995, *British Journal of Psychiatry*, 170, 5 (May 1997), pp. 467–72; P. Prior, 'Prisoner or patient?' The official debate on the criminal lunatic in nineteenth-century Ireland, *History of Psychiatry*, 15, 58 (Part 2) (June 2004), pp. 177–92; B.D. Kelly, 'The Mental Treatment Act 1945 in Ireland: an historical enquiry', *History of Psychiatry*, 19, 73(1) (March 2008), pp. 47–67.

52 Finnane, *Insanity and the Insane in Post-Famine Ireland*; M. Reuber, 'The architecture of psychological management: the Irish asylums (1801–1922)', *Psychological Medicine*, 26, 6 (November 1996), pp. 1179–89; M. Reuber, 'Moral management and the 'unseen eye': public lunatic asylums in Ireland, 1800–1845', in G. Jones and E. Malcolm (eds), *Medicine, Disease and the State in Ireland, 1650–1940* (Cork: Cork University Press, 1999), pp. 208–33.

53 B.D. Kelly, 'Mental health law in Ireland, 1821 to 1902: building the asylums', *Medico-Legal Journal*, 76, 1 (March 2008), pp. 19–25; B.D. Kelly, 'Mental health law in Ireland, 1821 to 1902: dealing with the "increase of insanity in Ireland"', *Medico-Legal Journal*, 76, 1 (March 2008), pp. 26–33; B.D. Kelly, 'Mental health law in Ireland, 1945 to 2001: reformation and renewal', *Medico-Legal Journal*, 76, 2 (June 2008), pp. 65–72; P. Prior, 'Dangerous lunacy: the misuse of mental health law in nineteenth-century Ireland', *Journal of Forensic Psychiatry and Psychology*, 14, 3 (September 2003), pp. 525–41.

54 A.W. Clare, 'St. Patrick's Hospital', *American Journal of Psychiatry*, 155, 11 (November 1998), p. 1599.

55 Malcolm, *Swift's Hospital: A History of St Patrick's Hospital, Dublin, 1746–1989*, p. 84.

56 Ibid., p. 83.

57 M. Guéret, *What the Doctor Saw* (Dublin: IMD, 2013), pp. 27–8.

58 O. Walsh, 'A lightness of mind': gender and insanity in nineteenth-century Ireland', in M. Kelleher and J.H. Murphy (eds), *Gender Perspectives in 19th Century Ireland: Public and Private Spheres* (Dublin: Irish Academic Press, 1997), pp. 159–67; Walsh, *Gender and Medicine in Ireland, 1700–1950*, pp. 69–85; Walsh, 'Asylums, Mental Health Care and the Irish, 1800–2010', pp. 246–70.

59 B.D. Kelly, 'Clinical and social characteristics of women committed to inpatient forensic psychiatric care in Ireland, 1868–1908', *Journal of Forensic Psychiatry and Psychology*, 19, 2 (June 2008), pp. 261–73; B.D. Kelly, 'Poverty, crime and mental illness', *Social History of Medicine*, 21, 2 (August 2008), pp. 311–28; Prior, *Madness and Murder: Gender, Crime and Mental Disorder in Nineteenth Century Ireland*.

60 D. Walsh, 'The birth and death of a diagnosis: monomania in France, Britain and in Ireland', *Irish*

Journal of Psychological Medicine, 31, 1 (1 March 2014), pp. 39–45.

61 McCarthy, *Irish Women's History*, pp. 115–36.

62 G.B. Risse and J.H. Warner, 'Reconstructing clinical activities', *Social History of Medicine*, 5, 2 (August 1992), pp. 183–205.

63 R. Porter, 'The patient's view: doing medical history from below', *Theory and Society*, 14, 2, (March 1985), pp. 175–98. See also: A. Bacopoulos-Viau and A. Fauvel, 'The Patient's Turn', *Medical History*, 60, 1 (January 2016), pp. 1–18. The January 2016 issue of *Medical History* presents several papers of interest, including: S. Chaney, "No "sane" person would have any idea': patients' involvement in late nineteenth-century British asylum psychiatry', *Medical History*, 60, 1 (January 2016), pp. 37–53; H. Morrison, 'Constructing patient stories: 'dynamic' case notes and clinical encounters at Glasgow's Gartnavel Mental Hospital, 1921–32', *Medical History*, 60, 1 (January 2016), pp. 67–86.

64 L. Smith, '"Your very thankful inmate': discovering the patients of an early county lunatic asylum', *Social History of Medicine*, 21, 2 (August 2008), pp. 237–52.

65 P. Bartlett, *The Poor Law of Lunacy: The Administration of Pauper Lunatics in Mid-Nineteenth-Century England* (London and Washington: Leicester University Press, 1999), p. 159.

66 D. Armstrong, 'The patient's view', *Social Science and Medicine*, 18, 9 (September 1984), pp. 737–44.

67 D. Walsh, 'The ups and downs of schizophrenia in Ireland', *Irish Journal of Psychiatry*, 13, 2 (Autumn 1992), pp. 12–6.

68 B.D. Kelly, 'Learning disability and forensic mental healthcare in nineteenth-century Ireland', *Irish Journal of Psychological Medicine*, 25, 3 (September 2008), pp. 116–18; B.D. Kelly, 'Intellectual disability, mental illness and offending behaviour: forensic cases from early twentieth-century Ireland', *Irish Journal of Medical Science*, 179, 3 (September 2010), pp. 409–16.

69 K. McNally, 'Letter to the editor', *Irish Journal of Psychological Medicine*, 30, 1 (1 March 2013), p. 91; D. Walsh, 'Letter to the editor', *Irish Journal of Psychological Medicine*, 30, 1 (1 March 2013), pp. 91–2.

70 F. Condrau, 'The patient's view meets the clinical gaze', *Social History of Medicine*, 20, 3 (December 2007), pp. 525–40.

71 See, for example: B. Majerus, 'Making Sense of the 'Chemical Revolution'', *Medical History*, 60, 1 (January 2016), pp. 54–66.

72 A. Beveridge, 'Voices of the mad: patients' letters from the Royal Edinburgh Asylum, 1873–1908', *Psychological Medicine*, 27, 4 (July 1997), pp. 899–908.

73 Smith, '"Your very thankful inmate"', *Social History of Medicine*, 21, 2 (August 2008), pp. 237–52.

74 L. Wannell, 'Patients' relatives and psychiatric doctors', *Social History of Medicine*, 20, 2 (August 2007), pp. 297–313.

75 C. Coleborne, '"His brain was wrong, his mind astray"', *Journal of Family History*, 31, 1 (January 2006), pp.

45–65; C. Coleborne, 'Families, patients and emotions: asylums for the insane in colonial Australia and New Zealand, c. 1880–1910', *Social History of Medicine*, 19, 3 (December 2006), pp. 425–42.

76 J.T. Perceval, *A Narrative of the Treatment Experienced by a Gentleman During a State of Mental Derangement Designed to Explain the Causes and Nature of Insanity, and to Expose the Injudicious Conduct Pursued Towards Many Unfortunate Sufferers under that Calamity* (London: Effingham Wilson, 1838); C.W. Beers, *A Mind That Found Itself: An Autobiography* (New York: Longmans, Green and Co., 1908); L. Feeney and B.D. Kelly, 'Mental health advocacy and *A Mind that Found Itself*', *Irish Psychiatrist*, 9, 1 (Spring 2008), pp. 19–22.

77 S. Cullen (ed.), *Climbing Mountains in our Minds: Stories and Photographs from St. Senan's Hospital, Enniscorthy* (Wexford: Wexford County Council, 2012). For a perspective on this book, see: S. McDaid, 'Book review: *Climbing Mountains in our Minds: Stories and Photographs from St. Senan's Hospital, Enniscorthy*', *Irish Journal of Psychological Medicine*, 30, 2 (June 2013), pp. 156–7. St Senan's, which opened in 1865, is one of the most striking asylum buildings standing in Ireland, built to a symmetrical plan and presenting a curious mix of traditional and non-traditional design features. See also: McCarthy, *Irish Women's History*, pp. 115–36.

78 P.M. Prior (ed.), 'Voices of mental health service users – poetry and prose', in P.M. Prior (ed.), *Asylums, Mental Health Care and the Irish, 1800–2010* (Dublin: Irish Academic Press, 2012), pp. 103–16.

79 G. McClelland, '*Speedwell* magazine: an insider view of Holywell Psychiatric Hospital, Antrim, 1959–1973', in P.M. Prior (ed.), *Asylums, Mental Health Care and the Irish, 1800–2010* (Dublin: Irish Academic Press, 2012), pp. 44–73.

80 McDermott, *St Mary's Hospital Castlebar: Serving Mayo Mental Health from 1866*, pp. 149–50, 179.

81 C. Duffy, *It Happened in Ireland* (New York: The Christian Press, 1944).

82 H. Greally, *Bird's Nest Soup* (Dublin: Allen Figgis and Co., 1971).

83 P. Casey and B.D. Kelly, *Fish's Clinical Psychopathology (Third Edition)* (London: Gaskell/Royal College of Psychiatrists, 2007).

84 Finnane, *Insanity and the Insane in Post-Famine Ireland*, p. 193.

85 B.D. Kelly, 'Murder, mercury, mental illness: infanticide in nineteenth-century Ireland', *Irish Journal of Medical Science*, 176, 3 (September 2007), pp. 149–52.

86 D. Penney and P. Stastny, *The Lives They Left Behind: Suitcases from a State Hospital Attic* (New York: Bellevue Literary Press, 2008).

87 D. Bolger, 'Forgotten relics of lives written off as 'lunatics' and 'imbeciles'', *Irish Daily Mail*, 14 August 2014; C. Murphy, 'It's time that dissenting voices were listened to', *Sunday Business Post*, 8 June 2014. An associated radio documentary, 'Ghosts of Grangegorman', produced

by Alan Counihan and Nicoline Greer, was broadcast on RTÉ Radio 1 on 5 September 2015 as part of the 'Documentary on One' series. See: www.alancounihan.net

88 P.M. Prior (ed.), 'Voices of doctors and officials', in P.M. Prior (ed.), *Asylums, Mental Health Care and the Irish, 1800–2010* (Dublin: Irish Academic Press, 2012), pp. 271–83.

89 J. Fogarty, 'The people who hear voices in their heads', *Irish Examiner*, 11 April 2015. See: www.voicesireland.com

90 J.C. Burnham, *What is Medical History?* (Cambridge and Malden, MA: Polity Press, 2005), pp. v, 9.

91 Committee on Lunacy Administration (Ireland), *First and Second Reports of the Committee Appointed by the Lord Lieutenant of Ireland on Lunacy Administration (Ireland)* (Edinburgh: Neill & Co. for Her Majesty's Stationery Office, 1891).

Chapter 1. The Birth of Psychiatry in Ireland

1 Committee on Lunacy Administration (Ireland), *First and Second Reports of the Committee Appointed by the Lord Lieutenant of Ireland on Lunacy Administration (Ireland)* (Edinburgh: Neill & Co. for Her Majesty's Stationery Office, 1891), p. 65.

2 P. Vandermeersch, '"*Les mythes d'origine*" in the history of psychiatry', in M.S. Micale and R. Porter (eds), *Discovering the History of Psychiatry* (New York and Oxford: Oxford University Press, 1994), pp. 219–31.

3 Burnham, *What is Medical History?*, p. 9.

4 Scull, *Madness in Civilization: A Cultural History of Insanity, From the Bible to Freud, From the Madhouse to Modern Medicine*, pp. 16–69. A version of some of the material in this section was published as: B.D. Kelly, 'A "Madman's Chair" and other ancient mental illness cures', *Irish Medical Times*, 31 July 2015. Material from the *Irish Medical Times* is reproduced by kind permission of the *Irish Medical Times*.

5 S.J. Arbuthnot (ed.), *Cóir Anmann: A Late Middle Irish Treatise on Personal Names* (London: Irish Texts Society, 2006), pp. 105, 142. See also: L. O'Brien, 'The magic wisp: a history of the mentally ill in Ireland', *Bulletin of the Menninger Clinic*, 31, 2 (March 1967), pp. 79–95; p. 79 (this paper by Liam O'Brien MD, Superintendent at State Hospital No. 2, St Joseph, Missouri, was accepted as a thesis in the Scientific Writing Course in the Menninger School of Psychiatry, and awarded first prize by the Alumni Association of the School, July 1962; presented to the History of Medicine Seminar, The Menninger Foundation, 22 May 1965); Robins, *Fools and Mad: A History of the Insane in Ireland*, pp. 5–6; J.A. Robins, 'The advent of the District Mental Hospital System', in E. Lonergan (ed.), *St Luke's Hospital, Clonmel, 1834–1984*

(Clonmel: South Eastern Health Board, 1984), pp. 13–21; p. 13.

6 T.P.C. Kirkpatrick, *A Note on the History of the Care of the Insane in Ireland up to the End of the Nineteenth Century* (Dublin: University Press, Ponsonby and Gibbs, 1931), p. 5. For more information regarding the remarkable T. Percy C. Kirkpatrick, MD LittD, Fellow and Registrar of the Royal College of Physicians of Ireland, see: M. O'Doherty, 'Irish medical historiography', in J.B. Lyons (ed.), *2000 Years of Irish Medicine* (Dublin: Eireann Healthcare Publications, 1999), pp. 145–8; p. 146.

7 These and other tales were explored in some depth by Eugene O'Curry in Lecture X of his published lecture series: E. O'Curry, *On the Manners and Customs of the Ancient Irish* (London: Williams and Norgate, 1873), pp. 203–29 (especially pp. 203–5).

8 Anonymous, 'Louth Ordnance Survey Letters (Continued)', *Journal of the County Louth Archaeological Society*, 5, 1 (December, 1921), pp. 28–34; p. 29; K. Chadbourne, 'Áine Chnoc Áine', *Proceedings of the Harvard Celtic Colloquium*, 20/21 (2000/2001), p. 176; Robins, *Fools and Mad: A History of the Insane in Ireland*, p. 9.

9 These stories clearly merit detailed study in a book of their own. Many relevant texts (e.g. Deirdre) are available online through CELT, the Corpus of Electronic Texts, Ireland's longest running Humanities Computing project (http://celt.ucc.ie/index.html), a fascinating, invaluable resource.

10 C. Plummer, *Bethada Náem Nérenn (Lives of Irish Saints)* (Oxford: Clarendon Press, 1922), p. 285.

11 T. Wright (ed.), *The Historical Works of Giraldus Cambrensis* (London: George Bell and Sons, 1894), p. 106.

12 F. Kelly, *A Guide to Early Irish Law* (Dublin: School of Celtic Studies, Dublin Institute for Advanced Studies, 2003), p. 93. See also: O'Brien, 'The magic wisp: a history of the mentally ill in Ireland', *Bulletin of the Menninger Clinic*, 31, 2 (March 1967), pp. 79–95; pp. 80–1.

13 F. Kelly, 'Medicine and early Irish law', in J.B. Lyons (ed.), *2000 Years of Irish Medicine* (Dublin: Eireann Healthcare Publications, 1999), pp. 15–19; p. 18.

14 Kirkpatrick, *A Note on the History of the Care of the Insane in Ireland up to the End of the Nineteenth Century*, p. 6.

15 Kelly, *A Guide to Early Irish Law*, pp. 92–4.

16 J. O'Donovan (transl.), *The Banquet of Dun na nGedh and the Battle of Magh Rath* (Dublin: The University Press, for the Irish Archaeology Society, 1842), pp. 231–3; Kirkpatrick, *A Note on the History of the Care of the Insane in Ireland up to the End of the Nineteenth Century*, p. 5.

17 K. Myer (ed.), *Anecdota Oxoniensia: Cath Finntrága* (Oxford: Clarendon Press, 1885), pp. 17–18.

18 S. Heaney, *Sweeney Astray* (London: Faber and Faber Ltd, 1984; first published by Field Day Theatre Company, 1983).

19   F. O'Brien, *At Swim-Two-Birds* (London: Penguin, 2001; first published by Longmans Green, 1939), pp. 64–72, 78–85, 88–91, 185, 216–19.

20   O'Donovan, *The Banquet of Dun na nGedh and the Battle of Magh Rath*, pp. 231–3.

21   Ibid., p. 235.

22   See, for example: Scull, *Madness in Civilization: A Cultural History of Insanity, From the Bible to Freud, From the Madhouse to Modern Medicine*, p. 69.

23   This story is linked with those of Sweeney and Bolcán, who fled to Glenn Bolcáin, which is identified with *Gleann na nGealt* (G.S. Mac Eoin, 'Gleann Bolcáin agus Gleann na nGealt', *Béaloideas*, 30 (1962), pp. 105–20; Kirkpatrick, *A Note on the History of the Care of the Insane in Ireland up to the End of the Nineteenth Century*, p. 5; M. Purcell, *A Time for Sowing: The History of St John of God Brothers in Ireland, 1879–1979* (Dublin: Hospitaller Brothers of St John of God, 1980), pp. 35–6).

24   B. O'Connell, 'Recovering well', *Irish Times*, 23 October 2012; R. Foley, 'Indigenous narratives of health: (re) placing folk-medicine within Irish health histories', *Journal of Medical Humanities*, 36, 1 (March 2015), pp. 5–18; p. 15. See also: S. MacDonagh, *The Dingle Peninsula* (Dingle: Utter Press, 2013), pp. 200–2.

25   N. Ishii, T. Terao, Y. Araki, K. Kohno, Y. Mizokami, I. Shiotsuki, K. Hatano, M. Makino, K. Kodama and N. Iwata, 'Low risk of male suicide and lithium in drinking water', *Journal of Clinical Psychiatry*, 76, 3 (March 2015), pp. 319–26.

26   Samples were collected by the author in August 2015. I am very grateful for the guidance and assistance of Dr Maria Fitzgibbon, Consultant Clinical Biochemist, Mater Misericordiae University Hospital, Dublin.

27   N.D. Kapusta, N. Mossaheb, E. Etzersdorfer, G. Hlavin, K. Thau, M. Willeit, N. Praschak-Rieder, G. Sonneck and K. Leithner-Dziubas, 'Lithium in drinking water and suicide mortality', *British Journal of Psychiatry*, 198, 5 (April 2011), pp. 346–50.

28   H. Ohgami, T. Terao, I. Shiotsuki, N. Ishii and N. Iwata, 'Lithium levels in drinking water and risk of suicide', *British Journal of Psychiatry*, 194, 5 (May 2009), pp. 464–5.

29   N.D. Kapusta and D. König, 'Naturally occurring low-dose lithium in drinking water', *Journal of Clinical Psychiatry*, 76, 3 (March 2015), pp. 373–4.

30   J. O'Donovan, *Ordnance Survey Letters (Donegal)* (1835) (Dublin: Four Masters Press, 2000), pp. 171–2; E. Ó Muirgheasa, 'The holy wells of Donegal', *Béaloideas*, 6, 2 (December 1936), pp. 143–62; p. 157.

31   Robins, *Fools and Mad: A History of the Insane in Ireland*, pp. 12–8; P. Logan, *The Holy Wells of Ireland* (Gerrards Cross, Buckinghamshire: Colin Smythe Ltd., 1981), p. 73.

32   J. McDermott, *St Mary's Hospital Castlebar: Serving Mayo Mental Health from 1866* (Castlebar: Western Health Board, 1999), p. 19.

33   C. McNeill, 'Hospital of S. John without the New Gate, Dublin', *The Journal of the Royal Society of Antiquaries of Ireland (Sixth Series)*, 15, 1 (June 1925), pp. 58–64; Kirkpatrick, *A Note on the History of the Care of the Insane in Ireland up to the End of the Nineteenth Century*, pp. 7–8.

34   Robins, *St Luke's Hospital, Clonmel, 1834–1984*, p. 13.

35   Kirkpatrick, *A Note on the History of the Care of the Insane in Ireland up to the End of the Nineteenth Century*, p. 7; O'Brien, 'The magic wisp: a history of the mentally ill in Ireland', *Bulletin of the Menninger Clinic*, 31, 2 (March 1967), pp. 79–95; p. 81; P. Pietikäinen, *Madness: A History* (London and New York: Routledge, 2015), p. 50.

36   Robins, *Fools and Mad: A History of the Insane in Ireland*, pp. 26–7.

37   Ibid.; Webb, *Trinity's Psychiatrists: From Serenity of the Soul to Neuroscience*, p. 16. For perspectives on this book, see: D. Walsh, 'Book review: *Trinity's Psychiatrists: From Serenity of the Soul to Neuroscience*', *Irish Journal of Psychological Medicine*, 29, 2 (June, 2012), pp. 136–7; B. O'Shea, 'Leaving a mark on Irish psychiatry', *Irish Medical Times*, 6 September 2013; A. Collins, 'Book review: *Trinity's Psychiatrists: From Serenity of the Soul to Neuroscience*', *Irish Journal of Psychological Medicine*, 33, 1 (March 2016), p. 65.

38   W. Donnelly, W.R. Wilde and E. Singleton, *The Census of Ireland for the Year 1851, Part III: Report on the Status of Disease* (Dublin: Thom and Sons for Her Majesty's Stationery Office, 1854), p. 62–3; Robins, *Fools and Mad: A History of the Insane in Ireland*, p. 45.

39   Kirkpatrick, *A Note on the History of the Care of the Insane in Ireland up to the End of the Nineteenth Century*, pp. 9–13.

40   T. Sheridan and J. Nichols (arranged and revised), *The Works of Rev. Jonathan Swift, D.D., Dean of St Patrick's Dublin, with Notes, Historical and Critical, Volume XVIII* (New York: William Durrell and Co., 1813), pp. 213–14.

41   Ibid., p. 214.

42   Kirkpatrick, *A Note on the History of the Care of the Insane in Ireland up to the End of the Nineteenth Century*, p. 14. Although Mercer's was, in part, intended to house the mentally ill, it was not a significant element in systematic provision for this group.

43   Sheridan and Nichols, *The Works of Rev. Jonathan Swift, D.D., Dean of St Patrick's, Dublin, with Notes, Historical and Critical, Volume XVIII*, pp. 215–18.

44   For a discussion, see: O'Brien, 'The magic wisp: a history of the mentally ill in Ireland', *Bulletin of the Menninger Clinic*, 31, 2 (March 1967), pp. 79–95; pp. 82–5.

45   Malcolm, *Swift's Hospital: A History of St Patrick's Hospital, Dublin, 1746–1989*, p. 20.

46   Ibid., p. 1; Malcolm, in this excellent book, provides a fascinating discussion of Swift and madness (pp. 1–31). See also: Robins, *Fools and Mad: A History of the Insane*

in Ireland, pp. 42–54; Webb, *Trinity's Psychiatrists: From Serenity of the Soul to Neuroscience*, pp. 19–28.

47 Torrey and Miller, *The Invisible Plague: The Rise of Mental Illness from 1750 to the Present*, p. 126.

48 A.W. Clare, 'Swift, mental illness and St Patrick's Hospital', *Irish Journal of Psychological Medicine*, 15, 3 (September 1998), pp. 100–4; pp. 100–1.

49 C. Arnold, *Bedlam: London and its Mad* (London: Simon & Schuster/Pocket Books, 2009), pp. 99–100.

50 Clare, 'Swift, mental illness and St Patrick's Hospital', *Irish Journal of Psychological Medicine*, 15, 3 (September 1998), pp. 100–4; p. 100.

51 Arnold, *Bedlam: London and its Mad*, p. 100.

52 Clare, 'Swift, mental illness and St Patrick's Hospital', *Irish Journal of Psychological Medicine*, 15, 3 (September 1998), pp. 100–4; p. 102.

53 Shorter, *A History of Psychiatry: From the Era of the Asylum to the Age of Prozac*, p. 5. See also: Scull, *The Most Solitary of Afflictions: Madness and Society in Britain, 1700–1900*, pp. 64–77.

54 Malcolm, *Swift's Hospital: A History of St Patrick's Hospital, Dublin, 1746–1989*, p. 23.

55 Ibid, pp. 1–3.

56 W.R. Wilde, *The Closing Years of Dean Swift's Life* (Dublin: Hodges and Smith, 1849), p. 78.

57 Malcolm, *Swift's Hospital: A History of St Patrick's Hospital, Dublin, 1746–1989*, p. 6. See also: Kirkpatrick, *A Note on the History of the Care of the Insane in Ireland up to the End of the Nineteenth Century*, p. 15; T.P.C. Kirkpatrick, 'Obituary: Richard Robert Leeper', *Journal of Mental Science*, 88, 372 (1 July 1942), pp. 480–1; p. 480.

58 Clare, 'Swift, mental illness and St Patrick's Hospital', *Irish Journal of Psychological Medicine*, 15, 3 (September 1998), pp. 100–4; p. 103; Malcolm, *Swift's Hospital: A History of St Patrick's Hospital, Dublin, 1746–1989*, pp. 3, 6.

59 A.G. Gordon, 'Swift's pocky quean', *Journal of the Royal Society of Medicine*, 92, 2 (February 1998), p. 102.

60 T.H. Bewley, 'The health of Jonathan Swift', *Journal of the Royal Society of Medicine*, 91, 11 (November 1998), pp. 602–5; T.H. Bewley, 'Swift's pocky quean', *Journal of the Royal Society of Medicine*, 92, 4 (April 1999), p. 216; Arnold, *Bedlam: London and its Mad*, p. 100; B.D. Kelly, *Custody, Care and Criminality: Forensic Psychiatry and Law in 19th Century Ireland* (Dublin: History Press Ireland, 2014), pp. 56, 158. See also: O'Brien, 'The magic wisp: a history of the mentally ill in Ireland', *Bulletin of the Menninger Clinic*, 31, 2 (March 1967), pp. 79–95; p. 83.

61 Clare, 'Swift, mental illness and St Patrick's Hospital', *Irish Journal of Psychological Medicine*, 15, 3 (September 1998), pp. 100–4; p. 103.

62 W.R. Brain, 'The illness of Dean Swift', *Irish Journal of Medical Science*, 320–1, 6 (August/September 1952), pp. 337–45.

63 See also: T.G. Wilson, 'Swift's deafness: And his last illness', *Irish Journal of Medical Science*, 14, 6 (June 1939),

pp. 241–56; T.G. Wilson, 'The mental and physical health of Dean Swift', *Medical History*, 2, 3 (July 1958), pp. 175–90; T.G. Wilson, 'Swift and the doctors', *Medical History*, 8, 3 (July 1964), pp. 199–216. For Professor Norman Moore's views, see: J.N.P. Moore, *Swift's Philanthropy* (Dublin: Governors of St Patrick's Hospital Dublin, 1967); J. Cooney, 'Contentions about Swift rejected', *Irish Times*, 24 October 1988; Webb, *Trinity's Psychiatrists: From Serenity of the Soul to Neuroscience*, p. 25. For a strongly psychoanalytic view of Swift, see: P. Greenacre, *Swift and Carroll: A Psychoanalytic Study of Two Lives* (New York: International Universities Press, 1955).

64 Clare, 'Swift, mental illness and St Patrick's Hospital', *Irish Journal of Psychological Medicine*, 15, 3 (September 1998), pp. 100–4; p. 104.

65 A.W. Clare, 'St. Patrick's Hospital', *American Journal of Psychiatry*, 155, 11 (November 1998), p. 1599.

66 Malcolm, *Swift's Hospital: A History of St Patrick's Hospital, Dublin, 1746–1989*, pp. 32, 54.

67 Kirkpatrick, *A Note on the History of the Care of the Insane in Ireland up to the End of the Nineteenth Century*, p. 16.

68 Malcolm, *Swift's Hospital: A History of St Patrick's Hospital, Dublin, 1746–1989*, pp. 87–93.

69 Reynolds, *Grangegorman: Psychiatric Care in Dublin since 1815*, p. 26.

70 Select Committee on the Lunatic Poor in Ireland, *Report from the Select Committee on the Lunatic Poor in Ireland with Minutes of Evidence Taken Before the Committee and an Appendix* (London: House of Commons, 1817), p. 3.

71 Ibid., p. 11. See also: Malcolm, *Swift's Hospital: A History of St Patrick's Hospital, Dublin, 1746–1989*, p. 88.

72 Select Committee on the Lunatic Poor in Ireland, *Report from the Select Committee on the Lunatic Poor in Ireland with Minutes of Evidence Taken Before the Committee and an Appendix*, pp. 45, 46.

73 Ibid. See also: Reynolds, *Grangegorman: Psychiatric Care in Dublin since 1815*, pp. 20–30.

74 Select Committee on the Lunatic Poor in Ireland, *Report from the Select Committee on the Lunatic Poor in Ireland with Minutes of Evidence Taken Before the Committee and an Appendix*, p. 45.

75 Ibid.

76 Ibid., p. 46. Transporting the mentally ill presented continual challenges; see: Robins, *Fools and Mad: A History of the Insane in Ireland*, pp. 39–41.

77 Select Committee on the Lunatic Poor in Ireland, *Report from the Select Committee on the Lunatic Poor in Ireland with Minutes of Evidence Taken Before the Committee and an Appendix*, p. 4.

78 Lunatic Asylums, Ireland, Commission, *Report of the Commissioners of Inquiry into the State of the Lunatic Asylums and Other Institutions for the Custody and Treatment of the Insane in Ireland: with Minutes of Evidence and Appendices (Part 1 – Report, Tables, and*

Returns) (Dublin: Thom and Sons, for Her Majesty's Stationery Office, 1858), p. 34.

79 Ibid., pp. 34–5.

80 O'Brien, 'The magic wisp: a history of the mentally ill in Ireland', *Bulletin of the Menninger Clinic*, 31, 2 (March 1967), pp. 79–95; p. 90.

81 Lunatic Asylums, Ireland, Commission, *Report of the Commissioners of Inquiry into the State of the Lunatic Asylums and Other Institutions for the Custody and Treatment of the Insane in Ireland: with Minutes of Evidence and Appendices (Part 1 – Report, Tables, and Returns)*, p. 35.

82 Ibid., p. 36.

83 Malcolm, *Swift's Hospital: A History of St Patrick's Hospital, Dublin, 1746–1989*, pp. 214–16.

84 B.D. Kelly, 'Dr William Saunders Hallaran and psychiatric practice in nineteenth-century Ireland', *Irish Journal of Medical Science*, 177, 1 (March 2008), pp. 79–84; B.D. Kelly, 'Introduction', in W.S. Hallaran, *An Enquiry into the Causes Producing the Extraordinary Addition to the Number of Insane Together with Extended Observations on the Cure of Insanity with Hints as to the Better Management of Public Asylums for Insane Persons* (Dublin: First Medical, 2008; Hallaran's book was first published in Cork by Edwards and Savage, 1810), pp. 3–11; Kelly, *Custody, Care and Criminality Forensic Psychiatry and Law in 19th Century Ireland*, pp. 27–35. (For a perspective on this book, see: B. O'Shea, 'The horrors of the old asylum', *Irish Medical Times*, 12 January 2015.) See also: Henry, *Our Lady's Psychiatric Hospital Cork*, pp. 9–13.

85 A. Williamson, 'The beginnings of state care for the mentally ill in Ireland', *Economic and Social Review*, 10, 1 (January 1970), pp. 280–91. See also: A.P. Williamson, 'The Origins of the Irish Mental Hospital Service, 1800–1843' (MLitt Thesis, Trinity College Dublin, 1970); Henry, *Our Lady's Psychiatric Hospital Cork*, pp. 16–23. 'In 1787, an Asylum was erected in connexion with the House of Industry in Cork' (W. Donnelly, W.R. Wilde and E. Singleton, *The Census of Ireland for the Year 1851, Part III: Report on the Status of Disease* (Dublin: Thom and Sons for Her Majesty's Stationery Office, 1854), p. 64).

86 Kirkpatrick, *A Note on the History of the Care of the Insane in Ireland up to the End of the Nineteenth Century*, p. 17.

87 W.S. Hallaran, *An Enquiry into the Causes Producing the Extraordinary Addition to the Number of Insane together with Extended Observations on the Cure of Insanity with Hints as to the Better Management of Public Asylums for Insane Persons* (Cork: Edwards and Savage, 1810) (hereafter 'Hallaran, *An Enquiry*').

88 R. Hunter and I. Macalpine, *Three Hundred Years of Psychiatry, 1535–1860: A History Presented in Selected English Texts* (London: Oxford University Press, 1963), pp. 648–55; P. Laffey, 'Two registers of madness in Enlightenment Britain. Part 2', *History of Psychiatry*, 14, 53 (Part 1) (March 2003), pp. 63–81.

89 Hallaran, *An Enquiry*, p. 1.

90 R. Blackmore, *A Treatise of the Spleen and Vapours, or, Hypocondriacal and Hysterical Affections: With Three Discourses on the Nature and Cure of the Cholick, Melancholy, and Palsies (Second Edition)* (London: J. Pemberton, 1726).

91 Hallaran, *An Enquiry*, pp. 2–4.

92 Ibid., p. 6.

93 Ibid., p. 8.

94 Stone, *Healing the Mind: A History of Psychiatry from Antiquity to the Present*, pp. 105, 121.

95 For more information about Cullen, see: E.T. Carlson and R.B. McFadden, 'Dr William Cullen on mania', *American Journal of Psychiatry*, 117, 5 (November 1960), pp. 463–5; W.F. Knoff, 'A history of the concept of neurosis, with a memoir of William Cullen', *American Journal of Psychiatry*, 127, 1 (July 1970), pp. 80–4.

96 A. Dörries and T. Beddies, 'The Wittenauer Heilstätten in Berlin: a case record study of psychiatric patients in Germany, 1919–1960' in R. Porter and D. Wright (eds), *The Confinement of the Insane: International Perspectives, 1800–1965* (Cambridge: Cambridge University Press, 2003), pp. 149–72; P.E. Prestwich, 'Family strategies and medical power: 'voluntary' committal in a Parisian asylum, 1876–1914', in R. Porter and D. Wright (eds), *The Confinement of the Insane: International Perspectives, 1800–1965* (Cambridge: Cambridge University Press, 2003), pp. 79–99.

97 D. Hayden, *Pox: Genius, Madness, and The Mysteries Of Syphilis* (New York: Basic Books, 2003).

98 W.S. Hallaran, *Practical Observations on the Causes and Cures of Insanity (Second Edition)* (Cork: Edwards and Savage, 1818), pp. 23–35; J.F. Fleetwood, *The History of Medicine in Ireland (Second Edition)* (Dublin: Skellig Press, 1983), p. 172.

99 See: E. Kraepelin, *Psychiatrie. Ein Lehrbuch für Studirende und Aerzte (Sixth Edition)* (Leipzig: Verlag von Johann Ambrosius Barth, 1899). See also: Shorter, *A History of Psychiatry: From the Era of the Asylum to the Age of Prozac*, pp. 100–9.

100 World Health Organisation, *International Classification of Mental and Behavioural Disorders (Volume 10)* (Geneva: World Health Organisation, 1992); American Psychiatric Association, *Diagnostic and Statistical Manual of Mental Disorders (Fifth Edition)* (Washington DC: American Psychiatric Association, 2013).

101 Hallaran, *An Enquiry*, p. 12.

102 Ibid., p. 13.

103 Ibid., p. 22. Religious fervour is discussed by Robins in *Fools and Mad: A History of the Insane in Ireland* (pp. 117–20).

104 Hallaran, *An Enquiry*, p. 14.

105 Kelly, *Custody, Care and Criminality: Forensic Psychiatry and Law in 19th Century Ireland*, pp. 35–47.

106 J. Wilde, *Ancient Cures, Charms, and Usages of Ireland* (London: Ward & Downey, 1890), p. 33. See also: Kirkpatrick, *A Note on the History of the Care of the*

Insane in Ireland up to the End of the Nineteenth Century, p. 10; O'Brien, 'The magic wisp: a history of the mentally ill in Ireland', *Bulletin of the Menninger Clinic*, 31, 2 (March 1967), pp. 79–95; p. 82.

107   Wilde, *Ancient Cures, Charms, and Usages of Ireland*, p. 34.

108   Ibid., pp. 34–5.

109   Ibid., pp. 35–7.

110   Stone, *Healing the Mind: A History of Psychiatry from Antiquity to the Present*, pp. 43, 49, 53, 121; I.H. Kerridge and M. Lowe, 'Bloodletting: the story of a therapeutic technique', *Medical Journal of Australia*, 163, 11–12 (December 1995), pp. 631–3; Millon, *Masters of the Mind: Exploring the Story of Mental Illness from Ancient Times to the New Millennium*, pp. 26–7, 237; T. Farmar, *Patients, Potions and Physicians: A Social History of Medicine in Ireland* (Dublin: A & A Farmar in association with the Royal College of Physicians of Ireland, 2004), pp. 43–4, 72–5, 98–9.

111   Hallaran, *An Enquiry*, p. 50. See also: Robins, *Fools and Mad: A History of the Insane in Ireland*, pp. 57–9.

112   W. Battie, *Treatise on Madness* (London: Whiston and White, 1758), p. 94.

113   Malcolm, *Swift's Hospital: A History of St Patrick's Hospital, Dublin, 1746–1989*, p. 89; Stone, *Healing the Mind: A History of Psychiatry from Antiquity to the Present*, pp. 48, 53, 121; Farmar, *Patients, Potions and Physicians: A Social History of Medicine in Ireland*, p. 74.

114   Hallaran, *An Enquiry*, pp. 51–2.

115   Battie, *Treatise on Madness*, p. 97.

116   M. Tuomy, *Treatise on the Principal Diseases of Dublin* (Dublin: William Folds, 1810).

117   Farmar, *Patients, Potions and Physicians: A Social History of Medicine in Ireland*, p. 75.

118   Hallaran, *An Enquiry*, p. 59.

119   Stone, *Healing the Mind: A History of Psychiatry from Antiquity to the Present*, p. 105; Porter, *Madmen: A Social History of Mad-houses, Mad-doctors and Lunatics*, pp. 223–4.

120   N.J. Wade, U. Norrsell and A. Presly, 'Cox's chair: 'a moral and a medical mean in the treatment of maniacs'', *History of Psychiatry*, 16, 61 (Part 1) (March 2005), pp. 73–88.

121   N.J. Wade, 'The original spin doctors: the meeting of perception and insanity', *Perception*, 34, 3 (2005), pp. 253–60.

122   Torrey and Miller, *The Invisible Plague: The Rise of Mental Illness from 1750 to the Present*, p. 45; Wade, Norrsell and Presly, 'Cox's chair: 'a moral and a medical mean in the treatment of maniacs'', *History of Psychiatry*, 16, 61 (Part 1) (March 2005), pp. 73–88.

123   J.M. Cox, *Practical Observations on Insanity* (London: Baldwin and Murray, 1804), p. 137.

124   Hallaran, *An Enquiry*, p. 59.

125   Ibid., p. 67.

126   Ibid., p. 61. See also: Henry, *Our Lady's Psychiatric Hospital Cork*, p. 538.

127   Hallaran, *An Enquiry*, pp. 63–4.

128   Ibid., p. 65.

129   Ibid., p. 67. See also: O'Brien, 'The magic wisp: a history of the mentally ill in Ireland', *Bulletin of the Menninger Clinic*, 31, 2 (March 1967), pp. 79–95; p. 82.

130   Hallaran, *An Enquiry*, p. 69.

131   United Nations, *Principles for the Protection of Persons with Mental Illness and the Improvement of Mental Health Care* (New York: United Nations, Secretariat Centre For Human Rights, 1991).

132   B.D. Kelly, 'Mental health and human rights: challenges for a new millennium', *Irish Journal of Psychological Medicine*, 18, 4 (December 2001), pp. 114–15; B.D. Kelly, *Dignity, Mental Health and Human Rights: Coercion and the Law* (Abingdon, Oxon: Routledge, 2015).

133   E.C. Leonard, Jr., 'Did some 18th and 19th century treatments for mental disorders act on the brain?', *Medical Hypotheses*, 62, 2 (February 2004), pp. 219–21; Farmar, *Patients, Potions and Physicians: A Social History of Medicine in Ireland*, p. 5.

134   Hallaran, *An Enquiry*, p. 76.

135   Ibid., p. 70.

136   E.C. Leonard, Jr., 'Did some 18th and 19th century treatments for mental disorders act on the brain?', *Medical Hypotheses*, 62, 2 (February 2004), pp. 219–21.

137   A. Breckenridge, 'William Withering's legacy', *Clinical Medicine*, 6, 4 (July–August, 2006), pp. 393–7.

138   M.M. Weber and H.M. Emrich, 'Current and historical concepts of opiate treatment in psychiatric disorders', *International Journal of Clinical Psychopharmacology*, 3, 3 (July 1988), pp. 255–66; Farmar, *Patients, Potions and Physicians: A Social History of Medicine in Ireland*, pp. 70, 72, 75.

139   Hallaran, *An Enquiry*, p. 81. Battie, in his *Treatise on Madness* (pp. 95–6), was notably cautious about opium.

140   W. Sneader, 'The prehistory of psychotherapeutic agents', *Journal of Psychopharmacology*, 4, 3 (May 1990), pp. 115–19.

141   Hallaran, *An Enquiry*, pp. 83–4.

142   D. Guthrie, *A History of Medicine* (London: Nelson, 1945), p. 204; H.H. Merrit, R. Adams and H.C. Solomon, *Neurosyphilis* (Oxford: Oxford University Press, 1946); Fleetwood, *The History of Medicine in Ireland (Second Edition)*, p. 100; Farmar, *Patients, Potions and Physicians: A Social History of Medicine in Ireland*, p. 75; E.M. Brown, 'Why Wagner-Jauregg won the Nobel Prize for discovering malaria therapy for general paralysis of the insane', *History of Psychiatry*, 11, 44 (October 2000), pp. 371–82.

143   Hallaran, *An Enquiry*, p. 92.

144   Scull, *Madness in Civilization: A Cultural History of Insanity, From the Bible to Freud, From the Madhouse to Modern Medicine*, pp. 272, 363; see also: Shorter, *A History of Psychiatry: From the Era of the Asylum to the Age of Prozac*, p. 37.

145   Hallaran, *An Enquiry*, p. 87.

146 Ibid., p. 86. A Turkish bath was installed in the Cork asylum in the 1860s; Dr James A. Eames later oversaw improvements of the baths and by 1881 approximately 400 inpatients were bathing weekly, but there was a gas explosion during the construction of a further bath (Henry, *Our Lady's Psychiatric Hospital Cork*, pp. 143, 168; see also: p. 162).

147 Robins, *Fools and Mad: A History of the Insane in Ireland*, p. 25.

148 C. Lucas, *Essay on Waters: In Three Parts, Treating, I. Of Simple Waters. II. Of Cold, Medicated Waters. III. Of Natural Baths* (London: A. Millar, 1756), pp. xv, 220. See also: J. Kelly, 'The life and significance of Charles Lucas (1713–1771)', *Irish Journal of Medical Science*, 184, 3 (September 2015), pp. 541–5.

149 C. Lucas and Dr Achmet, *The Theory and Uses of Baths, Being an Extract from the Essay on Waters by the Late Charles Lucas, Esq., MD, with Marginal Notes by Dr Achmet, Illustrated by Some Annexed Cases* (Dublin: J. Potts, 1772).

150 Robins, *Fools and Mad: A History of the Insane in Ireland*, pp. 25–6.

151 Lucas and Dr Achmet, *The Theory and Uses of Baths, being an Extract from the Essay on Waters by the Late Charles Lucas, Esq., MD, with Marginal Notes by Dr Achmet, Illustrated by Some Annexed Cases*, p. 80. In relation to baths, see also: D.A. Murphy, 'A long half-century, 1832–1885', in D.A. Murphy (ed.), *Tumbling Walls: The Evolution of a Community Institution over 150 Years* (Portlaoise: Midland Health Board, 1983), pp. 15–27; p. 26.

152 Hallaran, *An Enquiry*, p. 93.

153 Ibid., p. 95.

154 E. Lonergan, 'St Luke's, Clonmel, 1834–1984', in E. Lonergan (ed.), *St Luke's Hospital, Clonmel, 1834–1984* (Clonmel: South Eastern Health Board, 1984), pp. 22–83; p. 46; Finnane, *Insanity and the Insane in Post-Famine Ireland*, p. 203, 217–18; Henry, *Our Lady's Psychiatric Hospital Cork*, p. 145. For more on diet in general, see: Murphy, *Tumbling Walls: The Evolution of a Community Institution over 150 Years*, pp. 15–27; p. 22.

155 S. Scully, 'From minute to minute, 1886–1905' in D.A. Murphy (ed.), *Tumbling Walls: The Evolution of a Community Institution over 150 Years* (Portlaoise: Midland Health Board, 1983), pp. 28–33; p. 29.

156 Malcolm, *Swift's Hospital: A History of St Patrick's Hospital, Dublin, 1746–1989*, pp. 104–53; Cox, *Negotiating Insanity in the Southeast of Ireland, 1820–1900*, pp. 210–12.

157 A.P. Williamson, 'Psychiatry, moral management and the origins of social policy for mentally ill people in Ireland', *Irish Journal of Medical Science*, 161, 9 (September 1992), pp. 556–8; McCarthy, *Irish Women's History*, pp. 115–36; P. Prior, 'Prisoner or patient?' The official debate on the criminal lunatic in nineteenth-century Ireland, *History of Psychiatry*, 15, 58 (Part 2) (June 2004), pp.

177–92; Cox, *Negotiating Insanity in the Southeast of Ireland, 1820–1900*, pp. 212–13.

158 M. Reuber, *Staats- und Privatanstalten in Irland: Irre, Ärzte und Idioten (1600–1900)* (Köln: Verlag Josef Eul, 1994); M. Reuber, 'The architecture of psychological management: the Irish asylums (1801–1922)', *Psychological Medicine*, 26, 6 (November 1996), pp. 1179–89; Reuber, *Medicine, Disease and the State in Ireland, 1650–1940*, pp. 208–33.

159 H. Kazano, 'Asylum: the huge psychiatric hospital in the 19th century US', *Seishin Shinkeigaku Zasshi*, 114, 10 (2012), pp. 1194–200.

160 Hallaran, *An Enquiry*, p. 109.

161 E.N.M. O'Sullivan, *Textbook of Occupational Therapy with Chief Reference to Psychological Medicine* (London: H.K Lewis & Co. Ltd., 1955); G.O. Gabbard and J. Kay, 'The fate of integrated treatment: whatever happened to the biopsychosocial psychiatrist?', *American Journal of Psychiatry*, 158, 12 (December 2001), pp. 1956–63.

162 Arnold, *Bedlam: London and its Mad*, pp. 133–6.

163 L.D. Smith, *'Cure, Comfort and Safe Custody': Public Lunatic Asylums in Early Nineteenth-Century England* (London and New York: Leicester University Press, 1999), p. 14.

164 Battie, *Treatise on Madness*, pp. v–vi, 1–2, 68. Shorter, *A History of Psychiatry: From the Era of the Asylum to the Age of Prozac*, pp. 9–10.

165 Battie, *Treatise on Madness*, pp. v–vi.

166 Smith, *'Cure, Comfort and Safe Custody': Public Lunatic Asylums in Early Nineteenth-Century England*, p. 18.

167 S. Tuke, *Description of the Retreat, an Institution Near York, for Insane Persons of the Society of Friends: Containing an Account of its Origin and Progress, the Modes of Treatment, and a Statement of Cases* (Philadelphia: Isaac Pierce, 1813); Kirkpatrick, *A Note on the History of the Care of the Insane in Ireland up to the End of the Nineteenth Century*, p. 24; Torrey and Miller, *The Invisible Plague: The Rise of Mental Illness from 1750 to the Present*, p. 28.

168 Stone, *Healing the Mind: A History of Psychiatry from Antiquity to the Present*, p. 104.

169 Lieberman with Ogas, *Shrinks: The Untold Story of Psychiatry*, pp. 35–7. See also: Kirkpatrick, *A Note on the History of the Care of the Insane in Ireland up to the End of the Nineteenth Century*, pp. 20–2.

170 P. Pinel, *A Treatise on Insanity* (translated by D.D. Davis MD) (Sheffield: W. Todd for Messrs. Cadell and Davies, 1806).

171 Kirkpatrick, *A Note on the History of the Care of the Insane in Ireland up to the End of the Nineteenth Century*, p. 2.

172 D.B. Weiner, 'Philippe Pinel's "Memoir on Madness" of December 11, 1794', *American Journal of Psychiatry*, 149, 6 (June 1992), pp. 725–32. See also: D.B. Weiner, '"*Le geste de Pinel*": the history of a psychiatric myth', in M.S. Micale and R. Porter (eds), *Discovering the History of Psychiatry* (New York and Oxford: Oxford University Press, 1994), pp. 232–47.

173 Hallaran, *An Enquiry*, pp. 46–7.

174 M. Balter, 'Talking back to madness', *Science*, 343, 6176 (14 March 2014), pp. 1190–3; B.D. Kelly, 'Integrating psychological treatment approaches', *Science*, 344, 6181 (18 April 2014), pp. 254–5.

175 E. Williams, *A CBT Approach to Mental Health Problems in Psychosis* (London: Speechmark Publishing Ltd., 2013).

176 Shorter, *A History of Psychiatry: From the Era of the Asylum to the Age of Prozac*, p. 7.

177 G.N. Grob, *Mental Institutions in America: Social Policy to 1875* (New Brunswick and London: Transaction Publishers, 2009), p. 16.

178 Ibid., p. 27.

179 Ibid., p. 35.

180 Shorter, *A History of Psychiatry: From the Era of the Asylum to the Age of Prozac*, p. 6.

181 The plight of the homeless mentally ill is described in: Robins, *Fools and Mad: A History of the Insane in Ireland*, pp. 37–9.

182 Kirkpatrick, *A Note on the History of the Care of the Insane in Ireland up to the End of the Nineteenth Century*, p. 17.

183 Ibid., p. 22.

184 Ibid., p. 19.

185 J. Carr, *The Stranger in Ireland, or, A Tour in the Southern and Western Parts of that Country, in the Year 1805* (Philadelphia: T and G Palmer, 1806), p. 200.

186 Reynolds, *Grangegorman: Psychiatric Care in Dublin since 1815*, p. 17.

187 D. Walsh, 'Brief historical review', *Irish Journal of Psychiatry*, 13, 1 (Spring 1992), pp. 3–20; p. 3.

188 Battie, *Treatise on Madness*, p. 1.

189 Ibid., pp. v–vi.

190 Ibid., pp. 41–58.

191 Ibid., pp. 68–70.

192 Ibid., p. 93.

193 Ibid., pp. 94–7.

194 Shorter, *A History of Psychiatry: From the Era of the Asylum to the Age of Prozac*, p. 10.

Chapter 2. The Nineteenth Century: Growth of the Asylums

1 Lunatic Asylums, Ireland, Commission, *Report of the Commissioners of Inquiry into the State of the Lunatic Asylums and Other Institutions for the Custody and Treatment of the Insane in Ireland: with Minutes of Evidence and Appendices (Part 1 – Report, Tables, and Returns)* (Dublin: Thom and Sons, for Her Majesty's Stationery Office, 1858), p. 12.

2 R. Moran, 'The origin of insanity as a special verdict', *Law & Society Review*, 19, 3 (1985), pp. 487–519.

3 Kirkpatrick, *A Note on the History of the Care of the Insane in Ireland up to the End of the Nineteenth Century*, p. 23.

4 Robins, *Fools and Mad: A History of the Insane in Ireland*, pp. 62–4.

5 Reynolds, *Grangegorman: Psychiatric Care in Dublin since 1815*, pp. 21–3.

6 Kirkpatrick, *A Note on the History of the Care of the Insane in Ireland up to the End of the Nineteenth Century*, p. 26.

7 Ibid., p. 29.

8 Inspector of Lunatic Asylums, *Report of the District, Local and Private Lunatic Asylums in Ireland 1846* (Dublin: Alexander Thom, for Her Majesty's Stationery Office, 1847), p. 19.

9 Ibid., p. 51.

10 Tuke, *Description of the Retreat, an Institution Near York, for Insane Persons of the Society of Friends: Containing an Account of its Origin and Progress, the Modes of Treatment, and a Statement of Cases*; Robins, *Fools and Mad: A History of the Insane in Ireland*, p. 55; A.P. Williamson, 'Psychiatry, moral management and the origins of social policy for mentally ill people in Ireland', *Irish Journal of Medical Science*, 161, 9 (September 1992), pp. 556–8; Shorter, *A History of Psychiatry: From the Era of the Asylum to the Age of Prozac*, p. 20–1.

11 J.É. Esquirol, *Des Passions* (Paris: Didot Jeune, 1805). See also: A. Brigham, 'The moral treatment of insanity', *American Journal of Insanity*, 4, 1 (July 1847), pp. 1–15.

12 E.T. Carlson and N. Dain, 'The psychotherapy that was moral treatment', *American Journal of Psychiatry*, 117, 6 (December 1960), pp. 519–24.

13 Henry, *Our Lady's Psychiatric Hospital Cork*, pp. 528–35.

14 Finnane, *Insanity and the Insane in Post-Famine Ireland*, pp. 190–201; Cox, *Negotiating Insanity in the Southeast of Ireland, 1820–1900*, pp. 207–10; B.D. Kelly, *'He Lost Himself Completely': Shell Shock and its Treatment at Dublin's Richmond War Hospital, 1916–1919* (Dublin: Liffey Press, 2014), pp. 7–8.

15 M. Reuber, 'The architecture of psychological management: the Irish asylums (1801–1922)', *Psychological Medicine*, 26, 6 (November 1996), pp. 1179–89; Reuber, *Medicine, Disease and the State in Ireland, 1650–1940*, pp. 208–33. In relation to landscape, see: O. Walsh, 'Landscape and the Irish asylum' in Ú. Ní Bhroiméil and G. Hooper (eds), *Land and Landscape in Nineteenth-Century Ireland* (Dublin: Four Courts Press, 2008), pp. 156–70.

16 Reynolds, *Grangegorman: Psychiatric Care in Dublin since 1815*, pp. 46–9.

17 Ibid., p. 26. For some background to this initiative, see: Kirkpatrick, *A Note on the History of the Care of the Insane in Ireland up to the End of the Nineteenth Century*, pp. 24–6; L. O'Brien, 'The magic wisp: a history of the mentally ill in Ireland', *Bulletin of the Menninger Clinic*, 31, 2 (March 1967), pp. 79–95; pp. 87–8.

18 Finnane, *Insanity and the Insane in Post-Famine Ireland*, pp. 22–3: Newport had pressed for the establishment of provincial asylums in 1805, to no avail. See also: Robins,

Fools and Mad: A History of the Insane in Ireland, pp. 60–2; p. 65.

19   Select Committee on the Lunatic Poor in Ireland, *Report from the Select Committee on the Lunatic Poor in Ireland with Minutes of Evidence Taken Before the Committee and an Appendix* (London: House of Commons, 1817), p. 3.

20   Ibid., p. 4.

21   Finnane, *Insanity and the Insane in Post-Famine Ireland*, pp. 26–9.

22   Select Committee on the Lunatic Poor in Ireland, *Report from the Select Committee on the Lunatic Poor in Ireland with Minutes of Evidence Taken Before the Committee and an Appendix*, p. 9.

23   Ibid., p. 9.

24   Ibid., p. 24.

25   Ibid., p. 7.

26   Ibid., p. 12. See also: Robins, *Fools and Mad: A History of the Insane in Ireland*, pp. 64–7, 73–4; M.D. Grimsley-Smith, 'Politics, Professionalisation, and Poverty: Lunatic Asylums for the Poor in Ireland, 1817–1920' (PhD Thesis, University of Notre Dame, Indiana, 2011), pp. 28–31.

27   Select Committee on the Lunatic Poor in Ireland, *Report from the Select Committee on the Lunatic Poor in Ireland with Minutes of Evidence Taken Before the Committee and an Appendix*, p. 12.

28   Ibid., p. 13. Regarding Hallaran, see: Reynolds, *Grangegorman: Psychiatric Care in Dublin since 1815*, pp. 17–20, 29; B.D. Kelly, 'Dr William Saunders Hallaran and psychiatric practice in nineteenth-century Ireland', *Irish Journal of Medical Science*, 177, 1 (March 2008), pp. 79–84.

29   Select Committee on the Lunatic Poor in Ireland, *Report from the Select Committee on the Lunatic Poor in Ireland with Minutes of Evidence Taken Before the Committee and an Appendix*, p. 13.

30   Ibid., p. 14.

31   Ibid., pp. 14–15.

32   Ibid., p. 15.

33   Ibid., p. 5. See also: Kirkpatrick, *A Note on the History of the Care of the Insane in Ireland up to the End of the Nineteenth Century*, pp. 26–8.

34   Reynolds, *Grangegorman: Psychiatric Care in Dublin since 1815*, p. 16.

35   Select Committee on the Lunatic Poor in Ireland, *Report from the Select Committee on the Lunatic Poor in Ireland with Minutes of Evidence Taken Before the Committee and an Appendix*, p. 10. The general enthusiasm for the methods used at the Richmond was possibly over optimistic at this relatively early stage in the establishment's evolution, but it was a fair reflection of the governors' intent (Reynolds, *Grangegorman: Psychiatric Care in Dublin since 1815*, p. 31).

36   Reynolds, *Grangegorman: Psychiatric Care in Dublin since 1815*, p. 30. Rice, now a Member of Parliament for Limerick, was chief architect of the 1821 legislation (Robins, *Fools and Mad: A History of the Insane in Ireland*, p. 66). See also: Kirkpatrick, *A Note on the History of the Care of the Insane in Ireland up to the End of the Nineteenth Century*, p. 28.

37   Lunacy (Ireland) Act 1821, Section 2.

38   The Armagh asylum, established in 1825, was designed for 100 patients initially, with provision to extend for 150 (A.P. Williamson, 'Armagh District Lunatic Asylum', *Seanchas Ard Mhacha: Journal of the Armagh Diocesan Historical Society*, 8, 1 (1975/1976), pp. 111–20). See also: R.J. McClelland, 'The madhouses and mad doctors of Ulster', *The Ulster Medical Journal*, 57, 2 (October 1998), pp. 101–20; D. Walsh, 'The lunatic asylums of Ireland, 1825–1839', *Irish Journal of Psychological Medicine*, 25, 4 (December 2008), pp. 151–6.

39   M. Mulholland, *To Comfort Always: A History of Holywell Hospital, Antrim, 1898–1998* (Ballymena: Homefirst Community Trust, 1998); R. Delargy, 'The History of Belfast District Lunatic Asylum 1829–1921' (PhD Thesis, University of Ulster, 2002).

40   Torrey and Miller, *The Invisible Plague: The Rise of Mental Illness from 1750 to the Present*, p. 130.

41   Robins, *Fools and Mad: A History of the Insane in Ireland*, pp. 68–71.

42   Reynolds, *Grangegorman: Psychiatric Care in Dublin since 1815*, pp. 61–72. See also: Robins, *Fools and Mad: A History of the Insane in Ireland*, pp. 96–7, 135.

43   J. Mollan, 'Statistical report on the Richmond Lunatic Asylum', *Dublin Journal of Medical Science*, 13, 3 (July 1838), pp. 367–84.

44   Reynolds, *Grangegorman: Psychiatric Care in Dublin since 1815*, p. 67.

45   *Medical Press and Circular*, 21 September 1877.

46   Robins, *Fools and Mad: A History of the Insane in Ireland*, pp. 137–9.

47   J. Lalor, 'On the use of education and training in the treatment of the insane in public lunatic asylums', *Journal of the Statistical and Social Inquiry of Ireland*, 7, 54 (1878), pp. 361–73; p. 362.

48   Reynolds, *Grangegorman: Psychiatric Care in Dublin since 1815*, p. 141. See also: O'Brien, 'The magic wisp: a history of the mentally ill in Ireland', *Bulletin of the Menninger Clinic*, 31, 2 (March 1967), pp. 79–95; pp. 90–1; B.D. Kelly, *Custody, Care and Criminality: Forensic Psychiatry and Law in 19th Century Ireland*, (Dublin: History Press Ireland, 2014), pp. 182–3; Kelly, *'He Lost Himself Completely': Shell Shock and Its Treatment at Dublin's Richmond War Hospital, 1916–1919*, pp. 8–11.

49   Lalor, 'On the use of education and training in the treatment of the insane in public lunatic asylums', *Journal of the Statistical and Social Inquiry of Ireland*, 7, 54 (1878), pp. 361–73; pp. 367–8.

50   Ibid., p. 369.

51   D. Healy, 'Irish psychiatry. Part 2: use of the Medico-Psychological Association by its Irish members – *plus ça change!*', in G.E. Berrios and H. Freeman (eds), *150 Years of British Psychiatry, 1841–1991. Volume I* (London:

Gaskell/Royal College of Psychiatrists, 1991), pp. 314–20; p. 316.

52 O.R. McCarthy, 'Grandfather's choice – psychiatry in mid-Victorian Ireland', *Journal of Medical Biography*, 6, 3 (August 1998), pp. 141–8.

53 Reynolds, *Grangegorman: Psychiatric Care in Dublin since 1815*, pp. 144–50; Finnane, *Insanity and the Insane in Post-Famine Ireland*, pp. 67, 84.

54 J. Lalor, 'The President's address', *Journal of Mental Science*, 39, 7 (October 1861), pp. 318–26; Healy, *150 Years of British Psychiatry, 1841–1991. Volume I*, p. 316.

55 Lalor, 'On the use of education and training in the treatment of the insane in public lunatic asylums', *Journal of the Statistical and Social Inquiry of Ireland*, 7, 54 (1878), pp. 361–73; p. 370. See also: Finnane, *Insanity and the Insane in Post-Famine Ireland*, pp. 198–9.

56 D.H. Tuke, 'On the Richmond Asylum schools', *Journal of Mental Science*, 21, 95 (1 October 1875), pp. 467–74; pp. 467–8.

57 Anonymous, 'Obituary: Joseph Lalor, MD', *Journal of Mental Science*, 32, 139 (1 October 1886), pp. 462–3; p. 462.

58 *Irish Times*, 5 August 1886; Finnane, *Insanity and the Insane in Post-Famine Ireland*, p. 55.

59 Cox, *Negotiating Insanity in the Southeast of Ireland, 1820–1900*, p. 209. For more on physical treatments, custodial care and violence in the asylums, see: Finnane, *Insanity and the Insane in Post-Famine Ireland*, pp. 201–13, 218.

60 A. Halliday, *A General View of the Present State of Lunatic Asylums in Great Britain and Ireland and in Some Other Kingdoms* (London: Thomas & George Underwood, 1838), pp. 3–4.

61 D. Coakley, *Irish Masters of Medicine* (Dublin: Town House, 1992), pp. 64–71; J.F. Fleetwood, *The History of Medicine in Ireland (Second Edition)* (Dublin: Skellig Press, 1983), pp. 154–5.

62 J. Cheyne, *Essays on Partial Derangement of the Mind, in Supposed Connexion with Religion* (Dublin: William Curry Jun. and Company, 1843).

63 Webb, *Trinity's Psychiatrists: From Serenity of the Soul to Neuroscience*, pp. 32–5.

64 Cheyne, *Essays on Partial Derangement of the Mind, in Supposed Connexion with Religion*, p. 51.

65 Ibid.

66 Ibid., p. 52.

67 Ibid., p. 44.

68 A. Collins, 'Book review: Trinity's Psychiatrists: From Serenity of the Soul to Neuroscience', *Irish Journal of Psychological Medicine*, 33, 1 (March 2016), p. 65.

69 Cheyne, *Essays on Partial Derangement of the Mind, in Supposed Connexion with Religion*, pp. 61–2; Webb, *Trinity's Psychiatrists: From Serenity of the Soul to Neuroscience*, pp. 33–5. For a discussion of drunkenness, see: Finnane, *Insanity and the Insane in Post-Famine Ireland*, pp. 146–50.

70 Kirkpatrick, *A Note on the History of the Care of the Insane in Ireland up to the End of the Nineteenth Century*, p. 33. See also: Prior, *Madness and Murder: Gender, Crime and Mental Disorder in Nineteenth Century Ireland*, p. 27.

71 Inspectors of Lunatics, *The Forty-Second Report (With Appendices) of the Inspectors of Lunatics (Ireland)* (Dublin: Thom and Co. for Her Majesty's Stationery Office, 1893), p. 9.

72 P.M. Prior, 'Mental health law on the island of Ireland, 1800–2010', in P.M. Prior (ed.), *Asylums, Mental Health Care and the Irish, 1800–2010* (Dublin: Irish Academic Press, 2012), pp. 316–34.

73 J. Parry, 'Women and Madness in Nineteenth-Century Ireland' (MA Thesis, St Patrick's College, Maynooth (National University of Ireland), 1997), pp. 79–80.

74 Cox, *Negotiating Insanity in the Southeast of Ireland, 1820–1900*, pp. 76–7.

75 Kirkpatrick, *A Note on the History of the Care of the Insane in Ireland up to the End of the Nineteenth Century*, p. 30. See also: See also: L. O'Brien, 'The magic wisp: a history of the mentally ill in Ireland', *Bulletin of the Menninger Clinic*, 31, 2 (March 1967), pp. 79–95; p. 88; Prior, *Madness and Murder: Gender, Crime and Mental Disorder in Nineteenth Century Ireland*, pp. 27–9.

76 Reynolds, *Grangegorman: Psychiatric Care in Dublin since 1815*, pp. 75–6.

77 For a discussion of lunacy laws during this period, see: Robins, *Fools and Mad: A History of the Insane in Ireland*, pp. 143–56.

78 Finnane, *Insanity and the Insane in Post-Famine Ireland*, pp. 100, 231.

79 Ibid., p. 234.

80 Ibid.

81 Ibid., p. 222.

82 O. Walsh, "Tales from the big house': the Connaught District Lunatic Asylum in the late nineteenth-century', *History Ireland*, 13, 6 (November–December, 2005), pp. 21–5.

83 Finnane, *Insanity and the Insane in Post-Famine Ireland*, pp. 101–3.

84 Cox, *Negotiating Insanity in the Southeast of Ireland, 1820–1900*, pp. 77–87.

85 Lunacy (Ireland) Act 1867 (Section 10); Cox, *Negotiating Insanity in the Southeast of Ireland, 1820–1900*, pp. 85–6.

86 *Official Report of Dáil Éireann*, 29 November 1944.

87 Cox, *Negotiating Insanity in the Southeast of Ireland, 1820–1900*, pp. 73–6.

88 Torrey and Miller, *The Invisible Plague: The Rise of Mental Illness from 1750 to the Present*, p. 130.

89 Central Criminal Lunatic Asylum (Ireland) Act, 1845 (Prior, *Madness and Murder: Gender, Crime and Mental Disorder in Nineteenth Century Ireland*, pp. 30–3).

90 Walsh and Daly, *Mental Illness in Ireland 1750–2002: Reflections on the Rise and Fall of Institutional Care*, pp. 16–17. See also: Henry, *Our Lady's Psychiatric Hospital Cork*, pp. 47–87.

91 Cox, *Negotiating Insanity in the Southeast of Ireland, 1820–1900*, p. 41; Finnane, *Insanity and the Insane in Post-Famine Ireland*, p. 37; Robins, *Fools and Mad: A History of the Insane in Ireland*, pp. 79–80.

92 *Mayo Constitution*, 1 January 1861; *Irish Times*, 14 February and 10 October 1861 (Larcom Papers, National Library of Ireland, Ms. 7,776).

93 McDermott, *St Mary's Hospital Castlebar: Serving Mayo Mental Health from 1866*, p. 25.

94 Walsh and Daly, *Mental Illness in Ireland 1750–2002: Reflections on the Rise and Fall of Institutional Care*, p. 17; R. Boland, "Isolated from the mainstream': Portrane asylum in the 1950s', *Irish Times*, 10 June 2016.

95 *Building News and Engineering Journal*, 27 April 1900.

96 Walsh and Daly, *Mental Illness in Ireland 1750–2002: Reflections on the Rise and Fall of Institutional Care*, p. 17.

97 T. Bunbury, *800 Years of an Irish Castle* (Carlow: Carlow Town Council, 2013), p. 11.

98 Anonymous, *Hanover Park Asylum for the Recovery of Persons Labouring under Mental Derangement* (Carlow: Richard Price, 1815) [National Library of Ireland (P 1375(4))], p. i.

99 Ibid., p. ii–iii.

100 Ibid., pp. iii–iv.

101 Ibid. See also: W. Fitzgerald, 'Carlow Castle and its history', *Carlow Sentinel*, 17 September 1904; M. Murphy, *Carlow Castle* (Carlow: Carlow Town Council, 2013).

102 P.P.P. Middleton, *An Essay on Gout* (London: Baldwin & Company, 1827).

103 Cox, *Negotiating Insanity in the Southeast of Ireland, 1820–1900*, p. 2.

104 Robins, *Fools and Mad: A History of the Insane in Ireland*, pp. 81–2.

105 Kirkpatrick, *A Note on the History of the Care of the Insane in Ireland up to the End of the Nineteenth Century*, pp. 29–30. The legislation also made the Inspectors General of Prisons into Inspectors of Lunatic Asylums. See: Finnane, *Insanity and the Insane in Post-Famine Ireland*, pp. 118–19.

106 W. Harty, *Observations on an Act (5 and 6 Vict. c. 123) "For Amending the Law Relating to Private Lunatic Asylums in Ireland"* (Dublin: M.H. Gill, 1843). See also: Robins, *Fools and Mad: A History of the Insane in Ireland*, p. 85.

107 Cox, *Negotiating Insanity in the Southeast of Ireland, 1820–1900*, p. 21.

108 Henry, *Our Lady's Psychiatric Hospital Cork*, pp. 102–3.

109 A. Mauger, '"Confinement of the higher orders": The social role of private lunatic asylums in Ireland, c. 1820–60', *Journal of the History of Medicine and Allied Sciences*, 67, 2 (April 2012), pp. 281–317. See also: A. Mauger, "Confinement of the Higher Orders'? The Significance of Private Lunatic Asylums in Ireland, 1820–1860' (MA Dissertation, University College Dublin, 2009).

110 Robins, *Fools and Mad: A History of the Insane in Ireland*, pp. 80–7; p. 86.

111 Inspector of Mental Hospitals, *Annual Report of the Inspector of Mental Hospitals for the Year 1929* (Dublin: Department of Local Government and Public Health/Stationery Office, 1930), p. 26.

112 Henry, *Our Lady's Psychiatric Hospital Cork*, pp. 23–4.

113 Inspector of Mental Hospitals, *Annual Report of the Inspector of Mental Hospitals for the Year 1930* (Dublin: Department of Local Government and Public Health/Stationery Office, 1931), pp. 24–5.

114 Anonymous, 'Irish Division', *Journal of Mental Science*, 68, 282 (July 1922), p. 313.

115 Inspector of Mental Hospitals, *Annual Report of the Inspector of Mental Hospitals for the Year 1929* (Dublin: Department of Local Government and Public Health/Stationery Office, 1930), p. 29.

116 Inspector of Mental Hospitals, *Annual Report of the Inspector of Mental Hospitals for the Year 1933* (Dublin: Department of Local Government and Public Health/Stationery Office, 1934), p. 30.

117 Inspector of Mental Hospitals, *Annual Report of the Inspector of Mental Hospitals for the Year 1934* (Dublin: Department of Local Government and Public Health/Stationery Office, 1935), p. 29.

118 Anonymous, 'Irish Division', *Journal of Mental Science*, 95, 400 (supplement) (July 1949), pp. 8–9.

119 Inspector of Mental Hospitals, *Annual Report of the Inspector of Mental Hospitals for the Year 1949* (Dublin: Department of Health/Stationery Office, 1950), pp. 61–2.

120 Ibid., p. 35.

121 Ibid., pp. 61–2.

122 Brennan, *Irish Insanity, 1800–2000*, pp. 69–74.

123 Cox, *Negotiating Insanity in the Southeast of Ireland, 1820–1900*, pp. 12–4.

124 Robins, *Fools and Mad: A History of the Insane in Ireland*, pp. 105–8.

125 Lord Lieutenant and Council of Ireland, *General Rules for the Government of All the District Lunatic Asylums of Ireland, Made, Framed and Established by the Lord Lieutenant and Council of Ireland* (Dublin: Alexander Thom for her Majesty's Stationery Office, 1843).

126 Ibid., p. 9.

127 Ibid., p. 16.

128 Parry, 'Women and Madness in Nineteenth-Century Ireland', p. 48. See also: Finnane, *Insanity and the Insane in Post-Famine Ireland*, pp. 176–8; Cox, *Negotiating Insanity in the Southeast of Ireland, 1820–1900*, p. 18. For further discussion of the emergence of medical management of mental illness, see, among others: Pietikäinen, *Madness: A History*, pp. 107–33; and, in Ireland: Robins, *Fools and Mad: A History of the Insane in Ireland*, pp. 92–6.

129 Lord Lieutenant and Council of Ireland, *General Rules for the Government of All the District Lunatic Asylums of Ireland, Made, Framed and Established by the Lord Lieutenant and Council of Ireland*, p. 16.

130 Ibid., p. 17.

131 Ibid., p. 12.

132 The precise roles of many of these figures (as well as the 'fire brigade instructor', among others) are explored in: Henry, *Our Lady's Psychiatric Hospital Cork*, pp. 389–420. The wife of the gatekeeper was known as the 'female searcher', her job being to search the bags of female attendants as they entered and left the asylum (p. 414).

133 Lord Lieutenant and Council of Ireland, *Further Rules* (Dublin: Alexander Thom for her Majesty's Stationery Office, 1853), p. 4.

134 Lord Lieutenant and Council of Ireland, *General Rules for the Government of All the District Lunatic Asylums of Ireland, Made, Framed and Established by the Lord Lieutenant and Council of Ireland*, p. 7.

135 Ibid., p. 6.

136 For an account of Duncan, see: Webb, *Trinity's Psychiatrists: From Serenity of the Soul to Neuroscience*, pp. 38–43.

137 Kirkpatrick, *A Note on the History of the Care of the Insane in Ireland up to the End of the Nineteenth Century*, pp. 23–4.

138 Webb, *Trinity's Psychiatrists: From Serenity of the Soul to Neuroscience*, p. 38.

139 J.F. Duncan, 'President's Address at the Annual Meeting of the Medico-Psychological Association, held August 11th, 1875, at the Royal College of Physicians, Dublin', *Journal of Mental Science*, 21, 95 (October 1875), pp. 313–38; p. 338.

140 J.F. Duncan, *Medical Statistics, Their Force and Fallacies: A Lecture Delivered in Park Street School of Medicine, November 4th, 1846, Introductory to the Course on the Theory and Practice of Physic* (Dublin: McGlashan, 1847).

141 J.F. Duncan, *God in Disease, or, The Manifestations of Design in Morbid Phenomena* (Philadelphia: Lindsay and Blakiston, 1852).

142 Healy, *150 Years of British Psychiatry, 1841–1991. Volume I*, pp. 316–17.

143 Duncan, 'President's Address at the Annual Meeting of the Medico-Psychological Association, held August 11th, 1875, at the Royal College of Physicians, Dublin', *Journal of Mental Science*, 21, 95 (October 1875), pp. 313–38; pp. 315–6.

144 Ibid., p. 317.

145 Healy, *150 Years of British Psychiatry, 1841–1991. Volume I*, pp. 314–17.

146 Duncan, 'President's Address at the Annual Meeting of the Medico-Psychological Association, held August 11th, 1875, at the Royal College of Physicians, Dublin', *Journal of Mental Science*, 21, 95 (October 1875), pp. 313–38; p. 319.

147 Ibid., p. 329.

148 Ibid., pp. 329–30.

149 Ibid., p. 331.

150 Ibid., p. 332.

151 Ibid., p. 333.

152 Ibid., p. 336.

153 Ibid., p. 319.

154 Ibid., pp. 327–8.

155 Ibid., pp. 326–7.

156 M. Finnane, 'Irish psychiatry. Part 1: the formation of a profession', in G.E. Berrios and H. Freeman (eds), *150 Years of British Psychiatry, 1841–1991. Volume 1* (London: Gaskell/Royal College of Psychiatrists, 1991), pp. 306–13.

157 *British Medical Journal*, 13 April 1895; *The Medical Press*, 10 April 1895.

158 Select Committee of the House of Lords, *Report from the Select Committee of the House of Lords Appointed to Consider the State of the Lunatic Poor in Ireland and to Report Thereon to the House with the Minutes of Evidence, Appendix, and Index* (London: House of Commons, 1843), pp. ii–iii.

159 Ibid., p. iv.

160 Ibid., p. v.

161 Ibid., pp. v–vi.

162 Ibid., p. vii. See also: Robins, *Fools and Mad: A History of the Insane in Ireland*, p. 75.

163 It had been decided to establish an asylum in Clonmel in 1832 and the first meeting of the Board of Governors of Clonmel Lunatic Asylum took place on 15 November 1834 (Lonergan, *St Luke's Hospital, Clonmel, 1834–1984*, pp. 22–83; p. 24).

164 Select Committee of the House of Lords, *Report from the Select Committee of the House of Lords Appointed to Consider the State of the Lunatic Poor in Ireland and to Report Thereon to the House with the Minutes of Evidence, Appendix, and Index*, p. 88 (Appendix 1).

165 This was a strong feature of the Select Committee's findings; see: Reynolds, *Grangegorman: Psychiatric Care in Dublin since 1815*, pp. 84–5. See also: P. Prior, 'Dangerous lunacy: the misuse of mental health law in nineteenth-century Ireland', *Journal of Forensic Psychiatry and Psychology*, 14, 3 (September 2003), pp. 525–41; Kelly, *Custody, Care and Criminality: Forensic Psychiatry and Law in 19th Century Ireland*, p. 67.

166 Select Committee of the House of Lords, *Report from the Select Committee of the House of Lords Appointed to Consider the State of the Lunatic Poor in Ireland and to Report Thereon to the House with the Minutes of Evidence, Appendix and Index*, p. xxv.

167 Reynolds, *Grangegorman: Psychiatric Care in Dublin since 1815*, p. 85.

168 See also: Kirkpatrick, *A Note on the History of the Care of the Insane in Ireland up to the End of the Nineteenth Century*, p. 30.

169 F. McAuley, *Insanity, Psychiatry and Criminal Responsibility* (Dublin: Round Hall Press, 1993); D. Robinson, *Wild Beasts and Idle Humors: The Insanity Defense from Antiquity to the Present* (Cambridge, Massachusetts: Harvard University Press, 1998); S.A. Skålevåg, 'The matter of forensic psychiatry: a historical enquiry', *Medical History*, 50, 1 (January 2006), pp. 49–68; B.D. Kelly, 'Criminal insanity in nineteenth-century Ireland, Europe and the United States: cases, contexts and controversies',

International Journal of Law and Psychiatry, 32, 6 (November/December 2009), pp. 362–8.

170   F. Kelly, *A Guide to Early Irish Law* (Dublin: School of Celtic Studies, Dublin Institute for Advanced Studies, 2003), p. 92.

171   P. Gibbons, N. Mulryan and A. O'Connor, 'Guilty but insane: the insanity defence in Ireland, 1850–1995', *British Journal of Psychiatry*, 170, 5 (May 1997), pp. 467–72.

172   A. Hopkin and K. Bunney, *The Ship of Seven Murders: A True Story of Madness and Murder* (Cork: The Collins Press, 2010). See also: H. Kelleher Kahn, "Forced from this world': massacre on the Mary Russell', *History Ireland*, 17, 5 (September/October 2009), pp. 22–6. For an insightful, instructive, erudite and remarkably enlightening discussion of this case, see: L. Feeney, 'Book review: *The Ship of Seven Murders*', *Irish Journal of Psychological Medicine*, 27, 4 (December 2010), p. 220.

173   W. Scoresby, *Memorials of the Sea: The Mary Russell* (London: Longman, Brown, Green and Longmans, 1850), pp. 3–4.

174   Hopkin and Bunney, *The Ship of Seven Murders: A True Story of Madness and Murder*, p. 177.

175   Criminal Law (Insanity) Act 2006, Section 5(1). See also: Robins, *Fools and Mad: A History of the Insane in Ireland*, p. 59.

176   I. Ray, *A Treatise on the Medical Jurisprudence of Insanity [1838] [Reprint, W. Overholser (ed.)]* (Cambridge, MA: Harvard University Press, 1962).

177   R. Moran, *Knowing Right from Wrong: The Insanity Defense of Daniel McNaughtan* (New York: Free Press, 1981); McAuley, *Insanity, Psychiatry and Criminal Responsibility*; Prior, *Madness and Murder: Gender, Crime and Mental Disorder in Nineteenth Century Ireland*, pp. 55–9.

178   Kirkpatrick, *A Note on the History of the Care of the Insane in Ireland up to the End of the Nineteenth Century*, p. 31.

179   Central Criminal Lunatic Asylum (Ireland) Act 1845, Section 8.

180   Ibid., Section 11.

181   Ibid., Section 12. See also: J.W. Williams, 'Unsoundness of mind, in its medical and legal considerations', *Dublin Quarterly Journal of Medical Science*, 18, 2 (November 1854), pp. 260–87.

182   Central Criminal Lunatic Asylum (Ireland) Act 1845, Section 23.

183   Kirkpatrick, *A Note on the History of the Care of the Insane in Ireland up to the End of the Nineteenth Century*, pp. 32, 37. For a discussion of the Inspectorate, see: P.M. Prior, 'Overseeing the Irish asylums: the Inspectorate in Lunacy, 1845–1921' in P.M. Prior (ed.), *Asylums, Mental Health Care and the Irish, 1800–2010* (Dublin: Irish Academic Press, 2012), pp. 221–45.

184   Finnane, *Insanity and the Insane in Post-Famine Ireland*, p. 42.

185   Ibid., pp. 63–7; Reynolds, *Grangegorman: Psychiatric Care in Dublin since 1815*, pp. 144–9; Cox, *Negotiating Insanity in the Southeast of Ireland, 1820–1900*, pp. 9, 48. In relation to Nugent and Dundrum, see: Robins, *Fools and Mad: A History of the Insane in Ireland*, pp. 100–5.

186   Kirkpatrick, *A Note on the History of the Care of the Insane in Ireland up to the End of the Nineteenth Century*, p. 32.

187   C. Smith, 'The Central Mental Hospital, Dundrum, Dublin', in R. Bluglass and P. Bowden (eds), *Principles and Practice of Forensic Psychiatry* (Edinburgh: Churchill Livingstone, 1990), pp. 1351–3; p. 1352. See also: Robins, *Fools and Mad: A History of the Insane in Ireland*, pp. 147–51; Prior, *Madness and Murder: Gender, Crime and Mental Disorder in Nineteenth Century Ireland*, pp. 30–3.

188   P. Prior, 'Gender and criminal lunacy in nineteenth-century Ireland', in M.H. Preston and M. Ó hÓgartaigh (eds), *Gender and Medicine in Ireland, 1700–1950* (Syracuse, New York: Syracuse University Press, 2012), pp. 86–107; p. 88. See also: Prior, *Madness and Murder: Gender, Crime and Mental Disorder in Nineteenth Century Ireland*, pp. 33–46; Prior presents compelling case histories of 'men who killed women' (pp. 83–117), 'women who killed children' (pp. 118–48), 'women who killed men' (pp. 149–77) and 'family murders' (pp. 178–206).

189   B.D. Kelly, 'Clinical and social characteristics of women committed to inpatient forensic psychiatric care in Ireland, 1868–1908', *Journal of Forensic Psychiatry and Psychology*, 19, 2 (June 2008), pp. 261–73.

190   For more on child killing and infanticide, see: D. McLoughlin, (ed.), 'Infanticide in nineteenth-century Ireland', in A. Bourke, S. Kilfeather, M. Luddy, M. MacCurtain, G. Meaney, M. Ní Donnchadha, M. O'Dowd and C. Wills (eds), *Field Day Anthology of Irish Writing, Volume 4: Irish Women's Writing and Traditions* (Cork: Cork University Press, 2002), pp. 915–22; N. Mulryan, P. Gibbons and A. O'Connor, 'Infanticide and child murder: admissions to the Central Mental Hospital 1850–2000', *Irish Journal of Psychological Medicine*, 19, 1 (March 2002), pp. 8–12; A. Guilbride, 'Infanticide: the crime of motherhood', in P. Kennedy (ed.), *Motherhood in Ireland* (Cork: Mercier Press, 2004), pp. 170–80; H. Marland, *Dangerous Motherhood: Insanity and Childbirth in Victorian Britain* (Basingstoke: Palgrave MacMillan, 2004); B.D. Kelly, 'Murder, mercury, mental illness: infanticide in nineteenth-century Ireland', *Irish Journal of Medical Science*, 176, 3 (September 2007), pp. 149–52; B.D. Kelly, 'Clinical and social characteristics of women committed to inpatient forensic psychiatric care in Ireland, 1868–1908', *Journal of Forensic Psychiatry and Psychology*, 19, 2 (June 2008), pp. 261–73; B.D. Kelly, 'Poverty, crime and mental illness: female forensic psychiatric committal in Ireland, 1910–1948', *Social History of Medicine*, 21, 2 (August 2008), pp. 311–28; P.M. Prior, 'Psychiatry and the fate of women who killed

infants and young children, 1850–1900', in C. Cox and M. Luddy (eds), *Cultures of Care in Irish Medical History 1750–1950* (Basingstoke, Hampshire: Palgrave Macmillan, 2010), pp. 92–112; C. Rattigan, '"Half mad at the time": unmarried mothers and infanticide in Ireland, 1922–1950', in C. Cox and M. Luddy (eds), *Cultures of Care in Irish Medical History 1750–1950* (Basingstoke, Hampshire: Palgrave Macmillan, 2010), pp. 168–190; C. Rattigan, *What Else Could I Do? Single Mothers and Infanticide, Ireland 1900–1950* (Dublin: Irish Academic Press, 2011); E. Farrell, *'A Most Diabolical Deed': Infanticide and Irish Society, 1850–1900* (Manchester: Manchester University Press, 2013); Kelly, *Custody, Care and Criminality: Forensic Psychiatry and Law in 19th Century Ireland*, pp. 95–126.

191   B.D. Kelly, 'Poverty, crime and mental illness', *Social History of Medicine*, 21, 2 (August 2008), pp. 311–28.

192   For a discussion of discharges from Dundrum, see: Prior, *Madness and Murder: Gender, Crime and Mental Disorder in Nineteenth Century Ireland*, pp. 75–8, 207–24 (especially in relation to 'assisted' emigration schemes).

193   N. Mulryan, P. Gibbons and A. O'Connor, 'Infanticide and child murder: admissions to the Central Mental Hospital 1850–2000', *Irish Journal of Psychological Medicine*, 19, 1 (March 2002), pp. 8–12. See also: B.D. Kelly, 'Murder, mercury, mental illness', *Irish Journal of Medical Science*, 176, 3 (September 2007), pp. 149–52.

194   B.D. Kelly,*'Folie à plusieurs*: forensic cases from nineteenth-century Ireland', *History of Psychiatry*, 20, 77 (Part 1) (March 2009), pp. 47–60.

195   B.D. Kelly, 'Learning disability and forensic mental healthcare in nineteenth-century Ireland', *Irish Journal of Psychological Medicine*, 25, 3 (September 2008), pp. 116–18; B.D. Kelly, 'Intellectual disability, mental illness and offending behaviour: forensic cases from early twentieth-century Ireland', *Irish Journal of Medical Science*, 179, 3 (September 2010), pp. 409–16.

196   B.D. Kelly, 'Syphilis, psychiatry and offending behaviour: clinical cases from nineteenth-century Ireland', *Irish Journal of Medical Science*, 178, 1 (March 2009), pp. 73–7. See also: Finnane, *Insanity and the Insane in Post-Famine Ireland*, pp. 136–42.

197   B.D. Kelly, 'Tuberculosis in the nineteenth-century asylum: clinical cases from the Central Criminal Lunatic Asylum, Dundrum, Dublin', in P.M. Prior (ed.), *Asylums, Mental Health Care and the Irish, 1800–2010* (Dublin: Irish Academic Press, 2012), pp. 205–20.

198   P. Gibbons, N. Mulryan, A. McAleer and A. O'Connor, 'Criminal responsibility and mental illness in Ireland 1950–1995: fitness to plead', *Irish Journal of Psychological Medicine*, 196, 2 (June 1999), pp. 51–6.

199   Smith, *Principles and Practice of Forensic Psychiatry*, p. 1353.

200   P.M. Prior, 'Murder and madness: gender and the insanity defense in nineteenth-century Ireland', *New Hibernia Review*, 9, 4 (Winter 2005), pp. 19–36; P. Prior, 'Roasting a man alive: the case of Mary Rielly, criminal

lunatic', *Éire-Ireland*, 41, 1–2 (Spring/Summer 2006), pp. 169–91.

201   This was a problem not only in the 1800s and early 1900s, but also into the 1950s; see: Guéret, *What the Doctor Saw*, p. 28.

202   P. Froggatt, 'The demographic work of Sir William Wilde', *Irish Journal of Medical Science*, 40, 5 (May 1965), pp. 213–20; P. Froggatt, 'The demographic work of Sir William Wilde', *Irish Journal of Medical Science*, 185, 2 (May 2016), pp. 293–5.

203   T.G. Wilson, *Victorian Doctor: The Life of Sir William Wilde* (London: Methuen, 1942), pp. 221–2. See also: D. Coakley, 'William Wilde in the west of Ireland', *Irish Journal of Medical Science*, 185, 2 (May 2016), pp. 277–80; L. Geary, 'William Wilde: historian', *Irish Journal of Medical Science*, 185, 2 (May 2016), pp. 301–2.

204   W. Donnelly, W.R. Wilde and E. Singleton, *The Census of Ireland for the Year 1851, Part III: Report on the Status of Disease* (Dublin: Thom and Sons for Her Majesty's Stationery Office, 1854), p. 49.

205   Ibid.

206   Ibid., p. 53.

207   Ibid., pp. 58–9. For further discussion of diagnostic practices, see: Brennan, *Irish Insanity, 1800–2000*, pp. 85–9.

208   See, for example: Henry, *Our Lady's Psychiatric Hospital Cork*, pp. 261–2; D. Walsh and A. Daly, 'The socio-demographic and clinical profiles of patients admitted to the Sligo District Lunatic Asylum in the late 19th century with some modern comparisons', *Irish Journal of Psychological Medicine* 33, 1 (March 2016), pp. 43–54.

209   Donnelly, Wilde and Singleton, *The Census of Ireland for the Year 1851, Part III: Report on the Status of Disease*, pp. 62–6.

210   Ibid., p. 66.

211   Reynolds, *Grangegorman: Psychiatric Care in Dublin since 1815*, pp. 100–10.

212   J.C. Bucknill, 'Report of the Commissioners of Inquiry on the state of Lunatic Asylums and other Institutions for the Custody and Treatment of the Insane in Ireland: with Minutes of Evidence, and Appendices (State Paper, pp. 718)', *Journal of Mental Science*, 5, 28 (1 January 1859), pp. 222–45; p. 222.

213   Lunatic Asylums, Ireland, Commission, *Report of the Commissioners of Inquiry into the State of the Lunatic Asylums and Other Institutions for the Custody and Treatment of the Insane in Ireland: with Minutes of Evidence and Appendices (Part 1 – Report, Tables, and Returns)* (Dublin: Thom and Sons, for Her Majesty's Stationery Office, 1858).

214   Ibid., pp. 24–5: the Commissioners found the 'wretched inmates' in the Hardwicke Cells, connected with the House of Industry of the City of Dublin, to be 'in a most unsatisfactory state'.

215   Ibid., p. 2; the 'number of insane poor at large and unprovided for' was based on returns 'by the Constabulary and the Metropolitan Police'.

216   Ibid., p. 6.

217   Ibid., p. 7.

218   Ibid.

219   Ibid.

220   Ibid.

221   Ibid., p. 9.

222   Ibid.

223   Ibid., pp. 7–8.

224   Ibid., p. 8.

225   Ibid., pp. 10–1.

226   Ibid., p. 12.

227   Ibid.

228   Ibid., p. 5.

229   Ibid.

230   Ibid., p. 13.

231   Ibid., p. 14.

232   Ibid., p. 15.

233   Ibid., pp. 16–17.

234   '& c.': et cetera.

235   Ibid., p. 14.

236   Ibid., p. 18.

237   Ibid., p. 19: The workhouse asylums were to be restricted to 'quiet cases of imbecility or idiocy' only; 'no recent or acute case, or one for which there is any reasonable hope of cure, should ever be detained therein'.

238   Ibid., p. 19.

239   Ibid., p. 20.

240   Ibid., p. 26.

241   Ibid.

242   Ibid., pp. 28–32.

243   Ibid., pp. 9–10.

244   Ibid., pp. 32–6.

245   Ibid., pp. 36–9.

246   See also: D. Gladstone, 'The changing dynamic of institutional care: the Western Counties Idiot Asylum, 1864–1914' in D. Wright and A. Digby (eds), *From Idiocy to Mental Deficiency: Historical Perspectives on People with Learning Disabilities (Studies in the Social History of Medicine)* (London & New York: Routledge, 1996), pp. 134–60; M. Jackson, 'Institutional provision for the feeble-minded in Edwardian England: Sandlebridge and the scientific morality of permanent care', in D. Wright and A. Digby (eds), *From Idiocy to Mental Deficiency: Historical Perspectives on People with Learning Disabilities* (London and New York: Routledge, 1996), pp. 161–83.

247   Lunatic Asylums, Ireland, Commission, *Report of the Commissioners of Inquiry into the State of the Lunatic Asylums and Other Institutions for the Custody and Treatment of the Insane in Ireland: with Minutes of Evidence and Appendices (Part 1 – Report, Tables, and Returns)*, p. 17.

248   Ibid., pp. 17–18.

249   Ibid., p. 39.

250   Ibid., p. 12.

251   Lord Lieutenant and Council of Ireland, *General Rules for the Government of All the District Lunatic Asylums of Ireland, Made, Framed and Established by the Lord Lieutenant and Council of Ireland* (Dublin: Alexander Thom for her Majesty's Stationery Office, 1843); 12. Baths were used for both treatment and punishment (E.E.C. Kenny, *Short Hints and Observations on the Arrangement and Management of Lunatic Asylums* (Dublin: Philip Dixon Hardy & Sons, 1848), pp. 24, 31–3).

252   Ibid., p. 16.

253   Ibid.

254   A twill weave linen.

255   Ibid., pp. 16–17.

256   Reynolds, *Grangegorman: Psychiatric Care in Dublin since 1815*, pp. 34–5, 120.

257   Lunatic Asylums, Ireland, Commission, *Report of the Commissioners of Inquiry into the State of the Lunatic Asylums and Other Institutions for the Custody and Treatment of the Insane in Ireland: with Minutes of Evidence and Appendices (Part 1 – Report, Tables, and Returns)*, p. 17.

258   Ibid.

259   C. Haw and G. Yorston, 'Thomas Prichard and the non-restraint movement at the Northampton Asylum', *Psychiatric Bulletin*, 28, 4 (1 April 2004), pp. 140–2; p. 140.

260   G.N. Grob, *Mental Institutions in America: Social Policy to 1875* (New Brunswick and London: Transaction Publishers, 2009), pp. 206–10.

261   Select Committee of the House of Lords, *Report from the Select Committee of the House of Lords Appointed to Consider the State of the Lunatic Poor in Ireland and to Report Thereon to the House with the Minutes of Evidence, Appendix, and Index*, p. v.

262   J.C. Bucknill, 'Report of the Commissioners of Inquiry on the state of Lunatic Asylums and other Institutions for the Custody and Treatment of the Insane in Ireland: with Minutes of Evidence, and Appendices (State Paper, pp. 718)', *Journal of Mental Science*, 5, 28 (1 January 1859), pp. 222–45.

263   Reynolds, *Grangegorman: Psychiatric Care in Dublin since 1815*, p. 122.

264   Privy Council, *General Rules and Regulations for the Management of District Lunatic Asylums in Ireland* (Dublin: Alexander Thom for her Majesty's Stationery Office, 1862); see also: Reynolds, *Grangegorman: Psychiatric Care in Dublin since 1815*, pp. 127–9. For discussion of the role of the visiting physician, and associated conflicts, see: Finnane, *150 Years of British Psychiatry, 1841–1991. Volume I*, pp. 306–13; Robins, *Fools and Mad: A History of the Insane in Ireland*, pp. 96–100; McDermott, *St Mary's Hospital Castlebar: Serving Mayo Mental Health from 1866*, p. 44.

265   Privy Council, *General Rules and Regulations for the Management of District Lunatic Asylums in Ireland*, p. 6; Finnane, *Insanity and the Insane in Post-Famine Ireland*, p. 47. For more on the issues relating to the role of the 'visiting physician', see: Murphy, *Tumbling Walls: The Evolution of a Community Institution over 150 Years*, pp. 15–27.

266 *Journal of Mental Science*, 1 April 1862.

267 Lord Lieutenant of Ireland, *General Rules and Regulations for the Management of District Lunatic Asylums in Ireland* [1874] (Dublin: Pilkington, 1890) [National Library of Ireland (Ir 362 i 13)], paragraph XI.

268 Ibid., paragraph XVI.

269 Ibid., paragraph XVIII.

270 Ibid., paragraph XVII.

271 Ibid., paragraph XIX.

272 Ibid., paragraph XX.

273 Ibid., paragraph XXI.

274 Ibid., paragraph XXII.

275 J.A. Blake, *Defects in the Moral Treatment of Insanity in the Public Lunatic Asylums of Ireland* (Dublin: Churchill, 1862); see also: Robins, *Fools and Mad: A History of the Insane in Ireland*, pp. 135–6.

276 Torrey and Miller, *The Invisible Plague: The Rise of Mental Illness from 1750 to the Present*, p. 137; Finnane, *Insanity and the Insane in Post-Famine Ireland*, pp. 208–13, 219.

277 Ibid., p. 209.

278 Henry, *Our Lady's Psychiatric Hospital Cork*, pp. 218–19. In relation to patient violence in the Central Criminal Lunatic Asylum in Dundrum, see: Prior, *Madness and Murder: Gender, Crime and Mental Disorder in Nineteenth Century Ireland*, pp. 66–9.

279 Cox, *Negotiating Insanity in the Southeast of Ireland, 1820–1900*, pp. 226–9.

280 *British Medical Journal*, 15 June 1912.

281 B. Stoker, *Dracula* (London: Archibald Constable and Company, 1897). For explorations of the links between the vampire myth and psychiatry, see: B.D. Kelly, Z. Abood and D. Shanley, 'Vampirism and schizophrenia', *Irish Journal of Psychological Medicine*, 16, 3 (September 1999), pp. 114–15; B.D. Kelly, 'Diagnosis of a vampire', *Modern Medicine*, 41, 6 (2011), pp. 69–71; S. Mac Suibhne and B.D. Kelly, 'Vampirism as mental illness: myth, madness and the loss of meaning in psychiatry', *Social History of Medicine*, 24, 2 (August 2011), pp. 445–60.

282 C. Norman, 'The clinical features of beri-beri', *Transactions of the Royal Academy of Medicine in Ireland*, 17, 1 (1 December 1899), pp. 145–79.

283 Crawford, *Asylums, Mental Health Care and the Irish, 1800–2010*, pp. 185–204.

284 See also: A. Collins, 'Daniel Frederick Rambaut: 'Rugbanian' and innovative resident medical superintendent', *Irish Journal of Psychological Medicine* [published online ahead of print, 2016].

285 G. Jones, 'The campaign against tuberculosis in Ireland, 1899–1914' in G. Jones and E. Malcolm (eds), *Medicine, Disease and the State in Ireland, 1650–1940* (Cork: Cork University Press, 1999), pp. 158–76; pp. 159–60. See also: Kelly, *Custody, Care and Criminality: Forensic Psychiatry and Law in 19th Century Ireland*, pp. 94–5.

286 Finnane, *Insanity and the Insane in Post-Famine Ireland*, p. 137; B.D. Kelly, 'One hundred years ago: the Richmond Asylum, Dublin in 1907', *Irish Journal of Psychological*

Medicine, 24, 3 (September 2007), pp. 108–14; Kelly, *Asylums, Mental Health Care and the Irish, 1800–2010*, pp. 205–20.

287 P. McCandless, 'Curative asylum, custodial hospital: the South Carolina Lunatic Asylum and State Hospital, 1828–1920', in R. Porter and D. Wright (eds), *The Confinement of the Insane: International Perspectives, 1800–1965* (Cambridge: Cambridge University Press, 2003), pp. 173–92; p. 190.

288 Jones, *Medicine, Disease and the State in Ireland, 1650–1940*, pp. 158–76.

289 F.S L. Lyons, *Ireland Since the Famine* (London: Fontana, 1985), p. 79.

290 C.S. Breathnach and J.B. Moynihan, 'An Irish statistician's analysis of the national tuberculosis problem', *Irish Journal of Medical Science*, 172, 3 (July–September 2003), pp. 149–53.

291 Inspectors of Lunatics, *The Forty-Second Report (With Appendices) of the Inspectors of Lunatics (Ireland)* (Dublin: Thom and Co. for Her Majesty's Stationery Office, 1893), pp. 1, 5.

292 Ibid., p. 6.

293 Ibid., p. 145; B.D. Kelly, 'One hundred years ago: the Richmond Asylum, Dublin in 1907', *Irish Journal of Psychological Medicine*, 24, 3 (September 2007), pp. 108–14.

294 McCandless, *The Confinement of the Insane: International Perspectives, 1800–1965*, p. 189.

295 D. Wright, J.E. Moran and S. Gouglas, 'The confinement of the insane in Victorian Canada: the Hamilton and Toronto Asylums, c.1861–1891' in R. Porter and D. Wright (eds), *The Confinement of the Insane: International Perspectives, 1800–1965* (Cambridge: Cambridge University Press, 2003), pp. 100–28; p. 124.

296 P. Gibbons, N. Mulryan and A. O'Connor, 'Guilty but insane: the insanity defence in Ireland, 1850–1995', *British Journal of Psychiatry*, 170, 5 (May 1997), pp. 467–72.

297 N. Mulryan, P. Gibbons and A. O'Connor, 'Infanticide and child murder: admissions to the Central Mental Hospital 1850–2000', *Irish Journal of Psychological Medicine*, 19, 1 (March 2002), pp. 8–12.

298 D. Walsh and A. Daly, 'The socio-demographic and clinical profiles of patients admitted to the Sligo District Lunatic Asylum in the late 19th century with some modern comparisons', *Irish Journal of Psychological Medicine*, 33, 1 (March 2016), pp. 43–54.

299 C. Foley, *The Last Irish Plague: The Great Flu Epidemic in Ireland, 1918–19* (Dublin: Irish Academic Press, 2011).

300 Robins, *Fools and Mad: A History of the Insane in Ireland*, p. 180.

301 C. Norman, 'The domestic treatment of the insane', *Dublin Journal of Medical Science*, 101, 2 (February 1896), pp. 111–21; C. Norman, 'On the need for family care of persons of unsound mind in Ireland', *Journal of Mental Science*, 50, 210 (1 July 1904), pp. 461–73; C. Norman, 'The family care of the insane', *Medical Press and Circular*, 29 November–6 December 1905; Reynolds,

Grangegorman: Psychiatric Care in Dublin since 1815, p. 173.

302   Ibid., p. 250.

303   Finnane, *Insanity and the Insane in Post-Famine Ireland*, pp. 208–13, 219; Torrey and Miller, *The Invisible Plague: The Rise of Mental Illness from 1750 to the Present*, p. 137. In relation to patient suicide and the reported violence of an attendant towards a patient, resulting in a broken arm, see: Murphy, *Tumbling Walls: The Evolution of a Community Institution over 150 Years*, pp. 15–27; p. 25.

304   McDermott, *St Mary's Hospital Castlebar: Serving Mayo Mental Health from 1866*, p. 117.

305   Healy, *150 Years of British Psychiatry, 1841–1991. Volume I*, p. 316.

306   Finnane, *150 Years of British Psychiatry, 1841–1991. Volume I*, p. 309. See Norman's defence of this move: *Daily Independent*, 26 April 1892.

307   Finnane, *150 Years of British Psychiatry, 1841–1991. Volume I*, p. 308.

308   D. Enoch and H. Ball, *Uncommon Psychiatric Syndromes (Fourth Edition)* (London: Hodder Arnold, 2001), pp. 179–208.

309   C. Lasègue and J. Falret, 'La folie à deux ou folie communiquée', *Annales Medico-Psychologiques*, 18 (September 1877), pp. 321–55. See also: M.J. Nolan, 'Case of *folie á deux*', *Journal of Mental Science*, 35, 149 (April 1889), pp. 55–61.

310   W.W. Ireland, *The Blot upon the Brain: Studies in History and Psychology (First Edition)* (Edinburgh: Bell and Bradfute, 1885), pp. 201–8.

311   R. Mentjox, C.A. van Houten and C.G. Kooiman, 'Induced psychotic disorder: clinical aspects, theoretical considerations, and some guidelines for treatment', *Comprehensive Psychiatry*, 34, 2 (March–April, 1993), pp. 120–6.

312   A. Munro, *Delusional Disorder: Paranoia and Related Illnesses* (Cambridge: Cambridge University Press, 1999).

313   A. Bourke, *The Burning of Bridget Cleary: A True Story* (London: Pimlico, 1999); D. Walsh, '*Capgras à plusieurs*: the case of Brigid Cleary', *Irish Journal of Psychiatry*, 12, 1 (Spring 1991), pp. 10–2; D. Walsh, 'Burning of Bridget Cleary', *Irish Times*, 28 August 1999.

314   N.A.F. Kraya and C. Patrick, '*Folie à deux* in forensic setting', *Australian and New Zealand Journal of Psychiatry*, 31, 6 (December 1997), pp. 883–8; M. Mela, '*Folie à trois* in a multilevel security forensic treatment center: forensic and ethics-related implications', *Journal of the American Academy of Psychiatry and the Law*, 33, 3 (1 September 2005), pp. 310–6.

315   Enoch and Ball, *Uncommon Psychiatric Syndromes (Fourth Edition)*, p. 206.

316   M.L. Bourgeois, P. Duhamel and H. Verdoux, 'Delusional parasitosis: folie à deux and attempted murder of a family doctor', *British Journal of Psychiatry*, 161, 5 (1 November 1992), pp. 709–11.

317   Ireland, *The Blot upon the Brain: Studies in History and Psychology (First Edition)*, pp. 201–8.

318   These cases were previously discussed in: B.D. Kelly, '*Folie à plusieurs*: forensic cases from nineteenth-century Ireland', *History of Psychiatry*, 20, 77 (Part 1) (March 2009), pp. 47–60. For this work, a single researcher (BDK) studied medical case records of patients admitted to the Central Criminal Lunatic Asylum (Central Mental Hospital), Dublin, in the late 1800s and early 1900s. This formed part of a broader programme of historical and archival research based at the Department of Adult Psychiatry, Mater Misericordiae University Hospital, Dublin; the National Forensic Psychiatry Service, Central Mental Hospital, Dundrum, Dublin; and University College Dublin, Ireland. The programme of research was approved by the Health Service Executive (Dublin, Mid-Leinster) Research Ethics Committee. In order to maintain patient confidentiality, names were changed so as to render specific individuals unidentifiable. For further consideration of these cases, see: Kelly, *Custody, Care and Criminality: Forensic Psychiatry and Law in 19th Century Ireland*, pp. 129–41; P. Gibbons, N. Mulryan and A. O'Connor, 'Guilty but insane: the insanity defence in Ireland, 1850–1995', *British Journal of Psychiatry*, 170, 5 (May 1997), pp. 467–72; Prior, *Madness and Murder: Gender, Crime and Mental Disorder in Nineteenth Century Ireland*, pp. 178–206.

319   Ireland, *The Blot upon the Brain: Studies in History and Psychology (First Edition)*, pp. 201–8.

320   Anonymous, 'Obituary: Daniel Hack Tuke', *Lancet*, 145, 3733 (16 March 1895), pp. 718–19.

321   D.H. Tuke, 'Folie à deux', *Brain*, 10, 4 (1 January 1888), pp. 408–21.

322   A.P. Williamson, 'Psychiatry, moral management and the origins of social policy for mentally ill people in Ireland', *Irish Journal of Medical Science*, 161, 9 (September 1992), pp. 556–8; McCarthy, *Irish Women's History*, pp. 115–36.

323   M. Reuber, 'The architecture of psychological management: the Irish asylums (1801–1922)', *Psychological Medicine*, 26, 6 (November 1996), pp. 1179–89; Reuber, *Medicine, Disease and the State in Ireland, 1650–1940*, pp. 208–33.

324   P. Prior, 'Prisoner or patient? The official debate on the criminal lunatic in nineteenth-century Ireland', *History of Psychiatry*, 15, 58 (Part 2) (June 2004), pp. 177–92.

325   Inspectors of Lunatics, *The Forty-Second Report (With Appendices) of the Inspectors of Lunatics (Ireland)* (Dublin: Thom and Co. for Her Majesty's Stationery Office, 1893); Torrey and Miller, *The Invisible Plague: The Rise of Mental Illness from 1750 to the Present*; P. Prior, 'Dangerous lunacy: the misuse of mental health law in nineteenth-century Ireland', *Journal of Forensic Psychiatry and Psychology*, 14, 3 (September 2003), pp. 525–41; Kelly, *Asylums, Mental Health Care and the Irish, 1800–2010*, pp. 205–20.

326   O. Woods, 'The Presidential Address delivered at the Sixtieth Annual Meeting of the Medico-Psychological Association', *Journal of Mental Science*, 47, 199 (October

1901), pp. 645–58. See also: Henry, *Our Lady's Psychiatric Hospital Cork*, pp. 225–34; Webb, *Trinity's Psychiatrists: From Serenity of the Soul to Neuroscience*, pp. 45–6.

327   O.T. Woods, 'Notes of a case of folie à deux in five members of one family', *Journal of Mental Science*, 34, 148 (1 January 1889), pp. 535–9. See also: Kelly, *Custody, Care and Criminality: Forensic Psychiatry and Law in 19th Century Ireland*, pp. 134–41.

328   N.A.F. Kraya and C. Patrick, 'Folie à deux in forensic setting', *Australian and New Zealand Journal of Psychiatry*, 31, 6 (December 1997), pp. 883–8; M. Mela, 'Folie à trios in a multilevel security forensic treatment center', *Journal of the American Academy of Psychiatry and the Law*, 33, 3 (1 September 2005), pp. 310–6.

329   Enoch and Ball, *Uncommon Psychiatric Syndromes (Fourth Edition)*, pp. 205–6; Munro, *Delusional Disorder: Paranoia and Related Illnesses*, pp. 225–42.

330   McCarthy, *Irish Women's History*, pp. 115–36; P.M. Prior, 'Murder and madness: gender and the insanity defense in nineteenth-century Ireland', *New Hibernia Review*, 9, 4 (Winter 2005), pp. 19–36; P. Prior, 'Roasting a man alive: the case of Mary Rielly, criminal lunatic', *Éire-Ireland*, 41, 1–2 (Spring/Summer 2006), pp. 169–91; Prior, *Madness and Murder: Gender, Crime and Mental Disorder in Nineteenth Century Ireland*; Walsh, *Gender Perspectives in 19th Century Ireland*, pp. 159–67; O. Walsh, ''The designs of providence': race, religion and Irish insanity', in J. Melling and B. Forsythe (eds), *Insanity Institutions and Society, 1800–1914: A Social History of Madness in Comparative Perspective* (London and New York: Routledge, 1999), pp. 223–42; pp. 232–3; O. Walsh, 'Gender and insanity in nineteenth-century Ireland', in J. Andrews and A. Digby (eds), *Sex and Seclusion, Class and Custody: Perspectives on Gender and Class in the History of British and Irish Psychiatry* (Amsterdam: Editions Rodopi, 2004), pp. 69–93. See also: Kelly, *Custody, Care and Criminality: Forensic Psychiatry and Law in 19th Century Ireland*, pp. 95–8.

331   P. Gibbons, N. Mulryan and A. O'Connor, 'Guilty but insane: the insanity defence in Ireland, 1850–1995', *British Journal of Psychiatry*, 170, 5 (May 1997), pp. 467–72; N. Mulryan, P. Gibbons and A. O'Connor, 'Infanticide and child murder: admissions to the Central Mental Hospital 1850–2000', *Irish Journal of Psychological Medicine*, 19, 1 (March 2002), pp. 8–12.

332   B.D. Kelly, 'Clinical and social characteristics of women committed to inpatient forensic psychiatric care in Ireland, 1868–1908', *Journal of Forensic Psychiatry and Psychology*, 19, 2 (June 2008), pp. 261–73.

333   Prior, *Madness and Murder: Gender, Crime and Mental Disorder in Nineteenth Century Ireland*, pp. 126–8.

334   Parry, 'Women and Madness in Nineteenth-Century Ireland', pp. 74–5.

335   F. Churchill, 'On the mental disorders of pregnancy and childbed', *Dublin Quarterly Journal of Medical Science*,

9, 1 (February 1850), pp. 38–63; p. 39. See also: C. Breathnach, 'Medicalizing the female reproductive cycle in rural Ireland, 1926–56', *Historical Research*, 85, 230 (November 2012), pp. 674–90.

336   H. Maudsley, 'Homicidal insanity', *Journal of Mental Science*, 47, 9 (October 1863), pp. 327–43.

337   E. Meehan and K. MacRae, 'Legal implications of premenstrual syndrome', *Canadian Medical Association Journal*, 135, 6 (15 September 1986), pp. 601–8; A.D. Spiegel, 'Temporary insanity and premenstrual syndrome: medical testimony in an 1865 murder trial', *New York State Journal of Medicine*, 88, 9 (September 1988), pp. 482–92.

338   A.D. Spiegel and M.B. Spiegel, 'Was it murder or insanity? Reactions to a successful paroxysmal insanity plea in 1865', *Women and Health*, 18, 2 (1992), pp. 69–86.

339   I. Ray, *A Treatise on the Medical Jurisprudence of Insanity (Third Edition, with Additions)* (Cambridge, Massachusetts: Little, Brown and Company, 1853), p. 198.

340   Parry, 'Women and Madness in Nineteenth-Century Ireland', p. 37.

341   Ibid., p. 84. See also: O. Walsh, 'Gendering the asylums: Ireland and Scotland, 1847–1877', In T. Brotherstone, D. Simonton and O. Walsh (eds), *The Gendering of Scottish History: An International Approach* (Glasgow: Cruithne Press, 1999), pp. 199–215.

342   Inspectors of Lunatics, *The Fortieth Report (With Appendices) of the Inspectors of Lunatics (Ireland)* (Dublin: Thom and Co. for Her Majesty's Stationery Office, 1891), p. 6.

343   Ibid., p. 7.

344   E. Showalter, *The Female Malady: Women, Madness and English Culture, 1830–1980* (London: Virago, 1987); L. Appignanesi, *Mad, Bad and Sad: A History of Women and the Mind Doctors from 1800 to the Present* (London: Virago, 2008); for perspectives on this excellent, provocative book, see: H. Kureishi, 'None the wiser', *Financial Times (Magazine)*, 16/17 February 2008; P. Casey, 'Devil is in the dogma', *Sunday Business Post*, 17 February 2008.

345   L.K. Hanniffy, 'Changing terms in psychiatry', in D.A. Murphy (ed.), *Tumbling Walls: The Evolution of a Community Institution over 150 Years* (Portlaoise: Midland Health Board, 1983), pp. 93–9; p. 99.

346   McCarthy, *Irish Women's History*, pp. 115–36.

347   Parry, 'Women and Madness in Nineteenth-Century Ireland', p. 41.

348   See the work of Malcolm and Walsh for fascinating, penetrating perspectives on these matters; e.g.: E. Malcolm, 'Women and madness in Ireland, 1600–1850', in M. MacCurtain and M. O'Dowd (eds), *Women in Early Modern Ireland* (Edinburgh: Edinburgh University Press, 1991), pp. 318–34; Walsh, *Sex and Seclusion, Class and Custody: Perspectives on Gender and Class in the History of British and Irish Psychiatry*, pp. 69–93. Other

works by both of these authors and others are listed in the bibliography.

349 McDermott, *St Mary's Hospital Castlebar: Serving Mayo Mental Health from 1866*, p. 102; B.D. Kelly, 'One hundred years ago: the Richmond Asylum, Dublin in 1907', *Irish Journal of Psychological Medicine*, 24, 3 (September 2007), pp. 108–14; p. 110; B.D. Kelly, 'Intellectual disability, mental illness and offending behaviour: forensic cases from early twentieth-century Ireland', *Irish Journal of Medical Science*, 179, 3 (September 2010), pp. 409–16; p. 412. See also Chapter 4 of the present book.

350 J. Cooper, 'Children and the falling sickness, Ireland, 1850–1904' in A. Mac Lellan and A. Mauger (eds), *Growing Pains: Childhood Illness in Ireland, 1750–1950* (Dublin: Irish Academic Press, 2013), pp. 89–103.

Chapter 3. Psychiatry and Society in the 1800s

1 Lord Lieutenant and Council of Ireland, *General Rules for the Government of All the District Lunatic Asylums of Ireland, Made, Framed and Established by the Lord Lieutenant and Council of Ireland* (Dublin: Alexander Thom for her Majesty's Stationery Office, 1843), p. 17.

2 B.D. Kelly, 'Dr William Saunders Hallaran and psychiatric practice in nineteenth-century Ireland', *Irish Journal of Medical Science*, 177, 1 (March 2008), pp. 79–84; B.D. Kelly, 'Introduction', in W.S. Hallaran, *An Enquiry into the Causes Producing the Extraordinary Addition to the Number of Insane Together with Extended Observations on the Cure of Insanity with Hints as to the Better Management of Public Asylums for Insane Persons* (Dublin: First Medical, 2008; Hallaran's book was first published in Cork by Edwards and Savage, 1810), pp. 3–11.

3 P. Pinel, *A Treatise on Insanity* (translated by D.D. Davis MD) (Sheffield: W. Todd for Messrs. Cadell and Davies, 1806); Stone, *Healing the Mind: A History of Psychiatry from Antiquity to the Present*, p. 61.

4 Tuke, *Description of The Retreat, an Institution Near York, for Insane Persons of the Society of Friends: Containing an Account of its Origin and Progress, the Modes of Treatment, and a Statement of Cases*; Stone, *Healing the Mind: A History of Psychiatry from Antiquity to the Present*, p. 104.

5 L. Kennedy, P.S. Ell, E.M. Crawford and L.A. Clarkson, *Mapping the Great Irish Famine* (Dublin: Four Courts Press Ltd., 1999), p. 16.

6 Homelessness, for example, was a particular problem, in addition to starvation and disease: N.A. Kelly, 'Remembering homelessness in the Great Irish Famine', in D.A. Valone (ed.), *Ireland's Great Hunger: Relief, Representation, and Remembrance (Volume 2)* (Lanham, MD: University Press of America, 2010), pp. 140–60. As regards the asylum in Carlow, see: Cox, *Negotiating Insanity in the Southeast of Ireland, 1820–1900*, pp. 36–7.

7 B.D. Kelly, 'Mental illness in nineteenth century Ireland: a qualitative study of workhouse records', *Irish Journal of Medical Science*, 173, 1 (January 2004), pp. 53–5.

8 Cox, *Negotiating Insanity in the Southeast of Ireland, 1820–1900*, pp. 121–4.

9 H.W. Hoek, A.S. Brown and E. Susser, 'The Dutch famine and schizophrenia spectrum disorders', *Social Psychiatry and Psychiatric Epidemiology*, 33, 8 (August 1998), pp. 373–9.

10 B.D. Kelly, A. Lane, I. Agartz, K.M. Henriksson and T.F. McNeil, 'Craniofacial dysmorphology in Swedish schizophrenia patients', *Acta Psychiatrica Scandinavica*, 111, 3 (March 2005), pp. 202–7.

11 D. Walsh, 'Did the Great Irish Famine increase schizophrenia?', *Irish Journal of Psychological Medicine*, 29, 1 (January 2012), pp. 7–15.

12 Torrey and Miller, *The Invisible Plague: The Rise of Mental Illness from 1750 to the Present*, p. 133.

13 D. Walsh, 'The lunatic asylums of Ireland, 1825–1839', *Irish Journal of Psychological Medicine*, 25, 4 (December 2008), pp. 151–6.

14 Brennan, *Irish Insanity, 1800–2000*, pp. 130–1.

15 J. Mokyr, *Why Ireland Starved: A Quantitative and Analytical History of the Irish Economy, 1800–1850* (London: Unwin Hyman, 1985).

16 M. Grimsley-Smith, 'Revisiting a 'demographic freak': Irish asylums and hidden hunger', *Social History of Medicine*, 25, 2 (May 2012), pp. 307–23; see especially p. 315 and Figures 3 and 4 (p. 316).

17 Inspectors of Lunatics (Ireland), *The Sixty-Third Annual Report (With Appendices) of the Inspectors of Lunatics (Ireland), Being for the Year Ending 31st December 1913* (Dublin: Thom and Co. for His Majesty's Stationery Office, 1914), p. xvi. For further valuable discussion of this topic by Grimsley-Smith, see: M.D. Grimsley-Smith, 'Politics, Professionalisation, and Poverty: Lunatic Asylums for the Poor in Ireland, 1817–1920' (PhD Thesis, University of Notre Dame, IN, 2011), pp. 208–9. See also: Cox, *Negotiating Insanity in the Southeast of Ireland, 1820–1900*, pp. 38–9.

18 R. Porter and M.S. Micale, 'Introduction: reflections on psychiatry and its histories', in M.S. Micale and R. Porter (eds), *Discovering the History of Psychiatry* (New York and Oxford: Oxford University Press, 1994), pp. 3–36; p. 11; K. McNally, 'Letter to the editor', *Irish Journal of Psychological Medicine*, 30, 1 (March 2013), p. 91; D. Walsh, 'Letter to the editor', *Irish Journal of Psychological Medicine*, 30, 1 (March 2013), pp. 91–2.

19 E. Malcolm, ''The house of strident shadows': the asylum, the family and emigration in post-Famine rural Ireland' in G. Jones and E. Malcolm (eds), *Medicine, Disease and the State in Ireland, 1650–1940* (Cork: Cork University Press, 1999), pp. 177–91.

20 M. McDonagh, 'Impact of Great Famine on mental health examined at Science Week', *Irish Times*, 13 November 2013; O. Walsh, 'Nature or nurture: epigenetic change and the Great Famine in Ireland' in

C. Kinealy, C. Reilly and J. King (eds), *Women and the Great Hunger* (Hamden, CT: Quinnipiac University Press, 2017) (*in press*, forthcoming).

21   B.D. Kelly, 'Mental illness in nineteenth century Ireland: a qualitative study of workhouse records', *Irish Journal of Medical Science*, 173, 1 (January 2004), pp. 53–5.

22   M. Grimsley-Smith, 'Revisiting a 'demographic freak': Irish asylums and hidden hunger', *Social History of Medicine*, 25, 2 (May 2012), pp. 307–23; p. 318.

23   J.L.T. Birley, 'Famine: the distant shadow over French psychiatry', *British Journal of Psychiatry*, 180, 4 (April 2002), pp. 298–9.

24   D. McLellan, *Utopian Pessimist: The Life and Thought of Simone Weil* (London: Macmillan, 1989).

25   Torrey and Miller, *The Invisible Plague: The Rise of Mental Illness from 1750 to the Present*, pp. 70, 129–30, 195–6.

26   Ibid., p. 125; Reynolds, *Grangegorman: Psychiatric Care in Dublin since 1815*, pp. 2–3.

27   Robins, *Fools and Mad: A History of the Insane in Ireland*, pp. 28–9, 45–6.

28   Kelly, *Custody, Care and Criminality: Forensic Psychiatry and Law in 19th Century Ireland*, p. 56.

29   Finnane, *Insanity and the Insane in Post-Famine Ireland*, pp. 21–2, 66.

30   Walsh and Daly, *Mental Illness in Ireland 1750–2002: Reflections on the Rise and Fall of Institutional Care*, p. 14.

31   Finnane, *Insanity and the Insane in Post-Famine Ireland*, p. 24.

32   Ibid., p. 25.

33   Lunatic Asylums, Ireland, Commission, *Report of the Commissioners of Inquiry into the State of the Lunatic Asylums and Other Institutions for the Custody and Treatment of the Insane in Ireland: with Minutes of Evidence and Appendices (Part 1 – Report, Tables, and Returns)* (Dublin: Thom and Sons, for Her Majesty's Stationery Office, 1858), pp. 24–5. For a further account of the House of Industry of Dublin and, specifically, the 477 persons with mental disorder housed there when it closed, see: Kirkpatrick, *A Note on the History of the Care of the Insane in Ireland up to the End of the Nineteenth Century*, p. 29. See also: Reynolds, *Grangegorman: Psychiatric Care in Dublin since 1815*, pp. 10–4.

34   Kennedy, Ell, Crawford and Clarkson, *Mapping the Great Irish Famine*, p. 125.

35   M. Reuber, 'The architecture of psychological management: the Irish asylums (1801–1922)', *Psychological Medicine*, 26, 6 (November 1996), pp. 1179–89.

36   Walsh and Daly, *Mental Illness in Ireland 1750–2002: Reflections on the Rise and Fall of Institutional Care*, p. 20.

37   Finnane, *Insanity and the Insane in Post-Famine Ireland*, p. 129; Robins, *Fools and Mad: A History of the Insane in Ireland*, pp. 110–11.

38   Finnane, *Insanity and the Insane in Post-Famine Ireland*, p. 202.

39   Brennan, *Irish Insanity, 1800–2000*, pp. 136–7.

40   Walsh and Daly, *Mental Illness in Ireland 1750–2002: Reflections on the Rise and Fall of Institutional Care*, p. 20. See also: Robins, *Fools and Mad: A History of the Insane in Ireland*, pp. 159–61.

41   Brennan, *Irish Insanity, 1800–2000*, p. 44.

42   Ibid., p. 54.

43   Robins, *Fools and Mad: A History of the Insane in Ireland*, pp. 159–61, 177; Reynolds, *Grangegorman: Psychiatric Care in Dublin since 1815*, pp. 205, 208; Torrey and Miller, *The Invisible Plague: The Rise of Mental Illness from 1750 to the Present*, p. 130; N.A. Kelly, 'History by Proxy – Imaging the Great Irish Famine' (PhD Thesis, University of Amsterdam, 2010), pp. 210–12; N.A. Kelly, 'Narrating sites of history: workhouses and Famine memory', in O. Frawley (ed.), *Memory Ireland, Volume 3: The Famine and the Troubles* (Syracuse, NY: Syracuse University Press, 2014), pp. 152–73.

44   Select Committee on the Lunatic Poor in Ireland, *Report from the Select Committee on the Lunatic Poor in Ireland with Minutes of Evidence Taken Before the Committee and an Appendix*, p. 13.

45   Ballinrobe Poor Law Union, County Mayo, Minutes: 1845 to 1900; see: B.D. Kelly, 'Mental illness in nineteenth century Ireland: a qualitative study of workhouse records', *Irish Journal of Medical Science*, 173, 1 (January 2004), pp. 53–5; p. 54. See also: Kelly, *Custody, Care and Criminality: Forensic Psychiatry and Law in 19th Century Ireland*, pp. 47–54.

46   Cox, *Negotiating Insanity in the Southeast of Ireland, 1820–1900*, pp. 36–7.

47   Torrey and Miller, *The Invisible Plague: The Rise of Mental Illness from 1750 to the Present*, pp. 130, 138.

48   Cox, *Negotiating Insanity in the Southeast of Ireland, 1820–1900*, p. 173. Cox's discussion of the mentally ill in workhouses (pp. 169–94) is fascinating and insightful.

49   Ibid., p. 189. See also: Robins, *Fools and Mad: A History of the Insane in Ireland*, pp. 88–9, 202.

50   Cox, *Negotiating Insanity in the Southeast of Ireland, 1820–1900*, p. 175; D. Walsh, 'Brief historical review', *Irish Journal of Psychiatry*, 13, 1 (Spring 1992), pp. 3–20; p. 4.

51   Cox, *Negotiating Insanity in the Southeast of Ireland, 1820–1900*, pp. 181–2.

52   C. O'Mahony, *Cork's Poor Law Palace: Workhouse Life 1838–1890* (Monkstown, County Cork: Rosmathún Press, 2005), pp. 231–5.

53   Anonymous. 'Meeting of the Irish Division', *Journal of Mental Science*, 41, 174 (July 1895), pp. 547–55; p. 555.

54   D. Walsh, 'The Ennis District Lunatic Asylum and the Clare Workhouse Lunatic Asylums in 1901', *Irish Journal of Psychological Medicine*, 26, 4 (December 2010), pp. 206–11. See also: Robins, *Fools and Mad: A History of the Insane in Ireland*, p. 168.

55   Finnane, *Insanity and the Insane in Post-Famine Ireland*, p. 150.

56   Richmond Asylum Joint Committee, *Richmond Asylum*

Joint Committee Minutes (Dublin: Richmond Asylum, 1907), 31 January, pp. 92–3.

57 The industrial school in Youghal, County Cork was converted into an auxiliary asylum and opened in 1904 under the guidance of an order of nuns, the Poor Servants of the Mother of God (Henry, *Our Lady's Psychiatric Hospital Cork*, pp. 205–9).

58 B.D. Kelly, 'One hundred years ago: the Richmond Asylum, Dublin in 1907', *Irish Journal of Psychological Medicine*, 24, 3 (September 2007), pp. 108–14. See also: Kelly, *Custody, Care and Criminality: Forensic Psychiatry and Law in 19th Century Ireland*, pp. 83–5.

59 Richmond Asylum Joint Committee, *Richmond Asylum Joint Committee Minutes* (Dublin: Richmond Asylum, 1907), p. 8.

60 Ibid., p. 12.

61 Ibid., p. 14.

62 Ibid., p. 14.

63 Ibid., p. 15.

64 Ibid., p. 15.

65 This positive assessment of the South Dublin Union Workhouse was by no means universal; for discussions, see: Finnane, *Insanity and the Insane in Post-Famine Ireland*, p. 70; Reynolds, *Grangegorman: Psychiatric Care in Dublin since 1815*, p. 159.

66 Richmond Asylum Joint Committee, *Richmond Asylum Joint Committee Minutes* (Dublin: Richmond Asylum, 1907), p. 17.

67 Ibid., p. 18.

68 Reynolds, *Grangegorman: Psychiatric Care in Dublin since 1815*, p. 211.

69 Brennan, *Irish Insanity, 1800–2000*, pp. 137, 149.

70 B.D. Kelly, 'Intellectual disability, mental illness and offending behaviour: forensic cases from early twentieth-century Ireland', *Irish Journal of Medical Science*, 179, 3 (September 2010), pp. 409–16. See also: O. Walsh, "A person of the second order': the plight of the intellectually disabled in nineteenth-century Ireland', in L.M. Geary and O. Walsh (eds), *Philanthropy in Nineteenth-Century Ireland* (Dublin: Four Courts Press, 2014), pp. 161–80.

71 Lord Lieutenant and Council of Ireland, *General Rules for the Government of All the District Lunatic Asylums of Ireland, Made, Framed and Established by the Lord Lieutenant and Council of Ireland* (Dublin: Alexander Thom for her Majesty's Stationery Office, 1843), p. 6; Robins, *Fools and Mad: A History of the Insane in Ireland*, p. 158; see also, more generally: pp. 157–70.

72 Inspectors of Lunatics, *Special Report from the Inspectors of Lunatics to the Chief Secretary: Alleged Increasing Prevalence of Insanity in Ireland* (Dublin: Her Majesty's Stationery Office, 1894).

73 Robins, *Fools and Mad: A History of the Insane in Ireland*, p. 162.

74 C. Brady, *The Training of Idiotic and Feeble-Minded Children (Second Edition)* (Dublin: Hodges, Smith, and Co., 1865), pp. 5–6.

75 Robins, *Fools and Mad: A History of the Insane in Ireland*, p. 162.

76 Brady, *The Training of Idiotic and Feeble-Minded Children (Second Edition)*, pp. 35–6.

77 C.S. Breathnach, 'Henry Hutchinson Stewart (1798–1879)', *History of Psychiatry*, 9, 33 (March 1998), pp. 27–33; p. 29.

78 G.H. Kidd, *An Appeal on Behalf of the Idiotic and Imbecile Children of Ireland* (Dublin: John Falconer, 1865).

79 Breathnach, 'Henry Hutchinson Stewart (1798–1879)', *History of Psychiatry*, 9, 33 (March 1998), pp. 27–33; p. 28.

80 Lunatic Asylums, Ireland, Commission, *Report of the Commissioners of Inquiry into the State of the Lunatic Asylums and Other Institutions for the Custody and Treatment of the Insane in Ireland: with Minutes of Evidence and Appendices (Part 1 – Report, Tables, and Returns)*, pp. 24–5. See also: Kirkpatrick, *A Note on the History of the Care of the Insane in Ireland up to the End of the Nineteenth Century*, p. 29; Reynolds, *Grangegorman: Psychiatric Care in Dublin since 1815*, pp. 10–14.

81 Robins, *Fools and Mad: A History of the Insane in Ireland*, p. 163.

82 Breathnach, 'Henry Hutchinson Stewart (1798–1879)', *History of Psychiatry*, 9, 33 (March 1998), pp. 27–33; p. 29.

83 Robins, *Fools and Mad: A History of the Insane in Ireland*, p. 164.

84 Reynolds, *Grangegorman: Psychiatric Care in Dublin since 1815*, p. 86.

85 Inspectors of Lunatics, *Special Report from the Inspectors of Lunatics to the Chief Secretary: Alleged Increasing Prevalence of Insanity in Ireland*.

86 Great Britain Commissions for the Care and Control of the Feeble-Minded, *Report of the Royal Commission on the Care and Control of the Feeble-Minded* (London: Her Majesty's Stationery Office, 1908), p. 428.

87 Walsh, *Sex and Seclusion, Class and Custody: Perspectives on Gender and Class in the History of British and Irish Psychiatry*, pp. 69–93.

88 A. Digby, 'Contexts and perspectives', in D. Wright and A. Digby (eds), *From Idiocy to Mental Deficiency: Historical Perspectives on People with Learning Disabilities* (London & New York: Routledge, 1996), pp. 1–21. D. Atkinson, M. Jackson and J. Walmsley, 'Introduction: methods and themes', in D. Atkinson, M. Jackson and J. Walmsley (eds), *Forgotten Lives* (Worcestershire, UK: British Institute of Learning Disabilities (BILD), 1997), pp. 1–20; P. Dale and J. Melling, 'The politics of mental welfare: fresh perspectives on the history of institutional care for the mentally ill and disabled', in P. Dale and J. Melling (eds), *Mental Illness and Learning Disability Since 1850: Finding a Place for Mental Disorder in the United Kingdom* (London and New York: Routledge/ Taylor and Francis Group, 2006), pp. 1–23.

89 H.G. Simmons, 'Explaining social policy: the English Mental Deficiency Act of 1913', *Journal of Social History*,

11, 3 (Spring 1978), pp. 387–403; Gladstone, *From Idiocy to Mental Deficiency: Historical Perspectives on People with Learning Disabilities*, pp. 134–60.

90 M. Jackson, 'Institutional provision for the feeble-minded in Edwardian England: Sandlebridge and the scientific morality of permanent care', in D. Wright and A. Digby (eds), *From Idiocy to Mental Deficiency: Historical Perspectives on People with Learning Disabilities* (London and New York: Routledge, 1996), pp. 161–83.

91 A. Digby, 'Contexts and perspectives', in D. Wright and A. Digby (eds), *From Idiocy to Mental Deficiency: Historical Perspectives on People with Learning Disabilities* (London & New York: Routledge, 1996), pp. 1–21.

92 D. Walsh, 'Thomas Drapes, medical superintendent of the Enniscorthy Asylum', *British Journal of Psychiatry*, 199, 3 (September 2011), p. 218; B.D. Kelly, 'Asylum doctor extraordinaire: Dr Thomas Drapes (1847–1919)', *Irish Journal of Medical Science*, 184, 3 (September 2015), pp. 565–71.

93 Webb, *Trinity's Psychiatrists: From Serenity of the Soul to Neuroscience*, pp. 46–50.

94 W.R. Dawson, 'Obituary: Thomas Drapes, M.B. Dubl.: B. 1874 [*sic*]: D. 1919', *Journal of Mental Science*, 66, 273 (1 April 1920), pp. 83–7.

95 McCarthy, *Irish Women's History*, pp. 115–36.

96 Lord Lieutenant of Ireland, *General Rules and Regulations for the Management of District Lunatic Asylums in Ireland* [1874] (Dublin: Pilkington, 1890) [National Library of Ireland (Ir 362 i 13)], paragraph XXX.

97 Ibid., paragraph XXXI.

98 Ibid., paragraph XXXIII.

99 Ibid., paragraph XXXIV (see also paragraphs XLII and XLVI).

100 Ibid., paragraph XXXV.

101 Ibid., paragraph XXXVI.

102 Ibid., paragraph XXXVII.

103 Ibid., paragraph XXXVIII.

104 In 1876, 'Rules and Regulations for the Good Conduct and Management of the Central Lunatic Asylum at Dundrum' articulated regulations regarding inspections, complaints, annual reports, the 'Resident Physician and Governor', 'Visiting Physician', chaplains, and various other employees in Dundrum (Lord Lieutenant and Council of Ireland, *Rules and Regulations for the Good Conduct and Management of the Central Lunatic Asylum at Dundrum* (Dublin: Thom, 1876) [National Library of Ireland (Ir 362 I 13)]); e.g.: 'In order to effect the better management and control of the Central Asylum at Dundrum for the reception of insane persons charged with or convicted of offences in Ireland, the Inspectors of Lunatic Asylums shall visit that establishment together, or separately, once in each month, or oftener if they shall think proper' (paragraph 3); 'On no account whatever, without an express order in writing from the Chief or Under Secretary, will criminal lunatics be permitted to leave the precincts of the Asylum' (paragraph 88); and 'As lunatics charged with minor offences may be transferred from District Asylums to the Central Asylum, they shall, at the discretion of the Lord Lieutenant, and on the report of the Inspectors, be subject to be sent back to the Institutions from whence they came' (paragraph 89). The rules for Dundrum were similar in many respects to the 1874 rules for general asylums, outlining many of the same duties for the 'Resident Physician and Governor' in Dundrum as were outlined for RMSs.

105 Dawson, 'Obituary: Thomas Drapes, M.B. Dubl.: B. 1874 [*sic*]: D. 1919', *Journal of Mental Science*, 66, 273 (1 April 1920), pp. 83–7; p. 84.

106 Cox, *Negotiating Insanity in the Southeast of Ireland, 1820–1900*, p. xi.

107 Dawson, 'Obituary: Thomas Drapes, M.B. Dubl.: B. 1874 [*sic*]: D. 1919', *Journal of Mental Science*, 66, 273 (1 April 1920), pp. 83–7; p. 85.

108 Y. Delage (T. Drapes, transl.), 'Psychoanalysis, a new psychosis. Une psychose nouvelle: la psychoanalyse. Mercure de France, September 1st, 1916', *Journal of Mental Science*, 63, 260 (1 January 1917), pp. 61–76.

109 T. Drapes, 'On the alleged increase of insanity in Ireland', *Journal of Mental Science*, 40, 171 (1 October 1894), pp. 519–48.

110 T. Drapes, 'A case of acute hallucinatory insanity of traumatic origin', *Journal of Mental Science*, 50, 210 (1 July 1904), pp. 478–500.

111 T. Drapes, 'A note on psychiatric terminology and classification', *Journal of Mental Science*, 52, 216 (1 January 1906), pp. 75–84; p. 83.

112 E. Kraepelin, *Psychiatrie. Ein Lehrbuch für Studirende und Aerzte (Sixth Edition)* (Leipzig: Verlag von Johann Ambrosius Barth, 1899); T. Drapes, 'On the maniacal-depressive insanity of Kraepelin', *Journal of Mental Science*, 55, 228 (1 January 1909), pp. 58–64. See also: Shorter, *A History of Psychiatry: From the Era of the Asylum to the Age of Prozac*, pp. 100–9.

113 Shorter, *A History of Psychiatry: From the Era of the Asylum to the Age of Prozac*, pp. 104–9.

114 T. Drapes, 'The personal equation in alienism', *Journal of Mental Science*, 57, 239 (1 October 1911), pp. 598–617; p. 614.

115 R. Atkins, 'Report on nervous and mental diseases', *Dublin Journal of Medical Sciences*, 91, 1 (January 1891), pp. 54–70; Finnane, *150 Years of British Psychiatry, 1841–1991. Volume I*, p. 310.

116 C. Norman, 'Variations in form of mental affections in relation to the classification of insanity', *Dublin Journal of Medical Science*, 83, 3 (March 1887), pp. 228–35.

117 T. Drapes, 'Are punitive measures justifiable in asylums?', *Journal of Mental Science*, 45, 190 (1 July 1899), pp. 536–49.

118 Inspectors of Lunatics (Ireland), *The Sixty-Third Annual Report (With Appendices) of the Inspectors of Lunatics (Ireland), Being for the Year Ending 31st December 1913* (Dublin: Thom and Co. for His Majesty's Stationery Office, 1914), p. 92.

119 Inspectors of Lunatics (Ireland), *The Sixty-Sixth Annual Report (With Appendices) of the Inspectors of Lunatics (Ireland), Being for the Year Ending 31ˢᵗ December 1916* (Dublin: Thom and Co. for His Majesty's Stationery Office, 1917), pp. xx, 5, 12.

120 Anonymous, 'Irish Division', *Journal of Mental Science*, 63, 261 (1 April 1917), pp. 297–9; p. 299. See also: Kelly, *'He Lost Himself Completely': Shell Shock and its Treatment at Dublin's Richmond War Hospital, 1916–1919*, pp. 121–2.

121 N.C. Andreasen, *Brave New Brain: Conquering Mental Illness in the Era of the Genome* (Oxford and New York: Oxford University Press, 2001), pp. 25–37.

122 H. Marsh, *Do No Harm: Stories of Life, Death and Brain Surgery* (London: Weidenfeld & Nicolson, 2014), p. 271.

123 Anonymous, 'Notes and news: Irish division', *Journal of Mental Science*, 56, 234 (1 July 1910), pp. 577–81; p. 580.

124 For further information on eugenics and psychiatry in the US and Canada, see: I.R. Dowbiggin, *Keeping America Sane: Psychiatry and Eugenics in the United States and Canada, 1880–1940* (Ithaca and London: Cornell University Press, 1997).

125 Finnane, *150 Years of British Psychiatry, 1841–1991. Volume I*, p. 311; Healy, *150 Years of British Psychiatry. Volume II: The Aftermath*, pp. 268–91; p. 271. See also: Finnane, *Insanity and the Insane in Post-Famine Ireland*, pp. 79–81, 86; G. Jones, 'Eugenics in Ireland: the Belfast Eugenics Society, 1911–15', *Irish Historical Studies*, 28, 109 (May 1992), pp. 81–95.

126 Dawson, 'Obituary: Thomas Drapes, M.B. Dubl.: B. 1874 [*sic*]: D. 1919', *Journal of Mental Science*, 66, 273 (1 April 1920), pp. 83–7; p. 86.

127 Inspectors of Lunatics (Ireland), *The Sixty-Third Annual Report (With Appendices) of the Inspectors of Lunatics (Ireland), Being for the Year Ending 31ˢᵗ December 1913*, p. 93.

128 Dawson, 'Obituary: Thomas Drapes, M.B. Dubl.: B. 1874 [*sic*]: D. 1919', *Journal of Mental Science*, 66, 273 (1 April 1920), pp. 83–7; p. 87.

129 W.R. Dawson, 'The presidential address on the relation between the geographical distribution of insanity and that of certain social and other conditions in Ireland', *Journal of Mental Science*, 57, 239 (1 October 1911), pp. 571–97; Anonymous, 'Notes and news: The Medico-Psychological Association of Great Britain and Ireland', *Journal of Mental Science*, 57, 239 (1 October 1911), pp. 723–46; Webb, *Trinity's Psychiatrists: From Serenity of the Soul to Neuroscience*, pp. 50–4.

130 Anonymous, 'Notes and news: Irish division', *Journal of Mental Science*, 56, 234 (1 July 1910), pp. 577–81; p. 580.

131 Drapes, 'On the alleged increase of insanity in Ireland', *Journal of Mental Science*, 40, 171 (1 October 1894), pp. 519–48.

132 Torrey and Miller, *The Invisible Plague: The Rise of Mental Illness from 1750 to the Present*, pp. 124–60.

133 Hallaran, *An Enquiry into the Causes Producing the Extraordinary Addition to the Number of Insane together with Extended Observations on the Cure of Insanity with Hints as to the Better Management of Public Asylums for Insane Persons*, p. 10. See also: Kelly, *Custody, Care and Criminality: Forensic Psychiatry and Law in 19th Century Ireland*, pp. 28–33; B.D. Kelly, 'Dr William Saunders Hallaran and psychiatric practice in nineteenth-century Ireland', *Irish Journal of Medical Science*, 177, 1 (March 2008), pp. 79–84.

134 Hallaran, *An Enquiry into the Causes Producing the Extraordinary Addition to the Number of Insane together with Extended Observations on the Cure of Insanity with Hints as to the Better Management of Public Asylums for Insane Persons*, pp. 12,13.

135 Ibid., p. 14.

136 Ibid., p. 26.

137 Ibid., p. 27.

138 Ibid., pp. 17, 19.

139 Ibid., pp. 22–3.

140 Brennan, *Irish Insanity, 1800–2000*, pp. 123–14.

141 In relation to Nugent and Hatchell, see also: *The Dublin Gazette* (Number 15,356), 30 March 1860 (Larcom Papers, National Library of Ireland, Ms. 7,776).

142 Inspector of Lunatic Asylums, *The Thirty-Sixth Report on the District, Criminal and Private Lunatic Asylums in Ireland (With Appendices)* (Dublin: Thom and Co. for Her Majesty's Stationery Office, 1887), p. 5. 'Independent of ordinary lunatic inmates, Palmerston House may be essentially regarded as an establishment for imbeciles and idiots, admissible under a certain age and detainable for a limited period. Its management by the Board and under the immediate control of Dr Pim, has proved a great success. The interior arrangements and the system of tuition adopted in it are unexceptionable. One circumstance alone affects its progress and utility – It is not adequately supported.' (p. 21).

143 Ibid., pp. 7–8.

144 D. Walsh, 'Thomas Drapes, Medical Superintendent of the Enniscorthy Asylum', *British Journal of Psychiatry*, 199, 3 (September 2011), p. 218.

145 T. Drapes, 'On the alleged increase of insanity in Ireland', *Journal of Mental Science*, 40, 171 (1 October 1894), pp. 519–48; pp. 519–20.

146 Anonymous, 'Obituary: Daniel Hack Tuke', *Lancet*, 145, 3733 (16 March 1895), pp. 718–19.

147 D.H. Tuke, 'Alleged increase of insanity', *Journal of Mental Science*, 40, 169 (1 April 1894), pp. 219–34.

148 D.H. Tuke, 'Increase of insanity in Ireland', *Journal of Mental Science*, 40, 171 (1 October 1894), pp. 549–61; pp. 553–4.

149 Robins, *Fools and Mad: A History of the Insane in Ireland*, pp. 112–14.

150 US Bureau of the Census, *Historical Statistics of the United States, Colonial Times to 1970, Bicentennial Edition, Part 2* (Washington DC: GPO, 1975); Shorter, *A History of Psychiatry: From the Era of the Asylum to the Age of*

Prozac, p. 46; Torrey and Miller, *The Invisible Plague: The Rise of Mental Illness from 1750 to the Present*, pp. 193–214.

151 B.D. Kelly, 'Mental health law in Ireland, 1945 to 2001: reformation and renewal', *Medico-Legal Journal*, 76, 2 (June 2008), pp. 65–72.

152 F.B. Sanborn, 'Is American Insanity Increasing?', *Journal of Mental Science*, 40, 169 (1 April 1894), pp. 214–19.

153 Inspectors of Lunatics, *Special Report from the Inspectors of Lunatics to the Chief Secretary: Alleged Increasing Prevalence of Insanity in Ireland* (Dublin: Her Majesty's Stationery Office, 1894).

154 E. Hare, 'Was insanity on the increase? The fifty-sixth Maudsley Lecture', *British Journal of Psychiatry*, 142, 5 (1 May 1983), pp. 439–55; A. Scull, 'Was insanity increasing? A response to Edward Hare', *British Journal of Psychiatry*, 144, 4 (1 April 1984), pp. 432–6. For key perspectives, see also: E.D. O'Neill, *Increase of Lunacy and Special Reasons Applicable to Ireland* (Limerick: George McKern and Sons Limited, 1903); D. Walsh, 'The ups and downs of schizophrenia in Ireland', *Irish Journal of Psychiatry*, 13, 2 (Autumn 1992), pp. 12–16; Torrey and Miller, *The Invisible Plague: The Rise of Mental Illness from 1750 to the Present*, pp. 124–60; and Brennan, *Irish Insanity, 1800–2000*, pp. 58–92.

155 For an excellent discussion of this theme, see: Cox, *Negotiating Insanity in the Southeast of Ireland, 1820–1900*, pp. 53–64.

156 For a detailed dissection of the byzantine laws and practices governing 'lunacy' in Ireland in the 1800s, see: G.W. Abraham, *The Law and Practice of Lunacy in Ireland as Administered by the Lord Chancellor under the Sign Manual Together with a Compendium of the Law Relating to Establishments for the Care of the Insane* (Dublin: E. Ponsonby, 1886). See also: Finnane, *Insanity and the Insane in Post-Famine Ireland*, pp. 87–128; Prior, *Madness and Murder: Gender, Crime and Mental Disorder in Nineteenth Century Ireland*, pp. 27–9, 50–9.

157 See: B.D. Kelly, 'Mental health law in Ireland, 1821 to 1902: building the asylums', *Medico-Legal Journal*, 76, 1 (March 2008), pp. 19–25; B.D. Kelly, 'The apparent increase in insanity in Ireland in the 1800s: why and how?', *Irish Psychiatrist*, 2010, 11, 3 (Autumn 2010), pp. 140–4; B.D. Kelly, 'Enquiring into Ireland's asylums', *Irish Medical Times*, 5 September 2014; Kelly, *Custody, Care and Criminality: Forensic Psychiatry and Law in 19th Century Ireland*, pp. 64–73.

158 D. Walsh, 'The ups and downs of schizophrenia in Ireland', *Irish Journal of Psychiatry*, 13, 2 (Autumn 1992), pp. 12–16.

159 Tuke, 'Alleged increase of insanity', *Journal of Mental Science*, 40, 169 (1 April 1894), pp. 219–34.

160 K. Jones, *Lunacy, Law and Conscience: The Social History of the Care of the Insane* (London: Routledge and Kegan Paul, 1955); Torrey and Miller, *The Invisible Plague: The Rise of Mental Illness from 1750 to the Present*, pp. 6–123.

161 A.M. O'Neill, *Irish Mental Health Law* (Dublin: First Law, 2005), p. 8. See also: L. O'Brien, 'The magic wisp: a history of the mentally ill in Ireland', *Bulletin of the Menninger Clinic*, 31, 2 (March 1967), pp. 79–95; p. 86.

162 Reynolds, *Grangegorman: Psychiatric Care in Dublin since 1815*, p. 1. See also: B. O'Shea and J. Falvey, 'A history of the Richmond Asylum (St Brendan's Hospital), Dublin', in H. Freeman and G.E. Berrios (eds), *150 Years of British Psychiatry. Volume II: The Aftermath* (London: Athlone Press, 1996), pp. 407–33.

163 D. Walsh, 'The ups and downs of schizophrenia in Ireland', *Irish Journal of Psychiatry*, 13, 2 (Autumn 1992), pp. 12–16.

164 Tuke, 'Increase of insanity in Ireland', *Journal of Mental Science*, 40, 171 (1 October 1894), pp. 549–61.

165 D. Walsh, 'Two and two make five – multifactoriogenesis in mental illness in Ireland', *Irish Medical Journal*, 69, 16 (October 1976), pp. 417–22; Finnane, *Insanity and the Insane in Post-Famine Ireland*, pp. 161–19, 173; Walsh, *Sex and Seclusion, Class and Custody: Perspectives on Gender and Class in the History of British and Irish Psychiatry*, pp. 69–93.

166 A. Williamson, 'The beginnings of state care for the mentally ill in Ireland', *Economic and Social Review*, 10, 1 (January 1970), pp. 280–91.

167 Walsh, 'The ups and downs of schizophrenia in Ireland', *Irish Journal of Psychiatry*, 13, 2 (Autumn 1992), pp. 12–16.

168 Finnane, *Insanity and the Insane in Post-Famine Ireland*, pp. 14–15.

169 Scull, *The Most Solitary of Afflictions: Madness and Society in Britain, 1700–1900*, pp. 44–5.

170 P. Prior, 'Dangerous lunacy: the misuse of mental health law in nineteenth-century Ireland', *Journal of Forensic Psychiatry and Psychology*, 14, 3 (September 2003), pp. 525–41.

171 Walsh, 'The ups and downs of schizophrenia in Ireland', *Irish Journal of Psychiatry*, 13, 2 (Autumn 1992), pp. 12–16.

172 N. Mulryan, P. Gibbons and A. O'Connor, 'Infanticide and child murder: admissions to the Central Mental Hospital 1850–2000', *Irish Journal of Psychological Medicine*, 19, 1 (March 2002), pp. 8–12.

173 Walsh, 'The ups and downs of schizophrenia in Ireland', *Irish Journal of Psychiatry*, 13, 2 (Autumn 1992), pp. 12–16; p. 14.

174 This case is drawn from: B.D. Kelly, 'Mental health law in Ireland, 1821 to 1902: dealing with the "increase of insanity in Ireland"', *Medico-Legal Journal*, 76, 1 (March 2008), pp. 26–33. In order to maintain patient confidentiality, names were changed so as to render specific individuals unidentifiable. For further consideration of this case, see: Kelly, *Custody, Care and Criminality: Forensic Psychiatry and Law in 19th Century Ireland*, pp. 70–1.

175 Inspectors of Lunatics, *The Forty-Second Report (With Appendices) of the Inspectors of Lunatics (Ireland)* (Dublin: Thom and Co. for Her Majesty's Stationery Office, 1893).

176 Brennan, *Irish Insanity, 1800–2000*, pp. 69–74.

177 Lord Lieutenant of Ireland, *General Rules and Regulations for the Management of District Lunatic Asylums in Ireland* [1874] (Dublin: Pilkington, 1890) [National Library of Ireland (Ir 362 i 13)], paragraph XXIX.

178 Lords Justice and Privy Council in Ireland, *By the Lords Justice and Privy Council in Ireland* (Dublin: Council Chamber, 1885) [National Library of Ireland (Ir 362 i 13)].

179 For insightful discussions on the emergence of psychiatry as a profession in Ireland, see: Finnane, *150 Years of British Psychiatry, 1841–1991. Volume I*, pp. 306–13; Brennan, *Irish Insanity, 1800–2000*, pp. 69–83.

180 R. Powell, 'Observations upon the comparative prevalence of insanity at different periods', *Medical Transactions*, 4, 2 (1813), pp. 131–59.

181 Walsh, 'The ups and downs of schizophrenia in Ireland', *Irish Journal of Psychiatry*, 13, 2 (Autumn 1992), pp. 12–16; p. 12.

182 Inspectors of Lunatics, *Supplement to the Fifty-Fourth Report of the Inspectors of Lunatics on the District, Criminal, and Private Lunatic Asylums in Ireland. Being a Special Report on the Alleged Increase of Insanity* (Dublin: His Majesty's Stationery Office, 1906).

183 Robins, *Fools and Mad: A History of the Insane in Ireland*, pp. 122–3; Henry, *Our Lady's Psychiatric Hospital Cork*, p. 240.

184 Torrey and Miller, *The Invisible Plague: The Rise of Mental Illness from 1750 to the Present*; see, *inter alia*, pp. 314–33.

185 For a further discussion and a notably compelling analysis, see: Brennan, *Irish Insanity, 1800–2000*, pp. 117–21.

186 Ibid., pp. 120–1.

187 Cox, *Negotiating Insanity in the Southeast of Ireland, 1820–1900*, p. xiii. Cox's book is simply splendid.

188 Carlow District Lunatic Asylum, *Register of Patients ('Admission Book', 7 July 1848 to 21 February 1896, SDH/002/006)* (Archive of St Dympna's Hospital (Carlow), Delany Archive, Carlow College, College Street, Carlow).

189 For an exceptionally insightful discussion of 'mania' and 'melancholia' more generally, see: Finnane, *Insanity and the Insane in Post-Famine Ireland*, pp. 150–61.

190 J.F.G. Pieterson, 'Haematoma auris', in D.H. Tuke (ed.), *Dictionary of Psychological Medicine* (London: John Churchill, 1892), pp. 557–62. See also C.K. Mills and N.S. Yawger (eds), *Lippincott's Nursing Manuals and Care of Nervous and the Insane* (Philadelphia, Pennsylvania: J.B. Lipincott Company, 1915); E.H. Hare, 'Old familiar faces: some aspects of the asylum era in Britain. Part 1', *Psychiatric Developments*, 3, 3 (Autumn 1985), pp. 245–55. See also: G.J. Hearder, 'The treatment of haematoma auris', *Journal of Mental Science*, 22, 97 (April 1876), pp. 91–3.

191 B. Paterson, 'Restraint', in P. Barker (ed.), *Mental Health Ethics* (Abingdon, Oxon: Routledge, 2011), pp. 159–68; p. 163.

192 J. Cooney, 'Foreword', in Organising Committee (ed.), *St Canice's Hospital, 1852–2001* (Kilkenny: South Eastern Health Board, 2006), p. 3.

193 N. Griffin, 'St Canice's Hospital, Kilkenny, 1852–2001' in Organising Committee (ed.), *St Canice's Hospital, 1852–2001* (Kilkenny: South Eastern Health Board, 2001), pp. 7–9.

194 L. Feeney, A. Kavanagh, B.D. Kelly and M. Mooney, 'Moving to a purpose built acute psychiatric unit on a general hospital site: does the new environment produce change for the better?', *Irish Medical Journal*, 100, 3 (March 2007), pp. 391–3.

195 L.K. Hanniffy, 'Changing terms in psychiatry', in D.A. Murphy (ed.), *Tumbling Walls: The Evolution of a Community Institution over 150 Years* (Portlaoise: Midland Health Board, 1983), pp. 93–9.

196 D. Walsh and A. Daly, 'The socio-demographic and clinical profiles of patients admitted to the Sligo District Lunatic Asylum in the late 19th century with some modern comparisons', *Irish Journal of Psychological Medicine*, 33, 1 (March 2016), pp. 43–54.

197 Brennan, *Irish Insanity, 1800–2000*, pp. 85–9.

198 Ibid., pp. 65–6.

199 Kirkpatrick, *A Note on the History of the Care of the Insane in Ireland up to the End of the Nineteenth Century*, pp. 7–8; Robins, *Fools and Mad: A History of the Insane in Ireland*, pp. 16–18.

200 Finnane, *Insanity and the Insane in Post-Famine Ireland*, pp. 200–1, 217; Robins, *Fools and Mad: A History of the Insane in Ireland*, pp. 118–19; P.M. Prior and D.V. Griffiths, "The chaplaincy question': the Lord Lieutenant of Ireland versus the Belfast Lunatic Asylum', *Éire-Ireland*, 33, 2&3 (1997), pp.137–53; P.M. Prior and D.V. Griffiths, 'The 'chaplaincy question' at Belfast District Asylum, 1834–1870' in P.M. Prior (ed.), *Asylums, Mental Health Care and the Irish, 1800–2010* (Dublin: Irish Academic Press, 2012), pp. 167–84. In relation to religion at the mental hospital in Cork, see: Henry, *Our Lady's Psychiatric Hospital Cork*, pp. 548–57.

201 Robins, *Fools and Mad: A History of the Insane in Ireland*, p. 192–5.

202 Cox, *Negotiating Insanity in the Southeast of Ireland, 1820–1900*, p. 16.

203 Finnane, *Insanity and the Insane in Post-Famine Ireland*, pp. 75–6.

204 M. Purcell, *A Time for Sowing: The History of St John of God Brothers in Ireland, 1879–1979* (Dublin: Hospitaller Brothers of St John of God, 1979), p. 139.

205 Collins, *St Vincent's Hospital, Fairview: An Illustrated History, 1857–2007*. This is an excellent, insightful account of a fascinating hospital.

206 A. Collins, 'James Joyce and a North Dublin asylum', *Irish Journal of Psychological Medicine*, 19, 1 (March 2002), pp. 27–8.

207 J. Prunty, 'St Vincent's Hospital, Fairview, Dublin: from lunatic asylum to therapeutic intervention', in J. Prunty and L. Sullivan (eds), *The Daughters of Charity of St*

Vincent de Paul in Ireland: The Early Years (Dublin: Columba Press, 2014), pp. 95–119; p. 107.

208   Inspector of Mental Hospitals, *Report of the Inspector of Mental Hospitals for the year ending 31ˢᵗ December 1997*, p. 47.

209   E. Nolan, *Caring for the Nation: A History of the Mater Misericordiae University Hospital* (Dublin: Gill & Macmillan, 2013), p. 252. The Mater psychiatry service is provided collaboratively by the Mater Misericordiae University Hospital, Health Service Executive and St Vincent's Hospital (Fairview).

210   Nolan, *Caring for the Nation: A History of the Mater Misericordiae University Hospital*, pp. 127–8; McCabe, *Irish Families under Stress (Volume 7)*, p. 5.

211   Malcolm, *Swift's Hospital: A History of St Patrick's Hospital, Dublin, 1746–1989*, p. 1.

212   Kirkpatrick, *A Note on the History of the Care of the Insane in Ireland up to the End of the Nineteenth Century*, p. 24; Torrey and Miller, *The Invisible Plague: The Rise of Mental Illness from 1750 to the Present*, p. 28.

213   W. Donnelly, W.R. Wilde and E. Singleton, *The Census of Ireland for the Year 1851, Part III: Report on the Status of Disease* (Dublin: Thom and Sons for Her Majesty's Stationery Office, 1854), pp. 65–6; Douglas, Goodbody, Mauger and Davey, *Bloomfield: Bloomfield: A History, 1812–2012*, p. 17. For perspectives on this book, see: B. O'Shea, 'Mental healthcare is in full bloom', *Irish Medical Times*, 28 June 2013; T. Farmar, 'Book review: *Bloomfield: A History, 1812–2012*', *Irish Medical Journal*, 107, 7 (August 2014), p. 194. On this theme, see also: Webb, *Trinity's Psychiatrists: From Serenity of the Soul to Neuroscience*, pp. 29–32.

214   Kirkpatrick, *A Note on the History of the Care of the Insane in Ireland up to the End of the Nineteenth Century*, p. 24. See also: L. O'Brien, 'The magic wisp: a history of the mentally ill in Ireland', *Bulletin of the Menninger Clinic*, 31, 2 (March 1967), pp. 79–95; p. 87.

215   Douglas, Goodbody, Mauger and Davey, *Bloomfield: Bloomfield: A History, 1812–2012*, p. 35.

216   M. Lenihan, *Hidden Cork* (Cork: Mercier Press, 2009), p. 230.

217   Douglas, Goodbody, Mauger and Davey, *Bloomfield: Bloomfield: A History, 1812–2012*, p. 44.

218   For an interesting connection with George Bernard Shaw, see: Malcolm, *Swift's Hospital: A History of St Patrick's Hospital, Dublin, 1746–1989*, pp. 342–3.

219   Douglas, Goodbody, Mauger and Davey, *Bloomfield: Bloomfield: A History, 1812–2012*, p. 45.

220   Ibid., p. 59.

221   Ibid., p. 90.

222   Inspector of Mental Hospitals, *Report of the Inspector of Mental Hospitals for the year ending 31ˢᵗ December 1997*, p. 149.

223   Ibid., p. 150.

224   T.P.C. Kirkpatrick, 'Obituary: Richard Robert Leeper', *Journal of Mental Science*, 88, 372 (1 July 1942), pp. 480–1; p. 482.

225   Webb, *Trinity's Psychiatrists: From Serenity of the Soul to Neuroscience*, p. 67.

226   Inspector of Mental Hospitals, *Report of the Inspector of Mental Hospitals for the year ending 31ˢᵗ December 1997*, pp. 150–1.

227   J. Joyce, *Ulysses* (Franklin Centre, PA: Franklin Library, 1976; first published in full in Paris by Sylvia Beach, 1922), p. 506. Joycean historians of psychiatry might also be interested in Joyce's references to Conolly Norman (p. 6), St John of God Hospital (p. 307), mental disorder and the mentally ill (pp. 335, 706, 737), syphilis (pp. 6, 339), asylums (pp. 381, 780), Sir Thornley Stoker (p. 482), the Richmond Asylum (pp. 6, 544), (likely) psychiatric treatment (p. 683) and suicide (p. 693).

228   See, for example: E.F. O'Doherty and S.D. McGrath (eds), *The Priest and Mental Health*.

229   McDermott, *St Mary's Hospital Castlebar: Serving Mayo Mental Health from 1866*, pp. 121–5.

230   C. Norman, 'Cases illustrating the sedative effects of aceto-phenone (hypnone)', *Journal of Mental Science*, 32, 140 (1 January 1887), pp. 519–25. This paper was presented at the quarterly meeting of the Medico-Psychological Association in Dublin on 18 November 1886. See also: Mac Lellan, Nic Ghabhann and Byrne, *World Within Walls*, pp. 28–30.

231   Anonymous, 'Obituary: Conolly Norman, MD FRCPI', *British Medical Journal*, 1, 2461 (29 February 1908), p. 541. See also: *Irish Times*, 7 November 1894 and 23 May 1895. In relation to Rambaut, see: N.R. Phillips, 'Daniel Frederick Rambaut', *Journal of Mental Science*, 84, 348 (1 January 1938), pp. 1–2; A. Collins, 'Daniel Frederick Rambaut: 'Rugbanian' and innovative resident medical superintendent', *Irish Journal of Psychological Medicine* [published online ahead of print, 2016].

232   *Irish Times*, 29 February 1908. See also: Webb, *Trinity's Psychiatrists: From Serenity of the Soul to Neuroscience*, pp. 61–7.

233   D.B. Jacob, 'Restraint in lunatic asylums', *Irish Times*, 28 February 1908. See also: *Dublin Medical Press*, 8 July 1946 (p. 25); and, for more on Jacob: J. Robins, 'The advent of the district mental hospital system', in D.A. Murphy (ed.), *Tumbling Walls: The Evolution of a Community Institution over 150 Years* (Portlaoise: Midland Health Board, 1983), pp. 9–15; pp. 14–15; Murphy, *Tumbling Walls: The Evolution of a Community Institution over 150 Years*, pp. 15–27.

234   C. Haw and G. Yorston, 'Thomas Prichard and the non-restraint movement at the Northampton Asylum', *Psychiatric Bulletin*, 28, 4 (1 April 2004), pp. 140–2; p. 140.

235   H. Sturdy and W. Parry-Jones, 'Boarding-out insane patients: the significance of the Scottish system, 1857–1913' in P. Bartlett and D. Wright (eds), *Outside the Walls of the Asylum: The History of Care in the Community, 1750–2000* (London: Athlone Press, 1999), pp. 86–114.

236 Reynolds, *Grangegorman: Psychiatric Care in Dublin since 1815*, pp. 159–62, 203, 252; Robins, *Fools and Mad: A History of the Insane in Ireland*, pp. 139–40.

237 Scull, *Madness in Civilization: A Cultural History of Insanity, From the Bible to Freud, From the Madhouse to Modern Medicine*, p. 75–7. See also: O'Brien, 'The magic wisp: a history of the mentally ill in Ireland', *Bulletin of the Menninger Clinic*, 31, 2 (March 1967), pp. 79–95; p. 80.

238 C. Norman, 'On the need for family care of persons of unsound mind in Ireland', *Journal of Mental Science*, 50, 210 (1 July 1904), pp. 461–73; p. 464. See also: C. Norman, 'The domestic treatment of the insane', *Dublin Journal of Medical Science*, 101, 2 (February 1896), pp. 111–21; C. Norman, 'The family care of the insane', *Medical Press and Circular*, 29 November–6 December 1905; McDermott, *St Mary's Hospital Castlebar: Serving Mayo Mental Health from 1866*, pp. 121–2; Mac Lellan, Nic Ghabhann and Byrne, *World Within Walls*, p. 64.

239 Finnane, *Insanity and the Insane in Post-Famine Ireland*, pp. 185–9, 219–20.

240 B. Clarke, 'Mental illness and rehabilitation in early nineteenth-century Ireland: the case of Charles Stock', *Psychological Medicine*, 13, 4 (November 1983), pp. 727–34. See also: Malcolm, *Swift's Hospital: A History of St Patrick's Hospital, Dublin, 1746–1989*, p. 341.

241 C. Norman, 'Presidential address, delivered at the Royal College of Physicians, Dublin, June 12th, 1894', *Journal of Mental Science*, 40, 171 (1 October 1894), pp. 487–99.

242 C. Norman, 'The clinical features of beri-beri', *Transactions of the Royal Academy of Medicine in Ireland*, 17, 1 (1 December 1899), pp. 145–79. See also: Reynolds, *Grangegorman: Psychiatric Care in Dublin since 1815*, pp. 171–2.

243 For a discussion, see: Finnane, *150 Years of British Psychiatry, 1841–1991. Volume I*, p. 310.

244 Anonymous, 'Obituary: Conolly Norman, MD FRCPI', *British Medical Journal*, 1, 2461 (29 February 1908), p. 541.

245 C. Norman, 'Some points in Irish lunacy law', *Journal of Mental Science*, 31, 136 (1 January 1886), pp. 459–67.

246 T.C. Allbutt (ed.), *A System of Medicine* (London: Macmillan, 1896–99).

247 D.H. Tuke, *A Dictionary of Psychological Medicine* (London: Churchill, 1892).

248 I am indebted to Ms Harriet Wheelock, Keeper of Collections at the Royal College of Physicians of Ireland, for the inventory of Norman's library.

249 Anonymous, 'Obituary: Conolly Norman, MD FRCPI', *British Medical Journal*, 1, 2461 (29 February 1908), p. 541.

250 *Irish Times*, 19 October 1906.

251 *Irish Times*, 29 February 1908.

252 Norman's obituary in the *British Medical Journal* specifies that he suffered from angina pectoris (heart disease) (Anonymous, 'Obituary: Conolly Norman, MD FRCPI', *British Medical Journal*, 1, 2461 (29 February 1908), p. 541).

253 *Irish Times*, 29 February 1908.

254 Ibid.

255 *Irish Times*, 27 February 1908.

256 *Irish Times*, 28 February 1908. See also: Anonymous, 'Medico-Psychological Association of Great Britain and Ireland', *Journal of Mental Science*, 54, 227 (1 October 1908), pp. 780–98.

257 Joyce, *Ulysses*, p. 6.

258 *Irish Times*, 19 October 1910. See also: V. Jackson, *The Monuments in St Patrick's Cathedral Dublin* (Dublin: St Patrick's Cathedral, 1987), p. 35; A. Fenton, *Past Lives: The Memorials of Saint Patrick's Cathedral, Dublin* (Dublin: St Patrick's Cathedral, 2012), pp. 134–5.

259 Anonymous, 'The Conolly Norman memorial', *Journal of Mental Science*, 54, 226 (1 July 1908), p. 582; *Irish Times*, 11 April 1908 and 19 October 1910.

260 Anonymous, 'Obituary: Conolly Norman, MD FRCPI', *British Medical Journal*, 1, 2461 (29 February 1908), p. 541. See also: Kirkpatrick, *A Note on the History of the Care of the Insane in Ireland up to the End of the Nineteenth Century*, p. 38.

261 B.D. Kelly, 'Dr William Saunders Hallaran and psychiatric practice in nineteenth-century Ireland', *Irish Journal of Medical Science*, 177, 1 (March 2008), pp. 79–84.

262 A. Collins, 'Fleury, Eleonora Lilian', in J. McGuire and J. Quinn (eds), *Dictionary of Irish Biography* (Cambridge: Cambridge University Press, 2014).

263 Collins, 'Eleonora Fleury captured', *British Journal of Psychiatry*, 203, 1 (1 July 2013), p. 5. See also: B.D. Kelly, *Ada English: Patriot and Psychiatrist* (Dublin: Irish Academic Press, 2014), pp. 107–12.

264 M. Ó hÓgartaigh, '"Is there any need of you?" Women in medicine in Ireland and Australia', *Australian Journal of Irish Studies*, 4 (2004), pp. 162–71. See also: L. Kelly, *Irish Women in Medicine, c.1880s–1920s: Origins, Education and Careers* (Manchester and New York: Manchester University Press, 2012), p. 87.

265 Anonymous, 'Medical news', *British Medical Journal*, 1, 1786 (23 March 1895), p. 679; Anonymous, 'Erratum', *British Medical Journal*, 1, 1787 (30 March 1895), p. 738.

266 M. Ó hÓgartaigh, *Quiet Revolutionaries: Irish Women in Education, Sport and Medicine* (Dublin: The History Press Ireland, 2011), p. 147.

267 Reynolds, *Grangegorman: Psychiatric Care in Dublin since 1815*, pp. 20–30.

268 Robins, *Fools and Mad: A History of the Insane in Ireland*, pp. 128–42; B.D. Kelly, 'Mental health law in Ireland, 1821 to 1902: building the asylums', *Medico-Legal Journal*, 76, 1 (March 2008), pp. 19–25; B.D. Kelly, 'Mental health law in Ireland, 1821 to 1902: dealing with the "increase of insanity in Ireland"', *Medico-Legal Journal*, 76, 1 (March 2008), pp. 26–33.

269 Robins, *Fools and Mad: A History of the Insane in Ireland*, pp. 128–42.

270 A.J. Saris, 'The asylum in Ireland: a brief institutional history and some local effects', in A. Cleary and M.P.

Treacy (eds), *The Sociology of Health and Illness in Ireland* (Dublin: University College Dublin Press, 1997), pp. 208–23; p. 216.

271 Inspectors of Lunatics. *The Forty-Second Report (With Appendices) of the Inspectors of Lunatics (Ireland)* (Dublin: Thom and Co. for Her Majesty's Stationery Office, 1893), p. 9.

272 T. Bewley, *Madness to Mental Illness: A History of the Royal College of Psychiatrists* (London: RCPsych Publications, 2008), p. 10.

273 Healy, *150 Years of British Psychiatry, 1841–1991. Volume I*, p. 314: in 1862, the association had 200 members, of whom 26 were Irish; by 1875, this had risen to 30.

274 Finnane, *150 Years of British Psychiatry, 1841–1991. Volume I*, pp. 307–8.

275 Reynolds, *Grangegorman: Psychiatric Care in Dublin since 1815*, pp. 152–3; Bewley, *Madness to Mental Illness: A History of the Royal College of Psychiatrists*, p. 26.

276 Ibid., p. 27.

277 E.L. Fleury, 'Clinical note on agitated melancholia in women', *Journal of Mental Science*, 41, 174 (1 July 1895), pp. 548–54; p. 548.

278 Anonymous, 'Medical news', *British Medical Journal*, 1, 1786 (23 March 1895), p. 679; Anonymous, 'Erratum', *British Medical Journal*, 1, 1787 (30 March 1895), p. 738.

279 Reynolds, *Grangegorman: Psychiatric Care in Dublin since 1815*, p. 189.

280 *Medical Directory for 1905* (London: J. & A. Churchill, 1905), pp. 1414, 1417.

281 Kelly, *Ada English: Patriot and Psychiatrist*, pp. 107–17.

282 Reynolds, *Grangegorman: Psychiatric Care in Dublin since 1815*, p. 210.

283 Ibid., p. 229.

284 A. Matthews, *Renegades: Irish Republican Women 1900–1922* (Cork: Mercier Press, 2010), pp. 208–9. See also: M. Ó hÓgartaigh, *Kathleen Lynn: Patriot, Irishwoman, Doctor* (Dublin: Irish Academic Press, 2006), pp. 37–40; Kelly, *Ada English: Patriot and Psychiatrist*, pp. 61, 81–2, 112–17.

285 Witness Statement (Number 568) of Eilís Bean Uí Chonaill (Dublin: Bureau of Military History, 1913–21, File Number S.1846); pp. 53–4; Witness Statement (Number 624) of Mrs. Mary Flannery Woods (Dublin: Bureau of Military History, 1913–21, File Number S.1901); pp. 28–9. See also: Kelly, *Ada English: Patriot and Psychiatrist*, pp. 19–47.

286 A. Matthews, *Dissidents: Irish Republican Women 1923–1941* (Cork: Mercier Press, 2012); pp. 84–8, 90, 92, 96, 100–4; S. McCoole, *No Ordinary Women: Irish Female Activists in the Revolutionary Years 1900–1923* (Dublin: O'Brien Press, 2003); p. 117; *Irish Nation (Éire)*, 5 August 1923. See also: Kelly, *Ada English: Patriot and Psychiatrist*, pp. 27–31.

287 Mount Jerome Cemetery in Harold's Cross, Dublin is well worth a visit for historians of psychiatry: Norman and Fleury are both buried there, as is Sir William Wilde (1815–1876), the eye and ear surgeon, and distinguished author on the subjects of medicine, folklore, archaeology and mental disorder (W.R. Wilde, *The Closing Years of Dean Swift's Life: With an Appendix, Containing Several of his Poems Hitherto Unpublished, and Some Remarks on Stella* (Dublin: Hodges and Smith, 1849); W. Donnelly, W.R. Wilde and E. Singleton, *The Census of Ireland for the Year 1851, Part III: Report on the Status of Disease* (Dublin: Thom and Sons for Her Majesty's Stationery Office, 1854)).

288 Ó hÓgartaigh, *Kathleen Lynn: Patriot, Irishwoman, Doctor*.

289 A. Mac Lellan, 'Dr Dorothy Price and the eradication of TB in Ireland', *Irish Medical News*, 19 May 2008; A. Mac Lellan, 'Revolutionary doctors', in M. Mulvihill (ed.), *Lab Coats and Lace* (Dublin: Women in Technology and Science, 2009), pp. 86–101; A. Mac Lellan, *Dorothy Stopford Price: Rebel Doctor* (Dublin: Irish Academic Press, 2014).

290 J. Cowell, *A Noontide Blazing: Brigid Lyons Thornton – Rebel, Soldier, Doctor* (Dublin: Currach Press, 2005).

291 Kelly, *Irish Women in Medicine, c.1880s–1920s: Origins, Education and Careers*, pp. 160–7; B.D. Kelly, 'Irish women in medicine', *Irish Medial News*, 7 May 2013; *Irish Times*, 18 May 2013.

292 F. Clarke, 'English, Adeline ('Ada')', in J. McGuire and J. Quinn (eds), *Dictionary of Irish Biography: From the Earliest Times to the Year 2002 (Volume 3, D–F)* (Cambridge: Royal Irish Academy and Cambridge University Press, 2009), pp. 626–7; p. 626; Dickson: *Irish Times*, 12 March 1908.

293 *Irish Times*, 3 June 1895.

294 Quoted in: S.M. Macleod and H.N. McCullough, 'Social science education as a component of medical training', *Social Science and Medicine*, 39, 9 (November 1994), pp. 1367–73; p. 1367.

295 Kelly, *Ada English: Patriot and Psychiatrist*, pp. 112–17.

296 M. McDonagh, 'Impact of Great Famine on mental health examined at Science Week', *Irish Times*, 13 November 2013; O. Walsh, 'Nature or nurture: epigenetic change and the Great Famine in Ireland' in C. Kinealy, C. Reilly and J. King (eds), *Women and the Great Hunger* (Hamden, CT: Quinnipiac University Press, 2017) (*in press*, forthcoming).

297 C.C. Kelleher, J. Lynch, S. Harper, J.B. Tay and G. Nolan, 'Hurling alone? How social capital failed to save the Irish from cardiovascular disease in the United States', *American Journal of Public Health*, 94, 12 (December 2004), pp. 2162–9.

298 M.E. Daly, 'Death and disease in independent Ireland, c. 1920–1970: a research agenda', in C. Cox and M. Luddy (eds), *Cultures of Care in Irish Medical History 1750–1950* (Basingstoke, Hampshire: Palgrave Macmillan, 2010), pp. 229–50; p. 246.

299 Cox, *Negotiating Insanity in the Southeast of Ireland, 1820–1900*, p. 189. See also: Robins, *Fools and Mad: A History of the Insane in Ireland*, pp. 88–9, 202.

300 Cox, *Negotiating Insanity in the Southeast of Ireland,*

1820–1900, p. 175; D. Walsh, 'Brief historical review', *Irish Journal of Psychiatry*, 13, 1 (Spring 1992), pp. 3–20; p. 4.

301 Cox, *Negotiating Insanity in the Southeast of Ireland, 1820–1900*, pp. 181–2.

302 B.D. Kelly, 'Intellectual disability, mental illness and offending behaviour: forensic cases from early twentieth-century Ireland', *Irish Journal of Medical Science*, 179, 3 (September 2010), pp. 409–16.

303 Walsh, *Sex and Seclusion, Class and Custody: Perspectives on Gender and Class in the History of British and Irish Psychiatry*, pp. 69–93.

304 B.D. Kelly, 'Asylum doctor extraordinaire: Dr Thomas Drapes (1847–1919)', *Irish Journal of Medical Science*, 184, 3 (September 2015), pp. 565–71.

305 Drapes, 'On the alleged increase of insanity in Ireland', *Journal of Mental Science*, 40, 171 (1 October 1894), pp. 519–48.

306 Brennan, *Irish Insanity, 1800–2000*, pp. 123–4.

307 D. Walsh, 'Brief historical review', *Irish Journal of Psychiatry*, 13, 1 (Spring 1992), pp. 3–20; p. 3.

308 B.D. Kelly, 'Mental health law in Ireland, 1821 to 1902: building the asylums', *Medico-Legal Journal*, 76, 1 (March 2008), pp. 19–25; Kelly, *Custody, Care and Criminality: Forensic Psychiatry and Law in 19th Century Ireland*, pp. 64–73.

309 Reynolds, *Grangegorman: Psychiatric Care in Dublin since 1815*, pp. 179–85; Finnane, *Insanity and the Insane in Post-Famine Ireland*, p. 14.

310 R.J. McClelland, 'The madhouses and mad doctors of Ulster', *The Ulster Medical Journal*, 57, 2 (October 1998), pp. 101–20; p. 115.

311 C. Norman, 'On the need for family care of persons of unsound mind in Ireland', *Journal of Mental Science*, 50, 210 (1 July 1904), pp. 461–73; p. 464. See also: C. Norman, 'The domestic treatment of the insane', *Dublin Journal of Medical Science*, 101, 2 (February 1896), pp. 111–21; C. Norman, 'The family care of the insane', *Medical Press and Circular*, 29 November–6 December 1905; Mac Lellan, Nic Ghabhann and Byrne, *World Within Walls*, p. 64.

312 Bewley, *Madness to Mental Illness: A History of the Royal College of Psychiatrists*, pp. 26–7.

313 Kirkpatrick, *A Note on the History of the Care of the Insane in Ireland up to the End of the Nineteenth Century*, p. 33.

314 L. O'Brien, 'The magic wisp: a history of the mentally ill in Ireland', *Bulletin of the Menninger Clinic*, 31, 2 (March 1967), pp. 79–95; p. 89.

315 Cox, *Negotiating Insanity in the Southeast of Ireland, 1820–1900*, pp. 105–7.

316 J. O'Neill, 'The Portrayal of Madness in the Limerick Press, 1772–1845' (MA Thesis, Mary Immaculate College (University of Limerick), 2013), p. 105. Quotations used with permission.

317 Ibid., pp. 106–7.

318 Ibid., p. 110.

Chapter 4. Early Twentieth-Century Psychiatry

1 Committee on Lunacy Administration (Ireland), *First and Second Reports of the Committee Appointed by the Lord Lieutenant of Ireland on Lunacy Administration (Ireland)* (Edinburgh: Neill & Co. for Her Majesty's Stationery Office, 1891), p. 36.

2 Kirkpatrick, *A Note on the History of the Care of the Insane in Ireland up to the End of the Nineteenth Century*, p. 34.

3 Reynolds, *Grangegorman: Psychiatric Care in Dublin since 1815*, pp. 162–6.

4 Committee on Lunacy Administration (Ireland), *First and Second Reports of the Committee Appointed by the Lord Lieutenant of Ireland on Lunacy Administration (Ireland)*, p. 75.

5 G.W. Abraham, *The Law and Practice of Lunacy in Ireland as Administered by the Lord Chancellor under the Sign Manual Together with a Compendium of the Law Relating to Establishments for the Care of the Insane* (Dublin: E. Ponsonby, 1886). See also: Prior, *Madness and Murder: Gender, Crime and Mental Disorder in Nineteenth Century Ireland*, pp. 50–1.

6 Committee on Lunacy Administration (Ireland), *First and Second Reports of the Committee Appointed by the Lord Lieutenant of Ireland on Lunacy Administration (Ireland)*, p. 2.

7 Ibid., p. 8. See also: pp. 28–31.

8 Ibid., p. 15.

9 Ibid., pp. 14–28.

10 Ibid., pp. 33–42.

11 Ibid., p. 12.

12 Finnane, *Insanity and the Insane in Post-Famine Ireland*, pp. 67–8. See also: Reynolds, *Grangegorman: Psychiatric Care in Dublin since 1815*, pp. 162–6.

13 Healy, *150 Years of British Psychiatry. Volume II: The Aftermath*, pp. 268–91.

14 B.D. Kelly, 'One hundred years ago: the Richmond Asylum, Dublin in 1907', *Irish Journal of Psychological Medicine*, 24, 3 (September 2007), pp. 108–14.

15 Commission on the Relief of the Sick and Destitute Poor, Including the Insane Poor, *Report of the Commission on the Relief of the Sick and Destitute Poor, Including the Insane Poor* (Dublin: The Stationery Office, 1927).

16 Ibid., p. 93.

17 Ibid., pp. 97–8.

18 Ibid., p. 98.

19 Ibid., p. 99. See also: Robins, *Fools and Mad: A History of the Insane in Ireland*, pp. 187–90.

20 Anonymous, 'Increase in insanity', *American Journal of Insanity*, 18, 1 (July 1861), p. 95; Inspectors of Lunatics, *Special Report from the Inspectors of Lunatics to the Chief Secretary: Alleged Increasing Prevalence of Insanity in Ireland* (Dublin: Her Majesty's Stationery Office, 1894); D.H. Tuke, 'Increase of insanity in Ireland', *Journal of Mental Science*, 40, 171 (October 1894), pp. 549–61.

21   A.P. Williamson, 'Psychiatry, moral management and the origins of social policy for mentally ill people in Ireland', *Irish Journal of Medical Science*, 161, 9 (September 1992), pp. 556–8; Walsh, *Sex and Seclusion, Class and Custody: Perspectives on Gender and Class in the History of British and Irish Psychiatry*, pp. 69–93.

22   B.D. Kelly, 'Mental illness in nineteenth century Ireland: a qualitative study of workhouse records', *Irish Journal of Medical Science*, 173, 1 (January 2004), pp. 53–5; B.D. Kelly, 'One hundred years ago', *Irish Journal of Psychological Medicine*, 24, 3 (September 2007), pp. 108–14; D. Walsh, 'The Ennis District Lunatic Asylum and the Clare Workhouse Lunatic Asylums in 1901', *Irish Journal of Psychological Medicine*, 26, 4 (December 2010), pp. 206–11.

23   In December 2007, as part of a digitisation project, a census website was launched under the auspices of the National Archives of Ireland, along with various partners, and the resultant website now provides census data from 1901 for all 32 counties on the island of Ireland (www.census.nationalarchives.ie). These data are freely available to the public in a fully searchable, electronic format.

24   B.D. Kelly and N. Sherrard, 'Beyond the walls', *Irish Journal of Psychological Medicine*, 32, 3 (September 2015), pp. 275–82. Material in this section is drawn from this paper with the kind agreement of Ms N. Sherrard, ©College of Psychiatrists of Ireland, published by Cambridge University Press, reproduced with permission. Data in the table are derived from the 1901 census.

25   Census data can include inaccuracies for several possible reasons, including incorrect recording of data in the first place, compounded by the possibility that certain Irish households might have deliberately misled census enumerators. There might also have been incomplete enumeration in certain households or partial coverage of certain geographical areas. This is supported by the fact that the prevalence of mental disorder among individuals outside asylums, workhouses and other institutions identified in this study seems low, especially for certain counties. In addition, the design of the 1901 census form imposed certain limitations, including the fact that any person described as a 'lunatic' could not also be described an 'imbecile' or an 'idiot'.

26   S. Fisher, *Report on the Fourth Census of Canada 1901* (Ottawa: SE Dawson, Printer to the King's Most Excellent Majesty, 1902).

27   H.G. Simmons, 'Explaining social policy', *Journal of Social History*, 11, 3 (Spring 1978), pp. 387–403.

28   Brennan, *Irish Insanity, 1800–2000*, p. 124.

29   Walsh, *Sex and Seclusion, Class and Custody: Perspectives on Gender and Class in the History of British and Irish Psychiatry*, pp. 69–93; p. 74.

30   Ibid.

31   Cox, *Negotiating Insanity in the Southeast of Ireland, 1820–1900*, pp. 89–91.

32   C. Norman, 'The domestic treatment of the insane', *Dublin Journal of Medical Science*, 101, 2 (February

1896), pp. 111–21; C. Norman, 'The family care of the insane', *Medical Press and Circular*, 29 November–6 December 1905.

33   B.D. Kelly and N. Sherrard, 'Beyond the walls', *Irish Journal of Psychological Medicine*, 32, 3 (September 2015), pp. 275–82.

34   M. Hill, J. Lynch and F. Maguire, *Multitext Project in Irish History* (Cork: University College Cork, 2013).

35   Healy, *150 Years of British Psychiatry. Volume II: The Aftermath*, pp. 268–91.

36   Hallaran, *An Enquiry into the Causes producing the Extraordinary Addition to the Number of Insane together with Extended Observations on the Cure of Insanity with Hints as to the Better Management of Public Asylums for Insane Persons*, pp. 12, 13, 22.

37   M.J. Nolan, *The Increase in Insanity in Ireland and its Causes* (Dublin: Fannin & Co., 1906); Reynolds, *Grangegorman: Psychiatric Care in Dublin since 1815*, p. 203.

38   *Irish Times*, 26 November 1903.

39   E.D. O'Neill, *Increase of Lunacy and Special Reasons Applicable to Ireland* (Limerick: George McKern and Sons Limited, 1903), p. 3.

40   Ibid., p. 5.

41   Ibid., pp. 6–7.

42   Ibid., p. 9.

43   Ibid., p. 11.

44   Ibid., pp. 11–12. For a summary of O'Neill's paper, see: *Irish Times*, 26 November 1903.

45   For a summary of proceedings, see: Reynolds, *Grangegorman: Psychiatric Care in Dublin since 1815*, pp. 201–3; Healy, *150 Years of British Psychiatry. Volume II: The Aftermath*, pp. 270–4. See also: *Irish Times*, 27 November 1903 (especially in relation to 'criminal lunatics'); McDermott, *St Mary's Hospital Castlebar: Serving Mayo Mental Health from 1866*, pp. 44–5.

46   *Irish Times*, 26 November 1903.

47   C. Norman, 'Report of Dr Norman', in *Richmond Asylum Joint Committee Minutes* (Dublin: Richmond Asylum, 1907).

48   Walsh and Daly, *Mental Illness in Ireland, 1750–2002: Reflections on the Rise and Fall of Institutional Care*, p. 30.

49   O'Neill, *Irish Mental Health Law*, p. 19.

50   E. Boyd Barrett, 'Modern psycho-therapy and our asylums', *Studies*, 13, 49 (March 1924), pp. 29–43; pp. 31, 43.

51   Commission on the Relief of the Sick and Destitute Poor, Including the Insane Poor, *Report of the Commission on the Relief of the Sick and Destitute Poor, Including the Insane Poor*, pp. 131–3; see also: O'Neill, *Irish Mental Health Law*, p. 20. The Commission also reported on many other matters (see, for example: C. Breathnach, 'Lady Dudley's District Nursing Scheme and the Congested Districts Board, 1903–1923' in M.H. Preston and M. Ó hÓgartaigh (eds), *Gender and Medicine in Ireland, 1700–1950* (Syracuse, New York: Syracuse University Press, 2012), pp. 138–53; p. 152).

52 J. Gasser and G. Heller, 'The confinement of the insane in Switzerland, 1900–1970: Cery (Vaud) and Bel-Air (Geneva) asylums', in R. Porter and D. Wright (eds), *The Confinement of the Insane: International Perspectives, 1800–1965* (Cambridge: Cambridge University Press, 2003), pp. 54–78.

53 Prestwich, *The Confinement of the Insane: International Perspectives, 1800–1965*, pp. 79–99.

54 B.D. Kelly, 'The Mental Treatment Act 1945 in Ireland: an historical enquiry', *History of Psychiatry*, 19, 73(1) (March 2008), pp. 47–67.

55 This section draws upon: Richmond Asylum Joint Committee, *Richmond Asylum Joint Committee Minutes* (Dublin: Richmond Asylum, 1907), and B.D. Kelly, 'One hundred years ago: the Richmond Asylum, Dublin in 1907', *Irish Journal of Psychological Medicine*, 24, 3 (September 2007), pp. 108–14. See also: Kelly, *Custody, Care and Criminality: Forensic Psychiatry and Law in 19th Century Ireland*, pp. 74–87.

56 Richmond Asylum Joint Committee, *Richmond Asylum Joint Committee Minutes*, pp. 75–7.

57 Ibid., pp. 582–3.

58 J.M. Redington and P.J. Dwyer, 'Maniacal-depressive insanity amongst the male admissions to the Richmond District Asylum in the year 1907', *Journal of Mental Science*, 55, 228 (1 January 1909), pp. 56–8.

59 E. Kraepelin, *Psychiatrie. Ein Lehrbuch für Studirende und Aerzte (Sixth Edition)* (Leipzig: Verlag von Johann Ambrosius Barth, 1899).

60 T. Drapes, 'On the maniacal-depressive insanity of Kraepelin', *Journal of Mental Science*, 55, 228 (1 January 1909), pp. 58–64.

61 Richmond Asylum Joint Committee, *Richmond Asylum Joint Committee Minutes*, pp. 92–5.

62 Ibid., pp. 92–3.

63 Ibid., p. 14.

64 Reynolds, *Grangegorman: Psychiatric Care in Dublin since 1815*, p. 211.

65 Richmond Asylum Joint Committee, *Richmond Asylum Joint Committee Minutes*, p. 467.

66 Walsh and Daly, *Mental Illness in Ireland 1750–2002: Reflections on the Rise and Fall of Institutional Care*, p. 21.

67 Richmond Asylum Joint Committee, *Richmond Asylum Joint Committee Minutes*, p. 94.

68 Ibid., p. 468.

69 Ibid., p. 469.

70 Ibid., pp. 470–1.

71 Ibid., p. 472.

72 Ibid., pp. 472–3.

73 Ibid., p. 473.

74 Ibid., pp. 473–4.

75 Reynolds, *Grangegorman: Psychiatric Care in Dublin since 1815*, p. 141.

76 Richmond Asylum Joint Committee, *Richmond Asylum Joint Committee Minutes*, p. 208.

77 Ibid., p. 233.

78 Ibid., p. 114.

79 Ibid., pp. 80–1, 98–9, 234–5.

80 Ibid., p. 80.

81 Ibid., p. 81.

82 Ibid., p. 369.

83 Ibid., pp. 100–4.

84 Ibid., pp. 308–9.

85 S. Scully, 'From minute to minute, 1886–1905' in D.A. Murphy (ed.), *Tumbling Walls: The Evolution of a Community Institution over 150 Years* (Portlaoise: Midland Health Board, 1983), pp. 28–33; p. 30.

86 Richmond Asylum Joint Committee, *Richmond Asylum Joint Committee Minutes*, p. 557.

87 Ibid., p. 32.

88 Ibid., p. 33.

89 Ibid., p. 34.

90 Ibid., p. 33.

91 Ibid., p. 126.

92 Ibid., p. 201.

93 Ibid., pp. 204–5.

94 Ibid., pp. 31–2.

95 Ibid., p. 31.

96 Ibid., p. 116.

97 Ibid., p. 308.

98 Kelly, *Asylums, Mental Health Care and the Irish, 1800–2010*, pp. 205–20.

99 Richmond Asylum Joint Committee, *Richmond Asylum Joint Committee Minutes*, p. 307. See also: B.D. Kelly, 'Syphilis, psychiatry and offending behaviour: clinical cases from nineteenth-century Ireland', *Irish Journal of Medical Science*, 178, 1 (March 2009), pp. 73–7.

100 Richmond Asylum Joint Committee, *Richmond Asylum Joint Committee Minutes*, p. 31.

101 Ibid., p. 491.

102 Ibid., pp. 31–2.

103 Ibid., p. 200.

104 Ibid., p. 116.

105 Ibid., p. 98.

106 Ibid., p. 116.

107 Ibid. See also: Kelly, *Custody, Care and Criminality: Forensic Psychiatry and Law in 19th Century Ireland*, pp. 78–80.

108 J. McDermott, *St Mary's Hospital Castlebar: Serving Mayo Mental Health from 1866*, pp. 97–100.

109 This was a common problem; see, for example: Henry, *Our Lady's Psychiatric Hospital Cork*, pp. 142–3.

110 Richmond Asylum Joint Committee, *Richmond Asylum Joint Committee Minutes*, p. 156.

111 Ibid., p. 182.

112 Ibid., p. 548.

113 Ibid., pp. 152, 193, 237–9.

114 Ibid., pp. 250, 357, 391–2, 566–8.

115 Ibid., pp. 218, 239, 261–2, 322–4.

116 Ibid., p. 549.

117 Ibid., pp. 447–8.

118 S. Cherry and R. Munting, "Exercise is the thing'? Sport and the asylum c.1850–1950', *International Journal*

of the History of Sport, 22, 1 (2005), pp. 42–58. In relation to Portlaoise, see: Murphy, *Tumbling Walls: The Evolution of a Community Institution over 150 Years*, pp. 15–27; p. 25.

119 Richmond Asylum Joint Committee, *Richmond Asylum Joint Committee Minutes*, p. 157.

120 N.R. Phillips, 'Daniel Frederick Rambaut', *Journal of Mental Science*, 84, 348 (1 January 1938), pp. 1–2; A. Collins, 'Daniel Frederick Rambaut: 'Rugbanian' and innovative resident medical superintendent', *Irish Journal of Psychological Medicine* [published online ahead of print, 2016].

121 Richmond Asylum Joint Committee, *Richmond Asylum Joint Committee Minutes*, p. 151.

122 Anonymous, 'Obituary: Conolly Norman, MD FRCPI', *British Medical Journal*, 1, 2461 (29 February 1908), p. 541.

123 C. McCarthy, *Cumann na mBan and the Irish Revolution* (Dublin: The Collins Press, 2007), p. 53.

124 Material in this section is adapted from B.D. Kelly, *'He Lost Himself Completely': Shell Shock and its Treatment at Dublin's Richmond War Hospital, 1916–1919* (Dublin: Liffey Press, 2014), with kind permission of the publisher. For perspectives on this book, see: M. Guéret, 'Shell-shocked', *Sunday Independent*, 11 January 2015; E. Delaney, 'Fascinating tales of healing our forgotten war wounded', *Sunday Independent*, 15 February 2015.

125 B.D. Kelly, *Ada English: Patriot and Psychiatrist*, (Dublin: Irish Academic Press, 2014), pp. 20–4.

126 C.D. Greaves, *Liam Mellows and the Irish Revolution* (Belfast: An Ghlór Gafa, 2004).

127 A. Collins, 'The Richmond District Asylum and the 1916 Easter Rising', *Irish Journal of Psychological Medicine*, 30, 4 (December 2013), pp. 279–83; p. 279. Quotations from this paper are used with kind agreement of Dr Aidan Collins; ©College of Psychiatrists of Ireland, published by Cambridge University Press, reproduced with permission.

128 Dr Richard Leeper's report to the Governors of St Patrick's Hospital, 3 June 1916. Quoted in: E. Malcolm, *Swift's Hospital: A History of St Patrick's Hospital, Dublin, 1746–1989* (Dublin: Gill and Macmillan, 1989), pp. 326–7.

129 Webb, *Trinity's Psychiatrists: From Serenity of the Soul to Neuroscience*, pp. 75–6.

130 J. O'C. Donelon, Report to the Governors of the Richmond District Asylum, 1916, 11 May. Quoted in: Reynolds, *Grangegorman: Psychiatric Care in Dublin since 1815*, p. 217.

131 Collins, 'The Richmond District Asylum and the 1916 Easter Rising', *Irish Journal of Psychological Medicine*, 30, 4 (December 2013), pp. 279–83; p. 280.

132 Ibid., p. 281.

133 Dr Richard Leeper's report to the Governors of St Patrick's Hospital, 3 June 1916. Quoted in: Malcolm, *Swift's Hospital: A History of St Patrick's Hospital, Dublin, 1746–1989*, p. 326.

134 Hallaran, *An Enquiry into the Causes Producing the Extraordinary Addition to the Number of Insane together with Extended Observations on the Cure of Insanity with Hints as to the Better Management of Public Asylums for Insane Persons*, pp. 12–13.

135 Collins, 'The Richmond District Asylum and the 1916 Easter Rising', *Irish Journal of Psychological Medicine*, 30, 4 (December 2013), pp. 279–83; p. 281. See also: C.S. Myers, 'A contribution to the study of shell shock', *Lancet*, 185, 4772 (13 February 1915), pp. 316–20.

136 Witness Statement (Number 304) of Mr James Coughlan (Dublin: Bureau of Military History, 1913–21, File Number S.1337), pp. 26–8. I am very grateful to Dr Aidan Collins for drawing this witness statement to my attention.

137 D. Ferriter, *The Transformation of Ireland, 1900–2000* (London: Profile Books, 2004), p. 132. The precise figures are not known.

138 Material in this section is adapted from B.D. Kelly, *'He Lost Himself Completely': Shell Shock and its Treatment at Dublin's Richmond War Hospital, 1916–1919* (Dublin: Liffey Press, 2014), with kind permission of the publisher. For further reading, see: J. Bourke, 'Shellshock, psychiatry and the Irish soldier during the First World War', in: A. Gregory and S. Pašeta (eds), *Ireland and the Great War: 'A War To Unite Us All'?* (Manchester and New York: Manchester University Press, 2002), pp. 155–70; B.D. Kelly, 'Shell shock in Ireland: the Richmond War Hospital, Dublin (1916–19)', *History of Psychiatry*, 26, 1 (March 2015), pp. 50–63.

139 Reynolds, *Grangegorman: Psychiatric Care in Dublin since 1815*, p. 219.

140 Ibid., p. 217.

141 E. Jones, N.T. Fear and S. Wessely, 'Shell shock and mild traumatic brain injury: a historical review', *American Journal of Psychiatry*, 164, 11 (November 2007), pp. 1641–5.

142 C.S. Myers, 'A contribution to the study of shell shock', *Lancet*, 185, 4772 (13 February 1915), pp. 316–20; S.M. Archer, 'The racket and the fear', *History Today*, 66, 1 (January 2016), pp. 11–18.

143 Collins, 'The Richmond District Asylum and the 1916 Easter Rising', *Irish Journal of Psychological Medicine*, 30, 4 (December 2013), pp. 279–83.

144 Reynolds, *Grangegorman: Psychiatric Care in Dublin since 1815*, p. 217.

145 Ibid., pp. 217–18; B.D. Kelly, 'Political asylums', *History Today*, 66, 2 (February 2016), p. 66.

146 This case-history is drawn from: Richmond War Hospital Case Book (1918–1919) (BR/PRIV 1223 Richmond War) (National Archives, Bishop Street, Dublin, Ireland). The name, regiment, precise admission dates and other identifying details are not presented, in order to preserve anonymity. The programme of research upon which this section is based was approved by the Ethics Committee of the Health Service Executive, Dublin North City, Ireland (2014).

147 Anonymous, 'Irish Division', *Journal of Mental Science*, 63, 261 (1 April 1917), pp. 297–9. For more cases, see: Kelly, *'He Lost Himself Completely': Shell Shock and its Treatment at Dublin's Richmond War Hospital, 1916–1919*.

148 P. Howorth, 'The treatment of shell shock: cognitive therapy before its time', *Psychiatric Bulletin*, 24, 6 (June 2000), pp. 225–7.

149 This involved restructuring the way the soldier viewed and interpreted past experiences; see: W.H.R. Rivers, 'An address on the repression of war experience', *Lancet*, 191, 4927 (2 February 1918), pp. 173–7.

150 J. Bisson and M. Andrew, 'Psychological treatment of post-traumatic stress disorder (PTSD)', *Cochrane Database of Systematic Reviews*, 3, (18 July 2007), CD003388.

151 War Office Committee of Enquiry into 'Shell-Shock', *Report of the War Office Committee of Enquiry into "Shell-Shock"* (London: HMSO, 1922).

152 Reynolds, *Grangegorman: Psychiatric Care in Dublin since 1815*, pp. 218–19.

153 Anonymous, 'Irish Division', *Journal of Mental Science*, 63, 261 (1 April 1917), pp. 297–9.

154 J.T. Braslow, 'Punishment or therapy: patients, doctors, and somatic remedies in the early twentieth century', *Psychiatric Clinics of North America*, 17, 3 (September 1994), pp. 493–513.

155 War Office Committee of Enquiry into 'Shell-Shock', *Report of the War Office Committee of Enquiry into "Shell-Shock"*, p. 192.

156 K. Brune, 'The early history of non-opioid analgesics', *Acute Pain*, 1, 1 (December 1997), pp. 33–40.

157 W.H. Burt, *Physiological Materia Medica (Containing All that is Known of the Physiological Action of Our Remedies Together with their Characteristic Indications and Pharmacology) (Fifth Edition)* (Chicago: Gross & Delbridge Company, 1896), p. 321.

158 Shorter, *A History of Psychiatry: From the Era of the Asylum to the Age of Prozac*, pp. 201–2.

159 Anonymous, 'Reports and analyses and descriptions of new inventions in medicine, surgery, dietetics and the allied sciences', *British Medical Journal*, 1, 1109 (1 April 1882), pp. 464–5; D. Walker, 'Modern nerves, nervous moderns', in S.L. Goldberg and F.B. Smith (eds), *Australian Cultural History* (Cambridge: Cambridge University Press, 1988), pp. 123–37, p. 132.

160 R. Eager, 'A record of admissions to the mental section of the Lord Derby War Hospital, Warrington, from June 17th, 1916 to June 16th, 1917', *Journal of Mental Science*, 64, 266 (1 July 1918), pp. 272–96; p. 294.

161 Reynolds, *Grangegorman: Psychiatric Care in Dublin since 1815*, p. 219; Kelly, *'He Lost Himself Completely': Shell Shock and its Treatment at Dublin's Richmond War Hospital, 1916–1919*, p. 117.

162 For further discussion of this, see: D. Walsh, 'WW1 as "cause or associated factor" of mental illness', *Irish Medical Times*, 9 January 2015.

163 B.D. Kelly, 'The Mental Treatment Act 1945 in Ireland: an historical enquiry', *History of Psychiatry*, 19, 73(1) (March 2008), pp. 47–67.

164 P. Howorth, 'The treatment of shell shock: cognitive therapy before its time', *Psychiatric Bulletin*, 24, 6 (June 2000), pp. 225–7.

165 Shorter, *A History of Psychiatry: From the Era of the Asylum to the Age of Prozac*, pp. 93–4.

166 Howorth, 'The treatment of shell shock: cognitive therapy before its time', *Psychiatric Bulletin*, 24, 6 (June 2000), pp. 225–7.

167 Anonymous, 'Irish Division', *Journal of Mental Science*, 63, 261 (1 April 1917), pp. 297–9.

168 Ibid. p. 299; See also: Kelly, *'He Lost Himself Completely': Shell Shock and its Treatment at Dublin's Richmond War Hospital, 1916–1919*, pp. 121–12.

169 Other locations included Leopardstown Hospital, Dublin ('Victims of the War', *Irish Times*, 19 June 1924) and Hermitage Hospital, Lucan; see *Irish Times* (11 October 1918) in relation to the treatment of shell shock at the Hermitage, which reportedly achieved excellent results; see also: 'A grand Red Cross fete & horse jumping competition' (*Irish Times*, 9 August 1917).

170 L. O'Flaherty, *Return of the Brute* (London: The Mandrake Press, 1929).

171 See, for example: E. Byrne, 'We let them be forgotten', *Guardian*, 5 April 2014.

172 P. Gibbons, N. Mulryan, A. McAleer and A. O'Connor, 'Criminal responsibility and mental illness in Ireland 1950–1995: fitness to plead', *Irish Journal of Psychological Medicine*, 196, 2 (June 1999), pp. 51–6.

173 B.D. Kelly, '*Folie à plusieurs*: forensic cases from nineteenth-century Ireland', *History of Psychiatry*, 20, 77 (Part 1) (March 2009), pp. 47–60.

174 B.D. Kelly, 'Syphilis, psychiatry and offending behaviour: clinical cases from nineteenth-century Ireland', *Irish Journal of Medical Science*, 178, 1 (March 2009), pp. 73–7.

175 Kelly, *Asylums, Mental Health Care and the Irish, 1800–2010*, pp. 205–20.

176 B.D. Kelly, 'Intellectual disability, mental illness and offending behaviour: forensic cases from early twentieth-century Ireland', *Irish Journal of Medical Science*, 179, 3 (September 2010), pp. 409–16.

177 This case is drawn from: B.D. Kelly, 'Learning disability and forensic mental healthcare in nineteenth-century Ireland', *Irish Journal of Psychological Medicine*, 25, 3 (September 2008), pp. 116–18. Material from the *Irish Journal of Psychological Medicine* is used by kind permission of MedMedia Group (Dún Laoghaire, County Dublin, Ireland) and the College of Psychiatrists of Ireland. For further consideration of this case, see: Kelly, *Custody, Care and Criminality: Forensic Psychiatry and Law in 19th Century Ireland*, pp. 142–3.

178 A.P. Williamson, 'Psychiatry, moral management and the origins of social policy for mentally ill people in Ireland', *Irish Journal of Medical Science*, 161,

9 (September 1992), pp. 556–8; M. Reuber, 'The architecture of psychological management: the Irish asylums (1801–1922)', *Psychological Medicine*, 26, 6 (November 1996), pp. 1179–89; S. Cherry and R. Munting, '"Exercise is the thing"? Sport and the asylum c.1850–1950', *International Journal of the History of Sport*, 22, 1 (2005), pp. 42–58.

179 J.K. Aronson, *An Account of the Foxglove and Its Medical Uses, 1785–1985' (1785)* (Oxford: Oxford University Press, 1985); R.C. McGarry and P. McGarry, 'Please pass the strychnine: the art of Victorian pharmacy', *Canadian Medical Association Journal*, 161, 12 (December 1999), pp. 1556–8; B. Hodgson, *In the Arms of Morpheus: The Tragic History of Laudanum, Morphine, and Patent Medicines* (Buffalo, NY: Firefly Books (US) Inc., 2001); J. Buckingham, *Bitter Nemesis: The Intimate History of Strychnine* (Boca Raton, FL: CRC Press, Taylor and Francis Group, 2008).

180 Richmond Asylum Joint Committee, *Richmond Asylum Joint Committee Minutes*, pp. 469–70; B.D. Kelly, 'One hundred years ago: the Richmond Asylum, Dublin in 1907', *Irish Journal of Psychological Medicine*, 24, 3 (September 2007), pp. 108–14.

181 Robins, *Fools and Mad: A History of the Insane in Ireland*, pp. 157–70.

182 Walsh, *Sex and Seclusion, Class and Custody: Perspectives on Gender and Class in the History of British and Irish Psychiatry*, pp. 69–93.

183 H.G. Simmons, 'Explaining social policy', *Journal of Social History*, 11, 3 (Spring 1978), pp. 387–403; Digby, *From Idiocy to Mental Deficiency: Historical Perspectives on People with Learning Disabilities*, pp. 1–21; Atkinson, Jackson and Walmsley, *Forgotten Lives*, pp. 1–20; Gladstone, *From Idiocy to Mental Deficiency: Historical Perspectives on People with Learning Disabilities*, pp. 134–60; Dale and Melling, *Mental Illness and Learning Disability Since 1850: Finding a Place for Mental Disorder in the United Kingdom*, pp. 1–23; Jackson, *From Idiocy to Mental Deficiency: Historical Perspectives on People with Learning Disabilities*, pp. 161–83.

184 P. Chitsabesan, L. Kroll, S. Bailey, C. Kenning, S. Sneider, W. MacDonald and L. Theodosiou, 'Mental health needs of young offenders in custody and the community', *British Journal of Psychiatry*, 188, 6 (June 2006), pp. 534–40; V.C. Riches, T.R. Parmenter, M. Wiese and R.J. Stancliffe, 'Intellectual disability and mental illness in the NSW criminal justice system', *International Journal of Law and Psychiatry*, 29, 5 (September/October 2006), pp. 386–96; W.R. Lindsay, R.P. Hastings, D.M. Griffiths and S.C. Hayes, 'Trends and challenges in forensic research on offenders with intellectual disability', *Journal of Intellectual and Developmental Disability*, 32, 2 (June 2007), pp. 55–61.

185 Irish College of Psychiatrists, *People with a Learning Disability Who Offend: Forgiven but Forgotten? (Occasional Paper OP63)* (Dublin: Irish College of Psychiatrists, 2008), p. 7.

186 Expert Group on Mental Health Policy, *A Vision for Change* (Dublin: The Stationery Office, 2006), p. 141.

187 P. Leonard, A. Morrison, M. Delany-Warner and G.J. Calvert, 'A national survey of offending behaviour amongst intellectually disabled users of mental health services in Ireland', *Irish Journal of Psychological Medicine* [published online ahead of print, 2015], DOI: http://dx.doi.org/10.1017/ipm.2015.21.

188 M. Davoren, E.G. Breen and B.D. Kelly, 'Dr Adeline English: revolutionizing politics and psychiatry in Ireland', *Irish Psychiatrist*, 10, 4 (Winter 2009), pp. 260–2; M. Davoren, E.G. Breen and B.D. Kelly, 'Dr Ada English: patriot and psychiatrist in early twentieth-century Ireland', *Irish Journal of Psychological Medicine*, 28, 2 (June 2011), pp. 91–6; B.D. Kelly and M. Davoren, 'Dr Ada English', in M. Mulvihill (ed.), *Lab Coats and Lace* (Dublin: Women in Technology and Science, 2009), p. 97; B.D. Kelly, 'Dr Ada English (1875–1944): doctor, patriot, politician', *British Journal of Psychiatry*, 204, 1 (January 2014), p. 5; Much of this section is based on material in Kelly, *Ada English: Patriot and Psychiatrist*, and is used by kind permission of Irish Academic Press. For perspectives on this book, see: M. Guéret, 'The asylum years', *Sunday Independent*, 19 October 2014; S. McWilliams, 'Patriot and psychiatrist', *Irish Medical News*, 17 November 2014; C. Finnerty, 'Portrait of a revolutionary', *Ballinasloe Life*, December 2014–January 2015; M. Farrell, 'Ada English biography (book review of: *Ada English: Patriot and Psychiatrist)*', *Irish History Review*, 17 February 2015; M.M. Connerly, 'Book review: *Ada English: Patriot and Psychiatrist*', *Journal of International Women's Studies*, 16, 3 (July 2015), pp. 324–6.

189 Ó hÓgartaigh, *Kathleen Lynn: Patriot, Irishwoman, Doctor*.

190 A. Mac Lellan, 'Dr Dorothy Price and the eradication of TB in Ireland', *Irish Medical News*, 19 May 2008; Mac Lellan, *Lab Coats and Lace*, pp. 86–101; Mac Lellan, *Dorothy Stopford Price: Rebel Doctor*.

191 Cowell, *A Noontide Blazing: Brigid Lyons Thornton – Rebel, Soldier, Doctor*.

192 A. Collins, 'Eleonora Fleury captured', *British Journal of Psychiatry*, 203, 1 (1 July 2013), p. 5.

193 D. Kelly, *Between the Lines of History: People of Ballinasloe, Volume One* (Ballinasloe: Declan Kelly, 2000), p. 25.

194 F.O.C. Meenan, *Cecilia Street* (Dublin: Gill and Macmillan, 1987).

195 *Irish Independent*, 27 January 1944.

196 Clarke, *Dictionary of Irish Biography: From the Earliest Times to the Year 2002 (Volume 3, D–F)*, pp. 626–7; Kelly, *Between the Lines of History*, p. 25; M. McNamara and P. Mooney, *Women in Parliament: 1918–2000* (Dublin: Wolfhound Press, 2000), p. 79; M. Clancy, 'The "western outpost": local government and women's suffrage in county Galway 1898–1918' in G. Moran (ed.), *Galway: History and Society – Interdisciplinary Essays on the History of an Irish County* (Dublin:

Geography Publications, 1996), pp. 557–87; p. 562; Witness Statement (Number 568) of Eilís Bean Uí Chonaill (Dublin: Bureau of Military History, 1913–21, File Number S.1846), p. 55; Witness Statement (Number 1,752) of Mrs. McCarvill (Eileen McGrane) (Dublin: Bureau of Military History, 1913–21, File Number S.1434), p. 7; *Irish Press*, 28 January 1944; *East Galway Democrat*, 29 January 1944. For background, see also: McCarthy, *Cumann na mBan and the Irish Revolution*.

197 *Irish Press*, 28 January 1944.

198 McNamara and Mooney, *Women in Parliament: 1918–2000*, p. 79; *Irish Press*, 28 January 1944; *East Galway Democrat*, 29 January 1944.

199 *Irish Times*, 20 January 1921.

200 *Irish Times*, 25 February 1921; *Irish Times*, 12 March 1921.

201 General Register of Prisoners, Galway Prison, 1921 (National Archives, Bishop Street, Dublin, Ireland).

202 *East Galway Democrat*, 29 January 1944; War Office, 'Castle File No. 4168: Dr English, Ada' WO 35/206/75 (Kew, Richmond, Surrey: British National Archives), p. 1.

203 M. Clancy, 'Shaping the nation: women in the Free State parliament, 1923–1937' in Y. Galligan, E. Ward and R. Wilford (eds), *Contesting Politics: Women in Ireland, North and South* (Boulder, CO: Westview Press, 1999), pp. 201–18; p. 205.

204 *Official Report of Dáil Éireann*, 26 August 1921.

205 *Official Report of Dáil Éireann*, 4 January 1922.

206 McCoole, *No Ordinary Women: Irish Female Activists in the Revolutionary Years 1900–1923*, p. 86; G. Kearns, 'Mother Ireland and the revolutionary sisters', *Cultural Geographies*, 11, 4 (October 2004), pp. 443–67.

207 *Official Report of Dáil Éireann*, 4 January 1922.

208 *New York Times*, 18 June 1922.

209 *Irish Press*, 28 January 1944; McNamara and Mooney, *Women in Parliament: 1918–2000*, p. 79; Clarke, *Dictionary of Irish Biography: From the Earliest Times to the Year 2002 (Volume 3, D–F)*, p. 626.

210 *Irish Independent*, 27 January 1944.

211 *Irish Times*, 22 January 1929.

212 Kelly, *Ada English: Patriot and Psychiatrist*, pp. 129–33.

213 D. Kelly, *Ballinasloe: From Garbally Park to the Fairgreen* (Dublin: Nonsuch, 2007), p. 92.

214 *East Galway Democrat*, 29 January 1944.

215 Minutes of the Proceedings of the Committee of Management of Ballinasloe District Lunatic Asylum/Mental Hospital, 1904–1942 (Archives at St Brigid's Hospital, Ballinasloe, County Galway, Ireland) (referred to hereafter as 'Minutes'), 20 November 1939.

216 *East Galway Democrat*, 29 January 1944.

217 Minutes, 9 June 1942.

218 Minutes, 12 August 1940.

219 Lonergan, *St Luke's Hospital, Clonmel, 1834–1984*, pp. 22–83; p. 77.

220 Henry, *Our Lady's Psychiatric Hospital Cork*, pp. 149–55.

221 *Cork Constitution*, 1 February 1882.

222 J.A. Eames 'Presidential address, delivered at the Annual Meeting of the Medico-Psychological Association, held at Queen's College, Cork, August 4, 1885', *Journal of Mental Science*, 31, 135 (October 1885), p. 315–32.

223 Anonymous, 'Obituary: James Alexander Eames, MD', *Journal of Mental Science*, 32, 139 (1 October 1886), pp. 461–2.

224 *Irish Times*, 31 May 1913.

225 *Irish Press*, 28 January 1944; *East Galway Democrat*, 29 January 1944; McNamara and Mooney, *Women in Parliament: 1918–2000*, p. 79.

226 *East Galway Democrat*, 29 January 1944; *Irish Press*, 28 January 1944; McNamara and Mooney, *Women in Parliament: 1918–2000*, p. 79; Clarke, *Dictionary of Irish Biography: From the Earliest Times to the Year 2002 (Volume 3, D–F)*, p. 626; L. Kelly, *Irish Women in Medicine, c.1880s–1920s: Origins, Education and Careers*, p. 211.

227 Henry, *Our Lady's Psychiatric Hospital Cork*, pp. 146–9; Healy, *150 Years of British Psychiatry, 1841–1991. Volume I*, p. 318.

228 Finnane, *150 Years of British Psychiatry, 1841–1991. Volume I*, p. 309.

229 Webb, *Trinity's Psychiatrists: From Serenity of the Soul to Neuroscience*, pp. 56–60.

230 *East Galway Democrat*, 29 January 1944; McNamara and Mooney, *Women in Parliament: 1918–2000*, p. 79; Clarke, *Dictionary of Irish Biography: From the Earliest Times to the Year 2002 (Volume 3, D–F)*, p. 626.

231 Minutes, 10 June 1941.

232 Minutes, 11 August 1942.

233 *Westmeath Examiner*, 16 April 2016.

234 Ó hÓgartaigh, *Kathleen Lynn: Patriot, Irishwoman, Doctor*.

235 Mac Lellan, *Dorothy Stopford Price: Rebel Doctor*.

236 Cowell, *A Noontide Blazing: Brigid Lyons Thornton – Rebel, Soldier, Doctor*.

237 A. Collins, 'Eleonora Fleury captured', *British Journal of Psychiatry*, 203, 1 (1 July 2013), p. 5.

238 *Irish Times*, 24 October 1921.

239 Minutes, 14 August 1939.

240 *Official Report of Seanad Éireann (Houses of Oireachtas, Dublin, Ireland)* (Vol. 29 No. 25), 19 April 1945. See also: Kelly, *Ada English: Patriot and Psychiatrist*, pp. 131–2.

241 Finnane, *Insanity and the Insane in Post-Famine Ireland*, pp. 73–4. See also: Robins, *Fools and Mad: A History of the Insane in Ireland*, pp. 173–5.

242 Henry, *Our Lady's Psychiatric Hospital Cork*, p. 195.

243 Minutes, 12 June 1916.

244 Minutes, 11 July 1921.

245 Minutes, 14 February 1921.

246 Kelly, *Ada English: Patriot and Psychiatrist*, pp. 25–7, 58. Much of this section is based on material in Kelly, *Ada English: Patriot and Psychiatrist*, and is used by kind permission of Irish Academic Press.

247 Anonymous, 'Ballinasloe once more: Comic relief', *Journal of Mental Science*, 50, 210 (1 July 1904), pp. 597–8.

248 Henry, *Our Lady's Psychiatric Hospital Cork*, pp. 293, 296.

249 Witness Statement (Number 568) of Eilís Bean Uí Chonaill (Dublin: Bureau of Military History, 1913–21, File Number S.1846); pp. 53–4.

250 Witness Statement (Number 624) of Mrs. Mary Flannery Woods (Dublin: Bureau of Military History, 1913–21, File Number S.1901); pp. 28–9.

251 Ibid., p. 57.

252 Witness Statement (Number 250) of Mr William P. Corrigan (Dublin: Bureau of Military History, 1913–21, File Number S.378). I am very grateful to Dr Aidan Collins for bringing this witness statement to my attention.

253 L. Ó'Bróin, *W. E. Wylie and the Irish Revolution 1916–1921* (Dublin: Gill & Macmillan, 1989).

254 John Lynch, from Kilmallock, County Limerick, a republican member of Limerick County Council, was shot dead at the Royal Exchange Hotel on Parliament Street in Dublin in the early hours of Wednesday 22 September 1920 (B.P. Murphy, 'An unknown heroine who worked for Collins', *Irish Times*, 27 February 1997).

255 This meeting occurred on 26 September 1920 (C. Gallagher, 'How two lawyers ended up on opposing sides in 1916', *Irish Times*, 5 May 2014).

256 Witness Statement (Number 250) of Mr William P. Corrigan (Dublin: Bureau of Military History, 1913–21, File Number S.378). See also: S. Enright, *Easter Rising 1916: The Trials* (Dublin: Merrion/Irish Academic Press, 2013).

257 Matthews, *Dissidents: Irish Republican Women 1923–1941*, p. 90.

258 McCoole, *No Ordinary Women: Irish Female Activists in the Revolutionary Years 1900–1923*, p. 117.

259 Matthews, *Dissidents: Irish Republican Women 1923–1941*, pp. 84–8.

260 Ibid., p. 90.

261 Ibid., p. 92.

262 Ibid., p. 96.

263 Ibid., pp. 100–4.

264 *Irish Nation (Éire)*, 5 August 1923.

265 Cox, *Negotiating Insanity in the Southeast of Ireland, 1820–1900*, p. 17.

266 Lonergan, *St Luke's Hospital, Clonmel, 1834–1984*, pp. 176–7.

Chapter 5. Reformation and Renewal in the 1900s

1 E. Boyd Barrett, 'Modern psycho-therapy and our asylums', *Studies*, 13, 49 (March 1924), pp. 29–43; p. 29.

2 Ibid., pp. 29, 30.

3 For a fascinating account of the Carlow asylum in the 1800s, see: Cox, *Negotiating Insanity in the Southeast of Ireland, 1820–1900*.

4 Commission on the Relief of the Sick and Destitute Poor, Including the Insane Poor, *Report of the Commission on the Relief of the Sick and Destitute Poor, Including the Insane Poor*, p. 102.

5 L.G.E. Harris, *A Treatise on the Law and Practice in Lunacy in Ireland, Together with the Lunacy Regulation (Ireland) Act, 1871, and a Collection of Forms for Use in the Irish Free State and in Northern Ireland* (Dublin: Corrigan and Wilson, 1930).

6 Brennan, *Irish Insanity*, p. 125.

7 Inspector of Mental Hospitals, *Annual Report of the Inspector of Mental Hospitals for the Year 1929* (Dublin: Department of Local Government and Public Health/ Stationery Office, 1930), p. 5.

8 A neuropsychiatric disorder caused by late stage syphilis.

9 Inspector of Mental Hospitals, *Annual Report of the Inspector of Mental Hospitals for the Year 1929*, p. 7.

10 Kelly, *Custody, Care and Criminality: Forensic Psychiatry and Law in 19th Century Ireland*, p. 95.

11 Inspector of Mental Hospitals, *Annual Report of the Inspector of Mental Hospitals for the Year 1929*, p. 13.

12 Ibid., p. 14. In relation to overcrowding in Castlebar, see: McDermott, *St Mary's Hospital Castlebar: Serving Mayo Mental Health from 1866*, pp. 29, 70, 109.

13 Inspector of Mental Hospitals, *Annual Report of the Inspector of Mental Hospitals for the Year 1929*, pp. 15, 16, 19, 20.

14 Ibid., pp. 16, 17.

15 Ibid.

16 Ibid., pp. 18, 20.

17 Ibid., pp. 19.

18 Ibid., p. 14.

19 J.F. O'Dea, 'A day to remember', in E. Lonergan (ed.), *St Luke's Hospital, Clonmel, 1834–1984* (Clonmel: South Eastern Health Board, 1984), pp. 97–103.

20 Psychiatrist, 'Insanity in Ireland', *The Bell*, 7, 4 (January 1944), pp. 303–10.

21 Walsh and Daly, *Mental Illness in Ireland 1750–2002: Reflections on the Rise and Fall of Institutional Care*, p. 34.

22 D. Walsh, 'Brief historical review', *Irish Journal of Psychiatry*, 13, 1 (Spring 1992), pp. 3–20; pp. 18–19.

23 Richmond Asylum Joint Committee, *Richmond Asylum Joint Committee Minutes* (Dublin: Richmond Asylum, 1907), pp. 469–70.

24 E.E.C. Kenny, *Short Hints and Observations on the Arrangement and Management of Lunatic Asylums* (Dublin: Philip Dixon Hardy & Sons, 1848), p. 6.

25 Richmond Asylum Joint Committee, *Richmond Asylum Joint Committee Minutes*, p. 469.

26 Ibid., p. 470.

27 Great Britain Commissions for the Care and Control of the Feeble-Minded, *Report of the Royal Commission on the Care and Control of the Feeble-Minded*, p. 417.

28 Ibid., p. 428.

29 See also: Robins, *Fools and Mad: A History of the Insane in Ireland*, pp. 176–8.

30　Great Britain Commissions for the Care and Control of the Feeble-Minded, *Report of the Royal Commission on the Care and Control of the Feeble-Minded*, p. 418.

31　Ibid., p. 447.

32　Ibid.

33　Ibid., p. 451.

34　Ibid., pp. 456–8.

35　Ibid., pp. 458–65.

36　Ibid., pp. 466–7.

37　Ibid., pp. 467–8.

38　Ibid., pp. 468–70.

39　H.G. Simmons, 'Explaining social policy', *Journal of Social History*, 11, 3 (Spring 1978), pp. 387–403.

40　Commission on the Relief of the Sick and Destitute Poor, Including the Insane Poor, *Report of the Commission on the Relief of the Sick and Destitute Poor, Including the Insane Poor*, p. 101.

41　Ibid., p. 104.

42　Ibid., p. 131.

43　Ibid., pp. 131–3. See also: Reynolds, *Grangegorman*, pp. 131–6.

44　Commission on the Relief of the Sick and Destitute Poor, Including the Insane Poor, *Report of the Commission on the Relief of the Sick and Destitute Poor, Including the Insane Poor*, p. 110.

45　Ibid., p. 111.

46　Ibid., pp. 110–11.

47　Ibid., p. 111.

48　Robins, *Fools and Mad: A History of the Insane in Ireland*, pp. 192–5, 205–7. There were also developments in Northern Ireland: Muckamore Abbey Hospital in Antrim accepted its first patients, four teenage girls with intellectual disabilities, on 1 November 1949 (I. Montgomery with J. Armstrong, *From Specialist Care to Specialist Treatment: A History of Muckamore Abbey Hospital* (Belfast: Ulster Historical Foundation, 2009), p. 4).

49　L. O'Brien, 'The magic wisp: a history of the mentally ill in Ireland', *Bulletin of the Menninger Clinic*, 31, 2 (March 1967), pp. 79–95; pp. 94–5; Commission of Inquiry on Mental Handicap, *Commission of Inquiry on Mental Handicap: 1965 Report* (Dublin: The Stationery Office, 1965), p. xxvi.

50　Ibid., p. xiii.

51　Ibid., p. xiv.

52　Ibid., p. xv.

53　Ibid., p. xvi.

54　Ibid., p. xvii.

55　Ibid., p. xviii.

56　Ibid.

57　Ibid.

58　Ibid., p. xix.

59　Ibid., p. xxv.

60　Ibid., p. xxiii.

61　Browne, *Music and Madness*, p. 144; Reynolds, *Grangegorman: Psychiatric Care in Dublin since 1815*, pp. 301–2.

62　Mental Handicap Committee, *Planning Mental Handicap Services: Report of Mental Handicap Committee* (Dublin: Eastern Health Board, 1981), p. iv.

63　M. Mulcahy and A. Reynolds, *Census of Mental Handicap in the Republic of Ireland 1981* (Dublin: Medico-Social Research Board, 1984), p. 17.

64　D. Walsh, 'Brief historical review', *Irish Journal of Psychiatry*, 13, 1 (Spring 1992), pp. 3–20; p. 19.

65　A. Kelleher, D. Kavanagh and M. McCarthy, *Home Together: Study of Community Based Residencies in Ireland for People with Mental Handicap* (Dublin: Health Research Board, 1990); P. Finnegan, 'Medicine in Connaught', in J.B. Lyons (ed.), *2000 Years of Irish Medicine* (Dublin: Eireann Healthcare Publications, 1999), pp. 93–6; p. 96.

66　Review Group on Mental Handicap Services, *Needs and Abilities: A Policy for the Intellectually Disabled (Report of the Review Group on Mental Handicap Services)* (Dublin: Department of Health/Stationery Office, 1990); Expert Group on Mental Health Policy, *A Vision for Change*, pp. 124–34.

67　Mental Health Commission, *Mental Health Commission Annual Report 2007 Including Report of the Inspector of Mental Health Services* (Dublin: Mental Health Commission, 2008), p. 83.

68　Ibid., p. 84.

69　Richmond Asylum Joint Committee, *Richmond Asylum Joint Committee Minutes*, pp. 469–70.

70　P. Leonard, A. Morrison, M. Delany-Warner and G.J. Calvert, 'A national survey of offending behaviour amongst intellectually disabled users of mental health services in Ireland', *Irish Journal of Psychological Medicine* [published online ahead of print, 2015], DOI: http://dx.doi.org/10.1017/ipm.2015.21.

71　C. O'Reilly, 'Carers overlooked in disability debate', *Irish Times*, 15 June 2016.

72　B.D. Kelly, 'Mental health need amongst the intellectually disabled', *Irish Journal of Medical Science*, 182, 3 (September 2013), p. 539. See also: Working Group on Congregated Settings, *Time to Move on from Congregated Settings* (Dublin: Health Service Executive, 2011); *Irish Times*, 21 August 2015.

73　Richmond Asylum Joint Committee, *Richmond Asylum Joint Committee Minutes*, p. 156.

74　*Connaught Tribune*, 15 June 1929 (reporting on the meeting of the Committee of Management of the Ballinasloe Mental Hospital, 10 June 1929). See also: Kelly, *Ada English: Patriot and Psychiatrist*, pp. 64–6.

75　*East Galway Democrat*, 19 January 1929 (reporting on the meeting of the Committee of Management of the Ballinasloe Mental Hospital, 14 January 1929).

76　*East Galway Democrat*, 18 January 1930 (reporting on the meeting of the Committee of Management of the Ballinasloe Mental Hospital, 13 January 1930).

77　McDermott, *St Mary's Hospital Castlebar: Serving Mayo Mental Health from 1866*, pp. 101–2; Prior, *Madness and Murder: Gender, Crime and Mental Disorder in Nineteenth Century Ireland*, pp. 71–3.

78   Minutes of the Committee of Management of the Ballinasloe Mental Hospital, 11 November 1929.

79   *East Galway Democrat*, 16 November 1929.

80   A. McCabe and C. Mulholland, 'The red flag over the asylum', in P.M. Prior (ed.), *Asylums, Mental Health Care and the Irish, 1800–2010* (Dublin: Irish Academic Press, 2012), pp. 23–43.

81   Robins, *Fools and Mad: A History of the Insane in Ireland*, pp. 182–4.

82   A.J. Sheridan, 'The impact of political transition on psychiatric nursing – a case study of twentieth-century Ireland', *Nursing Inquiry*, 13, 4 (2006), pp. 289–99.

83   Robins, *Fools and Mad: A History of the Insane in Ireland*, pp. 174, 186–90. See also: Healy, *150 Years of British Psychiatry. Volume II: The Aftermath*, pp. 268–91; p. 276.

84   Cox, *Negotiating Insanity in the Southeast of Ireland, 1820–1900*, p. 207.

85   Lonergan, *St Luke's Hospital, Clonmel, 1834–1984*, p. 55.

86   Robins, *Fools and Mad: A History of the Insane in Ireland*, p. 184. See also: P. Walsh, 'Changing attitudes, changing times at the former Donegal District Lunatic Asylum', *Donegal Democrat*, 18 January 2011.

87   Henry, *Our Lady's Psychiatric Hospital Cork*, p. 480.

88   Ibid., pp. 482–7.

89   Ibid., pp. 487–517.

90   *Irish Times*, 16 July 1923.

91   For an interesting related discussion, see: D. Bates, 'Keepers to Nurses? A History of the Irish Asylum Workers' Trade Union 1917–1924' (MA Dissertation, University College Dublin, 2010).

92   *Irish Times*, 10 September 1924 and 16 February 1926.

93   *Irish Times*, 16 September 1924.

94   *The Times*, 10 September 1924. For further reports, see: *Nottingham Evening Post*, 9 September 1924; *Derby Daily Telegraph*, 9 and 10 September 1924; *Gloucester Citizen*, 9 September 1924; *Hull Daily Mail*, 9 September 1924.

95   Some of these disputes played themselves out in the courts; e.g. *Irish Independent*, 22 June, 23 and 25 January 1930. These issues were also repeatedly discussed at meetings of, for example, the Committee of Management of the Ballinasloe Mental Hospital (e.g. *Connaught Tribune*, 18 July 1931 (reporting on the meeting of the Committee of Management of the Ballinasloe Mental Hospital, 13 July 1931)).

96   *Irish Times*, 8 October 1938.

97   Henry, *Our Lady's Psychiatric Hospital Cork*, p. 514.

98   Reynolds, *Grangegorman: Psychiatric Care in Dublin since 1815*, pp. 252–5.

99   Ibid., p. 263.

100   L. MacGabhann, 'Dr Dunne retires after 45 years in St Brendan's', *Irish Times*, 31 December 1965; *Irish Times*, 1 January 1991.

101   Reynolds, *Grangegorman: Psychiatric Care in Dublin since 1815*, p. 237. See also: D. Healy, 'Interview: In conversation with Ivor Browne', *Psychiatric Bulletin*, 16, 1 (January 1992), pp. 1–9; pp. 2–3.

102   Shorter, *A History of Psychiatry: From the Era of the Asylum to the Age of Prozac*, pp. 53–6.

103   Ibid., pp. 192–4. See also: E. Cunningham Dax, *Modern Mental Treatment: A Handbook for Nurses* (London: Faber & Faber Ltd., 1947), pp. 51–61.

104   J. Dunne, 'The malarial treatment of general paralysis', *Journal of Mental Science*, 72, 298 (July 1926), pp. 343–6.

105   Reynolds, *Grangegorman: Psychiatric Care in Dublin since 1815*, p. 239.

106   Malcolm, *Swift's Hospital: A History of St Patrick's Hospital, Dublin, 1746–1989*, pp. 252–3. See also: Henry, *Our Lady's Psychiatric Hospital Cork*, p. 538.

107   *Irish Times*, 20 December 1928.

108   Ibid.

109   Reynolds, *Grangegorman: Psychiatric Care in Dublin since 1815*, p. 239.

110   *Irish Times*, 21 November 1929.

111   *Irish Times*, 22 May 1937.

112   Anonymous, 'Irish Division', *Journal of Mental Science*, 81, 335 (October 1935), pp. 1000–1. Dunne later hosted the Spring meeting of the Irish Division of the RMPA at Grangegorman in April 1942, and served as president of the Irish Division (*Irish Times*, 9 April 1943).

113   *Irish Times*, 1 January 1991.

114   *Irish Times*, 18 June 1937.

115   Reynolds, *Grangegorman: Psychiatric Care in Dublin since 1815*, p. 263.

116   *Irish Times*, 18 February 1938.

117   *Irish Times*, 4 March 1938; Reynolds, *Grangegorman: Psychiatric Care in Dublin since 1815*, pp. 266–7. Dr Pearse O'Malley provides an interesting account of a neuropsychiatric clinic established at the Mater Hospital in Belfast in 1946 (P. O'Malley, *Clinical Neuro-Psychiatry: Reflections on Neuro-Psychiatric Practice and Thought* (Dublin: Dunran Press, 2000)).

118   *Irish Times*, 9 July 1954.

119   D. Healy, 'Interview: In conversation with Tom Lynch', *Psychiatric Bulletin*, 16, 2 (February 1992), pp. 65–72; p. 67.

120   *Irish Times*, 1 January 1991.

121   J. Dunne, 'The contribution of the physical sciences to psychological medicine', *Journal of Mental Science*, 102, 427 (April 1956), pp. 209–20; pp. 217–20. See also: Healy, *150 Years of British Psychiatry, 1841–1991. Volume I*, pp. 314–20; B.D. Kelly, 'Physical sciences and psychological medicine: the legacy of Prof John Dunne', *Irish Journal of Psychological Medicine*, 22, 2 (June 2005), 67–72.' Kelly, *Custody, Care and Criminality: Forensic Psychiatry and Law in 19th Century Ireland*, pp. 180–93.

122   D. Dunne, 'Prescribing practices', *British Journal of Psychiatry*, 159, 1 (July 1991), p. 156.

123   I. Khan, 'Promoting the correct use of psychotropic drugs', *British Journal of Psychiatry*, 159, 5 (November 1991), pp. 731–2. For an account of Dunne using abreaction to treat a traumatised Garda, see: B. McCaffrey, 'Book review: *Music and Madness*', *Irish Psychiatrist*, 9, 2 (Summer 2008), pp. 117–18.

124 Webb, *Trinity's Psychiatrists: From Serenity of the Soul to Neuroscience*, pp. 76–8.

125 *Irish Times*, 1 January 1991.

126 *Irish Times*, 16 April 1962 and 29 April 1964.

127 J. Horgan, *Seán Lemass: The Enigmatic Patriot* (Dublin: Gill & Macmillan, 1999), image 22; Browne, *Music and Madness*, p. 128. For more on Dunne's political background, see: M. MacEvilly, *A Splendid Resistance: The Life of IRA Chief of Staff Dr Andy Cooney* (Blackrock, County Dublin: Edmund Burke Publisher), p. 315.

128 *Irish Times*, 20 October 1939, 31 July 1953, 21 June 1958 and 19 June 1959.

129 *Irish Times*, 21 October 1941.

130 *Irish Times*, 22 November 1946.

131 *Irish Times*, 16 May 1952.

132 *Irish Times*, 21 October 1949, 13 April 1956 and 15 October 1965.

133 *Irish Times*, 31 January 1958.

134 *Irish Times*, 20 August 1954.

135 L. MacGabhann, 'Dr Dunne retires after 45 years in St Brendan's', *Irish Times*, 31 December 1965.

136 *Irish Times*, 17 June 1943 and 23 May 1962.

137 *Irish Times*, 18 February 1961.

138 J. Dunne, 'Outpatient psychiatric clinic: report of two years' work', *Journal of the Irish Medical Association*, 64, 403 (7 January 1971), pp. 7–9.

139 D. Healy, 'Interview: In conversation with Desmond McGrath', *Psychiatric Bulletin*, 16, 3 (March 1992), pp. 129–37; p. 129.

140 Browne, *Music and Madness*, pp. 102–4.

141 Ibid., pp. 105–6.

142 Reynolds, *Grangegorman: Psychiatric Care in Dublin since 1815*, p. 280.

143 Ibid., pp. 263, 296–7; B.D. Kelly, 'Physical sciences and psychological medicine: the legacy of Prof John Dunne', *Irish Journal of Psychological Medicine*, 22, 2 (June 2005), pp. 67–72.

144 *Irish Times*, 1 January 1991.

145 *Irish Times*, 19 July 1957; Reynolds, *Grangegorman: Psychiatric Care in Dublin since 1815*, p. 293.

146 Reynolds, *Grangegorman: Psychiatric Care in Dublin since 1815*, pp. 263–4.

147 *Irish Times*, 5 April 1965.

148 Robins, *Fools and Mad: A History of the Insane in Ireland*, p. 197.

149 Finnane, *150 Years of British Psychiatry, 1841–1991. Volume I*, p. 310.

150 J. Hanaghan, *Society, Evolution and Revelation: An Original Insight into Man's Place in Creation* (Dublin: Runa Press, 1957); J. Hanaghan, *The Beast Factor: Forging Passion into Power* (Enniskerry, County Wicklow: Tansy Books from Egotist, 1979); R. Skelton, 'Jonathan Hanaghan: The founder of psychoanalysis in Ireland', *The Crane Bag*, 7, 2 (1983), pp. 183–90.

151 J. Hanaghan, 'Mental illness', *Irish Times*, 2 November 1963.

152 M. Fitzgerald, 'Psychoanalytic psychotherapy in Ireland', in M. Fitzgerald (ed.), *Irish Families under Stress (Volume 7)* (Dublin: South Western Area Health Board, 2003), pp. 115–19; p. 115; Robins, *Fools and Mad: A History of the Insane in Ireland*, p. 172.

153 Healy, *150 Years of British Psychiatry. Volume II: The Aftermath*, pp. 268–91; pp. 277–9; Webb, *Trinity's Psychiatrists: From Serenity of the Soul to Neuroscience*, pp. 74–5. See also: D. Healy, *Images of Trauma: From Hysteria to Post-Traumatic Stress Disorder* (London: Faber and Faber, 1993).

154 J.C. McQuaid, 'Introduction' in E.F. O'Doherty, and S.D. McGrath (eds), *The Priest and Mental Health* (New York: Alba House, 1963), pp. ix–xi; p. ix. See also: M. Viney, 'Psychiatry and the Irish', *Irish Times*, 30 October 1963.

155 J. Hanaghan, 'Mental illness', *Irish Times*, 2 November 1963. See also: J. Fitzgerald, 'Impervious to psychoanalysis?', *Conspiracies of Silence* (blog), 16 June 2016 (https://conspiraciesofsilence.wordpress.com/).

156 Malcolm, *Swift's Hospital: A History of St Patrick's Hospital, Dublin, 1746–1989*, pp. 252–3.

157 Millon, *Masters of the Mind: Exploring the Story of Mental Illness from Ancient Times to the New Millennium*, pp. 239–40.

158 K. Jones, 'Insulin coma therapy in schizophrenia', *Journal of the Royal Society of Medicine*, 93, 3 (March 2000), pp. 147–9. See also: Cunningham Dax, *Modern Mental Treatment: A Handbook for Nurses*, pp. 15–36.

159 Scull, *Madness in Civilization: A Cultural History of Insanity, From the Bible to Freud, From the Madhouse to Modern Medicine*, p. 310.

160 Ibid.

161 Shorter, *A History of Psychiatry: From the Era of the Asylum to the Age of Prozac*, p. 211; D. Healy, 'Interview: In conversation with Desmond McGrath', *Psychiatric Bulletin*, 16, 3 (March 1992), pp. 129–37; pp. 130–1.

162 Reynolds, *Grangegorman: Psychiatric Care in Dublin since 1815*, p. 264.

163 Mac Lellan, Nic Ghabhann and Byrne, *World Within Walls*, p. 92; M. Elliot, 'Inheriting New Opportunities for Women: Dr Eveleen O'Brien (1901–1981)' (MA Thesis, University College Dublin, 2003).

164 J. Dunne and E. O'Brien, 'Insulin therapy', *Journal of Mental Science*, 85, 356 (May 1939), pp. 498–504.

165 Mac Lellan, Nic Ghabhann and Byrne, *World Within Walls*, p. 93.

166 Henry, *Our Lady's Psychiatric Hospital Cork*, pp. 539–40.

167 J. Dunne, 'Survey of modern physical methods of treatment for mental illness carried out in Grangegorman Mental Hospital', *Journal of the Medical Association of Eire*, 27, 157 (July 1950), pp. 4–9; p. 5; J. Dunne, 'The contribution of the physical sciences to psychological medicine', *Journal of Mental Science*, 102, 427 (April 1956), pp. 209–20; B.D. Kelly, 'Physical sciences and psychological medicine: the legacy of Prof John Dunne', *Irish Journal of Psychological Medicine*, 22, 2 (July 2005), pp. 67–72.

168   D. Stafford-Clark, *Psychiatry To-day* (Harmondsworth, Middlesex: Penguin Books, 1952), p. 200.

169   L.B. Kalinowsky, 'Somatic therapy of depression', in J. Wortis (ed.), *Recent Advances in Biological Psychiatry* (New York and London: Grune and Stratton, 1960), pp. 236–47.

170   W. Sargant and E. Slater, *An Introduction to Physical Methods of Treatment in Psychiatry (Fourth Edition)* (Edinburgh and London: E&S Livingstone, 1963).

171   H. Bourne, 'The insulin myth', *Lancet*, 262, 6793 (7 November 1953), pp. 644–8.

172   D. Healy, 'Interview: In conversation with Tom Lynch', *Psychiatric Bulletin*, 16, 2 (February 1992), pp. 65–72; p. 66.

173   Scull, *Madness in Civilization: A Cultural History of Insanity, From the Bible to Freud, From the Madhouse to Modern Medicine*, p. 318.

174   P. Hays, *New Horizons in Psychiatry* (Harmondsworth, Middlesex: Penguin Books, 1964), p. 107.

175   Commission of Inquiry on Mental Illness, *Report of the Commission of Inquiry on Mental Illness* (Dublin: The Stationery Office, 1967), pp. 13–14.

176   J. El-Hai, *The Lobotomist: A Maverick Medical Genius and His Tragic Quest to Rid the World of Mental Illness* (Hoboken, NJ: Wiley and Sons, 2005). See also: B.D. Kelly, 'Therapism, self-reliance, and the mapping of the mind', *Irish Psychiatrist*, 6, 4 (August/September 2005), p. 168; E. Day, 'He was bad, so they put an ice pick in his brain ...', *Observer*, 13 January 2008.

177   Shorter, *A History of Psychiatry: From the Era of the Asylum to the Age of Prozac*, p. 248.

178   A. Scull, *Madhouse: A Tragic Tale of Megalomania and Modern Medicine* (New Haven and London: Yale University Press, 2005). See also: M. Gaffney, 'A fad insane', *Irish Times*, 14 January 2006.

179   Scull, *Madness in Civilization: A Cultural History of Insanity, From the Bible to Freud, From the Madhouse to Modern Medicine*, p. 311.

180   Shorter, *A History of Psychiatry: From the Era of the Asylum to the Age of Prozac*, pp. 207–17.

181   E. Shorter and D. Healy, *Shock Therapy: A History of Electroconvulsive Treatment in Mental Illness* (New Brunswick, NJ and London: Rutgers University Press, 2007), p. 22. For an interesting discussion of this book, see: H.R. Rollin, 'Book review: *Shock Therapy: A History of Electroconvulsive Treatment in Mental Illness*', *British Journal of Psychiatry*, 197, 2 (1 August 2010), p. 162–3.

182   M. Corry, 'Is there a place for ECT in today's psychiatry?', *Irish Medical Times*, 18 July 2008.

183   National Institute for Clinical Excellence, *Guidance on the Use of Electroconvulsive Therapy (Update: May 2010)* (London: National Institute for Clinical Excellence, 2010), p. 5.

184   M. Carolan, 'ECT treatment proves 'beneficial' for man who refused to eat', *Irish Times*, 11 June 2016.

185   Shorter, *A History of Psychiatry: From the Era of the Asylum to the Age of Prozac*, p. 214. See also: Cunningham

186   N. McCrae, '"A violent thunderstorm": Cardiazol treatment in British mental hospitals', *History of Psychiatry*, 17, 1 (March 2006), pp. 67–90.

187   L.J. Von Meduna, 'Versuche über die biologische Beeinflussung des Aflaubes der Schizophrenie', *Zeitschrift für die gesamte Neurologie und Psychiatrie*, 152, 1 (December 1935), pp. 235–62.

188   Henry, *Our Lady's Psychiatric Hospital Cork*, p. 539.

189   Kelly, *Ada English: Patriot and Psychiatrist*, pp. 59–61.

190   Minutes of the Proceedings of the Committee of Management of Ballinasloe District Lunatic Asylum/ Mental Hospital, 1904–1942 (Archives at St Brigid's Hospital, Ballinasloe, County Galway, Ireland) (hereafter referred to as 'Minutes'), 20 November 1939.

191   Kelly, *Ada English: Patriot and Psychiatrist*, pp. 60–1.

192   *East Galway Democrat*, 29 January 1944.

193   Minutes, 11 December 1939.

194   Reynolds, *Grangegorman: Psychiatric Care in Dublin since 1815*, p. 264.

195   Henry, *Our Lady's Psychiatric Hospital Cork*, pp. 540–2.

196   J. Dunne, 'Survey of modern physical methods of treatment for mental illness carried out in Grangegorman Mental Hospital', *Journal of the Medical Association of Eire*, 27, 157 (July 1950), pp. 4–9; p. 5.

197   McDermott, *St Mary's Hospital Castlebar: Serving Mayo Mental Health from 1866*, pp. 128–9.

198   Mac Lellan, Nic Ghabhann and Byrne, *World Within Walls*, p. 92.

199   O'Neill, *Irish Mental Health Law*, p. 277.

200   Suxamethonium chloride, a short term muscle relaxant used in anaesthesia

201   D. Healy, 'Interview: In conversation with Tom Lynch', *Psychiatric Bulletin*, 16, 2 (February 1992), pp. 65–72; p. 69.

202   R.H. Latey and T. Fahy, *Electroconvulsive Therapy in the Republic of Ireland, 1982* (Galway: Galway University Press, 1982), p. 41.

203   Ibid., p. 39.

204   P. Skrabanek, 'Convulsive therapy – a critical appraisal of its origins and value', *Irish Medical Journal*, 79, 6 (June 1986), pp. 157–65.

205   Mental Health Act 2001, Section 59.

206   R. Dunne and D.M. McLoughlin, 'Regional variation in electroconvulsive therapy use', *Irish Medical Journal*, 104, 3 (March 2011), pp. 84–7.

207   D. Walsh, 'Shock therapy must remain available to some', *Irish Times*, 28 December 2009; B.D. Kelly, 'Depressive psychosis, involuntary ECT and human rights', *Irish Medical Times*, 29 January 2010; C. O'Brien, 'A shock to the system of care', *Irish Times*, 2 February 2010; T. Bates, 'Patient's right to consent or refuse treatment has to be balanced with a professional duty of care', *Irish Times*, 2 February 2010; see also: *Irish Times*, 14 and 28 December 2009; 8, 12, 22, 25 and 26 January, and 16 March 2010; and 6 November 2014.

208   Mental Health Act 2001, Section 59(1).

209   Expert Group on the Review of the Mental Health Act 2001, *Report of the Expert Group on the Review of the Mental Health Act 2001* (Dublin: Department of Health, 2015), p. 61. *Declaration of Interest:* The present author (BDK) was nominated to the Expert Group on the Review of the Mental Health Act 2001 by the College of Psychiatrists of Ireland and appointed to the group by Minister Kathleen Lynch, Minister for Primary Care, Social Care (Disabilities & Older People) and Mental Health, in 2012. This book is written in a personal capacity, as a psychiatrist and historian, and views expressed here or elsewhere do not necessarily represent the views of the Expert Group on the Review of the Mental Health Act 2001, the College of Psychiatrists of Ireland or, indeed, any other individual or group.

210   P. Lynch, 'College of Psychiatry calls for ECT amendments', *Irish Medical News*, 22 March 2010.

211   Mental Health Commission, *The Administration of Electro-convulsive Therapy in Approved Centres: Activity Report 2012* (Dublin: Mental Health Commission, 2014), p. 27.

212   B.D. Kelly, 'Mental illness requires an all-of-society response', *Irish Times*, 13 April 2015.

213   G. Culliton, 'ECT data incomplete due to privacy concern', *Irish Medical Times*, 27 March 2015.

214   *Irish Times*, 5, 9 and 10 March 2015; *Irish Examiner*, 5 March 2015; coverage was thankfully aided in: J. Shannon, 'Moving on from the dark ages of mental health treatment', *Irish Medical Times*, 13 March 2015.

215   B.D. Kelly, 'Schizophrenia, but not as we know it', *Lancet Psychiatry*, 2, 7 (July 2015), p. 599.

216   Mental Health Commission, *Rules Governing the Use of Electro-Convulsive Therapy (Issued Pursuant to Section 59(2) of the Mental Health Act, 2001)* (Dublin: Mental Health Commission, 2009).

217   B. Shephard, *A War of Nerves: Soldiers and Psychiatrists, 1914–1994* (London: Pimlico, 2002); p. 338.

218   El-Hai, *The Lobotomist: A Maverick Medical Genius and His Tragic Quest to Rid the World of Mental Illness.* For an interesting perspective on this book, see: C.S. Breathnach, 'Walter Freeman – maverick medical genius?', *Irish Journal of Psychological Medicine*, 23, 3 (September 2006), pp. 124–5.

219   K.C. Larson, *Rosemary: The Hidden Kennedy Daughter* (New York: Houghton Mifflin Harcourt Publishing Company, 2015).

220   L.E. Hinsie and R.J. Campbell, *Psychiatric Dictionary (Fourth Edition)* (New York, London and Toronto: Oxford University Press, 1970), p. 438.

221   Stafford-Clark, *Psychiatry To-day*, p. 201.

222   Sargant and Slater, *An Introduction to Physical Methods of Treatment in Psychiatry (Fourth Edition)*, p. 134.

223   Shephard, *A War of Nerves: Soldiers and Psychiatrists, 1914–1994*, pp. 335–8; E. Jones and S. Wessely, *Shell Shock to PTSD: Military Psychiatry from 1900 to the Gulf War* (East Sussex, UK: Psychology Press (Taylor & Francis Group) on behalf of The Maudsley, 2005), p. 73.

224   Lieberman with Ogas, *Shrinks: The Untold Story of Psychiatry*, p. 162.

225   Scull, *Madness in Civilization: A Cultural History of Insanity, From the Bible to Freud, From the Madhouse to Modern Medicine*, pp. 314–15; See also: Cunningham Dax, *Modern Mental Treatment: A Handbook for Nurses*, pp. 45–50.

226   Reynolds, *Grangegorman: Psychiatric Care in Dublin since 1815*, pp. 264–5; Guéret, *What the Doctor Saw*, p. 143.

227   B. O'Donnell (ed.), *Irish Surgeons and Surgery in the Twentieth Century* (Dublin: Gill & Macmillan Ltd., 2008), pp. 384–5.

228   For a first-hand account, see: Browne, *Music and Madness*, pp. 49–51.

229   J. Dunne, 'Survey of modern physical methods of treatment for mental illness carried out in Grangegorman Mental Hospital', *Journal of the Medical Association of Eire*, 27, 157 (July 1950), pp. 4–9; pp. 7–8. See also: J.P. Malone, 'Problems arising from prefrontal leucotomy', *Irish Journal of Medical Science*, 22, 9 (September 1947), pp. 573–9.

230   Reynolds, *Grangegorman: Psychiatric Care in Dublin since 1815*, pp. 265, 280.

231   Dunne, 'Survey of modern physical methods of treatment for mental illness carried out in Grangegorman Mental Hospital', *Journal of the Medical Association of Eire*, 27, 157 (July 1950), pp. 4–9; p. 8.

232   Stafford-Clark, *Psychiatry To-day*, pp. 201–4.

233   Shorter, *A History of Psychiatry: From the Era of the Asylum to the Age of Prozac*, p. 228; Robins, *Fools and Mad: A History of the Insane in Ireland*, p. 197.

234   Hays, *New Horizons in Psychiatry*, p. 117.

235   El-Hai, *The Lobotomist: A Maverick Medical Genius and His Tragic Quest to Rid the World of Mental Illness*, pp. 305–7.

236   Lieberman with Ogas, *Shrinks: The Untold Story of Psychiatry*, p. 165; Shorter, *A History of Psychiatry: From the Era of the Asylum to the Age of Prozac*, p. 229; El-Hai, *The Lobotomist: A Maverick Medical Genius and His Tragic Quest to Rid the World of Mental Illness*, p. 312.

237   G.N. Grob, *Mental Illness and American Society, 1875–1940* (Princeton, NJ: Princeton University Press, 1983), p. 306.

238   D. Corless, 'Radio: Brain-salad surgery and Ronan's family cooking', *Irish Independent*, 7 June 2015.

239   Guéret, *What the Doctor Saw*, pp. 142–4.

240   B.D. Kelly, 'Book review: *What the Doctor Saw*', *Irish Journal of Psychological Medicine*, 31, 2 (June 2014), pp. 150–1.

241   Mental Health Act 2001, Section 58(6).

242   Ibid., Section 58(1).

243   Ibid., Section 58(2).

244   Ibid., Section 58(3)(a).

245 J. Luigjes, B.P. de Kwaasteniet, P.P. de Koning, M.S. Oudijn, P. van den Munckhof, P.R. Schuurman and D. Denys, 'Surgery for psychiatric disorders', *World Neurosurgery*, 80, 3–4 (S31) (September/October 2013), e17–28.

246 R. Thompson, 'The scope and limitations of modern physical methods of treatment in psychological medicine', *Irish Journal of Medical Science*, 25, 11 (November 1950), pp. 509–16; Shorter, *A History of Psychiatry: From the Era of the Asylum to the Age of Prozac*, p. 229; Lieberman with Ogas, *Shrinks: The Untold Story of Psychiatry*, p. 165.

247 E.N.M. O'Sullivan, *Textbook of Occupational Therapy with Chief Reference to Psychological Medicine* (London: H.K Lewis & Co. Ltd., 1955).

248 Hallaran, *An Inquiry into the Causes producing the Extraordinary Addition to the Number of Insane*, p. 109.

249 McDermott, *St Mary's Hospital Castlebar: Serving Mayo Mental Health from 1866*, pp. 135–41. For more on Rush, see: Shorter, *A History of Psychiatry: From the Era of the Asylum to the Age of Prozac*, pp. 15–16, 27–8, 333, 335.

250 J-É. Esquirol, *Des Passions* (Paris: Didot Jeune, 1805); E.T. Carlson and N. Dain, 'The psychotherapy that was moral treatment', *American Journal of Psychiatry*, 117, 6 (December 1960), pp. 519–24. See also: O. Walsh, 'Work and the Irish district asylums during the late nineteenth century', in E. Waltraud (ed.), *Work, Psychiatry and Society, c. 1750–2015* (Manchester: Manchester University Press, 2016), pp. 298–313. For an account of the asylum farm in Cork, see: Henry, *Our Lady's Psychiatric Hospital Cork*, pp. 570–2.

251 McDermott, *St Mary's Hospital Castlebar: Serving Mayo Mental Health from 1866*, pp. 135–6.

252 Robins, *Fools and Mad: A History of the Insane in Ireland*, pp. 128–42.

253 C. Prendiville and J. Pettigrew, 'Leisure occupations in the Central Criminal Lunatic Asylum 1890–1920', *Irish Journal of Occupational Therapy*, 43, 1 (Spring 2015), pp. 12–19. For a consideration of methodological themes, see: B. Dunne, J. Pettigrew and K. Robinson, 'Using historical documentary methods to explore the history of occupational therapy', *British Journal of Occupational Therapy*, 79, 6 (June 2016), pp. 376–84.

254 Kelly, *Ada English: Patriot and Psychiatrist*, pp. 54–6.

255 Shorter, *A History of Psychiatry: From the Era of the Asylum to the Age of Prozac*, pp. 69–112.

256 W. Fogarty, *Dr Eamonn O'Sullivan: A Man Before His Time* (Dublin: Wolfhound Press, 2007), pp. 191–7.

257 O'Sullivan, *Textbook of Occupational Therapy with Chief Reference to Psychological Medicine*.

258 McDermott, *St Mary's Hospital Castlebar: Serving Mayo Mental Health from 1866*, pp. 106–7.

259 Henry, *Our Lady's Psychiatric Hospital Cork*, pp. 519–27.

260 Reynolds, *Grangegorman: Psychiatric Care in Dublin since 1815*, pp. 252–5.

261 Inspector of Mental Hospitals, *Annual Report of the Inspector of Mental Hospitals for the Year 1935* (Dublin: Department of Local Government and Public Health/Stationery Office, 1936), p. 20.

262 Ibid., p. 21.

263 Inspector of Mental Hospitals, *Annual Report of the Inspector of Mental Hospitals for the Year 1949* (Dublin: Department of Health/Stationery Office, 1950), p. 24.

264 *East Galway Democrat*, 29 January 1944.

265 Minutes of the Proceedings of the Committee of Management of Ballinasloe District Lunatic Asylum/Mental Hospital, 1904–1942 (Archives at St Brigid's Hospital, Ballinasloe, County Galway, Ireland), 9 June 1942.

266 Anonymous, 'Irish Division', *Journal of Mental Science*, 63, 263 (1 October 1917), p. 620. For an interesting account of mental hospital farms, especially that in Castlebar, see: McDermott, *St Mary's Hospital Castlebar: Serving Mayo Mental Health from 1866*, pp. 55–67.

267 Kelly, *Ada English: Patriot and Psychiatrist*, pp. 56–9.

268 Minutes, 8 April 1940.

269 Mental Treatment Regulations (Statutory Instrument 261 of 1961), Section 12.

270 Reynolds, *Grangegorman: Psychiatric Care in Dublin since 1815*, pp. 291–2.

271 Mental Treatment Regulations (Statutory Instrument 261 of 1961), Section 13.

272 S. Cherry and R. Munting, '"Exercise is the thing"? Sport and the asylum c.1850–1950', *International Journal of the History of Sport*, 22, 1 (2005), pp. 42–58.

273 T. Mac Loughlin, *Ballinasloe Inniú agus Inné* (Ballinasloe: Tadgh Mac Loughlin, 1993), pp. 144–5.

274 Ibid., p. 144. Camogie was a feature at many mental hospitals; e.g. M. Hyland and T. Connolly, 'Elmville Camogie Club', in E. Lonergan (ed.), *St Luke's Hospital, Clonmel, 1834–1984* (Clonmel: South Eastern Health Board, 1984), pp. 133–7.

275 S. Cherry and R. Munting, '"Exercise is the thing"? Sport and the asylum c.1850–1950', *International Journal of the History of Sport*, 22, 1 (2005), pp. 42–58.

276 P. Heffernan, 'An Irish doctor's memories: Clonmel (1902–1905)', in E. Lonergan (ed.), *St Luke's Hospital, Clonmel, 1834–1984* (Clonmel: South Eastern Health Board, 1984), pp. 91–5.

277 E. Lonergan, 'An Olympic champion', in E. Lonergan (ed.), *St Luke's Hospital, Clonmel, 1834–1984* (Clonmel: South Eastern Health Board, 1984), pp. 119–23.

278 Carlow Mental Hospital Sports Entry Form (SDH/007/009) (Archive of St Dympna's Hospital (Carlow), Delany Archive, Carlow College, College Street, Carlow).

279 McDermott, *St Mary's Hospital Castlebar: Serving Mayo Mental Health from 1866*, pp. 145–8, 152–3.

280 Inspector of Mental Hospitals, *Annual Report of the Inspector of Mental Hospitals for the Year 1935*, pp. 20–1.

281 *East Galway Democrat*, 13 June 1914; Walsh, *Gender and Medicine in Ireland, 1700–1950*, p. 85.

282 Murphy, *Tumbling Walls: The Evolution of a Community Institution over 150 Years*, pp. 15–27; p. 25.

283 J.P. Hill, 'An RMS remembers', in D.A. Murphy (ed.), *Tumbling Walls: The Evolution of a Community Institution over 150 Years* (Portlaoise: Midland Health Board, 1983), pp. 54–7; p. 56.

284 M. Conroy, 'Inside stories', in D.A. Murphy (ed.), *Tumbling Walls: The Evolution of a Community Institution over 150 Years* (Portlaoise: Midland Health Board, 1983), pp. 51–3; p. 53.

285 B.D. Kelly, 'The Mental Treatment Act 1945 in Ireland: an historical enquiry', *History of Psychiatry*, 19, 73(1) (March 2008), pp. 47–67.

286 Healy, *150 Years of British Psychiatry. Volume II: The Aftermath*, pp. 268–91.

287 *Irish Times*, 1 January 1991.

288 Commission on the Relief of the Sick and Destitute Poor, Including the Insane Poor, *Report of the Commission on the Relief of the Sick and Destitute Poor, Including the Insane Poor*, p. 100.

289 *Official Report of Dáil Éireann*, 29 November 1944.

290 Reynolds, *Grangegorman: Psychiatric Care in Dublin since 1815*, pp. 275–7.

291 Mental Treatment Act, 1945, Part 15.

292 B.D. Kelly, 'The Mental Treatment Act 1945 in Ireland: an historical enquiry', *History of Psychiatry*, 19, 73(1) (March 2008), pp. 47–67.

293 Mental Treatment Act 1945, Sections 162, 177 and 184.

294 Robins, *Fools and Mad: A History of the Insane in Ireland*, pp. 195–7.

295 Mental Treatment Act 1945, Sections 239, 240 and 266.

296 Ibid., Section 266.

297 Constitution of Ireland (Bunreacht na hÉireann), Article 40.

298 T. Cooney and O. O'Neill, *Psychiatric Detention: Civil Commitment in Ireland* (Wicklow: Baikonur, 1996), p. 300.

299 Mental Treatment Act 1945, Section 260(1); J. Spellman, 'Section 260 of the Mental Treatment Act, 1945 reviewed', *Medico-Legal Journal of Ireland*, 4, 1 (1998), pp. 20–4.

300 *Blehein v. The Minister for Health and Children and others* [2008] IESC 40; E. Madden, 'Section of Mental Health Act was unconstitutional', *Irish Medical Times*, 27 July 2008.

301 L. O'Brien, 'The magic wisp: a history of the mentally ill in Ireland', *Bulletin of the Menninger Clinic*, 31, 2 (March 1967), pp. 79–95; p. 94.

302 J. Brown, 'The Legal Powers to Detain the Mentally Ill in Ireland: Medicalism or Legalism?' (PhD Thesis, Dublin City University, 2015), pp. 44, 47–8.

303 *Irish Times*, 18, 19 and 20 October and 17 December 1949.

304 *Official Report of Dáil Éireann*, 29 November 1944.

305 Walsh and Daly, *Mental Illness in Ireland 1750–2002: Reflections on the Rise and Fall of Institutional Care*, p. 33.

306 *Irish Times*, 19 October 1951.

307 D. Walsh, 'Mental illness in Ireland and its management', in D. McCluskey (ed.), H*ealth Policy and Practice in Ireland* (Dublin: University College Dublin Press, 2006), pp. 29–43; p. 34.

308 *Irish Times*, 21 March 1966.

309 Daly and Walsh, *Activities of Irish Psychiatric Services 2001*, p. 116.

310 Commission of Inquiry on Mental Illness, *Report of the Commission of Inquiry on Mental Illness* (Dublin: The Stationery Office, 1967) (hereafter 'Commission').

311 *Irish Times*, 16 November 1967.

312 L. O'Brien, 'The magic wisp: a history of the mentally ill in Ireland', *Bulletin of the Menninger Clinic*, 31, 2 (March 1967), pp. 79–95; pp. 94–5.

313 *Irish Times* Reporter, 'Ireland has high mental illness rate', *Irish Times*, 29 March 1967.

314 Commission, p. iii.

315 Ibid., p. xiii.

316 Ibid., p. xv.

317 Ibid., p. xiii.

318 Ibid., p. xv.

319 Ibid., p. xxi.

320 Ibid., p. xvi.

321 Ibid., p. xxii.

322 Ibid., p. xxvm.

323 Ibid., p. xxix.

324 Ibid., p. xxx.

325 Ibid., p. xxxi.

326 Ibid.

327 Ibid., p. xxxii. For further discussion of this aspect of the report, see: Webb, *Trinity's Psychiatrists: From Serenity of the Soul to Neuroscience*, pp. 101–3.

328 Commission, p. xxxi.

329 Ibid., p. xxxv.

330 Ibid., p. xxxvii.

331 Ibid., pp. xxxviii–xxxix.

332 Brennan, *Irish Insanity, 1800–2000*, pp. 100–1.

333 C. Norman, 'The domestic treatment of the insane', *Dublin Journal of Medical Science*, 101, 2 (February 1896), pp. 111–21.

334 C. Norman, 'The family care of the insane', *Medical Press and Circular*, 29 November–6 December 1905.

335 Department of Health and Social Security, *Royal Commission On The Law Relating To Mental Illness And Mental Deficiency. Cmnd 169* (London: Her Majesty's Stationery Office, 1957). But, in relation to community care in the UK, see also: D.J. Ward, 'Having breakfast with the late Enoch Powell', *Irish Medical Times*, 29 April 2016.

336 *Irish Times*, 30 March 1967.

337 Commission, p. xxxvii.

338 J.F. Reynolds, 'Mental illness', *Irish Times*, 5 April 1967.

339 J.C. Power, 'No admission', *Irish Times*, 29 April 1967.

340 M. Viney, '"Secret" justice and after', *Irish Times*, 9 February 1968.

341 M.D. Higgins, 'Mental illness', *Irish Times*, 19 March 1968.

342 *Irish Times*, 8 April 1967.

343 N.C. Browne, 'Best psychiatrist', *Irish Times*, 11 April 1967. See also: W.J. Coyne, 'Best psychiatrist', *Irish*

Times, 11 April 1967. For more information regarding Dr Browne and psychiatry (especially St Brendan's Hospital, Grangegorman), see: J. Horgan, *Noël Browne: Passionate Outsider* (Dublin: Gill & Macmillan, 2000), pp. 217–9; N. Browne, *Against the Tide* (Dublin: Gill & Macmillan, 1986), pp. 240–8.

344 Commission, p. xxxv.

345 Malcolm, *Swift's Hospital: A History of St Patrick's Hospital, Dublin, 1746–1989*, pp. 213–15.

346 D. Coakley, *Medicine in Trinity College Dublin: An Illustrated History* (Dublin: Trinity College Dublin, 2014), pp. 167–8 (for perspectives on this book, see: M. Houston, 'Three centuries of medicine at TCD', *Irish Medical Times*, 23 May 2014; J. Wallace, 'Medicine in Trinity', *Irish Medical News*, 20 October 2014; A. Collins, 'Book review: *Medicine in Trinity College Dublin: An Illustrated History*', *Irish Journal of Psychological Medicine*, 33, 2 (June 2016), p. 133); Webb, *Trinity's Psychiatrists: From Serenity of the Soul to Neuroscience*, p. 56.

347 T.P.C. Kirkpatrick, 'Obituary: Richard Robert Leeper', *Journal of Mental Science*, 88, 372 (1 July 1942), pp. 480–1; p. 480.

348 R. Thompson, 'Obituary: Richard Robert Leeper', *Journal of Mental Science*, 88, 372 (1 July 1942), pp. 481–4; p. 481.

349 Webb, *Trinity's Psychiatrists: From Serenity of the Soul to Neuroscience*, p. 67.

350 Malcolm, *Swift's Hospital: A History of St Patrick's Hospital, Dublin, 1746–1989*, pp. 216–57. See also: Webb, *Trinity's Psychiatrists: From Serenity of the Soul to Neuroscience*, pp. 67–70.

351 Thompson, 'Obituary: Richard Robert Leeper', *Journal of Mental Science*, 88, 372 (1 July 1942), pp. 481–4; p. 482.

352 D. Healy, 'Interview: In conversation with Tom Lynch', *Psychiatric Bulletin*, 16, 2 (February 1992), pp. 65–72; p. 67.

353 Malcolm, *Swift's Hospital: A History of St Patrick's Hospital, Dublin, 1746–1989*, pp. 222–3.

354 Thompson, 'Obituary: Richard Robert Leeper', *Journal of Mental Science*, 88, 372 (1 July 1942), pp. 481–4; p. 483.

355 Anonymous, 'Irish Division', *Journal of Mental Science*, 48, 203 (1 October 1902), pp. 805–6.

356 For an excellent discussion of Leeper's academic work, including views on the eugenics movement of this era, and further references, see: Webb, *Trinity's Psychiatrists: From Serenity of the Soul to Neuroscience*, pp. 67–70. For information on eugenics in Ireland, see: G. Jones, 'Eugenics in Ireland: the Belfast Eugenics Society, 1911–15', *Irish Historical Studies*, 28, 109 (May 1992), pp. 81–95. For further information on eugenics *and psychiatry* in Ireland, see: B.D. Kelly, 'Asylum doctor extraordinaire: Dr Thomas Drapes (1847–1919)', *Irish Journal of Medical Science*, 184, 3 (September 2015), pp. 565–71. For information on eugenics and psychiatry in the US and Canada, see: Dowbiggin, *Keeping America Sane: Psychiatry and Eugenics in the United States and Canada, 1880–1940*.

357 Later published as: D.F. Rambaut, 'Case-taking in large asylums', *Journal of Mental Science*, 49, 204 (1 January 1903), pp. 45–52.

358 R.R. Leeper, 'Some reflections on the progress of psychiatry: the presidential address at the ninetieth annual meeting of the Royal Medico-Psychological Association held in Dublin, July 8, 1931', *Journal of Mental Science*, 33, 319 (1 October 1931), pp. 683–91.

359 Malcolm, *Swift's Hospital: A History of St Patrick's Hospital, Dublin, 1746–1989*, p. 259.

360 A.W. Clare, 'Obituary: John Norman Parker Moore', *Psychiatric Bulletin*, 20, 12 (1 December 1996), pp. 771–3; p. 771.

361 C. Greenland, 'At the Crichton Royal with William Mayer-Gross (b. 15 Jan. 1889, d. 15 Feb. 1961)', *History of Psychiatry*, 13, 52 (October 2002), pp. 467–74.

362 Malcolm, *Swift's Hospital: A History of St Patrick's Hospital, Dublin, 1746–1989*, pp. 258–77, 282–4.

363 A.W. Clare, 'Obituary: John Norman Parker Moore', *Psychiatric Bulletin*, 20, 12 (1 December 1996), pp. 771–3, p. 772. See also: *Irish Times*, 29 July 1996.

364 For more details see: D. Healy, 'Interview: In conversation with Ivor Browne', *Psychiatric Bulletin*, 16, 1 (January 1992), pp. 1–9; p. 8; P. Gatenby, *The School of Physic, Trinity College Dublin: A Retrospective View* (Dublin: Trinity College, Faculty of Health Sciences, 1994), pp. 58, 64–5; Webb, *Trinity's Psychiatrists: From Serenity of the Soul to Neuroscience*, pp. 103–6; Coakley, *Medicine in Trinity College Dublin: An Illustrated History*, pp. 265–7.

365 Webb, *Trinity's Psychiatrists: From Serenity of the Soul to Neuroscience*, pp. 92–7.

366 Malcolm, *Swift's Hospital: A History of St Patrick's Hospital, Dublin, 1746–1989*, p. 276.

367 J. Wallace, 'Doctor Maurice O'Connor Drury, Wittgenstein's pupil', *Irish Journal of Psychological Medicine*, 17, 2 (1 June 2000), pp. 67–8; N. Malcolm, *Ludwig Wittgenstein: A Memoir* (Oxford: Oxford University Press, 2001; first published in 1958), pp. 62, 64, 83, 92, 106, 112, 113; M. O'C. Drury, *The Danger of Words and Writings on Wittgenstein* (Bristol: Thoemmes Press, 2003).

368 Webb, *Trinity's Psychiatrists: From Serenity of the Soul to Neuroscience*, pp. 84–7.

369 D. Healy, 'Interview: In conversation with Tom Lynch', *Psychiatric Bulletin*, 16, 2 (February 1992), pp. 65–72; p. 66.

370 Ibid., p. 67. See also: J.N.P. Moore, 'Perspective', *Bulletin of the Royal College of Psychiatrists*, 10, 11 (November 1986), pp. 298–302 (for Moore's reflections on psychiatry); D. Healy, 'Interview: In conversation with Desmond McGrath', *Psychiatric Bulletin*, 16, 3 (March 1992), pp. 129–37; pp. 133–4, 136.

371 'J.N.P. Moore' was listed as 'alienist' to the Meath Hospital, Dublin as of 31 December 1977 (Meath Hospital, *Annual Report* (Dublin: Brunswick Press Ltd., 1977), p. 2). I am very grateful to Professor Des O'Neill for this information.

372 Malcolm, *Swift's Hospital: A History of St Patrick's Hospital, Dublin, 1746–1989*, pp. 286–9, 317; P.J. Meehan, 'Psychiatry today – care, treatment and rehabilitation', in K. O'Sullivan (ed.), *All in the Mind: Approaches to Mental Health* (Dublin: Gill and Macmillan, 1986), pp. 11–15.

373 Malcolm, *Swift's Hospital: A History of St Patrick's Hospital, Dublin, 1746–1989*, pp. 287, 317; K. O'Sullivan (ed.), *All in the Mind: Approaches to Mental Health* (Dublin: Gill and Macmillan, 1986).

374 A. Clare, *Psychiatry in Dissent* (London: Tavistock Publications, 1976); R.M. Murray, 'Obituary: Professor Anthony Clare', *Psychiatric Bulletin*, 32, 3 (1 March 2008), pp. 118–19. Professor Clare narrated a DVD, titled 'Swift's Hospital, 1745–1995', produced and directed by Jim Sherwin (Sherwin Media Group, Delgany, County Wicklow).

375 P. McKeon, *Coping with Depression and Elation* (London: Sheldon Press, 1986); P. McKeon, 'Mood swings – depression and elation', in K. O'Sullivan (ed.), *All in the Mind: Approaches to Mental Health* (Dublin: Gill and Macmillan, 1986), pp. 34–42.

376 J. Lucey, *In My Room: The Recovery Journey as Encountered by a Psychiatrist* (Dublin: Gill and Macmillan, 2014). See also: Webb, *Trinity's Psychiatrists: From Serenity of the Soul to Neuroscience*, pp. 120–4.

377 See also: M. McDonagh, 'Independent mental health services', *Irish Medical News*, 29 March 2010.

378 The hospital has a long record of providing care in this area: J.A. Griffin, 'Eating disorders', in K. O'Sullivan (ed.), *All in the Mind: Approaches to Mental Health* (Dublin: Gill and Macmillan, 1986), pp. 106–9.

379 Inspector of Mental Health Services, *Report of the Inspector of Mental Health Services, 2013: St Patrick's University Hospital* (Dublin: Inspector of Mental Health Services, 2014), p. 1.

380 Malcolm, *Swift's Hospital: A History of St Patrick's Hospital, Dublin, 1746–1989*, p. 155.

381 Ibid., pp. 18–9.

Chapter 6. The Twentieth Century: Decline of the Institutions

1 Study Group on the Development of the Psychiatric Services, *The Psychiatric Services – Planning for the Future* (Dublin: Stationery Office, 1984), p. 4.

2 J. Foot, *The Man Who Closed the Asylums: Franco Basaglia and the Revolution in Mental Health Care* (London and New York: Verso, 2015). See also: N. Scheper-Hughes and A.M. Lovell (eds), *Psychiatry Inside Out: Selected Writings of Franco Basaglia* (New York: Columbia University Press, 1987); P. Guarnieri, 'The history of psychiatry in Italy', in M.S. Micale and R. Porter (eds), *Discovering the History of Psychiatry* (New York and Oxford: Oxford University Press, 1994), pp. 248–59; D.J. Ward, 'Having breakfast with the late Enoch Powell', *Irish Medical Times*, 29 April 2016 (in relation to the UK).

3 Daly and Walsh, *Activities of Irish Psychiatric Services 2001*, p. 116.

4 A. O'Hare and D. Walsh, *Activities of Irish Psychiatric Hospitals and Units 1965–1969* (Dublin: The Medico-Social Research Board, 1970), p. 13.

5 Walsh and Daly, *Mental Illness in Ireland 1750–2002: Reflections on the Rise and Fall of Institutional Care*, pp. 30–1.

6 A. Daly and D. Walsh, *Activities of Irish Psychiatric Units and Hospitals 2014* (Dublin: Health Research Board, 2015), p. 28.

7 Ibid., p. 20.

8 For an early (1947) discussion of the use of modern medication in psychiatry, see: Cunningham Dax, *Modern Mental Treatment: A Handbook for Nurses*, pp. 62–70.

9 Shorter, *A History of Psychiatry: From the Era of the Asylum to the Age of Prozac*, pp. 249–50. See also: Kelly, *'He Lost Himself Completely': Shell Shock and its Treatment at Dublin's Richmond War Hospital, 1916–1919*, pp. 102–3.

10 Sargant and Slater, *An Introduction to Physical Methods of Treatment in Psychiatry (Fourth Edition)*, p. 23.

11 Hinsie and Campbell, *Psychiatric Dictionary (Fourth Edition)*, p. 569.

12 R.P. Mackay, 'The neurology of motivation', in J. Wortis J (ed.), *Recent Advances in Biological Psychiatry* (New York and London: Grune and Stratton, 1960), pp. 2–13; p. 10.

13 Hays, *New Horizons in Psychiatry*, pp. 90–1. See also: B. Majerus, 'Making Sense of the 'Chemical Revolution'', *Medical History*, 60, 1 (January 2016), pp. 54–66.

14 *Irish Times*, 16 November 1956 and 6 December 1960.

15 *Irish Times*, 2 May 1961.

16 *Irish Times*, 11 November 1961 and 5 April 1965.

17 J.P. Hill, 'An RMS remembers', in D.A. Murphy (ed.), *Tumbling Walls: The Evolution of a Community Institution over 150 Years* (Portlaoise: Midland Health Board, 1983), pp. 54–7; p. 55. See also: Robins, *Fools and Mad: A History of the Insane in Ireland*, pp. 197–9.

18 McDermott, *St Mary's Hospital Castlebar: Serving Mayo Mental Health from 1866*, p. 129.

19 Henry, *Our Lady's Psychiatric Hospital Cork*, pp. 358, 544–5.

20 R. Boland, '"Isolated from the mainstream": Portrane asylum in the 1950s', *Irish Times*, 10 June 2016.

21 M. Viney, 'The opening door', *Irish Times*, 24 October 1963; Robins, *Fools and Mad: A History of the Insane in Ireland*, p. 199.

22 Ibid., p. 158; Commission of Inquiry on Mental Illness, *Report of the Commission of Inquiry on Mental Illness* (Dublin: The Stationery Office, 1967), p. 14; Henry, *Our Lady's Psychiatric Hospital Cork*, pp. 358, 544–5; Study Group on the Development of the Psychiatric Services, *The Psychiatric Services – Planning for the Future*, pp. 4–5.

23 D. Healy, 'Interview: In conversation with Tom Lynch', *Psychiatric Bulletin*, 16, 2 (February 1992), pp. 65–72; p. 70.

24 D. Walsh, 'Brief historical review', *Irish Journal of Psychiatry*, 13, 1 (Spring 1992), pp. 3–20; p. 9.

25 Commission of Inquiry on Mental Illness, *Report of the Commission of Inquiry on Mental Illness*, p. xv.

26 E. O'Sullivan and I. O'Donnell, 'Coercive confinement in the Republic of Ireland: the waning of a culture of control', *Punishment & Society*, 9, 1 (January 2007), pp. 27–48.

27 M. Viney, 'No room to move', *Irish Times*, 23 October 1963; M. Viney, 'The opening door', *Irish Times*, 24 October 1963; M. Viney, 'Patients with a purpose', *Irish Times*, 25 October 1963; M. Viney, 'Chance for a revolution', *Irish Times*, 26 October 1963; M. Viney, 'Children all their lives', *Irish Times*, 28 October 1963; M. Viney, 'Odd child out', *Irish Times*, 29 October 1963; M. Viney, 'Psychiatry and the Irish', *Irish Times*, 30 October 1963. These articles were reprinted as: M. Viney, *Mental Illness: An Inquiry* (Dublin: Irish Times, 1971). See also: E. O'Sullivan and I. O'Donnell (eds), *Coercive Confinement in Ireland: Patients, Prisoners and Penitents* (Manchester and New York: Manchester University Press, 2012), pp. 110–16.

28 For responses to Viney's *Irish Times* articles, see: 'Ex-Teacher', 'Mental illness', *Irish Times*, 2 November 1963; J. Hanaghan, 'Mental illness', *Irish Times*, 2 November 1963; J. Butler, 'Mental illness', *Irish Times*, 4 November 1963; 'Medicus', 'Mental illness', *Irish Times*, 5 November 1963; 'PHN', 'Mental illness', *Irish Times*, 8 November 1963; T. Ó Maoláin, 'Mental illness', *Irish Times*, 11 November 1963; 'Glencraig Parent', 'Mental illness', *Irish Times*, 16 November 1963.

29 H. Connolly, 'The scandal of the mental hospitals', *Magill*, October 1980.

30 Daly and Walsh, *Activities of Irish Psychiatric Services 2001*, p. 116.

31 E. Gillespie, 'No funds – no care?', *Irish Times*, 17 September 1981.

32 *Irish Times*, 16 April 1971.

33 Each mental hospital experienced change in a slightly different way; see, for example: P.A. Meehan, 'The changing face of psychiatry', in E. Lonergan (ed.), *St Luke's Hospital, Clonmel, 1834–1984* (Clonmel: South Eastern Health Board, 1984), pp. 85–9; S. Cullen (ed.), *Climbing Mountains in our Minds: Stories and Photographs from St. Senan's Hospital, Enniscorthy* (Wexford: Wexford County Council, 2012).

34 R. Porter, 'The patient's view: doing medical history from below', *Theory and Society*, 14, 2, (March 1985), pp. 175–98; K. Davies, "Silent and Censured Travellers'? Patients' narratives and patients' voices: perspectives on the history of mental illness since 1948', *Social History of Medicine*, 14, 2 (August 2001), pp. 267–92.

35 R. Porter, *A Social History of Madness: Stories of The Insane* (London: Phoenix Giants, 1987).

36 J.T. Perceval, *A Narrative of the Treatment Experienced by a Gentleman During a State of Mental Derangement Designed to Explain the Causes and Nature of Insanity, and to Expose the Injudicious Conduct Pursued Towards Many Unfortunate Sufferers under that Calamity* (London: Effingham Wilson, 1838).

37 C.W. Beers, *A Mind That Found Itself* (New York: Longmans, Green and Co., 1908).

38 L. Feeney and B.D. Kelly, 'Mental health advocacy and *A Mind that Found Itself*, *Irish Psychiatrist*, 9, 1 (Spring 2008), pp. 19–22.

39 C. Duffy, *It Happened in Ireland* (New York: The Christian Press, 1944).

40 H. Greally, *Bird's Nest Soup* (Dublin: Allen Figgis and Co., 1971).

41 Mac Lellan, Nic Ghabhann and Byrne, *World Within Walls*, p. 96.

42 While Duffy's book states that these events occurred in 1936, hospital records suggest it was 1937. (I am very grateful to Dr Anne Mac Lellan for her assistance in this matter.)

43 Greally, *Bird's Nest Soup*.

44 E. Ward, 'Security and asylum: the case of Hanna Greally', *Studies*, 95, 377 (Spring 2006), pp. 65–76.

45 Commemorative Book Committee, *The History of St Loman's Hospital in Changing Times* (Tullamore, County Offaly: Commemorative Book Committee, 2014).

46 See, for example: H. Greally, *Flown the Nest* (Cork: Attic Press, 2009).

47 This section of the book draws upon material within: B.D. Kelly, 'Homosexuality and Irish psychiatry: medicine, law and the changing face of Ireland', *Irish Journal of Psychological Medicine*, available on CJO 1st February 2016. doi:10.1017/ipm.2015.72, ©College of Psychiatrists of Ireland, published by Cambridge University Press, reproduced with permission.

48 American Psychiatric Association, *Diagnostic and Statistical Manual of Mental Disorders (First Edition)* (Washington DC: American Psychiatric Association, 1952), pp. 38–9.

49 American Psychiatric Association, *Diagnostic and Statistical Manual of Mental Disorders (Second Edition)* (Washington DC: American Psychiatric Association, 1968), p. 44.

50 Lieberman with Ogas, *Shrinks: The Untold Story of Psychiatry*, p. 123.

51 Shorter, *A History of Psychiatry: From the Era of the Asylum to the Age of Prozac*, p. 304.

52 Pietikäinen, *Madness: A History*, pp. 176–7.

53 T. Dickinson, *'Curing Queers': Mental Nurses and Their Patients, 1935–74* (Manchester: Manchester University Press, 2015), pp. 47–9. For perspectives on this fascinating book, see: S. Wise, "Curing Queers' – Review', *Guardian*, 3 June 2015; C. Hilton, 'Book review: *'Curing Queers': Mental Nurses and Their Patients, 1935–74*', *British Journal of Psychiatry*, 208, 6 (June 2016), p. 596.

54   K. Simpson, *Forensic Medicine (Eighth Edition)* (London: Edward Arnold (Publishers) Ltd., 1979), p. 214. This passage is used by kind permission of Taylor & Francis Group. I am grateful to Dr Aidan Collins for bringing this passage to my attention.

55   Pietikäinen, *Madness: A History*, p. 224; Scull, *Madness in Civilization: A Cultural History of Insanity, From the Bible to Freud, From the Madhouse to Modern Medicine*, p. 349; Dickinson, *'Curing Queers': Mental Nurses and Their Patients, 1935–74*, p. 22.

56   Lieberman with Ogas, *Shrinks: The Untold Story of Psychiatry*, pp. 122–3. For an interesting Irish perspective, see: C. Robson, 'Homosexuality', *Irish Times*, 18 September 1991.

57   Pietikäinen, *Madness: A History*, p. 234.

58   J.P. Joyce, 'A new normal', *History Today*, 66, 2 (February 2016), pp. 33–7.

59   Dickinson, *'Curing Queers': Mental Nurses and Their Patients, 1935–74*, p. 65.

60   Lieberman with Ogas, *Shrinks: The Untold Story of Psychiatry*, p. 123.

61   Dickinson, *'Curing Queers': Mental Nurses and Their Patients, 1935–74*, pp. 65–7.

62   M. King, G. Smith and A. Bartlett, 'Treatments of homosexuality in Britain since the 1950s – an oral history: the experience of professionals', *British Medical Journal*, 328, 7437 (21 February 2004), pp. 429–32.

63   D. Ferriter, *Occasions of Sin: Sex and Society in Modern Ireland* (London: Profile Books Ltd., 2009).

64   B. Lacey, *Terrible Queer Creatures: Homosexuality in Irish History* (Dublin: Wordwell Books, 2008).

65   Ferriter, *Occasions of Sin: Sex and Society in Modern Ireland*, p. 392.

66   *Irish Times*, 25 June 1980.

67   W.J. Murphy, 'Homosexuality', *Irish Times*, 13 July 1973.

68   E.F. O'Doherty, 'Sexual deviations', in E.F. O'Doherty, and S.D. McGrath (eds), *The Priest and Mental Health* (New York: Alba House, 1963), pp. 124–35; pp. 130–2. For a discussion of this book, see: Healy, *150 Years of British Psychiatry. Volume II: The Aftermath*, pp. 268–91; p. 279.

69   J. Dunne, 'Diseases of the mind', in E.F. O'Doherty, and S.D. McGrath (eds), *The Priest and Mental Health* (New York: Alba House, 1963), pp. 13–25; p. 19.

70   J.P.A. Ryan, 'Mental handicap and responsibility', in E.F. O'Doherty, and S.D. McGrath (eds), *The Priest and Mental Health* (New York: Alba House, 1963), pp. 190–7; p. 195.

71   *Irish Times*, 24 February 1964.

72   Commission of Inquiry on Mental Illness, p. 99.

73   Ibid., pp. xxix–xxx.

74   E. O'Brien, 'Dublin's mental health needs', *Irish Times*, 16 April 1971.

75   C. Murphy, 'Homosexuals – an oppressed minority?', *Irish Times*, 16 February 1974. See also: V.T. Greene, 'Homosexuality', in V.T. Greene (ed.), *Clinical Notes in Psychiatry* (Dublin: Royal College of Surgeons in Ireland, 1988), pp. 202–8; p. 207.

76   *Official Report of Seanad Éireann*, 10 April 1975. See also: *Irish Times*, 11 April 1975.

77   Ferriter, *Occasions of Sin: Sex and Society in Modern Ireland*, p. 489. In relation to Northern Ireland, see: M. Manning, 'Harassed gays fight for 20th century law', *Community Care*, 30 June 1976.

78   *Cork Examiner*, 14 and 17 June 1983.

79   N. McCafferty, 'Two consenting adults learn that it's an offence over here', *Irish Times*, 12 September 1975. See also: C. Gallagher and D. Conlon, 'Campaigner who started out as 'that wee Bogsider who hangs out with burglars'', *Irish Times*, 29 June 2015.

80   *Irish Times*, 8 March 1977. See also: D.P.B. Norris, 'Booklet on sexuality', *Evening Herald*, 21 April 1977.

81   Senator David Norris, Dublin (interview with the author in Dublin, 9 October 2015).

82   *Irish Times*, 5 August 1977; E. Gillespie, 'Gays reply to the Pope', *Irish Times*, 29 October 1979; D. McCarthy, "Let's celebrate the next generation of Irish people who can marry whomever they love", *Irish Examiner*, 29 May 2015.

83   Ferriter, *Occasions of Sin: Sex and Society in Modern Ireland*, p. 489.

84   B. O'Shea, 'The inconvenient truth around 'lunacy'', *Irish Medical Times*, 7 June 2014.

85   Neither have I come across the use of ECT for this purpose in any of the psychiatric archives I have studied (e.g. Central Criminal Lunatic Asylum, the Richmond District Asylum, or St Brigid's Hospital, Ballinasloe), although I only studied defined sections of these archives for other projects, and without this theme in mind. I am very grateful to the psychiatrists and clinical directors who discussed this matter with me as I prepared this book.

86   For a discussion of the challenges and opportunities in personal narrative study of Irish gay male lives, see: P. Ryan, 'Researching Irish gay male lives: reflections on disclosure and intellectual autobiography in the production of personal narratives', *Qualitative Research*, 6, 2 (May 2006), pp. 151–68.

87   For research from these perspectives in Britain, see: G. Smith, A. Bartlett and M. King, 'Treatments of homosexuality in Britain since the 1950s – an oral history: the experience of patients', *British Medical Journal*, 328, 7437 (21 February 2004), pp. 427–9; M. King, G. Smith and A. Bartlett, 'Treatments of homosexuality in Britain since the 1950s – an oral history: the experience of professionals', *British Medical Journal*, 328, 7437 (21 February 2004), pp. 429–32.

88   Committee on Homosexual Offences and Prostitution. *Report of the Committee on Homosexual Offences and Prostitution* (London: Her Majesty's Stationery Office, 1957), p. 115.

89   D. Norris, *A Kick Against the Pricks: The Autobiography* (London: Transworld Ireland, 2012), p. 116; *Irish Times*, 25 June 1980.

90   Senator David Norris, Dublin (interview with the author in Dublin, 9 October 2015).

91   *Irish Times*, 25 June 1980. See also: Norris, *A Kick Against the Pricks: The Autobiography*, p. 113. In addition, see Norris's account of a complaint upheld by the Broadcasting Complaints Commission regarding Norris's assertion on television in 1974 that he was not 'sick' by virtue of the fact of homosexuality (p. 86); and a very, very, very sad story about an unfortunate psychiatrist in Bavarian history (p. 133).

92   Norris, *A Kick Against the Pricks: The Autobiography*, p. 115.

93   *Irish Times*, 27 June 1980. See also: Norris, *A Kick Against the Pricks: The Autobiography*, p. 117.

94   *Irish Times*, 28 June 1980.

95   Norris, *A Kick Against the Pricks: The Autobiography*, p. 119.

96   Ibid., pp. 121–2.

97   Dickinson, *'Curing Queers': Mental Nurses and Their Patients, 1935–74*, pp. 205, 220.

98   C. Walsh, "Gay people don't have two heads", *Irish Times*, 28 September 1984.

99   R. Gallagher, 'Understanding the homosexual', *The Furrow*, 30, 9 (September 1979), pp. 555–69; p. 567.

100   H.M. Carlson and L.A. Baxter, 'Androgyny, depression, and self-esteem in Irish homosexual and heterosexual males and females', *Sex Roles*, 10, 5–6 (March 1984), pp. 457–67.

101   D.G. Patterson and E.G. O'Gorman, 'Psychosexual study of patients and non-patient homosexual groups', *IRCS Medical Science: Psychology & Psychiatry*, 12, 3–4 (March–April 1984), p. 243.

102   This change had been long awaited by the Irish Gay Rights Movement (*Irish Times*, 28 September 1984).

103   G. Egan, 'Father and son II', in G. O'Brien (ed.), *Coming Out* (Blackrock, County Dublin: Currach Press, 2003). For a perspective on this account, see: E. Collins, 'Back to the Future', *Gay Community News*, February 2004, p. 37.

104   W.T. Fielding, *Sissy Talk* (Dublin: William T. Fielding, 2012), p. 165.

105   K. Holmquist, 'Why are we so intolerant of difference?', *Irish Times*, 20 January 1990.

106   A.W. Clare, 'Homosexuality', *Irish Times*, 9 February 1990.

107   M. McAleese, 'Remarks by Mary McAleese, President of Ireland made at the International Association of Suicide Prevention XXIV Biennial Conference, August 31, 2007, Irish National Events Centre, Killarney, Co. Kerry, Ireland', *Crisis*, 29, 1 (January 2008), pp. 53–5.

108   P. Mayock, A. Bryan, N. Carr and K. Kitching, *Supporting LGBT Lives* (Dublin: Gay and Lesbian Equality Network (GLEN) and BeLonG To Youth Service, 2009). This research was commissioned by GLEN and BeLonG To Youth Service, and funded by the Health Service Executive's National Office for Suicide Prevention.

109   E. McCann , D. Sharek, A. Higgins, F. Sheerin, and M. Glacken, 'Lesbian, gay, bisexual and transgender older people in Ireland: mental health issues', *Aging & Mental Health*, 17, 3 (2013), pp. 358–65.

110   College of Psychiatry of Ireland (Public Education Committee) and Gay and Lesbian Equality Network (GLEN), *Lesbian, Gay & Bisexual Patients: The Issues for Mental Health Practice* (Dublin: College of Psychiatry of Ireland, GLEN, Health Service Executive, 2011), p. 3.

111   Ibid., p. 5.

112   Ibid., pp. 11–16.

113   In relation to psychiatry, see: B. McCormack, J. Tobin, H. Keeley, F. Yacoub, S. MacHale, M. Scully, W. Flannery, A. Ambikapathy, S. Monks, M. McLoughlin, G. Moynihan, R. Plunkett and H. Kennedy, 'Marriage referendum – countdown to polling day', *Irish Times*, 21 May 2015; D. Norris, 'Marriage referendum – countdown to polling day', *Irish Times*, 21 May 2015.

114   E. McCann and D. Sharek, 'Survey of lesbian, gay, bisexual, and transgender people's experiences of mental health services in Ireland', *International Journal of Mental Health Nursing*, 23, 2 (August 2014), pp. 118–27.

115   A. Higgins, L. Doyle, C. Downes, R. Murphy, D. Sharek, J. DeVries, T. Begley, E. McCann, F. Sheerin and S. Smyth, *The LGBTIreland Report: National Study of the Mental Health and Wellbeing of Lesbian, Gay, Bisexual, Transgender and Intersex People in Ireland* (Dublin: GLEN and BeLonG To, 2016), p. 23.

116   T. Drapes, 'On the alleged increase of insanity in Ireland', *Journal of Mental Science*, 40, 171 (1 October 1894), pp. 519–48.

117   Commission of Inquiry on Mental Illness, p. xiii.

118   Ibid., p. xiv.

119   Ibid., p. xv.

120   Anonymous, 'Economist with much to say on how Irish society works', *Irish Times*, 28 May 2016.

121   D. Walsh and B. Walsh, 'Hospitalized psychiatric morbidity in Ireland', *British Journal of Psychiatry*, 113, 499 (June 1967), pp. 675–6.

122   D. Walsh and B. Walsh, 'Some influences on the intercounty variation in Irish psychiatric hospitalization rates', *British Journal of Psychiatry*, 114, 506 (January 1968), pp. 15–20.

123   M.D. Higgins, 'Mental illness', *Irish Times*, 19 March 1968.

124   E.F. Torrey, M. McGuire, A. O'Hare, D. Walsh and M.P. Spellman, 'Endemic psychosis in western Ireland', *American Journal of Psychiatry*, 141, 8 (August 1984), pp. 966–70.

125   D. Walsh, A. O'Hare, B. Blake, J.V. Halpenny and P.F. O'Brien, 'The treated prevalence of mental illness in the Republic of Ireland – the three county case register study', *Psychological Medicine*, 10, 3 (August 1980), pp. 465–70.

126   This paper generated discussion: T.J. Fahy, 'Is psychosis endemic in western Ireland?', *American Journal of Psychiatry*, 142, 8 (August 1985), pp. 998–9; E.F. Torrey, 'Is psychosis endemic in western Ireland?', *American Journal of Psychiatry*, 142, 8 (August 1985), p. 999.

127   M.J. Kelleher, 'Possible differences in mental health needs between rural and urban society in Ireland', *Journal of*

the Irish Medical Association, 68, 14 (26 July 1975), pp. 337–9.

128 C. Keatinge, 'Psychiatric admissions for alcoholism, neuroses and schizophrenia in rural and urban Ireland', *International Journal of Social Psychiatry*, 34, 1 (March 1988), pp. 58–69.

129 C. Keatinge, 'Schizophrenia in rural Ireland: a case of service overutilisation', *International Journal of Social Psychiatry*, 33, 3 (September 1987), pp. 186–94. See also: C. Keatinge, 'Community factors influencing psychiatric hospital utilization in rural and urban Ireland', *Community Mental Health Journal*, 23, 3 (Fall 1987), pp. 192–203.

130 K.S. Kendler, M. McGuire, A.M. Gruenberg, A. O'Hare, M. Spellman and D. Walsh, 'The Roscommon Family Study: I. Methods, diagnosis of probands, and risk of schizophrenia in relatives', *Archives of General Psychiatry*, 50, 7 (July 1993), pp. 527–40.

131 E.F. Torrey, 'The prevalence of schizophrenia in Ireland', *Archives of General Psychiatry*, 51, 7 (July 1994), p. 513.

132 D. Walsh and K.S. Kendler, 'The prevalence of schizophrenia in Ireland', *Archives of General Psychiatry*, 51, 7 (July 1994), pp. 513–15.

133 J. Waddington, H.A. Youssef and A. Kinsella, 'The prevalence of schizophrenia in Ireland: readdressing the enigma', *Archives of General Psychiatry*, 52, 6 (June 1995), p. 509. See also: M.R. Cabot, 'The incidence and prevalence of schizophrenia in the Republic of Ireland', *Social Psychiatry and Psychiatric Epidemiology*, 25, 4 (July 1990), pp. 210–5; H.A. Youssef, A. Kinsella and J.L. Waddington, 'Evidence for geographical variation in the rate of schizophrenia in rural Ireland', *Archives of General Psychiatry*, 48, 3 (March 1991), pp. 254–8; D. Walsh, 'The prevalence of schizophrenia in Ireland: readdressing the enigma', *Archives of General Psychiatry*, 52, 6 (June 1995), p. 509.

134 For a further discussion of this theme, see: Robins, *Fools and Mad: A History of the Insane in Ireland*, pp. 200–4.

135 A. Clare, 'The mad Irish?', in C. Keane (ed.), *Mental Health in Ireland* (Dublin: Gill and Macmillan and Radio Telefís Éireann, 1991), pp. 4–17; pp. 4–6. See also: K. Holmquist, 'Studies show lower rate of schizophrenia', *Irish Times*, 19 October 1990.

136 J. McGrath, S. Saha, D. Chant and J. Welham, 'Schizophrenia: a concise overview of incidence, prevalence, and mortality', *Epidemiologic Reviews*, 30, 1 (1 November 2008), pp. 67–76.

137 N. Sartorius, A. Jablensky, A. Korten, G. Ernberg, M. Anker, J. E. Cooper and R. Day, 'Early manifestations and first-contact incidence of schizophrenia in different cultures: a preliminary report on the initial evaluation phase of the WHO Collaborative Study on determinants of outcome of severe mental disorders', *Psychological Medicine*, 16, 4 (November 1986), pp. 909–28.

138 See, for example: M. Webb, 'What's Irish about psychiatry?', *Irish Journal of Psychological Medicine*, 7, 1 (March 1990), pp. 7–16; pp. 7–8. Other key papers

include: A. O'Hare and D. Walsh, 'The three county schizophrenia study; a study of the prevalence and incidence of schizophrenia and an assessment of its clinical and social outcomes in the Republic of Ireland', in S.A. Mednick, A.E. Baert and B. Phillips Backmann (eds), *Prospective Longitudinal Research, An Empirical Basis for the Primary Prevention of Psychosocial Disorders* (Oxford: Oxford University Press on behalf of the World Health Organisation, 1981), pp. 247–9; B. Blake, J.V. Halpenny, P.F. O'Brien, M. Ní Nualláin, A. O'Hare and D. Walsh, 'The incidence of mental illness in Ireland: patients contacting psychiatric services in three Irish Counties', *Irish Journal of Psychiatry*, 5, 2 (Autumn 1984), p. 23–9; M.N. Ní Nualláin, A. O'Hare and D. Walsh, 'Incidence of schizophrenia in Ireland', *Psychological Medicine*, 17, 4 (November 1987), pp. 943–8; E. Kane, 'Stereotypes and Irish identity: mental illness as a cultural frame', *Studies*, 75, 300 (Winter 1986), pp. 539–51.

139 N. Scheper-Hughes, *Saints Scholars and Schizophrenics: Mental Illness in Rural Ireland (Twentieth Anniversary Edition)* (Berkeley: University of California Press, 2001); pp. 34–6, 39–42.

140 D. Nowlan, 'Death by suppression', *Irish Times*, 4 August 1979; M. Viney, 'Geared for a gale', *Irish Times*, 24 September 1980; N. Scheper-Hughes, 'Reply to 'Ballybran'', *Irish Times*, 21 February 1981; E. Kane, 'Reply to Ballybran', *Irish Times*, 13 April 1981; M. Viney, 'The yank in the corner', *Irish Times*, 6 August 1983; J.S. Bradshaw, 'The yank in the corner', *Irish Times*, 15 August 1983; P. Pye, 'The yank in the corner', *Irish Times*, 15 August 1983; K. Holmquist, 'Studies show lower rate of schizophrenia', *Irish Times*, 19 October 1990. See also: H. Brody, *Inishkillane: Change and Decline in the West of Ireland* (Harmondsworth: Penguin, 1973), pp. 86–108.

141 E. Kane, 'Is rural Ireland blighted?', *Irish Press*, 13 December 1979. See also: Healy, *150 Years of British Psychiatry. Volume II: The Aftermath*, pp. 268–91; p. 286.

142 A.J. Saris, 'An uncertain dominion: Irish psychiatry, methadone, and the treatment of opiate abuse', *Culture, Medicine and Psychiatry*, 32, 2 (June 2008), pp. 259–77; M. D'Arcy, 'The Hospital and the Holy Spirit: Psychotic Subjectivity and Institutional Returns in Dublin', paper delivered at the *Society for Psychological Anthropology*, Boston, MA, 10 April 2015. See also: A.J. Saris, 'Mad kings, proper houses, and an asylum in rural Ireland', *American Anthropologist*, 98, 3, (September 1996), pp. 539–54.

143 D. Walsh, 'The ups and downs of schizophrenia in Ireland', *Irish Journal of Psychiatry*, 13, 2 (Autumn 1992), pp. 12–16; p. 16.

144 Brennan, *Irish Insanity*, p. 117. See also: D. Brennan, 'A theoretical explanation of institution-based mental health care in Ireland', in P.M. Prior (ed.), *Asylums, Mental Health Care and the Irish, 1800–2010* (Dublin: Irish Academic Press, 2012), pp. 287–315.

145 B.D. Kelly, 'Mental health law in Ireland, 1945 to 2001: reformation and renewal', *Medico-Legal Journal*, 76, 2 (June 2008), pp. 65–72.

146 See: B.D. Kelly, 'Mental health law in Ireland, 1821 to 1902: building the asylums', *Medico-Legal Journal*, 76, 1 (March 2008), pp. 19–25; Kelly, *Custody, Care and Criminality: Forensic Psychiatry and Law in 19th Century Ireland*, pp. 64–73.

147 Walsh and Daly, *Mental Illness in Ireland 1750–2002: Reflections on the Rise and Fall of Institutional Care*, p. 100.

148 M. Jennings, 'A glimpse of psychiatric services in the past', *Irish Medical News*, 15–29 December 2008.

149 D. Healy, 'Interview: In conversation with Ivor Browne', *Psychiatric Bulletin*, 16, 1 (January 1992), pp. 1–9.

150 I. Browne, *Music and Madness* (Cork: Atrium/Cork University Press, 2008), pp. 49–51. For perspectives on this book, see: C. Benson, 'An elusive, unorthodox outsider', *Irish Times*, 19 April 2008; B. McCaffrey, 'Book review: *Music and Madness*', *Irish Psychiatrist*, 9, 2 (Summer 2008), pp. 117–18; B. O'Shea, 'Book review: *Music and Madness*', *Irish Psychiatrist*, 9, 2 (Summer 2008), pp. 118–20; B.D. Kelly, 'Book review: *Music and Madness*', *Scope*, 1, 1 (July 2008), pp. 43–4.

151 I. Browne, *The Writings of Ivor Browne – Steps Along the Road: The Evolution of a Slow Learner* (Cork: Atrium/Cork University Press, 2013).

152 J. Michael, *Report on a Study of Professor Ivor Browne's Experiential Psychotherapy Unit for the Committee Considering the Proposed National Trauma Unit (Second Draft)* (Dublin: No Publisher, 1993).

153 I.W. Browne and D. Walsh, *Psychiatric Services for the Dublin Area* (Dublin: I.W. Browne and D. Walsh, 1964); I. Browne, *Development of Psychiatric Services* (Dublin: Dublin Health Authority, 1966); I. Browne, *Development of Community Mental Health Services* (Dublin: Eastern Health Board, 1977), I. Browne, *The Psychiatric Services – Planning for the Future (Some Comments in Relation to Psychiatric Services in the Eastern Health Board)* (Dublin: I. Browne, 1985); I. Browne, *The Psychiatric Services – Planning for the Future (Preliminary Report of the Chief Psychiatrist to Advise the Board on the General Principles Necessary to the Development of a Community Psychiatric Service)* (Dublin: I. Browne, 1985).

154 See Tóibín's introduction to Browne's *Music and Madness* (pp. 1–8).

155 J. Waters, *Beyond Consolation: Or How We Became Too Clever For God … And Our Own Good* (London and New York: Continuum International Publishing Group Ltd., 2010), pp. 11–19. See also: J. Waters, 'Tears for fears: my drugs hell', *Sunday Independent*, 21 March 2010.

156 For these publications, and further references to Browne's academic work, see: Browne, *The Writings of Ivor Browne – Steps Along the Road: The Evolution of a Slow Learner*, pp. ix–x.

157 I. Browne, L. Liaropoulos, D. Lorenzen, T. Losavio, A. Maynard, P. Sakellaropoulos, Y. Tsiantis and G. Katzourakis, *Reform of Public Mental Health Care in Greece* (Brussels: Commission of the European Communities, 1984). See also: D. Healy, 'Interview: In conversation with Ivor Browne', *Psychiatric Bulletin*, 16, 1 (January 1992), pp. 1–9; p. 9.

158 Sahag Marg is a heart-based meditation system, a form of Raja Yoga.

159 See: F. O'Toole, 'Medical body censured Browne but ruled he acted for patient', *Irish Times*, 11 January 1997; Browne, *Music and Madness*, pp. 277–83.

160 Browne, *Music and Madness*, pp. 148–9.

161 I.W. Browne and D. Walsh, *Psychiatric Services for the Dublin Area* (Dublin: I.W. Browne and D. Walsh, 1964).

162 Commission of Inquiry on Mental Illness, p. 149.

163 Study Group on the Development of the Psychiatric Services, *The Psychiatric Services – Planning for the Future*, p. viii.

164 Expert Group on Mental Health Policy, *A Vision for Change*, p. 7.

165 E. F. Torrey, M. McGuire, A. O'Hare, D. Walsh and M.P. Spellman, 'Endemic psychosis in western Ireland', *American Journal of Psychiatry*, 141, 8 (August 1984), pp. 966–70; K.S. Kendler, M. McGuire, A.M. Gruenberg, A. O'Hare, M. Spellman and D. Walsh, 'The Roscommon Family Study: I. Methods, diagnosis of probands, and risk of schizophrenia in relatives', *Archives of General Psychiatry*, 50, 7 (July 1993), pp. 527–40.

166 D. Walsh, 'The lunatic asylums of Ireland, 1825–1839', *Irish Journal of Psychological Medicine*, 25, 4 (December 2008), pp. 151–6; D. Walsh, 'The Ennis District Lunatic Asylum and the Clare Workhouse Lunatic Asylums in 1901', *Irish Journal of Psychological Medicine*, 26, 4 (December 2010), pp. 206–11; D. Walsh, 'Psychiatric deinstitutionalisation in Ireland, 1960–2013', *Irish Journal of Psychological Medicine*, 32, 4 (December 2015), pp. 347–52.

167 D. Walsh, 'The ups and downs of schizophrenia in Ireland', *Irish Journal of Psychiatry*, 13, 2 (Autumn 1992), pp. 12–16.

168 D. Walsh, 'Mental health services in Ireland, 1959–2010' in P.M. Prior (ed.), *Asylums, Mental Health Care and the Irish, 1800–2010* (Dublin: Irish Academic Press, 2012), pp. 74–102. For perspectives on this book, including Walsh's chapter, see: E. O'Sullivan, 'Misery in Ireland's "massive mausoleums of madness"', *Irish Times*, 2 February 2013; M. Finnane, 'Book review: *Asylums, Mental Health Care and the Irish, 1800–2010*', *Bulletin of the History of Medicine*, 87, 2 (Summer 2013), pp. 289–90. See also: B.D. Kelly, 'History of mental health care', *Irish Medical News*, 30 July 2012; Anonymous, 'Monaghan soviet's success', *Books Ireland*, October 2012; R. Fitzpatrick, 'Our shameful asylums', *Irish Examiner*, 7 February 2013; I. Miller, 'Book review: *Asylums, Mental Health Care and the Irish, 1800–2010*', *Social History of Medicine*, 26, 3 (August 2013), pp. 581–3.

169 D. Walsh and A. Daly, *Mental Illness in Ireland 1750–2002: Reflections on the Rise and Fall of Institutional Care*

(Dublin: Health Research Board, 2004). This remarkable book is available to download free of charge from the website of Ireland's Health Research Board (www.hrb.ie). For a perspective on this book, see: T. Bates, 'A brief history of insanity', *Irish Times*, 7 December 2004.

170   D. Walsh, 'Stirrings in psychiatry', *Irish Journal of Psychiatry*, 13, 2 (Autumn 1992), pp. 1–2.

171   D. Walsh, 'Psychiatric illness – the extent of the problem and the response', *Irish Journal of Psychiatry*, 14, 1 (Spring 1993), pp. 1–2.

172   J. Shannon, 'Changing minds in Ireland', *Medical Independent*, 5 August 2010.

173   D. Walsh, 'Schizophrenia', in C. Keane (ed.), *Mental Health in Ireland* (Dublin: Gill and Macmillan and Radio Telefís Éireann, 1991), pp. 31–40.

174   D. Walsh, 'Mental illness in Ireland and its management', in D. McCluskey (ed.), *Health Policy and Practice in Ireland* (Dublin: University College Dublin Press, 2006), pp. 29–43.

175   D. Walsh, 'Private practice and the public good', *Irish Medical Times*, 30 September 2011.

176   D. Walsh, 'Irish College formed for psychiatrists (at last)', *Irish Medical Times*, 23 January 2009; D. Walsh, 'A College for Irish psychiatrists', *Irish Medical Times*, 30 January 2009; D. Walsh, 'College of Psychiatry for Ireland', *Irish Medical Times*, 6 February 2009.

177   D. Healy, 'Interview: In conversation with Tom Lynch', *Psychiatric Bulletin*, 16, 2 (February 1992), pp. 65–72; p. 68. See also: D. Healy, 'Interview: In conversation with Ivor Browne', *Psychiatric Bulletin*, 16, 1 (January 1992), pp. 1–9; p. 5; D. Healy, 'Interview: In conversation with Desmond McGrath', *Psychiatric Bulletin*, 16, 3 (March 1992), pp. 129–37; p. 135.

178   Daly and Walsh, *Activities of Irish Psychiatric Services 2001*, p. 116.

179   The Brothers of St John of God had a long history of assisting the mentally ill in France and elsewhere (Purcell, *A Time for Sowing: The History of St John of God Brothers in Ireland, 1879–1979*, pp. 37–44).

180   Purcell, *A Time for Sowing: The History of St John of God Brothers in Ireland, 1879–1979*, p. 54.

181   Ibid., pp. 82–5; *Irish Times*, 20 April 1950.

182   D. McGrath, 'Current developments in psychiatry', in E.F. O'Doherty, and S.D. McGrath (eds), *The Priest and Mental Health* (New York: Alba House, 1963), pp. 26–31; p. 28. For a background to this volume, see: D. Healy, 'Interview: In conversation with Desmond McGrath', *Psychiatric Bulletin*, 16, 3 (March 1992), pp. 129–37; p. 136.

183   J.P. Ryan, 'The open door system in the mental hospital', *Journal of the Irish Medical Association*, 39, 234 (December 1956), pp. 175–9; J.A. Koltes, 'Mental hospitals with open doors', *American Journal of Psychiatry*, 113, 3 (September 1956), pp. 250–3; Study Group on the Development of the Psychiatric Services, *The Psychiatric Services – Planning for the Future* (Dublin: Stationery Office, 1984), p. 5.

184   D. Healy, 'Interview: In conversation with Desmond McGrath', *Psychiatric Bulletin*, 16, 3 (March 1992), pp. 129–37.

185   Inspector of Mental Hospitals, *Report of the Inspector of Mental Hospitals for the year ending 31st December 1997* (Dublin: Department of Health and Children/The Stationery Office, 1998), pp. 146–7. In relation to Cluain Mhuire, see: Purcell, *A Time for Sowing: The History of St John of God Brothers in Ireland, 1879–1979*, pp. 122–3; D. Healy, 'Interview: In conversation with Desmond McGrath', *Psychiatric Bulletin*, 16, 3 (March 1992), pp. 129–37; p. 134.

186   I am grateful to Dr John Tobin for much of this information.

187   See, for example: Working Party on Services for the Elderly, *The Years Ahead ... A Policy for the Elderly* (Dublin: The Stationery Office, 1988), p. x.

188   J. Tobin, 'International human rights law and mental illness', *Irish Journal of Psychological Medicine*, 24, 1 (March 2007), pp. 31–9.

189   Commission of Inquiry on Mental Illness, *Report of the Commission of Inquiry on Mental Illness* (Dublin: The Stationery Office, 1967), p. xv.

190   D. Healy, 'Interview: In conversation with Tom Lynch', *Psychiatric Bulletin*, 16, 2 (February 1992), pp. 65–72; p. 68.

191   Study Group on the Development of the Psychiatric Services, *The Psychiatric Services – Planning for the Future*.

192   D. Pillay and B.D. Kelly, 'Acute psychiatric units in general hospitals: where are we now?', *Irish Medical Journal*, 102, 5 (May 2009), pp. 137–8.

193   Study Group on the Development of the Psychiatric Services, *The Psychiatric Services – Planning for the Future*, p. 51–2.

194   D. Walsh, 'General hospital psychiatric units in Ireland', *Irish Journal of Psychiatry*, 13, 2 (Autumn 1992), pp. 6–11; p. 8.

195   A. McGennis, 'Psychiatric units in general hospitals – the Irish experience', *Irish Journal of Psychological Medicine*, 9, 2 (November 1992), pp. 129–34; p. 130; P. Finnegan, 'Medicine in Connaught', in J.B. Lyons (ed.), *2000 Years of Irish Medicine* (Dublin: Eireann Healthcare Publications, 1999), pp. 93–6; p. 96.

196   M. O'Beirne and T.J. Fahy, 'The impact of a general hospital psychiatric unit on established patterns of psychiatric care', *Irish Journal of Psychological Medicine*, 5, 2 (September 1988), pp. 85–8.

197   D. Mitchell, *A 'Peculiar' Place: The Adelaide Hospital, Dublin, 1839 to 1989* (Dublin: Blackwater, 1989), p. 167; Healy, *150 Years of British Psychiatry. Volume II: The Aftermath*, pp. 268–91; p. 275; Webb, *Trinity's Psychiatrists: From Serenity of the Soul to Neuroscience*, p. 90.

198   Reynolds, *Grangegorman: Psychiatric Care in Dublin since 1815*, pp. 249–57.

199   Ibid., pp. 267–8.

200 Ibid., p. 295. See also: J. Dunne, 'Outpatient psychiatric clinic: report of two years' work', *Journal of the Irish Medical Association*, 64, 403 (7 January 1971), pp. 7–9.

201 Henry, *Our Lady's Psychiatric Hospital Cork*, pp. 600–1.

202 McDermott, *St Mary's Hospital Castlebar: Serving Mayo Mental Health from 1866*, p. 130.

203 Meehan, *St Luke's Hospital, Clonmel, 1834–1984*, pp. 85–9; p. 85.

204 Midland Health Board, 'The future', in D.A. Murphy (ed.), *Tumbling Walls: The Evolution of a Community Institution over 150 Years* (Portlaoise: Midland Health Board, 1983), pp. 84–93.

205 Healy, *150 Years of British Psychiatry. Volume II: The Aftermath*, pp. 268–91; p. 273.

206 Robins, *Fools and Mad: A History of the Insane in Ireland*, p. 201.

207 Brennan, *Irish Insanity, 1800–2000*, p. 125.

208 A. O'Connor and D. Walsh, *Activities of Irish Psychiatric Hospitals and Units 1988* (Dublin: Health Research Board, 1991), pp. 65–6, 68.

209 A. McGennis, 'Psychiatric units in general hospitals – the Irish experience', *Irish Journal of Psychological Medicine*, 9, 2 (November 1992), pp. 129–34; p. 132.

210 Ibid., p. 129.

211 L. Feeney, A. Kavanagh, B.D. Kelly, M. Mooney, 'Moving to a purpose built acute psychiatric unit on a general hospital site: does the new environment produce change for the better?', *Irish Medical Journal*, 100, 3 (March 2007), pp. 391–3.

212 D. Walsh, 'A revolution in mental care', *Irish Medical Times*, 30 March 2007.

213 A. Daly and D. Walsh, *Activities of Irish Psychiatric Services 2001* (Dublin: The Health Research Board, 2002), p. 116.

214 Health (Mental Services) Act 1981, Preamble.

215 An 'authorised officer' was 'an officer of a health board who is of a class designated by the Minister [for Health] for the purposes of this Act' (Health (Mental Services) Act 1981, Section 3).

216 Ibid., Section 15(2) (subject to Section 15(3)).

217 Ibid., Section 16(1).

218 Ibid., Section 19(3).

219 Ibid., Section 19(5)(b).

220 Ibid., Section 21.

221 Ibid., Section 22.

222 Ibid., Section 23(1).

223 Ibid., Section 23(2).

224 An 'authorised medical practitioner' 'means a registered medical practitioner holding an appointment or providing services as a consultant psychiatrist in a psychiatric centre' (Ibid., Section 3).

225 Ibid., Section 23(3).

226 Ibid., Section 13.

227 Ibid., Section 24.

228 Ibid., Section 19(6).

229 Ibid., Section 24(4).

230 Ibid., Section 26.

231 Ibid., Section 27.

232 Ibid., Section 28.

233 Ibid., Section 29.

234 Ibid., Section 30(2).

235 Ibid., Section 31.

236 Ibid., Section 32(1).

237 Ibid., Section 32(2).

238 Ibid., Part IV.

239 Ibid., Section 33.

240 Ibid., Section 34(2).

241 Ibid., Section 36.

242 Ibid., Section 37(2).

243 Ibid., Section 38(2).

244 Ibid., Section 38(3).

245 Ibid., Section 38(4).

246 Ibid., Section 38(5).

247 Ibid., Section 38(6).

248 Ibid., Section 39(1).

249 Ibid., Section 39(4).

250 Ibid., Section 39(5).

251 Ibid., Section 39(6).

252 Ibid., Section 40(1).

253 Ibid.

254 Ibid., Section 41(5).

255 Ibid., Section 42.

256 Ibid., Section 43.

257 Ibid., Section 44(1).

258 Health Act 1953, Section 4: '(1) Nothing in this Act or any instrument thereunder shall be construed as imposing an obligation on any person to avail himself or any service provided under this Act or to submit himself or any person for whom he is responsible to health examination or treatment. (2) Any person who avails himself of any service provided under this Act shall not be under any obligation to submit himself or any person for whom he is responsible to a health examination or treatment which is contrary to the teaching of his religion.'

259 Health (Mental Services) Act 1981, Section 44(2).

260 Ibid., Section 46(1).

261 Ibid., Part II.

262 Ibid., Section 12.

263 Ibid., Section 45.

264 A. O'Neill, 'Mental committal law leaves individual almost powerless', *Irish Times*, 3 April 1992.

265 K. Boyle, 'The right to information', *Irish Times*, 1 April 1985.

266 *Official Report of Dáil Éireann*, 23 April 1985.

267 Ibid. See also: *Irish Times*, 24 April 1985.

268 F. O'Toole, 'Simply ignoring the will of the people', *Irish Times*, 13 April 1989.

269 J. Dillon, 'Mental Health Act', *Irish Times*, 19 June 1991.

270 L. Keating, 'Psychiatric committal examinations leave system open to abuse', *Irish Times*, 1 January 1992.

271 N. Griffin, 'Psychiatric committal', *Irish Times*, 11 January 1992. See also: N. Fennell, 'Defeat of this Bill insults silent victims', *Irish Times*, 25 May 1992; D.J.

Ward, 'Mental health', *Irish Times*, 12 December 1980; O'Neill, *Irish Mental Health Law*, p. 24.

272 J.J. Wilson, 'Psychiatric committal', *Irish Times*, 17 January 1992.

273 N. Fennell, 'Psychiatric committal', *Irish Times*, 7 February 1992.

274 N. Fennell, 'Defeat of this Bill insults silent victims', *Irish Times*, 25 May 1992; O'Neill, *Irish Mental Health Law*, pp. 24–5.

275 O'Neill, *Irish Mental Health Law*, p. 25.

276 Department of Health, *White Paper: A New Mental Health Act* (Dublin: The Stationery Office, 1995), p. 13.

277 *Irish Times*, 26 August 1994.

278 B.D. Kelly, 'The Irish Mental Health Act 2001', *Psychiatric Bulletin*, 31, 1 (January 2007), pp. 21–4.

279 See: Finnane, *Insanity and the Insane in Post-Famine Ireland*, pp. 178–85; Robins, *Fools and Mad: A History of the Insane in Ireland*, pp. 180–6; Henry, *Our Lady's Psychiatric Hospital Cork*, pp. 87–91, 380–7, 453–79; D. Walsh, 'Brief historical review', *Irish Journal of Psychiatry*, 13, 1 (Spring 1992), pp. 3–20; pp. 14–15; J. McDermott, *St Mary's Hospital Castlebar: Serving Mayo Mental Health from 1866* (Castlebar: Western Health Board, 1999), pp. 67–96; A.J. Sheridan, 'Psychiatric nursing', in J. Robins (ed.), *Nursing and Midwifery in Ireland in the Twentieth Century* (Dublin: An Bord Altranais, 2000), pp. 141–61; A. Sheridan, 'Being a psychiatric nurse in Ireland in the 1950s', in G.M. Fealy (ed.), *Care to Remember: Nursing and Midwifery in Ireland* (Cork: Mercier Press, 2005), pp. 172–84; Commemorative Book Committee, *The History of St Loman's Hospital in Changing Times*, pp. 75–148; Brennan, *Irish Insanity, 1800–2000*, pp. 74–7; O. Walsh, 'Psychiatric nurses and their patients in the nineteenth century: the Irish perspective', in A. Borsay and P. Dale (eds), *Mental Health Nursing: The Working Lives of Paid Carers in the Nineteenth and Twentieth Centuries* (Manchester: Manchester University Press, 2015), pp. 28–53. For a methodological perspective, see: D. Brennan, '"Telling stories about ourselves': historical methodology and the creation of mental health nursing narratives', *Journal of Psychiatric and Mental Health Nursing*, 18, 8 (October 2011), pp. 657–63. In relation to intellectual disability nursing, see: F. Sheerin, 'Mental handicap nursing', in J. Robins (ed.), *Nursing and Midwifery in Ireland in the Twentieth Century* (Dublin: An Bord Altranais, 2000), pp. 163–75; J. Sweeney and D. Mitchell, 'A challenge to nursing: an historical review of intellectual disability nursing in the UK and Ireland', *Journal of Clinical Nursing*, 18, 19 (October 2009), pp. 2754–63.

280 P. Nolan and A. Sheridan, 'In search of the history of Irish psychiatric nursing', *International History of Nursing Journal*, 6, 2 (2001), pp. 35–43.

281 Robins, *Tumbling Walls: The Evolution of a Community Institution over 150 Years*, pp. 9–15; pp. 14–15. Cox, *Negotiating Insanity in the Southeast of Ireland, 1820–1900*, pp. 202–7.

282 Kirkpatrick, *A Note on the History of the Care of the Insane in Ireland up to the End of the Nineteenth Century*, p. 36.

283 P. Nolan, 'Mental health nursing in Great Britain', in H. Freeman and G.E. Berrios (eds), *150 Years of British Psychiatry. Volume II: The Aftermath* (London: Athlone Press, 1996), pp. 171–92; p. 176.

284 Prior, *Madness and Murder: Gender, Crime and Mental Disorder in Nineteenth Century Ireland*, pp. 65–6.

285 Robins, *Fools and Mad: A History of the Insane in Ireland*, p. 181.

286 Bewley, *Madness to Mental Illness: A History of the Royal College of Psychiatrists*, p. 111.

287 M. Arton, 'The Professionalisation of Mental Nursing in Great Britain, 1850–1950' (PhD Thesis, University College London, 1998), p. 126.

288 Henry, *Our Lady's Psychiatric Hospital, Cork*, p. 464.

289 McDermott, *St Mary's Hospital Castlebar: Serving Mayo Mental Health from 1866*, p. 122.

290 Nolan, *150 Years of British Psychiatry. Volume II: The Aftermath*, pp. 176–7. Finegan had a long standing interest in training; see, for example: Anonymous, 'Meeting of the Irish Division', *Journal of Mental Science*, 42, 178 (1 July 1896), pp. 656–60; pp. 658–9. For Finegan's role at the Conference of the Irish Asylums Committee at the Richmond Asylum in 1903, see: Reynolds, *Grangegorman: Psychiatric Care in Dublin since 1815*, p. 203.

291 N. Doheny, 'Psychiatric nurse training', in E. Lonergan (ed.), *St Luke's Hospital, Clonmel, 1834–1984* (Clonmel: South Eastern Health Board, 1984), pp. 105–11.

292 M. Canavan, 'Nurse training', in D.A. Murphy (ed.), *Tumbling Walls: The Evolution of a Community Institution over 150 Years* (Portlaoise: Midland Health Board, 1983), pp. 73–7; p. 73.

293 Reynolds, *Grangegorman: Psychiatric Care in Dublin since 1815*, pp. 189–90.

294 J. Robins, *Nursing and Midwifery in Ireland in the Twentieth Century* (Dublin: An Bord Altranais, 2000), p. 23.

295 Commemorative Book Committee, *The History of St Loman's Hospital in Changing Times*, p. 84. For more on staff-patient ratios (e.g. one male attendant to 17 patients in Sligo), see: Robins, *Fools and Mad: A History of the Insane in Ireland*, p. 181.

296 Canavan, *Tumbling Walls: The Evolution of a Community Institution over 150 Years*, pp. 73–7.

297 Arton, 'The Professionalisation of Mental Nursing in Great Britain, 1850–1950', p. 124.

298 A.J. Sheridan, 'The impact of political transition on psychiatric nursing – a case study of twentieth-century Ireland', *Nursing Inquiry*, 13, 4 (2006), pp. 289–99; p. 293. See also: Robins, *Nursing and Midwifery in Ireland in the Twentieth Century*, pp. 19–20. See also: Henry, *Our Lady's Psychiatric Hospital Cork*, p. 468.

299 P. Nolan, *A History of Mental Health Nursing* (London: Chapman & Hall, 1993), pp. 90, 110.

300 See: D. Healy, 'Interview: In conversation with Desmond McGrath', *Psychiatric Bulletin*, 16, 3 (March 1992), pp. 129–37; p. 136.

301 Robins, *Nursing and Midwifery in Ireland in the Twentieth Century*, p. 36.

302 Meehan, *St Luke's Hospital, Clonmel, 1834–1984*, pp. 85–9; p. 85. Other centres duly followed suit; e.g. Castlebar (McDermott, *St Mary's Hospital Castlebar: Serving Mayo Mental Health from 1866*, pp. 110, 156–8).

303 Commission of Inquiry on Mental Illness, p. xxxiii.

304 Ibid., pp. xxxiii–xxxiv.

305 Department of Health, *Psychiatric Nursing Services of Health Boards: Report of Working Party* (Dublin: The Stationery Office, 1972), p. 10.

306 Ibid., p. 11.

307 Ibid., pp. 11–12.

308 Ibid., p. 12.

309 A.J. Sheridan, 'The impact of political transition on psychiatric nursing – a case study of twentieth-century Ireland', *Nursing Inquiry*, 13, 4 (2006), pp. 289–99; p. 295.

310 Robins, *Nursing and Midwifery in Ireland in the Twentieth Century*, p. 38.

311 A.J. Sheridan, 'Psychiatric nursing', in J. Robins (ed.), *Nursing and Midwifery in Ireland in the Twentieth Century* (Dublin: An Bord Altranais, 2000), pp. 141–61.

312 D. Healy, 'Interview: In conversation with Tom Lynch', *Psychiatric Bulletin*, 16, 2 (February 1992), pp. 65–72; p. 72. See also: D. Healy, 'Interview: In conversation with Desmond McGrath', *Psychiatric Bulletin*, 16, 3 (March 1992), pp. 129–37; pp. 136–7.

313 Study Group on the Development of the Psychiatric Services, *The Psychiatric Services – Planning for the Future*.

314 South Eastern Health Board Sub-Committee, *Psychiatric Services* (Kilkenny: South Eastern Health Board, 1982), p. 2.

315 Ibid., p. 5.

316 Study Group on the Development of the Psychiatric Services, *The Psychiatric Services – Planning for the Future*, p. xi.

317 T. Crowley, O. Barry, M. Young, M. Shiel, R. Meyer Bridgers, C. McNulty, D. Boylan, C. Wade, J. Hynes, T. Brady, P. Reid and R. Kelly, 'Community care', *Irish Times*, 7 May 1986; O. Barry, 'Planning for the Future', *Irish Press*, 8 May 1985.

318 *Irish Press*, 6 March 1985; *Irish Times*, 6 March 1985.

319 Study Group on the Development of the Psychiatric Services, *The Psychiatric Services – Planning for the Future*, pp. xi–xii.

320 J. O'Boyle, 'Psychiatric services for the adult deaf', in Study Group on the Development of the Psychiatric Services (ed.), *The Psychiatric Services – Planning for the Future* (Dublin: Stationery Office, 1984), pp. 154–8.

321 Study Group on the Development of the Psychiatric Services, *The Psychiatric Services – Planning for the Future*, p. 21.

322 *Irish Press*, 6 March 1985; *Irish Times*, 6 March 1985.

323 O. Barry, 'Planning for the Future', *Irish Press*, 8 May 1985; J. Raftery, 'Mental health policy in Ireland: learning from the UK?', *Administration*, 35, 1 (1987), pp. 38–46; S. Butler, 'The Psychiatric Services: Planning for the Future – a critique', *Administration*, 35, 1 (1987), pp. 47–68.

324 D. Nowlan, 'The New Psychiatry, 1 – Releasing Grangegorman's 'lifers'', *Irish Times*, 1 July 1985; D. Nowlan, 'The New Psychiatry, 2 – Making the funny farm more fun', *Irish Times*, 2 July 1985; J.T. McNulty, 'The new psychiatry', *Irish Times*, 25 July 1985.

325 M. Leland, 'Doctor attacks psychiatric care', *Irish Times*, 13 May 1985.

326 P. O'Mahony, 'A 'blinkered' look at mental illness', *Irish Times*, 22 July 1985.

327 M. Maher, 'Mental health report rejected', *Irish Times*, 20 August 1985.

328 *Irish Times*, 23 October 1987.

329 *Irish Times*, 18 October 1985.

330 M. Maher, 'Simon warns on mental care move', *Irish Times*, 6 December 1985.

331 D. Nowlan, 'Court injunction curbs debate on psychiatry report', *Irish Times*, 30 October 1985; M. Maher, 'Turning our psychiatric patients out on the street', *Irish Times*, 6 November 1985.

332 E.F. Torrey, *American Psychosis: How the Federal Government Destroyed the Mental Illness Treatment System* (Oxford and New York: Oxford University Press, 2013).

333 D. Nowlan, 'Plans for psychiatric changes get backing', *Irish Times*, 16 June 1986.

334 Simon Community (ed.), *Institutions: Safety Belts or Strait-Jackets?* (Dublin: Simon Community, 1985).

335 M. Corry, 'Warehousing human problems', in Simon Community (ed.), *Institutions: Safety Belts or Strait-Jackets?* (Dublin: Simon Community, 1985), pp. 4–7.

336 P. Murphy, 'A place of one's own', in Simon Community (ed.), *Institutions: Safety Belts or Strait-Jackets?* (Dublin: Simon Community, 1985), pp. 11–16.

337 P. McLoone, 'Towards community care', in Simon Community (ed.), *Institutions: Safety Belts or Strait-Jackets?* (Dublin: Simon Community, 1985), pp. 8–10.

338 D. Hogan, 'Desmond says 2,000 patients should not be in hospital', *Irish Times*, 26 April, 1986.

339 *Irish Press*, 25 April 1987.

340 *Irish Times*, 9 April 1988.

341 K. Holmquist, 'Prisons bear cost of fewer psychiatric beds', *Irish Times*, 22 February 1990; P.J. Brady, 'Psychiatric service', *Irish Times*, 14 May 1990.

342 K. McGrath, 'Killings could shake belief in community-based services', *Irish Times*, 8 March 1997.

343 B.D. Kelly, 'Mental health policy in Ireland, 1984–2004: theory, overview and future directions', *Irish Journal of Psychological Medicine*, 21, 2 (June 2004), pp. 61–8.

344 Walsh, *Health Policy and Practice in Ireland*, p. 40.

345 Mental Health Commission, *Mental Health Commission Annual Report 2002* (Dublin: Mental Health Commission, 2003), p. 5.

346 G. Swanwick and B. Lawlor, 'Services for dementia sufferers and their carers: Implications for future development', in A.L. Leahy and M.M. Wiley (eds), *The Irish Health System In The 21st Century* (Dublin: Oak Tree Press, 1998), pp. 199–220.

347 A. Daly and D. Walsh, *Activities of Irish Psychiatric Services 2001* (Dublin: The Health Research Board, 2002), p. 2.

348 Ibid.

349 Ibid., p. 124.

350 Ibid., p. 116.

351 Mental Health Commission, *Mental Health Commission Annual Report 2002*, p. 22.

352 F. Keogh, A. Roche and D. Walsh, *"We Have No Beds ..." An Enquiry into the Availability and Use of Acute Psychiatric Beds in the Eastern Health Board Region* (Dublin: Health Research Board, 1999); V. O'Keane, A. Jeffers, E. Moloney and S. Barry, *"The Stark Facts" Irish Psychiatric Association Survey of Psychiatric Services in Ireland: A Regional Comparison of Clinical Resources and Affluence, and Specialist Services* (Dublin: The Irish Psychiatric Association, 2003).

353 Irish College of Psychiatrists, *Position Statement on Psychiatric Services for Adolescents* (Dublin: Irish College of Psychiatrists, 2002).

354 Swanwick and Lawlor, *The Irish Health System In The 21st Century*, pp. 199–220.

355 C. O'Neill, H. Sinclair, A. Kelly and H. Kennedy, 'Interaction of forensic and general psychiatric services in Ireland: learning the lessons or repeating the mistakes?', *Irish Journal of Psychological Medicine*, 19, 2 (June 2002), pp. 48–54; S. Linehan, D. Duffy, H. O'Neill, C. O'Neill and H.G. Kennedy, 'Irish travellers and forensic mental health', *Irish Journal of Psychological Medicine*, 19, 3 (September 2002), pp. 76–9.

356 L. Feeney, B.D. Kelly, P. Whitty and E. O'Callaghan, 'Mental illness in migrants: diagnostic and therapeutic challenges', *Irish Journal of Psychological Medicine*, 19, 1 (March 2002), pp. 29–31.

357 K. McKeon, *Mentally Ill and Homeless in Ireland: Facing the Reality, Finding Solutions* (Dublin: Disability Federation of Ireland, 1999); Amnesty International (Irish Section), *Mental Illness* (Dublin: Amnesty International (Irish Section), 2003).

358 C. O'Neill, H. Sinclair, A. Kelly and H. Kennedy, 'Interaction of forensic and general psychiatric services in Ireland: learning the lessons or repeating the mistakes?', *Irish Journal of Psychological Medicine*, 19, 2 (June 2002), pp. 48–54.

359 S. Linehan, D. Duffy, H. O'Neill, C. O'Neill and H.G. Kennedy, 'Irish travellers and forensic mental health', *Irish Journal of Psychological Medicine*, 19, 3 (September 2002), pp. 76–9.

360 Study Group on the Development of the Psychiatric Services, *The Psychiatric Services – Planning for the Future*, p. iii.

361 C. Newman, 'Delayed report on mental hospitals expected', *Irish Times*, 27 February 1992.

362 Expert Group on Mental Health Policy, *A Vision for Change*.

363 A. Crane, 'Radio psychiatrist who quizzed the famous', *Financial Times*, 31 October 2007.

364 *Irish Times*, 3 November 2007.

365 C. Richmond, 'Obituary: Anthony Clare', *Guardian*, 31 October 2007.

366 Webb, *Trinity's Psychiatrists: From Serenity of the Soul to Neuroscience*, pp. 120–3.

367 Richmond, 'Obituary: Anthony Clare', *Guardian*, 31 October 2007.

368 A.W. Clare, 'Diazepam, alcohol, and barbiturate abuse', *British Medical Journal*, 4, 5783 (6 November 1971), p. 340.

369 R.M. Murray, 'Obituary: Professor Anthony Clare', *Psychiatric Bulletin*, 32, 3 (1 March 2008), pp. 118–19.

370 Webb, *Trinity's Psychiatrists: From Serenity of the Soul to Neuroscience*, p. 121.

371 A. Clare, *Psychiatry in Dissent* (London: Tavistock Publications, 1976).

372 For some of Clare's later thoughts on this theme, see: A.W. Clare, 'Psychiatry's future', *Journal of Mental Health*, 8, 2 (1999), pp. 109–11.

373 S. Wessely, 'Ten books', *British Journal of Psychiatry*, 181, 1 (1 July 2002), pp. 81–4. See also: Richmond, 'Obituary: Anthony Clare', *Guardian*, 31 October 2007; J. Holmes, 'Ten books', *British Journal of Psychiatry*, 179, 5 (1 November 2001), pp. 468–71.

374 *Irish Times*, 3 November 2007.

375 A.W. Clare, '"The other half of medicine" and St Bartholomew's Hospital', *British Journal of Psychiatry*, 146, 2 (1 February 1985), pp. 120–6.

376 *Irish Times*, 3 November 2007.

377 A. Clare, *In the Psychiatrist's Chair* (London: Mandarin, 1993). See also: A. Clare, *In the Psychiatrist's Chair II* (London: Mandarin, 1996); A. Clare, *In the Psychiatrist's Chair III* (London: Sinclair-Stevenson Ltd., 1998).

378 A.W. Clare with S. Thompson, *Let's Talk About Me* (London: BBC Books, 1981). See also: C. Byrne, 'Warm tributes to man who changed face of psychiatry', *Irish Independent*, 31 October 2007.

379 J. Lucey, 'Dr Anthony Clare remembered', *Irish Medical Times*, 16 November 2007.

380 Webb, *Trinity's Psychiatrists: From Serenity of the Soul to Neuroscience*, p. 123.

381 S. Milligan and A. Clare, *Depression and How to Survive It* (London: Arrow Books, 1994); A. Clare, *On Men: Masculinity in Crisis* (London: Arrow Books/Random House Group, 2000).

382 *Medicine Weekly*, 19 March 2008.

383 Richmond, 'Obituary: Anthony Clare', *Guardian*, 31 October 2007.

384 *Irish Times*, 3 November 2007.

385   S. Cody, 'Anthony Clare', *Guardian*, 31 October 2007. See also: *Irish Times*, 3 November 2007.

386   C. Byrne, 'Warm tributes to man who changed face of psychiatry', *Irish Independent*, 31 October 2007; J. McEnroe, 'Tributes for doctor who "demystified psychiatry"', *Irish Examiner*, 31 October 2007.

387   P. Casey, 'Anthony Clare', *Guardian*, 31 October 2007; P. Casey, 'Farewell to a dear friend and kind mentor', *Irish Independent*, 31 October 2007; A. Crane, 'Radio psychiatrist who quizzed the famous', *Financial Times*, 31 October 2007; M. Houston, 'Prof Anthony Clare dies unexpectedly in Paris', *Irish Times*, 30 October 2007; J. Lucey, 'Dr Anthony Clare remembered', *Irish Medical Times*, 16 November 2007; R.M. Murray, 'Obituary: Professor Anthony Clare', *Psychiatric Bulletin*, 32, 3 (1 March 2008), pp. 118–19. See also: *Medicine Weekly*, 7 November 2007. For a particular example of Clare's collegial supportiveness and sense of justice, see: Browne, *Music and Madness*, pp. 282–3.

388   B.D. Kelly and L. Feeney, 'Psychiatry: no longer in dissent?', *Psychiatric Bulletin*, 30, 9 (1 September 2006), pp. 344–5.

389   A.W. Clare, Correspondence with the author (BK), 7 September 2005 (author's own collection).

390   A.W. Clare, Correspondence with the author (BK), 1 September 2006 (author's own collection).

391   R.M. Murray, 'Obituary: Professor Anthony Clare', *Psychiatric Bulletin*, 32, 3 (1 March 2008), pp. 118–19; p. 118.

392   D. Walsh, 'Brief historical review', *Irish Journal of Psychiatry*, 13, 1 (Spring 1992), pp. 3–20; p. 12.

393   United Nations, *Principles for the Protection of Persons with Mental Illness and the Improvement of Mental Health Care* (New York: United Nations, Secretariat Centre For Human Rights, 1991).

394   B.D. Kelly, 'Schizophrenia, mental health legislation and human rights', *Hospital Doctor of Ireland*, 21, 4 (May 2015), pp. 25–32.

395   Division of Mental Health and Prevention of Substance Abuse (World Health Organisation), *Mental Health Care Law: Ten Basic Principles* (Geneva: World Health Organisation, 1996).

396   Division of Mental Health and Prevention of Substance Abuse (World Health Organisation), *Guidelines for the Promotion of Human Rights of Persons with Mental Disorders* (Geneva: World Health Organisation, 1996).

397   World Health Organisation, *The World Health Report 2001. Mental Health: New Understanding, New Hope* (Geneva: World Health Organisation, 2001).

398   M.L. Perlin, A.S. Kanter, M.P. Treuthart, E. Szeli, and K. Gledhill, *International Human Rights and Comparative Mental Disability Law* (Durham, NC: Carolina Academic Press, 2006), pp. 891–4.

399   World Health Organisation, *WHO Resource Book on Mental Health, Human Rights and Legislation* (Geneva: World Health Organization, 2005). In relation to Ireland in particular, see: B.D. Kelly, 'Mental health legislation

and human rights in England, Wales and the Republic of Ireland', *International Journal of Law and Psychiatry*, 34, 6 (November–December 2011), pp. 439–54.

400   Council of Europe, *European Convention on Human Rights (Convention for the Protection of Human Rights and Fundamental Freedoms)* (Strasbourg: Council of Europe, 1950), preamble.

401   Ibid., Article 5(1).

402   Ibid., Article 5(4)

403   For example: *Winterwerp v Netherlands* (1979) 2 EHRR 387; *X v UK* (1981) 4 EHRR 188; *HL v UK (Bournewood)* (2004) 40 EHRR 761.

404   B.D. Kelly, 'Human rights in psychiatric practice: an overview for clinicians', *BJPsych Advances*, 21, 1 (January 2015), pp. 54–62.

405   P. Bartlett, O. Lewis and O. Thorold, *Mental Disability and the European Convention on Human Rights (International Studies in Human Rights, Volume 90)* (Leiden/Boston: Martinus Nijhoff Publishers, 2007), p. 1.

406   M.L. Perlin, A.S. Kanter, M.P. Treuthart, E. Szeli, and K. Gledhill, *International Human Rights and Comparative Mental Disability Law* (Durham, NC: Carolina Academic Press, 2006); M.L. Perlin, A.S. Kanter, M.P. Treuthart, E. Szeli, and K. Gledhill, *International Human Rights and Comparative Mental Disability Law: Documents Supplement* (Durham, NC: Carolina Academic Press, 2006).

407   Law Reform Committee, *Mental Health: The Case for Reform* (Dublin: The Law Society, 1999), p. 6.

408   Department of Health, *White Paper: A New Mental Health Act* (Dublin: The Stationery Office, 1995), p. 13.

409   Ibid., p. 15.

410   *Croke v Smith* [1994] 3 IR 529; *Croke v Smith (No. 2)* [1998] 1 IR 101; *Croke v Ireland* (2000) ECHR 680.

411   Health and Consumer Protectorate Director-General, *Improving the Mental Health of the Population: Towards a Strategy on Mental Health for the European Union* (Brussels: European Commission 2005).

412   B.D. Kelly, 'The emerging mental health strategy of the European Union: a multi-level work-in-progress', *Health Policy*, 85, 1 (January 2008), pp. 60–70.

413   European Union, *European Pact for Mental Health and Well-being* (Brussels: European Union, 2008).

414   T. Fahy, 'Obituary: Thomas Lynch', *Psychiatric Bulletin*, 29, 11 (November 2005), p. 438.

415   D. Healy, 'Interview: In conversation with Tom Lynch', *Psychiatric Bulletin*, 16, 2 (February 1992), pp. 65–72; p. 68.

416   D. Healy, 'Interview: In conversation with Desmond McGrath', *Psychiatric Bulletin*, 16, 3 (March 1992), pp. 129–37; p. 135.

417   D. Nowlan, 'Ireland's most successful Minister for Health', *Irish Times*, 18 November 1974.

418   On 16 November 1974, President Erskine Hamilton Childers collapsed (after delivering an emotional 20 minute speech about the overuse of medication) at the

first annual dinner of the Irish Division of the Royal College of Psychiatrists in the Royal College of Physicians in Dublin. He had suffered a myocardial infarction (heart attack) and, despite treatment at the Mater Misericordiae Hospital, died some hours later (E. Shanahan, 'President collapses after speech at medical event', *Irish Times*, 18 November 1974).

419 Healy, 'Interview: In conversation with Tom Lynch', *Psychiatric Bulletin*, 16, 2 (February 1992), pp. 65–72; p. 65.

420 T.J. Fahy, M.H. Irving and P. Millac, 'Severe head injuries: a six-year follow-up', *Lancet*, 290, 7514 (2 September 1967), pp. 475–9; T.J. Fahy, 'Is psychosis endemic in western Ireland?', American Journal of Psychiatry, 142, 8 (August 1985), pp. 998-9; D. O'Rourke, T.J. Fahy and P. Prescott, 'The Galway Study of Panic Disorder, IV: Temporal stability of diagnosis by present state examination test-retest', *British Journal of Psychiatry*, 169, 1 (July 1996), pp. 98–100; L. Conlon, T.J. Fahy and R. Conroy, 'PTSD in ambulant RTA victims: a randomized controlled trial of debriefing', *Journal of Psychosomatic Research*, 46, 1 (January 1999), pp. 37–44; T.J. Fahy, L. Mannion, M. Leonard and P. Prescott, 'Can suicides be identified from case records? A case control study using blind rating', *Archives of Suicide Research*, 8, 3 (2004), pp. 263–9.

421 T.J. Fahy, S. Brandon and R.F. Garside, 'Clinical syndromes in a sample of depressed patients', *Proceedings of the Royal Society of Medicine*, 62, 4 (April 1969), pp. 331–5.

422 I am very grateful to Professor Thomas Fahy for this information.

423 L. Emsell, A. Leemans, C. Langan, W. Van Hecke, G.J. Barker, P. McCarthy, B. Jeurissen, J. Sijbers, S. Sunaert, D.M. Cannon and C. McDonald, 'Limbic and callosal white matter changes in euthymic bipolar I disorder: an advanced diffusion MRI tractography study', *Biological Psychiatry*, 73, 2 (January 2013), pp. 194–201; M. Ahmed, D.M. Cannon, C. Scanlon, L. Holleran, H. Schmidt, J. McFarland, C. Langan, P. McCarthy, G.J. Barker, B. Hallahan and C. McDonald, 'Progressive brain atrophy and cortical thinning in schizophrenia after commencing clozapine treatment', *Neuropsychopharmacology*, 40, 10 (September 2015), pp. 2409–17.

424 Anonymous, 'Obituary: Dr Robert A. McCarthy', *Irish Medical Journal*, 107, 2 (February 2014), p. 62.

425 Anonymous, 'Psychiatrist who revolutionised care of mentally ill', *Irish Times*, 28 December 2013.

426 Reynolds, *Grangegorman: Psychiatric Care in Dublin since 1815*, p. 293. See also: Commemorative Book Committee, *The History of St Loman's Hospital in Changing Times*, pp. 240–3.

427 Henry, *Our Lady's Psychiatric Hospital Cork*, pp. 598–604.

428 *Irish Times*, 17 June 1966.

429 R.J. Daly, 'Samuel Pepys and post-traumatic stress disorder', *British Journal of Psychiatry*, 143, 1 (July 1983), pp. 64–8.

430 I.P. Burges Watson, L. Hoffman and G.V. Wilson, 'The neuropsychiatry of post-traumatic stress disorder', *British Journal of Psychiatry*, 152, 2 (February 1988), pp. 164–73.

431 M. Huckerby, 'Lasting injury to N.I. "hooding" victims', *Irish Times*, 9 July 1973; D. Musgrave, 'Drastic effects of NI torture methods described in survey', *Irish Times*, 13 May 1976.

432 M. Cowley, 'Torture hearing at Strasbourg resumes', *Irish Times*, 27 November 1973; M. Cowley, 'Rights Commission may visit North', *Irish Times*, 30 November 1973. See also: *Irish Times*, 11 December 1985. See: R.J. Daly, 'Compensation and rehabilitation of victims of torture', *Danish Medical Bulletin*, 27, 5 (November 1980), pp. 245–8.

433 *Irish Times*, 23 September 1981.

434 *Irish Times*, 14 August 1980.

435 N. Kiely, 'Psychiatrist accuses doctors of apathy in opposing torture', *Irish Times*, 17 October 1980.

436 M. Leland, "Why do I feel so awful when I should be feeling so glad", *Irish Times*, 22 February 1980.

437 E. Gillespie, 'Bursting with concern and tension', *Irish Times*, 15 September 1981.

438 E. Gillespie, 'No funds – no care?', *Irish Times*, 17 September 1981. See also: R.J. Daly, 'Community psychiatry and the National Institute of Mental Health', *Irish Journal of Psychological Medicine*, 7, 1 (March 1990), p. 5.

439 R.J. Daly and F.J. Kane, 'Two severe reactions to benzodiazepine compounds', *American Journal of Psychiatry*, 122, 5 (November 1965), pp. 577–8.

440 F.J. Kane, R.J. Daly, J. Ewing and M. Keeler, 'Mood and behavioural changes with progestational agents', *British Journal of Psychiatry*, 113, 496 (March 1967), pp. 265–8.

441 R.J. Daly, R. Aitken and S.V. Rosenthal, 'Flying phobia: phenomenological study', *Proceedings of the Royal Society of Medicine*, 63, 9 (September 1970), pp. 878–82.

442 *Irish Times*, 27 April 1994.

443 *Irish Times*, 4 March 1994, 27 April 1994; A. Cahill, 'The lull between war and peace', *Irish Times*, 14 June 1994.

444 Daly's other research outputs included papers in a variety of high impact journals; e.g. R.J. Daly, P.F. Duggan, P.J. Bracken, H.J. Doonan and N.J. Kelleher, 'Plasma levels of beta-endorphin in depressed patients with and without pain', *British Journal of Psychiatry*, 150, 2 (February 1987), pp. 224–7.

445 B. O'Shea and J. Falvey, *A Textbook of Psychological Medicine for the Irish Student* (Dublin: Eastern Health Board, 1985).

446 B. O'Shea (ed.), A *Textbook of Psychological Medicine: An Irish Perspective (Fourth Edition)* (Dublin: Eireann Healthcare Publications, 2002).

447 B. O'Shea (ed.), *Textbook of Psychological Medicine (Fifth Edition)* (Dublin: College of Psychiatry of Ireland, 2010).

448 Nolan, *Caring for the Nation: A History of the Mater Misericordiae University Hospital*, pp. 127–8.

449 I am very grateful to Professor Kevin Malone for this information.

450 Browne, *Music and Madness*, p. 141.

451 D. Nowlan, 'New Bureau to supervise all health education', *Irish Times*, 18 February 1975.

452 D. Nowlan, 'Addicts-to-be?', *Irish Times*, 19 December 1979.

453 D. Nowlan, 'Psychiatrists search for a better understanding of depression', *Irish Times*, 15 April 1974; J. Sheehan, M. Ryan, J. McKay, N. Walsh and D. O'Keeffe, 'Pain clinic attenders: an audit', *Irish Medical Journal*, 87, 2 (March–April 1994), pp. 52–3.

454 J. Cooney, 'Better aid needed for pregnant girls', *Irish Times*, 3 May 1975; L. Redmond, 'Abortion: not always the easiest way out', *Irish Times*, 19 April 1979.

455 D. Nowlan, 'Many doctors miss mental illness signs', *Irish Times*, 3 April 1976.

456 D. Nowlan, 'New psychiatric career structure proposed', *Irish Times*, 31 March 1977.

457 D. Nowlan, 'Updating sessions for doctors', *Irish Times*, 9 September 1977.

458 K. Holmquist, 'Psychiatry's role under scrutiny', *Irish Times*, 24 September 1988.

459 P.E. Garfinkel, D.M. Garner, J. Rose, P.L. Darby, J.S. Brandes, J. O'Hanlon and N. Walsh, 'A comparison of characteristics in the families of patients with anorexia nervosa and normal controls', *Psychological Medicine*, 13, 4 (November 1983), pp. 821–8.

460 K. Healy, R.M. Conroy and N. Walsh, 'The prevalence of binge-eating and bulimia in 1063 college students', *Journal of Psychiatric Research*, 19, 2–3 (1985), pp. 161–6.

461 B. Farragher and N. Walsh, 'Joint care admissions to a psychiatric unit: a prospective analysis', *General Hospital Psychiatry*, 20, 2 (March 1998), pp. 73–7.

462 T. Brugha, R. Conroy, N. Walsh, W. Delaney, J. O'Hanlon, E. Dondero, L. Daly, N. Hickey and G. Bourke, 'Social networks, attachments and support in minor affective disorders', *British Journal of Psychiatry*, 141, 3 (September 1982), pp. 249–55.

463 E. Donohoe, N. Walsh and J.A. Tracey, 'Pack-size legislation reduces severity of paracetamol overdoses in Ireland', *Irish Journal of Medical Science*, 175, 3 (July–September 2006), pp. 40–2.

464 D. Sloan, S. Browne, D. Meagher, A. Lane, C. Larkin, P. Casey, N. Walsh and E. O'Callaghan, 'Attitudes toward psychiatry among Irish final year medical students', *European Psychiatry*, 11, 8 (1996), pp. 407–11.

465 J. Sheehan, J. McKay, M. Ryan, N. Walsh and D. O'Keeffe, 'What cost chronic pain?', *Irish Medical Journal*, 89, 6 (November–December 1996), pp. 218–19.

466 M. Garland, D. Hickey, A. Corvin, J. Golden, P. Fitzpatrick, S. Cunningham and N. Walsh, 'Total serum cholesterol in relation to psychological correlates in parasuicide', *British Journal of Psychiatry*, 177, 1 (July 2000), pp. 77–83.

467 M.R. Garland, E. Lavelle, D. Doherty, L. Golden-Mason, P. Fitzpatrick, A. Hill, N. Walsh and C. O'Farrelly, 'Cortisol does not mediate the suppressive effects of psychiatric morbidity on natural killer cell activity: a cross-sectional study of patients with early breast cancer', *Psychological Medicine*, 34, 3 (April 2004), pp. 481–90.

468 M. Garland, D. Doherty, L. Golden-Mason, P. Fitzpatrick, N. Walsh and C. O'Farrelly, 'Stress-related hormonal suppression of natural killer activity does not show menstrual cycle variations: implications for timing of surgery for breast cancer', *Anticancer Research*, 23, 3B (May–June 2003), pp. 2531–5.

469 R. Cullivan, J. Crown and N. Walsh, 'The use of psychotropic medication in patients referred to a psycho-oncology service', *Psycho-Oncology*, 7, 4 (July–August 1998), pp. 301–6.

470 R. Murray and M. Cannon, 'Obituary: Professor Eadbhard O'Callaghan', *Psychiatric Bulletin*, 36, 5 (May 2012), pp. 198–9.

471 E. O'Callaghan, T. Gibson, H.A. Colohan, P. Buckley, D.G. Walshe, C. Larkin and J.L. Waddington, 'Risk of schizophrenia in adults born after obstetric complications and their association with early onset of illness: a controlled study', *British Medical Journal*, 305, 6864 (21 November 1992), pp. 1256–9.

472 E. O'Callaghan, P. Sham, N. Takei, G. Glover and R.M. Murray, 'Schizophrenia after prenatal exposure to 1957 A2 influenza epidemic', *Lancet*, 337, 8752 (25 May 1991), pp. 1248–50.

473 P. Murphy, 'Professor Eadbhard O'Callaghan, MD FRCPI, FRCPsych (1957–2011)', *The Consultant*, Autumn 2011, p. 88.

474 For example: B.D. Kelly, L. Feeney, E. O'Callaghan, R. Browne, M. Byrne, N. Mulryan, A. Scully, M. Morris, A. Kinsella, N. Takei, T. McNeil, D. Walsh and C. Larkin, 'Obstetric adversity and age at first presentation with schizophrenia: evidence of a dose-response relationship', *American Journal of Psychiatry*, 161, 5 (May 2004), pp. 920–2.

475 S. Hill, N. Turner, S. Barry and E. O'Callaghan, 'Client satisfaction among outpatients attending an Irish community mental health service', *Irish Journal of Psychological Medicine*, 26, 3 (September 2009), pp. 127–30.

476 Anonymous, 'UCD Newman professor and psychiatry leader', *Irish Times*, 2 July 2011.

477 B. O'Donoghue, J. Lyne, L. Renwick, K. Madigan, A. Kinsella, M. Clarke, N. Turner and E. O'Callaghan, 'A descriptive study of "non-cases" and referral rates to an early intervention for psychosis service', *Early Intervention in Psychiatry*, 6, 3 (August 2012), pp. 276–82.

478 Webb, *Trinity's Psychiatrists: From Serenity of the Soul to Neuroscience*.

479 J. Wallace, 'Doctor Maurice O'Connor Drury, Wittgenstein's pupil', *Irish Journal of Psychological Medicine*, 17, 2 (1 June 2000), pp. 67–8.

480 Webb, *Trinity's Psychiatrists: From Serenity of the Soul to Neuroscience*, pp. 103–6. See also: Browne, *Music and Madness*, pp. 141–2.

481 M.E. Martin, 'Puerperal mental illness; a follow-up study of 75 cases', *British Medical Journal*, 2, 5099 (27 September 1958), p. 773–7; M. Webb, 'Obituary: Mary Elizabeth Martin', *Psychiatric Bulletin*, 33, 5, (May 2009), p. 199.

482 G.E. Mullett, 'Schizophrenia today', in K. O'Sullivan (ed.), *All in the Mind: Approaches to Mental Health* (Dublin: Gill and Macmillan, 1986), pp. 27–33.

483 See also: M. Webb, 'Who becomes ill and why', in K. O'Sullivan (ed.), *All in the Mind: Approaches to Mental Health* (Dublin: Gill and Macmillan, 1986), pp. 1–10.

484 Coakley, *Medicine in Trinity College Dublin: An Illustrated History*, p. 267. See, for example: A.K. Merikangas, R. Segurado, P. Cormican, E.A. Heron, R.J. Anney, S. Moore, E. Kelleher, A. Hargreaves, H. Anderson-Schmidt, M. Gill, L. Gallagher and A. Corvin, 'The phenotypic manifestations of rare CNVs in schizophrenia', *Schizophrenia Research*, 158, 1–3 (September 2014), pp. 255–60.

485 Coakley, *Medicine in Trinity College Dublin: An Illustrated History*, p. 267.

486 Webb, *Trinity's Psychiatrists: From Serenity of the Soul to Neuroscience*, p. 125.

487 K.C. Murphy, L.A. Jones and M.J. Owen, 'High rates of schizophrenia in adults with velo-cardio-facial syndrome', *Archives of General Psychiatry*, 56, 10 (October 1999), pp. 940–5.

488 A. Ryan, *Walls of Silence* (Callan, County Kilkenny: Red Lion Press, 1999).

Chapter 7. The Twenty-First Century: New Policy, New Law

1 M. D'Arcy, 'The Hospital and the Holy Spirit: Psychotic Subjectivity and Institutional Returns in Dublin', paper delivered at the *Society for Psychological Anthropology*, Boston, MA, 10 April 2015 (used with permission).

2 Burnham, *What is Medical History?*, p. 3. See also: R. Porter and M.S. Micale, 'Introduction: reflections on psychiatry and its histories', in M.S. Micale and R. Porter (eds), *Discovering the History of Psychiatry* (New York and Oxford: Oxford University Press, 1994), pp. 3–36.

3 D. Walsh, 'Brief historical review', *Irish Journal of Psychiatry*, 13, 1 (Spring 1992), pp. 3–20; pp. 17–18.

4 Law Reform Committee, *Mental Health: The Case for Reform* (Dublin: The Law Society, 1999).

5 For background on mental health and human rights, see: B.D. Kelly, *Mental Illness, Human Rights and the Law* (London: RCPsych Publications, 2016), pp. 1–34.

6 Department of Health, *White Paper: A New Mental Health Act* (Dublin: The Stationery Office, 1995), p. 13.

7 Council of Europe, *European Convention on Human Rights (Convention for the Protection of Human Rights and Fundamental Freedoms)* (Strasbourg: Council of Europe, 1950).

8 Department of Health, *White Paper: A New Mental Health Act*, p. 15.

9 Ibid.

10 United Nations, *Principles for the Protection of Persons with Mental Illness and the Improvement of Mental Health Care* (New York: United Nations, Secretariat Centre For Human Rights, 1991).

11 Law Reform Committee, *Mental Health: The Case for Reform*, p. 6.

12 *Croke v Smith* [1994] 3 IR 529; *Croke v Smith (No. 2)* [1998] 1 IR 101; *Croke v Ireland* (2000) ECHR 680.

13 *Croke v Smith* [1994] 3 IR 529; A. Rutherdale, 'Detention in mental hospital after 6 month period without new order invalid', *Irish Times*, 26 September 1994; Department of Health, *White Paper: A New Mental Health Act*; *Croke v Smith (No. 2)* [1998] 1 IR 101.

14 C. Coulter, 'Legal rights of mental health sufferers ignored', *Irish Times*, 1 November 2005; B.D. Kelly, 'Irish mental health law', *Irish Psychiatrist*, 7, 1 (February/March 2006), pp. 29–30; J. Owens, 'Mental health services crying out for reform', *Irish Times*, 21 November 2005.

15 This might have started to change in 2015; see: P. Cullen, 'More monitoring of mentally ill patients sought', *Irish Times*, 17 April 2015.

16 Kelly, *Dignity, Mental Health and Human Rights: Coercion and the Law*, pp. 31–2.

17 United Nations, *Convention on the Rights of Persons with Disabilities* (Geneva: United Nations, 2006), Article 1.

18 B.D. Kelly, 'Dignity, human rights and the limits of mental health legislation', *Irish Journal of Psychological Medicine*, 31, 2 (June 2014), pp. 75–81; Kelly, *Dignity, Mental Health and Human Rights: Coercion and the Law*, pp. 18–24.

19 B.D. Kelly, 'Viewpoint: the Mental Health Act 2001', *Irish Medical Journal*, 95, 5 (May 2002), pp. 151–2; M. Keys, *Annotated Legislation: Mental Health Act 2001* (Dublin: Round Hall, Sweet and Maxwell, 2002); B.D. Kelly, 'The Irish Mental Health Act 2001', *Psychiatric Bulletin*, 31, 1 (January 2007), pp. 21–4; H. Kennedy, *The Annotated Mental Health Acts* (Dublin: Blackhall Publishing, 2007); D. Ryan, *The Mental Health Acts 2001–2009: Case Law and Commentary* (Dublin: Blackhall Publishing, 2010); D. Whelan, *Mental Health Law and Practice* (Dublin: Round Hall/Thomson Reuters, 2009).

20 Mental Health Act 2001, Section 3(2).

21 Ibid., Section 3(1); see also: *MR v Cathy Byrne, administrator, and Dr Fidelma Flynn, clinical director, Sligo Mental Health Services, Ballytivnan, Co. Sligo* [2007] IEHC 73.

22 Mental Health Act 2001, Section 3(1).

23 Mental Health Act 1983, Section 1(2).

24 Mental Health Act 2007, Section 1(2).

25   Expert Committee, *Review of the Mental Health Act 1983* (London: Department of Health, 1999), p. 38.

26   Mental Health Act Commission, *Placed Amongst Strangers: Twenty Years of the Mental Health Act 1983 and Future Prospects for Psychiatric Compulsion* (London: The Stationery Office, 2003), pp. 85–6.

27   D. Walsh, 'Brief historical review', *Irish Journal of Psychiatry*, 13, 1 (Spring 1992), pp. 3–20; p. 17.

28   Mental Health Act 2001, Section 8(2).

29   Ibid., Section 9(8).

30   Ibid., Section 9(2).

31   Ibid., Section 9(4).

32   Ibid., Sections 10(2) and 10(5).

33   Ibid., Section 13(1).

34   Ibid., Section 13(2); see also: *EF v The Clinical Director of St Ita's Hospital* [2007] JR 816; Health (Miscellaneous Provisions) Act 2009, Section 63.

35   Mental Health Act 2001, Section 13(3).

36   Ibid., Section 14(1).

37   Ibid., Section 15(1).

38   Ibid., Section 15(2); see also: *MD v Clinical Director of St Brendan's Hospital & Anor* [2007] IEHC 183.

39   Mental Health Act 2001, Section 15(3); see also: *JB v The Director of the Central Mental Hospital and Dr Ronan Hearne and the Mental Health Commission and the Mental Health Tribunal* [2007] IEHC 201; *MM v Clinical Director Central Mental Hospital* [2008] IESC 31.

40   Mental Health Act 2001, Section 17(1).

41   Ibid., Sections 23 and 24; see also: *Q v St Patrick's Hospital* [2006] O'Higgins J, *ex tempore*, 21 December 2006.

42   Mental Health Act 2001, Section 48(1).

43   Ibid., Section 48(3).

44   Ibid., Section 48(4).

45   Ibid., Section 18(1).

46   Ibid., Section 19(1).

47   Ibid., Section 19(16).

48   Ibid., Section 57(1).

49   Ibid., Section 58(1).

50   Ibid., Section 59(1).

51   Ibid., Section 60.

52   M. Wrigley, 'A State of unpreparedness', *Irish Medical Times*, 6 October 2006; J.A. Barnes, 'Red-letter day for mental health?', *Irish Medical News*, 6 November 2006; J. Shannon, 'Getting one's Act together', *Medicine Weekly*, 8 November 2006.

53   D. Whelan, 'Mental health tribunals', *Medico-Legal Journal of Ireland*, 10, 2 (2004), pp. 84–9; p. 87.

54   I. McGuinness, 'Tribunals to decide on legal representation', *Irish Medical Times*, 10 November 2006.

55   C. O'Brien, 'Reviews for mental patients in detention', *Irish Times*, 1 November 2006.

56   I. McGuinness, 'Consultants not to apply for mental health tribunal positions', *Irish Medical Times*, 11 March 2005.

57   E. Vize, 'Pay threat to psychiatrists over mental health tribunals', *Medicine Weekly*, 26 October 2005.

58   F. Ó Cionnaith, 'Consultants not responsible for harm under Act', *Medicine Weekly*, 8 November 2006.

59   K. Ganter, I. Daly and J. Owens, 'Implementing the Mental Health Act 2001: What should be done? What can be done?', *Irish Journal of Psychological Medicine*, 22, 3 (September 2005), pp. 79–82; B.D. Kelly and F. Lenihan, 'Attitudes towards the implementation of the Mental Health Act 2001', *Irish Journal of Psychological Medicine*, 23, 2 (June 2006), pp. 82–4.

60   K. Ganter, 'Funding for Mental Health Act is a human rights issue', *Medicine Weekly*, 6 April 2005.

61   J.A. Barnes, 'Mental health chief confident HSE will meet legal obligations', *Irish Medical News*, 31 October 2006.

62   I. McGuinness, 'Tribunals revoke 12 per cent of detentions', *Irish Medical Times*, 26 October 2007.

63   *D Han v The President of the Circuit Court and Doctor Malcolm Garland and Doctor Richard Blennerhassett and Doctor Conor Farren and Professor Patrick McKeon and the Mental Health Commission and the Mental Health Tribunal* [2008] IEHC 160; pp. 10–11; Kelly, *Mental Illness, Human Rights and the Law*, pp. 111–22.

64   Mental Health Act 2001, Section 2(1).

65   H. Kennedy, "Libertarian' groupthink not helping mentally ill', *Irish Times*, 12 September 2012. In relation to the Mental Health Act 2008, see: E. Cummings and O. O'Conor, 'The SM Judgment and The Mental Health Act 2008', *Irish Medical Journal*, 102, 7 (2009); *SM v The Mental Health Commissioner, The Mental Health Tribunal, The Clinical Director of St Patrick's Hospital, Dublin, Attorney General and the Human Rights Commission* [2008] JR 749; M. Carolan, 'Psychiatric patient takes case against involuntary detention in hospital', *Irish Times*, 16 October 2008; S. Collins, 'Emergency mental health law rushed through Dáil', *Irish Times*, 31 October 2008; M. Carolan, 'Woman's hospital detention ruled unlawful by court', *Irish Times*, 1 November 2008; C. Coulter, 'Government and judge combine to clear up loophole', *Irish Times*, 1 November 2008; Kelly, *Mental Illness, Human Rights and the Law*, pp. 118–20. See also: N. Nolan, 'Case law on the MHA 2001', *Irish Psychiatrist*, 9, 3 (Autumn 2008), pp. 176–82; D. Whelan, 'Legacy of unresolved legal issues on mental health', *Irish Times*, 4 November 2008.

66   Á. Ní Mhaoláin and B.D. Kelly, 'Ireland's Mental Health Act 2001: where are we now?', *Psychiatric Bulletin*, 33, 5 (May 2009), pp. 161–4.

67   For various studies and perspectives, see: B.D. Kelly, 'The Mental Health Act 2001', *Irish Medical News*, 18 May 2009; Á. Ní Mhaoláin and B.D. Kelly, 'Ireland's Mental Health Act 2001', *Psychiatric Bulletin*, 33, 5 (May 2009), pp. 161–4; F. Jabbar, B.D. Kelly and P. Casey, 'National survey of psychiatrists' responses to implementation of the Mental Health Act 2001 in Ireland', *Irish Journal of Medical Science*, 179, 2 (June 2010), pp. 291–4; B. O'Donoghue, J. Lyne, M. Hill, C. Larkin, L. Feeney and E. O'Callaghan, 'Involuntary admission from the

patients' perspective', *Social Psychiatry and Psychiatric Epidemiology*, 45, 6 (June 2010), pp. 631–8.; F. Jabbar, A.M. Doherty, M. Aziz and B.D. Kelly, 'Implementing the Mental Health Act 2007 in British general practice: lessons from Ireland', *International Journal of Law and Psychiatry*, 34, 6 (November/December 2011), pp. 414–18; H. Ramsay, E. Roche and B. O'Donoghue, 'Five years after implementation: a review of the Irish Mental Health Act 2001', *International Journal of Law and Psychiatry*, 36, 1 (January/February 2013), pp. 83–91; F. Jabbar, M. Aziz and B.D. Kelly, 'Implementing the Mental Health Act 2001 in Ireland: views of Irish general practitioners', *Irish Journal of Psychological Medicine*, 30, 4 (December 2013), pp. 255–9; A.M. Doherty, F. Jabbar and B.D. Kelly, 'Attitudes and experiences of nursing staff to the Mental Health Act 2001: lessons for future mental health legislation', *Irish Journal of Psychological Medicine*, 31, 2 (June 2014), pp. 83–7; V. Ranieri, K. Madigan, E. Roche, E. Bainbridge, D. McGuinness, K. Tierney, L. Feeney, B. Hallahan, C. McDonald and B. O'Donoghue, 'Caregivers' perceptions of coercion in psychiatric hospital admission', *Psychiatry Research*, 228, 3 (August 2015), pp. 380–5; I. Georgieva, E. Bainbridge, D. McGuinness, M. Keys, L. Brosnan, H. Felzmann, J. Maguire, K. Murphy, A. Higgins, C. McDonald and B. Hallahan, 'Opinions of key stakeholders concerning involuntary admission of patients under the Mental Health Act 2001', *Irish Journal of Psychological Medicine* [published online ahead of print, 2016]; B. O'Donoghue, E. Roche, J. Lyne, K. Madigan and L. Feeney, 'Service users' perspective of their admission: a report of study findings', *Irish Journal of Psychological Medicine* [published online ahead of print, 2016].

68   B. O'Donoghue and P. Moran, 'Consultant psychiatrists' experiences and attitudes following the introduction of the Mental Health Act 2001: a national survey', *Irish Journal of Psychological Medicine*, 26, 1 (March 2009), pp. 23–6.

69   D. Smith, E. Roche, K. O'Loughlin, D. Brennan, K. Madigan, J. Lyne, L. Feeney and B. O'Donoghue, 'Satisfaction with services following voluntary and involuntary admission', *Journal of Mental Health*, 23, 1 (February 2014), pp. 38–45.

70   Expert Group on Mental Health Policy, *A Vision for Change* (Dublin: The Stationery Office, 2006).

71   Study Group on the Development of the Psychiatric Services, *The Psychiatric Services – Planning for the Future*.

72   S. Guruswamy and B.D. Kelly, 'A change of vision? Mental health policy', *Irish Medical Journal*, 99, 6 (June 2006), pp. 164–6.

73   Mental Health Commission, *Mental Health Commission Annual Report 2002* (Dublin: Mental Health Commission, 2003), p. 5; B.D. Kelly, 'Mental health policy in Ireland, 1984–2004: theory, overview and future directions', *Irish Journal of Psychological Medicine*, 21, 2 (June 2004), pp. 61–8.

74   C. O'Neill, H. Sinclair, A. Kelly and H. Kennedy, 'Interaction of forensic and general psychiatric services in Ireland: learning the lessons or repeating the mistakes?', *Irish Journal of Psychological Medicine*, 19, 2 (June 2002), pp. 48–54; V. O'Keane, A. Jeffers, E. Moloney and S. Barry, 'Irish Psychiatric Association survey of psychiatric services in Ireland', *Psychiatric Bulletin*, 28, 10 (October 2004), pp. 364–7; Inspector of Mental Health Services, *Report of the Inspector of Mental Health Services 2005* (Dublin: The Stationery Office, 2005).

75   F. Keogh, A. Roche and D. Walsh, *"We Have No Beds ..." An Enquiry into the Availability and Use of Acute Psychiatric Beds in the Eastern Health Board Region* (Dublin: Health Research Board, 1999), pp. 5–7.

76   Amnesty International (Irish Section), *Mental Illness* (Dublin: Amnesty International (Irish Section), 2003), pp. 114–15.

77   Mental Health Commission, *Mental Health Commission Annual Report 2002*, p. 5.

78   P. MacÉinrí, *Immigration into Ireland* (Cork: Irish Centre For Migration Studies, 2001).

79   Department of Health, *Shaping A Healthier Future: A Strategy for Effective Healthcare in the 1990s* (Dublin: The Stationery Office, 1987), pp. 10–1.

80   Department of Health and Children, *Quality and Fairness: A Health System for You* (Dublin: The Stationery Office, 2001), pp. 17–19.

81   World Health Organisation, *The World Health Report 2001. Mental Health: New Understanding, New Hope* (Geneva: World Health Organisation, 2001).

82   D.L. Sackett, W.M. Rosenberg, J.A. Gray, R.B. Haynes and W.S. Richardson, 'Evidence based medicine: what it is and what it isn't', *British Medical Journal*, 312, 7023 (January 1996), pp. 71–2; B.D. Kelly, 'Evidence based medicine: what it is and why it matters', *Irish Psychiatrist*, 3, 4 (August/September, 2002), pp. 133–8.

83   Mental Health Commission, *Mental Health Commission Annual Report 2002*, p. 4; B.D. Kelly, 'The Irish Mental Health Act 2001', *Psychiatric Bulletin*, 31, 1 (January 2007), pp. 21–4.

84   Expert Group on Mental Health Policy, *A Vision for Change*, p. 8.

85   Ibid., p. 95.

86   Ibid., p. 77.

87   Ibid., p. 73.

88   Health Service Executive, National Suicide Review Group and Department of Health and Children, *Reach Out: National Strategy for Action on Suicide Prevention, 2005–2014* (Dublin: Health Service Executive, 2005).

89   Expert Group on Mental Health Policy, *A Vision for Change*, pp. 168–9.

90   Ibid., p. 181.

91   Ibid., p. 189.

92   Ibid., pp. 208–9.

93   S. Guruswamy and B.D. Kelly, 'A change of vision?', *Irish Medical Journal*, 99, 6 (June 2006), pp. 164–6.

94 World Health Organisation, *The World Health Report 2001. Mental Health: New Understanding, New Hope*, pp. xi, xii, 77–84, 103, 104–6.

95 Study Group on the Development of the Psychiatric Services, *The Psychiatric Services – Planning for the Future*, pp. 9–15.

96 Expert Group on Mental Health Policy, *A Vision for Change*, p. 218.

97 Ibid., p. 140.

98 Department of Health, *Shaping A Healthier Future: A Strategy for Effective Healthcare in the 1990s*, p. 10; Department of Health and Children, *Quality and Fairness: A Health System for You*, p. 17.

99 C. O'Neill, H. Sinclair, A. Kelly and H. Kennedy, 'Interaction of forensic and general psychiatric services in Ireland: learning the lessons or repeating the mistakes?', *Irish Journal of Psychological Medicine*, 19, 2 (June 2002), pp. 48–54.

100 S.L. George, N.J. Shanks and L. Westlake, 'Census of single homeless people in Sheffield', *British Medical Journal*, 302, 6789 (June 1991), pp. 1387–9; T.W. Holohan, 'Health and homelessness in Dublin', *Irish Medical Journal*, 93, 2 (March/April 2000), pp. 41–3; A. O'Carroll and F. O'Reilly, 'Health of the homeless in Dublin', *European Journal of Public Health*, 18, 5 (October 2008), pp. 448–53.

101 R.M. Duffy and B.D. Kelly, 'Psychiatric assessment and treatment of survivors of torture', *BJPsych Advances*, 21, 2 (March 2015), pp. 106–15.

102 B. Gavin, B.D. Kelly, A. Lane and E. O'Callaghan, 'The mental health of migrants', *Irish Medical Journal*, 94, 8 (September 2001), pp. 229–30.

103 F.E. Wilson, E. Hennessy, B. Dooley, B.D. Kelly and D.A. Ryan, 'Trauma and PTSD rates in an Irish psychiatric population: a comparison of native and immigrant samples', *Disaster Health*, 1, 2 (December 2013), pp. 74–83.

104 N. Crumlish and K. O'Rourke, 'A systematic review of treatments for post-traumatic stress disorder among refugees and asylum-seekers', *Journal of Nervous and Mental Disease*, 198, 4 (April 2010), pp. 237–51.

105 D.A. Ryan, C.A. Benson and B.A. Dooley, 'Psychological distress and the asylum process: a longitudinal study of forced migrants in Ireland', *Journal of Nervous and Mental Disease*, 196, 1 (January 2008), pp. 37–45.

106 Health Service Executive, *National Intercultural Health Strategy, 2007–2012* (Dublin: Health Service Executive, 2008).

107 A. Yung, L. Phillips and P.D. McGorry, *Treating Schizophrenia in the Prodromal Phase* (London: Taylor & Francis, 2004).

108 B. O'Donoghue, J. Lyne, L. Renwick, K. Madigan, A. Kinsella, M. Clarke, N. Turner and E. O'Callaghan, 'A descriptive study of "non-cases" and referral rates to an early intervention for psychosis service', *Early Intervention in Psychiatry*, 6, 3 (August 2012), pp. 276–82.

109 C. O'Neill, H. Sinclair, A. Kelly and H. Kennedy, 'Interaction of forensic and general psychiatric services in Ireland: learning the lessons or repeating the mistakes?', *Irish Journal of Psychological Medicine*, 19, 2 (June 2002), pp. 48–54; V. O'Keane, A. Jeffers, E. Moloney and S. Barry, 'Irish Psychiatric Association survey of psychiatric services in Ireland', *Psychiatric Bulletin*, 28, 10 (October 2004), pp. 364–7; Inspector of Mental Health Services, *Report of the Inspector of Mental Health Services 2005*.

110 Expert Group on Mental Health Policy, *A Vision for Change*, pp. 202–10.

111 Ibid., p. 146.

112 J. Barry, C. Farren, E. Keenan, F. Nangle-O'Connor, A. Quigley, S. Rooney, B. Smyth and J. Treacy, 'Excluding addiction from mental health services', *Irish Times*, 15 December 2006. See also: A. Leahy, 'Addiction and mental health', *Irish Times*, 28 December 2006.

113 E. Donnellan, 'Mental hospitals to close over 10-year phase', *Irish Times*, 25 January 2006; M. Houston, 'Milestone in development of a new mental health policy', *Irish Times*, 25 January 2006; T. Bates, 'Vision of mental health', *Irish Times*, 31 January 2006.

114 *Irish Times*, 14 March 2006.

115 L. Kanner, *Child Psychiatry* (Springfield, IL: C.C. Thomas Publishing, 1935).

116 D. Coghill, S. Bonnar, S.L. Duke, J. Graham and S. Seth, *Child and Adolescent Psychiatry* (Oxford: Oxford University Press, 2009), p. 2.

117 For overviews, see: M. Fitzgerald, 'The child and the family', in: C. Keane (ed.), *Mental Health in Ireland* (Dublin: Gill and Macmillan and Radio Telefís Éireann, 1991), pp. 41–52; D. Walsh, 'Brief historical review', *Irish Journal of Psychiatry*, 13, 1 (Spring 1992), pp. 3–20; pp. 16–17.

118 A. McCabe, 'A brief history of the early development of social work in child psychiatry in Ireland', in M. Fitzgerald (ed.), *Irish Families under Stress (Volume 7)* (Dublin: South Western Area Health Board, 2003), pp. 1–15; p. 4. See also: D. Healy, 'Interview: In conversation with Desmond McGrath', *Psychiatric Bulletin*, 16, 3 (March 1992), pp. 129–37; pp. 133, 137.

119 J. Stack, 'History of child psychiatry in Ireland', in M. Fitzgerald (ed.), *Irish Families under Stress (Volume 7)* (Dublin: South Western Area Health Board, 2003), pp. 35–6. This invaluable account was recorded by Professor Michael Fitzgerald in the mid-1980s and published in 2003.

120 Commission of Inquiry on Mental Handicap, *Commission of Inquiry on Mental Handicap: 1965 Report* (Dublin: The Stationery Office, 1965), p. 179.

121 *Irish Times*, 27 May 1998. See also: M. Nolan, 'Professor John McKenna', in M. Fitzgerald (ed.), *Irish Families under Stress (Volume 7)* (Dublin: South Western Area Health Board, 2003), pp. 33–4.

122 Stack, *Irish Families under Stress (Volume 7)*, p. 36.

123 E. Nolan, *Caring for the Nation* (Dublin: Gill & Macmillan, 2013), pp. 127–8; McCabe, *Irish Families under Stress (Volume 7)*, p. 5.

124 Personal communication: Dr Paul McQuaid, by email (27 November 2015).

125 McCabe, *Irish Families under Stress (Volume 7)*, p. 6.

126 Commission of Inquiry on Mental Illness, p. xxiv.

127 Indeed, the report stated that 'the whole problem of industrial schools should be examined' (Ibid., p. xxiv).

128 Ibid., p. xxv.

129 McCabe, *Irish Families under Stress (Volume 7)*, pp. 7–8.

130 Study Group on the Development of the Psychiatric Services, *The Psychiatric Services – Planning for the Future*, pp. 91–103; p. 102.

131 McCabe, *Irish Families under Stress (Volume 7)*, p. 8.

132 Ibid., pp. 9–10.

133 Ibid., p. 13.

134 M. Lawlor and D. Macintyre, 'The *Stay Safe* programme', in M. Fitzgerald (ed.), *Irish Families under Stress (Volume 7)* (Dublin: South Western Area Health Board, 2003), pp. 18–29.

135 O. Higgins, 'Child care workers in child psychiatry in Ireland', in M. Fitzgerald (ed.), *Irish Families under Stress (Volume 7)* (Dublin: South Western Area Health Board, 2003), pp. 37–8.

136 V. Foley, 'The history of speech and language therapy in Ireland', in M. Fitzgerald (ed.), *Irish Families under Stress (Volume 7)* (Dublin: South Western Area Health Board, 2003), pp. 30–2.

137 See, for example: M. Fitzgerald, *Autism and Creativity: Is There a Link between Autism in Men and Exceptional Ability?* (Hove: Brunner-Routledge, 2004).

138 In 2002 the Irish Division of the Royal College of Psychiatrists became the Irish College of Psychiatrists.

139 Irish College of Psychiatrists, *A Better Future Now: Position Statement on Psychiatric Services for Children and Adolescents in Ireland (Occasional Paper OP60)* (Dublin: Irish College of Psychiatrists, 2005).

140 Expert Group on Mental Health Policy, *A Vision for Change*, p. 90.

141 Mental Health Commission, *Mental Health Commission Annual Report 2013 Including Report of the Inspector of Mental Health Services* (Dublin: Mental Health Commission, 2014), p. 34.

142 D. Bradley, 'Hospital tells mother of suicidal boy 'ring guards'', *Galway City Tribune*, 29 May 2015.

143 Mental Health Commission, *Mental Health Commission Annual Report 2013 Including Report of the Inspector of Mental Health Services*, p. 7.

144 Mental Health Commission, *Mental Health Commission Annual Report 2014 Including Report of the Inspector of Mental Health Services* (Dublin: Mental Health Commission, 2015), p. 8.

145 S. Bardon, '50 children in adult psychiatric units', *Irish Times*, 10 August 2015; B.D. Kelly, 'Mental health services for children', *Irish Times*, 12 August 2015.

146 E. Keogh, 'Hospital sees "exponential" self-harm rise in teenagers', *Irish Times*, 18 August 2015.

147 Mental Health Commission, *Mental Health Commission Annual Report 2015 Including Report of the Inspector of Mental Health Services* (Dublin: Mental Health Commission, 2016), pp. 8, 36–40, 64–6.

148 *Irish Medical Times*, 22 April 2016. See also: C. O'Brien, 'Children with mental health issues admitted into adult units', *Irish Times*, 31 October 2014.

149 E. Loughlin and F. Ó Cionnaith, 'Taskforce for youth mental health to get green light', *Irish Examiner*, 27 July 2016.

150 B.D. Kelly, 'The *Irish Journal of Psychological Medicine* and the College of Psychiatry of Ireland', *Irish Journal of Psychological Medicine*, 29, 1 (January 2012), pp. 3–6. This section of the book draws upon material from this paper; ©College of Psychiatrists of Ireland, published by Cambridge University Press, reproduced with permission.

151 A. McGennis, 'Obituary: Mark Hartman', *Psychiatric Bulletin*, 18, 7 (July 1994), p. 442.

152 Webb, *Trinity's Psychiatrists: From Serenity of the Soul to Neuroscience*, p. 103.

153 R. McClelland, 'An appreciation of Dr Mark Hartman, founder and editor-in-chief of the Irish Journal of Psychological Medicine', *Irish Journal of Psychological Medicine*, 11, 1 (March 1994), p. 4.

154 L. Redmond, 'Suicide', *Irish Times*, 29 January (1979), p. 10.

155 B.A. Lawlor, 'Quo vadis?', *Irish Journal of Psychological Medicine*, 11, 3 (September 1994), p. 107.

156 Reynolds, *Grangegorman: Psychiatric Care in Dublin since 1815*, pp. 262–277; B.D. Kelly, 'Physical sciences and psychological medicine: the legacy of Prof John Dunne', *Irish Journal of Psychological Medicine*, 22, 2 (June 2005), pp. 67–72.

157 B.D. Kelly, 'The Irish Journal of Psychological Medicine: looking to the future', *Irish Journal of Psychological Medicine*, 27, 4 (December 2010); pp. 170–1.

158 B.D. Kelly, 'Investing in the future', *Irish Journal of Psychological Medicine*, 21, 4 (December 2004), p. 111.

159 D. Walsh, 'Brief historical review', *Irish Journal of Psychiatry*, 13, 1 (Spring 1992), pp. 3–20; p. 12.

160 For an interesting discussion of the balance between professionalism and nationalism in Irish psychiatry's relations with the Royal College of Psychiatrists, see: Healy, *150 Years of British Psychiatry, 1841–1991. Volume I*, p. 319.

161 C. H., 'Dr Kate Ganter – 1948–2012', *Irish Medical Times*, 14 September 2012. See also: B. O'Shea, 'Appreciation: Kate Ganter (née Dempsey; 1948–2012)', *Psychiatry Professional*, 1, 3 (Autumn, 2012), p. 12.

162 College of Psychiatrists of Ireland, *Constitution (revised)* (Dublin: College of Psychiatrists of Ireland, 2013).

163 R.J. Daly, 'Community psychiatry and the National Institute of Mental Health', *Irish Journal of Psychological Medicine*, 7, 1 (March 1990), p. 5; M. Hartman, 'An Irish National Institute of Mental Health', *Irish Journal of Psychological Medicine*, 7, 1 (March 1990), p. 5; A. Clare, R.J. Daly, T.G. Dinan, D. King, B.E. Leonard, C. O'Boyle, J. O'Connor, J. Waddington, N. Walsh and M. Webb, 'Advancement of psychiatric research in Ireland:

proposal for a national body', *Irish Journal of Psychological Medicine*, 7, 2 (September 1990), p. 93.

164 M.D. Higgins, 'Editorial – Remarks by President Michael D. Higgins, The College of Psychiatry of Ireland, Research and Innovation, Winter Conference, 2012', *Irish Journal of Psychological Medicine*, 2013, 30, 1 (March 2013), pp. 1–5. See also: M.D. Higgins, 'Mental illness', *Irish Times*, 19 March 1968.

165 B.D. Kelly, 'Head shop drugs: they haven't gone away', *Irish Journal of Psychological Medicine*, 28, 1 (March 2011), p. S1.

166 J. Lyne and M. Cannon, 'A special issue: highlighting the youth mental health agenda', *Irish Journal of Psychological Medicine*, 32, 1 (March 2015), pp. 1–3.

167 B.D. Kelly, 'The *Irish Journal of Psychological Medicine*: expanding horizons, moving on', *Irish Journal of Psychological Medicine*, 33, 1 (March 2016), pp. 1–2.

168 J. Lyne, 'An exciting new chapter for the *Irish Journal of Psychological Medicine*', *Irish Journal of Psychological Medicine*, 33, 2 (June 2016), pp. 71–2.

169 B.D. Kelly, 'Mental health policy in Ireland: a decade after *A Vision for Change*, where are we now?', *Irish Medical Journal*, 108, 10 (November/December 2015), p. 293.

170 Commission of Inquiry on Mental Illness, p. xv.

171 Ibid., p. xiii.

172 Brennan, *Irish Insanity, 1800–2000*, p. 126.

173 M. Bowe, P. Devitt, and F. Kelly, *Changing Minds – Home not Hospital* (Dublin: TAF Publishing, 2011).

174 Mac Lellan, Nic Ghabhann and Byrne, *World Within Walls*, pp. 136–8. (This essay, by Dr John Owens, October 2014, provides a fascinating overview of developments in Cavan and Monaghan.)

175 B.D. Kelly, 'Obituary: James Maguire', *Psychiatric Bulletin*, 32, 6 (June 2008), p. 236.

176 S. Barry and P. Murphy (on behalf of the Faculty of Clinical Directors of the College of Psychiatry of Ireland), *A Gloomy View: Rhetoric or reality in relation to the advancement of A Vision for Change* (Dublin: College of Psychiatry of Ireland, 2009).

177 Ibid., p. 17.

178 Indecon International Consultants, *Review of Government Spending on Mental Health and Assessment of Progress on Implementation of A Vision for Change* (Dublin: Indecon/Amnesty International, 2009), pp. x–xi.

179 Independent Monitoring Group, *A Vision for Change: Sixth Annual Report on Implementation (2011)* (Dublin: Department of Health, 2012), p. 3. For some background, see: D. Walsh, 'Vision must not become a mirage', *Irish Medical Times*, 15 June 2007.

180 Independent Monitoring Group, *A Vision for Change: Sixth Annual Report on Implementation (2011)*, p. 3.

181 Ibid., p. 95.

182 Ibid., pp. 3–4.

183 Ibid., pp. 103–8.

184 Ibid., p. 103.

185 H. Johnston, *All Vision but No Change? Determinants of Implementation: The Case of Ireland and Mental Health*

Policy (Dublin: Institute of Public Administration, 2014), pp. 60, 81.

186 Ibid., p. 101.

187 M. Browne, 'Marrying the strategic with the operational', *The Clinical Care Journal*, 2015, pp. 85–6.

188 G. Culliton, '23 clinical programme posts filled to date', *Irish Medical Times*, 26 March 2015.

189 Mental Health Commission, *Mental Health Commission Annual Report 2013 Including Report of the Inspector of Mental Health Services*, p. 6.

190 Ibid., p. 7.

191 P. Prior, 'Mad, not bad: crime, mental disorder and gender in nineteenth-century Ireland', in I. O'Donnell and F. McAuley (eds), *Criminal Justice History* (Dublin: Four Courts Press, 2003), pp. 66–82; p. 82.

192 *British Medical Journal*, 29 November 1902.

193 J.W. Taylor, *Guilty but Insane: J. C. Bowen-Colthurst – Villain or Victim?* (Cork: Mercier Press, 2016).

194 Commission on the Relief of the Sick and Destitute Poor, Including the Insane Poor, *Report of the Commission on the Relief of the Sick and Destitute Poor, Including the Insane Poor*, p. 102.

195 Guéret, *What the Doctor Saw*, pp. 27–8.

196 Personal communication: Dr Michael Reynolds, by email (22 and 23 June 2015).

197 E. O'Brien, 'Helping minds to work again', *Irish Times*, 10 April 1967.

198 Personal communication: Dr Michael Reynolds, by email (22 and 23 June 2015).

199 Health Act 1970, Section 44.

200 Personal communication: Dr Liam Daly, interview (27 June 2015).

201 N. Sheppard and E. Hardiman, 'Treatment of the mentally ill offender in Ireland', *Irish Journal of Psychiatry*, 7, 1 (Spring 1986), pp. 13–19.

202 M. Stokes and A. O'Connor, 'Deaths in the Central Mental Hospital', *Irish Journal of Psychological Medicine*, 6, 2 (September 1989), pp. 144–6.

203 A. O'Connor and H. O'Neill, 'Male prison transfers to the Central Mental Hospital, a special hospital (1983–1988)', *Irish Journal of Psychological Medicine*, 7, 2 (September 1990), pp. 118–20.

204 A. O'Connor and H. O'Neill, 'Female prison transfers to the Central Mental Hospital, a special hospital (1983–1988)', *Irish Journal of Psychological Medicine*, 8, 2 (September 1991), pp. 122–3.

205 T. Hegarty, 'Study finds 5% of prison inmates are mentally ill', *Irish Times*, 24 March 1993.

206 C. O'Neill, H. Sinclair, A. Kelly and H. Kennedy, 'Interaction of forensic and general psychiatric services in Ireland: learning the lessons or repeating the mistakes?', *Irish Journal of Psychological Medicine*, 19, 2 (June 2002), pp. 48–54.

207 For an interesting consideration of criminal insanity in Ireland in 1993, see: F. McAuley, *Insanity, Psychiatry and Criminal Responsibility* (Dublin: Round Hall Press, 1993).

208 S. Linehan, D. Duffy, H. O'Neill, C. O'Neill and H.G. Kennedy, 'Irish travellers and forensic mental health', *Irish Journal of Psychological Medicine*, 19, 3 (September 2002), pp. 76–9.

209 C. O'Neill, P. Heffernan, R. Goggins, C. Corcoran, S. Linehan, D. Duffy, H. O'Neill, C. Smith and H.G. Kennedy, 'Long-stay forensic psychiatric inpatients in the Republic of Ireland: aggregated needs assessment', *Irish Journal of Psychological Medicine*, 20, 4 (December 2003), pp. 119–25.

210 S. Linehan, D.M. Duffy B. Wright, K. Curtin, S. Monks and H.G. Kennedy, 'Psychiatric morbidity in a cross-sectional sample of male remanded prisoners', *Irish Journal of Psychological Medicine*, 22, 4 (December 2005), pp. 128–32; D. Duffy, S. Linehan and H.G. Kennedy, 'Psychiatric morbidity in the male sentenced Irish prisons population', *Irish Journal of Psychological Medicine*, 23, 2 (June 2006), pp. 54–62.

211 B. Wright, D. Duffy, K. Curtin, S. Linehan, S. Monks and H.G. Kennedy, 'Psychiatric morbidity among women prisoners newly committed and amongst remanded and sentenced women in the Irish prison system', *Irish Journal of Psychological Medicine*, 23, 2 (June 2006), pp. 47–53.

212 H.G. Kennedy, 'The future of forensic mental health services in Ireland', *Irish Journal of Psychological Medicine*, 23, 2 (June 2006), pp. 45–6.

213 D. Bergin, 'Dundrum chief blasts Mental Health Commission report', *Irish Medical News*, 6 June 2006; P. Mulholland, 'Location, location, location', *Irish Medical News*, 23 June 2008.

214 C. Coulter, 'North Dublin site selected for prison complex', *Irish Times*, 27 January 2005; L. Mudiwa, 'Mary Robinson hits out at CMH relocation', *Medicine Weekly*, 12 July 2006.

215 L. Hutchinson and A. O'Connor, 'Unfit to plead in Ireland', *Irish Journal of Psychological Medicine*, 12, 3 (September 1995), pp. 112–14; J. Brophy, 'Progress of Criminal Insanity Bill not matched by promises of funding', *Irish Times*, 14 March 2003.

216 Interdepartmental Committee on Mentally Ill and Maladjusted Persons, *Third Interim Report of the Interdepartmental Committee on Mentally Ill and Maladjusted Persons: Treatment and Care of Persons Suffering From Mental Disorder Who Appear Before the Courts on Criminal Charges* (Dublin: The Stationery Office, 1978).

217 Kennedy, *The Annotated Mental Health Acts*; see also: *Irish Times*, 26 June 2006; Criminal Law (Insanity) Act 2010.

218 H.G. Kennedy, 'Foreword', in: B.D. Kelly, *Custody, Care and Criminality: Forensic Psychiatry and Law in 19th Century Ireland* (Dublin: History Press Ireland, 2014), pp. 6–14; p. 13.

219 C. O'Brien, 'Corridors of the mind', *Irish Times*, 11 August 2007; K. Sheridan, 'A voice behind closed doors', *Irish Times*, 29 November 2008; H. Kennedy and S. Thompson, 'It's an ethical challenge, choosing which prisoners we can take', *Irish Times*, 7 April 2015. See also: Mental Health Commission, *Mental Health Commission Annual Report 2004 Including the Report of the Inspector of Mental Health Services* (Dublin: Mental Health Commission, 2005): 'The plans to relocate the Central Mental Hospital to a new, purpose-designed building should progress as quickly as possible' (p. 504).

220 J.A. Barnes, '25% of Mountjoy prisoners former psychiatric patients', *Irish Medical Times*, 5 September 2005.

221 B.D. Kelly, 'Penrose's Law in Ireland: an ecological analysis of psychiatric inpatients and prisoners', *Irish Medical Journal*, 100, 2 (February 2007), pp. 373–4.

222 L.S. Penrose, 'Mental disease and crime: outlines of a comparative study of European statistics', *British Journal of Medical Psychology*, 18, 1 (March 1939), pp. 1–15. This relationship tends to be supported by ecological (group-level) studies, rather than cohort (individual-level, follow-up) studies (P. Winkler, B. Barrett, P. McCrone, L. Csémy, M. Janoušková and C. Höschl, 'Deinstitutionalised patients, homelessness and imprisonment: systematic review', *British Journal of Psychiatry*, 208, 5 (May 2016), pp. 421–8).

223 C. McInerney , M. Davoren, G. Flynn, D. Mullins, M. Fitzpatrick, M. Caddow, F. Caddow, S. Quigley, F. Black, H.G. Kennedy and C. O'Neill, 'Implementing a court diversion and liaison scheme in a remand prison by systematic screening of new receptions', *International Journal of Mental Health Systems*, 7 (June 2013), 18; J. Humphreys, 'The prison trap', *Irish Times*, 14 September 2014.

224 M. Houston, 'Mountjoy team wins top psychiatric care award', *Irish Times*, 6 October 2011; D. Gantly, 'The 'Joy of innovation', *Medicine Weekly*, 25 November 2011.

225 See, for example: M. Davoren, S. O'Dwyer, Z. Abidin, L. Naughton, O. Gibbons, E. Doyle, K. McDonnell, S. Monks and H.G. Kennedy, 'Prospective in-patient cohort study of moves between levels of therapeutic security; the DUNDRUM-1 triage security, DUNRDUM-3 programme completion and DUNDRUM-4 recovery scales and the HCR-20', *BMC Psychiatry*, 12 (July 2012), 80; M. Davoren, S. Hennessy, C. Conway, S. Marrinan, P. Gill and H.G. Kennedy, 'Recovery and concordance in a secure forensic psychiatry hospital – the self-rated DUNDRUM-3 programme completion and DUNDRUM-4 recovery scales', *BMC Psychiatry*, 15 (March 2015), 61. See also: H.G. Kennedy, 'The future of forensic mental health services in Ireland', *Irish Journal of Psychological Medicine*, 23, 2 (June 2006), pp. 45–6.

226 H. Kennedy, 'Prisons now a dumping ground for mentally ill young men', *Irish Times*, 18 May 2016.

227 *Irish Times*, 4 June 2015.

228 L. Mudiwa, 'Decision on forensic hospital is 'hugely significant'', *Irish Medical Times*, 12 June 2015.

229 G. Cullitan, 'Budget moves claims rejected', *Irish Medical Times*, 13 May 2016.

230 I am very grateful to Dr Margaret du Feu for much of the information in this section.

231 M. du Feu and C. Chovaz, *Mental Health and Deafness* (Oxford and New York: Oxford University Press, 2014), pp. 132–4.

232 J. O'Boyle, 'Psychiatric services for the adult deaf', in Study Group on the Development of the Psychiatric Services (ed.), *The Psychiatric Services – Planning for the Future* (Dublin: Stationery Office, 1984), pp. 154–8; p. 154.

233 Ibid., p. 155.

234 Ibid., p. 156.

235 Ibid., p. 158.

236 *Irish Times*, 24 May 1971 (p. 5: 'Seminar on problems of deaf').

237 I am very grateful to Dr Jim O'Boyle for this information.

238 D. Dunne, 'Obituary: Irene Veronica Josephine Aherne', *Psychiatric Bulletin*, 28, 9 (September 2004), p. 347.

239 I am very grateful to Dr Paul McQuaid for this information.

240 Expert Group on Mental Health Policy, *A Vision for Change*, p. 40.

241 Ibid., pp. 40–1.

242 I am very grateful to Dr Margaret du Feu for this information.

243 I am very grateful to Dr Lorcan Martin for this information.

244 M. O'Regan, 'Mental illness still carries stigma, says TD', *Irish Times*, 28 January 2016.

245 Steering Group on the Review of the Mental Health Act 2001, *Interim Report of the Steering Group on the Review of the Mental Health Act 2001* (Dublin: Department of Health, 2012).

246 Expert Group on the Review of the Mental Health Act 2001, *Report of the Expert Group on the Review of the Mental Health Act 2001* (Dublin: Department of Health, 2015) (hereafter 'Expert Group'). See: B.D. Kelly, 'Revising, reforming, reframing: *Report of the Expert Group on the Review of the Mental Health Act 2001* (2015)', *Irish Journal of Psychological Medicine*, 32, 2 (June 2015), pp. 161–6.

247 G. Culliton, 'Review of Act is to be built on "human rights"', *Irish Medical Times*, 27 May 2011.

248 Expert Group, p. 15.

249 Mental Health Act 2001, Section 4(1).

250 B.D. Kelly, 'Dignity, human rights and the limits of mental health legislation', *Irish Journal of Psychological Medicine*, 31, 2 (June 2014), pp. 75–81. See also: B.D. Kelly, 'Schizophrenia, mental health legislation and human rights', *Hospital Doctor of Ireland*, 21, 4 (May 2015), pp. 25–32.

251 Expert Group, p. 17. In relation to intellectual disability, see: M. Hilliard, 'Concern over Mental Health Act change', *Irish Times*, 18 March 2016.

252 Mental Health Act 2007, Section 1(2).

253 Expert Group, p. 22.

254 Mental Health Act 2001, Section 3.

255 Expert Group, p. 37. See also: B.D. Kelly, 'Report of the Expert Group on the Review of the Mental Health Act 2001: what does it mean for social workers?', *The Irish Social Worker*, (Spring 2016), pp. 41–4.

256 Mental Health Act 2001, Section 9; Mental Treatment Act 1945, Sections 162, 177 and 184.

257 Expert Group, p. 37.

258 F. Jabbar, M. Aziz and B.D. Kelly, 'Implementing the Mental Health Act 2001 in Ireland: views of Irish general practitioners', *Irish Journal of Psychological Medicine*, 30, 4 (December 2013), pp. 255–9.

259 Steering Group on the Review of the Mental Health Act 2001, *Interim Report of the Steering Group on the Review of the Mental Health Act 2001*, p. 30.

260 O'Neill, *Irish Mental Health Law*, p. 11.

261 P. Prior, 'Dangerous lunacy: the misuse of mental health law in nineteenth-century Ireland', *Journal of Forensic Psychiatry and Psychology*, 14, 3 (September 2003), pp. 525–41; B.D. Kelly, 'Mental health law in Ireland, 1821 to 1902: building the asylums', *Medico-Legal Journal*, 76, 1 (March 2008), pp. 19–25.

262 B.D. Kelly, 'Stigma and mental illness', *Irish Medical Journal*, 98, 2 (February 2005), p. 37.

263 Expert Group, p. 37.

264 *Irish Times*, 5, 9 and 10 March 2015; *Irish Examiner*, 5 March 2015; coverage was broader in: J. Shannon, 'Moving on from the dark ages of mental health treatment', *Irish Medical Times*, 13 March 2015.

265 P. Lynch, 'College of Psychiatry calls for ECT amendments', *Irish Medical News*, 22 March 2010.

266 Expert Group, p. 15; see also: B.D. Kelly, 'Mental illness requires an all-of-society response', *Irish Times*, 13 April 2015.

267 B.D. Kelly, 'Best interests, mental capacity legislation and the UN Convention on the Rights of Persons with Disabilities', *BJPsych Advances*, 21, 3 (May 2015), pp. 188–95.

268 Mental Capacity Bill 2014, Section 2(2).

269 Ibid., Section 7(6).

270 Ibid., Section 7(7). See also: Kelly, *Mental Illness, Human Rights and the Law*, pp. 63–103.

271 Mental Health Act 2007, Section 8. See also: Kelly, *Mental Illness, Human Rights and the Law*, pp. 47–58.

272 Mental Health (Care and Treatment) (Scotland) Act 2003, Section 1(3)(f). See also: Kelly, *Mental Illness, Human Rights and the Law*, pp. 132–70.

273 Review Group, *Limited Review of the Mental Health (Care and Treatment) (Scotland) Act 2003* (Edinburgh: Scottish Government, 2009).

Chapter 8. The Future of Psychiatry in Ireland

1 Commission of Inquiry on Mental Illness, *Report of the Commission of Inquiry on Mental Illness* (Dublin: The Stationery Office, 1967), p. 14.

2   Expert Group on Mental Health Policy, *A Vision for Change*.

3   B.D. Kelly, 'Mental health services in Ireland – justice, history and human rights explored', *Irish Medical Times*, 18 November 2011.

4   J. Waters, *Jiving at the Crossroads (Updated Edition)* (London: Transworld Ireland, 2011), pp. 86, 192, 216–17.

5   D. Walsh, 'Brief historical review', *Irish Journal of Psychiatry*, 13, 1 (Spring 1992), pp. 3–20; p. 14.

6   Robins, *Fools and Mad: A History of the Insane in Ireland*, p. 203.

7   S. Barry, *The Secret Scripture* (London: Faber and Faber Limited, 2008).

8   D. Clarke, '*My Name is Emily* review: a teen road movie that's well worth the mileage', *Irish Times*, 8 April 2016.

9   S. Fitzmaurice, 'Lights, camera, nerves: how can I direct a film when I can't speak?', *Irish Times*, 31 March 2016.

10 A. Daly and D. Walsh, *Activities of Irish Psychiatric Units and Hospitals 2011* (Dublin: Health Research Board, 2012), p. 23.

11 Ibid., p. 17; A. Daly and D. Walsh, *Activities of Irish Psychiatric Units and Hospitals 2014* (Dublin: Health Research Board, 2015), p. 20.

12 D.A. Sisti, A.G. Segal and E.J. Emmanuel, 'Improving long-term psychiatric care: bring back the asylum', *Journal of the American Medical Association*, 313, 3 (20 January 2015), pp. 243–4.

13 P.M. Prior, 'Mental health law on the island of Ireland, 1800–2010', in P.M. Prior (ed.), *Asylums, Mental Health Care and the Irish, 1800–2010* (Dublin: Irish Academic Press, 2012), pp. 316–34; p. 333.

14 H. Kennedy, 'Prisons now a dumping ground for mentally ill young men', *Irish Times*, 18 May 2016.

15 M. Finnegan, 'I would rather get cancer again than be a patient in the Irish mental health service', *Irish Times*, 29 April 2016.

16 C. D'Arcy, 'Protests over cuts to funding for mental health services', *Irish Times*, 29 April 2016. See also: C. O'Sullivan, "Mental health fund cuts disgust me, minister", *Irish Examiner*, 31 May 2016; M. O'Regan, 'McEntee says commitment to more funds for mental health', *Irish Times*, 3 June 2016.

17 A. Culhane and T. Kearns, *An Impact Evaluation of 'Vision for Change' (Mental Health Policy) on Mental Health Service Provision: A National Descriptive Evaluation Project* (Dublin: Psychiatric Nurses Association and Royal College of Surgeons in Ireland, Faculty of Nursing and Midwifery, 2016), pp. 4–5; *Irish Times*, 23 June 2016.

18 D. Walsh, 'Planning for a 21st century mental health service', *Irish Medical Times*, 15 April 2016.

19 N. Mullen, 'Psychoanalytic field still misrepresented', *Irish Medical Times*, 22 April 2016.

20 Expert Group on the Review of the Mental Health Act 2001, *Report of the Expert Group on the Review of the Mental Health Act 2001*, p. 38.

21 Mental Health Commission, *Mental Health Commission Annual Report 2013 Including Report of the Inspector of Mental Health Services*, p. 40.

22 Health and Social Care Information Centre, *Inpatients Formally Detained in Hospitals under the Mental Health Act 1983, and Patients Subject to Supervised Community Treatment: Annual Report, England, 2013* (Leeds: Health and Social Care Information Centre/National Statistics, 2013), p. 26.

23 Commission of Inquiry on Mental Illness, *Report of the Commission of Inquiry on Mental Illness*, p. xxi.

24 T. Lynch, *Beyond Prozac: Healing Mental Distress* (Dublin: Marino, 2001); for a response, see: B.D. Kelly, 'Healing mental suffering', *Irish Medical News*, 10 June 2002. See also: D. Healy, *The Creation of Psychopharmacology* (Cambridge, Massachusetts and London: Harvard University Press, 2002); I. Kirsch, B.J. Deacon, T.B. Huedo-Medina, A. Scoboria, T.J. Moore and B.T. Johnson, 'Initial severity and antidepressant benefits: a meta-analysis of data submitted to the Food and Drug Administration', *PLoS Medicine*, 5, 2 (February 2008), p. e45; for a response, see: B.D. Kelly, 'Do new-generation antidepressants work?', *Irish Medical Journal*, 101, 5, (May 2008), p. 155.

25 D. Lewer, C. O'Reilly, R. Mojtabai and S. Evans-Lacko, 'Antidepressant use in 27 European countries: associations with sociodemographic, cultural and economic factors', *British Journal of Psychiatry*, 207, 3 (September 2015), pp. 221–6.

26 National Advisory Committee on Drugs and Public Health Information and Research Branch, *Drug Use in Ireland and Northern Ireland: First Results from the 2010/2011 Drug Prevalence Survey* (Dublin and Belfast: National Advisory Committee on Drugs and Public Health Information and Research Branch, 2012), pp. 13, 20.

27 College of Psychiatrists of Ireland, *The Use of Psychotropic Medication in Vulnerable Populations* (Dublin: College of Psychiatrists of Ireland, 2015).

28 C. Shanahan, 'Our €40m drug problem', *Irish Examiner*, 19 March 2015; B.D. Kelly, 'Polarised public debate about anti-depressants deeply unhelpful', *Irish Independent*, 1 June 2015. Psychiatrists have repeatedly called for more judicious use of medication; e.g. College of Psychiatrists of Ireland, *The Use of Psychotropic Medication in Vulnerable Populations* (Dublin: College of Psychiatrists of Ireland, 2015).

29 American Psychiatric Association, *Diagnostic and Statistical Manual of Mental Disorders (Fifth Edition)* (Washington DC: American Psychiatric Association, 2013).

30 World Health Organisation, *International Classification of Mental and Behavioural Disorders (Volume 10)* (Geneva: World Health Organisation, 1992).

31 See, for example: M. Hennessy, 'Warning over rise in ADHD [attention deficit hyperactivity disorder] misdiagnosis', *Irish Times*, 6 November 2013.

32 American Psychiatric Association, *Diagnostic and Statistical Manual of Mental Disorders (Fifth Edition)*, p. 19.

33 World Health Organisation, *International Classification of Mental and Behavioural Disorders (Volume 10)*, p. 2.

34 B.D. Kelly, 'Compassion, cognition and the illusion of self: Buddhist notes towards more skilful engagement with diagnostic classification systems in psychiatry', in E. Shonin, W. Van Gordon and M.D. Griffiths (eds), *Mindfulness and Buddhist-Derived Approaches in Mental Health and Addiction* (Heidelberg: Springer, 2015), pp. 9–28.

35 R. Jowell and Central Coordinating Team, *European Social Survey 2006/2007: Technical Report* (London: Centre for Comparative Social Surveys, City University, 2007). The European Social Survey is an academically driven, cross-national survey conducted across Europe since 2001. Every two years, face-to-face interviews are conducted with newly selected, cross-sectional samples, measuring the attitudes, beliefs and behaviour patterns of diverse populations in over thirty nations. Data are available on an open-access basis (www.europeansocialsurvey.org). See also: A.M. Doherty and B.D. Kelly, 'Social and psychological correlates of happiness in seventeen European countries: analysis of data from the European Social Survey', *Irish Journal of Psychological Medicine*, 27, 3 (September 2010), pp. 130–4.

36 A.M. Doherty and B.D. Kelly, 'When Irish eyes are smiling: income and happiness in Ireland, 2003–2009', *Irish Journal of Medical Science*, 182, 1 (March 2013), pp. 113–19.

37 B.D. Kelly and A.M. Doherty, 'Impact of recent economic problems on mental health in Ireland', *International Psychiatry*, 10, 1 (February 2013), pp. 6–8.

38 J. Helliwell, R. Layard and J. Sachs (eds)., *World Happiness Report 2016, Update (Volume 1)* (New York: Sustainable Development Solutions Network, 2016); M. Hilliard, 'Ireland ranks 19th in happiness report', *Irish Times*, 17 March 2016.

39 K. Gaynor, *Protecting Mental Health* (Dublin: Veritas Publications, 2015).

40 Kelly, *Mental Illness, Human Rights and the Law*, pp. 171–216.

41 A. O'Carroll and F. O'Reilly, 'Health of the homeless in Dublin: has anything changed in the context of Ireland's economic boom?', *European Journal of Public Health*, 18, 5 (October 2008), pp. 448–53.

42 T. Carey, *Mountjoy* (Cork: Collins Press, 2000), pp. 97–100, 244; S. Linehan, D.M. Duffy B. Wright, K. Curtin, S. Monks and H.G. Kennedy, 'Psychiatric morbidity in a cross-sectional sample of male remanded prisoners', *Irish Journal of Psychological Medicine*, 22, 4 (December 2005), pp. 128–32; B.D. Kelly, 'Penrose's Law in Ireland: an ecological analysis of psychiatric inpatients and prisoners', *Irish Medical Journal*, 100, 2 (February 2007), pp. 373–4;

43 C. Edwards, G. Harold and S. Kilcommins, *Access to Justice for People with Disabilities as Victims of Crime in Ireland* (University College Cork: School of Applied Social Studies and Centre for Criminal Justice and Human Rights, Faculty of Law, 2012), p. 58.

44 A. Bailey, *The Grangegorman Murders: Dean Lyons, Mark Nash and the Story Behind the Grangegorman Murders* (Dublin: Gill & Macmillan, 2015).

45 P. Byrne, 'Stigma of mental illness', *British Journal of Psychiatry*, 174, 1 (January 1999), pp. 1–2; P. Byrne, 'Stigma of mental illness and ways of diminishing it', *Advances in Psychiatric Treatment*, 6, 1 (January 2000), pp. 65–72; B.D. Kelly, 'Stigma and mental illness', *Irish Medical Journal*, 98, 2 (February 2005), p. 37.

46 B.D. Kelly, 'Structural violence and schizophrenia', *Social Science and Medicine*, 61, 3 (August 2005), pp. 721–30. For background to this concept, see: P. Farmer, 'Pathologies of power: rethinking health and human rights', *American Journal of Public Health*, 89, 10 (October 1999), pp. 1486–96; P. Farmer, *Pathologies of Power: Human Rights and the New War on the Poor* (Berkeley: University of California Press, 2003). In the Irish context, see: National Economic and Social Forum, *Mental Health and Social Inclusion (Report 36)* (Dublin: National Economic and Social Forum, 2007); National Economic and Social Forum, *Mental Health in the Workplace* (Dublin: National Economic and Social Forum, 2007).

47 W.R. Dawson, 'The presidential address on the relation between the geographical distribution of insanity and that of certain social and other conditions in Ireland', *Journal of Mental Science*, 57, 239 (1 October 1911), pp. 571–97; pp. 580, 587. See also: Finnane, *150 Years of British Psychiatry, 1841–1991. Volume I*, p. 311.

48 B.D. Kelly, 'The power gap: freedom, power and mental illness', *Social Science and Medicine*, 63, 8 (October 2006), pp. 2118–28; *Irish Times*, 23 June 2016.

49 B.D. Kelly, 'Voting and mental illness: the silent constituency', *Irish Journal of Psychological Medicine*, 31, 4 (December 2014), pp. 225–7.

50 C. Crump, M.A. Winkleby, K. Sundquist and J. Sundquist, 'Comorbidities and mortality in persons with schizophrenia: a Swedish national cohort study', *American Journal of Psychiatry*, 170, 3 (March 2013), pp. 324–33.

51 Independent Monitoring Group, *A Vision for Change: Sixth Annual Report on Implementation (2011)*, p. 3; Johnston, *All Vision but No Change? Determinants of Implementation: The Case of Ireland and Mental Health Policy*, pp. 60, 81; B.D. Kelly, 'Mental health policy in Ireland: a decade after *A Vision for Change*, where are we now?', *Irish Medical Journal*, 108, 10 (November/December 2015), p. 293.

52 Expert Group on Mental Health Policy, *A Vision for Change*, pp. 178, 180.

53 College of Psychiatrists of Ireland, *Budget Submission 2016: Press Statement: 9th October 2015* (Dublin: College of Psychiatrists of Ireland, 2015). For more

details, see: College of Psychiatrists of Ireland, *Budget Submission 2016* (Dublin: College of Psychiatrists of Ireland, 2015).

54 M. O'Regan, 'Mental-health services in Donegal collapsing, says Independent TD', *Irish Times*, 10 December 2015.

55 S. McDaid, 'Voters can make mental health an election issue', *Irish Times*, 28 December 2015; B.D. Kelly, 'Making mental health an election issue' *Irish Times*, 30 December 2015.

56 M. Brennan, 'FF manifesto promises mental health authority', *Sunday Business Post*, 24 January 2016.

57 Mental Health Reform, *Our State of Mind* (Dublin: Mental Health Reform, 2016).

58 United Nations, *Principles for the Protection of Persons with Mental Illness and the Improvement of Mental Health Care* (New York: United Nations, Secretariat Centre For Human Rights, 1991).

59 World Health Organisation, *WHO Resource Book on Mental Health, Human Rights and Legislation*, pp. 119–54.

60 B.D. Kelly, 'Mental health legislation and human rights in England, Wales and the Republic of Ireland', *International Journal of Law and Psychiatry*, 34, 6 (November–December 2011), pp. 439–54.

61 Expert Group on the Review of the Mental Health Act 2001, *Report of the Expert Group on the Review of the Mental Health Act 2001*, pp. 88–105.

62 Mental Health (Amendment) Act 2015, Section 2. See also: B.D. Kelly, 'Don't deny them this treatment', *Sunday Independent*, 22 November 2015; G. Culliton, 'ECT Bill "respects patients' wishes"', *Irish Medical Times*, 11 December 2015; B.D. Kelly, 'We need to change how we think about ECT', *Irish Medical Times*, 11 December 2015.

63 Mental Health (Amendment) Act 2015, Section 3.

64 Expert Group on the Review of the Mental Health Act 2001, *Report of the Expert Group on the Review of the Mental Health Act 2001* (Dublin: Department of Health, 2015), p. 22.

65 B.D. Kelly, 'An end to psychiatric detention? Implications of the United Nations Convention on the Rights of Persons with Disabilities', *British Journal of Psychiatry*, 204, 3 (March 2014), pp. 174–5.

66 United Nations, *Convention on the Rights of Persons with Disabilities* (Geneva: United Nations, 2006); P. Bartlett, O. Lewis and O. Thorold, *Mental Disability and the European Convention on Human Rights (International Studies in Human Rights, Volume 90)* (Leiden/Boston: Martinus Nijhoff Publishers, 2007).

67 Convention on the Rights of Persons with Disabilities, Article 1.

68 B.D. Kelly, 'An end to psychiatric detention? Implications of the United Nations Convention on the Rights of Persons with Disabilities', *British Journal of Psychiatry*, 204, 3 (March 2014), pp. 174–5.

69 B.D. Kelly, *Mental Illness, Human Rights and the Law* (London: RCPsych Publications, 2016), p. 30.

70 Convention on the Rights of Persons with Disabilities, Preamble.

71 G. Lee and M. Raley, 'State has long neglected those with a disability', *Irish Times*, 30 March 2015.

72 Convention on the Rights of Persons with Disabilities, Article 14.

73 United Nations High Commissioner for Human Rights. *Annual Report* (Geneva: United Nations, 2009), Paragraph 49.

74 M. Donnelly, *Healthcare Decision-Making and the Law: Autonomy, Capacity and the Limits of Liberalism* (Cambridge: Cambridge University Press, 2010); D. Madden, *Medicine, Ethics and the Law in Ireland (Second Edition)* (Haywards Heath, West Sussex and Dublin: Bloomsbury Professional, 2011), pp. 363–426.

75 K. Doyle, 'President signs new asylum law after concerns', *Irish Independent*, 31 December 2015; B.D. Kelly, 'Assisted Decision-Making Bill', *Irish Independent*, 2 January 2016.

76 B.D. Kelly, 'The Assisted Decision-Making (Capacity) Bill: content, commentary, controversy', *Irish Journal of Medical Science*, 184, 1 (March 2015), pp. 31–46.

77 Assisted Decision-Making (Capacity) Act 2015, Sections 2 and 8. See also: B.D. Kelly, 'The Assisted Decision-Making (Capacity) Act 2015: what it is and why it matters', *Irish Journal of Medical Science* [published online ahead of print, 2016].

78 Assisted Decision-Making (Capacity) Act 2015, Section 3.

79 Ibid., Section 8(7)(e).

80 Ibid., Parts 3–5.

81 Ibid., Part 7.

82 Ibid., Part 8.

83 Ibid., 85(7). For further consideration of these matters, including advance healthcare directives for persons detained under the Mental Health Act 2001, see the comments of Minister Kathleen Lynch in Seanad Éireann: K. Lynch, 'Assisted Decision-Making (Capacity) Bill 2013: Report and Final Stages', *Seanad Éireann Debate*, 244, 9 (15 December 2015).

84 B.D. Kelly, 'An end to psychiatric detention? Implications of the United Nations Convention on the Rights of Persons with Disabilities', *British Journal of Psychiatry*, 204, 3 (March 2014), pp. 174–5.

85 B.D. Kelly, 'The Assisted Decision-Making (Capacity) Bill: content, commentary, controversy', *Irish Journal of Medical Science*, 184, 1 (March 2015), pp. 31–46.

86 Healthcare Pricing Office, *Activity in Acute Public Hospitals in Ireland* (Dublin: Health Service Executive, 2014), p. vi.

87 G.S. Owen, G. Szmukler, G. Richardson, A.S. David, V. Raymont, F. Freyenhagen, W. Martin and M. Hotopf, 'Decision-making capacity for treatment in psychiatric and medical in-patients: cross-sectional, comparative study', *British Journal of Psychiatry*, 203, 6 (December 2013), pp. 461–7; p. 463.

88   N. Bilanakis, A. Vratsista, E. Athanasiou, D. Niakas and V. Peritogiannis, 'Medical patients' treatment decision-making capacity: a report from a general hospital in Greece', *Clinical Practice & Epidemiology in Mental Health*, 10 (November 2014), pp. 133–9; p. 133.

89   Daly and Walsh, *Activities of Irish Psychiatric Units and Hospitals 2014*, p. 20.

90   D. Okai, G. Owen, H. McGuire, S. Singh, R. Churchill and M. Hotopf, 'Mental capacity in psychiatric patients: systematic review', *British Journal of Psychiatry*, 191, 4 (October 2007), pp. 291–7; p. 291.

91   BDO, *Health's Ageing Crisis* (Dublin: BDO, 2014), p. iii.

92   K. Christensen, A. Haroun, L.J. Schneiderman and D.V. Jeste, 'Decision-making capacity for informed consent in the older population', *Bulletin of the American Academy of Psychiatry and the Law*, 23, 3 (September 1995), pp. 353–65; p. 360.

93   Expert Group on Mental Health Policy, *A Vision for Change*, p. 133.

94   Richmond Asylum Joint Committee, *Richmond Asylum Joint Committee Minutes* (Dublin: Richmond Asylum, 1907), pp. 469–70.

95   S. McDaid and A. Higgins, 'Introduction', in A. Higgins and S. McDaid (eds), *Mental Health in Ireland: Policy, Practice and Law* (Dublin: Gill and Macmillan, 2014), pp. 1–10; p. 2. For a perspective on this book, see: B. Joy, 'Book review: *Mental Health in Ireland: Policy, Practice and Law*', *The Irish Social Worker*, (Spring 2016), p. 78.

96   D. Healy, 'Interview: In conversation with Tom Lynch', *Psychiatric Bulletin*, 16, 2 (February 1992), pp. 65–72; p. 71.

97   T. Fahy, 'Obituary: Thomas Lynch', *Psychiatric Bulletin*, 29, 11 (November 2005), p. 438.

98   D. Lyons, K. Collins and C. Hayes, 'Offering support to the general public by building CBT-based life skills', *Irish Journal of Psychological Medicine* [published online ahead of print, 2016].

99   *Irish Times*, 21 January 2012.

100   J. Fogarty, 'The people who hear voices in their heads', *Irish Examiner*, 11 April 2015.

101   I am very grateful to Dr Shari McDaid (Director, Mental Health Reform) for this information.

102   Expert Group on Mental Health Policy, *A Vision for Change*, p. 178.

103   P. Bracken, *Trauma: Culture, Meaning and Philosophy* (London and Philadelphia, PA: Whurr Publishers Ltd., 2002).

104   P. Bracken, P. Thomas, S. Timimi, E. Asen, G. Behr, C. Beuster, S. Bhunnoo, I. Browne, N. Chhina, D. Double, S. Downer, C. Evans, S. Fernando, M.R. Garland, W. Hopkins, R. Huws, B. Johnson, B. Martindale, H. Middleton, D. Moldavsky, J. Moncrieff, S. Mullins, J. Nelki, M. Pizzo, J. Rodger, M. Smyth, D. Summerfield, J. Wallace and D. Yeomans, 'Psychiatry beyond the current paradigm', *British Journal of Psychiatry*, 201, 6 (December 2012), pp. 430–4.

105   P. Thomas and P. Bracken, 'Critical psychiatry in practice', *Advances in Psychiatric Treatment*, 10, 5 (August 2004), pp. 361–70.

106   P. Bracken and P. Thomas, *Postpsychiatry: Mental Health in a Postmodern World* (Oxford: Oxford University Press, 2005).

107   P. Bracken and P. Thomas, 'Postpsychiatry: a new direction for mental health', *British Medical Journal*, 322, 7288 (24 March 2001), pp. 724–7.

108   L. Appleby, 'Suicide and self-harm', in R. Murray, P. Hill and P. McGuffin (eds), *The Essentials of Postgraduate Psychiatry (Third Edition)* (Cambridge: Cambridge University Press, 1997), pp. 551–62; p. 551.

109   See: N. Walsh and D. McGrath, 'Self-poisoning and psycho-historical change in Ireland', *Irish Medical Journal*, 68, 14 (July 1975), pp. 343–50; D. Walsh, 'A century of suicide in Ireland', *Journal of the Irish Medical Association*, 69, 6 (1976), pp. 144–52; T. Brugha and D. Walsh, 'Suicide past and present – the temporal constancy of under-reporting', *British Journal of Psychiatry*, 132, 2 (February 1978), pp. 177–9; D. Walsh, 'The recent increase in reported suicide in Ireland', *Irish Medical Journal*, 71, 18 (December 1978), pp. 613–6; C. Smyth, M. MacLachlan and A. Clare, *Cultivating Suicide? Destruction of Self in a Changing Ireland* (Dublin: Liffey Press, 2003).

110   T. Fahy, 'Suicide and the Irish: from sin to serotonin', in C. Keane (ed.), *Mental Health in Ireland* (Dublin: Gill & Macmillan and Radio Teilifís Éireann, 1991), pp. 18–30; p. 19.

111   M. McGoff-McCann, *Melancholy Madness: A Coroner's Casebook* (Cork: Mercier Press, 2003), pp. 109–38.

112   G. Laragy, 'Narratives of poverty in Irish suicides between the Great Famine and the First World War, 1845–1914' in A. Gestrich, E. Hurren and S. King (eds), *Poverty and Sickness in Modern Europe: Narratives of the Sick Poor, 1780–1938* (London and New York: Continuum International Publishing Group, 2012), pp. 143–59. See also: G. Laragy, 'Suicide and insanity in post-Famine Ireland', in C. Cox and M. Luddy (eds), *Cultures of Care in Irish Medical History 1750–1950* (Basingstoke, Hampshire: Palgrave Macmillan, 2010), pp. 79–91; G. Laragy, '"A peculiar species of felony": suicide, medicine, and the law in Victorian Britain and Ireland', *Journal of Social History*, 46, 3 (Spring 2013), pp. 732–43.

113   M.J. Kelleher, *Suicide and the Irish* (Cork and Dublin: Mercier Press, 1996), pp. 11–13.

114   M.J. Kelleher, 'Suicide in Ireland', *Irish Medical Journal*, 84, 2 (June 1991), pp. 40–1.

115   M. Osman and A.C. Parnell, 'Effect of the First World War on suicide rates in Ireland: an investigation of the 1864–1921 suicide trends', *British Journal of Psychiatry Open*, 1, 2 (November 2015), pp. 164–5.

116   Central Statistics Office, *Tuarascáil an Ard-Chláraitheora 1952* (Dublin: Stationery Office, 1954), p. 8.

117   G.R. Swanwick and A.W. Clare, 'Suicide in Ireland 1945–1992: social correlates', *Irish Medical Journal*, 90, 3 (April/May 1997), pp. 106–8.

118 F. Bowers, *Suicide in Ireland* (Dublin: Irish Medical Organisation, 1994), p. 7.

119 McDermott, *St Mary's Hospital Castlebar: Serving Mayo Mental Health from 1866*, p. 162.

120 Health Service Executive, National Suicide Review Group and Department of Health and Children, *Reach Out: National Strategy for Action on Suicide Prevention, 2005–2014* (Dublin: Health Service Executive, 2005).

121 National Office for Suicide Prevention, *Annual Report 2014* (Dublin: Health Service Executive, 2015), pp. 63–9.

122 C. D'Arcy, 'Suicide rates are 'stabilising' after increasing during recession', *Irish Times*, 23 April 2016.

123 B.D. Kelly and A.M. Doherty, 'Impact of recent economic problems on mental health in Ireland', *International Psychiatry*, 10, 1 (February 2013), pp. 6–8; C. O'Brien, 'Almost 500 additional suicides linked to recession', *Irish Times*, 16 March 2015; D. Walsh, 'Rethinking the link between the recession and increased 'economic suicides'', *Irish Medical Times*, 5 June 2015.

124 O.C. Murphy, C. Kelleher and K.M. Malone, 'Demographic trends in suicide in the UK and Ireland, 1980–2010', *Irish Journal of Medical Science*, 184, 1 (March 2015), pp. 227–35.

125 K.M. Malone, L. Quinlivan, S. McGuinness, F. McNicholas and C. Kelleher, 'Suicide in children over two decades: 1993–2008', *Irish Medical Journal*, 105, 7 (July–August 2012), pp. 231–3.

126 National Office for Suicide Prevention, *Annual Report 2013* (Dublin: Health Service Executive, 2014), p. 69.

127 College of Psychiatry of Ireland, *Antidepressant Medication – Clarification* (Dublin: College of Psychiatry of Ireland, 2010).

128 Healthy Ireland, Department of Health, Health Service Executive and National Office for Suicide Prevention, *Connecting for Life: Ireland's National Strategy to Reduce Suicide, 2015–2020* (Dublin: Department of Health, 2015).

129 L. Mudiwa, 'A programme for Health', *Irish Medical Times*, 22 January 2016.

130 D. Beattie and P. Devitt, *Suicide: A Modern Obsession* (Dublin: Liberties Press, 2015).

131 D. Murray, 'Is it time to abandon suicide risk assessment?', *British Journal of Psychiatry Open*, 2, 1 (February 2016), pp. e1–2.

132 S. Bardon, 'Kenny and Martin deal on Seanad', *Irish Times*, 28 May 2016.

133 M. O'Regan, 'Mental illness still carries stigma, says TD', *Irish Times*, 28 January 2016. See also: E. Byrne, 'Do we really need 232 suicide charities?', *Sunday Business Post*, 26 June 2016.

134 Mental Health Commission, *A Vision for a Recovery Model in Irish Mental Health Services: Discussion Paper* (Dublin: Mental Health Commission, 2005), p. 15.

135 C. Griffin and Mental Health Commission, *A Vision for a Recovery Model in Irish Mental Health Services: A Qualitative Analysis of Submissions to the Mental Health Commission* (Dublin: Mental Health Commission, 2007).

136 A. Higgins and Mental Health Commission, *A Recovery Approach Within the Irish Mental Health Services: A Framework for Development* (Dublin: Mental Health Commission, 2008), p. 14.

137 P. Collins and L. Naughton, *Advancing Recovery in Ireland. A National Conversation: Opening Thoughts* (Dublin: National Office for Advancing Recovery in Ireland, Health Service Executive, Mental Health Division, 2015).

138 S. Thompson, 'Eolas offers integrated, innovative map of mental health services', *Irish Times*, 23 June 2015; A. Higgins, D. Hevey, P. Gibbons, C. O'Connor, F. Boyd, P. McBennett and M. Monahan, 'A participatory approach to the development of a co-produced and co-delivered information programme for users of services and family members: the EOLAS programme (paper 1)', *Irish Journal of Psychological Medicine* [published online ahead of print, 2016]; A. Higgins, D. Hevey, P. Gibbons, C. O'Connor, F. Boyd, P. McBennett and M. Monahan, 'Impact of co-facilitated information programmes on outcomes for service users and family members: the EOLAS programmes (paper 2)', *Irish Journal of Psychological Medicine* [published online ahead of print, 2016].

139 J. Hough, 'Call to "rip up" mental health services', *Irish Examiner*, 12 November 2015.

140 N. Salter, 'Mental health and children', *Irish Times*, 22 August 2015 (in response to: B.D. Kelly, 'Mental health services for children', *Irish Times*, 12 August 2015).

141 Cox, *Negotiating Insanity in the Southeast of Ireland, 1820–1900*, pp. 60–2.

142 E. Malcolm, 'Between habitual drunkards and alcoholics: inebriate women and reformatories in Ireland, 1899–1919', in M.H. Preston and M. Ó hÓgartaigh (eds), *Gender and Medicine in Ireland, 1700–1950* (Syracuse, New York: Syracuse University Press, 2012), pp. 108–22. See also: Robins, *Fools and Mad: A History of the Insane in Ireland*, pp. 113–16.

143 Richmond Asylum Joint Committee, *Richmond Asylum Joint Committee Minutes*, pp. 557–8.

144 L. O'Brien, 'The magic wisp: a history of the mentally ill in Ireland', *Bulletin of the Menninger Clinic*, 31, 2 (March 1967), pp. 79–95; pp. 91–2.

145 E. Malcolm, *'Ireland Sober, Ireland Free'. Drink and Temperance in Nineteenth-Century Ireland* (Dublin: Gill and Macmillan, 1986); E. Malcolm, 'Between habitual drunkards and alcoholics: inebriate women and reformatories in Ireland, 1899–1919', in M.H. Preston and M. Ó hÓgartaigh (eds), *Gender and Medicine in Ireland, 1700–1950* (Syracuse, New York: Syracuse University Press, 2012), pp. 108–22.

146 G. Bretherton, 'Irish inebriate reformatories, 1899–1902: an experiment in coercion', in I. O'Donnell and F. McAuley (eds), *Criminal Justice History: Themes and Controversies from Pre-Independence Ireland* (Dublin: Four Courts Press, 2003), pp. 214–32.

147 Finnane, *Insanity and the Insane in Post-Famine Ireland*, pp. 146–50, 171.

148 S. Butler, *Benign Anarchy: Alcoholics Anonymous in Ireland* (Dublin: Irish Academic Press, 2010), p. 66.

149 M. Webb, 'Alcohol excess – the curse of the drinking classes', in: C. Keane (ed.), *Mental Health in Ireland* (Dublin: Gill and Macmillan and Radio Telefís Éireann, 1991), pp. 99–111; Kelleher, *Suicide and the Irish*, pp. 43–4, 59–68.

150 Malcolm, *Swift's Hospital: A History of St Patrick's Hospital, Dublin, 1746–1989*, p. 288; J.G. Cooney, 'The problem drinker', in K. O'Sullivan (ed.), *All in the Mind: Approaches to Mental Health* (Dublin: Gill and Macmillan, 1986), pp. 100–5.

151 R. Shelley, 'Dr Pat Tubridy, 1936–2013', *The Consultant*, Summer 2013, p. 101. See also: D. Healy, 'Interview: In conversation with Desmond McGrath', *Psychiatric Bulletin*, 16, 3 (March 1992), pp. 129–37; pp. 136–7; B. O'Shea, 'Appreciation – Dr Pat Tubridy (1936–2013)', *Irish Medical Times*, 15 February 2013.

152 F. Murray, 'The price of alcohol', *Irish Times*, 12 December 2015.

153 B.D. Kelly, 'Should we legalise or decriminalise cannabis?', *Irish Times*, 27 November 2015.

154 Expert Group on Mental Health Policy, *A Vision for Change*, p. 146.

155 J. Barry, C. Farren, E. Keenan, F. Nangle-O'Connor, A. Quigley, S. Rooney, B. Smyth and J. Treacy, 'Excluding addiction from mental health services', *Irish Times*, 15 December 2006.

156 L. Douglas and L. Feeney, 'Thirty years of referrals to a community mental health service', *Irish Journal of Psychological Medicine*, 33, 2 (June 2016), pp. 105–9.

157 E. Shorter, *How Everyone Became Depressed: The Rise and Fall of the Nervous Breakdown* (Oxford and New York: Oxford University Press, 2013).

158 C. Collins, M.T. O'Shea, P. Finegan, J. Cunniffe, D. Collier, M. Curran and M. Kearns, *Mental Health Consultations in a General Practice Out of Hours Service – Informing the Future Direction of Services* (Dublin: Irish College of General Practitioners, 2016).

159 MacÉinrí, *Immigration into Ireland* (Cork: Irish Centre For Migration Studies, 2001).

160 F.E. Wilson, E. Hennessy, B. Dooley, B.D. Kelly and D.A. Ryan, 'Trauma and PTSD rates in an Irish psychiatric population: a comparison of native and immigrant samples', *Disaster Health*, 1, 2 (December 2013), pp. 74–83; B.D. Kelly, 'Psychiatric admission in Ireland: the role of country of origin', in M. Donnelly and C. Murray (eds), *Ethical and Legal Debates in Irish Healthcare: Confronting Complexities* (Manchester: Manchester University Press, 2016), pp. 194–207.

161 X.T. Ng and B.D. Kelly, 'Voluntary and involuntary care: three-year study of demographic and diagnostic admission statistics at an inner-city adult psychiatry unit', *International Journal of Law and Psychiatry*, 35, 4 (July–August 2012), pp. 317–26; B.D. Kelly, A. Emechebe, C. Anamdi, R. Duffy, N. Murphy and C. Rock, 'Custody, care and country of origin: demographic and diagnostic admission statistics at an inner-city adult psychiatry unit', *International Journal of Law and Psychiatry*, 38, 1 (January–February 2015), pp. 1–7.

162 A. Curley, E. Agada, A. Emechebe, C. Anamdi, X.T. Ng, R. Duffy and B.D. Kelly, 'Exploring and explaining involuntary care: the relationship between psychiatric admission status, gender and other demographic and clinical variables', *International Journal of Law and Psychiatry* [published online ahead of print, 2016].

163 A. Hearns, 'Dealing with the aftermath of torture', *Forum*, 33, 1 (January 2016), pp. 17–18.

164 Health Service Executive, *National Intercultural Health Strategy, 2007–2012* (Dublin: Health Service Executive, 2008).

165 S. Linehan, D. Duffy, H. O'Neill, C. O'Neill and H.G. Kennedy, 'Irish travellers and forensic mental health', *Irish Journal of Psychological Medicine*, 19, 3 (September 2002), pp. 76–9; C. McGorrian, N.A. Hamid, P. Fitzpatrick, L. Daly, K.M. Malone and C. Kelleher, 'Frequent mental distress (FMD) in Irish Travellers: discrimination and bereavement negatively influence mental health in the All Ireland Traveller Health Study', *Transcultural Psychiatry*, 50, 4 (August 2013), pp. 559–78.

166 Mental Health Reform, *Ethnic Minorities and Mental Health: A Position Paper* (Dublin: Mental Health Reform, 2014).

167 B.D. Kelly, 'Migrants need support but they also need dignity', *Irish Times*, 16 September 2015.

168 M. O'Connell, R. Duffy and N. Crumlish, 'Refugees, the asylum system and mental healthcare in Ireland', *BJPsych International*, 13, 2 (May 2016), pp. 35–7.

169 D. Walsh, 'Brief historical review', *Irish Journal of Psychiatry*, 13, 1 (Spring 1992), pp. 3–20; p. 16.

170 Working Party on Services for the Elderly, *The Years Ahead ... A Policy for the Elderly* (Dublin: The Stationery Office, 1988).

171 Inter-Departmental Subcommittee on the Care of the Aged, *The Care of the Aged* (Dublin: The Stationery Office, 1968), p. 13.

172 Working Party on Services for the Elderly, *The Years Ahead ... A Policy for the Elderly*, p. 16.

173 Ibid., pp. 1–11.

174 Ibid., pp. 10–11.

175 D. Walsh, 'The elderly and handicapped in psychiatric hospitals', *Irish Journal of Psychiatry*, 12, 1 (Spring 1991), p. 2.

176 H. Ruddle, F. Donoghue and R. Mulvihill, The Years Ahead *Report: A Review of the Implementation of its Recommendations* (Dublin: National Council on Ageing and Older People, 1998).

177 D. O'Neill and S. O'Keeffe, 'Health care for older people in Ireland', *Journal of the American Geriatric Society*, 51, 9 (September 2003), pp. 1280–6.

178 Expert Group on Mental Health Policy, *A Vision for Change*, p. 116.

179 C. Jagger, F.E. Matthews, P. Wohland, T. Fouweather, B.C.M Stephan, L. Robinson, A. Arthur and C. Brayne, on behalf of the Medical Research Council Cognitive Function and Ageing Collaboration, 'A comparison of health expectancies over two decades in England: results of the Cognitive Function and Ageing Study I and II', *Lancet*, 387, 10020 (20 February 2016), pp. 779–86. See also: D. O'Neill, 'Playing constituency politics to the detriment of our hospitals', *Irish Times*, 8 March 2016.

180 C. Kelly, *Annual Report of the National Intellectual Disability Database Committee 2014* (Dublin: Health Research Board, 2015); D. Barron, 'Intellectual disability needs increasing as cohort ages', *Irish Medical News*, 24 November 2015.

181 Department of Health and Healthy Ireland, *The National Positive Ageing Strategy* (Dublin: Department of Health, 2013), p. 20.

182 Ibid., pp. 28–9.

183 College of Psychiatrists of Ireland, *Workforce Planning Report 2013–2023* (Dublin: College of Psychiatrists of Ireland, 2013), pp. 9–11.

184 Ibid., p. 2.

185 Ibid., p. 4.

186 R.J. Daly, 'Community psychiatry and the National Institute of Mental Health', *Irish Journal of Psychological Medicine*, 7, 1 (March 1990), p. 5; M. Hartman, 'An Irish National Institute of Mental Health', *Irish Journal of Psychological Medicine*, 7, 1 (March 1990), p. 5; A. Clare, R.J. Daly, T.G. Dinan, D. King, B.E. Leonard, C. O'Boyle, J. O'Connor, J. Waddington, N. Walsh and M. Webb, 'Advancement of psychiatric research in Ireland: proposal for a national body', *Irish Journal of Psychological Medicine*, 7, 2 (September 1990), p. 93.

187 D. Meagher, N. O'Regan, D. Ryan, W. Connolly, E. Boland, R. O'Caoimhe, J. Clare, J. McFarland, S. Tighe, M. Leonard, D. Adamis, P.T. Trzepacz and S. Timmons, 'Frequency of delirium and subsyndromal delirium in an adult acute hospital population', *British Journal of Psychiatry*, 205, 6 (December 2014), pp. 478–85.

188 D. Meagher, 'Dr Maeve Leonard (Ryan) 1968–2015', *Irish Journal of Psychological Medicine*, 33, 1 (March 2016), pp. 67–8.

189 A.K. Merikangas, R. Segurado, P. Cormican, E.A. Heron, R.J. Anney, S. Moore, E. Kelleher, A. Hargreaves, H. Anderson-Schmidt, M. Gill, L. Gallagher and A. Corvin, 'The phenotypic manifestations of rare CNVs in schizophrenia', *Schizophrenia Research*, 158, 1–3 (September 2014), pp. 255–60.

190 L. Emsell, A. Leemans, C. Langan, W. Van Hecke, G.J. Barker, P. McCarthy, B. Jeurissen, J. Sijbers, S. Sunaert, D.M. Cannon and C. McDonald, 'Limbic and callosal white matter changes in euthymic bipolar I disorder: an advanced diffusion MRI tractography study', *Biological Psychiatry*, 73, 2 (January 2013), pp. 194–201; M. Ahmed, D.M. Cannon, C. Scanlon, L. Holleran, H. Schmidt, J. McFarland, C. Langan, P. McCarthy, G.J. Barker, B. Hallahan and C. McDonald, 'Progressive brain atrophy and cortical thinning in schizophrenia after commencing clozapine treatment', *Neuropsychopharmacology*, 40, 10 (September 2015), pp. 2409–17.

191 See, for example: M.C. Clarke, A. Tanskanen, M.O. Huttunen, M. Clancy, D.R. Cotter and M. Cannon, 'Evidence for shared susceptibility to epilepsy and psychosis: a population-based family study', *Biological Psychiatry*, 71, 9 (May 2012), pp. 836–9; A.M. Doherty, F. Jabbar, B.D. Kelly and P. Casey, 'Distinguishing between adjustment disorder and depressive episode in clinical practice: the role of personality disorder', *Journal of Affective Disorders*, 168 (October 2014), pp. 78–85; V. O'Keane, T. Frodl and T.G. Dinan, 'A review of atypical depression in relation to the course of depression and changes in HPA axis organization', *Psychoneuroendocrinology*, 37, 10 (October 2012), pp. 1589–99; M. Semkovska, S. Landau, R. Dunne, E. Kolshus, A. Kavanagh, A. Jelovac, M. Noone, M. Carton, S. Lambe, C. McHugh, and D. M. McLoughlin, 'Bitemporal versus high-dose unilateral twice-weekly electroconvulsive therapy for depression (EFFECT-Dep): a pragmatic, randomized, non-inferiority trial', *American Journal of Psychiatry*, 173, 4 (1 April 2016), pp. 408–17.

192 S.R. Foley and B.D. Kelly, 'Psychological concomitants of capital punishment: thematic analysis of last statements from death row', *American Journal of Forensic Psychiatry*, 28, 4 (2007), pp. 7–13; B.D. Kelly and S.R. Foley, 'The price of life', *British Medical Journal*, 335, 7626 (3 November 2007), p. 938; B.D. Kelly and S.R. Foley, 'Love, spirituality and regret: thematic analysis of last statements from death row, Texas (2006–2011)', *Journal of the American Academy of Psychiatry and the Law*, 41, 4 (December 2013), pp. 540–50.

193 S. McWilliams, *The Witchdoctor of Chisale* (Guildford, Surrey: Grosvenor House Publishing Ltd., 2006); S. McWilliams, *Fiction and Physicians: Medicine Through the Eyes of Writers* (Dublin: Liffey Press, 2012).

194 C. Farren, *Overcoming Alcohol Misuse: A 28-Day Guide* (Blackrock, County Dublin: Kite Books/Blackhall Publishing, 2011); C. Farren, *The U-Turn: A Guide to Happiness* (Blackrock, County Dublin: Orpen Press, 2013).

195 A. Mac Lellan, N. Nic Ghabhann and F. Byrne, *World Within Walls* (Monaghan: Health Service Executive and Stair: An Irish Public History Company Ltd., 2015).

196 For example, a discussion of homosexuality in the history of psychiatry on *History Show*, RTÉ Radio 1, 20 March 2016.

197 D. Lynch, 'A look at what we tried not to see', *Irish Independent*, 25 September 2005.

198 M. Raftery, 'Revealing the horrific past of psychiatric hospitals', *Irish Times*, 5 September 2011; B. Harrison, 'One forensic documentary beats two cliché-ridden cop dramas', *Irish Times*, 17 September 2011; A. Connors, 'Mental Health Minister claims that our services "have

come a long way"', *Irish Medical Times*, 23 September 2011.

199   D. McManus, 'Irish documentary provides fascinating insight into history of mental health care in Ireland', *Irish Independent*, 17 September 2014.

200   K. Millett, *The Loony Bin Trip* (London: Virago, 1991).

201   A. Scott (edited by S. Dolamore), *Is That Me? My Life with Schizophrenia* (Dublin: A. & A. Farmar, 2002). For a perspective on this book, see: B.D. Kelly, 'True stories of illness', *Irish Psychiatrist*, 6, 1 (February–March 2005), p. 23.

202   M. Maddock and J. Maddock, *Soul Survivor: A Personal Encounter with Psychiatry* (Sheffield: Asylum Books, 2006).

203   V. Grattan, *Hidden Grief: Words From A Journey of Hopelessness to a Pathway to Hope and Survival* (Dublin: Betaprint Limited, 2005).

204   É. Walshe, *Cissie's Abattoir* (Cork: The Collins Press, 2009); pp. 65–81, 107–8.

205   F. Cleary, *In A World Apart* (Donegal: Fergus Cleary, 2015).

206   M. Hawkins, *Restless Spirit: The Story of Rose Quinn* (Cork: Mercier Press, 2006).

207   T. Dooley, *The Decline and Fall of the Dukes of Leinster, 1872–1948: Love, War, Debt and Madness* (Dublin: Four Courts Press, 2014). For a perspective on this book, see: D. Walsh, 'The grand young Duke of Leinster', *Irish Medical Times*, 9 October 2015.

208   N.C. Andreasen, 'James Joyce. A portrait of the artist as a schizoid', *Journal of the American Medical Association*, 224, 1 (April 1973), pp. 67–71; J.B. Lyons, *Thrust Syphilis Down to Hell and Other Rejoyceana: Studies in the Border-lands of Literature and Medicine* (Dún Laoghaire: Irish Books and Media, 1988); A. Collins, 'James Joyce and a North Dublin asylum', *Irish Journal of Psychological Medicine*, 19, 1 (March 2002), pp. 27–8).

209   J.M. Synge, *Collected Works, Volume II, Prose* (Oxford: Oxford University Press, 1966), pp. 209–11, 216–20.

210   W.B. Yeats, *Collected Poems* (Ware, Hertfordshire: Wordsworth Editions Limited, 1994), pp. 217–22.

211   S. Beckett, *Malone Meurt* (Paris: Les Éditions de Minuit, 1951).

212   Torrey and Miller, *The Invisible Plague: The Rise of Mental Illness from 1750 to the Present*, pp. 150–7. See also: S. O'Casey, *Drums Under the Windows. Autobiography: Book 3, 1906–1916* (London: Pan Books Limited, 1972; first published by Macmillan and Company Limited, 1945), pp. 54–65; Finnane, *Insanity and the Insane in Post-Famine Ireland*, p. 129.

213   K. O'Brien, *Presentation Parlour* (London: Heinemann, 1963).

214   W. Trevor, *Two Lives* (London: Viking, 1991); Healy, *150 Years of British Psychiatry. Volume II: The Aftermath*, pp. 286–7.

215   L. O'Flaherty, *Return of the Brute* (London: The Mandrake Press, 1929).

216   T. Murphy, *The Wake* (London: Bloomsbury Methuen Drama, 1998), pp.87–8.

217   S. Barry, *The Secret Scripture* (London: Faber and Faber Limited, 2008).

218   K. Barry, 'Roethke in the Bughouse', *Irish Times*, 8 August 2015.

219   C. Maturin, *Melmoth the Wanderer* (Edinburgh: Archibald Constable and Company, and Hurst, Robinson and Co., Cheapside, 1820).

220   Malcolm, *Swift's Hospital: A History of St Patrick's Hospital, Dublin, 1746–1989*, p. 341. See also: D. Kramer, *Charles Robert Maturin (Twayne's English Authors Series)* (New York: Twayne, 1973).

221   D. Tighe, 'Start making sense', in A. Harpin and J. Foster (eds), *Performance, Madness and Psychiatry: Isolated Acts* (Basingstoke, Hampshire: Palgrave Macmillan, 2014), pp. 111–36.

222   B.D. Kelly, 'Psychiatry and cinema', *Irish Psychiatrist*, 2, 5 (October/November 2001), pp. 267–72; B.D. Kelly, 'Psychiatry in contemporary Irish cinema: a qualitative study', *Irish Journal of Psychological Medicine*, 23, 2 (June 2006), pp. 74–9.

223   D. Bolger, 'Forgotten relics of lives written off as 'lunatics' and 'imbeciles'', *Irish Daily Mail*, 14 August 2014.

224   J. Fagan, '€7m for Sligo's four-star Clarion Hotel', *Irish Times*, 28 October 2015.

225   C. O'Brien, 'Goodbye Grangegorman', *Irish Times*, 23 February 2013.

226   D. Walsh, 'Grangegorman development misses the point', *Irish Medical Times*, 19 June 2009.

227   B.D. Kelly, 'Walking through the past in today's Sligo', *Irish Medical Times*, 1 October 2010.

228   F. O'Toole, 'Neglect of archives shows contempt for citizens', *Irish Times*, 10 April 2010; M. Tighe, 'Call for cash to preserve asylum files', *Sunday Times*, 18 April 2010; P. Crooks, 'Archives in crisis', *History Ireland*, 18, 3 (May/June 2010), pp. 10–1; D. Walsh, 'Preserving the history of old asylums', *Irish Medical Times*, 22 October 2010.

229   L.S. Penrose, 'Mental disease and crime: outlines of a comparative study of European statistics', *British Journal of Medical Psychology*, 18, 1 (March 1939), pp. 1–15; B.D. Kelly, 'Penrose's Law in Ireland: an ecological analysis of psychiatric inpatients and prisoners', *Irish Medical Journal*, 100, 2 (February 2007), pp. 373–4; W.S. Chow and S. Priebe, 'How has the extent of institutional mental healthcare changed in Western Europe? Analysis of data since 1990', *British Medical Journal Open*, 6, 4 (29 April 2016), e010188.

230   T. Taylor Salisbury and G. Thornicroft, 'Deinstitutionalisation does not increase imprisonment or homelessness', *British Journal of Psychiatry*, 208, 5 (May 2016), pp. 412–13; P. Winkler, B. Barrett, P. McCrone, L. Csémy, M. Janoušková and C. Höschl, 'Deinstitutionalised patients, homelessness and imprisonment: systematic review', *British Journal of Psychiatry*, 208, 5 (May 2016), pp. 421–8.

231 S. Kilcommins, I. O'Donnell, E. O'Sullivan and B. Vaughan, *Crime Punishment and the Search for Order in Ireland* (Dublin: Institute of Public Administration, 2004), p. 80; see also: M. Ignatieff, *A Just Measure of Pain* (London: Peregrine, 1978), pp. 214–15).

232 E. Malcolm, 'Between habitual drunkards and alcoholics: inebriate women and reformatories in Ireland, 1899–1919', in M.H. Preston and M. Ó hÓgartaigh (eds), *Gender and Medicine in Ireland, 1700–1950* (Syracuse, New York: Syracuse University Press, 2012), pp. 108–22.

233 S. Kilcommins, I. O'Donnell, E. O'Sullivan and B. Vaughan, *Crime Punishment and the Search for Order in Ireland*, p. 21.

234 M. Raftery, 'Psychiatric profession at it again', *Irish Times*, 25 May 2005.

235 C. Halpin, 'Psychiatrists, involuntary committals, and the Mental Health Act', *Irish Times*, 30 May 2005; S. Barry and B. Cassidy, 'Consultant psychiatrists making a principled stand', *Irish Medical Times*, 10 June 2005.

236 More broadly, see: M. Corry and Á. Tubridy, *Going Mad? Understanding Mental Illness* (Dublin: Newleaf/Gill and Macmillan Ltd., 2001).

237 P. Cullen, 'Apology from HSE on assault allegations', *Irish Times*, 5 February 2016.

238 F. O'Toole, 'Uncomfortable truths of old mental hospital system', *Irish Times*, 12 March 2013. See also: F. O'Toole, 'Dark stain of Irish gulag system not yet addressed', *Irish Times*, 25 September 2012; C. O'Brien, 'Call to extend inquiry to mental homes', *Irish Times*, 16 June 2014.

239 C. O'Brien, 'Psychiatric care and the gap in our social history', *Irish Times*, 16 June 2014.

240 See, for example: C. Smith, 'A future for our mentally ill?', in: C. Keane (ed.), *Mental Health in Ireland* (Dublin: Gill and Macmillan and Radio Telefís Éireann, 1991), pp. 112–24; pp. 122–3.

241 K. Crowe, Irish Advocacy Network on behalf of the Expert Group on Mental Health Policy, *What We Heard* (Dublin: Department of Health, 2004), p. 8. See also: Carr Communications on behalf of the Expert Group on Mental Health Policy, *Speaking Your Mind* (Dublin: Department of Health, 2004).

242 D. Brennan, 'Let those damaged by Irish asylum system tell their stories', *Irish Examiner*, 28 June 2014.

243 N. Breslin, *Me and My Mate Jeffrey: A Story of Big Dreams, Tough Realities and Facing My Demons Head On* (Dublin: Hachette Books Ireland, 2015).

244 L. Bailey, *Because We Are Bad: OCD and a Girl Lost in Thought* (Kingston upon Thames, Surrey: Canbury Press, 2016); A. Wallace, "Getting better is really scary ...", *Irish Times*, 11 June 2016.

245 F. Kennedy, 'I don't want to hear anyone else 'opening up' about their 'battle' with depression', *Irish Times*, 5 May 2016.

246 B.D. Kelly, 'Dignity, human rights and the limits of mental health legislation', *Irish Journal of Psychological Medicine*, 31, 2 (June 2014), pp. 75–81.

247 P. Casey, 'Any review of past abuses must extend to asylums', *Irish Independent*, 16 June 2014.

248 See, for example: Webb, *Trinity's Psychiatrists: From Serenity of the Soul to Neuroscience*, pp. 108–16. Webb also provides a fascinating account of the life and career of Dr Edward Armstrong Bennett (1888–1977), psychiatrist and Jungian analyst (pp. 80–4).

249 Commission on Lunacy, *Report on Insanity and Idiocy in Massachusetts* (Boston: William White, 1855), p. 62; W.H. Davenport, 'Blackwell's Island Lunatic Asylum', *Harper's New Monthly Magazine*, 32, 189 (February 1866), pp. 273–94; Robins, *Fools and Mad: A History of the Insane in Ireland*, pp. 121–7; Torrey and Miller, *The Invisible Plague: v*, pp. 98, 147, 240–1, 329; Walsh and Daly, *Mental Illness in Ireland 1750–2002: Reflections on the Rise and Fall of Institutional Care*, pp. 85–6; E. Malcolm, "A most miserable looking object': The Irish in English asylums, 1851–1901: migration, poverty and prejudice', in J. Belchem and K. Tenfelde (eds), *Irish and Polish Migration in Comparative Perspective* (Essen: Klartext Verlag, 2003), pp. 115–23; E. Malcolm, 'Irish emigrants in a Colonial Asylum during the Australian Gold Rushes, 1848–1869' in P.M. Prior (ed.), *Asylums, Mental Health Care and the Irish, 1800–2010* (Dublin: Irish Academic Press, 2012), pp. 119–48; A. McCarthy, 'Transitional ties to home: Irish migrants in New Zealand asylums, 1860–1926', in P.M. Prior (ed.), *Asylums, Mental Health Care and the Irish, 1800–2010* (Dublin: Irish Academic Press, 2012), pp. 149–66; C. Cox and H. Marland (eds), *Migration, Health and Ethnicity in the Modern World* (Basingstoke, Hampshire: Palgrave Macmillan, 2013); Pietikäinen, *Madness: A History*, 94, 117; C. Cox and H. Marland, "A burden on the county': madness, institutions of confinement and the Irish patient in Victorian Lancashire', *Social History of Medicine*, 28, 2 (May 2015), pp. 263–87. The issue of stigma against the Irish abroad is also worthy of mention: J. McCurry, 'Xenophobic Seoul job rejection hard to swallow', *Guardian*, 8 November 2014.

250 See, for example: M. Carolan, 'Young woman in UK psychiatric unit to come home', *Irish Times*, 8 July 2015.

251 F. Stonor Saunders, *The Woman Who Shot Mussolini* (London: Faber and Faber, 2010), p. 324; for perspectives on this book, see: L. Hughes-Hallett, 'God's chosen instrument', *Guardian*, 27 February 2010; B. Brennan, 'Society lady with a violent mission', *Irish Independent*, 6 March 2010; T. Barber, 'A flawed assassin', *Financial Times*, 3 April 2010. See also: F. McNally, 'An Irishman's Diary', *Irish Times*, 9 April 2016.

252 C. Loeb Shloss, *Lucia Joyce: To Dance in the Wake* (London: Bloomsbury, 2004), p. 455.

253 P.M. Prior, "Where lunatics abound': a history of mental health services in Northern Ireland', in H. Freeman and G.E. Berrios (eds), *150 Years of British Psychiatry. Volume II: The Aftermath* (London: Athlone Press, 1996), pp. 292–308; P.P. O'Malley, 'Attempted suicide before and after the communal violence in Belfast, August 1969',

Journal of the Irish Medical Association, 65, 5 (4 March 1972), pp. 109–13; P.P. O'Malley, 'Attempted suicide, suicide and communal violence', *Journal of the Irish Medical Association*, 68, 5 (8 March 1975), pp. 103–9; O'Malley, *Clinical Neuro-Psychiatry: Reflections on Neuro-Psychiatric Practice and Thought*, pp. 42–57; P. Hayes and J. Campbell, *Bloody Sunday: Trauma Pain and Politics* (London, Dublin and Ann Arbor, MI: Pluto Press, 2005); F. Ferry, B. Bunting, S. Murphy, S. O'Neill, D. Stein and K. Koenen, 'Traumatic events and their relative PTSD burden in Northern Ireland: a consideration of the impact of the 'Troubles', *Social Psychiatry and Psychiatric Epidemiology*, 49, 3 (March 2014), pp. 435–46; A. Turkington, M. Duffy, S. Barrett, R. McCaul, R. Anderson, S.J. Cooper, T. Rushe and C. Mulholland, 'Exposure to political violence in Northern Ireland and outcome of first episode psychosis', *Schizophrenia Bulletin*, 42, 3 (May 2016), pp. 626–32.

254   D.A. Sisti, A.G. Segal and E.J. Emmanuel, 'Improving long-term psychiatric care: bring back the asylum', *Journal of the American Medical Association*, 313, 3 (20 January 2015), pp. 243–4; W.S. Chow and S. Priebe, 'How has the extent of institutional mental healthcare changed in Western Europe? Analysis of data since 1990', *British Medical Journal Open*, 6, 4 (29 April 2016), e010188. See also: C. O'Brien, 'Vulnerable patients living in 'mini-institutions', *Irish Times*, 24 June 2014; Mental Health Commission, *Mental Health Commission Annual Report 2015 Including Report of the Inspector of Mental Health Services* (Dublin: Mental Health Commission, 2016), pp. 7, 34, 66–9.

255   See: Healy, *150 Years of British Psychiatry. Volume II: The Aftermath*, pp. 268–91.

256   G. Cullitan, 'Budget moves claims rejected', *Irish Medical Times*, 13 May 2016.

257   Walsh and Daly, *Mental Illness in Ireland 1750–2002: Reflections on the Rise and Fall of Institutional Care*, pp. 34, 88–90.

258   College of Psychiatrists of Ireland, *Budget Submission 2016: Press Statement: 9th October 2015* (Dublin: College of Psychiatrists of Ireland, 2015).

259   N. Tomes, 'Feminist histories of psychiatry', in M.S. Micale and R. Porter (eds), *Discovering the History of Psychiatry* (New York and Oxford: Oxford University Press, 1994), pp. 348–83.

260   M. Foucault, *History of Madness* (Abingdon, Oxon.: Routledge, 2006; first published as *Folie et Déraison: Histoire de la Folie à l'Âge Classique* in Paris by Librarie Plon, 1961).

261   Healy, *150 Years of British Psychiatry. Volume II: The Aftermath*, pp. 268–91.

262   Fitzgerald, *Irish Families under Stress (Volume 7)*, p. 115.

263   Healy, *150 Years of British Psychiatry. Volume II: The Aftermath*, pp. 268–91; Walsh, *Insanity Institutions and Society, 1800–1914: A Social History of Madness in Comparative Perspective*, pp. 228–9; Á.F. Lorié, *Secular Health and Sacred Belief? A Study of Religion and Mental Illness in Modern Irish Society* (Bern: Peter Lang, 2013), pp. 32–47; Cox, *Negotiating Insanity in the Southeast of Ireland, 1820–1900*, pp. 16–17.

264   P. Heffernan, 'An Irish doctor's memories: Clonmel (1902–1905)', in E. Lonergan (ed.), *St Luke's Hospital, Clonmel, 1834–1984* (Clonmel: South Eastern Health Board, 1984), pp. 91–5.

265   See, for example: Malcolm, ''The house of strident shadows': the asylum, the family and emigration in post-Famine rural Ireland', in G. Jones and E. Malcolm (eds), *Medicine, Disease and the State in Ireland, 1650–1940* (Cork: Cork University Press, 1999), pp. 177–91; p. 179; M.J. Breslin and E. Best, *Saints, Scholars and Schizophrenics Revisited: A Twenty-First Century Perspective on Religion and Mental Health in Ireland* (Bedford: Amazon/ CreateSpace Independent Publishing Platform, 2013).

266   O. Walsh, 'Gendering the asylums: Ireland and Scotland, 1847–1877' In T. Brotherstone, D. Simonton and O. Walsh (eds), *The Gendering of Scottish History: An International Approach* (Glasgow: Cruithne Press, 1999), pp. 199–215.

267   Brennan, *Irish Insanity, 1800–2000*, p. 103; C. O'Brien, 'Vulnerable patients living in 'mini-institutions', *Irish Times*, 24 June 2014.

268   S. Chaney, ''No "sane" person would have any idea': patients' involvement in late nineteenth-century British asylum psychiatry', *Medical History*, 60, 1 (January 2016), pp. 37–53.

269   O. Walsh, 'Lunatic and criminal alliances in nineteenth-century Ireland', in P. Bartlett and D. Wright (eds), *Outside the Walls of the Asylum: The History of Care in the Community, 1750–2000* (London: Athlone Press, 1999), pp. 132–52; p. 152.

270   L.D. Smith, *'Cure, Comfort and Safe Custody': Public Lunatic Asylums in Early Nineteenth-Century England* (London and New York: Leicester University Press, 1999), p. 5 (©Leonard D. Smith (1999), *'Cure, Comfort and Safe Custody': Public Lunatic Asylums in Early Nineteenth-Century England* (Leicester University Press, an imprint of Bloomsbury Publishing Plc). Used with permission.).

271   Ibid., p. 94 (© Leonard D. Smith (1999), *'Cure, Comfort and Safe Custody': Public Lunatic Asylums in Early Nineteenth-Century England* (Leicester University Press, an imprint of Bloomsbury Publishing Plc). Used with permission.).

272   Cox, *Negotiating Insanity in the Southeast of Ireland, 1820–1900*, pp. xviii, 97–132. See also: M. Finnane, 'Asylums, families and the State', *History Workshop Journal*, 20, 1 (Autumn 1985), pp. 134–48.

273   Cox, *Negotiating Insanity in the Southeast of Ireland, 1820–1900*, pp. 153–61. For an excellent discussion of families in this context, see: Finnane, *Insanity and the Insane in Post-Famine Ireland*, pp. 161–9, 173. In relation to families, see also: D. Walsh, 'Two and two make five – multifactoriogenesis in mental illness in Ireland', *Irish Medical Journal*, 69, 16 (October 1976), pp. 417–22.

274 E. Malcolm, "Ireland's crowded madhouses': the institutional confinement of the insane in nineteenth- and twentieth-century Ireland', in R. Porter and D. Wright (eds), *The Confinement of the Insane: International Perspectives, 1800–1965* (Cambridge: Cambridge University Press, 2003), pp. 315–33; pp. 330–2. See also: Brennan, *Irish Insanity, 1800–2000*, pp. 83–5.

275 E. Goffman, *Asylums: Essays on the Social Situation of Mental Patients and Other Inmates* (New York: Anchor Books, Doubleday and Company, 1961), p. 130. See also: S. Mac Suibhne, 'Medical classics: *Asylums: Essays on the Social Situation of Mental Patients and Other Inmates*', *British Medical Journal*, 339, 7725 (10 October 2009), p. 867; S. Mac Suibhne, 'Erving Goffman's *Asylums* 50 years on', *British Journal of Psychiatry*, 198, 1 (January 2011), pp. 1–2; J. Adlam, I. Gill, S.N. Glackin, B.D. Kelly, C. Scanlon and S. Mac Suibhne, 'Perspectives on Erving Goffman's "Asylums" fifty years on', *Medicine, Health Care and Philosophy*, 16, 3 (August 2013), pp. 605–13.

276 A. Scull, 'Rethinking the history of asylumdom', in J. Melling and B. Forsythe (eds), *Insanity Institutions and Society, 1800–1914: A Social History of Madness in Comparative Perspective* (London and New York: Routledge, 1999), pp. 295–315; p. 309; Pietikäinen, *Madness: A History*, pp. 155–6.

277 B.D. Kelly, 'Focus on mental health services', *Irish Times*, 14 July 2016.

Epilogue: Psychiatry in History

1 G.O. Gabbard and K. Gabbard, *Psychiatry and the Cinema (Second Edition)* (Washington, DC and London: American Psychiatric Publishing, 1999); B.D. Kelly, 'Psychiatry and cinema', *Irish Psychiatrist*, 2, 5 (October/November 2001), pp. 267–72; B.D. Kelly, 'Festival of film', *Irish Psychiatrist*, 3, 2 (April/May 2002), p. 66; B.D. Kelly, 'Psychiatry in contemporary Irish cinema: a qualitative study', *Irish Journal of Psychological Medicine*, 23, 2 (June 2006), pp. 74–9; D. Wedding, M.A. Boyd and R.M. Niemiec, *Movies and Mental Illness 3 (Third Edition)* (Cambridge, MA: Hogrefe Publishing, 2010); B.D. Kelly, 'Celluloid psychiatry', *Modern Medicine: Scope*, 43, 3 (March 2013), pp. 55–6; B.D. Kelly, 'Psychiatry at the movies', *Psychiatry Professional*, 2, 2 (Summer 2013), p. 12. For an affecting cinematic treatment of suicide in Ireland, see 'I Used to Live Here' (Write Direction Films, 2014); see also: D. Clarke, 'Live and don't let die', *Irish Times*, 3 April 2015; D. Clarke, 'Tallaght tale', *Irish Times*, 6 April 2015.

2 For interesting perspectives on this remarkable film, see: T. Brady, 'Sculpted in anguish', *Irish Times*, 20 June 2014; N. Andrews, 'Camille Claudel 1915', *Financial Times (Life and Arts)*, 21/22 June 2014.

3 E.K. Mahon, *Scandalous Women: The Lives and Loves of History's Most Notorious Women* (New York: Perigree/

Penguin Books, 2011), p. 213. See also: B. Cooper, 'Camille Claudel: trajectory of a psychosis', *Medical Humanities*, 34, 1 (June 2008), pp. 25–9; D. Walsh, 'Hammer and chisel to old asylum system', *Irish Medical Times*, 5 February 2016.

4 Mahon, *Scandalous Women: The Lives and Loves of History's Most Notorious Women*, p. 214.

5 A similar case in St Ita's, Portrane is outlined in the Introduction; see also: R. Boland, "Isolated from the mainstream': Portrane asylum in the 1950s', *Irish Times*, 10 June 2016.

6 D. Walsh, 'Brief historical review', *Irish Journal of Psychiatry*, 13, 1 (Spring 1992), pp. 3–20; p. 19.

7 In relation to the early twenty-first century, see: B.D. Kelly, 'Psychiatry cannot provide neat solutions on suicide', *Irish Times*, 17 July 2013; D. Beattie and P. Devitt, *Suicide: A Modern Obsession* (Dublin: Liberties Press, 2015), pp. 75–84. For an historico-philosophical perspective, see: P. Bracken, 'On *Madness and Civilisation: A History of Insanity in the Age of Reason* (1961), by Michel Foucault', *British Journal of Psychiatry*, 207, 5 (November 2015), p. 434.

8 Walsh, *Asylums, Mental Health Care and the Irish, 1800-2010*, pp. 252–62.

9 Walsh, *Health Policy and Practice in Ireland*, pp. 29–43; B.D. Kelly, 'The Mental Treatment Act 1945 in Ireland: an historical enquiry', *History of Psychiatry*, 19, 73(1) (March 2008), pp. 47–67.

10 D. Walsh, 'Mental illness in Ireland and its management', in D. McCluskey (ed.), *Health Policy and Practice in Ireland* (Dublin: University College Dublin Press, 2006), pp. 29–43; p. 34; B.D. Kelly, 'The Mental Treatment Act 1945 in Ireland: an historical enquiry', *History of Psychiatry*, 19, 73(1) (March 2008), pp. 47–67.

11 Walsh, *Gender and Medicine in Ireland, 1700-1950*, pp. 69–85.

12 J. Mills, *Conference of the Irish Asylum Committees* (Dublin: Dollard Printing House, 1904), pp. 55–6; Finnane, *Insanity and the Insane in Post-Famine Ireland*, pp. 175, 213; D. Healy, 'Interview: In conversation with Ivor Browne', *Psychiatric Bulletin*, 16, 1 (January 1992), pp. 1–9; D. Healy, 'Irish psychiatry in the twentieth century', in H. Freeman and G.E. Berrios (eds), *150 Years of British Psychiatry. Volume II: The Aftermath* (London: Athlone Press, 1996), pp. 268–91; p. 173.

13 Reynolds, *Grangegorman: Psychiatric Care in Dublin since 1815*, p. 78; McCarthy, *Irish Women's History*, pp. 123–6; B.D. Kelly, 'Clinical and social characteristics of women committed to inpatient forensic psychiatric care in Ireland, 1868-1908', *Journal of Forensic Psychiatry and Psychology*, 19, 2 (June 2008), pp. 261–73; B.D. Kelly, 'Poverty, crime and mental illness', *Social History of Medicine*, 21, 2 (August 2008), pp. 311–28; Guéret, *What the Doctor Saw*, p. 28.

14 B.D. Kelly, '*Folie à plusieurs*: forensic cases from nineteenth-century Ireland', *History of Psychiatry*, 20, 77 (Part 1) (March 2009), pp. 47–60; p. 51.

15 Finnane, *Insanity and the Insane in Post-Famine Ireland*, p. 188.

16 C. Norman, 'Presidential address, delivered at the Royal College of Physicians, Dublin, June 12th, 1894', *Journal of Mental Science*, 40, 171 (1 October 1894), pp. 487–99; C. Norman, 'The domestic treatment of the insane', *Dublin Journal of Medical Science*, 101, 2 (February 1896), pp. 111–21; C. Norman, 'On the need for family care of persons of unsound mind in Ireland', *Journal of Mental Science*, 50, 210 (1 July 1904), pp. 461–73; C. Norman, 'The family care of the insane', *Medical Press and Circular*, 29 November–6 December 1905.

17 Richmond Asylum Joint Committee, *Richmond Asylum Joint Committee Minutes* (Dublin: Richmond Asylum, 1907), pp. 92–3; B.D. Kelly, 'One hundred years ago: the Richmond Asylum, Dublin in 1907', *Irish Journal of Psychological Medicine*, 24, 3 (September 2007), pp. 108–14.

18 In relation to asylums, see, *inter alia*: E. Malcolm, 'Asylums and other "total institutions" in Ireland: recent studies', *Éire-Ireland*, 22, 3 (Fall 1987), pp. 151–60.

19 B.D. Kelly, 'One hundred years ago: the Richmond Asylum, Dublin in 1907', *Irish Journal of Psychological Medicine*, 24, 3 (September 2007), pp. 108–14; p.111.

20 A. O'Neill, P. Casey and R. Minton, 'The homeless mentally ill: an audit from an inner city hospital', *Irish Journal of Psychological Medicine*, 24, 2 (1 June 2007), pp. 62–6.

21 Porter and Micale, *Discovering the History of Psychiatry*, pp. 8–11.

22 Health and Social Care Information Centre, *Inpatients Formally Detained in Hospitals under the Mental Health Act 1983, and Patients Subject to Supervised Community Treatment: Annual Report, England, 2013* (Leeds: Health and Social Care Information Centre/National Statistics, 2013), p. 26.

23 A. Daly and D. Walsh, *Activities of Irish Psychiatric Units and Hospitals 2013* (Dublin: Health Research Board, 2014), p. 17.

24 M. Finnegan, 'I would rather get cancer again than be a patient in the Irish mental health service', *Irish Times*, 29 April 2016; H. Kennedy, 'Prisons now a dumping ground for mentally ill young men', *Irish Times*, 18 May 2016.

25 J. Fogarty, 'The people who hear voices in their heads', *Irish Examiner*, 11 April 2015.

26 M.M. Kłapciński and J. Rymaszewska, 'Open Dialogue approach – about the phenomenon of Scandinavian psychiatry', *Psychiatria Polska*, 49, 6 (2015), pp. 1179–90; Á. Quinlan, 'A fresh approach to mental health', *Irish Examiner*, 2 May 2016.

27 Expert Group on the Review of the Mental Health Act 2001, *Report of the Expert Group on the Review of the Mental Health Act 2001*. See also: B.D. Kelly, 'Mental illness requires an all-of-society response', *Irish Times*, 13 April 2015.

28 Expert Group on Mental Health Policy, *A Vision for Change*; B.D. Kelly, 'Depression – "them and us"', *Irish Times*, 15 May 2015.

29 C. O'Brien, 'Vulnerable patients living in "mini-institutions"', *Irish Times*, 24 June 2014; Z. Kelly, 'Within these walls ...' *Medical Independent*, 14 May 2015; A. Cullen, 'Psychotic patients left on trolleys in crisis-hit A&E', *Irish Independent*, 24 June 2015; A.A. Muhammad, 'Back to the land of serenity', *Irish Medical Times*, 29 January 2016; Kelly, *Mental Illness, Human Rights and the Law*, pp. 171–216.

30 O'Dúill, Fr Piaras, interview (18 May 2016). Fr O'Dúill was chaplain at St Brendan's in Grangegorman, Dublin, for over four decades and recalls many funerals at which hospital staff were the only mourners. See also: Henry, *Our Lady's Psychiatric Hospital Cork*, p. 594; R. Boland, "Isolated from the mainstream": Portrane asylum in the 1950s', *Irish Times*, 10 June 2016.

Chronology: Key Events in the History of Psychiatry in Ireland

1 D.H. Tuke, 'Alleged increase of insanity', *Journal of Mental Science*, 40, 169 (1 April 1894), pp. 219–34.

2 D. Brennan, *Irish Insanity, 1800–2000* (Abingdon, Oxon.: Routledge, 2014), pp. 123–4.

3 A. Collins, 'The Richmond District Asylum and the 1916 Easter Rising', *Irish Journal of Psychological Medicine*, 30, 4 (December 2013), pp. 279–83.

4 D. Walsh, 'Mental illness in Ireland and its management', in D. McCluskey (ed.), *Health Policy and Practice in Ireland* (Dublin: University College Dublin Press, 2006), pp. 29–43; p. 34.

5 Brennan, *Irish Insanity, 1800–2000*, pp. 125, 142.

6 *Croke v Smith* [1994] 3 IR 529; *Croke v Smith (No. 2)* [1998] 1 IR 101; *Croke v Ireland* (2000) ECHR 680.

7 Independent Monitoring Group, *A Vision for Change: Sixth Annual Report on Implementation (2011)* (Dublin: Department of Health, 2012), p. 3.

8 National Office for Suicide Prevention, *Annual Report 2014* (Dublin: Health Service Executive, 2015), pp.63–9.

9 A. Daly and D. Walsh, *Activities of Irish Psychiatric Units and Hospitals 2014* (Dublin: Health Research Board, 2015), p.28.

10 L. Douglas and L. Feeney, 'Thirty years of referrals to a community mental health service', *Irish Journal of Psychological Medicine*, 33, 2 (June 2016), pp.105–9.

BIBLIOGRAPHY

Primary Sources

MANUSCRIPT

Anonymous, *Hanover Park Asylum for the Recovery of Persons Labouring under Mental Derangement* (Carlow: Richard Price, 1815) [National Library of Ireland (P 1375(4))].

Ballinrobe Poor Law Union, County Mayo, Minutes: 1845 to 1900.

Browne, I., *The Psychiatric Services – Planning for the Future (Some Comments in Relation to Psychiatric Services in the Eastern Health Board)* (Dublin: I. Browne, 1985).

Browne, I., *The Psychiatric Services – Planning for the Future (Preliminary Report of the Chief Psychiatrist to Advise the Board on the General Principles Necessary to the Development of a Community Psychiatric Service)* (Dublin: I. Browne, 1985).

Browne, I.W. and D. Walsh, *Psychiatric Services for the Dublin Area* (Dublin: I.W. Browne and D. Walsh, 1964).

Bureau of Military History 1913–21 Collection Witness Statements (Military Archives, Cathal Brugha Barracks, Dublin):

- Witness Statement (Number 250) of Mr William P. Corrigan (File Number S.378).
- Witness Statement (Number 304) of Mr James Coughlan (File Number S.1337).
- Witness Statement (Number 568) of Eilís Bean Uí Chonaill (File Number S.1846).
- Witness Statement (Number 624) of Mrs Mary Flannery Woods (File Number S.1901).
- Witness Statement (Number 1,752) of Mrs McCarvill (Eileen McGrane) (File Number S.1434).

Carlow District Lunatic Asylum, Register of Patients ('Admission Book', 7 July 1848 to 21 February 1896, SDH/002/006) (Archive of St Dympna's Hospital (Carlow), Delany Archive, Carlow College, College Street, Carlow).

Carlow Mental Hospital Sports Entry Form (SDH/007/009) (Archive of St Dympna's Hospital (Carlow), Delany Archive, Carlow College, College Street, Carlow).

Central Mental Hospital (Central Criminal Lunatic Asylum), Medical Case Books and Case Registers (mid-1800s to early1900s) (Central Mental Hospital, Dundrum, Dublin).

Clare, A.W., Correspondence with the author (BK), 7 September 2005 (author's own collection).

Clare, A.W., Correspondence with the author (BK), 1 September 2006 (author's own collection).

General Register of Prisoners, Galway Prison, 1921 (National Archives, Bishop Street, Dublin, Ireland).

Larcom Papers, National Library of Ireland (Ms. 7,775 and 7,776). [This is a treasure trove of letters, minutes, regulations and cuttings about asylums, lunacy law and various issues relating to mental disorder in Ireland. Sir Thomas Aiskew Larcom (1801–1879) was Assistant Supervisor of the Ordnance Survey of Ireland (1828–48) and Under-Secretary of State for Ireland (1853–69)].

Lord Lieutenant of Ireland, *General Rules and Regulations for the Management of District Lunatic Asylums in Ireland* [1874] (Dublin: Pilkington, 1890) [National Library of Ireland (Ir 362 i 13)].

Lord Lieutenant and Council of Ireland, *General Rules for the Government of All the District Lunatic Asylums of Ireland, Made, Framed and Established by the Lord Lieutenant and Council of Ireland* (Dublin: Alexander Thom for her Majesty's Stationery Office, 1843).

Lord Lieutenant and Council of Ireland, *Further Rules* (Dublin: Alexander Thom for her Majesty's Stationery Office, 1853).

Lord Lieutenant and Council of Ireland, *Rules and Regulations for the Good Conduct and Management of the Central Lunatic Asylum at Dundrum* (Dublin: Thom, 1876) [National Library of Ireland (Ir 362 i 13)]).

Lords Justice and Privy Council in Ireland, *By the Lords Justice and Privy Council in Ireland* (Dublin: Council Chamber, 1885) [National Library of Ireland (Ir 362 i 13)].

Medical Directory for 1905 (London: J. and A. Churchill, 1905).

Michael, J., *Report on a Study of Professor Ivor Browne's Experiential Psychotherapy Unit for the Committee Considering the Proposed National Trauma Unit (Second Draft)* (Dublin: No Publisher, 1993).

Minutes of the Proceedings of the Committee of Management of Ballinasloe District Lunatic Asylum/Mental Hospital, 1904–42 (Archives at St Brigid's Hospital, Ballinasloe, County Galway, Ireland).

Norman, C., 'Report of Dr Norman' in *Richmond Asylum Joint Committee Minutes* (Dublin: Richmond Asylum, 1907).

Official Report of Dáil Éireann (Houses of Oireachtas, Dublin, Ireland).

Official Report of Seanad Éireann (Houses of Oireachtas, Dublin, Ireland).

Privy Council, *General Rules and Regulations for the Management of District Lunatic Asylums in Ireland* (Dublin: Alexander Thom for her Majesty's Stationery Office, 1862).

Richmond Asylum Joint Committee, *Richmond Asylum Joint Committee Minutes* (Dublin: Richmond Asylum, 1907).

Richmond War Hospital Case Book (1918–1919) (BR/PRIV 1223 Richmond War) (National Archives, Bishop Street, Dublin, Ireland).

War Office, 'Castle File No. 4168: Dr English, Ada' WO 35/206/75 (Kew, Richmond, Surrey: British National Archives).

UNIVERSITY THESES

Arton, M., 'The Professionalisation of Mental Nursing in Great Britain, 1850–1950' (PhD Thesis, University College London, 1998).

Bates, D., 'Keepers to Nurses? A History of the Irish Asylum Workers' Trade Union 1917–1924' (MA Dissertation, University College Dublin, 2010).

Brown, J., 'The Legal Powers to Detain the Mentally Ill in Ireland: Medicalism or Legalism?' (PhD Thesis, Dublin City University, 2015).

Delargy, R., 'The History of Belfast District Lunatic Asylum 1829–1921' (PhD Thesis, University of Ulster, 2002).

Elliot, M., 'Inheriting New Opportunities for Women: Dr Eveleen O'Brien (1901–1981)' (MA Thesis, University College Dublin, 2003).

Grimsley-Smith, M.D., 'Politics, Professionalisation, and Poverty: Lunatic Asylums for the Poor in Ireland, 1817–1920' (PhD Thesis, University of Notre Dame, Indiana, 2011).

Kelly, N.A., 'History by Proxy – Imaging the Great Irish Famine' (PhD Thesis, University of Amsterdam, 2010).

Mauger, A., '"Confinement of the Higher Orders"? The Significance of Private Lunatic Asylums in Ireland, 1820–1860' (MA Dissertation, University College Dublin, 2009).

O'Neill, J., 'The Portrayal of Madness in the Limerick Press, 1772–1845' (MA Thesis, Mary Immaculate College (University of Limerick), 2013).

Parry, J., 'Women and Madness in Nineteenth-Century Ireland' (MA Thesis, St Patrick's College, Maynooth (National University of Ireland), 1997).

Williamson, A.P., 'The Origins of the Irish Mental Hospital Service, 1800–1843' (MLitt Thesis, Trinity College Dublin, 1970).

PRINTED (pre-1970)

Abraham, G.W., *The Law and Practice of Lunacy in Ireland as Administered by the Lord Chancellor under the Sign Manual Together with a Compendium of the Law Relating to Establishments for the Care of the Insane* (Dublin: E. Ponsonby, 1886).

Allbutt, T.C. (ed.), *A System of Medicine* (London: Macmillan, 1896–99).

American Psychiatric Association, *Diagnostic and Statistical Manual of Mental Disorders (First Edition)* (Washington DC: American Psychiatric Association, 1952).

American Psychiatric Association, *Diagnostic and Statistical Manual of Mental Disorders (Second Edition)* (Washington DC: American Psychiatric Association, 1968).

Anonymous, 'Increase in insanity', *American Journal of Insanity*, 18, 1 (July 1861).

Anonymous, 'Reports and analyses and descriptions of new inventions in medicine, surgery, dietetics and the allied sciences', *British Medical Journal*, 1, 1109 (1 April 1882), 464–5.

Anonymous, 'Obituary: James Alexander Eames, MD', *Journal of Mental Science*, 32, 139 (1 October 1886), 461–2.

Anonymous, 'Obituary: Joseph Lalor, MD', *Journal of Mental Science*, 32, 139 (1 October 1886), 462–3.

Anonymous, 'Obituary: Daniel Hack Tuke', *Lancet*, 145, 3733 (16 March 1895), 718–19.

Anonymous, 'Medical news', *British Medical Journal*, 1, 1786 (23 March 1895), 679.

Anonymous, 'Erratum', *British Medical Journal*, 1, 1787 (30 March 1895), 738.

Anonymous, 'Meeting of the Irish Division', *Journal of Mental Science*, 42, 178 (1 July 1896), 656–60.

Anonymous, 'Irish Division', *Journal of Mental Science*, 48, 203 (1 October 1902), 805–6.

Anonymous, 'Ballinasloe once more: Comic relief', *Journal of Mental Science*, 50, 210 (1 July 1904), 597–8.

Anonymous, 'Obituary: Conolly Norman, MD FRCPI', *British Medical Journal*, 1, 2461 (29 February 1908), 541.

Anonymous, 'The Conolly Norman memorial', *Journal of Mental Science*, 54, 226 (1 July 1908), 582.

Anonymous, 'Medico-Psychological Association of Great Britain and Ireland', *Journal of Mental Science*, 54, 227 (1 October 1908), 780–98.

Anonymous, 'Notes and news: Irish division', *Journal of Mental Science*, 56, 234 (1 July 1910), 577–81.

Anonymous, 'Notes and news: The Medico-Psychological Association of Great Britain and Ireland', *Journal of Mental Science*, 57, 239 (1 October 1911), 723–46.

Anonymous, 'Irish Division', *Journal of Mental Science*, 63, 261 (1 April 1917), 297–9.

Anonymous, 'Irish Division', *Journal of Mental Science*, 63, 263 (1 October 1917), 620.

Anonymous, 'Louth Ordnance Survey Letters (Continued)', *Journal of the County Louth Archaeological Society*, 5, 1 (December 1921), 28–34.

Anonymous, 'Irish Division', *Journal of Mental Science*, 68, 282 (July 1922), 313.

Anonymous, 'Irish Division', *Journal of Mental Science*, 81, 335 (October 1935), 1000–1.

Anonymous, 'Irish Division', *Journal of Mental Science*, 95, 400 (supplement) (July 1949), 8–9.

Ashe, I., 'Some observations on general paralysis', *Journal of Mental Science*, 22, 97 (April 1876), 82–91.

Atkins, R., 'Report on nervous and mental disease', *Dublin Journal of Medical Sciences*, 91, 1 (January 1891), 54–70.

Battie, W., *Treatise on Madness* (London: Whiston and White, 1758).

Beckett, S., *Malone Meurt* (Paris: Les Éditions de Minuit, 1951).

Beers, C.W., *A Mind That Found Itself: An Autobiography* (New York: Longmans, Green and Co., 1908).

Blackmore, R., *A Treatise of the Spleen and Vapours, or, Hypocondriacal and Hysterical Affections: With Three Discourses on the Nature and Cure of the Cholick, Melancholy, and Palsies (Second Edition)* (London: J. Pemberton, 1726).

Blake, J.A., *Defects in the Moral Treatment of Insanity in the Public Lunatic Asylums of Ireland* (Dublin: Churchill, 1862).

Bourne, H., 'The insulin myth', *Lancet*, 262, 6793 (7 November 1953), 644–8.

Boyd Barrett, E., 'Modern psycho-therapy and our asylums', *Studies*, 13, 49 (March 1924), 29–43.

Brady, C., *The Training of Idiotic and Feeble-Minded Children (Second Edition)* (Dublin: Hodges, Smith, and Co., 1865).

Brain, W.R., 'The illness of Dean Swift', *Irish Journal of Medical Science*, 320–1, 6 (August/September 1952), 337–45.

Brigham, A., 'The moral treatment of insanity', *American Journal of Insanity*, 4, 1 (July 1847), 1–15.

Browne, I., *Development of Psychiatric Services* (Dublin: Dublin Health Authority, 1966).

Browne, N.C., 'Best psychiatrist', *Irish Times*, 11 April 1967.

Bucknill, J.C., 'Report of the Commissioners of Inquiry on the state of Lunatic Asylums and other Institutions for the Custody and Treatment of the Insane in Ireland: with Minutes of Evidence, and Appendices (State Paper, p. 718)', *Journal of Mental Science*, 5, 28 (1 January 1859), 222–45.

Burt, W.H., *Physiological Materia Medica (Containing All that is Known of the Physiological Action of Our Remedies Together with their Characteristic Indications and Pharmacology) (Fifth Edition)* (Chicago: Gross and Delbridge Company, 1896).

Butler, J., 'Mental illness', *Irish Times*, 4 November 1963.

Carlson, E.T. and N. Dain, 'The psychotherapy that was moral treatment', *American Journal of Psychiatry*, 117, 6 (December 1960), 519–24.

Carlson, E.T. and R.B. McFadden, 'Dr William Cullen on mania', *American Journal of Psychiatry*, 117, 5 (November 1960), 463–5.

Carr, J., *The Stranger in Ireland, or, A Tour in the Southern and Western Parts of that Country, in the Year 1805* (Philadelphia: T and G Palmer, 1806).

Central Statistics Office, *Tuarascáil an Ard-Chláraitheora 1952* (Dublin: Stationery Office, 1954).

Cheyne, J., *Essays on Partial Derangement of the Mind, in Supposed Connexion with Religion* (Dublin: William Curry Jun. and Company, 1843).

Churchill, F., 'On the mental disorders of pregnancy and childbed', *Dublin Quarterly Journal of Medical Science*, 9, 1 (February 1850), 38–63.

Commission of Inquiry on Mental Handicap, *Commission of Inquiry on Mental Handicap: 1965 Report* (Dublin: The Stationery Office, 1965).

Commission of Inquiry on Mental Illness, *Report of the Commission of Inquiry on Mental Illness* (Dublin: The Stationery Office, 1967).

Commission on Lunacy, *Report on Insanity and Idiocy in Massachusetts* (Boston, MA: William White, 1855).

Commission on the Relief of the Sick and Destitute Poor, Including the Insane Poor, *Report of the Commission on the Relief of the Sick and Destitute Poor, Including the Insane Poor* (Dublin: The Stationery Office, 1927).

Committee on Homosexual Offences and Prostitution. *Report of the Committee on Homosexual Offences and Prostitution* (London: Her Majesty's Stationery Office, 1957).

Committee on Lunacy Administration (Ireland), *First and Second Reports of the Committee Appointed by the Lord Lieutenant of Ireland on Lunacy Administration (Ireland)* (Edinburgh: Neill & Co. for Her Majesty's Stationery Office, 1891).

Council of Europe, *European Convention on Human Rights (Convention for the Protection of Human Rights and Fundamental Freedoms)* (Strasbourg: Council of Europe, 1950).

Cox, J.M., *Practical Observations on Insanity* (London: Baldwin and Murray, 1804).

Coyne, W.J., 'Best psychiatrist', *Irish Times*, 11 April 1967.

Cunningham Dax, E., *Modern Mental Treatment: A Handbook for Nurses* (London: Faber and Faber Ltd., 1947).

Daly, R.J. and F.J. Kane, 'Two severe reactions to benzodiazepine compounds', *American Journal of Psychiatry*, 122, 5 (November 1965), 577–8.

Davenport, W.H., 'Blackwell's Island Lunatic Asylum', *Harper's New Monthly Magazine*, 32, 189 (February 1866), 273–94.

Dawson, W.R., 'The presidential address on the relation between the geographical distribution of insanity and that of certain social and other conditions in Ireland', *Journal of Mental Science*, 57, 239 (1 October 1911), 571–97.

Dawson, W.R., 'Obituary: Thomas Drapes, M.B. Dubl.: B. 1874 [*sic*]: D. 1919', *Journal of Mental Science*, 66, 273 (1 April 1920), 83–7.

Delage, Y. (T. Drapes, transl.), 'Psychoanalysis, a new psychosis. Une psychose nouvelle: la psychoanalyse. Mercure de France, September 1st, 1916', *Journal of Mental Science*, 63, 260 (1 January 1917), 61–76.

Department of Health and Social Security, *Royal Commission On The Law Relating To Mental Illness And Mental Deficiency. Cmnd 169* (London: Her Majesty's Stationery Office, 1957).

Donnelly, W., W.R. Wilde and E. Singleton, *The Census of Ireland for the Year 1851, Part III: Report on the Status of Disease* (Dublin: Thom and Sons for Her Majesty's Stationery Office, 1854).

Drapes, T., 'On the alleged increase of insanity in Ireland', *Journal of Mental Science*, 40, 171 (1 October 1894), 519–48.

Drapes, T., 'Are punitive measures justifiable in asylums?', *Journal of Mental Science*, 45, 190 (1 July 1899), 536–49.

Drapes, T., 'A case of acute hallucinatory insanity of traumatic origin', *Journal of Mental Science*, 50, 210 (1 July 1904), 478–500.

Drapes, T., 'A note on psychiatric terminology and classification', *Journal of Mental Science*, 52, 216 (1 January 1906), 75–84.

Drapes, T., 'On the maniacal-depressive insanity of Kraepelin', *Journal of Mental Science*, 55, 228 (1 January 1909), 58–64.

Drapes, T., 'The personal equation in alienism', *Journal of Mental Science*, 57, 239 (1 October 1911), 598–617.

Duffy, C., *It Happened in Ireland* (New York: The Christian Press, 1944).

Duncan, J.F., *Medical Statistics, Their Force and Fallacies: A Lecture Delivered in Park Street School of Medicine, November 4th, 1846, Introductory to the Course on the Theory and Practice of Physic* (Dublin: McGlashan, 1847).

Duncan, J.F., *God in Disease, or, The Manifestations of Design in Morbid Phenomena* (Philadelphia: Lindsay and Blakiston, 1852).

Duncan, J.F., 'President's Address at the Annual Meeting of the Medico-Psychological Association, held August 11th, 1875, at the Royal College of Physicians, Dublin', *Journal of Mental Science*, 21, 95 (October 1875), 313–38.

Dunne, J., 'The malarial treatment of general paralysis', *Journal of Mental Science*, 72, 298 (July 1926), 343–6.

Dunne, J., 'Survey of modern physical methods of treatment for mental illness carried out in Grangegorman Mental Hospital', *Journal of the Medical Association of Eire*, 27, 157 (July 1950), 4–9.

Dunne, J., 'The contribution of the physical sciences to psychological medicine', *Journal of Mental Science*, 102, 427 (April 1956), 209–20.

Dunne, J., 'Diseases of the mind' in E.F. O'Doherty, and S.D. McGrath (eds), *The Priest and Mental Health* (New York: Alba House, 1963), 13–25.

Dunne, J. and E. O'Brien, 'Insulin therapy', *Journal of Mental Science*, 85, 356 (May 1939), 498–504.

Eager, R., 'A record of admissions to the mental section of the Lord Derby War Hospital, Warrington, from June 17th, 1916 to June 16th, 1917', *Journal of Mental Science*, 64, 266 (1 July 1918), 272–96.

Eames, J.A., 'Presidential address, delivered at the Annual Meeting of the Medico-Psychological Association, held at Queen's College, Cork, August 4, 1885', *Journal of Mental Science*, 31, 135 (October 1885), 315–32.

Esquirol, J.É., *Des Passions* (Paris: Didot Jeune, 1805).

'Ex-Teacher', 'Mental illness', *Irish Times*, 2 November 1963.

Fahy, T.J., S. Brandon and R.F. Garside, 'Clinical syndromes in a sample of depressed patients', *Proceedings of the Royal Society of Medicine*, 62, 4 (April 1969), 331–5.

Fahy, T.J., M.H. Irving and P. Millac, 'Severe head injuries: a six-year follow-up', *Lancet*, 290, 7514 (2 September 1967), 475–9.

Fisher, S., *Report on the Fourth Census of Canada 1901* (Ottawa: SE Dawson, Printer to the King's Most Excellent Majesty, 1902).

Fitzgerald, W., 'Carlow Castle and its history', *Carlow Sentinel*, 17 September 1904.

Fleury, E.L., 'Clinical note on agitated melancholia in women', *Journal of Mental Science*, 41, 174 (1 July 1895), 548–54.

Foucault, M., *History of Madness* (Abingdon, Oxon.: Routledge, 2006; first published as *Folie et Déraison: Histoire de la Folie à l'Âge Classique* in Paris by Librarie Plon, 1961).

Froggatt, P., 'The demographic work of Sir William Wilde', *Irish Journal of Medical Science*, 40, 5 (May 1965), 213–20.

'Glencraig Parent', 'Mental illness', *Irish Times*, 16 November 1963.

Goffman, E., *Asylums: Essays on the Social Situation of Mental Patients and Other Inmates* (New York: Anchor Books, Doubleday and Company, 1961).

Great Britain Commissions for the Care and Control of the Feeble-Minded, *Report of the Royal Commission on the Care and Control of the Feeble-Minded* (London: Her Majesty's Stationery Office, 1908).

Greenacre, P., *Swift and Carroll: A Psychoanalytic Study of Two Lives* (New York: International Universities Press, 1955).

Guthrie, D., *A History of Medicine* (London: Nelson, 1945).

Hallaran, W.S., *An Enquiry into the Causes Producing the Extraordinary Addition to the Number of Insane together with Extended Observations on the Cure of Insanity with Hints as to the Better Management of Public Asylums for Insane Persons* (Cork: Edwards and Savage, 1810).

Hallaran, W.S., *Practical Observations on the Causes and Cures of Insanity (Second Edition)* (Cork: Edwards and Savage, 1818).

Halliday, A., *A General View of the Present State of Lunatic Asylums in Great Britain and Ireland and in Some Other Kingdoms* (London: Thomas & George Underwood, 1838).

Hanaghan, J., *Society, Evolution and Revelation*: A*n Original Insight into Man's Place in Creation* (Dublin: Runa Press, 1957).

Hanaghan, J., 'Mental illness', *Irish Times*, 2 November 1963.

Harris, L.G.E., *A Treatise on the Law and Practice in Lunacy in Ireland, Together with the Lunacy Regulation (Ireland) Act, 1871, and a Collection of Forms for Use in the Irish Free State and in Northern Ireland* (Dublin: Corrigan and Wilson, 1930).

Harty, J., *Observations on an Act (5 and 6 Vict. c. 123) "For Amending the Law Relating to Private Lunatic Asylums in Ireland"* (Dublin: M.H. Gill, 1843).

Hays, P., *New Horizons in Psychiatry* (Harmondsworth, Middlesex: Penguin Books, 1964).

Hearder, G.J., 'The treatment of haematoma auris', *Journal of Mental Science*, 22, 97 (April 1876), 91–3.

Higgins, M.D., 'Mental illness', *Irish Times*, 19 March 1968.

Hunter, R. and I. Macalpine, *Three Hundred Years of Psychiatry, 1535–1860: A History Presented in Selected English Texts* (London: Oxford University Press, 1963).

Inspector of Lunatic Asylums, *Report of the District, Local and Private Lunatic Asylums in Ireland 1846* (Dublin: Alexander Thom, for Her Majesty's Stationery Office, 1847).

Inspector of Lunatic Asylums, *The Thirty-Sixth Report on the District, Criminal and Private Lunatic Asylums in Ireland (With Appendices)* (Dublin: Thom and Co. for Her Majesty's Stationery Office, 1887).

Inspectors of Lunatics, *The Fortieth Report (With Appendices) of the Inspectors of Lunatics (Ireland)* (Dublin: Thom and Co. for Her Majesty's Stationery Office, 1891).

Inspectors of Lunatics, *The Forty-Second Report (With Appendices) of the Inspectors of Lunatics (Ireland)* (Dublin: Thom and Co. for Her Majesty's Stationery Office, 1893).

Inspectors of Lunatics, *Special Report from the Inspectors of Lunatics to the Chief Secretary: Alleged Increasing Prevalence of Insanity in Ireland* (Dublin: Her Majesty's Stationery Office, 1894).

Inspectors of Lunatics, *Supplement to the Fifty-Fourth Report of the Inspectors of Lunatics on the District, Criminal, and Private Lunatic Asylums in Ireland. Being a Special Report on the Alleged Increase of Insanity* (Dublin: His Majesty's Stationery Office, 1906).

Inspectors of Lunatics (Ireland), *The Sixty-Third Annual Report (With Appendices) of the Inspectors of Lunatics (Ireland), Being for the Year Ending 31ˢᵗ December 1913* (Dublin: Thom and Co. for His Majesty's Stationery Office, 1914).

Inspectors of Lunatics (Ireland), *The Sixty-Sixth Annual Report (With Appendices) of the Inspectors of Lunatics (Ireland), Being for the Year Ending 31ˢᵗ December 1916* (Dublin: Thom and Co. for His Majesty's Stationery Office, 1917).

Inspector of Mental Hospitals, *Annual Report of the Inspector of Mental Hospitals for the Year 1929* (Dublin: Department of Local Government and Public Health/Stationery Office, 1930).

Inspector of Mental Hospitals, *Annual Report of the Inspector of Mental Hospitals for the Year 1930* (Dublin: Department of Local Government and Public Health/Stationery Office, 1931).

Inspector of Mental Hospitals, *Annual Report of the Inspector of Mental Hospitals for the Year 1933* (Dublin: Department of Local Government and Public Health/Stationery Office, 1934).

Inspector of Mental Hospitals, *Annual Report of the Inspector of Mental Hospitals for the Year 1934* (Dublin: Department of Local Government and Public Health/Stationery Office, 1935).

Inspector of Mental Hospitals, *Annual Report of the Inspector of Mental Hospitals for the Year 1935* (Dublin: Department of Local Government and Public Health/Stationery Office, 1936).

Inspector of Mental Hospitals, *Annual Report of the Inspector of Mental Hospitals for the Year 1949* (Dublin: Department of Health/Stationery Office, 1950).

Inter-Departmental Subcommittee on the Care of the Aged, *The Care of the Aged* (Dublin: The Stationery Office, 1968).

Ireland, W.W., *Blot upon the Brain: Studies in History and Psychology (First Edition)* (Edinburgh: Bell and Bradfute, 1885).

Irish Times Reporter, 'Ireland has high mental illness rate', *Irish Times*, 29 March 1967.

Jacob, D.B., 'Restraint in lunatic asylums', *Irish Times*, 28 February 1908.

Jones, K., *Lunacy, Law and Conscience: The Social History of the Care of the Insane* (London: Routledge and Keegan Paul, 1955).

Joyce, J., *Ulysses* (Franklin Centre, Pennsylvania: Franklin Library, 1976; first published in full in Paris by Sylvia Beach, 1922).

Kalinowsky, L.B., 'Somatic therapy of depression' in J. Wortis (ed.), *Recent Advances in Biological Psychiatry* (New York and London: Grune and Stratton, 1960), 236–47.

Kane, F.J., R.J. Daly, J. Ewing and M. Keeler, 'Mood and behavioural changes with progestational agents', *British Journal of Psychiatry*, 113, 496 (March 1967), 265–8.

Kanner, L., *Child Psychiatry* (Springfield, Illinois: C.C. Thomas Publishing, 1935).

Kenny, E.E.C., *Short Hints and Observations on the Arrangement and Management of Lunatic Asylums* (Dublin: Philip Dixon Hardy & Sons, 1848).

Kidd, G.H., *An Appeal on Behalf of the Idiotic and Imbecile Children of Ireland* (Dublin: John Falconer, 1865).

Kirkpatrick, T.P.C., *A Note on the History of the Care of the Insane in Ireland up to the End of the Nineteenth Century* (Dublin: University Press, Ponsonby and Gibbs, 1931).

Kirkpatrick, T.P.C., 'Obituary: Richard Robert Leeper', *Journal of Mental Science*, 88, 372 (1 July 1942), 480–1.

Koltes, J.A., 'Mental hospitals with open doors', *American Journal of Psychiatry*, 113, 3 (September 1956), 250–3.

Kraepelin, E., *Psychiatrie. Ein Lehrbuch für Studirende und Aerzte (Sixth Edition)* (Leipzig: Verlag von Johann Ambrosius Barth, 1899).

Lalor, J., 'The President's address', *Journal of Mental Science*, 39, 7 (October 1861), 318–26.

Lalor, J., 'On the use of education and training in the treatment of the insane in public lunatic asylums', *Journal of the Statistical and Social Inquiry of Ireland*, 7, 54 (1878), 361–73.

Lasègue, C. and J. Falret, 'La folie à deux ou folie communiquée', *Annales Medico-Psychologiques*, 18 (September 1877), 321–55.

Leeper, R.R., 'Some reflections on the progress of psychiatry', *Journal of Mental Science*, 33, 319 (1 October 1931), 683–91.

Lucas, C., *Essay on Waters: In Three Parts, Treating, I. Of Simple Waters. II. Of Cold, Medicated Waters. III. Of Natural Baths* (London: A. Millar, 1756).

Lucas, C. and Dr Achmet, *The Theory and Uses of Baths, Being an Extract from the Essay on Waters by the Late Charles Lucas, Esq., MD, with Marginal Notes by Dr Achmet, Illustrated by Some Annexed Cases* (Dublin: J. Potts, 1772).

Lunatic Asylums, Ireland, Commission, *Report of the Commissioners of Inquiry into the State of the Lunatic Asylums and Other Institutions for the Custody and Treatment of the Insane in Ireland: with Minutes of Evidence and Appendices (Part 1 – Report, Tables, and Returns)* (Dublin: Thom and Sons, for Her Majesty's Stationery Office, 1858).

Mac Eoin, G.S., 'Gleann Bolcáin agus Gleann na nGealt', *Béaloideas*, 30 (1962), 105–20.

MacGabhann, L., 'Dr Dunne retires after 45 years in St Brendan's', *Irish Times*, 31 December 1965.

Mackay, R.P., 'The neurology of motivation' in J. Wortis J (ed.), *Recent Advances in Biological Psychiatry* (New York and London: Grune and Stratton, 1960), 2–13.

Malone, J.P., 'Problems arising from prefrontal leucotomy', *Irish Journal of Medical Science*, 22, 9 (September 1947), 573–9.

Martin, M.E., 'Puerperal mental illness; a follow-up study of 75 cases', *British Medical Journal*, 2, 5099 (27 September 1958), 773–7.

Maturin, C., *Melmoth the Wanderer* (Edinburgh: Archibald Constable and Company, and Hurst, Robinson and Co., Cheapside, 1820).

Maudsley, H., 'Homicidal insanity', *Journal of Mental Science*, 47, 9 (October 1863), 327–43.

McGrath, D., 'Current developments in psychiatry' in E.F. O'Doherty, and S.D. McGrath (eds), *The Priest and Mental Health* (New York: Alba House, 1963), 26–31.

McNeill, C., 'Hospital of S. John without the New Gate, Dublin', *The Journal of the Royal Society of Antiquaries of Ireland (Sixth Series)*, 15, 1 (June 1925), 58–64.

McQuaid, J.C., 'Introduction' in E.F. O'Doherty, and S.D. McGrath (eds), *The Priest and Mental Health* (New York: Alba House, 1963), ix–xi.

'Medicus', 'Mental illness', *Irish Times*, 5 November 1963.

Meduna, L.J. Von, 'Versuche über die biologische Beeinflussung des Aflaubes der Schizophrenie', *Zeitschrift für die gesamte Neurologie und Psychiatrie*, 152, 1 (December 1935), 235–62.

Merrit, H.H., R. Adams and H.C. Solomon, *Neurosyphilis* (Oxford: Oxford University Press, 1946).

Middleton, P.P.P., *An Essay on Gout* (London: Baldwin and Company, 1827).

Mills, J., *Conference of the Irish Asylum Committees* (Dublin: Dollard Printing House, 1904), 55–6.

Mills, C.K. and N.S. Yawger (eds), *Lippincott's Nursing Manuals and Care of Nervous and the Insane* (Philadelphia, Pennsylvania: J.B. Lippincott Company, 1915).

Mollan, J., 'Statistical report on the Richmond Lunatic Asylum', *Dublin Journal of Medical Science*, 13, 3 (July 1838), 367–84.

Moore, J.N.P., *Swift's Philanthropy* (Dublin: Governors of St Patrick's Hospital Dublin, 1967).

Myer, K. (ed.), *Anecdota Oxoniensia: Cath Finntrága* (Oxford: Clarendon Press, 1885).

Myers, C.S., 'A contribution to the study of shell shock', *Lancet*, 185, 4772 (13 February 1915), 316–20.

Nolan, M.J., 'Case of folie á deux', *Journal of Mental Science*, 35, 149 (April 1889), 55–61.

Nolan, M.J., *The Increase in Insanity in Ireland and its Causes* (Dublin: Fannin & Co., 1906).

Norman, C., 'Some points in Irish lunacy law', *Journal of Mental Science*, 31, 136 (1 January 1886), 459–67.

Norman, C., 'Cases illustrating the sedative effects of aceto-phenone (hypnone)', *Journal of Mental Science*, 32, 140 (1 January 1887), 519–25.

Norman, C., 'Variations in form of mental affections in relation to the classification of insanity', *Dublin Journal of Medical Science*, 83, 3 (March 1887), 228–35.

Norman, C., 'Presidential address, delivered at the Royal College of Physicians, Dublin, June 12th, 1894', *Journal of Mental Science*, 40, 171 (1 October 1894), 487–99.

Norman, C., 'The domestic treatment of the insane', *Dublin Journal of Medical Science*, 101, 2 (February 1896), 111–21.

Norman, C., 'The clinical features of beri-beri', *Transactions of the Royal Academy of Medicine in Ireland*, 17, 1 (1 December 1899), 145–79.

Norman, C., 'On the need for family care of persons of unsound mind in Ireland', *Journal of Mental Science*, 50, 210 (1 July 1904), 461–73.

Norman, C., 'The family care of the insane', *Medical Press and Circular*, 29 November–6 December 1905.

O'Brien, E., 'Helping minds to work again', *Irish Times*, 10 April 1967.

O'Brien, F., *At Swim-Two-Birds* (London: Penguin, 2001; first published by Longmans Green, 1939).

O'Brien, K., *Presentation Parlour* (London: Heinemann, 1963).

O'Brien, L., 'The magic wisp: a history of the mentally ill in Ireland', *Bulletin of the Menninger Clinic*, 31, 2 (March 1967), 79–95.

O'Curry, E., *On the Manners and Customs of the Ancient Irish* (London: Williams and Norgate, 1873).

O'Doherty, E.F. and S.D. McGrath (eds), *The Priest and Mental Health* (New York: Alba House, 1963).

O'Doherty, E.F., 'Sexual deviations' in E.F. O'Doherty, and S.D. McGrath (eds), *The Priest and Mental Health* (New York: Alba House, 1963), 124–35.

O'Donovan, J. (transl.), *The Banquet of Dun na nGedh and the Battle of Magh Rath* (Dublin: The University Press, for the Irish Archaeology Society, 1842).

O'Donovan, J., *Ordnance Survey Letters (Donegal)* (1835) (Dublin: Four Masters Press, 2000).

O'Flaherty, L., *Return of the Brute* (London: The Mandrake Press, 1929).

Ó Maoláin, T., 'Mental illness', *Irish Times*, 11 November 1963.

Ó Muirgheasa, E., 'The holy wells of Donegal', *Béaloideas*, 6, 2 (December 1936), 143–62.

O'Neill, E.D., *Increase of Lunacy and Special Reasons Applicable to Ireland* (Limerick: George McKern and Sons Limited, 1903).

O'Sullivan, E.N.M., *Textbook of Occupational Therapy with Chief Reference to Psychological Medicine* (London: H.K Lewis and Co. Ltd., 1955).

Penrose, L.S., 'Mental disease and crime: outlines of a comparative study of European statistics', *British Journal of Medical Psychology*, 18, 1 (March 1939), 1–15.

Perceval, J.T., *A Narrative of the Treatment Experienced by a Gentleman During a State of Mental Derangement Designed to Explain the Causes and Nature of Insanity, and to Expose the Injudicious Conduct Pursued Towards Many Unfortunate Sufferers under that Calamity* (London: Effingham Wilson, 1838).

Phillips, N.R., 'Daniel Frederick Rambaut', *Journal of Mental Science*, 84, 348 (1 January 1938), 1–2.

'PHN', 'Mental illness', *Irish Times*, 8 November 1963.

Pieterson, J.F.G., 'Haematoma auris' in D.H. Tuke (ed.), *Dictionary of Psychological Medicine* (London: John Churchill, 1892).

Pinel, P., *A Treatise on Insanity* (translated by D.D. Davis MD) (Sheffield: W. Todd for Messrs. Cadell and Davies, 1806).

Plummer, C., *Bethada Náem Nérenn (Lives of Irish Saints)* (Oxford: Clarendon Press, 1922).

Powell, R., 'Observations upon the comparative prevalence of insanity at different periods', *Medical Transactions*, 4, 2 (1813), 131–59.

Power, J.C., 'No admission', *Irish Times*, 29 April 1967.

Psychiatrist, 'Insanity in Ireland', *The Bell*, 7, 4 (January 1944), 303–10.

Rambaut, D.F., 'Case-taking in large asylums', *Journal of Mental Science*, 49, 204 (1 January 1903), 45–52.

Ray, I., *A Treatise on the Medical Jurisprudence of Insanity [1838] [Reprint, W. Overholser (ed.)]* (Cambridge, MA: Harvard University Press, 1962).

Ray, I., *A Treatise on the Medical Jurisprudence of Insanity (Third Edition, with Additions)* (Cambridge, MA: Little, Brown and Company, 1853).

Redington, J.M. and P.J. Dwyer, 'Maniacal-depressive insanity amongst the male admissions to the Richmond District Asylum in the year 1907', *Journal of Mental Science*, 55, 228 (1 January 1909), 56–8.

Reynolds, J.F., 'Mental illness', *Irish Times*, 5 April 1967.

Rivers, W.H.R., 'An address on the repression of war experience', *Lancet*, 191, 4927 (2 February 1918), 173–7.

Ryan, J.P., 'The open door system in the mental hospital', *Journal of the Irish Medical Association*, 39, 234 (December 1956), 175–9.

Ryan, J.P.A., 'Mental handicap and responsibility' in E.F. O'Doherty, and S.D. McGrath (eds), *The Priest and Mental Health* (New York: Alba House, 1963).

Sanborn, F.B., 'Is American Insanity Increasing?', *Journal of Mental Science*, 40, 169 (1 April 1894), 214–9.

Sargant, W. and E. Slater, *An Introduction to Physical Methods of Treatment in Psychiatry (Fourth Edition)* (Edinburgh and London: E. and S. Livingstone, 1963).

Scoresby, W., *Memorials of the Sea: The Mary Russell* (London: Longman, Brown, Green and Longmans, 1850).

Select Committee on the Lunatic Poor in Ireland, *Report from the Select Committee on the Lunatic Poor in Ireland with Minutes of Evidence Taken Before the Committee and an Appendix* (London: House of Commons, 1817).

Select Committee of the House of Lords, *Report from the Select Committee of the House of Lords Appointed to Consider the State of the Lunatic Poor in Ireland and to Report Thereon to the House with the Minutes of Evidence, Appendix, and Index* (London: House of Commons, 1843).

Sheridan, T. and J. Nichols (arranged and revised), *The Works of Rev. Jonathan Swift, D.D., Dean of St Patrick's, Dublin, with Notes, Historical and Critical, Volume XVIII* (New York: William Durrell and Co., 1813).

Stafford-Clark, D., *Psychiatry To-day* (Harmondsworth, Middlesex: Penguin Books, 1952).

Stoker, B., *Dracula* (London: Archibald Constable and Company, 1897).

Synge, J.M., *Collected Works, Volume II, Prose* (Oxford: Oxford University Press, 1966).

Thompson, R., 'Obituary: Richard Robert Leeper', *Journal of Mental Science*, 88, 372 (1 July 1942), 481–4.

Thompson, R., 'The scope and limitations of modern physical methods of treatment in psychological medicine', *Irish Journal of Medical Science*, 25, 11 (November 1950), 509–16.

Tuke, D.H., 'On the Richmond Asylum schools', *Journal of Mental Science*, 21, 95 (1 October 1875), 467–74.

Tuke, D.H., 'Folie à deux', *Brain*, 10, 4 (1 January 1888), 408–21.

Tuke, D.H., *A Dictionary of Psychological Medicine* (London: Churchill, 1892).

Tuke, D.H., 'Alleged increase of insanity', *Journal of Mental Science*, 40, 169 (1 April 1894), 219–34.

Tuke, D.H., 'Increase of insanity in Ireland', *Journal of Mental Science*, 40, 171 (1 October 1894), 549–61.

Tuke, S., *Description of the Retreat, an Institution Near York, for Insane Persons of the Society of Friends: Containing an Account of its Origin and Progress, the Modes of Treatment, and a Statement of Cases* (Philadelphia: Isaac Pierce, 1813).

Tuomy, M., *Treatise on the Principal Diseases of Dublin* (Dublin: William Folds, 1810).

Viney, M., 'No room to move', *Irish Times*, 23 October 1963.

Viney, M., 'The opening door', *Irish Times*, 24 October 1963.

Viney, M., 'Patients with a purpose', *Irish Times*, 25 October 1963.

Viney, M., 'Chance for a revolution', *Irish Times*, 26 October 1963.

Viney, M., 'Children all their lives', *Irish Times*, 28 October 1963.

Viney, M., 'Odd child out', *Irish Times*, 29 October 1963.

Viney, M., 'Psychiatry and the Irish', *Irish Times*, 30 October 1963.

Viney, M., '"Secret" justice and after', *Irish Times*, 9 February 1968.

Walsh, D. and B. Walsh, 'Hospitalized psychiatric morbidity in Ireland', *British Journal of Psychiatry*, 113, 499 (June 1967), 675–6.

Walsh, D. and B. Walsh, 'Some influences on the intercounty variation in Irish psychiatric hospitalization rates', *British Journal of Psychiatry*, 114, 506 (January 1968), 15–20.

War Office Committee of Enquiry into 'Shell-Shock', *Report of the War Office Committee of Enquiry into "Shell-Shock"* (London: HMSO, 1922).

Wilde, J., *Ancient Cures, Charms, and Usages of Ireland* (London: Ward and Downey, 1890).

Wilde, W.R., *The Closing Years of Dean Swift's Life: With an Appendix, Containing Several of his Poems Hitherto Unpublished, and Some Remarks on Stella* (Dublin: Hodges and Smith, 1849).

Williams, J.W., 'Unsoundness of mind, in its medical and legal considerations', *Dublin Quarterly Journal of Medical Science*, 18, 2 (November 1854), 260–87.

Wilson, T.G., 'Swift's deafness: And his last illness', *Irish Journal of Medical Science*, 14, 6 (June 1939), 241–56.

Wilson, T.G., *Victorian Doctor: The Life of Sir William Wilde* (London: Methuen, 1942).

Wilson, T.G., 'The mental and physical health of Dean Swift', *Medical History*, 2, 3 (July 1958), 175–90.

Wilson, T.G., 'Swift and the doctors', *Medical History*, 8, 3 (July 1964), 199–216.

Woods, O., 'The presidential address delivered at the Sixtieth Annual Meeting of the Medico-Psychological Association', *Journal of Mental Science*, 47, 199 (October 1901), 645–58.

Woods, O.T., 'Notes of a case of folie à deux in five members of one family', *Journal of Mental Science*, 34, 148 (1 January 1889), 535–9.

Wright, T. (ed.), *The Historical Works of Giraldus Cambrensis* (London: George Bell and Sons, 1894).

NEWSPAPERS

Ballinasloe Life
Building News and Engineering Journal
Connaught Tribune
Cork Constitution
Daily Independent
Derby Daily Telegraph
Donegal Democrat
Dublin Gazette
East Galway Democrat
Financial Times
Galway City Tribune
Gay Community News

Gloucester Citizen
Guardian
Hull Daily Mail
Irish Daily Mail
Irish Examiner
Irish Independent
Irish Medical News
Irish Medical Times
Irish Nation (Éire)
Irish Press
Irish Times
Mayo Constitution
Medical Independent
Medical Press
Medical Press and Circular
Medicine Weekly
New York Times
Nottingham Evening Post
Observer
Sunday Business Post
Sunday Independent
The Times

PERSONAL COMMUNICATIONS

Daly, Dr Liam, interview (27 June 2015).
Du Feu, Dr Margaret, by email (21, 22 and 24 April, and 8 May 2016).
Fahy, Professor Thomas, by email (25, 27 and 28 August 2015).
McDaid, Dr Shari, by email (12 August 2015).
McQuaid, Dr Paul, by email (27 November 2015 and 3 May 2016).
Malone, Professor Kevin, by email (17 August 2015).
Martin, Dr Lorcan, by email (6 and 7 May 2016).
Norris, Senator David, interview (9 October 2015).
O'Boyle, Dr Jim, by email (2 and 8 May, 12, 17 and 21 June 2016).
O'Dúill, Fr Piaras, interview (18 May 2016).
Reynolds, Dr Michael, by email (22 and 23 June 2015).
Tobin, Dr John, by email (1 March and 21 September 2015).
Walsh, Dr Elizabeth, by email (30 August and 28 November 2015).

Secondary Sources (1970 onwards)

Adlam, J., I. Gill, S.N. Glackin, B.D. Kelly, C. Scanlon and S. Mac Suibhne, 'Perspectives on Erving Goffman's "Asylums" fifty years on', *Medicine, Health Care and Philosophy,* 16, 3 (August 2013), 605–13.

Ahmed, M., D.M. Cannon, C. Scanlon, L. Holleran, H. Schmidt, J. McFarland, C. Langan, P. McCarthy, G.J. Barker, B. Hallahan and C. McDonald, 'Progressive brain atrophy and cortical thinning in schizophrenia after commencing clozapine treatment', *Neuropsychopharmacology,* 40, 10 (September 2015), 2409–17.

American Psychiatric Association, *Diagnostic and Statistical Manual of Mental Disorders (Fifth Edition)* (Washington DC: American Psychiatric Association, 2013).

Amnesty International (Irish Section), *Mental Illness* (Dublin: Amnesty International (Irish Section), 2003).

Andreasen, N.C., 'James Joyce. A portrait of the artist as a schizoid', *Journal of the American Medical Association,* 224, 1 (April 1973), 67–71.

Andreasen, N.C., *Brave New Brain: Conquering Mental Illness in the Era of the Genome* (Oxford and New York: Oxford University Press, 2001).

Andrews, N., 'Camille Claudel 1915', *Financial Times (Life and Arts),* 21/22 June 2014.

Anonymous, 'UCD Newman professor and psychiatry leader', *Irish Times,* 2 July 2011.

Anonymous, 'Monaghan soviet's success', *Books Ireland*, October 2012.

Anonymous, 'Psychiatrist who revolutionised care of mentally ill', *Irish Times*, 28 December 2013.

Anonymous, 'Obituary: Dr Robert A. McCarthy', *Irish Medical Journal*, 107, 2 (February 2014), 62.

Anonymous, 'Economist with much to say on how Irish society works', *Irish Times*, 28 May 2016.

Appignanesi, L., *Mad, Bad and Sad: A History of Women and the Mind Doctors from 1800 to the Present* (London: Virago, 2008).

Appleby, L., 'Suicide and self-harm', in R. Murray, P. Hill and P. McGuffin (eds), *The Essentials of Postgraduate Psychiatry (Third Edition)* (Cambridge: Cambridge University Press, 1997), 551–62.

Arbuthnot, S.J. (ed.), *Cóir Anmann: A Late Middle Irish Treatise on Personal Names* (London: Irish Texts Society, 2006).

Archer, S.M., 'The racket and the fear', *History Today*, 66, 1 (January 2016), 11–18.

Armstrong, D., 'The patient's view', *Social Science and Medicine*, 18, 9 (September 1984), 737–44.

Arnold, C., *Bedlam: London and its Mad* (London: Simon and Schuster/Pocket Books, 2009).

Aronson, J.K., *An Account of the Foxglove and Its Medical Uses, 1785–1985* (Oxford: Oxford University Press, 1985).

Atkinson, D., M. Jackson and J. Walmsley, 'Introduction: methods and themes' in D. Atkinson, M. Jackson and J. Walmsley (eds), *Forgotten Lives* (Worcestershire, UK: British Institute of Learning Disabilities (BILD), 1997), 1–20.

Bacopoulos-Viau, A. and A. Fauvel, 'The Patient's Turn', *Medical History*, 60, 1 (January 2016), 1–18.

Bailey, A., *The Grangegorman Murders: Dean Lyons, Mark Nash and the Story Behind the Grangegorman Murders* (Dublin: Gill and Macmillan, 2015).

Bailey, L., *Because We Are Bad: OCD and a Girl Lost in Thought* (Kingston upon Thames, Surrey: Canbury Press, 2016).

Balter, M., 'Talking back to madness', *Science*, 343, 6176 (14 March 2014), 1190–3.

Barber, T., 'A flawed assassin', *Financial Times*, 3 April 2010.

Bardon, S., '50 children in adult psychiatric units', *Irish Times*, 10 August 2015.

Bardon, S., 'Kenny and Martin deal on Seanad', *Irish Times*, 28 May 2016.

Barnes, J.A., '25% of Mountjoy prisoners former psychiatric patients', *Irish Medical Times*, 5 September 2005.

Barnes, J.A., 'Mental health chief confident HSE will meet legal obligations', *Irish Medical News*, 31 October 2006.

Barnes, J.A., 'Red-letter day for mental health?', *Irish Medical News*, 6 November 2006.

Barron, D., 'Intellectual disability needs increasing as cohort ages', *Irish Medical News*, 24 November 2015.

Barry, J., C. Farren, E. Keenan, F. Nangle-O'Connor, A. Quigley, S. Rooney, B. Smyth and J. Treacy, 'Excluding addiction from mental health services', *Irish Times*, 15 December 2006.

Barry, K., 'Roethke in the Bughouse', *Irish Times*, 8 August 2015.

Barry, O., 'Planning for the Future', *Irish Press*, 8 May 1985.

Barry, S., *The Secret Scripture* (London: Faber and Faber Limited, 2008).

Barry, S. and B. Cassidy, 'Consultant psychiatrists making a principled stand', *Irish Medical Times*, 10 June 2005.

Barry, S. and P. Murphy (on behalf of the Faculty of Clinical Directors of the College of Psychiatry of Ireland), *A Gloomy View: Rhetoric or reality in relation to the advancement of A Vision for Change* (Dublin: College of Psychiatry of Ireland, 2009).

Bartlett, P., *The Poor Law of Lunacy: The Administration of Pauper Lunatics in Mid-Nineteenth-Century England* (London and Washington: Leicester University Press, 1999).

Bartlett, P., O. Lewis and O. Thorold, *Mental Disability and the European Convention on Human Rights (International Studies in Human Rights, Volume 90)* (Leiden/Boston: Martinus Nijhoff Publishers, 2007).

Bates, T., 'A brief history of insanity', *Irish Times*, 7 December 2004.

Bates, T., 'Vision of mental health', *Irish Times*, 31 January 2006.

Bates, T., 'Patient's right to consent or refuse treatment has to be balanced with a professional duty of care', *Irish Times*, 2 February 2010.

BDO, *Health's Ageing Crisis* (Dublin: BDO, 2014).

Beattie, D. and P. Devitt, *Suicide: A Modern Obsession* (Dublin: Liberties Press, 2015).

Benson, C., 'An elusive, unorthodox outsider', *Irish Times*, 19 April 2008.

Bergin, D., 'Dundrum chief blasts Mental Health Commission report', *Irish Medical News*, 6 June 2006.

Beveridge, A., 'Voices of the mad: patients' letters from the Royal Edinburgh Asylum, 1873–1908', *Psychological Medicine*, 27, 4 (July 1997), 899–908.

Bewley, T., *Madness to Mental Illness: A History of the Royal College of Psychiatrists* (London: RCPsych Publications, 2008).

Bewley, T.H., 'The health of Jonathan Swift', *Journal of the Royal Society of Medicine*, 91, 11 (November 1998), 602–5.

Bewley, T.H., 'Swift's pocky quean', *Journal of the Royal Society of Medicine*, 92, 4 (April 1999), 216.

Bilanakis, N., A. Vratsista, E. Athanasiou, D. Niakas and V. Peritogiannis, 'Medical patients' treatment decision-making capacity: a report from a general hospital in Greece', *Clinical Practice and Epidemiology in Mental Health*, 10 (November 2014), 133–9.

Birley, J.L.T., 'Famine: the distant shadow over French psychiatry', *British Journal of Psychiatry*, 180, 4 (April 2002), 298–9.

Bisson, J. and M. Andrew, 'Psychological treatment of post-traumatic stress disorder', *Cochrane Database of Systematic Reviews*, 3, (18 July 2007), CD003388.

Blake, B., J.V. Halpenny, P.F. O'Brien, M. Ní Nualláin, A. O'Hare and D. Walsh, 'The incidence of mental illness in Ireland: patients contacting psychiatric services in three Irish Counties', *Irish Journal of Psychiatry*, 5, 2 (Autumn 1984), 23–9.

Boland, R., '"Isolated from the mainstream": Portrane asylum in the 1950s', *Irish Times*, 10 June 2016.

Bolger, D., 'Forgotten relics of lives written off as 'lunatics' and 'imbeciles'', *Irish Daily Mail*, 14 August 2014.

Bourgeois, M. L., P. Duhamel and H. Verdoux, 'Delusional parasitosis: folie à deux and attempted murder of a family doctor', *British Journal of Psychiatry*, 161, 5 (1 November 1992), 709–11.

Bourke, A., *The Burning of Bridget Cleary: A True Story* (London: Pimlico, 1999).

Bourke, J., 'Shellshock, psychiatry and the Irish soldier during the First World War', in A. Gregory and S. Pašeta (eds), *Ireland and the Great War: 'A War to Unite Us All'?* (Manchester and New York: Manchester University Press, 2002).

Bowe, M., P. Devitt, and F. Kelly, *Changing Minds – Home not Hospital* (Dublin: TAF Publishing, 2011).

Bowers, F., *Suicide in Ireland* (Dublin: Irish Medical Organisation, 1994).

Boyle, K., 'The right to information', *Irish Times*, 1 April 1985.

Bracken, P., *Trauma: Culture, Meaning and Philosophy* (London and Philadelphia, PA: Whurr Publishers Ltd., 2002).

Bracken, P., 'On *Madness and Civilisation: A History of Insanity in the Age of Reason* (1961), by Michel Foucault', *British Journal of Psychiatry*, 207, 5 (November 2015), 434.

Bracken, P. and P. Thomas, 'Postpsychiatry: a new direction for mental health', *British Medical Journal*, 322, 7288 (24 March 2001), 724–7.

Bracken, P. and P. Thomas, *Postpsychiatry: Mental Health in a Postmodern World* (Oxford: Oxford University Press, 2005).

Bracken, P., P. Thomas, S. Timimi, E. Asen, G. Behr, C. Beuster, S. Bhunnoo, I. Browne, N. Chhina, D. Double, S. Downer, C. Evans, S. Fernando, M.R. Garland, W. Hopkins, R. Huws, B. Johnson, B. Martindale, H. Middleton, D. Moldavsky, J. Moncrieff, S. Mullins, J. Nelki, M. Pizzo, J. Rodger, M. Smyth, D. Summerfield, J. Wallace and D. Yeomans, 'Psychiatry beyond the current paradigm', *British Journal of Psychiatry*, 201, 6 (December 2012), 430–4.

Bradley, D., 'Hospital tells mother of suicidal boy 'ring guards'', *Galway City Tribune*, 29 May 2015.

Bradshaw, J.S., 'The yank in the corner', *Irish Times*, 15 August 1983.

Brady, P.J., 'Psychiatric service', *Irish Times*, 14 May 1990.

Brady, T., 'Sculpted in anguish', *Irish Times*, 20 June 2014.

Braslow, J.T., 'Punishment or therapy: patients, doctors, and somatic remedies in the early twentieth century', *Psychiatric Clinics of North America*, 17, 3 (September 1994), 493–513.

Breathnach, C., 'Lady Dudley's District Nursing Scheme and the Congested Districts Board, 1903–1923' in M.H. Preston and M. Ó hÓgartaigh (eds), *Gender and Medicine in Ireland, 1700–1950* (Syracuse, New York: Syracuse University Press, 2012).

Breathnach, C., 'Medicalizing the female reproductive cycle in rural Ireland, 1926–56', *Historical Research*, 85, 230 (November 2012), 674–90.

Breathnach, C. and B.D. Kelly, 'Perspectives on patienthood, practitioners and pedagogy' *Medical Humanities*, 42, 2 (June 2016), 73–5.

Breathnach, C.S., 'Henry Hutchinson Stewart (1798–1879)', *History of Psychiatry*, 9, 33 (March 1998), 27–33.

Breathnach, C.S., 'Walter Freeman', *Irish Journal of Psychological Medicine*, 23, 3 (September 2006), 124–5.

Breathnach, C. S. and J.B. Moynihan, 'An Irish statistician's analysis of the national tuberculosis problem', *Irish Journal of Medical Science*, 172, 3 (July–September 2003), 149–53.

Breckenridge, A., 'William Withering's legacy', *Clinical Medicine*, 6, 4 (July–August, 2006), 393–7.

Brennan, B., 'Society lady with a violent mission', *Irish Independent*, 6 March 2010.

Brennan, D., '"Telling stories about ourselves": historical methodology and the creation of mental health nursing narratives', *Journal of Psychiatric and Mental Health Nursing*, 18, 8 (October 2011), 657–63.

Brennan, D., 'A theoretical explanation of institution-based mental health care in Ireland', in P.M. Prior (ed.), *Asylums, Mental Health Care and the Irish, 1800–2010* (Dublin: Irish Academic Press, 2012).

Brennan, D., *Irish Insanity, 1800–2000* (Abingdon, Oxon.: Routledge, 2014).

Brennan, D., 'Let those damaged by Irish asylum system tell their stories', *Irish Examiner*, 28 June 2014.

Brennan, M., 'FF manifesto promises mental health authority', *Sunday Business Post*, 24 January 2016.

Breslin, M.J. and E. Best, *Saints, Scholars and Schizophrenics Revisited: A Twenty-First Century Perspective on Religion and Mental Health in Ireland* (Bedford: Amazon/CreateSpace Independent Publishing Platform, 2013).

Breslin, N., *Me and My Mate Jeffrey: A Story of Big Dreams, Tough Realities and Facing My Demons Head On* (Dublin: Hachette Books Ireland, 2015).

Bretherton, G., 'Irish inebriate reformatories, 1899–1902: an experiment in coercion' in I. O'Donnell and F. McAuley (eds), *Criminal Justice History: Themes and Controversies from Pre-Independence Ireland* (Dublin: Four Courts Press, 2003).

Brody, H., *Inishkillane: Change and Decline in the West of Ireland* (Harmondsworth: Penguin, 1973).

Brophy, J., 'Progress of Criminal Insanity Bill not matched by promises of funding', *Irish Times*, 14 March 2003.

Brown, E.M., 'Why Wagner-Jauregg won the Nobel Prize for discovering malaria therapy for general paralysis of the insane', *History of Psychiatry*, 11, 44 (October 2000), 371–82.

Browne, I., *Development of Community Mental Health Services* (Dublin: Eastern Health Board, 1977).

Browne, I., *Music and Madness* (Cork: Atrium/Cork University Press, 2008).

Browne, I., *The Writings of Ivor Browne – Steps Along the Road: The Evolution of a Slow Learner* (Cork: Atrium/Cork University Press, 2013).

Browne, I., L. Liaropoulos, D. Lorenzen, T. Losavio, A. Maynard, P. Sakellaropoulos, Y. Tsiantis and G. Katzourakis, *Reform of Public Mental Health Care in Greece* (Brussels: Commission of the European Communities, 1984).

Browne, M., 'Marrying the strategic with the operational', *The Clinical Care Journal*, (2015), 85–6.

Browne, N., *Against the Tide* (Dublin: Gill and Macmillan, 1986).

Brugha, T., R. Conroy, N. Walsh, W. Delaney, J. O'Hanlon, E. Dondero, L. Daly, N. Hickey and G. Bourke, 'Social networks, attachments and support in minor affective disorders', *British Journal of Psychiatry*, 141, 3 (September 1982), 249–55.

Brugha, T. and D. Walsh, 'Suicide past and present – the temporal constancy of under-reporting', *British Journal of Psychiatry*, 132, 2 (February 1978), 177–9.

Brune, K., 'The early history of non-opioid analgesics', *Acute Pain*, 1, 1 (December 1997), 33–40.

Buckingham, J., *Bitter Nemesis: The Intimate History of Strychnine* (Boca Raton, FL: CRC Press, Taylor and Francis Group, 2008).

Buckley, S.A., 'Certified in the 19th century', *Irish Times*, 9 March 2013.

Bunbury, T., *800 Years of an Irish Castle* (Carlow: Carlow Town Council, 2013).

Burges Watson, I.P., L. Hoffman and G.V. Wilson, 'The neuropsychiatry of post-traumatic stress disorder', *British Journal of Psychiatry*, 152, 2 (February 1988), 164–73.

Burnham, J.C., *What is Medical History?* (Cambridge and Malden, MA: Polity Press, 2005).

Butler, S., 'The Psychiatric Services: Planning for the Future – a critique', *Administration*, 35, 1 (1987), 47–68.

Butler, S., *Benign Anarchy: Alcoholics Anonymous in Ireland* (Dublin: Irish Academic Press, 2010).

Byrne, C., 'Warm tributes to man who changed face of psychiatry', *Irish Independent*, 31 October 2007.

Byrne, E., 'We let them be forgotten', *Guardian*, 5 April 2014.

Byrne, E., 'Do we really need 232 suicide charities?', *Sunday Business Post*, 26 June 2016.

Byrne, P., 'Stigma of mental illness', *British Journal of Psychiatry*, 174, 1 (January 1999), 1–2.

Byrne, P., 'Stigma of mental illness and ways of diminishing it', *Advances in Psychiatric Treatment*, 6, 1 (January 2000), 65–72.

Cabot, M.R., 'The incidence and prevalence of schizophrenia in the Republic of Ireland', *Social Psychiatry and Psychiatric Epidemiology*, 25, 4 (July 1990), 210–15.

Cahill, A., 'The lull between war and peace', *Irish Times*, 14 June 1994.

Canavan, M., 'Nurse training' in D.A. Murphy (ed.), *Tumbling Walls: The Evolution of a Community Institution over 150 Years* (Portlaoise: Midland Health Board, 1983).

Carlson, H.M. and L.A. Baxter, 'Androgyny, depression, and self-esteem in Irish homosexual and heterosexual males and females', *Sex Roles*, 10, 5–6 (March 1984), 457–67.

Carolan, M., 'Psychiatric patient takes case against involuntary detention in hospital', *Irish Times*, 16 October 2008.

Carolan, M., 'Woman's hospital detention ruled unlawful by court', *Irish Times*, 1 November 2008.

Carolan, M., 'Young woman in UK psychiatric unit to come home', *Irish Times*, 8 July 2015.

Carolan, M., 'ECT treatment proves 'beneficial' for man who refused to eat', *Irish Times*, 11 June 2016.

Carr Communications on behalf of the Expert Group on Mental Health Policy, *Speaking Your Mind* (Dublin: Department of Health, 2004).

Casey, P., 'Anthony Clare', *Guardian*, 31 October 2007.

Casey, P. 'Farewell to a dear friend and kind mentor', *Irish Independent*, 31 October 2007.

Casey, P., 'Devil is in the dogma', *Sunday Business Post*, 17 February 2008.

Casey, P., 'Any review of past abuses must extend to asylums', *Irish Independent*, 16 June 2014.

Casey, P. and B.D. Kelly, *Fish's Clinical Psychopathology (Third Edition)* (London: Gaskell/Royal College of Psychiatrists, 2007).

Chadbourne, K., 'Áine Chnoc Áine', *Proceedings of the Harvard Celtic Colloquium*, 20/21 (2000/2001), 176.

Chaney, S., "No "sane" person would have any idea': patients' involvement in late nineteenth-century British asylum psychiatry', *Medical History*, 60, 1 (January 2016), 37–53.

Cherry, S. and R. Munting, "Exercise is the thing'? Sport and the asylum c.1850–1950', *International Journal of the History of Sport*, 22, 1 (2005), 42–58.

Chitsabesan, P., L. Kroll, S. Bailey, C. Kenning, S. Sneider, W. MacDonald and L. Theodosiou, 'Mental health needs of young offenders in custody and the community', *British Journal of Psychiatry*, 188, 6 (June 2006), 534–40.

Chow, W.S. and S. Priebe, 'How has the extent of institutional mental healthcare changed in Western Europe? Analysis of data since 1990', *British Medical Journal Open*, 6, 4 (29 April 2016), e010188.

Christensen, K., A. Haroun, L.J. Schneiderman and D.V. Jeste, 'Decision-making capacity for informed consent in the older population', *Bulletin of the American Academy of Psychiatry and the Law*, 23, 3 (September 1995), 353–65.

Clancy, M., 'The "western outpost": local government and women's suffrage in county Galway 1898–1918' in G. Moran (ed.), *Galway: History and Society – Interdisciplinary Essays on the History of an Irish County* (Dublin: Geography Publications, 1996).

Clancy, M., 'Shaping the nation: women in the Free State parliament, 1923–1937' in Y. Galligan, E. Ward and R. Wilford (eds), *Contesting Politics: Women in Ireland, North and South* (Boulder, Colorado: Westview Press, 1999).

Clare, A., *Psychiatry in Dissent* (London: Tavistock Publications, 1976).

Clare, A., 'The mad Irish?' in C. Keane (ed.), *Mental Health in Ireland* (Dublin: Gill and Macmillan and Radio Telefís Éireann, 1991).

Clare, A., *In the Psychiatrist's Chair* (London: Mandarin, 1993).

Clare, A., 'Psychological medicine' in P. Kumar and M. Clark (eds), *Clinical Medicine: A Textbook for Medical Students and Doctors (Third Edition)* (London: Ballière Tindall, 1994).

Clare, A., *In the Psychiatrist's Chair II* (London: Mandarin, 1996).

Clare, A., *In the Psychiatrist's Chair III* (London: Sinclair-Stevenson Ltd., 1998).

Clare, A., *On Men: Masculinity in Crisis* (London: Arrow Books/Random House Group, 2000).

Clare, A., R.J. Daly, T.G. Dinan, D. King, B.E. Leonard, C. O'Boyle, J. O'Connor, J. Waddington, N. Walsh and M. Webb, 'Advancement of psychiatric research in Ireland: proposal for a national body', *Irish Journal of Psychological Medicine*, 7, 2 (September 1990), 93.

Clare, A.W., 'Diazepam, alcohol, and barbiturate abuse', *British Medical Journal*, 4, 5783 (6 November 1971), 340.

Clare, A.W., '"The other half of medicine" and St Bartholomew's Hospital', *British Journal of Psychiatry*, 146, 2 (1 February 1985), 120–6.

Clare, A.W., 'Homosexuality', *Irish Times*, 9 February 1990.

Clare, A.W., 'Obituary: John Norman Parker Moore', *Psychiatric Bulletin*, 20, 12 (1 December 1996), 771–3.

Clare, A.W., 'Swift, mental illness and St Patrick's Hospital', *Irish Journal of Psychological Medicine*, 15, 3 (September 1998), 100–4.

Clare, A.W., 'St. Patrick's Hospital', *American Journal of Psychiatry*, 155, 11 (November 1998), 1599.

Clare, A.W., 'Psychiatry's future', *Journal of Mental Health*, 8, 2 (1999), 109–11.

Clare, A.W. with S. Thompson, *Let's Talk About Me* (London: BBC Books, 1981).

Clarke, B., 'Mental illness and rehabilitation in early nineteenth-century Ireland: the case of Charles Stock', *Psychological Medicine*, 13, 4 (November 1983), 727–34.

Clarke, D., 'Live and don't let die', *Irish Times*, 3 April 2015.

Clarke, D., 'Tallaght tale', *Irish Times*, 6 April 2015.

Clarke, D., '*My Name is Emily* review: a teen road movie that's well worth the mileage', *Irish Times*, 8 April 2016.

Clarke, F., 'English, Adeline ('Ada')' in J. McGuire and J. Quinn (eds), *Dictionary of Irish Biography: From the Earliest Times to the Year 2002 (Volume 3, D–F)* (Cambridge: Royal Irish Academy and Cambridge University Press, 2009).

Clarke, M.C., A. Tanskanen, M.O. Huttunen, M. Clancy, D.R. Cotter and M. Cannon, 'Evidence for shared susceptibility to epilepsy and psychosis: a population-based family study', *Biological Psychiatry*, 71, 9 (May 2012), 836–9.

Cleary, F., *In A World Apart* (Donegal: Fergus Cleary, 2015).

Coakley, D., *Irish Masters of Medicine* (Dublin: Town House, 1992).

Coakley, D., *Medicine in Trinity College Dublin: An Illustrated History* (Dublin: Trinity College Dublin, 2014).

Coakley, D., 'William Wilde in the West of Ireland', *Irish Journal of Medical Science*, 185, 2 (May 2016), 277–80.

Cody, S., 'Anthony Clare', *Guardian*, 31 October 2007.

Coghill, D., S. Bonnar, S.L. Duke, J. Graham and S. Seth, *Child and Adolescent Psychiatry* (Oxford: Oxford University Press, 2009).

Coleborne, C., '"His brain was wrong, his mind astray"', *Journal of Family History*, 31, 1 (January 2006), 45–65.

Coleborne, C., 'Families, patients and emotions: asylums for the insane in colonial Australia and New Zealand, c. 1880–1910', *Social History of Medicine*, 19, 3 (December 2006), 425–42.

College of Psychiatry of Ireland, *Antidepressant Medication – Clarification* (Dublin: College of Psychiatry of Ireland, 2010).

College of Psychiatrists of Ireland, *Constitution (Revised)* (Dublin: College of Psychiatrists of Ireland, 2013).

College of Psychiatrists of Ireland, *Workforce Planning Report 2013–2023* (Dublin: College of Psychiatrists of Ireland, 2013).

College of Psychiatrists of Ireland, *Budget Submission 2016: Press Statement: 9th October 2015* (Dublin: College of Psychiatrists of Ireland, 2015).

College of Psychiatrists of Ireland, *Budget Submission 2016* (Dublin: College of Psychiatrists of Ireland, 2015).

College of Psychiatrists of Ireland, *The Use of Psychotropic Medication in Vulnerable Populations* (Dublin: College of Psychiatrists of Ireland, 2015).

College of Psychiatry of Ireland (Public Education Committee) and Gay and Lesbian Equality Network (GLEN), *Lesbian, Gay and Bisexual Patients: The Issues for Mental Health Practice* (Dublin: College of Psychiatry of Ireland, GLEN, Health Service Executive, 2011).

Collins, A., 'James Joyce and a North Dublin asylum', *Irish Journal of Psychological Medicine*, 19, 1 (March 2002), 27–8.

Collins, A., *St Vincent's Hospital, Fairview: An Illustrated History, 1857–2007* (Dublin: Albertine Kennedy Publishing with Duke Kennedy Sweetman, 2007).

Collins, A., 'Eleonora Fleury captured', *British Journal of Psychiatry*, 203, 1 (1 July 2013), 5.

Collins, A. 'The Richmond District Asylum and the 1916 Easter Rising', *Irish Journal of Psychological Medicine*, 30, 4 (December 2013), 279–83.

Collins, A., 'Fleury, Eleonora Lilian' in J. McGuire and J. Quinn (eds), *Dictionary of Irish Biography* (Cambridge: Cambridge University Press, 2014).

Collins, A., 'Book review: *Trinity's Psychiatrists: From Serenity of the Soul to Neuroscience*', *Irish Journal of Psychological Medicine*, 33, 1 (March 2016), 65.

Collins, A., 'Book review: *Medicine in Trinity College Dublin: An Illustrated History*', *Irish Journal of Psychological Medicine*, 33, 2 (June 2016), 133.

Collins, A., 'Daniel Frederick Rambaut: 'Rugbanian' and innovative resident medical superintendent', *Irish Journal of Psychological Medicine* [published online ahead of print, 2016].

Collins, C., M.T. O'Shea, P. Finegan, J. Cunniffe, D. Collier, M. Curran and M. Kearns, *Mental Health Consultations in a General Practice Out of Hours Service – Informing the Future Direction of Services* (Dublin: Irish College of General Practitioners, 2016).

Collins, E., 'Back to the Future', *Gay Community News*, February 2004.

Collins, P. and L. Naughton, *Advancing Recovery in Ireland. A National Conversation: Opening Thoughts* (Dublin: National Office for Advancing Recovery in Ireland, Health Service Executive, Mental Health Division, 2015).

Collins, S., 'Emergency mental health law rushed through Dáil', *Irish Times*, 31 October 2008.

Commemorative Book Committee, *The History of St Loman's Hospital in Changing Times* (Tullamore, County Offaly: Commemorative Book Committee, 2014).

Condrau, F., 'The patient's view meets the clinical gaze', *Social History of Medicine*, 20, 3 (December 2007), 525–40.

Conlon, L., T.J. Fahy and R. Conroy, 'PTSD in ambulant RTA victims: a randomized controlled trial of debriefing', *Journal of Psychosomatic Research*, 46, 1 (January 1999), 37–44.

Connerly, M.M., 'Book review: *Ada English: Patriot and Psychiatrist*', *Journal of International Women's Studies*, 16, 3 (July 2015), 324–6.

Connolly, H., 'The scandal of the mental hospitals.', *Magill*, October 1980.

Connors, A., 'Mental Health Minister claims that our services "have come a long way"', *Irish Medical Times*, 23 September 2011.

Conroy, M., 'Inside stories', in D.A. Murphy (ed.), *Tumbling Walls: The Evolution of a Community Institution over 150 Years* (Portlaoise: Midland Health Board, 1983).

Cooney, J., 'Better aid needed for pregnant girls', *Irish Times*, 3 May 1975.

Cooney, J., 'Contentions about Swift rejected', *Irish Times*, 24 October 1988.

Cooney, J., 'Foreword', in Organising Committee (ed.), *St Canice's Hospital, 1852–2001* (Kilkenny: South Eastern Health Board, 2006).

Cooney, J.G., 'The problem drinker' in K. O'Sullivan (ed.), *All in the Mind: Approaches to Mental Health* (Dublin: Gill and Macmillan, 1986).

Cooney, T. and O. O'Neill, *Psychiatric Detention: Civil Commitment in Ireland* (Wicklow: Baikonur, 1996).

Cooper, B., 'Camille Claudel: trajectory of a psychosis', *Medical Humanities*, 34, 1 (June 2008), 25–9.

Cooper, J., 'Children and the falling sickness, Ireland, 1850–1904' in A. Mac Lellan and A. Mauger (eds), *Growing Pains: Childhood Illness in Ireland, 1750–1950* (Dublin: Irish Academic Press, 2013).

Corless, D., 'Radio: Brain-salad surgery and Ronan's family cooking', *Irish Independent*, 7 June 2015.

Corry, M., 'Warehousing human problems', in Simon Community (ed.), *Institutions: Safety Belts or Strait-Jackets?* (Dublin: Simon Community, 1985), 4–7.

Corry, M., 'Is there a place for ECT in today's psychiatry?', *Irish Medical Times*, 18 July 2008.

Corry, M. and Á. Tubridy, *Going Mad? Understanding Mental Illness* (Dublin: Newleaf/Gill and Macmillan Ltd., 2001).

Coulter, C., 'North Dublin site selected for prison complex', *Irish Times*, 27 January 2005.

Coulter, C., 'Legal rights of mental health sufferers ignored', *Irish Times*, 1 November 2005.

Coulter, C., 'Government and judge combine to clear up loophole', *Irish Times*, 1 November 2008.

Cowell, J., *A Noontide Blazing: Brigid Lyons Thornton – Rebel, Soldier, Doctor* (Dublin: Currach Press, 2005).

Cowley, M., 'Torture hearing at Strasbourg resumes', *Irish Times*, 27 November 1973.

Cowley, M., 'Rights Commission may visit North', *Irish Times*, 30 November 1973.

Cox, C., *Negotiating Insanity in the Southeast of Ireland, 1820–1900* (Manchester and New York: Manchester University Press, 2012).

Cox, C. and H. Marland (eds), *Migration, Health and Ethnicity in the Modern World* (Basingstoke, Hampshire: Palgrave Macmillan, 2013).

Cox, C. and H. Marland, '"A burden on the county': madness, institutions of confinement and the Irish patient in Victorian Lancashire', *Social History of Medicine*, 28, 2 (May 2015), 263–87.

Crane, A., 'Radio psychiatrist who quizzed the famous', *Financial Times*, 31 October 2007.

Crawford, E.M., 'A mysterious malady in an Irish asylum: the Richmond epidemic of the late nineteenth century', in P.M. Prior (ed.), *Asylums, Mental Health Care and the Irish, 1800–2010* (Dublin: Irish Academic Press, 2012).

Crooks, P., 'Archives in crisis', *History Ireland*, 18, 3 (May/June 2010), 10–1.

Crowe, K., Irish Advocacy Network on behalf of the Expert Group on Mental Health Policy, *What We Heard* (Dublin: Department of Health, 2004).

Crowley, T., O. Barry, M. Young, M. Shiel, R. Meyer Bridgers, C. McNulty, D. Boylan, C. Wade, J. Hynes, T. Brady, P. Reid and R. Kelly, 'Community care', *Irish Times*, 7 May 1986.

Crumlish, N. and K. O'Rourke, 'A systematic review of treatments for post-traumatic stress disorder among refugees and asylum-seekers', *Journal of Nervous and Mental Disease*, 198, 4 (April 2010), 237–51.

Crump, C., M.A. Winkleby, K. Sundquist and J. Sundquist, 'Comorbidities and mortality in persons with schizophrenia: a Swedish national cohort study', *American Journal of Psychiatry*, 170, 3 (March 2013), 324–33.

Culhane, A. and T. Kearns, *An Impact Evaluation of 'Vision for Change' (Mental Health Policy) on Mental Health Service Provision: A National Descriptive Evaluation Project* (Dublin: Psychiatric Nurses Association and Royal College of Surgeons in Ireland, Faculty of Nursing and Midwifery, 2016).

Cullen, A., 'Psychotic patients left on trolleys in crisis-hit A&E', *Irish Independent*, 24 June 2015.

Cullen, P., 'More monitoring of mentally ill patients sought', *Irish Times*, 17 April 2015.

Cullen, P., 'Apology from HSE on assault allegations', *Irish Times*, 5 February 2016.

Cullen, S. (ed.), *Climbing Mountains in our Minds: Stories and Photographs from St. Senan's Hospital, Enniscorthy* (Wexford: Wexford County Council, 2012).

Culliton, G., 'Review of Act is to be built on "human rights"', *Irish Medical Times*, 27 May 2011.

Culliton, G., '23 clinical programme posts filled to date', *Irish Medical Times*, 26 March 2015.

Culliton, G., 'ECT data incomplete due to privacy concern', *Irish Medical Times*, 27 March 2015.

Culliton, G., 'ECT Bill "respects patients' wishes"', *Irish Medical Times*, 11 December 2015.

Cullitan, G., 'Budget moves claims rejected', *Irish Medical Times*, 13 May 2016.

Cullivan, R., J. Crown and N. Walsh, 'The use of psychotropic medication in patients referred to a psycho-oncology service', *Psycho-Oncology*, 7, 4 (July–August1998), 301–6.

Cummings, E. and O. O'Conor, 'The SM Judgment and The Mental Health Act 2008', *Irish Medical Journal*, 102, 7 (2009), 234.

Curley, A., E. Agada, A. Emechebe, C. Anamdi, X.T. Ng, R. Duffy and B.D. Kelly, 'Exploring and explaining involuntary care: the relationship between psychiatric admission status, gender and other demographic and clinical variables', *International Journal of Law and Psychiatry* [published online ahead of print, 2016].

Dale, P. and J. Melling, 'The politics of mental welfare: fresh perspectives on the history of institutional care for the mentally ill and disabled' in P. Dale and J. Melling (eds), *Mental Illness and Learning Disability Since 1850: Finding a Place for Mental Disorder in the United Kingdom* (London and New York: Routledge/Taylor and Francis Group, 2006).

Daly, A. and D. Walsh, *Activities of Irish Psychiatric Services 2001* (Dublin: The Health Research Board, 2002).

Daly, A. and D. Walsh, *Activities of Irish Psychiatric Units and Hospitals 2011* (Dublin: Health Research Board, 2012).

Daly, A. and D. Walsh, *Activities of Irish Psychiatric Units and Hospitals 2013* (Dublin: Health Research Board, 2014).

Daly, A. and D. Walsh, *Activities of Irish Psychiatric Units and Hospitals 2014* (Dublin: Health Research Board, 2015).

Daly, M.E., 'Death and disease in independent Ireland, c. 1920–1970: a research agenda' in C. Cox and M. Luddy (eds), *Cultures of Care in Irish Medical History 1750–1950* (Basingstoke, Hampshire: Palgrave Macmillan, 2010).

Daly, R.J., 'Compensation and rehabilitation of victims of torture', *Danish Medical Bulletin*, 27, 5 (November 1980), 245–8.

Daly, R.J., 'Samuel Pepys and post-traumatic stress disorder', *British Journal of Psychiatry*, 143, 1 (July 1983), 64–8.

Daly, R.J., 'Community psychiatry and the National Institute of Mental Health', *Irish Journal of Psychological Medicine*, 7, 1 (March 1990), 5.

Daly, R.J., R. Aitken and S.V. Rosenthal, 'Flying phobia: phenomenological study', *Proceedings of the Royal Society of Medicine*, 63, 9 (September 1970), 878–82.

Daly, R.J., P.F. Duggan, P.J. Bracken, H.J. Doonan and N.J. Kelleher, 'Plasma levels of beta-endorphin in depressed patients with and without pain', *British Journal of Psychiatry*, 150, 2 (February 1987), 224–7.

D'Arcy, C., 'Suicide rates are 'stabilising' after increasing during recession', *Irish Times*, 23 April 2016.

D'Arcy, C., 'Protests over cuts to funding for mental health services', *Irish Times*, 29 April 2016.

D'Arcy, M., 'The Hospital and the Holy Spirit: Psychotic Subjectivity and Institutional Returns in Dublin', paper delivered at the *Society for Psychological Anthropology*, Boston, MA, 10 April 2015.

Davies, K., '"Silent and Censured Travellers'? Patients' narratives and patients' voices: perspectives on the history of mental illness since 1948', *Social History of Medicine*, 14, 2 (August 2001), 267–92.

Davoren, M., E.G. Breen and B.D. Kelly, 'Dr Adeline English: revolutionizing politics and psychiatry in Ireland', *Irish Psychiatrist*, 10, 4 (Winter 2009), 260–2.

Davoren, M., E.G. Breen and B.D. Kelly, 'Dr Ada English: patriot and psychiatrist in early twentieth-century Ireland', *Irish Journal of Psychological Medicine*, 28, 2 (June 2011), 91–6.

Davoren, M., S. Hennessy, C. Conway, S. Marrinan, P. Gill and H.G. Kennedy, 'Recovery and concordance in a secure forensic psychiatry hospital – the self-rated DUNDRUM-3 programme completion and DUNDRUM-4 recovery scales', *BMC Psychiatry*, 15 (March 2015), 61.

Davoren, M., S. O'Dwyer, Z. Abidin, L. Naughton, O. Gibbons, E. Doyle, K. McDonnell, S. Monks and H.G. Kennedy, 'Prospective in-patient cohort study of moves between levels of therapeutic security; the DUNDRUM-1 triage security, DUNDRUM-3 programme completion and DUNDRUM-4 recovery scales and the HCR-20', *BMC Psychiatry*, 12 (July 2012), 80.

Day, E., 'He was bad, so they put an ice pick in his brain...', *Observer*, 13 January 2008.

Delaney, E., 'Fascinating tales of healing our forgotten war wounded', *Sunday Independent*, 15 February 2015.

Department of Health, *Psychiatric Nursing Services of Health Boards: Report of Working Party* (Dublin: The Stationery Office, 1972).

Department of Health, *Shaping A Healthier Future: A Strategy for Effective Healthcare in the 1990s* (Dublin: The Stationery Office, 1987).

Department of Health, *White Paper: A New Mental Health Act* (Dublin: The Stationery Office, 1995).

Department of Health and Children, *Quality and Fairness: A Health System for You* (Dublin: The Stationery Office, 2001).

Department of Health and Healthy Ireland, *The National Positive Ageing Strategy* (Dublin: Department of Health, 2013).

Dickinson, T., *'Curing Queers': Mental Nurses and Their Patients, 1935–74* (Manchester: Manchester University Press, 2015).

Digby, A., 'Contexts and perspectives', in D. Wright and A. Digby (eds), *From Idiocy to Mental Deficiency: Historical Perspectives on People with Learning Disabilities* (London and New York: Routledge, 1996), 1–21.

Dillon, J., 'Mental Health Act', *Irish Times*, 19 June 1991.

Division of Mental Health and Prevention of Substance Abuse (World Health Organisation), *Mental Health Care Law: Ten Basic Principles* (Geneva: World Health Organisation, 1996).

Division of Mental Health and Prevention of Substance Abuse (World Health Organisation), *Guidelines for the Promotion of Human Rights of Persons with Mental Disorders* (Geneva: World Health Organisation, 1996).

Doheny, N., 'Psychiatric nurse training', in E. Lonergan (ed.), *St Luke's Hospital, Clonmel, 1834–1984* (Clonmel: South Eastern Health Board, 1984), 105–11.

Doherty, A.M., F. Jabbar and B.D. Kelly, 'Attitudes and experiences of nursing staff to the Mental Health Act 2001: lessons for future mental health legislation', *Irish Journal of Psychological Medicine*, 31, 2 (June 2014), 83–7.

Doherty, A.M., F. Jabbar, B.D. Kelly and P. Casey, 'Distinguishing between adjustment disorder and depressive episode in clinical practice: the role of personality disorder', *Journal of Affective Disorders*, 168 (October 2014), 78–85.

Doherty, A.M. and B.D. Kelly, 'Social and psychological correlates of happiness in seventeen European countries: analysis of data from the European Social Survey', *Irish Journal of Psychological Medicine*, 27, 3 (September 2010), 130–4.

Doherty, A.M. and B.D. Kelly, 'When Irish eyes are smiling: income and happiness in Ireland, 2003–2009', *Irish Journal of Medical Science*, 182, 1 (March 2013), 113–19.

Donnellan, E., 'Mental hospitals to close over 10-year phase', *Irish Times*, 25 January 2006.

Donnelly, M., *Healthcare Decision-Making and the Law: Autonomy, Capacity and the Limits of Liberalism* (Cambridge: Cambridge University Press, 2010).

Donohoe, E., N. Walsh and J.A. Tracey, 'Pack-size legislation reduces severity of paracetamol overdoses in Ireland', *Irish Journal of Medical Science*, 175, 3 (July–September 2006), 40–2.

Dooley, T., *The Decline and Fall of the Dukes of Leinster, 1872–1948: Love, War, Debt and Madness* (Dublin: Four Courts Press, 2014).

Dörries, A. and T. Beddies, 'The Wittenauer Heilstätten in Berlin: a case record study of psychiatric patients in Germany, 1919–1960' in R. Porter and D. Wright (eds), *The Confinement of the Insane: International Perspectives, 1800–1965* (Cambridge: Cambridge University Press, 2003).

Douglas, G., R. Goodbody, A. Mauger and J. Davey, *Bloomfield: A History, 1812–2012* (Dublin: Ashfield Press, 2012).

Douglas, L. and L. Feeney, 'Thirty years of referrals to a community mental health service', *Irish Journal of Psychological Medicine*, 33, 2 (June 2016), 105–9.

Dowbiggin, I.R., *Keeping America Sane: Psychiatry and Eugenics in the United States and Canada, 1880–1940* (Ithaca and London: Cornell University Press, 1997).

Doyle, K., 'President signs new asylum law after concerns', *Irish Independent*, 31 December 2015.

Drury, M. O'C., *The Danger of Words and Writings on Wittgenstein* (Bristol: Thoemmes Press, 2003).

Du Feu, M. and C. Chovaz, *Mental Health and Deafness* (Oxford and New York: Oxford University Press, 2014).

Duffy, D., S. Linehan and H.G. Kennedy, 'Psychiatric morbidity in the male sentenced Irish prisons population', *Irish Journal of Psychological Medicine*, 23, 2 (June 2006), 54–62.

Duffy, R.M. and B.D. Kelly, 'Psychiatric assessment and treatment of survivors of torture', *BJPsych Advances*, 21, 2 (March 2015), 106–15.

Dunne, B., J. Pettigrew and K. Robinson, 'Using historical documentary methods to explore the history of occupational therapy', *British Journal of Occupational Therapy*, 79, 6 (June 2016), 376–84.

Dunne, D., 'Prescribing practices', *British Journal of Psychiatry*, 159, 1 (July 1991), 156.

Dunne, D., 'Obituary: Irene Veronica Josephine Aherne', *Psychiatric Bulletin*, 28, 9 (September 2004), 347.

Dunne, J., 'Outpatient psychiatric clinic: report of two years' work', *Journal of the Irish Medical Association*, 64, 403 (7 January 1971), 7–9.

Dunne, R. and D.M. McLoughlin, 'Regional variation in electroconvulsive therapy use', *Irish Medical Journal*, 104, 3 (March 2011), 84–7.

Edwards, C., G. Harold and S. Kilcommins, *Access to Justice for People with Disabilities as Victims of Crime in Ireland* (University College Cork: School of Applied Social Studies and Centre for Criminal Justice and Human Rights, Faculty of Law, 2012).

Egan, G., 'Father and son II', in G. O'Brien (ed.), *Coming Out* (Blackrock, County Dublin: Currach Press, 2003).

El-Hai, J., *The Lobotomist: A Maverick Medical Genius and His Tragic Quest to Rid the World of Mental Illness* (Hoboken, New Jersey: Wiley and Sons, 2005).

Emsell, L., A. Leemans, C. Langan, W. Van Hecke, G.J. Barker, P. McCarthy, B. Jeurissen, J. Sijbers, S. Sunaert, D.M. Cannon and C. McDonald, 'Limbic and callosal white matter changes in euthymic bipolar I disorder: an advanced diffusion MRI tractography study', *Biological Psychiatry*, 73, 2 (January 2013), 194–201.

Enoch, D. and H. Ball, *Uncommon Psychiatric Syndromes (Fourth Edition)* (London: Hodder Arnold, 2001).

Enright, S., *Easter Rising 1916: The Trials* (Dublin: Merrion/Irish Academic Press, 2013).

European Union, *European Pact for Mental Health and Well-being* (Brussels: European Union, 2008).

Expert Committee, *Review of the Mental Health Act 1983* (London: Department of Health, 1999).

Expert Group on Mental Health Policy, *A Vision for Change* (Dublin: The Stationery Office, 2006).

Expert Group on the Review of the Mental Health Act 2001, *Report of the Expert Group on the Review of the Mental Health Act 2001* (Dublin: Department of Health, 2015).

Fagan, J., '€7m for Sligo's four-star Clarion Hotel', *Irish Times*, 28 October 2015.

Fahy, T., 'Suicide and the Irish: from sin to serotonin', in C. Keane (ed.), *Mental Health in Ireland* (Dublin: Gill and Macmillan and Radio Teilifís Éireann, 1991).

Fahy, T., 'Obituary: Thomas Lynch', *Psychiatric Bulletin*, 29, 11 (November 2005), 438.

Fahy, T.J., 'Is psychosis endemic in western Ireland?', *American Journal of Psychiatry*, 142, 8 (August 1985), 998–9.

Fahy, T.J., L. Mannion, M. Leonard and P. Prescott, 'Can suicides be identified from case records? A case control study using blind rating', *Archives of Suicide Research*, 8, 3 (2004), 263–9.

Farmar, T., *Patients, Potions and Physicians: A Social History of Medicine in Ireland* (Dublin: A and A Farmar in association with the Royal College of Physicians of Ireland, 2004).

Farmar, T., 'Book review: *Bloomfield: A History, 1812–2012*', *Irish Medical Journal*, 107, 7 (August 2014), 194.

Farmer, P., 'Pathologies of power: rethinking health and human rights', *American Journal of Public Health*, 89, 10 (October 1999), 1486–96.

Farmer, P., *Pathologies of Power: Human Rights and the New War on the Poor* (Berkeley: University of California Press, 2003).

Farragher, B. and N. Walsh, 'Joint care admissions to a psychiatric unit: a prospective analysis', *General Hospital Psychiatry*, 20, 2 (March 1998), 73–7.

Farrell, E., *'A Most Diabolical Deed': Infanticide and Irish Society, 1850–1900* (Manchester: Manchester University Press, 2013).

Farrell, M., 'Ada English biography (book review of: *Ada English: Patriot and Psychiatrist*)', *Irish History Review*, 17 February 2015.

Farren, C., *Overcoming Alcohol Misuse: A 28-Day Guide* (Blackrock, County Dublin: Kite Books/Blackhall Publishing, 2011).

Farren, C., *The U-Turn: A Guide to Happiness* (Blackrock, County Dublin: Orpen Press, 2013).

Feeney, L., 'Book review: *The Ship of Seven Murders*', *Irish Journal of Psychological Medicine*, 27, 4 (December 2010), 220.

Feeney, L., A. Kavanagh, B.D. Kelly and M. Mooney, 'Moving to a purpose built acute psychiatric unit on a general hospital site: does the new environment produce change for the better?', *Irish Medical Journal*, 100, 3 (March 2007), 391–3.

Feeney, L. and B.D. Kelly, 'Mental health advocacy and *A Mind that Found Itself*', *Irish Psychiatrist*, 9, 1 (Spring 2008), 19–22.

Feeney, L., B.D. Kelly, P. Whitty and E. O'Callaghan, 'Mental illness in migrants: diagnostic and therapeutic challenges', *Irish Journal of Psychological Medicine*, 19, 1 (March 2002), 29–31.

Fennell, N., 'Psychiatric committal', *Irish Times*, 7 February 1992.

Fennell, N., 'Defeat of this Bill insults silent victims', *Irish Times*, 25 May 1992.

Fenton, A., *Past Lives: The Memorials of Saint Patrick's Cathedral, Dublin* (Dublin: St Patrick's Cathedral, 2012).

Ferriter, D., *The Transformation of Ireland, 1900–2000* (London: Profile Books, 2004).

Ferriter, D., *Occasions of Sin: Sex and Society in Modern Ireland* (London: Profile Books Ltd., 2009).

Ferry, F., B. Bunting, S. Murphy, S. O'Neill, D. Stein and K. Koenen, 'Traumatic events and their relative PTSD burden in Northern Ireland: a consideration of the impact of the 'Troubles'', *Social Psychiatry and Psychiatric Epidemiology*, 49, 3 (March 2014), 435–46.

Fielding, W.T., *Sissy Talk* (Dublin: William T. Fielding, 2012).

Finnane, M., *Insanity and the Insane in Post-Famine Ireland* (London: Croom Helm, 1981).

Finnane, M., 'Asylums, families and the State', *History Workshop Journal*, 20, 1 (Autumn 1985), 134–48.

Finnane, M., 'Irish psychiatry. Part 1: the formation of a profession', in G.E. Berrios and H. Freeman (eds), *150 Years of British Psychiatry, 1841–1991. Volume I* (London: Gaskell/Royal College of Psychiatrists, 1991), 306–13.

Finnane, M., 'Book review: *Asylums, Mental Health Care and the Irish, 1800–2010*', *Bulletin of the History of Medicine*, 87, 2 (Summer 2013), 289–90.

Finnegan, M., 'I would rather get cancer again than be a patient in the Irish mental health service', *Irish Times*, 29 April 2016.

Finnegan, P., 'Medicine in Connaught', in J.B. Lyons (ed.), *2000 Years of Irish Medicine* (Dublin: Eireann Healthcare Publications, 1999), 93–6.

Finnerty, C., 'Portrait of a revolutionary', *Ballinasloe Life*, December 2014–January 2015.

Fitzgerald, J., 'Impervious to psychoanalysis?', *Conspiracies of Silence* (blog), 16 June 2016 (https://conspiraciesofsilence.wordpress.com/).

Fitzgerald, M., 'The child and the family', in C. Keane (ed.), *Mental Health in Ireland* (Dublin: Gill and Macmillan and Radio Telefís Éireann, 1991).

Fitzgerald, M., 'Psychoanalytic psychotherapy in Ireland', in M. Fitzgerald (ed.), *Irish Families under Stress (Volume 7)* (Dublin: South Western Area Health Board, 2003), 115–19.

Fitzgerald, M., *Autism and Creativity: Is There a Link between Autism in Men and Exceptional Ability?* (Hove: Brunner-Routledge, 2004).

Fitzmaurice, S., 'Lights, camera, nerves: how can I direct a film when I can't speak?', *Irish Times*, 31 March 2016.

Fitzpatrick, R., 'Our shameful asylums', *Irish Examiner*, 7 February 2013.

Fleetwood, J.F., *The History of Medicine in Ireland (Second Edition)* (Dublin: Skellig Press, 1983).

Fogarty, J., 'The people who hear voices in their heads', *Irish Examiner*, 11 April 2015.

Fogarty, W., *Dr Eamonn O'Sullivan: A Man Before His Time* (Dublin: Wolfhound Press, 2007).

Foley, C., *The Last Irish Plague: The Great Flu Epidemic in Ireland, 1918–19* (Dublin: Irish Academic Press, 2011).

Foley, R., 'Indigenous narratives of health: (re)placing folk-medicine within Irish health histories', *Journal of Medical Humanities*, 36, 1 (March 2015), 5–18.

Foley, S.R. and B.D. Kelly, 'Psychological concomitants of capital punishment: thematic analysis of last statements from death row', *American Journal of Forensic Psychiatry*, 28, 4 (2007), 7–13.

Foley, V., 'The history of speech and language therapy in Ireland' in M. Fitzgerald (ed.), *Irish Families under Stress (Volume 7)* (Dublin: South Western Area Health Board, 2003), 30–2.

Foot, J., *The Man Who Closed the Asylums: Franco Basaglia and the Revolution in Mental Health Care* (London and New York: Verso, 2015).

Froggatt, P., 'The demographic work of Sir William Wilde', *Irish Journal of Medical Science*, 185, 2 (May 2016), 293–5.

Gabbard, G.O. and J. Kay, 'The fate of integrated treatment: whatever happened to the biopsychosocial psychiatrist?', *American Journal of Psychiatry*, 158, 12 (December 2001), 1956–63.

Gaffney, M., 'A fad insane', *Irish Times*, 14 January 2006.

Gallagher, C., 'How two lawyers ended up on opposing sides in 1916', *Irish Times*, 5 May 2014.

Gallagher, C. and D. Conlon, 'Campaigner who started out as 'that wee Bogsider who hangs out with burglars'', *Irish Times*, 29 June 2015.

Gallagher, R., 'Understanding the homosexual', *The Furrow*, 30, 9 (September 1979), 555–69.

Ganter, K., 'Funding for Mental Health Act is a human rights issue', *Medicine Weekly*, 6 April 2005.

Ganter, K., I. Daly and J. Owens, 'Implementing the Mental Health Act 2001: What should be done? What can be done?', *Irish Journal of Psychological Medicine*, 22, 3 (September 2005), 79–82.

Gantly, D., 'The 'Joy of innovation', *Medicine Weekly*, 25 November 2011.

Garfinkel, P.E., D.M. Garner, J. Rose, P.L. Darby, J.S. Brandes, J. O'Hanlon and N. Walsh, 'A comparison of characteristics in the families of patients with anorexia nervosa and normal controls', *Psychological Medicine*, 13, 4 (November 1983), 821–8.

Garland, M., D. Doherty, L. Golden-Mason, P. Fitzpatrick, N. Walsh and C. O'Farrelly, 'Stress-related hormonal suppression of natural killer activity does not show menstrual cycle variations: implications for timing of surgery for breast cancer', *Anticancer Research*, 23, 3B (May–June 2003), 2531–5.

Garland, M., D. Hickey, A. Corvin, J. Golden, P. Fitzpatrick, S. Cunningham and N. Walsh, 'Total serum cholesterol in relation to psychological correlates in parasuicide', *British Journal of Psychiatry*, 177, 1 (July 2000), 77–83.

Garland, M.R., E. Lavelle, D. Doherty, L. Golden-Mason, P. Fitzpatrick, A. Hill, N. Walsh and C. O'Farrelly. 'Cortisol does not mediate the suppressive effects of psychiatric morbidity on natural killer cell activity: a cross-sectional study of patients with early breast cancer', *Psychological Medicine*, 34, 3 (April 2004), 481–90.

Gasser, J. and G. Heller, 'The confinement of the insane in Switzerland, 1900–1970: Cery (Vaud) and Bel-Air (Geneva) asylums' in R. Porter and D. Wright (eds), *The Confinement of the Insane: International Perspectives, 1800–1965* (Cambridge: Cambridge University Press, 2003).

Gatenby, P., *The School of Physic, Trinity College Dublin: A Retrospective View* (Dublin: Trinity College, Faculty of Health Sciences, 1994).

Gavin, B., B.D. Kelly, A. Lane and E. O'Callaghan, 'The mental health of migrants', *Irish Medical Journal*, 94, 8 (September 2001), 229–30.

Gaynor, K., *Protecting Mental Health* (Dublin: Veritas Publications, 2015).

Geary, L., 'William Wilde: historian', *Irish Journal of Medical Science*, 185, 2 (May 2016), 301–2.

Geary, L.M., *Medicine and Charity in Ireland, 1718–1851* (Dublin: University College Dublin Press, 2004).

George, S.L., N.J. Shanks and L. Westlake, 'Census of single homeless people in Sheffield', *British Medical Journal*, 302, 6789 (June 1991), 1387–9.

Georgieva, I., E. Bainbridge, D. McGuinness, M. Keys, L. Brosnan, H. Felzmann, J. Maguire, K. Murphy, A. Higgins, C. McDonald and B. Hallahan, 'Opinions of key stakeholders concerning involuntary admission of patients under the Mental Health Act 2001', *Irish Journal of Psychological Medicine* [published online ahead of print, 2016].

Gibbons, P., N. Mulryan, A. McAleer and A. O'Connor, 'Criminal responsibility and mental illness in Ireland 1950–1995: fitness to plead', *Irish Journal of Psychological Medicine*, 196, 2 (June 1999), 51–6.

Gibbons, P., N. Mulryan and A. O'Connor, 'Guilty but insane: the insanity defence in Ireland, 1850–1995', *British Journal of Psychiatry*, 170, 5 (May 1997), 467–72.

Gillespie, E., 'Gays reply to the Pope', *Irish Times*, 29 October 1979.

Gillespie, E., 'Bursting with concern and tension', *Irish Times*, 15 September 1981.

Gillespie, E., 'No funds – no care?', *Irish Times*, 17 September 1981.

Gladstone, D., 'The changing dynamic of institutional care: the Western Counties Idiot Asylum, 1864–1914' in D. Wright and A. Digby (eds), *From Idiocy to Mental Deficiency: Historical Perspectives on People with Learning Disabilities* (London and New York: Routledge, 1996), 134–60.

Gordon, A.G., 'Swift's pocky quean', *Journal of the Royal Society of Medicine*, 92, 2 (February 1998), 102.

Grattan, V., *Hidden Grief: Words From A Journey of Hopelessness to a Pathway to Hope and Survival* (Dublin: Betaprint Limited, 2005).

Greally, H., *Bird's Nest Soup* (Dublin: Allen Figgis and Co., 1971).

Greally, H., *Flown the Nest* (Cork: Attic Press, 2009).

Greaves, C.D., *Liam Mellows and the Irish Revolution* (Belfast: An Ghlór Gafa, 2004).

Greene, V.T., 'Homosexuality', in V.T. Greene (ed.), *Clinical Notes in Psychiatry* (Dublin: Royal College of Surgeons in Ireland, 1988), 202–8.

Greenland, C., 'At the Crichton Royal with William Mayer-Gross (b. 15 Jan. 1889, d. 15 Feb. 1961)', *History of Psychiatry*, 13, 52 (October 2002), 467–74.

Griffin, C. and Mental Health Commission, *A Vision for a Recovery Model in Irish Mental Health Services: A Qualitative Analysis of Submissions to the Mental Health Commission* (Dublin: Mental Health Commission, 2007).

Griffin, J.A., 'Eating disorders' in K. O'Sullivan (ed.), *All in the Mind: Approaches to Mental Health* (Dublin: Gill and Macmillan, 1986).

Griffin, N., 'Psychiatric committal', *Irish Times*, 11 January 1992.

Griffin, N., 'St Canice's Hospital, Kilkenny, 1852–2001' in *Organising Committee* (ed.), St Canice's Hospital, 1852–2001 (Kilkenny: South Eastern Health Board, 2001).

Grimsley-Smith, M., 'Revisiting a 'demographic freak': Irish asylums and hidden hunger', *Social History of Medicine*, 25, 2 (May 2012), 307–23.

Grob, G.N., *Mental Illness and American Society, 1875–1940* (Princeton, New Jersey: Princeton University Press, 1983).

Grob, G.N., *Mental Institutions in America: Social Policy to 1875* (New Brunswick and London: Transaction Publishers, 2009).

Guarnieri, P., 'The history of psychiatry in Italy', in M.S. Micale and R. Porter (eds), *Discovering the History of Psychiatry* (New York and Oxford: Oxford University Press, 1994).

Guéret, M., *What the Doctor Saw* (Dublin: IMD, 2013).

Guéret, M., 'The asylum years', *Sunday Independent*, 19 October 2014.

Guéret, M., 'Shell-shocked', *Sunday Independent*, 11 January 2015.

Guilbride, A., 'Infanticide: the crime of motherhood', in P. Kennedy (ed.), *Motherhood in Ireland* (Cork: Mercier Press, 2004).

Guruswamy, S. and B.D. Kelly, 'A change of vision? Mental health policy', *Irish Medical Journal*, 99, 6 (1 June 2006), 164–6.

H., C., 'Dr Kate Ganter – 1948–2012', *Irish Medical Times*, 14 September 2012.

Halpin, C., 'Psychiatrists, involuntary committals, and the Mental Health Act', *Irish Times*, 30 May 2005.

Hanaghan, J., *The Beast Factor: Forging Passion into Power* (Enniskerry, County Wicklow: Tansy Books from Egotist, 1979).

Hanniffy, L.K., 'Changing terms in psychiatry' in D.A. Murphy (ed.), *Tumbling Walls: The Evolution of a Community Institution over 150 Years* (Portlaoise: Midland Health Board, 1983).

Hare, E., 'Was insanity on the increase? The fifty-sixth Maudsley Lecture', *British Journal of Psychiatry*, 142, 5 (1 May 1983), 439–55.

Hare, E.H., 'Old familiar faces: some aspects of the asylum era in Britain. Part 1', *Psychiatric Developments*, 3, 3 (Autumn 1985), 245–55.

Harrison, B., 'One forensic documentary beats two cliché-ridden cop dramas', *Irish Times*, 17 September 2011.

Hartman, M., 'An Irish National Institute of Mental Health', *Irish Journal of Psychological Medicine*, 7, 1 (March 1990), 5.

Haw, C. and G. Yorston, 'Thomas Prichard and the non-restraint movement at the Northampton Asylum', *Psychiatric Bulletin*, 28, 4 (1 April 2004), 140–2.

Hawkins, M., *Restless Spirit: The Story of Rose Quinn* (Cork: Mercier Press, 2006).

Hayden, D., *Pox: Genius, Madness, and The Mysteries Of Syphilis* (New York: Basic Books, 2003).

Hayes, P. and J. Campbell, *Bloody Sunday: Trauma Pain and Politics* (London, Dublin and Ann Arbor, Michigan: Pluto Press, 2005).

Health and Consumer Protectorate Director-General, *Improving the Mental Health of the Population: Towards a Strategy on Mental Health for the European Union* (Brussels: European Commission 2005).

Health and Social Care Information Centre, *Inpatients Formally Detained in Hospitals under the Mental Health Act 1983, and Patients Subject to Supervised Community Treatment: Annual Report, England, 2013* (Leeds: Health and Social Care Information Centre/ National Statistics, 2013).

Health Service Executive, *National Intercultural Health Strategy, 2007–2012* (Dublin: Health Service Executive, 2008).

Health Service Executive, National Suicide Review Group and Department of Health and Children, *Reach Out: National Strategy for Action on Suicide Prevention, 2005–2014* (Dublin: Health Service Executive, 2005).

Healthcare Pricing Office, *Activity in Acute Public Hospitals in Ireland* (Dublin: Health Service Executive, 2014).

Healthy Ireland, Department of Health, Health Service Executive and National Office for Suicide Prevention, *Connecting for Life: Ireland's National Strategy to Reduce Suicide, 2015–2020* (Dublin: Department of Health, 2015).

Healy, D., 'Irish psychiatry. Part 2: use of the Medico-Psychological Association by its Irish members – *plus ça change!*', in G.E. Berrios and H. Freeman (eds), *150 Years of British Psychiatry, 1841–1991. Volume I* (London: Gaskell/Royal College of Psychiatrists, 1991), 314–20.

Healy, D., 'Interview: In conversation with Ivor Browne', *Psychiatric Bulletin*, 16, 1 (January 1992), 1–9.

Healy, D., 'Interview: In conversation with Tom Lynch', *Psychiatric Bulletin*, 16, 2 (February 1992), 65–72.

Healy, D., 'Interview: In conversation with Desmond McGrath', *Psychiatric Bulletin*, 16, 3 (March 1992), 129–37.

Healy, D., *Images of Trauma: From Hysteria to Post-Traumatic Stress Disorder* (London: Faber and Faber, 1993).

Healy, D., 'Irish psychiatry in the twentieth century', in H. Freeman and G.E. Berrios (eds), *150 Years of British Psychiatry. Volume II: The Aftermath* (London: Athlone Press, 1996), 268–91.

Healy, D., *The Creation of Psychopharmacology* (Cambridge, MA and London: Harvard University Press, 2002).

Healy, K., R.M. Conroy and N. Walsh, 'The prevalence of binge-eating and bulimia in 1063 college students', *Journal of Psychiatric Research*, 19, 2–3 (1985), 161–6.

Heaney, S., *Sweeney Astray* (London: Faber and Faber Ltd, 1984; first published by Field Day Theatre Company, 1983).

Hearns, A., 'Dealing with the aftermath of torture', *Forum*, 33, 1 (January 2016), 17–18.

Heffernan, P., 'An Irish doctor's memories: Clonmel (1902–1905)' in E. Lonergan (ed.), *St Luke's Hospital, Clonmel, 1834–1984* (Clonmel: South Eastern Health Board, 1984).

Hegarty, T., 'Study finds 5% of prison inmates are mentally ill', *Irish Times*, 24 March 1993.

Helliwell, J., R. Layard and J. Sachs (eds)., *World Happiness Report 2016, Update (Volume 1)* (New York: Sustainable Development Solutions Network, 2016).

Hennessy, M., 'Warning over rise in ADHD [attention deficit hyperactivity disorder] misdiagnosis', *Irish Times*, 6 November 2013.

Henry, H.M., *Our Lady's Psychiatric Hospital Cork* (Cork: Haven Books, 1989).

Higgins, A., L. Doyle, C. Downes, R. Murphy, D. Sharek, J. DeVries, T. Begley, E. McCann, F. Sheerin and S. Smyth, *The LGBTIreland Report: National Study of the Mental Health and Wellbeing of Lesbian, Gay, Bisexual, Transgender and Intersex People in Ireland* (Dublin: GLEN and BeLonG To, 2016).

Higgins, A., D. Hevey, P. Gibbons, C. O'Connor, F. Boyd, P. McBennett and M. Monahan, 'A participatory approach to the development of a co-produced and co-delivered information programme for users of services and family members: the EOLAS programme (paper 1)', *Irish Journal of Psychological Medicine* [published online ahead of print, 2016].

Higgins, A., D. Hevey, P. Gibbons, C. O'Connor, F. Boyd, P. McBennett and M. Monahan, 'Impact of co-facilitated information programmes on outcomes for service users and family members: the EOLAS programmes (paper 2)', *Irish Journal of Psychological Medicine* [published online ahead of print, 2016].

Higgins, A. and Mental Health Commission, *A Recovery Approach Within the Irish Mental Health Services: A Framework for Development* (Dublin: Mental Health Commission, 2008).

Higgins, M.D., 'Editorial – Remarks by President Michael D. Higgins, The College of Psychiatry of Ireland, Research and Innovation, Winter Conference, 2012', *Irish Journal of Psychological Medicine*, 30, 1 (March 2013), 1–5.

Higgins, O., 'Child care workers in child psychiatry in Ireland' in M. Fitzgerald (ed.), *Irish Families under Stress (Volume 7)* (Dublin: South Western Area Health Board, 2003).

Hill, J.P., 'An RMS remembers' in D.A. Murphy (ed.), *Tumbling Walls: The Evolution of a Community Institution over 150 Years* (Portlaoise: Midland Health Board, 1983).

Hill, M., J. Lynch and F. Maguire, *Multitext Project in Irish History* (Cork: University College Cork, 2013).

Hill, S., N. Turner, S. Barry and E. O'Callaghan, 'Client satisfaction among outpatients attending an Irish community mental health service', *Irish Journal of Psychological Medicine*, 26, 3 (September 2009), 127–30.

Hilliard, M., 'Ireland ranks 19th in happiness report', *Irish Times*, 17 March 2016.

Hilliard, M., 'Concern over Mental Health Act change', *Irish Times*, 18 March 2016.

Hilton, C., 'Book review: *'Curing Queers': Mental Nurses and Their Patients, 1935–74*', *British Journal of Psychiatry*, 208, 6 (June 2016), 596.

Hinsie, L.E. and R.J. Campbell, *Psychiatric Dictionary (Fourth Edition)* (New York, London and Toronto: Oxford University Press, 1970).

Hodgson, B., *In the Arms of Morpheus: The Tragic History of Laudanum, Morphine, and Patent Medicines* (Buffalo, NY: Firefly Books (US) Inc., 2001).

Hoek, H.W., A.S. Brown and E. Susser, 'The Dutch famine and schizophrenia spectrum disorders', *Social Psychiatry and Psychiatric Epidemiology*, 33, 8 (August 1998), 373–9.

Hogan, D., 'Desmond says 2,000 patients should not be in hospital', *Irish Times*, 26 April, 1986.

Holmes, J., 'Ten books', *British Journal of Psychiatry*, 179, 5 (1 November 2001), 468–71.

Holmquist, K., 'Psychiatry's role under scrutiny', *Irish Times*, 24 September 1988.

Holmquist, K., 'Why are we so intolerant of difference?', *Irish Times*, 20 January 1990.

Holmquist, K., 'Prisons bear cost of fewer psychiatric beds', *Irish Times*, 22 February 1990.

Holmquist, K., 'Studies show lower rate of schizophrenia', *Irish Times*, 19 October 1990.

Holohan, T.W., 'Health and homelessness in Dublin', *Irish Medical Journal*, 93, 2 (March/April 2000), 41–3.

Hopkin, A. and K. Bunney, *The Ship of Seven Murders: A True Story of Madness and Murder* (Cork: The Collins Press, 2010).

Horgan, J., *Seán Lemass: The Enigmatic Patriot* (Dublin: Gill and Macmillan, 1999).

Horgan, J., *Noël Browne: Passionate Outsider* (Dublin: Gill and Macmillan, 2000).

Horowitz, A.V., *Creating Mental Illness* (Chicago and London: University of Chicago Press, 2002).

Hough, J., 'Call to "rip up" mental health services', *Irish Examiner*, 12 November 2015.

Houston, M., 'Milestone in development of a new mental health policy', *Irish Times*, 25 January 2006.

Houston, M., 'Prof Anthony Clare dies unexpectedly in Paris', *Irish Times*, 30 October 2007.

Houston, M., 'Mountjoy team wins top psychiatric care award', *Irish Times*, 6 October 2011.

Houston, M., 'Three centuries of medicine at TCD', *Irish Medical Times*, 23 May 2014.

Howorth, P., 'The treatment of shell shock: cognitive therapy before its time', *Psychiatric Bulletin*, 24, 6 (June 2000), 225–7.

Huckerby, M., 'Lasting injury to N.I. "hooding" victims', *Irish Times*, 9 July 1973.

Hughes-Hallett, L., 'God's chosen instrument', *Guardian*, 27 February 2010.

Humphreys, J., 'The prison trap', *Irish Times*, 14 September 2014.

Hutchinson, L. and A. O'Connor, 'Unfit to plead in Ireland', *Irish Journal of Psychological Medicine*, 12, 3 (September 1995), 112–14.

Hyland, M. and T. Connolly, 'Elmville Camogie Club' in E. Lonergan (ed.), *St Luke's Hospital, Clonmel, 1834–1984* (Clonmel: South Eastern Health Board, 1984).

Ignatieff, M., *A Just Measure of Pain* (London: Peregrine, 1978).

Indecon International Consultants, *Review of Government Spending on Mental Health and Assessment of Progress on Implementation of A Vision for Change* (Dublin: Indecon/Amnesty International, 2009).

Independent Monitoring Group, *A Vision for Change: Sixth Annual Report on Implementation (2011)* (Dublin: Department of Health, 2012).

Inspector of Mental Hospitals, *Report of the Inspector of Mental Hospitals for the year ending 31ˢᵗ December 1997* (Dublin: Department of Health and Children/The Stationery Office, 1998).

Inspector of Mental Health Services, *Report of the Inspector of Mental Health Services 2005* (Dublin: The Stationery Office, 2005).

Interdepartmental Committee on Mentally Ill and Maladjusted Persons, *Third Interim Report of the Interdepartmental Committee on Mentally Ill and Maladjusted Persons: Treatment and Care of Persons Suffering From Mental Disorder Who Appear Before the Courts on Criminal Charges* (Dublin: The Stationery Office, 1978).

Irish College of Psychiatrists, *Position Statement On Psychiatric Services For Adolescents* (Dublin: Irish College of Psychiatrists, 2002).

Irish College of Psychiatrists, *A Better Future Now: Position Statement on Psychiatric Services for Children and Adolescents in Ireland (Occasional Paper OP60)* (Dublin: Irish College of Psychiatrists, 2005).

Irish College of Psychiatrists, *People with a Learning Disability Who Offend: Forgiven but Forgotten? (Occasional Paper OP63)* (Dublin: Irish College of Psychiatrists, 2008).

Ishii, N., T. Terao, Y. Araki, K. Kohno, Y. Mizokami, I. Shiotsuki, K. Hatano, M. Makino, K. Kodama and N. Iwata, 'Low risk of male suicide and lithium in drinking water', *Journal of Clinical Psychiatry*, 76, 3 (March 2015), 319–26.

Jabbar, F., M. Aziz and B.D. Kelly, 'Implementing the Mental Health Act 2001 in Ireland: views of Irish general practitioners', *Irish Journal of Psychological Medicine*, 30, 4 (December 2013), 255–9.

Jabbar, F., A.M. Doherty, M. Aziz and B.D. Kelly, 'Implementing the Mental Health Act 2007 in British general practice: lessons from Ireland', *International Journal of Law and Psychiatry*, 34, 6 (November/December 2011), 414–18.

Jabbar, F., B.D. Kelly and P. Casey, 'National survey of psychiatrists' responses to implementation of the Mental Health Act 2001 in Ireland', *Irish Journal of Medical Science*, 179, 2 (June 2010), 291–4.

Jackson, M., 'Institutional provision for the feeble-minded in Edwardian England: Sandlebridge and the scientific morality of permanent care' in D. Wright and A. Digby (eds), *From Idiocy to Mental Deficiency: Historical Perspectives on People with Learning Disabilities* (London and New York: Routledge, 1996).

Jackson, V., *The Monuments in St Patrick's Cathedral Dublin* (Dublin: St Patrick's Cathedral, 1987).

Jagger, C., F.E. Matthews, P. Wohland, T. Fouweather, B.C.M Stephan, L. Robinson, A. Arthur and C. Brayne, on behalf of the Medical Research Council Cognitive Function and Ageing Collaboration, 'A comparison of health expectancies over two decades in England: results of the Cognitive Function and Ageing Study I and II', *Lancet*, 387, 10020 (20 February 2016), 779–86.

Jennings, M., 'A glimpse of psychiatric services in the past', *Irish Medical News*, 15–29 December 2008.

Johnston, H., *All Vision but No Change? Determinants of Implementation: The Case of Ireland and Mental Health Policy* (Dublin: Institute of Public Administration, 2014).

Jones, E., N.T. Fear and S. Wessely, 'Shell shock and mild traumatic brain injury: a historical review', *American Journal of Psychiatry*, 164, 11 (November 2007), 1641–5.

Jones, E. and S. Wessely, *Shell Shock to PTSD: Military Psychiatry from 1900 to the Gulf War* (East Sussex, UK: Psychology Press (Taylor and Francis Group) on behalf of The Maudsley, 2005).

Jones, G., 'Eugenics in Ireland: the Belfast Eugenics Society, 1911–15', *Irish Historical Studies*, 28, 109 (May 1992), 81–95.

Jones, G., 'The campaign against tuberculosis in Ireland, 1899–1914' in G. Jones and E. Malcolm (eds), *Medicine, Disease and the State in Ireland, 1650–1940* (Cork: Cork University Press, 1999), 158–76.

Jones, K., 'Scull's dilemma', *British Journal of Psychiatry*, 141, 3 (September 1982), 221–6.

Jones, K., 'Insulin coma therapy in schizophrenia', *Journal of the Royal Society of Medicine*, 93, 3 (March 2000), 147–9.

Jowell, R. and Central Coordinating Team, *European Social Survey 2006/2007: Technical Report* (London: Centre for Comparative Social Surveys, City University, 2007).

Joy, B., 'Book review: *Mental Health in Ireland: Policy, Practice and Law*', *The Irish Social Worker* (Spring 2016), 78.

Joyce, J.P., 'A new normal', *History Today*, 66, 2 (February 2016), 33–7.

Kane, E., 'Is rural Ireland blighted?', *Irish Press*, 13 December 1979.

Kane, E., 'Reply to Ballybran', *Irish Times*, 13 April 1981.

Kane, E., 'Stereotypes and Irish identity: mental illness as a cultural frame', *Studies*, 75, 300 (Winter 1986), 539–51.

Kapusta, N.D. and D. König, 'Naturally occurring low-dose lithium in drinking water', *Journal of Clinical Psychiatry*, 76, 3 (March 2015), 373–4.

Kapusta, N.D., N. Mossaheb, E. Etzersdorfer, G. Hlavin, K. Thau, M. Willeit, N. Praschak-Rieder, G. Sonneck and K. Leithner-Dziubas, 'Lithium in drinking water and suicide mortality', *British Journal of Psychiatry*, 198, 5 (April 2011), 346–50.

Kazano, H., 'Asylum: the huge psychiatric hospital in the 19th century US', *Seishin Shinkeigaku Zasshi*, 114, 10 (2012), 1194–200.

Kearns, G., 'Mother Ireland and the revolutionary sisters', *Cultural Geographies*, 11, 4 (October 2004), 443–67.

Keating, L., 'Psychiatric committal examinations leave system open to abuse', *Irish Times*, 1 January 1992.

Keatinge, C., 'Community factors influencing psychiatric hospital utilization in rural and urban Ireland', *Community Mental Health Journal*, 23, 3 (Fall 1987), 192–203.

Keatinge, C., 'Schizophrenia in rural Ireland: a case of service overutilisation', *International Journal of Social Psychiatry*, 33, 3 (September 1987), 186–94.

Keatinge, C., 'Psychiatric admissions for alcoholism, neuroses and schizophrenia in rural and urban Ireland', *International Journal of Social Psychiatry*, 34, 1 (March 1988), 58–69.

Kelleher, A., D. Kavanagh and M. McCarthy, *Home Together: Study of Community Based Residencies in Ireland for People with Mental Handicap* (Dublin: Health Research Board, 1990).

Kelleher, C.C., J. Lynch, S. Harper, J.B. Tay and G. Nolan, 'Hurling alone? How social capital failed to save the Irish from cardiovascular disease in the United States', *American Journal of Public Health*, 94, 12 (December 2004), 2162–9.

Kelleher, M.J., 'Possible differences in mental health needs between rural and urban society in Ireland', *Journal of the Irish Medical Association*, 68, 14 (26 July 1975), 337–9.

Kelleher, M.J., 'Suicide in Ireland', *Irish Medical Journal*, 84, 2 (June 1991), 40–1.

Kelleher, M.J., *Suicide and the Irish* (Cork and Dublin: Mercier Press, 1996).

Kelleher Kahn, H., ''Forced from this world': massacre on the Mary Russell', *History Ireland*, 17, 5 (September/October 2009), 22–6.

Kelly, B.D., 'Psychiatry and cinema', *Irish Psychiatrist*, 2, 5 (October/November 2001), 267–72.

Kelly, B.D., 'Mental health and human rights: challenges for a new millennium', *Irish Journal of Psychological Medicine*, 18, 4 (December 2001), 114–15.

Kelly, B.D., 'Festival of film', *Irish Psychiatrist*, 3, 2 (April/May 2002), 66.

Kelly, B.D., 'Viewpoint: the Mental Health Act 2001', *Irish Medical Journal*, 95, 5 (May 2002), 151–2.

Kelly, B.D., 'Healing mental suffering', *Irish Medical News*, 10 June 2002.

Kelly, B.D., 'Evidence based medicine: what it is and why it matters', *Irish Psychiatrist*, 3, 4 (August/September, 2002), 133–8.

Kelly, B.D., 'Mental illness in nineteenth century Ireland: a qualitative study of workhouse records', *Irish Journal of Medical Science*, 173, 1 (January 2004), 53–5.

Kelly, B.D., 'Mental health policy in Ireland, 1984–2004: theory, overview and future directions', *Irish Journal of Psychological Medicine*, 21, 2 (June 2004), 61–8.

Kelly, B.D., 'Investing in the future', *Irish Journal of Psychological Medicine*, 21, 4 (December 2004), 111.

Kelly, B.D., 'Stigma and mental illness', *Irish Medical Journal*, 98, 2 (February 2005), 37.

Kelly, B.D., 'True stories of illness', *Irish Psychiatrist*, 6, 1 (February–March 2005), 23.

Kelly, B.D., 'Physical sciences and psychological medicine: the legacy of Prof John Dunne', *Irish Journal of Psychological Medicine*, 22, 2 (June 2005), 67–72.

Kelly, B.D., 'Structural violence and schizophrenia', *Social Science and Medicine*, 61, 3 (August 2005), 721–30.

Kelly, B.D., 'Therapism, self-reliance, and the mapping of the mind', *Irish Psychiatrist*, 6, 4 (August/September 2005), 168.

Kelly, B.D., 'Irish mental health law', *Irish Psychiatrist*, 7, 1 (February/March 2006), 29–30.

Kelly, B.D., 'Psychiatry in contemporary Irish cinema: a qualitative study', *Irish Journal of Psychological Medicine*, 23, 2 (June 2006), 74–9.

Kelly, B.D., 'The power gap: freedom, power and mental illness', *Social Science and Medicine*, 63, 8 (October 2006), 2118–28.

Kelly, B.D., 'The Irish Mental Health Act 2001', *Psychiatric Bulletin*, 31, 1 (January 2007), 21–4.

Kelly, B.D., 'Penrose's Law in Ireland: an ecological analysis of psychiatric inpatients and prisoners', *Irish Medical Journal*, 100, 2 (February 2007), 373–4.

Kelly, B.D., 'The historical swing of Foucault's pendulum', *Medicine Weekly*, 22 August 2007.

Kelly, B.D., 'Murder, mercury, mental illness: infanticide in nineteenth-century Ireland', *Irish Journal of Medical Science*, 176, 3 (September 2007), 149–52.

Kelly, B.D., 'One hundred years ago: the Richmond Asylum, Dublin in 1907', *Irish Journal of Psychological Medicine*, 24, 3 (September 2007), 108–14.

Kelly, B.D., 'Book review: *St Vincent's Hospital, Fairview: An Illustrated History, 1857–2007*', *Irish Journal of Psychological Medicine*, 24, 4 (December 2007), 163.

Kelly, B.D., 'Introduction' in W.S. Hallaran, *An Enquiry into the Causes Producing the Extraordinary Addition to the Number of Insane Together with Extended Observations on the Cure of Insanity with Hints as to the Better Management of Public Asylums for Insane Persons* (Dublin: First Medical, 2008; Hallaran's book was first published in Cork by Edwards and Savage, 1810).

Kelly, B.D., 'The emerging mental health strategy of the European Union: a multi-level work-in-progress', *Health Policy*, 85, 1 (January 2008), 60–70.

Kelly, B.D., 'Dr William Saunders Hallaran and psychiatric practice in nineteenth-century Ireland', *Irish Journal of Medical Science*, 177, 1 (March 2008), 79–84.

Kelly, B.D., 'The Mental Treatment Act 1945 in Ireland: an historical enquiry', *History of Psychiatry*, 19, 73(1) (March 2008), 47–67.

Kelly, B.D., 'Mental health law in Ireland, 1821 to 1902: building the asylums', *Medico-Legal Journal*, 76, 1 (March 2008), 19–25.

Kelly, B.D., 'Mental health law in Ireland, 1821 to 1902: dealing with the "increase of insanity in Ireland"', *Medico-Legal Journal*, 76, 1 (March 2008), 26–33.

Kelly, B.D., 'Do new-generation antidepressants work?', *Irish Medical Journal*, 101, 5, (May 2008), 155.

Kelly, B.D., 'Clinical and social characteristics of women committed to inpatient forensic psychiatric care in Ireland, 1868–1908', *Journal of Forensic Psychiatry and Psychology*, 19, 2 (June 2008), 261–73.

Kelly, B.D., 'Mental health law in Ireland, 1945 to 2001: reformation and renewal', *Medico-Legal Journal*, 76, 2 (June 2008), 65–72.

Kelly, B.D., 'Obituary: James Maguire', *Psychiatric Bulletin*, 32, 6 (June 2008), 236.

Kelly, B.D., 'Book review: *Music and Madness*', *Scope*, 1, 1 (July 2008), 43–4.

Kelly, B.D., 'Poverty, crime and mental illness: female forensic psychiatric committal in Ireland, 1910–1948', *Social History of Medicine*, 21, 2 (August 2008), 311–28.

Kelly, B.D., 'Learning disability and forensic mental healthcare in nineteenth-century Ireland', *Irish Journal of Psychological Medicine*, 25, 3 (September 2008), 116–18.

Kelly, B.D., '*Folie à plusieurs:* forensic cases from nineteenth-century Ireland', *History of Psychiatry*, 20, 77 (Part 1) (March 2009), 47–60.

Kelly, B.D., 'Syphilis, psychiatry and offending behaviour: clinical cases from nineteenth-century Ireland', *Irish Journal of Medical Science*, 178, 1 (March 2009), 73–7.

Kelly, B.D., 'The Mental Health Act 2001', *Irish Medical News*, 18 May 2009.

Kelly, B.D., 'Criminal insanity in nineteenth-century Ireland, Europe and the United States: cases, contexts and controversies', *International Journal of Law and Psychiatry*, 32, 6 (November/December 2009), 362–8.

Kelly, B.D., 'Depressive psychosis, involuntary ECT and human rights', *Irish Medical Times*, 29 January 2010.

Kelly, B.D., 'The apparent increase in insanity in Ireland in the 1800s: why and how?', *Irish Psychiatrist*, 11, 3 (Autumn 2010), 140–4.

Kelly, B.D., 'Intellectual disability, mental illness and offending behaviour: forensic cases from early twentieth-century Ireland', *Irish Journal of Medical Science*, 179, 3 (September 2010), 409–16.

Kelly, B.D., 'Walking through the past in today's Sligo', *Irish Medical Times*, 1 October 2010.

Kelly, B.D., '*The Irish Journal of Psychological Medicine*: looking to the future', *Irish Journal of Psychological Medicine*, 27, 4 (December 2010), 170–1.

Kelly, B.D., 'Diagnosis of a vampire', *Modern Medicine*, 41, 6 (2011), 69–71.

Kelly, B.D., 'Head shop drugs: they haven't gone away', *Irish Journal of Psychological Medicine*, 28, 1 (March 2011), S1.

Kelly, B.D., 'Mental health services in Ireland – justice, history and human rights explored', *Irish Medical Times*, 18 November 2011.

Kelly, B.D., 'Mental health legislation and human rights in England, Wales and the Republic of Ireland', *International Journal of Law and Psychiatry*, 34, 6 (November–December 2011), 439–54.

Kelly, B.D., 'Tuberculosis in the nineteenth-century asylum: clinical cases from the Central Criminal Lunatic Asylum, Dundrum, Dublin' in P.M. Prior (ed.), *Asylums, Mental Health Care and the Irish, 1800–2010* (Dublin: Irish Academic Press, 2012).

Kelly, B.D., 'The *Irish Journal of Psychological Medicine* and the College of Psychiatry of Ireland', *Irish Journal of Psychological Medicine*, 29, 1 (January 2012), 3–6.

Kelly, B.D., 'History of mental health care', *Irish Medical News*, 30 July 2012.

Kelly, B.D., 'Celluloid psychiatry', *Modern Medicine: Scope*, 43, 3 (March 2013), 55–6.

Kelly, B.D., 'Irish women in medicine', *Irish Medial News*, 7 May 2013.

Kelly, B.D., 'Book review: *Negotiating Insanity in the Southeast of Ireland, 1820–1900*', *Irish Journal of Psychological Medicine*, 30, 2 (June 2013), 159–60.

Kelly, B.D., 'Psychiatry cannot provide neat solutions on suicide', *Irish Times*, 17 July 2013.

Kelly, B.D., 'Psychiatry at the movies', *Psychiatry Professional*, 2, 2 (Summer 2013), 12.

Kelly, B.D., 'Book review: *Gender and Medicine in Ireland, 1700–1950*', *Irish Journal of Psychological Medicine*, 30, 3 (September 2013), 227.

Kelly, B.D., 'Mental health need amongst the intellectually disabled', *Irish Journal of Medical Science*, 182, 3 (September 2013), 539.

Kelly, B.D., *Ada English: Patriot and Psychiatrist* (Dublin: Irish Academic Press, 2014).

Kelly, B.D., *Custody, Care and Criminality: Forensic Psychiatry and Law in 19th-Century Ireland* (Dublin: History Press Ireland, 2014).

Kelly, B.D., '*He Lost Himself Completely': Shell Shock and Its Treatment at Dublin's Richmond War Hospital, 1916–1919* (Dublin: Liffey Press, 2014).

Kelly, B.D., 'Dr Ada English (1875–1944): doctor, patriot, politician', *British Journal of Psychiatry*, 204, 1 (January 2014), 5.

Kelly, B.D., 'An end to psychiatric detention? Implications of the United Nations Convention on the Rights of Persons with Disabilities', *British Journal of Psychiatry*, 204, 3 (March 2014), 174–5.

Kelly, B.D., 'An important story', *Irish Medical News*, 31 March 2014.

Kelly, B.D., 'Integrating psychological treatment approaches', *Science*, 344, 6181 (18 April 2014), 254–5.

Kelly, B.D., 'Dignity, human rights and the limits of mental health legislation', *Irish Journal of Psychological Medicine*, 31, 2 (June 2014), 75–81.

Kelly, B.D., 'Book review: *What the Doctor Saw*', *Irish Journal of Psychological Medicine*, 31, 2 (June 2014), 150–1.

Kelly, B.D., 'Enquiring into Ireland's asylums', *Irish Medical Times*, 5 September 2014.

Kelly, B.D., 'Voting and mental illness: the silent constituency', *Irish Journal of Psychological Medicine*, 31, 4 (December 2014), 225–7.

Kelly, B.D., *Dignity, Mental Health and Human Rights: Coercion and the Law* (Abingdon, Oxon: Routledge, 2015).

Kelly, B.D., 'Compassion, cognition and the illusion of self: Buddhist notes towards more skilful engagement with diagnostic classification systems in psychiatry' in E. Shonin, W. Van Gordon and M.D. Griffiths (eds), *Mindfulness and Buddhist-Derived Approaches in Mental Health and Addiction* (Heidelberg: Springer, 2015), 9–28.

Kelly, B.D., 'Human rights in psychiatric practice: an overview for clinicians', *BJPsych Advances*, 21, 1 (January 2015), 54–62.

Kelly, B.D., 'Shell shock in Ireland: the Richmond War Hospital, Dublin (1916–19)', *History of Psychiatry*, 26, 1 (March 2015), 50–63.

Kelly, B.D., 'The Assisted Decision-Making (Capacity) Bill: content, commentary, controversy', *Irish Journal of Medical Science*, 184, 1 (March 2015), 31–46.

Kelly, B.D., 'Mental illness requires an all-of-society response', *Irish Times*, 13 April 2015.

Kelly, B.D., 'Schizophrenia, mental health legislation and human rights', *Hospital Doctor of Ireland*, 21, 4 (May 2015), 25–32.

Kelly, B.D., 'Best interests, mental capacity legislation and the UN Convention on the Rights of Persons with Disabilities', *BJPsych Advances*, 21, 3 (May 2015), 188–95.

Kelly, B.D., 'Schizophrenia, mental health legislation and human rights', *Hospital Doctor of Ireland*, 21, 4 (May 2015), 25–32.

Kelly, B.D., 'Depression – 'them and us'', *Irish Times*, 15 May 2015.

Kelly, B.D., 'Revising, reforming, reframing: *Report of the Expert Group on the Review of the Mental Health Act 2001* (2015)', *Irish Journal of Psychological Medicine*, 32, 2 (June 2015), 161–6.

Kelly, B.D., 'Polarised public debate about anti-depressants deeply unhelpful', *Irish Independent*, 1 June 2015.

Kelly, B.D., 'Schizophrenia, but not as we know it', *Lancet Psychiatry*, 2, 7 (July 2015), 599.

Kelly, B.D., 'A "Madman's Chair" and other ancient mental illness cures', *Irish Medical Times*, 31 July 2015.

Kelly, B.D., 'Mental health services for children', *Irish Times*, 12 August 2015.

Kelly, B.D., 'Asylum doctor extraordinaire: Dr Thomas Drapes (1847–1919)', *Irish Journal of Medical Science*, 184, 3 (September 2015), 565–71.

Kelly, B.D., 'Migrants need support but they also need dignity', *Irish Times*, 16 September 2015.

Kelly, B.D., 'Don't deny them this treatment', *Sunday Independent*, 22 November 2015.

Kelly, B.D., 'Should we legalise or decriminalise cannabis?', *Irish Times*, 27 November 2015.

Kelly, B.D., 'Mental health policy in Ireland: a decade after *A Vision for Change*, where are we now?', *Irish Medical Journal*, 108, 10 (November/December 2015), 293.

Kelly, B.D., 'We need to change how we think about ECT', *Irish Medical Times*, 11 December 2015.

Kelly, B.D., 'Making mental health an election issue' *Irish Times*, 30 December 2015.

Kelly, B.D., *Mental Illness, Human Rights and the Law* (London: RCPsych Publications, 2016).

Kelly, B.D., 'Psychiatric admission in Ireland: the role of country of origin' in M. Donnelly and C. Murray (eds), *Ethical and Legal Debates in Irish Healthcare: Confronting Complexities* (Manchester: Manchester University Press, 2016).

Kelly, B.D., 'Assisted Decision-Making Bill', *Irish Independent*, 2 January 2016.

Kelly, B.D., 'Political asylums', *History Today*, 66, 2 (February 2016), 66.

Kelly, B.D., 'Homosexuality and Irish psychiatry: medicine, law and the changing face of Ireland', *Irish Journal of Psychological Medicine*, available on CJO 1st February 2016.

Kelly, B.D., 'The *Irish Journal of Psychological Medicine*: expanding horizons, moving on', *Irish Journal of Psychological Medicine*, 33, 1 (March 2016), 1–2.

Kelly, B.D., 'Report of the Expert Group on the Review of the Mental Health Act 2001: what does it mean for social workers?', *The Irish Social Worker* (Spring 2016), 41–4.

Kelly, B.D., 'Searching for the patient's voice in the Irish asylums', *Medical Humanities*, 42, 2 (June 2016), 87–91.

Kelly, B.D., 'Focus on mental health services', *Irish Times*, 14 July 2016.

Kelly, B.D., 'The Assisted Decision-Making (Capacity) Act 2015: what it is and why it matters', *Irish Journal of Medical Science* [published online ahead of print, 2016].

Kelly, B.D., Z. Abood and D Shanley, 'Vampirism and schizophrenia', *Irish Journal of Psychological Medicine*, 16, 3 (September 1999), 114–15.

Kelly, B.D. and M. Davoren, 'Dr Ada English', in M. Mulvihill (ed.), *Lab Coats and Lace* (Dublin: Women in Technology and Science, 2009), 97.

Kelly, B.D. and A.M. Doherty, 'Impact of recent economic problems on mental health in Ireland', *International Psychiatry*, 10, 1 (February 2013), 6–8.

Kelly, B.D., A. Emechebe, C. Anamdi, R. Duffy, N. Murphy and C. Rock, 'Custody, care and country of origin: demographic and diagnostic admission statistics at an inner-city adult psychiatry unit', *International Journal of Law and Psychiatry*, 38, 1 (January–February 2015), 1–7.

Kelly, B.D. and L. Feeney, 'Psychiatry: no longer in dissent?', *Psychiatric Bulletin*, 30, 9 (1 September 2006), 344–5.

Kelly, B.D., L. Feeney, E. O'Callaghan, R. Browne, M. Byrne, N. Mulryan, A. Scully, M. Morris, A. Kinsella, N. Takei, T. McNeil, D. Walsh and C. Larkin, 'Obstetric adversity and age at first presentation with schizophrenia: evidence of a dose-response relationship', *American Journal of Psychiatry*, 161, 5 (May 2004), 920–2.

Kelly, B.D. and S.R. Foley, 'The price of life', *British Medical Journal*, 335, 7626 (3 November 2007), 938.

Kelly, B.D. and S.R. Foley, 'Love, spirituality and regret: thematic analysis of last statements from death row, Texas (2006–2011)', *Journal of the American Academy of Psychiatry and the Law*, 41, 4 (December 2013), 540–50.

Kelly, B.D., A. Lane, I. Agartz, K.M. Henriksson and T.F. McNeil, 'Craniofacial dysmorphology in Swedish schizophrenia patients', *Acta Psychiatrica Scandinavica*, 111, 3 (March 2005), 202–7.

Kelly, B.D. and F. Lenihan, 'Attitudes towards the implementation of the Mental Health Act 2001', *Irish Journal of Psychological Medicine*, 23, 2 (June 2006), 82–4.

Kelly, B.D. and N. Sherrard, 'Beyond the walls', *Irish Journal of Psychological Medicine*, 32, 3 (September 2015), 275–82.

Kelly, C., *Annual Report of the National Intellectual Disability Database Committee 2014* (Dublin: Health Research Board, 2015).

Kelly, C., 'From quacks to Freud to Quaaludes', *Sunday Independent*, 29 March 2015.

Kelly, D., *Between the Lines of History: People of Ballinasloe, Volume One* (Ballinasloe: Declan Kelly, 2000).

Kelly, D., *Ballinasloe: From Garbally Park to the Fairgreen* (Dublin: Nonsuch, 2007).

Kelly, F., 'Medicine and early Irish law' in J.B. Lyons (ed.), *2000 Years of Irish Medicine* (Dublin: Eireann Healthcare Publications, 1999).

Kelly, F., *A Guide to Early Irish Law* (Dublin: School of Celtic Studies, Dublin Institute for Advanced Studies, 2003).

Kelly, J., 'The life and significance of Charles Lucas (1713–1771)', *Irish Journal of Medical Science*, 184, 3 (September 2015), 541–5.

Kelly, L., *Irish Women in Medicine, c.1880s–1920s: Origins, Education and Careers* (Manchester and New York: Manchester University Press, 2012).

Kelly, N.A., 'Remembering homelessness in the Great Irish Famine' in D.A. Valone (ed.), *Ireland's Great Hunger: Relief, Representation, and Remembrance (Volume 2)* (Lanham, Maryland: University Press of America, ® Inc., 2010).

Kelly, N.A., 'Narrating sites of history: workhouses and Famine memory', in O. Frawley (ed.), *Memory Ireland, Volume 3: The Famine and the Troubles* (Syracuse, New York: Syracuse University Press, 2014), 152–73.

Kelly, Z., 'Within these walls...' *Medical Independent*, 14 May 2015.

Kendler, K.S., M. McGuire, A.M. Gruenberg, A. O'Hare, M. Spellman and D. Walsh, 'The Roscommon Family Study: I. Methods, diagnosis of probands, and risk of schizophrenia in relatives', *Archives of General Psychiatry*, 50, 7 (July 1993), 527–40.

Kennedy, F., 'I don't want to hear anyone else 'opening up' about their 'battle' with depression', *Irish Times*, 5 May 2016.

. Kennedy, H., *The Annotated Mental Health Acts* (Dublin: Blackhall Publishing, 2007).

Kennedy, H., 'Book review: *Madness and Murder: Gender, Crime and Mental Disorder in Nineteenth-Century Ireland*', *Journal of Forensic Psychiatry and Psychology*, 20, 4 (2009), 602–4.

Kennedy, H., "Libertarian' groupthink not helping mentally ill', *Irish Times*, 12 September 2012.

Kennedy, H., 'Prisons now a dumping ground for mentally ill young men', *Irish Times*, 18 May 2016.

Kennedy, H. and S. Thompson, 'It's an ethical challenge, choosing which prisoners we can take', *Irish Times*, 7 April 2015.

Kennedy, H.G., 'The future of forensic mental health services in Ireland', *Irish Journal of Psychological Medicine*, 23, 2 (June 2006), 45–6.

Kennedy, H.G., 'Foreword', in B. Kelly, *Custody, Care and Criminality: Forensic Psychiatry and Law in 19th-Century Ireland* (Dublin: History Press Ireland, 2014), 6–14.

Kennedy, L., P.S. Ell, E.M. Crawford and L.A. Clarkson, *Mapping the Great Irish Famine* (Dublin: Four Courts Press Ltd., 1999).

Keogh, E., 'Hospital sees "exponential" self-harm rise in teenagers', *Irish Times*, 18 August 2015.

Keogh, F., A. Roche and D. Walsh, *"We Have No Beds..." An Enquiry into the Availability and Use of Acute Psychiatric Beds in the Eastern Health Board Region* (Dublin: Health Research Board, 1999).

Kerridge, I.H. and M. Lowe, 'Bloodletting: the story of a therapeutic technique', *Medical Journal of Australia*, 163, 11–2 (December 1995), 631–3.

Keys, M., *Annotated Legislation: Mental Health Act 2001* (Dublin: Round Hall, Sweet and Maxwell, 2002).

Khan, I., 'Promoting the correct use of psychotropic drugs', *British Journal of Psychiatry*, 159, 5 (November 1991), 731–2.

Kiely, N., 'Psychiatrist accuses doctors of apathy in opposing torture', *Irish Times*, 17 October 1980.

Kilcommins, S., I. O'Donnell, E. O'Sullivan and B. Vaughan, *Crime Punishment and the Search for Order in Ireland* (Dublin: Institute of Public Administration, 2004).

King, M., G. Smith and A. Bartlett, 'Treatments of homosexuality in Britain since the 1950s – an oral history: the experience of professionals', *British Medical Journal*, 328, 7437 (21 February 2004), 429–32.

Kirsch, I., B.J. Deacon, T.B. Huedo-Medina, A. Scoboria, T.J. Moore and B.T. Johnson, 'Initial severity and antidepressant benefits: a meta-analysis of data submitted to the Food and Drug Administration', *PLoS Medicine*, 5, 2 (February 2008), 45.

Kłapciński, M.M. and J. Rymaszewska, 'Open Dialogue approach – about the phenomenon of Scandinavian psychiatry', *Psychiatria Polska*, 49, 6 (2015), 1179–90.

Knoff, W.F., 'A history of the concept of neurosis, with a memoir of William Cullen', *American Journal of Psychiatry*, 127, 1 (July 1970), 80–4.

Kramer, D., *Charles Robert Maturin (Twayne's English Authors Series)* (New York: Twayne, 1973).

Kraya, N.A.F. and C. Patrick, '*Folie à deux* in forensic setting', *Australian and New Zealand Journal of Psychiatry*, 31, 6 (December 1997), 883–8.

Kureishi, H., 'None the wiser', *Financial Times (Magazine)*, 16/17 February 2008.

Lacey, B. *Terrible Queer Creatures: Homosexuality in Irish History* (Dublin: Wordwell, 2008).

Laffey, P., 'Two registers of madness in Enlightenment Britain. Part 2', *History of Psychiatry*, 14, 53 (Part 1) (March 2003), 63–81.

Laragy, G., 'Suicide and insanity in post-Famine Ireland', in C. Cox and M. Luddy (eds), *Cultures of Care in Irish Medical History 1750–1950* (Basingstoke, Hampshire: Palgrave Macmillan, 2010), 79–91.

Laragy, G., 'Narratives of poverty in Irish suicides between the Great Famine and the First World War, 1845–1914' in A. Gestrich, E. Hurren and S. King (eds), *Poverty and Sickness in Modern Europe: Narratives of the Sick Poor, 1780–1938* (London and New York: Continuum International Publishing Group, 2012), 143–59.

Laragy, G., ''A peculiar species of felony': suicide, medicine, and the law in Victorian Britain and Ireland', *Journal of Social History*, 46, 3 (Spring 2013), 732–43.

Larson, K.C., *Rosemary: The Hidden Kennedy Daughter* (New York: Houghton Mifflin Harcourt Publishing Company, 2015).

Latey, R.H., and T. Fahy, *Electroconvulsive Therapy in the Republic of Ireland, 1982* (Galway: Galway University Press, 1982).

Law Reform Committee, *Mental Health: The Case for Reform* (Dublin: The Law Society, 1999).

Lawlor, B.A., 'Quo vadis?', *Irish Journal of Psychological Medicine*, 11, 3 (September 1994), 107.

Lawlor, M. and D. Macintyre, 'The *Stay Safe* programme' in M. Fitzgerald (ed.), *Irish Families under Stress (Volume 7)* (Dublin: South Western Area Health Board, 2003).

Leahy, A., 'Addiction and mental health', *Irish Times*, 28 December 2006.

Lee, G. and M. Raley, 'State has long neglected those with a disability', *Irish Times*, 30 March 2015.

Leland, M., "Why do I feel so awful when I should be feeling so glad", *Irish Times*, 22 February 1980.

Leland, M., 'Doctor attacks psychiatric care', *Irish Times*, 13 May 1985.

Lenihan, M., *Hidden Cork* (Cork: Mercier Press, 2009).

Leonard, E.C. Jr., 'Did some 18th and 19th century treatments for mental disorders act on the brain?', *Medical Hypotheses*, 62, 2 (February 2004), 219–21.

Leonard, P., A. Morrison, M. Delany-Warner and G.J. Calvert, 'A national survey of offending behaviour amongst intellectually disabled users of mental health services in Ireland', *Irish Journal of Psychological Medicine* [published online ahead of print, 2015].

Lewer, D., C. O'Reilly, R. Mojtabai and S. Evans-Lacko, 'Antidepressant use in 27 European countries: associations with sociodemographic, cultural and economic factors', *British Journal of Psychiatry*, 207, 3 (September 2015), 221–6.

Lieberman, J.A. with O. Ogas, *Shrinks: The Untold Story of Psychiatry* (London: Weidenfeld and Nicolson, 2015).

Lindsay, W.R., R.P. Hastings, D.M. Griffiths and S.C. Hayes, 'Trends and challenges in forensic research on offenders with intellectual disability', *Journal of Intellectual and Developmental Disability* 32, 2 (June 2007), 55–61.

Linehan, S., D. Duffy, H. O'Neill, C. O'Neill and H.G. Kennedy, 'Irish travellers and forensic mental health', *Irish Journal of Psychological Medicine*, 19, 3 (September 2002), 6–9.

Linehan, S., D.M. Duffy B. Wright, K. Curtin, S. Monks and H.G. Kennedy, 'Psychiatric morbidity in a cross-sectional sample of male remanded prisoners', *Irish Journal of Psychological Medicine*, 22, 4 (December 2005), 128–32.

Loeb Shloss, C., *Lucia Joyce: To Dance in the Wake* (London: Bloomsbury, 2004).

Logan, P., *The Holy Wells of Ireland* (Gerrards Cross, Buckinghamshire: Colin Smythe Ltd., 1981).

Lonergan, E. (ed.), *St Luke's Hospital, Clonmel, 1834–1984* (Clonmel: South Eastern Health Board, 1984).

Lonergan, E., 'St Luke's, Clonmel, 1834–1984' in E. Lonergan (ed.), *St Luke's Hospital, Clonmel, 1834–1984* (Clonmel: South Eastern Health Board, 1984), 22–83.

Lonergan, E., 'An Olympic champion', in E. Lonergan (ed.), *St Luke's Hospital, Clonmel, 1834–1984* (Clonmel: South Eastern Health Board, 1984), 119–23.

Lorié, Á.F., *Secular Health and Sacred Belief? A Study of Religion and Mental Illness in Modern Irish Society* (Bern: Peter Lang, 2013).

Loughlin, E. and F. Ó Cionnaith, 'Taskforce for youth mental health to get green light', Irish Examiner, 27 July 2016.

Lucey, J., 'Dr Anthony Clare remembered', *Irish Medical Times*, 16 November 2007.

Lucey, J., *In My Room: The Recovery Journey as Encountered by a Psychiatrist* (Dublin: Gill and Macmillan, 2014).

Luigjes, J., B.P. de Kwaasteniet, P.P. de Koning, M.S. Oudijn, P. van den Munckhof, P.R. Schuurman and D. Denys, 'Surgery for psychiatric disorders', *World Neurosurgery*, 80, 3–4 (S31) (September/October 2013), e17–28.

Lynch, D., 'A look at what we tried not to see', *Irish Independent*, 25 September 2005.

Lynch, K., 'Assisted Decision-Making (Capacity) Bill 2013: Report and Final Stages', *Seanad Éireann Debate*, 244, 9 (15 December 2015).

Lynch, P., 'College of Psychiatry calls for ECT amendments', *Irish Medical News*, 22 March 2010.

Lynch, T., *Beyond Prozac: Healing Mental Distress* (Dublin: Marino, 2001).

Lyne, J., 'An exciting new chapter for the *Irish Journal of Psychological Medicine*', *Irish Journal of Psychological Medicine*, 33, 2 (June 2016), 71–2.

Lyne, J. and M. Cannon, 'A special issue: highlighting the youth mental health agenda', *Irish Journal of Psychological Medicine*, 32, 1 (March 2015), 1–3.

Lyons, D., K. Collins and C. Hayes, 'Offering support to the general public by building CBT-based life skills', *Irish Journal of Psychological Medicine* [published online ahead of print, 2016].

Lyons, F.S.L., *Ireland Since the Famine* (London: Fontana, 1985).

Lyons, J.B., *Thrust Syphilis Down to Hell and Other Rejoyceana: Studies in the Border-lands of Literature and Medicine* (Dún Laoghaire: Irish Books and Media, 1988).

Mac Lellan, A., 'Dr Dorothy Price and the eradication of TB in Ireland', *Irish Medical News*, 19 May 2008.

Mac Lellan, A., 'Revolutionary doctors' in M. Mulvihill (ed.), *Lab Coats and Lace:* (Dublin: Women in Technology and Science, 2009).

Mac Lellan, A., *Dorothy Stopford Price: Rebel Doctor* (Dublin: Irish Academic Press, 2014).

Mac Lellan, A., N. Nic Ghabhann and F. Byrne, *World Within Walls* (Monaghan: Health Service Executive and Stair: An Irish Public History Company Ltd., 2015).

Mac Loughlin, T., *Ballinasloe Inniú agus Inné* (Ballinasloe: Tadgh Mac Loughlin, 1993).

Mac Suibhne, S., 'Medical classics: *Asylums: Essays on the Social Situation of Mental Patients and Other Inmates*', *British Medical Journal*, 339, 7725 (10 October 2009), 867.

Mac Suibhne, S., 'Erving Goffman's *Asylums* 50 years on', *British Journal of Psychiatry*, 198, 1 (January 2011), 1–2.

Mac Suibhne, S. and B.D. Kelly, 'Vampirism as mental illness: myth, madness and the loss of meaning in psychiatry', *Social History of Medicine*, 24, 2 (August 2011), 445–60.

MacDonagh, S., *The Dingle Peninsula* (Dingle: Utter Press, 2013).

MacÉinrí, P., *Immigration into Ireland* (Cork: Irish Centre For Migration Studies, 2001).

MacEvilly, M., *A Splendid Resistance: The Life of IRA Chief of Staff Dr Andy Cooney* (Blackrock, County Dublin: Edmund Burke Publisher).

Macleod, S.M. and H.N. McCullough, 'Social science education as a component of medical training', *Social Science and Medicine*, 39, 9 (November 1994), 1367–73.

Madden, D., *Medicine, Ethics and the Law in Ireland (Second Edition)* (Haywards Heath, West Sussex and Dublin: Bloomsbury Professional, 2011).

Madden, E., 'Section of Mental Health Act was unconstitutional', *Irish Medical Times*, 27 July 2008.

Maddock, M. and J. Maddock, *Soul Survivor: A Personal Encounter with Psychiatry* (Sheffield: Asylum Books, 2006).

Maher, M., 'Mental health report rejected', *Irish Times*, 20 August 1985.

Maher, M., 'Turning our psychiatric patients out on the street', *Irish Times*, 6 November 1985.

Maher, M., 'Simon warns on mental care move', *Irish Times*, 6 December 1985.

Mahon, E.K., *Scandalous Women: The Lives and Loves of History's Most Notorious Women* (New York: Perigree/Penguin Books, 2011).

Majerus, B., 'Making Sense of the 'Chemical Revolution'', *Medical History*, 60, 1 (January 2016), 54–66.

Malcolm, E., *'Ireland Sober, Ireland Free': Drink and Temperance in Nineteenth-Century Ireland* (Dublin: Gill and Macmillan, 1986).

Malcolm, E., 'Asylums and other 'total institutions' in Ireland: recent studies', *Éire-Ireland*, 22, 3 (Fall 1987), 151–60.

Malcolm, E. *Swift's Hospital: A History of St Patrick's Hospital, Dublin, 1746–1989* (Dublin: Gill and Macmillan, 1989).

Malcolm, E., 'Women and madness in Ireland, 1600–1850', in M. MacCurtain and M. O'Dowd (eds), *Women in Early Modern Ireland* (Edinburgh: Edinburgh University Press, 1991).

Malcolm, E., '"The house of strident shadows": the asylum, the family and emigration in post-Famine rural Ireland' in G. Jones and E. Malcolm (eds), *Medicine, Disease and the State in Ireland, 1650–1940* (Cork: Cork University Press, 1999).

Malcolm, E., '"A most miserable looking object": The Irish in English asylums, 1851–1901: migration, poverty and prejudice' in J. Belchem and K. Tenfelde (eds), *Irish and Polish Migration in Comparative Perspective* (Essen: Klartext Verlag, 2003).

Malcolm, E., '"Ireland's crowded madhouses': the institutional confinement of the insane in nineteenth-and twentieth-century Ireland' in R. Porter and D. Wright (eds), *The Confinement of the Insane: International Perspectives, 1800–1965* (Cambridge: Cambridge University Press, 2003).

Malcolm, E., 'Irish emigrants in a Colonial Asylum during the Australian Gold Rushes, 1848–1869' in P.M. Prior (ed.), *Asylums, Mental Health Care and the Irish, 1800–2010* (Dublin: Irish Academic Press, 2012).

Malcolm, E., 'Between habitual drunkards and alcoholics: inebriate women and reformatories in Ireland, 1899–1919' in M.H. Preston and M. Ó hÓgartaigh (eds), *Gender and Medicine in Ireland, 1700–1950* (Syracuse, New York: Syracuse University Press, 2012).

Malcolm, N., *Ludwig Wittgenstein: A Memoir* (Oxford: Oxford University Press, 2001; first published in 1958).

Malone, K.M., L. Quinlivan, S. McGuinness, F. McNicholas and C. Kelleher, 'Suicide in children over two decades: 1993–2008', *Irish Medical Journal*, 105, 7 (July–August 2012), 231–3.

Manning, M., 'Harassed gays fight for 20th century law', *Community Care*, 30 June 1976.

Marland, H., *Dangerous Motherhood: Insanity and Childbirth in Victorian Britain* (Basingstoke: Palgrave MacMillan, 2004).

Marsh, H., *Do No Harm: Stories of Life, Death and Brain Surgery* (London: Weidenfeld and Nicolson, 2014).

Matthews, A., *Renegades: Irish Republican Women 1900–1922* (Cork: Mercier Press, 2010).

Matthews, A., *Dissidents: Irish Republican Women 1923–1941* (Cork: Mercier Press, 2012).

Mauger, A., '"Confinement of the higher orders": The social role of private lunatic asylums in Ireland, c. 1820–60', *Journal of the History of Medicine and Allied Sciences*, 67, 2 (April 2012), 281–317.

Mayo Mental Health Services Arts Committee, *St Mary's Hospital, Castlebar: 'Snapshots in Time'* (Castlebar: Galway Mayo Institute of Technology, 2005).

Mayock, P., A. Bryan, N. Carr and K. Kitching, *Supporting LGBT Lives* (Dublin: Gay and Lesbian Equality Network (GLEN) and BeLonG To Youth Service, 2009).

McAleese, M., 'Remarks by Mary McAleese, President of Ireland made at the International Association of Suicide Prevention XXIV Biennial Conference, August 31, 2007, Irish National Events Centre, Killarney, Co. Kerry, Ireland', *Crisis*, 29, 1 (January 2008), 53–5.

McAuley, F., *Insanity, Psychiatry and Criminal Responsibility* (Dublin: Round Hall Press, 1993).

McCabe, A., 'A brief history of the early development of social work in child psychiatry in Ireland' in M. Fitzgerald (ed.), *Irish Families under Stress (Volume 7)* (Dublin: South Western Area Health Board, 2003).

McCabe, A. and C. Mulholland, 'The red flag over the asylum' in P.M. Prior (ed.), *Asylums, Mental Health Care and the Irish, 1800–2010* (Dublin: Irish Academic Press, 2012).

McCafferty, N., 'Two consenting adults learn that it's an offence over here', *Irish Times*, 12 September 1975.

McCaffrey, B. 'Book review: *Music and Madness*', *Irish Psychiatrist*, 9, 2 (Summer 2008), 117–18.

McCandless, P., 'Curative asylum, custodial hospital: the South Carolina Lunatic Asylum and State Hospital, 1828–1920' in R. Porter and D. Wright (eds), *The Confinement of the Insane: International Perspectives, 1800–1965* (Cambridge: Cambridge University Press, 2003), 173–92.

McCann, E., D. Sharek, A. Higgins, F. Sheerin, and M. Glacken, 'Lesbian, gay, bisexual and transgender older people in Ireland: mental health issues', *Aging and Mental Health*, 17, 3 (2013), 358–65.

McCann, E. and D. Sharek, 'Survey of lesbian, gay, bisexual, and transgender people's experiences of mental health services in Ireland', *International Journal of Mental Health Nursing*, 23, 2 (August 2014), 118–27.

McCarthy, Á., 'Hearths, bodies and minds: gender ideology and women's committal to Enniscorthy Lunatic Asylum, 1916–1925' in A. Hayes and D. Urquhart (eds), *Irish Women's History* (Dublin: Irish Academic Press, 2004), 115–36.

McCarthy, A., 'Transitional ties to home: Irish migrants in New Zealand asylums, 1860–1926', in P.M. Prior (ed.), *Asylums, Mental Health Care and the Irish, 1800–2010* (Dublin: Irish Academic Press, 2012), 149–66.

McCarthy, C., *Cumann na mBan and the Irish Revolution* (Dublin: The Collins Press, 2007).

McCarthy, D., "Let's celebrate the next generation of Irish people who can marry whomever they love", *Irish Examiner*, 29 May 2015.

McCarthy, O.R., 'Grandfather's choice – psychiatry in mid-Victorian Ireland', *Journal of Medical Biography*, 6, 3 (August 1998), 141–8.

McClelland, G., '*Speedwell* magazine: an insider view of Holywell Psychiatric Hospital, Antrim, 1959–1973' in P.M. Prior (ed.), *Asylums, Mental Health Care and the Irish, 1800–2010* (Dublin: Irish Academic Press, 2012).

McClelland, R., 'An appreciation of Dr Mark Hartman, founder and editor-in-chief of the Irish Journal of Psychological Medicine', *Irish Journal of Psychological Medicine*, 11, 1 (March 1994), 4.

McClelland, R.J., 'The madhouses and mad doctors of Ulster', *The Ulster Medical Journal*, 57, 2 (October 1998), 101–20.

McCoole, S., *No Ordinary Women: Irish Female Activists in the Revolutionary Years 1900–1923* (Dublin: O'Brien Press, 2003).

McCormack, B., J. Tobin, H. Keeley, F. Yacoub, S. MacHale, M. Scully, W. Flannery, A. Ambikapathy, S. Monks, M. McLoughlin, G. Moynihan, R. Plunkett and H. Kennedy, 'Marriage referendum – countdown to polling day', *Irish Times*, 21 May 2015.

McCrae, N., '"A violent thunderstorm": Cardiazol treatment in British mental hospitals', *History of Psychiatry*, 17, 1 (March 2006), 67–90.

McCurry, J., 'Xenophobic Seoul job rejection hard to swallow', *Guardian*, 8 November 2014.

McDaid, S., 'Book review: *Climbing Mountains in our Minds: Stories and Photographs from St. Senan's Hospital, Enniscorthy*', *Irish Journal of Psychological Medicine*, 30, 2 (June 2013), 156–7.

McDaid, S., 'Voters can make mental health an election issue', *Irish Times*, 28 December 2015.

McDaid, S., and A. Higgins, 'Introduction', in A. Higgins and S. McDaid (eds), *Mental Health in Ireland: Policy, Practice and Law* (Dublin: Gill and Macmillan, 2014).

McDermott, J., *St Mary's Hospital Castlebar: Serving Mayo Mental Health from 1866* (Castlebar: Western Health Board, 1999).

McDonagh, M., 'Independent mental health services', *Irish Medical News*, 29 March 2010.

McDonagh, M., 'Impact of Great Famine on mental health examined at Science Week', *Irish Times*, 13 November 2013.

McEnroe, J., 'Tributes for doctor who "demystified psychiatry"', *Irish Examiner*, 31 October 2007.

McGarry, R.C. and P. McGarry, 'Please pass the strychnine: the art of Victorian pharmacy', *Canadian Medical Association Journal*, 161, 12 (December 1999), 1556–8.

McGennis, A., 'Psychiatric units in general hospitals – the Irish experience', *Irish Journal of Psychological Medicine*, 9, 2 (November 1992), 129–34.

McGennis, A., 'Obituary: Mark Hartman', *Psychiatric Bulletin*, 18, 7 (July 1994), 442.

McGoff-McCann, M., *Melancholy Madness: A Coroner's Casebook* (Cork: Mercier Press, 2003).

McGorrian, C., N.A. Hamid, P. Fitzpatrick, L. Daly, K.M. Malone and C. Kelleher, 'Frequent mental distress (FMD) in Irish Travellers: discrimination and bereavement negatively influence mental health in the All Ireland Traveller Health Study', *Transcultural Psychiatry*, 50, 4 (August 2013), 559–78.

McGrath, J., S. Saha, D. Chant and J. Welham, 'Schizophrenia: a concise overview of incidence, prevalence, and mortality', *Epidemiologic Reviews*, 30, 1 (1 November 2008), 67–76.

McGrath, K., 'Killings could shake belief in community-based services', *Irish Times*, 8 March 1997.

McGuinness, I., 'Consultants not to apply for mental health tribunal positions', *Irish Medical Times*, 11 March 2005.

McGuinness, I., 'Tribunals to decide on legal representation', *Irish Medical Times*, 10 November 2006.

McGuinness, I., 'Tribunals revoke 12 per cent of detentions', *Irish Medical Times*, 26 October 2007.

McInerney, C., M. Davoren, G. Flynn, D. Mullins, M. Fitzpatrick, M. Caddow, F. Caddow, S. Quigley, F. Black, H.G. Kennedy and C. O'Neill, 'Implementing a court diversion and liaison scheme in a remand prison by systematic screening of new receptions', *International Journal of Mental Health Systems*, 7 (June 2013), 18.

McKeon, K., *Mentally Ill And Homeless In Ireland: Facing The Reality, Finding Solutions* (Dublin: Disability Federation of Ireland, 1999).

McKeon, P., 'Mood swings – depression and elation', in K. O'Sullivan (ed.), *All in the Mind: Approaches to Mental Health* (Dublin: Gill and Macmillan, 1986).

McKeon, P., *Coping with Depression and Elation* (London: Sheldon Press, 1986).

McLellan, D., *Utopian Pessimist: The Life and Thought of Simone Weil* (London: Macmillan, 1989).

McLoone, P., 'Towards community care', in Simon Community (ed.), *Institutions: Safety Belts or Strait-Jackets?* (Dublin: Simon Community, 1985), 8–10.

McLoughlin, D. (ed.), 'Infanticide in nineteenth-century Ireland', in A. Bourke, S. Kilfeather, M. Luddy, M. Mac Curtin, G. Meaney, M. Ní Donnchadha, M. O'Dowd and C. Wills (eds), *Field Day Anthology of Irish Writing, Volume 4: Irish Women's Writing and Traditions* (Cork: Cork University Press, 2002).

McManus, D., 'Irish documentary provides fascinating insight into history of mental health care in Ireland', *Irish Independent*, 17 September 2014.

McNally, F., 'An Irishman's Diary', *Irish Times*, 9 April 2016.

McNally, K., 'Letter to the editor', *Irish Journal of Psychological Medicine*, 30, 1 (March 2013), 91.

McNamara, M. and Mooney, P., *Women in Parliament: 1918-2000* (Dublin: Wolfhound Press, 2000).

McNulty, J.T., 'The new psychiatry', *Irish Times*, 25 July 1985.

McWilliams, S., *The Witchdoctor of Chisale* (Guildford, Surrey: Grosvenor House Publishing Ltd., 2006).

McWilliams, S., *Fiction and Physicians: Medicine Through the Eyes of Writers* (Dublin: Liffey Press, 2012).

McWilliams, S., 'Patriot and psychiatrist', *Irish Medical News*, 17 November 2014.

Meagher, D., 'Dr Maeve Leonard (Ryan) 1968-2015', *Irish Journal of Psychological Medicine*, 33, 1 (March 2016), 67-8.

Meagher, D., N. O'Regan, D. Ryan, W. Connolly, E. Boland, R. O'Caoimhe, J. Clare, J. McFarland, S. Tighe, M. Leonard, D. Adamis, P.T. Trzepacz and S. Timmons, 'Frequency of delirium and subsyndromal delirium in an adult acute hospital population', *British Journal of Psychiatry*, 205, 6 (December 2014), 478–85.

Meath Hospital, *Annual Report* (Dublin: Brunswick Press Ltd., 1977).

Meehan, E. and K. MacRae, 'Legal implications of premenstrual syndrome', *Canadian Medical Association Journal*, 135, 6 (15 September 1986), 601-8.

Meehan, P.A., 'The changing face of psychiatry', in E. Lonergan (ed.), *St Luke's Hospital, Clonmel, 1834-1984* (Clonmel: South Eastern Health Board, 1984), 85-9.

Meehan, P.J., 'Psychiatry today – care, treatment and rehabilitation', in K. O'Sullivan (ed.), *All in the Mind: Approaches to Mental Health* (Dublin: Gill and Macmillan, 1986).

Meenan, F.O.C., *Cecilia Street* (Dublin: Gill and Macmillan, 1987).

Mela, M., '*Folie à trois* in a multilevel security forensic treatment center: forensic and ethics-related implications', *Journal of the American Academy of Psychiatry and the Law*, 33, 3 (1 September 2005), 310-6.

Mental Handicap Committee, *Planning Mental Handicap Services: Report of Mental Handicap Committee* (Dublin: Eastern Health Board, 1981).

Mental Health Act Commission, *Placed Amongst Strangers: Twenty Years of the Mental Health Act 1983 and Future Prospects for Psychiatric Compulsion* (London: The Stationery Office, 2003).

Mental Health Commission, *Mental Health Commission Annual Report 2002* (Dublin: Mental Health Commission, 2003).

Mental Health Commission, *Mental Health Commission Annual Report 2004 Including the Report of the Inspector of Mental Health Services* (Dublin: Mental Health Commission, 2005).

Mental Health Commission, *A Vision for a Recovery Model in Irish Mental Health Services: Discussion Paper* (Dublin: Mental Health Commission, 2005).

Mental Health Commission, *Mental Health Commission Annual Report 2007 Including Report of the Inspector of Mental Health Services* (Dublin: Mental Health Commission, 2008).

Mental Health Commission, *Rules Governing the Use of Electro-Convulsive Therapy (Issued Pursuant to Section 59(2) of the Mental Health Act, 2001)* (Dublin: Mental Health Commission, 2009).

Mental Health Commission, *Mental Health Commission Annual Report 2013 Including Report of the Inspector of Mental Health Services* (Dublin: Mental Health Commission, 2014).

Mental Health Commission, *The Administration of Electro-convulsive Therapy in Approved Centres: Activity Report 2012* (Dublin: Mental Health Commission, 2014).

Mental Health Commission, *Mental Health Commission Annual Report 2014 Including Report of the Inspector of Mental Health Services* (Dublin: Mental Health Commission, 2015).

Mental Health Commission, *Mental Health Commission Annual Report 2015 Including Report of the Inspector of Mental Health Services* (Dublin: Mental Health Commission, 2016).

Mental Health Reform, *Ethnic Minorities and Mental Health: A Position Paper* (Dublin: Mental Health Reform, 2014).

Mental Health Reform, *Our State of Mind* (Dublin: Mental Health Reform, 2016).

Mentjox, R., C.A. van Houten and C.G. Kooiman, 'Induced psychotic disorder: clinical aspects, theoretical considerations, and some guidelines for treatment', *Comprehensive Psychiatry*, 34, 2 (March-April, 1993), 120-6.

Merikangas, A.K., R. Segurado, P. Cormican, E.A. Heron, R.J. Anney, S. Moore, E. Kelleher, A. Hargreaves, H. Anderson-Schmidt, M. Gill, L. Gallagher and A. Corvin, 'The phenotypic manifestations of rare CNVs in schizophrenia', *Schizophrenia Research*, 158, 1–3 (September 2014), 255–60.

Midland Health Board, 'The future' in D.A. Murphy (ed.), *Tumbling Walls: The Evolution of a Community Institution over 150 Years* (Portlaoise: Midland Health Board, 1983).

Miller, I., 'Book review: *Asylums, Mental Health Care and the Irish, 1800–2010*', *Social History of Medicine*, 26, 3 (August 2013), 581–3.

Millett, K., *The Loony Bin Trip* (London: Virago, 1991).

Milligan, S. and A. Clare, *Depression and How to Survive It* (London: Arrow Books, 1994).

Millon, T., *Masters of the Mind: Exploring the Story of Mental Illness from Ancient Times to the New Millennium* (Hoboken, New Jersey: John Wiley and Sons, Inc., 2004).

Mitchell, D., *A 'Peculiar' Place: The Adelaide Hospital, Dublin, 1839 to 1989* (Dublin: Blackwater, 1989).

Mokyr, J., *Why Ireland Starved: A Quantitative and Analytical History of the Irish Economy, 1800–1850* (London: Unwin Hyman, 1985).

Mollan, C., 'Maniacs, melancholics and others', *Irish Times*, 25 July 1981.

Montgomery, I. with J. Armstrong, *From Specialist Care to Specialist Treatment: A History of Muckamore Abbey Hospital* (Belfast: Ulster Historical Foundation, 2009).

Moore, J.N.P., 'Perspective', *Bulletin of the Royal College of Psychiatrists*, 10, 11 (November 1986), 298–302.

Moran, R., *Knowing Right from Wrong: The Insanity Defense of Daniel McNaughtan* (New York: Free Press, 1981).

Moran, R., 'The origin of insanity as a special verdict', *Law and Society Review*, 19, 3 (1985), 487–519.

Morrison, H., 'Constructing patient stories: 'dynamic' case notes and clinical encounters at Glasgow's Gartnavel Mental Hospital, 1921–32', *Medical History*, 60, 1 (January 2016), 67–86.

Mudiwa, L., 'Mary Robinson hits out at CMH relocation', *Medicine Weekly*, 12 July 2006.

Mudiwa, L., 'Decision on forensic hospital is 'hugely significant'', *Irish Medical Times*, 12 June 2015.

Mudiwa, L., 'A programme for Health', *Irish Medical Times*, 22 January 2016.

Muhammad, A.A., 'Back to the land of serenity', *Irish Medical Times*, 29 January 2016.

Mulcahy, M. and A. Reynolds, *Census of Mental Handicap in the Republic of Ireland 1981* (Dublin: Medico-Social Research Board, 1984).

Mulholland, M., *To Comfort Always: A History of Holywell Hospital, Antrim, 1898-1998* (Ballymena: Homefirst Community Trust, 1998).

Mulholland, P., 'Location, location, location', *Irish Medical News*, 23 June 2008.

Mullen, N., 'Psychoanalytic field still misrepresented', *Irish Medical Times*, 22 April 2016.

Mullett, G.E., 'Schizophrenia today' in K. O'Sullivan (ed.), *All in the Mind: Approaches to Mental Health* (Dublin: Gill and Macmillan, 1986).

Mulryan, N., P. Gibbons and A. O'Connor, 'Infanticide and child murder: admissions to the Central Mental Hospital 1850–2000', *Irish Journal of Psychological Medicine*, 19, 1 (March 2002), 8–12.

Munro, A., *Delusional Disorder: Paranoia and Related Illnesses* (Cambridge: Cambridge University Press, 1999).

Murphy, B.P., 'An unknown heroine who worked for Collins', *Irish Times*, 27 February 1997.

Murphy, C., 'Homosexuals – an oppressed minority?', *Irish Times*, 16 February 1974.

Murphy, C., 'It's time that dissenting voices were listened to', *Sunday Business Post*, 8 June 2014.

Murphy, D.A. (ed.), *Tumbling Walls: The Evolution of a Community Institution over 150 Years* (Portlaoise: Midland Health Board, 1983).

Murphy, D.A., 'A long half-century, 1832–1885' in D.A. Murphy (ed.), *Tumbling Walls: The Evolution of a Community Institution over 150 Years* (Portlaoise: Midland Health Board, 1983).

Murphy, K.C., L.A. Jones and M.J. Owen, 'High rates of schizophrenia in adults with velo-cardio-facial syndrome', *Archives of General Psychiatry*, 56, 10 (October 1999), 940–5.

Murphy, M., *Carlow Castle* (Carlow: Carlow Town Council, 2013).

Murphy, O.C., C. Kelleher and K.M. Malone, 'Demographic trends in suicide in the UK and Ireland, 1980–2010', *Irish Journal of Medical Science*, 184, 1 (March 2015), 227–35.

Murphy, P., 'A place of one's own', in Simon Community (ed.), *Institutions: Safety Belts or Strait-Jackets?* (Dublin: Simon Community, 1985).

Murphy, P., 'Professor Eadbhard O'Callaghan, MD FRCPI, FRCPsych (1957–2011)', *The Consultant*, Autumn 2011, 88.

Murphy, T., *The Wake* (London: Bloomsbury Methuen Drama, 1998).

Murphy, W.J., 'Homosexuality', *Irish Times*, 13 July 1973.

Murray, D., 'Is it time to abandon suicide risk assessment?', *British Journal of Psychiatry Open*, 2, 1 (February 2016), 1–2.

Murray, F., 'The price of alcohol', *Irish Times*, 12 December 2015.

Murray, R. and M. Cannon, 'Obituary: Professor Eadbhard O'Callaghan', *Psychiatric Bulletin*, 36, 5 (May 2012), 198–9.

Murray, R.M., 'Obituary: Professor Anthony Clare', *Psychiatric Bulletin*, 32, 3 (1 March 2008), 118–19.

Musgrave, D., 'Drastic effects of NI torture methods described in survey', *Irish Times*, 13 May 1976.

National Advisory Committee on Drugs and Public Health Information and Research Branch. *Drug Use in Ireland and Northern Ireland: First Results from the 2010/2011 Drug Prevalence Survey* (Dublin and Belfast: National Advisory Committee on Drugs and Public Health Information and Research Branch, 2012).

National Economic and Social Forum, *Mental Health and Social Inclusion (Report 36)* (Dublin: National Economic and Social Forum, 2007).

National Economic and Social Forum, *Mental Health in the Workplace* (Dublin: National Economic and Social Forum, 2007).

National Institute for Clinical Excellence, *Guidance on the Use of Electroconvulsive Therapy (Update: May 2010)* (London: National Institute for Clinical Excellence, 2010).

National Office for Suicide Prevention, *Annual Report 2013* (Dublin: Health Service Executive, 2014).

National Office for Suicide Prevention, *Annual Report 2014* (Dublin: Health Service Executive, 2015).

Newman, C., 'Delayed report on mental hospitals expected', *Irish Times*, 27 February 1992.

Ng, X.T. and B.D. Kelly, 'Voluntary and involuntary care: three-year study of demographic and diagnostic admission statistics at an inner-city adult psychiatry unit', *International Journal of Law and Psychiatry*, 35, 4 (July–August 2012), 317–26.

Ní Mhaoláin, Á. and B.D. Kelly, 'Ireland's Mental Health Act 2001: where are we now?', *Psychiatric Bulletin*, 33, 5 (May 2009), 161–4.

Ní Nualláin, M.N., A. O'Hare and D. Walsh, 'Incidence of schizophrenia in Ireland', *Psychological Medicine*, 17, 4 (November 1987), 94–8.

Nolan, E., *Caring for the Nation: A History of the Mater Misericordiae University Hospital* (Dublin: Gill and Macmillan, 2013).

Nolan, M., 'Professor John McKenna' in M. Fitzgerald (ed.), *Irish Families under Stress (Volume 7)* (Dublin: South Western Area Health Board, 2003).

Nolan, N., 'Case law on the Mental Health Act 2001', *Irish Psychiatrist*, 9, 3 (Autumn 2008), 176–82; 177.

Nolan, P., *A History of Mental Health Nursing* (London: Chapman and Hall, 1993).

Nolan, P., 'Mental health nursing in Great Britain', in H. Freeman and G.E. Berrios (eds), *150 Years of British Psychiatry. Volume II: The Aftermath* (London: Athlone Press, 1996), 171–92.

Nolan, P. and A. Sheridan, 'In search of the history of Irish psychiatric nursing', *International History of Nursing Journal*, 6, 2 (2001), 35–43.

Norris, D., *A Kick Against the Pricks: The Autobiography* (London: Transworld Ireland, 2012).

Norris, D., 'Marriage referendum – countdown to polling day', *Irish Times*, 21 May 2015.

Norris, D.P.B., 'Booklet on sexuality', *Evening Herald*, 21 April 1977.

Nowlan, D., 'Psychiatrists search for a better understanding of depression', *Irish Times*, 15 April 1974.

Nowlan, D., 'Ireland's most successful Minister for Health', *Irish Times*, 18 November 1974.

Nowlan, D., 'New Bureau to supervise all health education', *Irish Times*, 18 February 1975.

Nowlan, D., 'Many doctors miss mental illness signs', *Irish Times*, 3 April 1976.

Nowlan, D., 'New psychiatric career structure proposed', *Irish Times*, 31 March 1977.

Nowlan, D., 'Updating sessions for doctors', *Irish Times*, 9 September 1977.

Nowlan, D., 'Death by suppression', *Irish Times*, 4 August 1979.

Nowlan, D., 'Addicts-to-be?', *Irish Times*, 19 December 1979.

Nowlan, D., 'The New Psychiatry, 1 – Releasing Grangegorman's 'lifers'', *Irish Times*, 1 July 1985.

Nowlan, D., 'The New Psychiatry, 2 – Making the funny farm more fun', *Irish Times*, 2 July 1985.

Nowlan, D., 'Court injunction curbs debate on psychiatry report', *Irish Times*, 30 October 1985.

Nowlan, D., 'Plans for psychiatric changes get backing', *Irish Times*, 16 June 1986.

Ó hÓgartaigh, M., '"Is there any need of you?" Women in medicine in Ireland and Australia', *Australian Journal of Irish Studies*, 4 (2004), 162–71.

Ó hÓgartaigh, M., *Kathleen Lynn: Patriot, Irishwoman, Doctor* (Dublin: Irish Academic Press, 2006).

Ó hÓgartaigh, M., *Quiet Revolutionaries: Irish Women in Education, Sport and Medicine* (Dublin: The History Press Ireland, 2011).

O'Beirne, M. and T.J. Fahy, 'The impact of a general hospital psychiatric unit on established patterns of psychiatric care', *Irish Journal of Psychological Medicine*, 5, 2 (September 1988), 85–8.

O'Boyle, J., 'Psychiatric services for the adult deaf' in Study Group on the Development of the Psychiatric Services (ed.), *The Psychiatric Services – Planning for the Future* (Dublin: Stationery Office, 1984).

O'Brien, C., 'Reviews for mental patients in detention', *Irish Times*, 1 November 2006.

O'Brien, C., 'Corridors of the mind', *Irish Times*, 11 August 2007.

O'Brien, C., 'A shock to the system of care', *Irish Times*, 2 February 2010.

O'Brien, C., 'Goodbye Grangegorman', *Irish Times*, 23 February 2013.

O'Brien, C., 'Call to extend inquiry to mental homes', *Irish Times*, 16 June 2014.

O'Brien, C., 'Psychiatric care and the gap in our social history', *Irish Times*, 16 June 2014.

O'Brien, C., 'Vulnerable patients living in 'mini-institutions'', *Irish Times*, 24 June 2014.

O'Brien, C., 'Children with mental health issues admitted into adult units', *Irish Times*, 31 October 2014.

O'Brien, C., 'Almost 500 additional suicides linked to recession', *Irish Times*, 16 March 2015.

O'Brien, E., 'Dublin's mental health needs', *Irish Times*, 16 April 1971.

Ó'Bróin, L., *W. E. Wylie and the Irish Revolution 1916–1921* (Dublin: Gill & Macmillan, 1989).

O'Callaghan, E., T. Gibson, H.A. Colohan, P. Buckley, D.G. Walshe, C. Larkin and J.L. Waddington, 'Risk of schizophrenia in adults born after obstetric complications and their association with early onset of illness: a controlled study', *British Medical Journal*, 305, 6864 (21 November 1992), 1256–9.

O'Callaghan, E., P. Sham, N. Takei, G. Glover and R.M. Murray, 'Schizophrenia after prenatal exposure to 1957 A2 influenza epidemic', *Lancet*, 337, 8752 (25 May 1991), 1248–50.

O'Carroll, A. and F. O'Reilly, 'Health of the homeless in Dublin: has anything changed in the context of Ireland's economic boom?', *European Journal of Public Health*, 18, 5 (October 2008), 448–53.

O'Casey, S., *Drums Under the Windows. Autobiography: Book 3, 1906–1916* (London: Pan Books Limited, 1972; first published by Macmillan and Company Limited, 1945).

Ó Cionnaith, F, 'Consultants not responsible for harm under Act', *Medicine Weekly*, 8 November 2006.

O'Connell, B., 'Recovering well', *Irish Times*, 23 October 2012.

O'Connell, M., R. Duffy and N. Crumlish, 'Refugees, the asylum system and mental healthcare in Ireland', *BJPsych International*, 13, 2 (May 2016), 35–7.

O'Connor, A. and H. O'Neill, 'Male prison transfers to the Central Mental Hospital, a special hospital (1983–1988)', *Irish Journal of Psychological Medicine*, 7, 2 (September 1990), 118–20.

O'Connor, A. and H. O'Neill, 'Female prison transfers to the Central Mental Hospital, a special hospital (1983–1988)', *Irish Journal of Psychological Medicine*, 8, 2 (September 1991), 122–3.

O'Connor, A. and D. Walsh, *Activities of Irish Psychiatric Hospitals and Units 1988* (Dublin: Health Research Board, 1991).

O'Dea, J.F., 'A day to remember' in E. Lonergan (ed.), *St Luke's Hospital, Clonmel, 1834–1984* (Clonmel: South Eastern Health Board, 1984).

O'Doherty, M., 'Irish medical historiography' in J.B. Lyons (ed.), *2000 Years of Irish Medicine* (Dublin: Eireann Healthcare Publications, 1999).

O'Donnell, B. (ed.), *Irish Surgeons and Surgery in the Twentieth Century* (Dublin: Gill and Macmillan Ltd., 2008).

O'Donoghue, B., J. Lyne, M. Hill, C. Larkin, L. Feeney and E. O'Callaghan, 'Involuntary admission from the patients' perspective', *Social Psychiatry and Psychiatric Epidemiology*, 45, 6 (June 2010), 631–8.

O'Donoghue, B., J. Lyne, L. Renwick, K. Madigan, A. Kinsella, M. Clarke, N. Turner and E. O'Callaghan, 'A descriptive study of "non-cases" and referral rates to an early intervention for psychosis service', *Early Intervention in Psychiatry*, 6, 3 (August 2012), 276–82.

O'Donoghue, B. and P. Moran, 'Consultant psychiatrists' experiences and attitudes following the introduction of the Mental Health Act 2001: a national survey', *Irish Journal of Psychological Medicine*, 26, 1 (March 2009), 23–6.

O'Donoghue, B., E. Roche, J. Lyne, K. Madigan and L. Feeney, 'Service users' perspective of their admission: a report of study findings', *Irish Journal of Psychological Medicine* [published online ahead of print, 2016].

O'Hare, A. and D. Walsh, *Activities of Irish Psychiatric Hospitals and Units 1965–1969* (Dublin: The Medico-Social Research Board, 1970).

O'Hare, A. and D. Walsh, 'The three county schizophrenia study; a study of the prevalence and incidence of schizophrenia and an assessment of its clinical and social outcomes in the Republic of Ireland' in S.A. Mednick, A.E. Baert and B. Phillips Backmann (eds), *Prospective Longitudinal Research. An Empirical Basis for the Primary Prevention of Psychosocial Disorders* (Oxford: Oxford University Press on behalf of the World Health Organisation, 1981).

O'Keane, V., T. Frodl and T.G. Dinan, 'A review of atypical depression in relation to the course of depression and changes in HPA axis organization', *Psychoneuroendocrinology*, 37, 10 (October 2012), 1589–99.

O'Keane, V, A. Jeffers, E. Moloney and S. Barry, *The Stark Facts Irish Psychiatric Association Survey of Psychiatric Services in Ireland: A Regional Comparison of Clinical Resources and Affluence, and Specialist Services* (Dublin: The Irish Psychiatric Association, 2003).

O'Keane, V., A. Jeffers, E. Moloney and S. Barry, 'Irish Psychiatric Association survey of psychiatric services in Ireland', *Psychiatric Bulletin*, 28, 10 (October 2004), 364–7.

O'Mahony, C., *Cork's Poor Law Palace: Workhouse Life 1838–1890* (Monkstown, County Cork: Rosmathún Press, 2005).

O'Malley, P., *Clinical Neuro-Psychiatry: Reflections on Neuro-Psychiatric Practice and Thought* (Dublin: Dunran Press, 2000).

O'Malley, P.P., 'Attempted suicide before and after the communal violence in Belfast, August 1969', *Journal of the Irish Medical Association*, 65, 5 (4 March 1972), 109–13.

O'Malley, P.P., 'Attempted suicide, suicide and communal violence', *Journal of the Irish Medical Association*, 68, 5 (8 March 1975), 103–9.

O'Neill, A., 'Mental committal law leaves individual almost powerless', *Irish Times*, 3 April 1992.

O'Neill, A., P. Casey and R. Minton, 'The homeless mentally ill: an audit from an inner city hospital', *Irish Journal of Psychological Medicine*, 24, 2 (1 June 2007), 62–6.

O'Neill, A.M., *Irish Mental Health Law* (Dublin: First Law, 2005).

O'Neill, C., P. Heffernan, R. Goggins, C. Corcoran, S. Linehan, D. Duffy, H. O'Neill, C. Smith and H.G. Kennedy, 'Long-stay forensic psychiatric inpatients in the Republic of Ireland: aggregated needs assessment', *Irish Journal of Psychological Medicine*, 20, 4 (December 2003), 119–25.

O'Neill, C., H. Sinclair, A. Kelly and H. Kennedy, 'Interaction of forensic and general psychiatric services in Ireland: learning the lessons or repeating the mistakes?', *Irish Journal of Psychological Medicine*, 19, 2 (June 2002), 48–54.

O'Neill, D., 'Playing constituency politics to the detriment of our hospitals', *Irish Times*, 8 March 2016.

O'Neill, D. and S. O'Keeffe, 'Health care for older people in Ireland', *Journal of the American Geriatric Society*, 51, 9 (September 2003), 1280–6.

O'Regan, M., 'Mental-health services in Donegal collapsing, says Independent TD', *Irish Times*, 10 December 2015.

O'Regan, M., 'Mental illness still carries stigma, says TD', *Irish Times*, 28 January 2016.

O'Regan, M., 'McEntee says commitment to more funds for mental health', *Irish Times*, 3 June 2016.

O'Reilly, C., 'Carers overlooked in disability debate', *Irish Times*, 15 June 2016.

O'Rourke, D., T.J. Fahy and P. Prescott, 'The Galway Study of Panic Disorder, IV: Temporal stability of diagnosis by present state examination test-retest', *British Journal of Psychiatry*, 169, 1 (July 1996), 98–100.

O'Shea, B. (ed.), A *Textbook of Psychological Medicine: An Irish Perspective (Fourth Edition)* (Dublin: Eireann Healthcare Publications, 2002).

O'Shea, B., 'Book review: *Music and Madness*', *Irish Psychiatrist*, 9, 2 (Summer 2008), 118–20.

O'Shea, B. (ed.), *Textbook of Psychological Medicine (Fifth Edition)* (Dublin: College of Psychiatry of Ireland, 2010).

O'Shea, B., 'Appreciation: Kate Ganter (née Dempsey; 1948–2012)', *Psychiatry Professional*, 1, 3 (Autumn, 2012), 12.

O'Shea, B., 'Appreciation – Dr Pat Tubridy (1936–2013)', *Irish Medical Times*, 15 February 2013.

O'Shea, B., 'Mental healthcare is in full bloom', *Irish Medical Times*, 28 June 2013.

O'Shea, B., 'Leaving a mark on Irish psychiatry', *Irish Medical Times*, 6 September 2013.

O'Shea, B., 'The inconvenient truth around 'lunacy'', *Irish Medical Times*, 7 June 2014.

O'Shea, B., 'The horrors of the old asylum', *Irish Medical Times*, 12 January 2015.

O'Shea, B. and J. Falvey, *A Textbook of Psychological Medicine for the Irish Student* (Dublin: Eastern Health Board, 1985).

O'Shea, B. and J. Falvey, 'A history of the Richmond Asylum (St Brendan's Hospital), Dublin', in H. Freeman and G.E. Berrios (eds), *150 Years of British Psychiatry. Volume II: The Aftermath* (London: Athlone Press, 1996).

O'Sullivan, C., "Mental health fund cuts disgust me, minister", *Irish Examiner*, 31 May 2016.

O'Sullivan, E., 'Misery in Ireland's "massive mausoleums of madness"', *Irish Times*, 2 February 2013.

O'Sullivan, E. and I. O'Donnell, 'Coercive confinement in the Republic of Ireland: the waning of a culture of control', *Punishment and Society*, 9, 1 (January 2007), 27–48.

O'Sullivan, E. and I. O'Donnell (eds), *Coercive Confinement in Ireland: Patients, Prisoners and Penitents* (Manchester and New York: Manchester University Press, 2012).

O'Sullivan, K. (ed.), *All in the Mind: Approaches to Mental Health* (Dublin: Gill and Macmillan, 1986).

O'Toole, F., 'Simply ignoring the will of the people', *Irish Times*, 13 April 1989.

O'Toole, F., 'Medical body censured Browne but ruled he acted for patient', *Irish Times*, 11 January 1997.

O'Toole, F., 'Neglect of archives shows contempt for citizens', *Irish Times*, 10 April 2010.

O'Toole, F., 'Dark stain of Irish gulag system not yet addressed', *Irish Times*, 25 September 2012.

O'Toole, F., 'Uncomfortable truths of old mental hospital system', *Irish Times*, 12 March 2013.

Ohgami, H., T. Terao, I. Shiotsuki, N. Ishii and N. Iwata, 'Lithium levels in drinking water and risk of suicide', *British Journal of Psychiatry*, 194, 5 (May 2009), 464–5.

Okai, D., G. Owen, H. McGuire, S. Singh, R. Churchill and M. Hotopf, 'Mental capacity in psychiatric patients: systematic review', *British Journal of Psychiatry*, 191, 4 (October 2007), 291–7.

Osman, M. and A.C. Parnell, 'Effect of the First World War on suicide rates in Ireland: an investigation of the 1864–1921 suicide trends', *British Journal of Psychiatry Open*, 1, 2 (November 2015), 164–5.

Owen, G.S., G. Szmukler, G. Richardson, A.S. David, V. Raymont, F. Freyenhagen, W. Martin and M. Hotopf, 'Decision-making capacity for treatment in psychiatric and medical in-patients: cross-sectional, comparative study', *British Journal of Psychiatry*, 203, 6 (December 2013), 461–7.

Owens, J., 'Mental health services crying out for reform', *Irish Times*, 21 November 2005.

Paterson, B., 'Restraint' in P. Barker (ed.), *Mental Health Ethics* (Abingdon, Oxon: Routledge, 2011).

Patterson, D.G. and E.G. O'Gorman, 'Psychosexual study of patients and non-patient homosexual groups', *IRCS Medical Science: Psychology and Psychiatry*, 12, 3–4 (March–April 1984), 243.

Pearsall, J. and B. Trumble, (eds), *The Oxford Reference English Dictionary (Second Edition)* (Oxford and New York: Oxford University Press, 1996).

Penney, D. and P. Stastny, *The Lives They Left Behind: Suitcases from a State Hospital Attic* (New York: Bellevue Literary Press, 2008).

Perlin, M.L., A.S. Kanter, M.P. Treuthart, E. Szeli, and K. Gledhill, *International Human Rights and Comparative Mental Disability Law* (Durham, NC: Carolina Academic Press, 2006).

Perlin, M.L., A.S. Kanter, M.P. Treuthart, E. Szeli, and K. Gledhill, *International Human Rights and Comparative Mental Disability Law: Documents Supplement* (Durham, NC: Carolina Academic Press, 2006).

Pietikäinen, P., *Madness: A History* (London and New York: Routledge, 2015).

Pillay, D. and B.D. Kelly, 'Acute psychiatric units in general hospitals: where are we now?', *Irish Medical Journal*, 102, 5 (May 2009), 137–8.

Porter, R., 'The patient's view: doing medical history from below', *Theory and Society*, 14, 2, (March 1985), 175–98.

Porter, R., *A Social History of Madness: Stories Of The Insane* (London: Phoenix Giants, 1987).

Porter, R. *Madmen: A Social History of Mad-houses, Mad-doctors and Lunatics* (Gloucestershire, United Kingdom: Tempus, 2004).

Porter, R. and M.S. Micale, 'Introduction: reflections on psychiatry and its histories' in M.S. Micale and R. Porter (eds), *Discovering the History of Psychiatry* (New York and Oxford: Oxford University Press, 1994).

Prendiville, C. and J. Pettigrew, 'Leisure occupations in the Central Criminal Lunatic Asylum 1890–1920', *Irish Journal of Occupational Therapy*, 43, 1 (Spring 2015), 12–19.

Prestwich, P.E., 'Family strategies and medical power: "voluntary" committal in a Parisian asylum, 1876–1914', in R. Porter and D. Wright (eds), *The Confinement of the Insane: International Perspectives, 1800–1965* (Cambridge: Cambridge University Press, 2003).

Prior, P., 'Mad, not bad: crime, mental disorder and gender in nineteenth-century Ireland' in I. O'Donnell and F. McAuley (eds), *Criminal Justice History: Themes and Controversies from Pre-Independence Ireland* (Dublin: Four Courts Press, 2003).

Prior, P., 'Dangerous lunacy: the misuse of mental health law in nineteenth-century Ireland', *Journal of Forensic Psychiatry and Psychology*, 14, 3 (September 2003), 525–41.

Prior, P., 'Prisoner or patient? The official debate on the criminal lunatic in nineteenth-century Ireland', *History of Psychiatry*, 15, 58 (Part 2) (June 2004), 177–92.

Prior, P., 'Roasting a man alive: the case of Mary Rielly, criminal lunatic', *Éire-Ireland*, 41, 1–2 (Spring/Summer 2006), 169–91.

Prior, P., 'Gender and criminal lunacy in nineteenth-century Ireland' in M.H. Preston and M. Ó hÓgartaigh (eds), *Gender and Medicine in Ireland, 1700–1950* (Syracuse, New York: Syracuse University Press, 2012).

Prior, P.M., "Where lunatics abound': a history of mental health services in Northern Ireland' in H. Freeman and G.E. Berrios (eds), *150 Years of British Psychiatry. Volume II: The Aftermath* (London: Athlone Press, 1996).

Prior, P.M., 'Murder and madness: gender and the insanity defense in nineteenth-century Ireland', *New Hibernia Review*, 9, 4 (Winter 2005), 19–36.

Prior, P.M., *Madness and Murder: Gender, Crime and Mental Disorder in Nineteenth Century Ireland* (Dublin: Irish Academic Press, 2008).

Prior, P.M, 'Psychiatry and the fate of women who killed infants and young children, 1850–1900' in C. Cox and M. Luddy (eds), *Cultures of Care in Irish Medical History 1750–1950* (Basingstoke, Hampshire: Palgrave Macmillan, 2010).

Prior, P.M. (ed.), 'Voices of mental health service users – poetry and prose' in P.M. Prior (ed.), *Asylums, Mental Health Care and the Irish, 1800–2010* (Dublin: Irish Academic Press, 2012).

Prior, P.M., 'Overseeing the Irish asylums: the Inspectorate in Lunacy, 1845–1921' in P.M. Prior (ed.), *Asylums, Mental Health Care and the Irish, 1800-2010* (Dublin: Irish Academic Press, 2012).

Prior, P.M., 'Mental health law on the island of Ireland, 1800–2010' in P.M. Prior (ed.), *Asylums, Mental Health Care and the Irish, 1800–2010* (Dublin: Irish Academic Press, 2012).

Prior, P.M. (ed.), 'Voices of doctors and officials' in P.M. Prior (ed.), *Asylums, Mental Health Care and the Irish, 1800–2010* (Dublin: Irish Academic Press, 2012).

Prior, P.M. and D.V. Griffiths, "The chaplaincy question': the Lord Lieutenant of Ireland versus the Belfast Lunatic Asylum', *Éire-Ireland*, 33, 2&3 (1997), 137–53.

Prior, P.M. and D.V. Griffiths, 'The "chaplaincy question" at Belfast District Asylum, 1834–1870' in P.M. Prior (ed.), *Asylums, Mental Health Care and the Irish, 1800–2010* (Dublin: Irish Academic Press, 2012).

Prunty, J., 'St Vincent's Hospital, Fairview, Dublin: from lunatic asylum to therapeutic intervention', in J. Prunty and L. Sullivan (eds), *The Daughters of Charity of St Vincent de Paul in Ireland: The Early Years* (Dublin: Columba Press, 2014).

Purcell, M., *A Time for Sowing: The History of St John of God Brothers in Ireland, 1879–1979* (Dublin: Hospitaller Brothers of St John of God, 1979).

Pye, P., 'The yank in the corner', *Irish Times*, 15 August 1983.

Quinlan, Á., 'A fresh approach to mental health', *Irish Examiner*, 2 May 2016.

Raftery, J., 'Mental health policy in Ireland: learning from the UK?', *Administration*, 35, 1 (1987), 38–46.

Raftery, M., 'Psychiatric profession at it again', *Irish Times*, 25 May 2005.

Raftery, M., 'Revealing the horrific past of psychiatric hospitals', *Irish Times*, 5 September 2011.

Ramsay, H., E. Roche and B. O'Donoghue, 'Five years after implementation: a review of the Irish Mental Health Act 2001', *International Journal of Law and Psychiatry*, 36, 1 (January/February 2013), 83–91.

Ranieri, V., K. Madigan, E. Roche, E. Bainbridge, D. McGuinness, K. Tierney, L. Feeney, B. Hallahan, C. McDonald and B. O'Donoghue, 'Caregivers' perceptions of coercion in psychiatric hospital admission', *Psychiatry Research*, 228, 3 (August 2015), 380–5.

Rattigan, C., '"Half mad at the time": unmarried mothers and infanticide in Ireland, 1922–1950', in C. Cox and M. Luddy (eds), *Cultures of Care in Irish Medical History 1750–1950* (Basingstoke, Hampshire: Palgrave Macmillan, 2010).

Rattigan, C., *What Else Could I Do? Single Mothers and Infanticide, Ireland 1900–1950* (Dublin: Irish Academic Press, 2011).

Redmond, L., 'Suicide: act of destruction or cry of despair?', *Irish Times*, 29 January 1979.

Redmond, L., 'Abortion: not always the easiest way out', *Irish Times*, 19 April 1979.

Reuber, M., *Staats- und Privatanstalten in Irland: Irre, Ärzte und Idioten (1600–1900)* (Köln: Verlag Josef Eul, 1994).

Reuber, M., 'The architecture of psychological management: the Irish asylums (1801–1922)', *Psychological Medicine*, 26, 6 (November 1996), 1179–89.

Reuber, M., 'Moral management and the 'unseen eye': public lunatic asylums in Ireland, 1800–1845' in G. Jones and E. Malcolm (eds), *Medicine, Disease and the State in Ireland, 1650–1940* (Cork: Cork University Press, 1999).

Review Group, *Limited Review of the Mental Health (Care and Treatment) (Scotland) Act 2003* (Edinburgh: Scottish Government, 2009).

Review Group on Mental Handicap Services, *Needs and Abilities: A Policy for the Intellectually Disabled (Report of the Review Group on Mental Handicap Services)* (Dublin: Department of Health/Stationery Office, 1990).

Reynolds, J., *Grangegorman: Psychiatric Care in Dublin since 1815* (Dublin: Institute of Public Administration in association with Eastern Health Board, 1992).

Riches, V.C., T.R. Parmenter, M. Wiese and R.J. Stancliffe, 'Intellectual disability and mental illness in the NSW [New South Wales] criminal justice system', *International Journal of Law and Psychiatry*, 29, 5 (September/October 2006), 386–96.

Richmond, C., 'Obituary: Anthony Clare', *Guardian*, 31 October 2007.

Risse, G.B. and J.H. Warner, 'Reconstructing clinical activities', *Social History of Medicine*, 5, 2 (August 1992), 183–205.

Robins, J., 'The advent of the district mental hospital system' in D.A. Murphy (ed.), *Tumbling Walls: The Evolution of a Community Institution over 150 Years* (Portlaoise: Midland Health Board, 1983).

Robins, J., *Fools and Mad: A History of the Insane in Ireland* (Dublin: Institute of Public Administration, 1986).

Robins, J., 'A house for fools and mad', *Irish Times*, 3 February 1990.

Robins, J., *Nursing and Midwifery in Ireland in the Twentieth Century* (Dublin: An Bord Altranais, 2000).

Robins, J.A., 'The advent of the District Mental Hospital System' in E. Lonergan (ed.), *St Luke's Hospital, Clonmel, 1834–1984* (Clonmel: South Eastern Health Board, 1984).

Robinson, D., *Wild Beasts and Idle Humors: The Insanity Defense from Antiquity to the Present* (Cambridge, MA: Harvard University Press, 1998).

Robson, C., 'Homosexuality', *Irish Times*, 18 September 1991.

Rollin, H.R., 'Book review: *Shock Therapy: A History of Electroconvulsive Treatment in Mental Illness*', *British Journal of Psychiatry*, 197, 2 (1 August 2010), 162–3.

Ruddle, H., F. Donoghue and R. Mulvihill, The Years Ahead *Report: A Review of the Implementation of its Recommendations* (Dublin: National Council on Ageing and Older People, 1998).

Rutherdale, A., 'Detention in mental hospital after 6 month period without new order invalid', *Irish Times*, 26 September 1994.

Ryan, A., *Walls of Silence* (Callan, County Kilkenny: Red Lion Press, 1999).

Ryan, D., *The Mental Health Acts 2001–2009: Case Law and Commentary* (Dublin: Blackhall Publishing, 2010).

Ryan, D.A., C.A. Benson and B.A. Dooley, 'Psychological distress and the asylum process: a longitudinal study of forced migrants in Ireland', *Journal of Nervous and Mental Disease*, 196, 1 (January 2008), 37–45.

Ryan, P., 'Researching Irish gay male lives: reflections on disclosure and intellectual autobiography in the production of personal narratives', *Qualitative Research*, 6, 2 (May 2006), 151–68.

Sackett, D.L., W.M. Rosenberg, J.A. Gray, R.B. Haynes and W.S. Richardson, 'Evidence based medicine: what it is and what it isn't', *British Medical Journal*, 312, 7023 (January 1996), 71–2.

Salter, N., 'Mental health and children', *Irish Times*, 22 August 2015.

Saris, A.J., 'Mad kings, proper houses, and an asylum in rural Ireland', *American Anthropologist*, 98, 3, (September 1996), 539–54.

Saris, A.J., 'The asylum in Ireland: a brief institutional history and some local effects', in A. Cleary and M.P. Treacy (eds), *The Sociology of Health and Illness in Ireland* (Dublin: University College Dublin Press, 1997).

Saris, A.J., 'An uncertain dominion: Irish psychiatry, methadone, and the treatment of opiate abuse', *Culture, Medicine and Psychiatry*, 32, 2 (June 2008), 259–77.

Sartorius, N., A. Jablensky, A. Korten, G. Ernberg, M. Anker, J.E. Cooper and R. Day, 'Early manifestations and first-contact incidence of schizophrenia in different cultures: a preliminary report on the initial evaluation phase of the WHO Collaborative Study on determinants of outcome of severe mental disorders', *Psychological Medicine*, 16, 4 (November 1986), 909–28.

Scheper-Hughes, N., 'Reply to 'Ballybran'', *Irish Times*, 21 February 1981.

Scheper-Hughes, N., *Saints Scholars and Schizophrenics: Mental Illness in Rural Ireland (Twentieth Anniversary Edition)* (Berkeley: University of California Press, 2001).

Scheper-Hughes, N. and A.M. Lovell (eds), *Psychiatry Inside Out: Selected Writings of Franco Basaglia* (New York: Columbia University Press, 1987).

Scott, A. (edited by S. Dolamore), *Is That Me? My Life with Schizophrenia* (Dublin: A. and A. Farmar, 2002).

Scull, A., *Decarceration: Community Treatment and the Deviant – A Radical View* (Englewood Cliffs, New Jersey: Prentice-Hall, 1977).

Scull, A., *Museums of Madness: Social Organization of Insanity in 19th Century England* (New York: St Martin's Press, 1979).

Scull, A., 'Was insanity increasing? A response to Edward Hare', *British Journal of Psychiatry*, 144, 4 (1 April 1984), 432–6.

Scull, A., *The Most Solitary of Afflictions: Madness and Society in Britain, 1700–1900* (New Haven and London: Yale University Press, 1993).

Scull, A., 'Rethinking the history of asylumdom', in J. Melling and B. Forsythe (eds), *Insanity Institutions and Society, 1800–1914: A Social History of Madness in Comparative Perspective* (London and New York: Routledge, 1999).

Scull, A., *Madhouse: A Tragic Tale of Megalomania and Modern Medicine* (New Haven and London: Yale University Press, 2005).

Scull, A., 'Scholarship of fools', *Times Literary Supplement*, 23 March 2007.

Scull, A., *Madness in Civilization: A Cultural History of Insanity, From the Bible to Freud, From the Madhouse to Modern Medicine* (London: Thames and Hudson Ltd., 2015).

Scully, S., 'From minute to minute, 1886–1905' in D.A. Murphy (ed.), *Tumbling Walls: The Evolution of a Community Institution over 150 Years* (Portlaoise: Midland Health Board, 1983).

Semkovska, M., Landau, S., Dunne, R., Kolshus, E., Kavanagh, A., Jelovac, A., Noone, M., Carton, M., Lambe, S., McHugh, C. and D. M. McLoughlin, 'Bitemporal versus high-dose unilateral twice-weekly electroconvulsive therapy for depression (EFFECT-Dep): a pragmatic, randomized, non-inferiority trial', *American Journal of Psychiatry*, 173, 4 (1 April 2016), 408–17.

Shanahan, C., 'Our €40m drug problem', *Irish Examiner*, 19 March 2015.

Shanahan, E., 'President collapses after speech at medical event', *Irish Times*, 18 November 1974.

Shannon, J, 'Getting one's Act together', *Medicine Weekly*, 8 November 2006.

Shannon, J., 'Changing minds in Ireland', *Medical Independent*, 5 August 2010.

Shannon, J., 'Moving on from the dark ages of mental health treatment', *Irish Medical Times*, 13 March 2015.

Sheehan, J., J. McKay, M. Ryan, N. Walsh and D. O'Keeffe, 'What cost chronic pain?', *Irish Medical Journal*, 89, 6 (November–December 1996), 218–19.

Sheehan, J., M. Ryan, J. McKay, N. Walsh and D. O'Keeffe, 'Pain clinic attenders: an audit', *Irish Medical Journal*, 87, 2 (March–April 1994), 52–3.

Sheerin, F., 'Mental handicap nursing' in J. Robins (ed.), *Nursing and Midwifery in Ireland in the Twentieth Century* (Dublin: An Bord Altranais, 2000).

Shelley, R., 'Dr Pat Tubridy, 1936–2013', *The Consultant*, Summer 2013, 101.

Shephard, B., *A War of Nerves: Soldiers and Psychiatrists, 1914–1994* (London: Pimlico, 2002).

Sheppard, N. and E. Hardiman, 'Treatment of the mentally ill offender in Ireland', *Irish Journal of Psychiatry*, 7, 1 (Spring 1986), 13–19.

Sheridan, A., 'Being a psychiatric nurse in Ireland in the 1950s', in G.M. Fealy (ed.), *Care to Remember: Nursing and Midwifery in Ireland* (Cork: Mercier Press, 2005).

Sheridan, A.J., 'Psychiatric nursing' in J. Robins (ed.), *Nursing and Midwifery in Ireland in the Twentieth Century* (Dublin: An Bord Altranais, 2000).

Sheridan, A.J., 'The impact of political transition on psychiatric nursing – a case study of twentieth-century Ireland', *Nursing Inquiry*, 13, 4 (2006), 289–99.

Sheridan, K., 'A voice behind closed doors', *Irish Times*, 29 November 2008.

Shorter, E., *A History of Psychiatry: From the Era of the Asylum to the Age of Prozac* (New York: John Wiley and Sons, 1997).

Shorter, E., *How Everyone Became Depressed: The Rise and Fall of the Nervous Breakdown* (Oxford and New York: Oxford University Press, 2013).

Shorter, E. and D. Healy, *Shock Therapy: A History of Electroconvulsive Treatment in Mental Illness* (New Brunswick, New Jersey and London: Rutgers University Press, 2007).

Showalter, E., *The Female Malady: Women, Madness and English Culture, 1830–1980* (London: Virago, 1987).

Simmons, H.G., 'Explaining social policy: the English Mental Deficiency Act of 1913', *Journal of Social History*, 11, 3 (Spring 1978), 387–403.

Simon Community (ed.), *Institutions: Safety Belts or Strait-Jackets?* (Dublin: Simon Community, 1985).

Simpson, K., *Forensic Medicine (Eighth Edition)* (London: Edward Arnold (Publishers) Ltd., 1979).

Sisti, D.A., A.G. Segal and E.J. Emmanuel, 'Improving long-term psychiatric care: bring back the asylum', *Journal of the American Medical Association*, 313, 3 (20 January 2015), 243–4.

Skålevåg, S.A., 'The matter of forensic psychiatry: a historical enquiry', *Medical History*, 50, 1 (January 2006), 49–68.

Skelton, R., 'Jonathan Hanaghan: The founder of psychoanalysis in Ireland', *The Crane Bag*, 7, 2 (1983), 183–90.

Skrabanek, P., 'Convulsive therapy – a critical appraisal of its origins and value', *Irish Medical Journal*, 79, 6 (June 1986), 157–65.

Sloan, D., S. Browne, D. Meagher, A. Lane, C. Larkin, P. Casey, N. Walsh and E. O'Callaghan, 'Attitudes toward psychiatry among Irish final year medical students', *European Psychiatry*, 11, 8 (1996), 407–11.

Smith, C., 'The Central Mental Hospital, Dundrum, Dublin' in R. Bluglass and P. Bowden (eds), *Principles and Practice of Forensic Psychiatry* (Edinburgh: Churchill Livingstone, 1990).

Smith, C., 'A future for our mentally ill?' in C. Keane (ed.), *Mental Health in Ireland* (Dublin: Gill and Macmillan and Radio Telefís Éireann, 1991).

Smith, C., 'Living with insanity: narratives of poverty, pauperism and sickness in asylum records, 1840–76' in A. Gestrich, E. Hurren and S. King (eds), *Poverty and Sickness in Modern Europe: Narratives of the Sick Poor, 1780-1938* (London and New York: Continuum International Publishing Group, 2012).

Smith, D., E. Roche, K. O'Loughlin, D. Brennan, K. Madigan, J. Lyne, L. Feeney and B. O'Donoghue, 'Satisfaction with services following voluntary and involuntary admission', *Journal of Mental Health*, 23, 1 (February 2014), 38–45.

Smith, G., A. Bartlett and M. King, 'Treatments of homosexuality in Britain since the 1950s – an oral history: the experience of patients', *British Medical Journal*, 328, 7437 (21 February 2004), 427–9.

Smith, L., '"Your very thankful inmate": discovering the patients of an early county lunatic asylum', *Social History of Medicine*, 21, 2 (August 2008), 237–52.

Smith, L.D., *'Cure, Comfort and Safe Custody': Public Lunatic Asylums in Early Nineteenth-Century England* (London and New York: Leicester University Press, 1999).

Smyth, C., M. MacLachlan and A. Clare, *Cultivating Suicide? Destruction of Self in a Changing Ireland* (Dublin: Liffey Press, 2003).

Sneader, W., 'The prehistory of psychotherapeutic agents', *Journal of Psychopharmacology*, 4, 3 (May 1990), 115–19.

South Eastern Health Board Sub-Committee, *Psychiatric Services* (Kilkenny: South Eastern Health Board, 1982).

Spellman, J., 'Section 260 of the Mental Treatment Act, 1945 reviewed', *Medico-Legal Journal of Ireland*, 4, 1 (1998), 20–4.

Spiegel, A.D., 'Temporary insanity and premenstrual syndrome: medical testimony in an 1865 murder trial', *New York State Journal of Medicine*, 88, 9 (September 1988), 482–92.

Spiegel, A.D. and M.B. Spiegel, 'Was it murder or insanity? Reactions to a successful paroxysmal insanity plea in 1865', *Women and Health*, 18, 2 (1992), 69–86.

Stack, J., 'History of child psychiatry in Ireland' in M. Fitzgerald (ed.), *Irish Families under Stress (Volume 7)* (Dublin: South Western Area Health Board, 2003).

Steering Group on the Review of the Mental Health Act 2001, *Interim Report of the Steering Group on the Review of the Mental Health Act 2001* (Dublin: Department of Health, 2012).

Stokes, M. and A. O'Connor, 'Deaths in the Central Mental Hospital', *Irish Journal of Psychological Medicine*, 6, 2 (September 1989), 144–6.

Stone, M.H., *Healing the Mind: A History of Psychiatry from Antiquity to the Present* (London: Pimlico, 1998).

Stonor Saunders, F., *The Woman Who Shot Mussolini* (London: Faber and Faber, 2010).

Study Group on the Development of the Psychiatric Services, *The Psychiatric Services – Planning for the Future* (Dublin: Stationery Office, 1984).

Sturdy, H. and W. Parry-Jones, 'Boarding-out insane patients: the significance of the Scottish system, 1857–1913' in P. Bartlett and D. Wright (eds), *Outside the Walls of the Asylum: The History of Care in the Community, 1750–2000* (London: Athlone Press, 1999).

Swanwick, G. and B. Lawlor, 'Services for dementia sufferers and their carers: Implications for future development' in A.L. Leahy and M.M. Wiley (eds), *The Irish Health System In The 21st Century* (Dublin: Oak Tree Press, 1998).

Swanwick, G.R. and A.W. Clare, 'Suicide in Ireland 1945–1992: social correlates', *Irish Medical Journal*, 90, 3 (April/May 1997), 106–8.

Sweeney, J. and D. Mitchell, 'A challenge to nursing: an historical review of intellectual disability nursing in the UK and Ireland', *Journal of Clinical Nursing*, 18, 19 (October 2009), 2754–63.

Taylor, J.W., *Guilty but Insane: J. C. Bowen-Colthurst – Villain or Victim?* (Cork: Mercier Press, 2016).

Taylor Salisbury, T. and G. Thornicroft, 'Deinstitutionalisation does not increase imprisonment or homelessness', *British Journal of Psychiatry*, 208, 5 (May 2016), 412–13.

Thomas, P. and P. Bracken, 'Critical psychiatry in practice', *Advances in Psychiatric Treatment*, 10, 5 (August 2004), 361–70.

Thompson, S., 'Eolas offers integrated, innovative map of mental health services', *Irish Times*, 23 June 2015.

Tighe, D., 'Start making sense' in A. Harpin and J. Foster (eds), *Performance, Madness and Psychiatry: Isolated Acts* (Basingstoke, Hampshire: Palgrave Macmillan, 2014).

Tighe, M., 'Call for cash to preserve asylum files', *Sunday Times*, 18 April 2010.

Tobin, J., 'International human rights law and mental illness', *Irish Journal of Psychological Medicine*, 24, 1 (March 2007), 31–9.

Tomes, N., 'Feminist histories of psychiatry' in M.S. Micale and R. Porter (eds), *Discovering the History of Psychiatry* (New York and Oxford: Oxford University Press, 1994).

Torrey, E.F., 'Is psychosis endemic in western Ireland?', *American Journal of Psychiatry*, 142, 8 (August 1985), 999.

Torrey, E.F., 'The prevalence of schizophrenia in Ireland', *Archives of General Psychiatry*, 51, 7 (July 1994), 513.

Torrey, E.F., *American Psychosis: How the Federal Government Destroyed the Mental Illness Treatment System* (Oxford and New York: Oxford University Press, 2013).

Torrey, E.F., M. McGuire, A. O'Hare, D. Walsh and M.P. Spellman, 'Endemic psychosis in western Ireland', *American Journal of Psychiatry*, 141, 8 (August 1984), 966–70.

Torrey, E.F. and J. Miller, *The Invisible Plague: The Rise of Mental Illness from 1750 to the Present* (New Jersey: Rutgers University Press, 2001).

Trevor, W., *Two Lives* (London: Viking, 1991).

Turkington, A., M. Duffy, S. Barrett, R. McCaul, R. Anderson, S.J. Cooper, T. Rushe and C. Mulholland, 'Exposure to political violence in Northern Ireland and outcome of first episode psychosis', *Schizophrenia Bulletin*, 42, 3 (May 2016), 626–32.

Tyrer, P., 'Book review: *Shrinks: The Untold Story of Psychiatry*', *British Journal of Psychiatry*, 208, 4 (April 2016), 401.

United Nations, *Principles for the Protection of Persons with Mental Illness and the Improvement of Mental Health Care* (New York: United Nations, Secretariat Centre For Human Rights, 1991).

United Nations, *Convention on the Rights of Persons with Disabilities* (Geneva: United Nations, 2006).

United Nations High Commissioner for Human Rights. *Annual Report* (Geneva: United Nations, 2009).

US Bureau of the Census, *Historical Statistics of the United States, Colonial Times to 1970, Bicentennial Edition, Part 2* (Washington, DC: GPO, 1975).

Vandermeersch, P., '"*Les mythes d'origine*" in the history of psychiatry' in M.S. Micale and R. Porter (eds), *Discovering the History of Psychiatry* (New York and Oxford: Oxford University Press, 1994).

Viney, M., *Mental Illness: An Inquiry* (Dublin: *Irish Times*, 1971).

Viney, M., 'Geared for a gale', *Irish Times*, 24 September 1980.

Viney, M., 'The yank in the corner', *Irish Times*, 6 August 1983.

Vize, E., 'Pay threat to psychiatrists over mental health tribunals', *Medicine Weekly*, 26 October 2005.

Waddington, J.L., H.A. Youssef and A. Kinsella, 'The prevalence of schizophrenia in Ireland: readdressing the enigma', *Archives of General Psychiatry*, 52, 6 (June 1995), 509.

Wade, N.J., 'The original spin doctors: the meeting of perception and insanity', *Perception*, 34, 3 (2005), 253–60.

Wade N.J., U. Norrsell and A. Presly, 'Cox's chair: 'a moral and a medical mean in the treatment of maniacs'', *History of Psychiatry*, 16, 61 (Part 1) (March 2005), 73–88.

Walker, D., 'Modern nerves, nervous moderns' in S.L. Goldberg and F.B. Smith (eds), *Australian Cultural History* (Cambridge: Cambridge University Press, 1988).

Wallace, A., "Getting better is really scary...", *Irish Times*, 11 June 2016.

Wallace, J., 'Doctor Maurice O'Connor Drury, Wittgenstein's pupil', *Irish Journal of Psychological Medicine*, 17, 2 (1 June 2000), 67–8.

Wallace, J., 'Medicine in Trinity', *Irish Medical News*, 20 October 2014).

Walsh, C., "Gay people don't have two heads", *Irish Times*, 28 September 1984.

Walsh, D., 'Two and two make five – multifactoriogenesis in mental illness in Ireland', *Irish Medical Journal*, 69, 16 (October 1976), 417–22.

Walsh, D., 'A century of suicide in Ireland', *Journal of the Irish Medical Association*, 69, 6 (1976), 144–52.

Walsh, D., 'The recent increase in reported suicide in Ireland', *Irish Medical Journal*, 71, 18 (December 1978), 613–6.

Walsh, D., 'Schizophrenia' in C. Keane (ed.), *Mental Health in Ireland* (Dublin: Gill and Macmillan and Radio Telefís Éireann, 1991).

Walsh, D., 'The elderly and handicapped in psychiatric hospitals', *Irish Journal of Psychiatry*, 12, 1 (Spring 1991), 2.

Walsh, D., '*Capgras à plusieurs*: the case of Brigid Cleary', *Irish Journal of Psychiatry*, 12, 1 (Spring 1991), 10–2.

Walsh, D., 'Brief historical review', *Irish Journal of Psychiatry*, 13, 1 (Spring 1992), 3–20.

Walsh, D., 'Stirrings in psychiatry', *Irish Journal of Psychiatry*, 13, 2 (Autumn 1992), 1–2.

Walsh, D., 'General hospital psychiatric units in Ireland', *Irish Journal of Psychiatry*, 13, 2 (Autumn 1992), 6–11.

Walsh, D., 'The ups and downs of schizophrenia in Ireland', *Irish Journal of Psychiatry*, 13, 2 (Autumn 1992), 12–6.

Walsh, D., 'Book review: *Grangegorman: Psychiatric Care in Dublin since 1815*', *Irish Journal of Psychiatry*, 13, 2 (Autumn 1992), 17.

Walsh, D., 'Psychiatric illness – the extent of the problem and the response', *Irish Journal of Psychiatry*, 14, 1 (Spring 1993), 1–2.

Walsh, D., 'The prevalence of schizophrenia in Ireland: readdressing the enigma', *Archives of General Psychiatry*, 52, 6 (June 1995), 509.

Walsh, D., 'Burning of Bridget Cleary', *Irish Times*, 28 August 1999.

Walsh, D., 'Mental illness in Ireland and its management', in D. McCluskey (ed.), *Health Policy and Practice in Ireland* (Dublin: University College Dublin Press, 2006), 29–43.

Walsh, D., 'A revolution in mental care', *Irish Medical Times*, 30 March 2007.

Walsh, D., 'Vision must not become a mirage', *Irish Medical Times*, 15 June 2007.

Walsh, D., 'The lunatic asylums of Ireland, 1825–1839', *Irish Journal of Psychological Medicine*, 25, 4 (December 2008), 151–6.

Walsh, D., 'Irish College formed for psychiatrists (at last)', *Irish Medical Times*, 23 January 2009.

Walsh, D., 'A College for Irish psychiatrists', *Irish Medical Times*, 30 January 2009.

Walsh, D., 'College of Psychiatry for Ireland', *Irish Medical Times*, 6 February 2009.

Walsh, D., 'Grangegorman development misses the point', *Irish Medical Times*, 19 June 2009.

Walsh, D., 'Shock therapy must remain available to some', *Irish Times*, 28 December 2009.

Walsh, D., 'Preserving the history of old asylums', *Irish Medical Times*, 22 October 2010.

Walsh, D., 'The Ennis District Lunatic Asylum and the Clare Workhouse Lunatic Asylums in 1901', *Irish Journal of Psychological Medicine*, 26, 4 (December 2010), 206–11.

Walsh, D., 'Thomas Drapes, medical superintendent of the Enniscorthy Asylum', *British Journal of Psychiatry*, 199, 3 (September 2011), 218.

Walsh, D., 'Private practice and the public good', *Irish Medical Times*, 30 September 2011.

Walsh, D., 'Mental health services in Ireland, 1959–2010' in P.M. Prior (ed.), *Asylums, Mental Health Care and the Irish, 1800–2010* (Dublin: Irish Academic Press, 2012).

Walsh, D., 'Did the Great Irish Famine increase schizophrenia?', *Irish Journal of Psychological Medicine*, 29, 1 (January 2012), 7–15.

Walsh, D., 'Book review: *Trinity's Psychiatrists: From Serenity of the Soul to Neuroscience*', *Irish Journal of Psychological Medicine*, 29, 2 (June, 2012), 136–7.

Walsh, D., 'Letter to the editor', *Irish Journal of Psychological Medicine*, 30, 1 (March 2013), 91–2.

Walsh, D., 'The birth and death of a diagnosis: monomania in France, Britain and in Ireland', *Irish Journal of Psychological Medicine*, 31, 1 (1 March 2014), 39–45.

Walsh, D., 'WW1 as "cause or associated factor" of mental illness', *Irish Medical Times*, 9 January 2015.

Walsh, D., 'Rethinking the link between the recession and increased 'economic suicides'', *Irish Medical Times*, 5 June 2015.

Walsh, D., 'The grand young Duke of Leinster', *Irish Medical Times*, 9 October 2015.

Walsh, D., 'Psychiatric deinstitutionalisation in Ireland, 1960–2013', *Irish Journal of Psychological Medicine*, 32, 4 (December 2015), 347–52.

Walsh, D., 'Hammer and chisel to old asylum system', *Irish Medical Times*, 5 February 2016.

Walsh, D., 'Planning for a 21st century mental health service', *Irish Medical Times*, 15 April 2016.

Walsh, D. and A. Daly, *Mental Illness in Ireland 1750–2002: Reflections on the Rise and Fall of Institutional Care* (Dublin: Health Research Board, 2004).

Walsh, D. and A. Daly, 'The socio-demographic and clinical profiles of patients admitted to the Sligo District Lunatic Asylum in the late 19th century with some modern comparisons', *Irish Journal of Psychological Medicine*, 33, 1 (March 2016), 43–54.

Walsh, D. and K.S. Kendler, 'The prevalence of schizophrenia in Ireland', *Archives of General Psychiatry*, 51, 7 (July 1994), 513–15.

Walsh, D., A. O'Hare, B. Blake, J.V. Halpenny and P.F. O'Brien, 'The treated prevalence of mental illness in the Republic of Ireland – the three county case register study', *Psychological Medicine*, 10, 3 (August 1980), 465–70.

Walsh, N. and D. McGrath, 'Self-poisoning and psycho-historical change in Ireland', *Irish Medical Journal*, 68, 14 (July 1975), 343–50.

Walsh, O., "A lightness of mind': gender and insanity in nineteenth-century Ireland' in M. Kelleher and J.H. Murphy (eds), *Gender Perspectives in Nineteenth-Century Ireland: Public and Private Spheres* (Dublin: Irish Academic Press, 1997).

Walsh, O., "The designs of providence': race, religion and Irish insanity' in J. Melling and B. Forsythe (eds), *Insanity Institutions and Society, 1800–1914: A Social History of Madness in Comparative Perspective* (London and New York: Routledge, 1999).

Walsh, O., 'Gendering the asylums: Ireland and Scotland, 1847–1877' in T. Brotherstone, D. Simonton and O. Walsh (eds), *The Gendering of Scottish History: An International Approach* (Glasgow: Cruithne Press, 1999).

Walsh, O., 'Lunatic and criminal alliances in nineteenth-century Ireland' in P. Bartlett and D. Wright (eds), *Outside the Walls of the Asylum: The History of Care in the Community, 1750–2000* (London: Athlone Press, 1999).

Walsh, O., 'Gender and insanity in nineteenth-century Ireland' in J. Andrews and A. Digby (eds), *Sex and Seclusion, Class and Custody: Perspectives on Gender and Class in the History of British and Irish Psychiatry* (Amsterdam: Editions Rodopi, 2004).

Walsh, O., "Tales from the big house': the Connaught District Lunatic Asylum in the late nineteenth-century', *History Ireland*, 13, 6 (November–December, 2005), 21–5.

Walsh, O., 'Landscape and the Irish asylum' in Ú. Ní Bhroiméil and G. Hooper (eds), *Land and Landscape in Nineteenth-Century Ireland* (Dublin: Four Courts Press, 2008).

Walsh, O., 'Cure or custody: therapeutic philosophy at the Connaught District Lunatic Asylum' in M.H. Preston and M. Ó hÓgartaigh (eds), *Gender and Medicine in Ireland, 1700–1950* (Syracuse, New York: Syracuse University Press, 2012).

Walsh, O., 'A perfectly ordered establishment: Connaught District Lunatic Asylum (Ballinasloe)' in P.M. Prior (ed.), *Asylums, Mental Health Care and the Irish, 1800–2010* (Dublin: Irish Academic Press, 2012).

Walsh, O., "A person of the second order': the plight of the intellectually disabled in nineteenth-century Ireland' in L.M. Geary and O. Walsh (eds), *Philanthropy in Nineteenth-Century Ireland* (Dublin: Four Courts Press, 2014).

Walsh, O., 'Psychiatric nurses and their patients in the nineteenth century: the Irish perspective' in A. Borsay and P. Dale (eds), *Mental Health Nursing: The Working Lives of Paid Carers in the Nineteenth and Twentieth Centuries* (Manchester: Manchester University Press, 2015).

Walsh, O., 'Work and the Irish district asylums during the late nineteenth century' in E. Waltraud (ed.), *Work, Psychiatry and Society, c. 1750–2015* (Manchester: Manchester University Press, 2016).

Walsh, O., 'Nature or nurture: epigenetic change and the Great Famine in Ireland' in C. Kinealy, C. Reilly and J. King (eds), *Women and the Great Hunger* (Hamden, Connecticut: Quinnipiac University Press, 2017) (*in press*, forthcoming).

Walsh, P., 'Changing attitudes, changing times at the former Donegal District Lunatic Asylum', *Donegal Democrat*, 18 January 2011.

Walshe, É., *Cissie's Abattoir* (Cork: The Collins Press, 2009).

Wannell, L., 'Patients' relatives and psychiatric doctors: letter writing in the York Retreat, 1875–1910', *Social History of Medicine*, 20, 2 (August 2007), 297–313.

Ward, D.J., 'Mental health', *Irish Times*, 12 December 1980.

Ward, D.J., 'Having breakfast with the late Enoch Powell', *Irish Medical Times*, 29 April 2016.

Ward, E., 'Security and asylum: the case of Hanna Greally', *Studies*, 95, 377 (Spring 2006), 65–76.

Waters, J., *Beyond Consolation: Or How We Became Too Clever For God...And Our Own Good* (London and New York: Continuum International Publishing Group Ltd., 2010).

Waters, J., 'Tears for fears: my drugs hell', *Sunday Independent*, 21 March 2010.

Waters, J., *Jiving at the Crossroads (Updated Edition)* (London: Transworld Ireland, 2011).

Watters, E., *Crazy Like Us: The Globalization of the American Psyche* (New York: Free Press, 2010).

Webb, M., 'Who becomes ill and why' in K. O'Sullivan (ed.), *All in the Mind: Approaches to Mental Health* (Dublin: Gill and Macmillan, 1986).

Webb, M., 'What's Irish about psychiatry?', *Irish Journal of Psychological Medicine*, 7, 1 (March 1990), 7–16.

Webb, M., 'Alcohol excess – the curse of the drinking classes' in C. Keane (ed.), *Mental Health in Ireland* (Dublin: Gill and Macmillan and Radio Telefís Éireann, 1991).

Webb, M., 'Obituary: Mary Elizabeth Martin', *Psychiatric Bulletin*, 33, 5, (May 2009), 199.

Webb, M., *Trinity's Psychiatrists: From Serenity of the Soul to Neuroscience* (Dublin: Trinity College, 2011).

Weber, M.M. and H.M. Emrich, 'Current and historical concepts of opiate treatment in psychiatric disorders', *International Journal of Clinical Psychopharmacology*, 3, 3 (July 1988), 255–66.

Wedding, D., M.A. Boyd and R.M. Niemiec, *Movies and Mental Illness 3 (Third Edition)* (Cambridge, MA: Hogrefe Publishing, 2010).

Weiner, D.B., 'Philippe Pinel's "Memoir on Madness" of December 11, 1794', *American Journal of Psychiatry*, 149, 6 (June 1992), 725–32.

Weiner, D.B., "'Le geste de Pinel': the history of a psychiatric myth' in M.S. Micale and R. Porter (eds), *Discovering the History of Psychiatry* (New York and Oxford: Oxford University Press, 1994).

Wessely, S., 'Ten books', *British Journal of Psychiatry*, 181, 1 (1 July 2002), 81–4.

Whelan, D., 'Mental health tribunals', *Medico-Legal Journal of Ireland*, 10, 2 (2004), 84–9.

Whelan, D., 'Legacy of unresolved legal issues on mental health', *Irish Times*, 4 November 2008.

Whelan, D., *Mental Health Law and Practice* (Dublin: Round Hall/Thomson Reuters, 2009).

Williams, E., *A CBT Approach to Mental Health Problems in Psychosis* (London: Speechmark Publishing Ltd., 2013).

Williamson, A., 'The beginnings of state care for the mentally ill in Ireland', *Economic and Social Review*, 10, 1 (January 1970), 280–91.

Williamson, A.P., 'Armagh District Lunatic Asylum', *Seanchas Ard Mhacha: Journal of the Armagh Diocesan Historical Society*, 8, 1 (1975/1976), 111–20.

Williamson, A.P., 'Psychiatry, moral management and the origins of social policy for mentally ill people in Ireland', *Irish Journal of Medical Science*, 161, 9 (September 1992), 556–8.

Wilson, F.E., E. Hennessy, B. Dooley, B.D. Kelly and D.A. Ryan, 'Trauma and PTSD rates in an Irish psychiatric population: a comparison of native and immigrant samples', *Disaster Health*, 1, 2 (December 2013), 74–83.

Wilson, J.J., 'Psychiatric committal', *Irish Times*, 17 January 1992.

Winkler, P., B. Barrett, P. McCrone, L. Csémy, M. Janoušková and C. Höschl, 'Deinstitutionalised patients, homelessness and imprisonment: systematic review', *British Journal of Psychiatry*, 208, 5 (May 2016), 421–8.

Wise, S. 'Demon Doctors', *Financial Times*, 21/22 March 2015.

Wise, S., '"Curing Queers' – Review', *Guardian*, 3 June 2015.

Working Group on Congregated Settings, *Time to Move on from Congregated Settings* (Dublin: Health Service Executive, 2011).

Working Party on Services for the Elderly, *The Years Ahead ... A Policy for the Elderly* (Dublin: The Stationery Office, 1988).

World Health Organisation, *International Classification of Mental and Behavioural Disorders (Volume 10)* (Geneva: World Health Organisation, 1992).

World Health Organisation, *The World Health Report 2001. Mental Health: New Understanding, New Hope* (Geneva: World Health Organisation, 2001).

World Health Organisation, *WHO Resource Book on Mental Health, Human Rights and Legislation* (Geneva: World Health Organization, 2005).

Wright, B., D. Duffy, K. Curtin, S. Linehan, S. Monks and H.G. Kennedy, 'Psychiatric morbidity among women prisoners newly committed and amongst remanded and sentenced women in the Irish prison system', *Irish Journal of Psychological Medicine*, 23, 2 (June 2006), 47–53.

Wright, D., 'Delusions of gender? Lay identification and clinical diagnosis of insanity in Victorian England', in J. Andrews and A. Digby (eds), *Sex and Seclusion, Class and Custody: Perspectives on Gender and Class in the History of British and Irish Psychiatry* (Amsterdam: Editions Rodopi, 2004), 149–76.

Wright, D., J.E. Moran and S. Gouglas, 'The confinement of the insane in Victorian Canada: the Hamilton and Toronto Asylums, c.1861–1891' in R. Porter and D. Wright (eds), *The Confinement of the Insane: International Perspectives, 1800–1965* (Cambridge: Cambridge University Press, 2003).

Wrigley, M., 'A State of unpreparedness', *Irish Medical Times*, 6 October 2006.

Yeats, W.B., *Collected Poems* (Ware, Hertfordshire: Wordsworth Editions Limited, 1994).

Youssef, H.A., A. Kinsella and J.L. Waddington, 'Evidence for geographical variation in the rate of schizophrenia in rural Ireland', *Archives of General Psychiatry*, 48, 3 (March 1991), 254–8.

Yung, A., L. Phillips and P.D. McGorry, *Treating Schizophrenia in the Prodromal Phase* (London: Taylor and Francis, 2004).

Acknowledgements

Many people assisted and advised me as I wrote this book. I am deeply indebted to all the colleagues and friends who answered my emails and calls, and discussed various themes with me as the project progressed.

Once again, I greatly appreciate the support and guidance of Mr Conor Graham, Ms Fiona Dunne and all at Irish Academic Press in the preparation of this book. I am deeply grateful to Professor Edward Shorter for writing the foreword.

Particular thanks once again to Dr Larkin Feeney (for his advice and guidance on this and various other manuscripts) and Dr Aidan Collins (for his invaluable guidance on numerous aspects of this and other projects).

I am also very grateful to Professor Veronica O'Keane, Professor Aiden Corvin, Professor Michael Gill, Professor Louise Gallagher, Dr Anne Mac Lellan, Dr Fiona Byrne, Dr Ciara Breathnach, Professor Oonagh Walsh, Professor Patricia Casey, Professor John Sheehan, Dr Eugene Breen, Professor Harry Kennedy, Professor Carol Fitzpatrick, Professor Fiona McNicholas, Professor Tim Lynch, Professor Kevin Malone, Professor Thomas Fahy, Professor James Lucey, Dr Susan Finnerty, Dr Pauline Moloney, Dr Margaret du Feu, Dr John Tobin, Dr Tony Carney, Dr Fionnuala O'Loughlin, Dr Dermot Walsh, Professor Ivor Browne, Mr David Givens (Liffey Press), Mr Dermot Mulligan (Museum Curator, Carlow County Museum), Dr Brian O'Shea, Dr Pat Gibbons, Dr William Flannery, Dr Martha Finnegan, Dr Pat Bracken, Dr Robert Daly, Professor Robert Daly, Professor Noel Walsh, Dr Elizabeth Walsh, Dr Ciaran Corcoran, Professor Colm McDonald, Professor David Meagher, Professor Ted Dinan, Professor Kieran Murphy, Professor Des O'Neill, Dr Peter Whitty, Dr Maria Fitzgibbon, Dr Brian Hallahan, Dr Michael Reynolds, Dr Liam Daly, Dr Desmond McGrath, Dr Paul McQuaid, Dr Maurice Guéret, Dr Shari McDaid (Director, Mental Health Reform), Mr Brian Hartnett (Hearing Voices Ireland), Dr Michael D'Arcy, Professor Thomas Pruzinsky, Dr Lorcan Martin, Dr Martin Mahon, Dr Éibhear Walshe, Mr Dara Gantly (*Irish Medical Times*), Mr John O'Neill, Mr Alan Gilsenan, Ms Joanne Parry, Ms Virginia O'Callaghan, Dr Patrice Murphy, Dr Jim O'Boyle, Mr Ned Kelly, Senator David Norris, Dr Maura Cronin, Dr John Bruzzi, Dr John Cooney, Mr Declan Jones, Mr Jonny Dillon (National Folklore Collection), Dr Fionnuala Lynch, Dr Liam Hanniffy, Councillor Ruth Illingworth, Dr Catherine Cox, Professor Damien Brennan, Professor David Healy, Dr Siobhan Barry, Ms Natalie Sherrard, Mr John O'Neill,' Ms Bernie Deasy (archivist, Delany Archive, Carlow College, Carlow), Ms Patricia Gilheaney, Ms Sheila Ahern, Professor Tom O'Dowd, Professor Joe Barry, Mr Dick Bennett, Fr Piaras O'Dúill, Ms Carmel Kitching (HSE), Mr Alan Counihan, Ms Úna Spain, Health Service Executive (CH09, Dublin North City), Carlow County Museum, McKerns Printing (Limerick) Ltd., Mr Brendan Culleton, Ms Irina Maldea,

Grangegorman Art Group (Health Service Executive, Dublin North City) and the Clinical Photography Department, Mater Misericordiae University Hospital.

I am very grateful for the assistance of Mrs Jane Hogan Clare and Mr Sebastian Clare.

I remain extremely grateful to Professor Sharlene Walbaum, her family, colleagues and students at Quinnipiac University, Connecticut. Shar's wisdom, enthusiasm and hospitality have added greatly to my historical work.

I am also grateful for the assistance and support of Ms Miriam Silke (College of Psychiatrists of Ireland), Dr Roy Browne, Dr Margo Wrigley, Mr Sean Tone, Mr Gerry Devine (Health Service Executive, Dublin), Mr Brian Donnelly (National Archives of Ireland); Dr Peter Reid (University College Dublin); Ms Harriet Wheelock (Heritage Centre, Royal College of Physicians of Ireland); and Ms Úna Fowler.

My historical work would not have been possible without the earlier support of Dr Cathy Smith and Professor Jon Stobart at the University of Northampton.

I owe a long standing debt of gratitude to my teachers at Scoil Chaitríona, Renmore, Galway; St Joseph's Patrician College, Nun's Island, Galway (especially my history teacher, Mr Ciaran Doyle); and the School of Medicine at NUI Galway.

Finally, and above all else, I deeply appreciate the support of my wife (Regina), children (Eoin and Isabel), parents (Mary and Desmond), sisters (Sinéad and Niamh) and nieces (Aoife and Aisling).

Permissions

Quotations from the Minutes of the Proceedings of the Committee of Management of Ballinasloe District Lunatic Asylum and the Minutes of the Meeting of the Commissioner Administering the Affairs of the Ballinasloe Mental Hospital are taken from the Minute Books in the archives at St Brigid's Hospital, Ballinasloe, County Galway, Ireland. I am deeply grateful to Mr John Dair, Mr Adrian Ahern and Dr Kieran Power for their cooperation and assistance.

Quotations from the *Official Report of Dáil Éireann* and *Official Report of Seanad Éireann* are Copyright Houses of Oireachtas. This book contains Irish public sector information re-used under the Licence to Re-Use Public Sector Information Under the European Communities (Re-Use of Public Sector Information) Regulations 2005 (SI 279/2005). This book also contains public sector information licensed under the Open Government Licences v.1.0, v.2.0 and v.3.0 (England), and Scottish Parliamentary information licensed under the Open Scottish Parliament Licence v.1.0.

I am very grateful to the following for permission to reproduce published material:

- Material from the *Irish Medical Times* is reproduced by kind permission of the *Irish Medical Times*.
- Material from B.D. Kelly, 'Dr William Saunders Hallaran and psychiatric practice in nineteenth-century Ireland', *Irish Journal of Medical Science*, *177*, 1 (March 2008), pp. 79–84, is used with kind permission from Springer Science+Business Media: *Irish Journal of Medical Science*, Dr William Saunders Hallaran and psychiatric practice in nineteenth-

century Ireland, Volume: 177, Year of publication: 2008, Pages: 79–84, Author: Brendan D Kelly.

- Material from A. Clare, 'Psychological medicine' in P. Kumar and M. Clark (eds), *Clinical Medicine: A Textbook for Medical Students and Doctors (Third Edition)* (London: Ballière Tindall, 1994), pp. 957–91, is Copyright Elsevier 1994, and reproduced by kind permission of Elsevier.

- Material from the *Journal of Mental Science* and *Psychiatric Bulletin* is reproduced by kind permission of the Royal College of Psychiatrists.

- Material from *Studies: An Irish Quarterly Review* is reproduced by kind permission of the editor of *Studies: An Irish Quarterly Review*.

- Material from *The Irish Journal of Psychiatry* is reproduced by kind permission of Dr Dermot Walsh.

- Material from the *Irish Times* is reproduced by kind permission of the *Irish Times*.

- Material from the *Irish Independent* is reproduced by kind permission of the *Irish Independent*.

- Material from the *Irish Journal of Psychological Medicine* is reproduced by kind permission of Cambridge University Press and the College of Psychiatrists of Ireland. Material from the *Irish Journal of Psychological Medicine* prior to Cambridge University Press is reproduced by kind permission of MedMedia Group (Dún Laoghaire, County Dublin, Ireland) and the College of Psychiatrists of Ireland.

- Material from *'He Lost Himself Completely': Shell Shock and its Treatment at Dublin's Richmond War Hospital, 1916–1919* by Brendan Kelly (Liffey Press, 2014) is used by kind permission of Liffey Press.

- Material from *Swift's Hospital: A History of St Patrick's Hospital, Dublin, 1746–1989* by Elizabeth Malcolm (Gill and Macmillan, 1989) is reproduced by kind permission of Gill and Macmillan.

- Material from 'The Portrayal of Madness in the Limerick Press, 1772–1845' by John O'Neill (MA Thesis, Mary Immaculate College (University of Limerick), 2013) is used by kind permission of Mr John O'Neill.

- Material from 'Women and Madness in Nineteenth-Century Ireland' by Joanne Parry (MA Thesis, St Patrick's College, Maynooth (National University of Ireland), 1997) is used by kind permission of Ms Joanne Parry.

- Material from *Grangegorman: Psychiatric Care in Dublin since 1815* by Joseph Reynolds (Institute of Public Administration in association with Eastern Health Board, 1992) is reproduced by kind permission of the Institute of Public Administration.

- Material from *Ada English: Patriot and Psychiatrist* by Brendan Kelly (Irish Academic Press, 2014) is used by kind permission of Irish Academic Press.

- Material from the *Journal of the Statistical and Social Inquiry of Ireland* is reproduced by kind permission of the *Journal of the Statistical and Social Inquiry of Ireland*.

- Material from *What the Doctor Saw* by Maurice Guéret (Dublin: IMD, 2013) is used by kind permission of the author, Dr Maurice Guéret, and IMD.

- Material from *Forensic Medicine (Eighth Edition)* by Keith Simpson (London: Edward Arnold, 1979; p. 214) is used by kind permission of Taylor & Francis Group.

- Material from *Drums Under the Windows. Autobiography: Book 3, 1906–1916* by Sean O'Casey (London: Pan Books Limited, 1972; first published by Macmillan and Company Limited, 1945) (pp. 55–6) is reproduced by kind permission of the Estate of Sean O'Casey.

- Material from *'Cure, Comfort and Safe Custody': Public Lunatic Asylums in Early Nineteenth-Century England* by Leonard D. Smith (London and New York: Leicester University Press, 1999) is reproduced by kind permission of Leicester University Press, an imprint of Bloomsbury Publishing Plc., and with the agreement of Dr L.D. Smith (©Leonard D. Smith (1999), *'Cure, Comfort and Safe Custody': Public Lunatic Asylums in Early Nineteenth-Century England* (Leicester University Press, an imprint of Bloomsbury Publishing Plc.)).

- Material from 'The Hospital and the Holy Spirit: Psychotic Subjectivity and Institutional Returns in Dublin' by Michael D'Arcy (paper delivered at the *Society for Psychological Anthropology*, Boston, Massachusetts, 10 April 2015) is used by kind permission of the author.

- Material from the following papers is reproduced by kind permission of SAGE Publications:
  - Kelly, B.D., 'Mental health law in Ireland, 1821 to 1902: building the asylums', *Medico-Legal Journal*, 76, 1 (March 2008), pp. 19–25 (doi: 10.1258/rsmmlj.76.1.19).
  - Kelly, B.D., 'Mental health law in Ireland, 1821 to 1902: dealing with the "increase of insanity in Ireland"', *Medico-Legal Journal*, 76, 1 (March 2008), pp. 26–33. (doi: 10.1258/rsmmlj.76.1.26).
  - Kelly, B.D., 'Mental health law in Ireland, 1945 to 2001: reformation and renewal', *Medico-Legal Journal*, 76, 2 (June 2008), pp. 65–72. (doi: 10.1258/rsmmlj.76.2.65).
  - Kelly, B.D., 'The Mental Treatment Act 1945 in Ireland: an historical enquiry', *History of Psychiatry*, 19, 73(1) (March 2008), pp. 47–67. (doi: 10.1177/0957154X06075949).
  - Kelly, B.D., *'Folie à plusieurs*: forensic cases from nineteenth-century Ireland', *History of Psychiatry*, 20, 77 (Part 1) (March 2009), pp. 47–60. (doi: 10.1177/0957154X08094236).

The Introduction contains material adapted by permission from BMJ Publishing Group Limited: 'Searching for the patient's voice in the Irish asylums', *Medical Humanities*, B.D. Kelly, Volume 42, No. 2 (June 2016), pp. 87–91; published Online First: 5 January 2016; doi:10.1136/medhum-2015-010825 ©2016. Chapter 6 draws upon material within: B.D. Kelly, 'Homosexuality and Irish psychiatry: medicine, law and the changing face of Ireland', *Irish Journal of Psychological Medicine*, available on CJO 1st February 2016. doi:10.1017/ipm.2015.72 ©, College of Psychiatrists of Ireland, published by Cambridge University Press, reproduced with permission.

I am very grateful to the editors, publishers, authors and copyright holders of these publications for permitting re-use of material in this book. All reasonable efforts have been made to contact the copyright holders for all texts quoted and images used in this book. If any have been omitted, please contact the publisher.

INDEX

Printed in Great Britain
by Amazon

48446697R00280